The Human Shield

50p from the sale of this book will go towards a memorial to those who suffered in hiding in Kuwait or as a hostage of the Iraqis, most notably to the six who died.

1991

The Human Shield

– British hostages in the Gulf and the work of the Gulf Support Group

Other books by Tim Lewis:
Pisspote's Progress
Moonlight Sonata
Coventry Voices

British Library Cataloguing in Publication Data
Lewis, Tim Richard, *1953*-
The human shield: British hostages in the Gulf and the work of the Gulf Support Group
953.670530922
ISBN 0 9517381 1 9

Cover design Tim Lewis
Photographs copyright Tim Lewis, unless otherwise stated.
Published by Leomansley Press, Lichfield, Staffordshire.
Printed and bound by The Bath Press, Lower Bristol Road, Bath.
Distributed by Turnaround, 27 Horsell Road, London.

To

The Forgotten Ones

– the hostages, their relatives and friends

especially

Douglas Crosgery

William Atack

Jamail Sultan Saleem

Alex Duncan

Tony Duffy

Don Majors

Clive Stringer

and

their families

Thanks to

Stephen Brookes, Joanna and Jonathan Copley,
Tony Moorby, Lynda Pickup, Lollo Murthwaite,
Rob Hayward MP, Tony Benn MP, Kathy Ludbrook,
Ted Heath MP, Robert Vaudry, Dr Jeffrey Easton,
Andrew and Carolyn Stevenson, Christopher Denne,
Betty and Andrew Stevenson, Maureen Evans,
Maureen and John Chappell Jnr, Mark Lennox-Boyd MP,
Sir Harold Walker, Tom and Gilly Colclough,
Cathy Willis, Lawrence and Bernice MacDonald,
Mike and Lesley Devey, Brenda Richardson, Christine
Willatt, Joe Wild, Claire and David Shattock,
Cynthia Hill, Cliff Lindley, John Petty, Ivan Manning,
Norma and Nigel Armstrong, Anne Mansell,
Dr Corky McGuiness, Lichfield Library,
Barbara and Stewart Griffiths, Carol Kirkby,
Jane and Jim McAlindin, Hazel Martin,
Maureen Evans, David Cunningham, Hamish Ross,
the Foreign Office Emergency Unit staff,
Brian Jarman and Genevieve Eckenstein at Gulf Link,
Ian Barrett, Richard Barnes, Clem Prothero,
Andy Charles and Nicola Benwell, Carole Bevis,
Sue and Dave Dorrington, Margaret Hanson,
Margaret and George Parkin, Lesley and Frank Kerfoot,
Cynthia Hill, Anne Hill and Sir Michael Weston.

Introduction

It all began for me and Stephen with a phone call. Our dear friend, Wen Li, rang desperate for news of her husband, Eric Watson. We had known Eric for years. Stephen had been best man at his wedding and Eric had given him power of attorney to sell his flat in Coventry.

Eric was on BA Flight 149 to Singapore, calling in at Kuwait to refuel and change crews, and had been caught at the airport by the Iraqis. We were stunned by the news, but immediately phoned everyone we could think of for information: British Airways, the emergency centre at Heathrow, the Foreign Office, MPs, the BBC, Stephen's contacts from his aerospace days, anyone. None of them had any news whatsoever. We even tried to phone Kuwait, but the international lines had been cut off.

The Iraqi invasion of Kuwait had been headlines for several days, but now it hit us between the eyes. We were so angry, so bitter, so frustrated at the lack of news, we were galvanised into action. We felt our loved ones had been forgotten as headlines concentrated on the price of oil and the American military response. Someone had to do something to get those innocent people freed.

Joanna Copley and her husband and brother set up a helpline in London. Rob Hayward MP had established one in Bristol with the help of several volunteers, including Sue Brownlow. Dorothy Croft, a trained counsellor, had put one into action in Derbyshire, and we set up our operation in Coventry. None of us had any idea how big it would become. We all thought it would be over in a matter of days. In fact, the next four months of our lives were totally dominated by one thing - the Gulf Support Group - as the crisis dragged on until December - and beyond.

In those first days, we gave out our phone number for people to contact. We had no idea what the response would be. In fact, thousands of people phoned, all as anxious and distraught for their friends and family as we were. It was overwhelming. We realised rapidly that we would have to become far more organised. We began compiling file indexes and computer lists of families and hostages, keeping track of people as they phoned. We asked for volunteers to staff our phone lines. British Telecom put in more lines. We converted a bedroom into an office. Our whole lives became dominated by the crisis.

It was the same for Rob Hayward and Joanna Copley. The London operation soon merged with Bristol and moved into, firstly the Connaught Rooms, then Alexandra House, in the West End. There, they had several large rooms with fax machines, telephone lines, computers, refreshments, and even a Reuter line. Soon afterwards, we set up the Gulf Support Trust to handle donations and help pay some of the enormous expenses of running a support group. From the beginning, we all had a nagging feeling the hostage crisis could turn out like the Terry Waite episode, lasting for years. It added further imperative to our work.

For us all, those months represented day after day of no sleep, no rest, no escape from worry or dealing with the thousands of problems people had. Families caught over here on holiday had no money, no houses, no clothes, no jobs. Their children couldn't go back to their schools, they had no uniforms, no winter coats, and they met with lack of understanding from government departments. Although many had grandparents who could offer support, and those months brought many families very close together, they felt desperately alone.

People rallied around. Dozens of volunteers put in hundreds of hours of work. I found immense joy at being able to give to so many people and being of help to them. There were so many mothers, fathers, brothers, wives, sisters, friends, and children suffering. We were all having to make such desperately difficult decisions. When the women and children were able to leave Kuwait in September, many were hopelessly torn at leaving their husbands behind. Families were shattered. Lives were torn apart and destroyed.

Even when the men followed their families out in December, their problems weren't over. In fact, for many, they were just beginning. Once the new year began, we started getting phone calls and letters from relatives of soldiers and civilians in Saudi Arabia and other Gulf states, anxious about their relatives and friends, so our work still hadn't finished, even then. As all the other helplines had been closed down, we were forced to struggle on alone.

For those who had undergone a particularly bad time, things deteriorated over the next six months. We found ourselves having to offer counselling and advice on housing, finance, benefits, and a plethora of other issues. Our work never seemed to stop. I had to tour the country talking to people, counselling them, trying to help them readjust. It was evident that there were many hidden problems.

It was important to get help for these people and so Stephen and I drew up a report into the emotional and psycholgical after-effects in an attempt to get a centre set up to deal with post-traumatic stress. Meanwhile, a medical report into the trauma of the hostages and those in hiding was conducted by Drs Easton and Turner, which discovered that most had suffered from loss events, many had been traumatised by witnessing people being tortured or shot, and some had been raped or beaten up. For them, the struggle to regain some normality is still, even eighteen months after their release, going on. Eventually, trauma centres were established at the Maudsley and Middlesex Hospitals.

As the crisis was unfolding, I began to realise how important it would be to record what we all were all going through. Stephen and I took detailed notes, kept all letters and information and I began a detailed diary. After the hostages had returned and the Gulf War had been fought we were able to catch our breath. I approached Tim Lewis to write a book on the people held hostage and in hiding, their relatives and friends, and the work of the Gulf Support Group. We have now worked together on it for a year, to produce what we hope will be a fitting testimony.

One point that stands out for me is that, no matter what colour of skin people are, no matter what religion, nationality or culture, that crisis united human beings. Whilst the world was tearing itself apart preparing for war, whilst people were being maimed and a tiny country was being torn asunder, there was one heart-beat of humanity still alive. The work we were all able to achieve through the Gulf Support Group, by giving aid and comfort to thousands of people in deep distress, the comfort, the counselling, the consoling, stands out for me as a spark of human warmth and spirit which gives me such hope for the future. I hope this thread of love will continue to grow and that every person, everywhere, in their own way, will always remember the pain of separation, persevere to make the quality of life for us and our children strong, and make this world a place of love and peace.

My great wish is that this book will help the people caught up in the Gulf Crisis find the peace and strength to go forward with their lives. I also hope that world leaders will learn from it that hostage-taking serves no useful purpose whatsoever. In fact, it only firms people's resolve to fight against it at all costs. There have to be other ways to solve major disputes without using innocent men, women and children to achieve political gain.

Above all, this book its a testimony to the strength and suffering of the people who endured the hostage crisis. They have received no other national recognition, although they suffered a higher rate of casualties - six out of three thousand - than were suffered by British forces in the Gulf. As a result, 50p from every copy sold of this book will go towards a memorial at Coventry Cathedral, to commemorate the members of the human shield who died and the suffering we all endured during those four terrible months in 1990.

Finally, I would like to give a personal thanks to my husband, Stephen, who has borne with me and whose strength and hope guided me through the crisis.

Notes on the Text

Throughout this book, the terms 'hostages' and 'human shield' have been used, not just to refer to those captured by the Iraqis and put into installations, but to those who were forced into hiding as well. They were as one. Many spent time both in hiding and on strategic sites. Several installations were actually in Kuwait, some of them in the heart of the city. Crucially, the Iraqis allowed those people in hiding to stay in the emirate because they were an effective human shield against attack in Kuwait. The Iraqis billeted their soldiers in blocks they knew housed foreigners, or in schools near to villas occupied by foreigners. Their troops were dispersed amongst the civilian population, which acted just as much as a shield as those at dams or armaments factories.

Arabic names are notoriously difficult to translate into the Roman alphabet. Many places have a variety of spellings, even on road signs in their area. Accordingly, this book employs the spellings used by the Kuwaiti Ministry of Information, as printed on their maps of Kuwait.

Contents

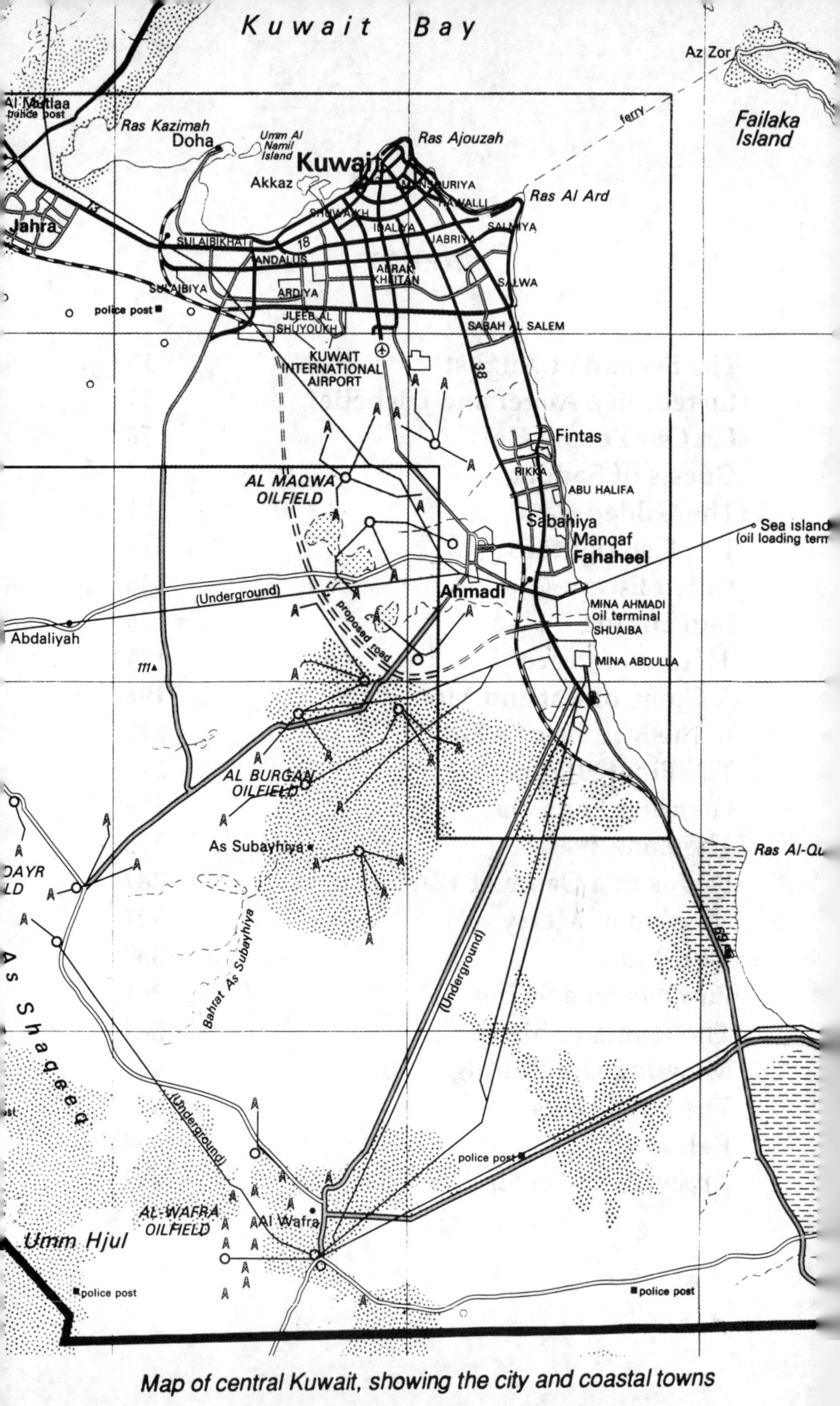

Map of central Kuwait, showing the city and coastal towns

The Second of August

"He was distracted by a rumbling noise to the north. It grew louder and louder for five minutes, before the first of a huge column of tanks emerged around a bend and clattered and squeaked past him in continuous file... The Iraqis were moving forward as fast as their tanks could carry them."

"The British embassy in Kuwait is instructing British nationals in Kuwait to keep their heads down. As in most countries, there is a contingency plan to evacuate British citizens in Kuwait in a time of crisis. We are not looking to put that plan into effect."
A Foreign Office spokesman, Thursday 2nd August

At ten-thirty on the morning of 26th July 1990, Josie Brookes was desperate to find her close friend Eric Watson. He and his son Tim were due to fly out to Singapore to rejoin his wife, Wen Li.

"I've got to find him. I've got to tell him. He mustn't go. He just mustn't go."

The urge of the premonition engulfed her as she drove from work to the flat in Coventry where he lived. She speeded up. Once there, she threw the car into the nearest parking space and rushed to the security door. She waved frantically to someone inside, who opened it for her, as she swept past and banged repeatedly on the button for the lift.

"He can't go. It's too much of a risk. Something's going to happen to the flight, I know it. You can't just pack up and leave everything. It's too final."

The unchangeability of it swept over her. She pushed into the lift and repeatedly pressed the button for Eric's floor. The doors wouldn't shut. When they did, the lift was so slow. Someone else stopped it and entered. It seemed an eternity before she reached the right level and was able to run to his door. She paused for a second to catch her breath, then rang his bell - long and incessantly. As she waited, she flicked her ginger hair back into place.

"Oh, come on Eric. You mustn't go, you mustn't." She rang again, even longer, then knocked hard. The effort calmed her slightly.

She knew that how she was feeling and acting was very strange. She knew Wen Li was waiting for Eric, that he had a bright new life as a musical director in Singapore, that he desperately wanted to be out there with her. "Oh, he'll hate me for this," she mumbled, staring up at the ceiling. "Come on, come on." She knocked again. Leaning her back on his door, she picked nervously at a nail. Turning and bending, she peered through the letter box. But no one came. The flat remained silent. "Oh, Eric, there's something very wrong. Delay it, delay it. You can't go. Listen to me!" She screamed this out, as if he could hear it, then looked through the little slit in the door again. "Oh, God, he's not there. What'm I going to do?" She felt so stupid and so defeated. She slipped down onto her knees and cried.

Westinghouse Radome was about three times the size of a barrage balloon and was sited at Abdaly on the Kuwait-Iraq border. It was flown high into the sky, tethered by wires and communication cables to an information station on the ground. Being a highly sophisticated observation post equipped with radar, infra-red and other imaging devices it had direct links to both the Kuwaiti government and to satellites. It gave the Kuwaitis visibility eighty to a hundred kilometres inside Iraq. For a week now, they had observed whole units of Iraq soldiers moving into position and columns of tanks deploying just across the border.

The night the Iraqis invaded, the staff manning the information station could see everything that happened. They watched Iraqi sappers and reconnaissance groups coming across the border in the late evening of 1st August. They watched the Iraqi armour start rolling several hours before midnight. They watched lorries and coaches full of troops driving straight across the desert and down the Basra road towards them. A Frenchman was working with the Kuwaitis. He warned them what was happening but, in his own words, "And what did they do? They stuck their fingers up their bottoms and just sat down."

The tanks streamed across the border down the road to Jahra, followed by the troops. They came straight past the radome at Abdaly, leaving it in their wake, not bothering to destroy it. They had no need to. They knew the Kuwaiti army was unready, that most of its Chieftain tanks were stood down and that no foreign troops could arrive in time. They were supremely confident of an easy victory.

The landing was perfectly normal - as everything appeared at that early hour - except, it seemed strange that there were no other planes in the airport. Some passengers disembarked to stretch their legs in the early morning dark, waiting for the plane to refuel, change crews and take off again. The cleaners came on. Eric Watson and his son Tim stared out at the lights of the terminal building before trying to get some more fitful sleep. David and Claire Shattock and their family, James and Natalie, also tried to sleep. David worked for British Airways and knew the airport terminal well. There was little to do there. Maureen Chappell dozed off, her head leaning on her husband John's shoulder. He was a senior electronics engineer and the whole family was going out with him to his work in India. For half an hour everything was quiet and calm.

At about five-twenty Maureen was woken by an air stewardess.

"I'm sorry, but can you all leave the plane?"

"Why?"

"It's just a routine precaution. We might be delayed here a little longer than usual." She was deliberately calm and non-committal.

In fact, the relief pilot, Captain Peter Clark, announced that the airplane would be delayed for two hours. Barely five minutes later there was an explosion as a bomb landed near them and rocked the plane. The captain immediately told the passengers to disembark. He was horrified to see fighter aircraft bombing and strafing the runway and the military airfield in the distance.

"Can you all leave the plane as quickly as possible," the stewardesses instructed. A hasty announcement came from the captain over the tannoy. "Will everyone leave the plane immediately and calmly."

The people on the plane didn't need telling twice. They hurriedly clambered down the plane's steps and ran across the tarmac to the terminal. As they headed towards the lights and glass of the modern departure lounge, two jets screamed low in the distance, followed by a series of dull thuds and flashes against the early dawn horizon. There was a strong smell of burning.

"Oh, heavens, the engine's on fire," Maureen Chappell complained to her fifteen year old son John. "We'll be here for hours." She held the hand of her daughter Jenny tightly. But it was not an engine. It was cordite from the Iraqi jets bombarding the military air base on the far side of the airport. As they entered the departure lounge, more jets seared low across the dawn sky.

"Oh," Maureen added, out of breath, "that's interesting." She pointed to a shape in the distance.

"What is it?"

"I think it's a tank."

They began to run again and managed to reach the comparative safety of the building. But they still felt very vulnerable. The spacious lounge was surrounded by large, plate-glass windows, through which they could witness most of what was happening. The series of explosions, jets and flashes of light against the dawn sky continued as the Iraqis bombed the military airfield and attacked the retreating Kuwaiti units who were putting up stiff resistance to the south. The passengers were moved into a part of the terminal away from the glass windows. David Shattock remembers feeling a dull sense of unreality, as though it was some thriller on the television. He wasn't scared at that point, more deeply concerned, especially for the children. It was impossible to believe it was really happening - and happening to them. His son, James, and another boy started kicking a football around.

It was a quarter to six. The Iraqis had continued rolling across the Kuwaiti border since their first incursion at midnight. From the Westinghouse Radome and its own satellites, the Pentagon had known that a full-scale invasion was under way by two o'clock that morning. They had known the invasion was imminent before midnight, Kuwaiti time, as their satellite pictures showed Iraqi armour moving up towards the border. President Bush's advisers were called to the White House in the next few hours. The President was informed that an invasion had begun. Richard Haass, his Special Adviser, recalled how they were all in a state of alert from 8.30pm (Washington time, 3.30am Kuwait time), through until 2.30am the next morning. "What we had was, in effect, a running council meeting." By 10.30pm (6.30am in Kuwait), Thomas Pickering, the US ambassador to the UN, knew the invasion was under way and had also been called to the White House.

However, it would seem that the British government did not know, though that seems too incredible to accept, for it failed to inform British Airways of any danger in the region until much later. Its embassy in Kuwait was even closed for the Arabic weekend - Thursday and Friday - despite the obvious danger. By three o'clock, an hour before BA Flight 149 landed at the airport, an Iraqi column had reached Jahra, eighty kilometres inside Kuwait and barely twenty from Kuwait City, having just encountered the first real resistance from some Chieftain tanks as they came down Mutlaa Ridge. At 3.10, Kuwaiti diplomats had informed Reuter of the invasion, so the Foreign Office must have known soon after - an hour before the plane landed. Half an hour before the plane came in, Iraqi helicopters had landed at the Emir's palace and fighters had attacked a key communications centre near Fahaheel, twenty kilometres south of the airport. As the plane was cleared to land (in itself incredible), Iraqi troops had entered the city and were taking over the Defence Ministry, and the Kuwaiti royal family and government ministers were fleeing. Kuwaitis in the Ministries were destroying their computer records and files.

Everyone in the country had ID cards, including all foreign nationals and all members of the Kuwaiti armed forces and security forces, with their fingerprints, blood samples, addresses, home addresses, work places, and personal details and photograph. If the Iraqis had gained possession of them, it would have been a disaster. A copy of the electoral registers were taken out of the country, to preserve records of property ownership and prevent a massive expulsion of Kuwaitis and replacement by Iraqis and Palestinians, similar to the Nazi treatment of the Poles. As the plane taxied along the runway at 4.20am and came to a halt by the terminal building, Iraqi tanks were within a few kilometres of the airport.

The flight had been over two hours late leaving Heathrow. It was bound for Madras and Kuala Lumpur, and due merely to change crews at Kuwait. As they waited in London, the pilot and co-pilot were certainly nervous about stopping there and checked repeatedly with ground control before leaving. Many of the passengers on the plane were aware of the Iraqi military build-up on the Kuwaiti border and were apprehensive. Ground control was in constant contact with the British embassy in Kuwait. Both gave the plane clearance to take off and no news of any invasion was relayed to them as they entered Kuwaiti air space although the Kuwaitis had known an invasion was imminent five hours before it landed and at least four hours, and possibly more, had passed since the Pentagon had known that Iraqi troops had crossed the border.

Maureen ordered her son John away from the window and drew the heavy curtains across it. Flight Captain Clark called everyone together. He told them he had phoned the BA operations room at Heathrow to inform it of what was going on. According to BA, it still hadn't heard anything from the British embassy or the government in London. He told the assembled passengers that Kuwait had been invaded and that the Iraqis were already in Kuwait City, but not to worry, as they would probably be allowed to leave fairly soon.

There were anxious questions from some of the passengers, most of whom were Indians or Malaysians on their way home or to visit their families. One shouted out, "Let's get out of here, before we're taken away."

"We can't," the pilot replied. "We have to wait for clearance."

"Is the plane ready to go?"

"Yes. It's been refuelled. All the joining passengers have been cleared through. If we'd been just fifteen minutes earlier we could have flown out, but now it's too dangerous. We've all seen the jets and tanks, but there could be ground-to-air missiles out there too. We can't take that risk."

Some passengers still wanted the plane to take off, but it would obviously have been suicidal. More Iraqi jets screamed over as they discussed the point. There were tanks around the perimeter of the airport and more were probably blocking the runways. They were trapped.

Meanwhile, the Iraqi government was busy issuing statements to explain the invasion. At 5.45am, Baghdad Radio announced that a group of Kuwaitis had launched an attempt to overthrow the corrupt government of the al-Sabahs and warned against foreign intervention. At 6.00am it declared that the revolutionaries had overthrown the Kuwaiti government and that Iraqi troops had entered the country to help the new rulers. At 6.30am, Reuter reported that Kuwait international airport was closed, after having been bombed.

As they sat around, most passengers tried to relax and not grow too anxious. Many were hoping, indeed joked, that the crisis would soon be over, that it was nothing more than a local takeover, a typical Third World coup. It may last a day or two, but they would soon be allowed out, once the fighting had died down.

Eric Watson stared across the tarmac. The plane was so near! It had been refuelled and restocked with food. The relief crew was ready. It would be so easy to board it and for it to taxi to the runway and be away. They could be clear of Kuwaiti air space within half an hour.

The passengers could do nothing but sit. Eric turned back to his son Tim and sat down beside him. He smiled and shook his head. He is a very affable man and soon fell into conversation with some other British people. Maureen and John Chappell tried to keep their two children's minds off what was happening by keeping them occupied. They had a pack of cards and played Snap as mortar bombs went off outside. After a while, the airport staff brought some telephones into the lounge for people to phone out. At that time, the international lines were still working. They broke out cans of Pepsi from the drinks machines and sandwiches from a kiosk to give to the passengers. Some stewards risked going back onto the plane to salvage it's overnight supply of food and drink, as well as the medical kit.

By now the bombing was much heavier. Mortar fire could be heard on every side of the airport. Tanks crashed through the perimeter fences. Others were shelling key buildings in the city to the north and east. A major battle was raging to the west and south as Kuwaiti forces tried to withdraw to the Saudi border and defend a military airport and missile site. The Chieftain tanks from the military academy in Jahra which had put up stiff resistance, destroying a number of Iraqi tanks as they came down Mutlaa Ridge, had soon ran out of ammunition and been forced to retreat. The rest of the Kuwaiti tanks, about a hundred Chieftains, were to the south of Kuwait, but hadn't been refuelled or stocked with shells. They took no part in the battle.

The passengers sat nervously in the departure lounge, trying to keep calm. Maureen hoped that once the Iraqis had secured the airfield and the fighters were no longer going over, they would let them get on their way. However, two hours after they were taken off the plane, at about eight o'clock, they were ordered to the nearby Airport Hotel. They didn't know by whom. They thought by the Kuwaitis.

As the passengers rose, they picked up their meagre possessions. Their baggage, with all their clothes and personal possessions, was still in the hold of the plane. Eric Watson blinked as they filed out to some waiting airport buses. The sky was quite light by now and it was already getting hot as they reluctantly clambered aboard. They noticed several platoons of soldiers with heavy machine guns around the terminal and digging in along the runway. Most thought they must be Kuwaitis preparing to defend the airport. They had no special markings, flags or distinguishing uniforms.

In fact, it seems, they were Iraqis. So quickly had they invaded and so ineffectual had resistance been from the Kuwaiti army, small anyway, much of it on leave, and the rest caught napping by an invasion on the eve of a Friday, the Moslem holy day, that within a few hours the Iraqis had taken the city and most of the country. The main resistance to the invasion had initially occurred in pockets. At the military training school near Jahra, at the royal palaces, at the naval base at al-Julayah, and the army officers' club on Misila Beach. Otherwise, the stiffest resistance was put up when the retreating Kuwaiti forces were engaged south west of the international airport, down to the Saudi border. One Iraqi column had swept in from the west, circling the city from the south, and had reached the coast road. It was now heading north into the city to try and trap the Kuwaiti army and royal family. However, some of the army escaped and most of the al-Sabahs had left hours before dawn, although at least two were still in the city, one leading the resistance in the Bayan Palace, the other a princess who spent the next few months in hiding in the city.

Cliff Lindley was woken early that morning by two jets screaming overhead. 'Damn Kuwaiti air force,' he thought. 'Can't they practice at more civilised times?' He was in charge of the design and modifications office with Kuwaiti Airlines and worked in a large block of offices within the international airport complex. He had been in Kuwait since 1987. As he dozed, thinking nothing more of the incident, his alarm clock ticked towards half past five, when it went off. He rose, as he always did, and after breakfast read the *Arab Times*. It had a headline on the Jeddah talks between Iraq, Kuwait and other oil states. Iraq was bitter about Kuwait over-producing oil and forcing its price down on the world market. It also had grievances over the border with Kuwait. During the Iran-Iraq war, Kuwait had pushed it northwards until it crossed the Rumillah oil field and promptly drilled a number of wells into it. Iraq angrily accused Kuwait of stealing its oil. But there was nothing unusual in the paper, nothing warning of an Iraqi attack. In fact, the article suggested the talks were starting to get somewhere.

As he drove from his villa in Mushrif, a suburb of Kuwait City, the few miles to the airport, Cliff noticed how few cars there were on the highway. He thought nothing of it. It was Thursday, the start of the Arab weekend, and was normally quieter than during the week. As he drove down the Sixth Ring Road he noticed to the west and south that the desert sand was being blown high into the air. This too seemed strange, as there was no wind.

Kuwait City is ringed by seven major roads linking the coast road in the east with the western suburbs of the city. The innermost one, the First Ring Road, skirts the city centre, whilst the seventh is twelve kilometres to the south, half way to Ahmadi. This dual carriageway comes down from the Jahra Road and sweeps eastwards, south of the international airport, to the coast road. It was of key strategic importance on the day of the invasion.

Cliff turned down International Airport Road, showed his security pass, and entered the airport. To his surprise, his was the only car parked there. It was not until he was in his office and had received a phone call that he was told the Iraqis had invaded. Several Kuwaitis had also turned up for work. One turned round and walked straight out when he heard the news and never returned.

"What's happened?" Cliff asked the other.

"They came about midnight. The airport runway has been bombed. You'd better get out of here." Cliff did so. He had not noticed a single soldier or tank on his way to work. Looking out to the airfield, he noticed machine gun emplacements and some armoured vehicles, but thought they were Kuwaiti. He was certain that the Kuwaiti army, which was well equipped and highly trained, though small, could keep the Iraqis at bay for at least for a day or two. It had a very good air force, stockpiles of missiles and had a reputation for efficiency. It was with the idea of sauntering back to his villa, stocking up with water, packing his things and filling his XJS with petrol that he left. 'Plenty of time,' he thought.

Fortunately, his wife Wendy and two sons were on holiday in Wolverhampton at the time. Only his twenty-one-year-old daughter Jane was living in Kuwait, where she worked. He drove to the bank at Misila, but the dispenser was shut. He went to another in Salmiya, and that was also closed. He finally found one open closer to the city centre. He had to queue at it for an hour. Then he queued for another hour at a petrol station, before getting back to his villa. By now, he noticed a lot of Kuwaitis leaving in cars or stocking up with food. He was beginning to feel more anxious and decided to buy some provisions in. He headed for the local co-operative. Mushrif is a Kuwaiti part of the city, as opposed to a Palestinian enclave or ex-pat area, and there were hundreds of local people queuing for food. In their usual, very polite way with Westerners, they waved Cliff through to the front and gave him more of everything than the locals were receiving.

It was mid-morning. Soldiers began to appear everywhere. Cliff, thinking they were Kuwaitis, waved to them and cheered them on. "Go get the b......s!" he shouted, raising his fingers in a victory salute. He drove back to his villa to phone his wife. The international phone lines were still open and he managed to reach Wendy. As he talked, the sky above him suddenly filled with helicopters flying low over the apartment block, roaring just a few feet above him, drowning out his voice. At the time he thought they were Kuwaiti. It was not until much later, in hiding, that he reflected that they, like the two jets which had woken him earlier, were in fact Iraqi. They were probably targeting the Bayan Palace, which was nearby. The palace, originally built as a conference centre, had been transformed into a residence for the Emir and his family. The Iraqis homed in on it straight away and it was one of the few places the Kuwaitis put up any resistance. It was guarded by the Emir's own National Guard and held out for several days. No-one came out alive. All surrendering Kuwaiti soldiers were shot. The Emir's brother was in there. His body was allegedly dragged onto the street and driven over by a tank. When Cliff next saw the palace, the gun emplacements on its roof had been blown away and several huge holes had been blasted through its walls, as if it had been pounded remorselessly.

Helicopters continued to buzz across the city, looking for cars or soldiers fleeing from the palace. The noise was deafening.

"There' helicopters everywhere."

Wendy began to cry with worry.

"Listen, we'll be OK. I have to get Jane's passport from the airport. The Kuwaitis'll keep the Iraqis out, don't worry." He couldn't hear himself speak at times, but again assured Wendy they would be all right and would try to get out of Kuwait if they had to. He rang Jane's number several times and eventually got through. He discussed the situation with her, still not realising the seriousness of the position, and told her he would drive back to the airport and pick up her passport. He had been organising a visa for her and had left it in his desk at work.

After putting the phone down, Cliff climbed into his car and drove back along the Sixth Ring Road. He had no idea that the airport had been taken by the Iraqis. At the junction with International Airport Road, he was stopped by a large body of soldiers, rifles pointing at him. Again, he thought they were Kuwaitis. They could be aggressive at times and wore the same indistinct battledress fatigues as all Arab armies. He pointed to his pass and explained in Arabic that he worked for Kuwaiti Airlines. They brusquely waved him through the traffic lights.

After a sharp exchange with the soldiers guarding the airport, Cliff was accompanied to his office and allowed to pick up Jane's passport. Once back out of the complex, he decided not to risk the soldiers on the Sixth Ring Road again. 'You never know with these Kuwaitis, they can be a bit funny,' he thought. So he drove along the motorway to the south, but this route took him smack into the middle of the main Iraqi column which had skirted the city to the south. It was even more heavily congested with troops. There were tanks everywhere, nose to tail along the road. Cliff counted thirty-two of them, before giving up. Once again, he waved to them, giving them the thumbs up. They were heading north, he thought, to defend the border with Iraq. There were no markings to tell him they were Iraqis, no flags, just small pennants on the aerials of the tanks.

He turned north up the al-Safr Motorway and rejoined the Sixth Ring Road. It was jammed with cars and trucks slowly trying to weave between lorry loads of troops. He saw a tank collide with a car and the car's owner jump out and start remonstrating with the hulk of metal. No-one bothered to appear from the tank and it simply rolled on past. Everywhere, people were arguing, shouting or driving on the wrong side of the street, in desperation to get out of the city. It took him another hour to make his way through the chaos to his villa.

Stewart Griffiths was not so fortunate to escape arrest. He and his wife Barbara had lived in Kuwait for five years. They were both in their late forties and thinking of retiring to Cheshire once Stewart had finished his latest contract.

Stewart worked on a group of oil installations on the northern border of Kuwait, near Abdaly. He left their apartment in Manqaf as usual at half-five in the morning, as dawn was breaking. He left the town and turned north along the motorway towards Kuwait City, turned onto the Sixth Ring Road and joined Route 73 to Jahra, a town several kilometres west of the city, on the main road northwards towards Iraq. It is a modern dual carriageway and is the main highway linking Iraq and Kuwait. It was the one the Iraqis had poured down at midnight in their old buses and troop carriers.

As Stewart neared Jahra, he noticed some plumes of smoke in the far distance. He thought little of it. At the approach to the town, some Kuwaiti police were directing traffic off the main road onto a diversion through the back streets. Stewart followed it round, eventually emerging just beyond the town. Nothing had been said to him by the police. He still had no idea that the invasion had actually taken place and that the Iraqis were already in the city. In fact, for the next few days, the Kuwaiti police continued to work directing traffic and patrolling. On some occasions, they actually directed columns of Iraqi tanks and troop lorries. It was not until several days after the invasion that the Kuwaiti police suddenly disappeared into hiding.

Stewart rejoined Route 73 and started the climb up Mutlaa Ridge, the long sandstone escarpment which overlooks the Bay of Kuwait and divides the city from the northern border of the country. He was soon flagged down by some soldiers. Again, he took them to be Kuwaitis who had set up a temporary road block. At first, the soldier spoke in Arabic, until Stewart crudely explained he was English.

"Where you go?"

"Abdaly. I work on the pipeline." Stewart showed him his pass. "The Umm al-Aish camp."

The soldier showed it to his officer, who glanced at the pass and handed it back to Stewart. He waved him on. Stewart drove to the top of the ridge, where he was stopped by some more soldiers.

"Off."

"What?"

The officer pointed to the keys in the ignition. A dozen armed soldiers encircled the car, their rifles pointing at him. He turned off the engine.

"Step out, please." The officer, wielding a pistol, pulled open the door. Stewart reluctantly climbed out, to find himself staring into the raised barrels of several semi-automatic AK47s.

"Go. Over there." He was waved around the front of his car and led to the roadside. Everywhere, soldiers eyed him suspiciously. Three Indian civilians who happened to work on the same installation as Stewart were there, and were just as perplexed and worried.

"What's happening?"

"We don't know."

Stewart turned to the Iraqi officer. "What's happening?"

"You are our prisoners. You have been captured."

"What do you mean, captured? Whose prisoners?"

"Of the Iraqi army."

"Of the...?"

"We have entered Kuwait to support the new Kuwaiti Revolutionary Council."

"The what?"

"The al-Sabahs are overthrown. The Kuwaiti peoples now rule Kuwait.

The great Iraqi Army, led by the great military giant the Saddam Hussein, has freed the peoples of Kuwait from the oppression."

"Oh, good heavens!" It suddenly dawned on Stewart what had happened. But not that he would be separated from his wife and not see or hear from her until December, other than over a crackling shortwave radio.

Looking back, both he and Barbara had suspected something was in the air for about a month. They had been aware of the large troop build-up on the Iraqi border and had suspected the possibility of them crossing if they didn't get their way at the Jeddah talks. But the speed of the invasion had taken them, and everyone else, completely by surprise.

The four prisoners stood around as Iraqi troops poured passed. On reflection, Stewart realised that the 'Kuwaiti' soldiers who had beckoned him through the roadblock at Jahra may well have been Iraqi, as there was very little Kuwaiti resistance in evidence. As he watched, two large grain wagons growled down the Abdaly road towards Kuwait City. They screeched to a halt just beyond him. Their backs were lowered and dozens of Iraqi soldiers jumped down and dispersed over the nearby scrub and desert, then headed down the ridge towards Jahra.

"What's going to happen to us? What'll you do to with us?" Stewart asked another officer. But all he heard in reply was, "Wait here, wait here."

He was distracted by a rumbling noise to the north. It grew louder and louder for five minutes, before the first of a huge column of tanks emerged around a bend and clattered and squeaked past him in continuous file. It was seven o'clock in the morning. They were seventy-five kilometres from Iraq and barely twenty from the outskirts of Kuwait City. Stewart was astounded at the rapidity of the advance. There was virtually no resistance. The Iraqis were moving forward as fast as their tanks could carry them.

The four prisoners were suddenly ordered into their cars and told to drive a couple of kilometres up towards Iraq. Once there, they were ordered out of their cars and told to kneel down in the desert. The soldiers were very impatient, their eyes were stern and their fingers nervously played on the triggers of their rifles. Stewart was very aware of how easy it would be to simply shoot them and bury them in some shallow desert grave. No one would ever know what had happened.

As they crouched, the flow of tanks went on and on, interspersed with armoured cars, battered lorries and coaches full of soldiers. Sounds of firing and explosions could be heard below the ridge and around the city. A group of captured Kuwaiti soldiers was being guarded nearby. More Arab civilians were ordered to crouch down with them. Stewart and the Indians were given a banana between them and some dirty water. A minibus came up from the ridge and an Iraqi soldier was carried out, covered in blood. He had been shot in the stomach. They commandeered one of the Arabs' cars. The driver was ordered to take the injured soldier up towards Iraq.

Stewart was kneeling in the desert for about an hour and a half. The sun was high and hot in the sky by now. They had no water and were unprotected from the intense heat. Still tanks and lorries thundered past. Small arms fire came from the south. An Iraqi officer pointed to Stewart's car. The middle-aged British man stood and said it was his, so was beckoned over.

"Take me down," he ordered, pointing towards the south. His English, as that of many Iraqi officers, was good. So Stewart drove him a few kilometres back down the road to a radio post set up on the central reservation between the carriageways of the road. Around it motorbikes with telephones were parked and soldiers relaxed. As Stewart pulled up by it, a squadron of Iraqi helicopters swept past, low across the desert, over the ridge and down towards the city. Suddenly, a Kuwaiti Mirage appeared to the west. It fired two missiles, both direct hits on helicopters, and veered sharply to the south as the Iraqis around the communications post opened up with their rifles and machine guns. For several seconds it was bedlam and Stewart was rushed towards a petrol tanker, where he was ordered to hide. He refused, not wanting to be burnt to death if it was hit.

As the firing continued around him, helicopters cascaded from the sky and exploded as they hit the desert. He tried to make a run for it and dashed into the desert. Two bullets whizzed over his head, so he stopped. As he turned, the Iraqi officer ran up to him and roughly manhandled him back towards the troop trucks by the road. He was pushed under one and told to lie still. There he stayed until the firing had ceased and the Mirage disappeared.

Those few moments were the worst in Stewart's life. He felt very close to death. As he talked about it nearly a year later, his body and voice were tense with nervousness. He shuffled about on the sofa, holding his neck, extending and retracting his arms, twisting his hands back and forth as he emphasised points, waving them, wiping back his greying hair, scratching his neck, crossing and recrossing his legs and wiping water from his eyes. His voice was crackly, interrupted by frequent sighs, and he seemed constantly on the verge of tears. For a man in middle age, the trauma of those few minutes was something he had never before experienced and which will never leave him.

He went on with his account. "The firing ceased. This officer told me to take him back to where he had been before. So I drove back. Again, I was told to crawl down in the desert. Maybe another hour went by. A couple of Turkish lorry drivers had joined us by now. We were all taken to our vehicles, each escorted by two Iraqi soldiers and organised into a small convoy of eight cars. We were told to proceed up to Abdaly, on the Iraqi border.

"I was petrified. I've never been so scared in all my life. Literally, I had no idea what would happen next. My mouth started going dry. I was just looking round wondering what I was going to do."

As they drove up to Abdaly, they passed several burnt-out tanks and some armoured personnel carriers which had careered into them. Near a petrol station another helicopter was burning so fiercely it had almost melted. The bodies of the crew were on fire. The Iraqis had brought up a bulldozer and were pushing the blazing wreckage off the road so the rest of the convoy could come down.

As they drove northwards, tanks were coming onto their carriageway to pass the obstruction. Several steered the other way and careered into a petrol station, knocking over the pumps, completely unconcerned about the damage they were doing. Soldiers were looting equipment from the offices of the ar-Rawdatayn water bottling plant, taking everything. They were coming out with typewriters, chairs, clocks, computer screens, water coolers, telephones, everything. These were not a rabble. They were front-line troops, supposedly disciplined. But the sight of such wealth was too tempting.

Eventually, the little convoy of cars reached the old Iraqi border. There was still a customs post on the Iraqi side but they drove straight past it, through Safwan, and ended up at a military installation. In the compound they were given some water. Stewart was asked for his passport. He explained that he didn't have it. It was back in Kuwait, as were those for the other prisoners. They were told they would have to go back to the border post and register that they had come through. So the eight cars drove back to the border and went through the farce of passport control. The Indians were allowed to go, but Stewart was held for what seemed ages. By four or five in the afternoon, only he and the two Turkish long distance lorry drivers were left. "We were told to get into the back of a covered wagon. I said, 'My car's there. It's a brand new car.' 'Oh, you come back tomorrow. Tomorrow.' So I climbed into this covered wagon and we drove maybe fifteen kilometres into Iraq, to a different military installation. There, the two Turkish lorry drivers were told to get out. I was told to stay in. I asked to see someone in charge."

An officer came out. "What is the problem?"

"If Britain's at war with Iraq, OK, I'm your prisoner, but if we're not, I want to see somebody from the embassy. My wife's in Kuwait, she's no idea where I am. She must be worried sick. I'm told I'm going back tomorrow. Is that true?"

"*Bookra, Insh'Allah, bookra.* Maybe tomorrow, God willing, maybe you go back tomorrow. Tonight we keep you, for your safety. We take you to our army camp."

As Stewart spoke to me, possibly going into such detail for the first time since it had happened, his wife Barbara sat listening. Much of it was clearly new to her as well. Like many hostages, they had found it very hard, if not impossible, to talk about the most traumatic moments they had gone through. Even at the time of the occupation, many men had tried to shield their wives from their worst suffering. Those separated from their families often wrote up-beat letters saying they were OK, despite going through an inner hell. When they were eventually let back home they still tried to hide it. But, instead of slowly drifting into their past, for some the trauma simply festered.

I felt that, even though it was hard for Stewart to talk to me, it did make him feel better, as though, at last, he was able to get some of this private, non-verbalised pain out of his system by sharing it.

The irony of his four months' captivity was not lost on Frank Kerfoot. He had been employed by the Kuwaitis as a unit operator at Doha West power station on the outskirts of Kuwait City, and during his internment the Iraqis shuffled him between Iraqi power stations.

Doha is a barren spot on a narrow peninsula west of the city. To get to it, Frank had to travel along the Jahra Road which lead, eventually, to the Iraqi border. On the 2nd August he had been due to finish his night shift at 6am, but his relief was late, not arriving until eight. By then everyone knew about the invasion and he was instructed not to leave until it was felt to be safe. That was not until twelve.

If he had left at eight, he might have made it home, but by midday the Iraqis were firmly in control and had set up their road blocks. Frank was stopped at one. Thinking they wouldn't bother with him, he flashed his ID card and tried to drive past. The Iraqi soldier ordered him to stop. He was illiterate, but handed the pass to his officer, who immediately realised Frank was British and ordered him out of his car. He was searched and the Iraqis went through his vehicle with great care. He had the barrel of a rifle pointing at his chest the whole time. They looked in the boot, under the seats, under the bonnet, in the glove compartment and even under the floor pan. Perhaps they thought he was a British soldier trying to escape, or was carrying arms for the Kuwaiti army.

Meanwhile, helicopters blared overhead, swooping towards central Kuwait City. The palace at Dasman in the city centre was being destroyed by rockets and tanks blasting its walls with shells. Like the Bayan Palace, it was guarded by the élite National Guard and was a major centre of resistance. Frank was forced to cower under an Iraqi tank for two hours as more armour and troop lorries rolled passed. He was so close to his home! Why had they taken him? Iraq was not at war with Britain. Perhaps these illiterate soldiers believed he was a spy, or a fleeing Kuwaiti soldier. Why else would he be on that road at that time?

After two hours, he was marched off and forced to climb into a truck with a number of Kuwaiti prisoners of war. He was driven with them to an occupied military installation in Basra. They were held under armed guard with semi-automatic rifles pointing at them the whole time. At the barracks, they were taken to a room. It was like a cell, devoid of furniture except a wooden billet, with bare walls and no windows. They were given nothing at all to eat, though some water to drink. Panic swept through him. He realised they *had* mistaken him for a Kuwaiti, but in plain clothes, and thus a spy. He could be taken out and summarily shot. He had heard so many rumours of Iraqi brutality during their war with Iran, he believed them capable of anything.

"Hey!" he shouted at the Iraqi guards in the cell. "I'm British! I'm a

British citizen!" He went up to them to emphasis his point, but they took no notice. They simply swore at him and told him to wait for the officer to arrive.

Nabil and Marie[1] arrived in Kuwait four days before the Iraqis invaded. They moved into Nabil's parents' flat in the Salmiya district of Kuwait City. It was a moderately sized apartment to accommodate his large family. It had two bedrooms and two living rooms. In it were Nabil's parents, one of his sisters, his brother, his brother-in-law and Nabil and Marie. The block of flats was not what Marie had expected of Kuwait. The one blessing it had was air-conditioning.

The couple's delight at being in Kuwait lasted less than a week. On the day of the invasion, Nabil was woken early by a phone call from his brother, who strongly urged him to go out and buy plenty of food.

"Why?"

"The Iraqis have come. They're in the city already."

"You're kidding me. Stop playing games." He put the phone down and went back to his bedroom. Out of curiosity he strolled over to the window and pulled back the curtain. Outside, hundreds of people were running to the shops, shouting and squabbling in queues which were already long. Nabil stood there horrified as the reality of the situation sank in. "My God, Marie," he shouted. "We're at war!" He ran to tell his mother, who refused to believe him. They turned the television on, but it was the normal bland programme of dancing and folk singing. By that time it was about half-nine. The whole family was roused and were phoning friends to find out what was going on. One of the people Nabil phoned was an acquaintance who owned a jewellery shop. But he couldn't talk to him.

"Why not?"

"Because there' hundreds of Iraqi soldiers around. All the shopkeepers are closing their shops and packing away their things. I have to get my jewellery out before they take it all."

Nabil put the phone down, mumbling to himself, rambling, "This is war, this is war." His staring eyes betrayed the confusion of his thoughts. He had no idea what to do.

Nabil's father reacted more quickly. He realised they needed to stock up with food immediately and instructed his family to visit the supermarkets. Marie went too, agreeing to wear an *abaya*. It was so awkward, she soon wished she hadn't. The hood kept slipping off her head and she repeatedly tripped over the front of it, causing people to stare and laugh at her.

By mid-morning the shops were jam-packed and some had closed their doors against anyone else getting in. They eventually found a grocer's selling rice and decided to stock up with it. As they queued, helicopters swooped overhead, heading for the Bayan Palace. A Kuwaiti

[1]Their names have been changed.

flag lay in the dust of the road. Nobody dared touch it, not even some Kuwaiti soldiers who were standing around watching the queues. These soldiers even refused to shoot at the helicopters, which were flying low over the apartment blocks. They had given up the fight completely.

The family's search for food was not very successful. Fortunately, Nabil's brother brought his van around at about twelve o'clock. It was full of fresh fruit and vegetables. Once they had unloaded it, the two brothers made their way onto the roof to watch the fighting, despite Marie's concern for their safety. By now, she was petrified, on the verge of hysterics. She wrote in her diary, "Bombs are going off around us. Planes are flying past. It's been quite scary. Sue from work phoned, so did Mum and Dad. Today I want to go home."

Nabil was acting as calmly as he could, observing the fighting in the distance. Their apartment was situated close to the Gulf Road so the two young men could see the Iraqi tanks rolling down it into the city centre. They saw jets bombing and strafing and great plumes of smoke billowing up from the Dasman and Bayan Palaces. They watched as tanks pounded city centre buildings and shells exploded along the coast and beach.

Most of the initial fighting took place along the coast road and beach because the majority of the key buildings in Kuwait, such as the National Assembly building, the Foreign Ministry and Council of Ministers, were right on the seafront. The main road from Iraq entered the city from the west and passed the harbour, Seif Palace and state buildings. It then made its way straight through the central commercial district of the city, past the American and British embassies, before turning south east and eventually reaching Saudi Arabia. The first Iraqi column pushed eastwards along it into the city centre, whilst the second swept southwards to join it near Misila and enter the city from the south, effectively cutting the city off from the rest of the country. It was obvious to the two men as they stared in bitter amazement, that the fighting was not going to last very long, the Iraqis had such superior numbers and resistance was so slight.

Nabil's father came in from a visit to Shuwaikh, an industrial area near the port and to the west of the city. He reported that it was full of Kuwaiti soldiers running away. None of them were putting up any resistance. Everywhere was packed with civilians trying to flee or get supplies whilst the Iraqis drove past in columns of tanks and trucks. They discussed whether to make a run for it as well, but the fear of being caught outweighed the fear of staying. A lot of Kuwaitis were being rounded up and dragged from their cars as they tried to drive away. Where they were taken, nobody knew, but to be a Kuwaiti on the streets of the city that first morning was extremely dangerous.

Bernice and Lawrence MacDonald had moved house from Mushrif to Bayan, just a few kilometres up the road towards Kuwait City, on 1st August. They awoke on the second amidst packing cases, rolled up carpets and assorted pieces of furniture.

Lawrence, in his early forties, slim, with slightly greying hair and burdened with a Liverpudlian accent, dug around for his shaving equipment. Once he had located it and blearily removed his stubble, he made himself a makeshift breakfast from whatever packets of food he could find. Soon afterwards he set off for work at the Arab Bank. He never made it.

As he drove along the al-Fahaheel Expressway towards central Kuwait, Lawrence passed dozens of tanks and troop lorries lining the route, facing northwards. Meanwhile, civilian cars were speeding recklessly southwards. The Kuwaitis were always bad drivers, but even they didn't usually drive over central reservations or down the wrong side of dual-carriageways. He was eventually stopped by what he took to be a Kuwaiti road block. The soldiers said nothing about what had happened. They simply informed him that the road ahead was closed and pointed him down a side street. They didn't say a word about the Iraqi invasion. Lawrence still had no idea what had happened.

Some way along this diversion he came across another road block. Once again he was diverted, this time along Arabian Gulf Street which ran along the Bay of Kuwait. Because it was a dual-carriageway he had to head south, away from work, until he could find a junction to turn around. To his horror, drivers on this road were behaving even more erratically. They were driving like maniacs, many in panic. As he waited at a red light, cars were hurtling past whilst others mounted the central reservation to get onto the other carriageway. They were deciding to drive south along the north-bound carriageway because it was largely deserted apart from tanks. Several smashed into each other. One hit a tank. Others were simply abandoned in the middle of the road, slewed across the lanes. Lawrence watched in utter amazement.

By now, the horizon was sullied by columns of smoke rising from the city centre. As he waited at the red light, cars zipping past him, one eventually drew up alongside. Lawrence leaned out of his window and shouted across to the driver.

"Hey mate, wha's going on?"

"They come, they come!"

"Who's come?"

"The Iraqis, they come."

Still Lawrence didn't understand. So what, he thought. If an Iraqi delegation had arrived, the negotiations over the oil price and possession of the Rumillah oil field could go ahead successfully. What was everyone worried about? There was more chance of a treaty being signed, more chance of peace. He smiled at the Kuwaiti. "Terrific!" he shouted.

"No, no, they invade!"

Lawrence went white. "Oh shit!"

Not far down the road was the Kuwaiti Officers' Club and the Misila Palace, situated between the Misila Beach Hotel and the SAS Hotel. It and several other buildings were ablaze and a major engagement was in progress. Once again, the National Guard was fighting to the death. Tanks were streaming northwards past him in a long column. He thought they must be Kuwaiti, going to reinforce the capital. In fact, it was the Iraqi column which had skirted the city to the south and was now entering the city along every major road northwards.

On seeing the troops, Lawrence actually felt safer. As he turned and drove northwards he passed the tanks and waved at soldiers whom he thought were Kuwaitis. He cheered them on from his car window, shouting out, "Go get'em lads, give'em hell!" He raised a clenched fist in solidarity.

Lawrence eventually reached Bernice after several diversions, road blocks and short-cuts. They sat sipping home-made wine, discussing what to do. There were too many troops around to risk attempting an immediate escape. They could be picked up at any of a hundred road blocks. The road south was heavy with armour and they had no idea whether the border had been sealed off or not. What confirmed their decision was a repeated broadcast the next day over the World Service from the Foreign Office warning them to stay low and not to risk crossing the border.

The couple tried not to panic. They decided that the crisis would soon blow over. It would only last a few days at the most. Tension had been rising for the previous few days and they had suspected the Iraqis might try to invade. As a precaution, Lawrence had made his mind up to transfer his savings into a bank in Britain after the weekend. Now it was too late. Even so they, like the majority of the British community believed, and this had been confirmed to them by the embassy, that if the Iraqis did invade they would only take the northern oilfield of ar-Rawdatayn and would stop at Mutlaa Ridge. They had never thought the Iraqis would take Kuwait City itself.

The phone rang. A friend was anxious about them, and relieved to find that Lawrence was safe. He said the whole of central Kuwait City was cordoned off, with fighting flaring up everywhere. As Bernice asked him what was going on, both she and Lawrence instinctively ducked. A flight of helicopters shrieked low overhead. Lawrence ran up onto the roof, followed by Bernice. They were in time to see about fifty - they counted them - Iraqi helicopter gunships circling the Bayan Palace and firing rockets into it. The palace was just behind them and the whole sky seemed full of gunfire and explosions as helicopters roared over and turned away. Several were hit. One came down in a fireball nearby, crashing into the road and exploding. The palace was being peppered with holes as rockets took out the defenders one by one.

Tom and Gilly Colclough were living in the Marafi compound, a group of apartment blocks between the Misila Beach Hotel and the Misila Palace, right on the beach front. They occupied a large villa owned by Tom's company, ICL. He was the country manager, so his house was a very pleasant villa in one of the nicest settings in Kuwait.

At half past five on the morning of 2nd August, Issam, one of Tom's workforce, rang him up.

"Mr Tom, it is on the news."

"What is, Issam?"

"You are right. They say it instead of the call to prayers."

"What is *who* saying?"

"The people from the North. They are here."

"For heaven's sake, Issam, *who* are *where*?"

"The Iraqi soldiers. On the radio. It calls all military people to the barracks from their holidays."

Tom only partly absorbed this confused news. Gilly had been woken by the call and he told her what he thought had happened. He rose from bed and switched on the radio. Everything sounded as normal. There were no special news broadcasts or even blank screens. Simply the usual religious calls to prayer. He made himself a coffee and lit a cigarette. What should he do?

There was no point in panicking. He didn't know either how well the Kuwaitis would resist or how far the Iraqis would push. He briefly considered escaping immediately, but had his staff and Carmen, their Filipino maid, to look after. They must remain his chief responsibility. He discussed heading for the border with Gilly, but she wouldn't go. She wasn't prepared to leave all their possessions for someone to rob. Some in their group of villas did flee as soon as they heard the news that first morning. A number of Americans who worked on the al-Wafra oilfield close to the Saudi Arabian border had no hesitation in going south across the desert tracks and escaping.

Misila Beach was soon crawling with Iraqis and there was heavy fighting less than a kilometre away at the Misila Palace. It was obvious to Tom that they would have to find a safer place to hide quickly and tried to think of somewhere. It was not easy.

Once taken, the palace and the entire stretch of Misila Beach became a key strategic area for the Iraqis who feared an invasion from the sea. The Iraqis had themselves used a marine invasion to capture vital positions in the centre of the city and further south along the coast. Several witnesses reported seeing an Iraqi marine commando land opposite the American embassy at two in the morning, close to the Seif Palace and key ministry buildings.

At the beginning of July, Tom and a senior British army officer, a general who had worked in military logistics for Kuwait in 1963 and was a member of ICL's defence systems department, were discussing the possibility of an Iraqi invasion. They went over what had happened when the Iraqis had last tried to invade but been repulsed by a combined British and Arab force. This time, the general believed that, once the Iraqis had amassed seventy-five thousand troops on the border, they would move in. They would thrust through Jahra before sweeping around the city in two columns, one along the Jahra road towards the city centre and the other flanking to the south along the Seventh Ring Road.

So concerned had Tom been about the Iraqi build-up that by mid-July he had finalised an evacuation plan for his staff in Kuwait. Tension had been growing daily in the region. Although there were talks going on, Iraqi belligerence was unsettling. A few days before the invasion he had contacted the British embassy and co-ordinated with them a visit to the northern border. He had gone to check on troop movements and the state of Kuwaiti readiness. When he had returned he had reported back to the embassy. From what he had seen, it was clear that the Iraqis were moving artillery and tanks into emplacements from which they could move into Kuwait. That had been on the twenty-seventh of July.

Not only did the British embassy in Kuwait seem to have this information, it presumably had satellite pictures of the build-up from the Americans and access to the constant stream of information from the Westinghouse Radome. Within a few days, thirty thousand Iraqis became a hundred thousand, clearly preparing to invade. The embassy didn't warn its community. Although it did tell the embassy wardens to stock up with food and water, it told the wardens *not* to pass this on to the community. It felt confident that the Iraqis, if they did invade, would only come as far as Mutlaa Ridge, and not enter Kuwait City. According to several Britons there, it even told people not to worry because the Iraqi build-up "is just a training exercise".

I asked Tom what he thought of the British embassy during the weeks leading up to the invasion, considering he had been working so closely with its staff.

"Hopeless. My senior contact there had no idea of the significance of the information I was imparting to him. I repeatedly warned him, *'This invasion is going to happen.'* A few signals went backwards and forwards, but the embassy was sceptical. 'There isn't any evidence that the Iraqis intend to move in,' the staff told me. 'We're not getting any signals from the Iraqi troops which suggest they are going to invade. There's no evidence of any military activity.' It wasn't surprising. It is normal military procedure to observe radio silence before a major operation. Even when they came in, the Iraqis used few communications. The manoeuvres had been preset, there was no need to talk over their radios."

"Had the embassy staff gone home for the weekend?" I asked Tom.

"Yes. There was an answering machine on." He laughed nervously. "Incredible, isn't it."

"Did they rush back when they heard of the invasion?"

"You're kidding, aren't you?"

I wasn't, and the point was made.

Just as the general had predicted, the Iraqis swarmed over Mutlaa Ridge, took Jahra and split into two columns. But at Jahra and on the Seventh Ring Road they met heavy resistance. The major tank battle of the invasion started at Jahra and swept south of the international airport as the Kuwaiti tanks ran out of ammunition and withdrew. The Iraqis came across retreating Kuwaiti units pulling out from the city. There was a missile base, a military airfield and an army base, all of which came in for heavy artillery fire and air bombardment.

The Foreign Office admitted that both it and the embassy in Kuwait were caught completely off guard by the invasion. None of their personnel thought the Iraqis would cross the border, despite all the secret military information the Foreign Office was receiving. It was in a far better position to judge the situation than most ordinary members of the British community in Kuwait. Surely it could see the military build-up and could have warned people?

"Although we all knew there were Iraqi forces on the frontier," a very senior British diplomat in the Gulf at the time told me, "it was assumed that it was a piece of bluster." So nothing was done and the embassy duly closed for the weekend.

Eric and Tim Watson, Maureen and John Chappell and their children, together with the other passengers of BA Flight 149, spent the rest of that day and evening in the Airport Hotel. BA 149 was the only flight caught at the airport, although there were some passengers due out on a Kuwaiti Airlines flight that morning. The last flight before 149 to leave had been a flight from Delhi which had left the airport at midnight. They had passed that aircraft on the way into Kuwait, and the two pilots had actually conversed over the radio to check that everything was all right in the tiny Gulf state.

There were about three hundred and seventy passengers from the plane, plus the crew and their reliefs. Most were Indians and Malays. It was far too many for the facilities at the small hotel. Whilst modern and well-equipped, it was essentially a place of transit where people stayed for one night either before or after their flight. It did not have enough facilities for a horde of long-term residents.

The hotel was chaotic. Soldiers were everywhere, though nearly all remained outside, and most of the hotel staff had fled. Those who had stayed where frightened out of their wits. It was still not clear to the passengers whether the soldiers were Iraqis or Kuwaitis. In fact, they were Iraqis, who had no idea what to do with the foreign nationals they found themselves warding, nor how many rooms there were in the hotel. Normal Iraqi incompetence was exaggerated by ignorance and the numbers involved. Rooms were gradually allocated, but on a completely indiscriminate basis. The Chappells were lucky enough to get two, with enough beds for each of them, and the Shattocks had one for the four of them, but in some rooms people were sharing with total strangers, sleeping on the floors, four or even six together, or had to make do with a couch in the lobby.

This fiasco did show two regular features of the Iraqis. Firstly, their love of children and respect for the family. Because they were a unit, the Chappells automatically received better treatment. Secondly, it demonstrated the largely haphazard, undirected and capricious way the Iraqis decided things. The hostages were constantly at the mercy of their whims. And that, with these very professional soldiers waving guns, could be very, very scary.

Once they checked in and went up to their bedroom, Eric and Tim Watson made their way back downstairs to have breakfast. They hadn't eaten since the in-flight meal the night before. They found the dining room full of Iraqi soldiers and had to wait for them to finish. Eventually, they were ushered into the dining room for breakfast as more tanks rolled up and further groups of soldiers wandered in. The airport was obviously one of the most strategic installations the Iraqis had targeted in their invasion and was rapidly becoming one of the most heavily defended. Claire Shattock described her feelings of unreality. "As we finished breakfast, we saw all these tanks outside. We thought they were Kuwaiti, but someone said, no, they're Iraqi. We couldn't believe it. It was quite a shock."

The hotel was so crowded, there was not enough tables in the dining room for them all and the Iraqis asked people to stay in their rooms. The remaining hotel staff did the best they could for their 'guests'. With the aid of the BA crew, they served a good meal in the circumstances. They had boiled eggs, made bread and brewed coffee. Eric and Tim were starving and ate well, but some passengers, such as Maureen Chappell, were too apprehensive to eat.

Throughout that day, there were more explosions and gunfire going off, continuing from when they had fled the plane. None of the passengers were allowed out of the hotel. They had to sit around twiddling their thumbs, talking about the situation, passing the time. Some Malaysian consular staff arrived and took details of their nationals, but there was no sign of anyone from the British embassy.

The British passengers kept fairly quiet. The kids got to know each other. To them it was an adventure, and even the adults were not unduly worried. They thought the heavy military presence would quickly diminish and they would soon be back on the plane. Being in a hotel so close to the airplane, with the crews still with them, ready to fly out as soon as they were given clearance, reassured them that it would not be long before they were allowed to go.

Lunch time came and went. Again, it was an adequate meal in the circumstances, mainly rice and vegetables. They tried watching some television, but the English and Arabic programmes from Bahrain were jammed. When they eventually came on, they were long celebrations, full of cheering processions, dancing, music and songs. There was no news amongst it and the passengers had no idea what was going on outside the walls of the hotel. They were totally cut off.

Tim Watson found a tennis ball, but wasn't allowed to take it outside to play. Instead, he wandered the corridors of the hotel and stared out of the windows at the activity in the airport. Below him an Iraqi soldier stopped patrolling to rest against a wall and have a cigarette. He saw Tim and smiled. Tim waved back, with the tennis ball in his hand. The Iraqi saw it and indicated for him to throw it down. Tim did. The soldier threw it back up, and so began a game, tossing the ball harder and further, smiling, trying to converse in basic English and rudimentary sign language, until it was time for dinner.

After the meal, the passengers drifted off to bed and tried to sleep. In the morning, they had breakfast then sat around for more long hours. By now, the meals were being prepared by the British Airways crews. Only the cook amongst the hotel's kitchen staff hadn't gone into hiding. With having to feed hundreds of Iraqis as well, the food was rapidly running out. There was much less of a selection than on the first morning. There was no choice, just chicken pieces and they had to queue up through the kitchens to be served as in a school. But at least it meant everyone received something. From that day on, until their eventual release, food was a problem for the passengers. For the men, it was to remain so for four and a half months and was to get far, far worse.

The Iraqis finally let the BA crew return to the plane and get the hand luggage, but not the suitcases from the aircraft's hold. Whilst it meant that at least the passengers had their passports and documents, they still had none of their clothes. They had been in the same ones for three hot, sweaty, dusty days since leaving England and were starting to smell. Despite frequent pleading, the Iraqis refused to change their minds. The passengers were never to see their luggage again. It all went up with the plane when it was blown apart during the allied invasion the following January.

Most annoyingly of all, there was still no news coming in and no sign of anyone from the British embassy. On the first day, some phone calls had reached the hotel, and some had got out. Occasionally, the tannoy would call people to the phone. But after that first day they dried up. None were from the embassy.

On the day of the invasion there were seventy-seven members of a special force of military advisers and technicians, the British Liaison Team, plus their families, stationed in Kuwait. It was not a functioning military unit, but a low-profile group of army and air force men including the Royal Signals, Royal Electrical and Mechanical Engineers (REME) and RAF personnel attached to the Kuwaiti armed forces. They were out there to service Kuwaiti military equipment, especially a hundred or so Chieftain tanks, and to train the Kuwaiti armed forces. They were all Warrant Officers or above. Their numbers had dwindled over the years, until there were only a handful left. Their commanding officer was Colonel Bruce Duncan. He, like most of the senior officers of the team, was not stationed in the camp but was living with his wife, daughter and two teenage sons, Alex and Rory, in civilian accommodation. They shared the Mazuk Pearl Building, a big block of flats on the sea front in Salmiya.

The rest of the team, about thirty-five men and their families, were stationed in a comfortable, converted oil workers' camp, known as the IBI camp, situated in the centre of the main Kuwaiti oil refinery, close to the terminal at Mina Ahmadi on the coast road, half way between Kuwait City and the Saudi Arabian border.

The invasion came as a complete shock to the British soldiers and their families, especially the speed of the take-over. They had been given no warning and were given no instructions to escape. The Iraqis only reached the camp on the second day of the invasion, as they pushed south towards the coastal towns and the Saudi border. The shock was rapidly merged with frustration because they had known of the Iraqi build-up and many of them suspected something might happen. Some had even asked the Kuwaitis if they could 'bomb up' the Chieftains with fuel and shells, ready for immediate action, but had been turned down.

According to one warden, a few days before the invasion the BLT men had been instructed by the embassy to stay in the IBI camp to help with the evacuation of British personnel in the event of an invasion. Otherwise, they would have been out of Kuwait before the camp was overrun and, in the event, they were unable to give any help. What was even more frustrating for them was that they had two high speed motorboats waiting on the shoreline which they could have used at ten minutes notice to evacuate the whole camp. On top of that, they had a host of four-wheel drives they could have used to escape across the desert.

Many British caught in Kuwait felt the embassy must have strongly suspected an invasion, despite its denials. And there are certain questions its position leaves unanswered. Did it receive *none* of the tactical information from the Kuwaitis or the satellites? Did it *really* imagine 100,000 heavily armed Iraqis on the border posed no more than a threat - "sabre rattling" as one Foreign Office official put it? Why did it instruct the British Liaison Team to help with an evacuation if it didn't believe Iraq would invade? And why did it warn its wardens to stock up with food and water?

The team had close and friendly ties with the rest of the British ex-pat community. There had been a sailing club operating from the nearby shore for years. A scout group was based there, and there were close links both through the clubhouse in the camp, the golf club at Ahmadi and the children. The camp held a disco on Wednesdays, so parents from outside the camp would take their children down on the Wednesday and let them stay over with their friends on the Thursday/Friday weekend.

The weekend of the invasion, one of the families was having a birthday party and disco, so had invited a whole number of children to stay overnight in the camp. The eldest was a lad of fourteen. On the third, one of the first places the Iraqis moved into was the oil terminal and the IBI camp, so these children were trapped there, away from their parents, surrounded by armed Iraqi troops and tanks. When all the men were taken away the next day by the Iraqis, the fourteen-year-old boy was the eldest British male on the camp. Their only contact with the outside world and the rest of the community was through a few wardens, including Mike Devey, who kept the embassy informed about their situation. Otherwise, the camp was cut off. Some parents of the children staying over in the camp had no idea what had happened to them throughout the first month of the crisis, until they, like their mothers and siblings, were allowed to go home. It was an extremely worrying time for them all.

Fortunately for the officers up at Salmiya, the Iraqis believed they had captured the entire British team. They were unaware of the others living in the city. Those men and their families were able to go into hiding and most managed to avoid capture. Those who were caught were able to convince the Iraqis they were normal British civilian contract workers. Some felt Salmiya was to unsafe and moved into other areas. All were helped in some way by the Kuwaiti Resistance, as well as by the wardens and embassy, who were very anxious to keep them out of Iraqi hands.

Some British decided to flee Kuwait immediately they realised the scope of the invasion. On the day of the invasion, Ian McDonald, an oil rig worker, went to work as normal. There were no Iraqis around that day but, by the next morning, Friday the third, there were Iraqi troops everywhere. After returning home and discussing the situation with his wife Eleanor and friends, he decided to leave with their twenty month old son Scott, and a handful of other Britons.

"We went into the office on Friday morning. That was the first time we noticed troops where we were living. From what we saw in the area where we worked, the Iraqis had moved into it in force. We knew they would have to start foraging for food, and once they started to come into the homes, it could lead to some pretty nasty situations. We weren't so much frightened as, visualising the situation a few days ahead, could see that we might not have an escape route. We tried to persuade others to come with us. There were several British and Australian families in the large block where we lived and we spoke to most of them. Some decided to leave and some decided to stay. It was a personal decision we all made. The invasion took everyone by surprise. No-one had a clue. On Wednesday evening, I was confidently saying there was no way the Iraqis would come in. It took everyone by surprise."

There was a great deal of confusion about whether the border was closed in the first two or three days. There still is. Different people give different stories. Some tried and were turned back. But many more were successful. Amongst those who made a dash for freedom on the first afternoon of the invasion were a number of Americans who dodged numerous roadblocks and columns of tanks as they sped south.

Rumours and reports were rife. To many, it seemed far safer to stay where they were rather than run the risk of being shot or held in the desert for days. However, there were definitely routes out. Even several weeks after the invasion people were escaping. GEC Matrix organised a successful convoy of its workers. A group of sixty Americans managed to escape. Some crossed without visas or passports. Thousands of Kuwaitis were fleeing. So many were coming through that the Saudis dispensed with border formalities in order to cope with the flood.

Within a few hours of the invasion the United States consulate in Dhahran sent staff to the Saudi Arabian border with Kuwait to meet people escaping. By Friday morning they had been joined by Canadian, European and British missions. There were no hotels anywhere near the border region and the British consular team arrived with camping equipment in case of a lengthy stay. The situation seemed so confusing to them and the staff in the Kuwait embassy that they advised the Foreign Office to warn people not to attempt to cross the border. Because of that advice, a British diplomat in London issued the following statement: "We are advising people in Kuwait to stay put." The World Service put out the Foreign Office's position that British citizens should not attempt to cross the border, but should remain where they were, and "keep their heads down". This decision was to cause a lot of resentment amongst members of the British community who felt that, otherwise, they could have escaped. They were to have four and a half months to dwell upon it.

The Foreign and Commonwealth Office (FCO) tried to explain its position. "There was the question of whether people should stay in Kuwait or whether they should be advised to try and get out. We thought about this very carefully. So did the embassy in Kuwait. And we concluded that it was just too risky to advise people to leave. We knew people were getting into their cars, the resourceful ones particularly. Those who had four-wheel drive vehicles were getting into their Land Rovers and so forth, and shooting across the desert. Most of them got out to Saudi Arabia. We reckoned it was just too risky to advise people to do that. We came to the conclusion that to give people that advice would, frankly, have been irresponsible. If we had said give it a try, it would have been a signal to the Iraqis to police the border extremely vigorously. Also, there would have been some who were not really equipped to make the journey and who would have got into serious trouble. And, of course, we know that there was at least one tragedy. Mr Crosgery was shot."

The Foreign Office insists that the Iraqis had declared the border closed the day of the invasion, which it had. However, that was extremely wishful thinking on the Iraqis' part. The border was virtually impossible to patrol until masses of Iraqi soldiers and armour had been moved in. Furthermore, the Iraqis were very anxious to placate Western governments, so were being very friendly and waved people leaving through the border posts. Unfortunately, the Foreign Office listened to the Iraqi announcements, taking them at face value, whereas the reality of the situation was quite different.

The advice to stay put in Kuwait is severely criticised by a great many of the community who felt the embassy had rapidly lost touch with the reality of the situation. Many of them had to watch thousands of Kuwaitis and other nationals flee the new, 'legitimate', 'democratic' government of Kuwait to the Saudi border, where they were allowed through without the need for customs checks, visas or even passports. Typical of those who escaped were a group sixty Americans. But hundreds of others made it across the border. Despite the Foreign Office advice to "stay put", those who did make a dash for safety were able to get through, where they were met by British consular officials from Dhahran. Nor did they need four-wheel drives, because many of the escapees were heading straight down the main road. Although road blocks were being set up, most people were not being stopped.

Nor is it legitimate to use Mr Crosgery's death in support of the case for staying put. Doug Crosgery was not shot until two weeks into the invasion when, essentially in response to the American and British determination to oppose the annexation, the United Nations sanctions, and the start of the military build-up, the Iraqis replied by closing the border. Not only was it this build-up which completely changed the Iraqis' initially very friendly attitude to Westerners, but it was the prime cause of the border being effectively sealed, not a few thousand Westerners making a bolt for it. In the first few days, the Iraqis believed they would get away with the invasion. They were anxious to portray themselves as responding to a call from Kuwaiti democratic fighters who had taken power. They wanted to appear civilised and compassionate to the rest of the world. They repeatedly said they would withdraw within a few days. Although this was undoubtedly bluff, it was reflected in the soldiers' attitudes. In the first days, they were actually waving people through the border posts. Even up to the sixth, it seems, the main road south was clear and people could drive straight through.

However, the FCO could still foresee people being killed. The community tended to blame it for taking a decision. In fact, quite a few of the British in those first days didn't take the invasion seriously. They stocked up with food and water but otherwise, for some, it was a joke. It would all be over in a few days. There was nothing to worry about, and certainly not to panic over. Their attitude was to stay calm and ride the storm. The one thing Doug's death did do was change all that. "It took away the holiday atmosphere and made people realise it was serious," explained one Briton who remained in hiding until he was caught in November. But by then it was too late for most people.

Ironically, Doug's death didn't stop people planning escapes, but rather made them more desperate to get out. Unfortunately, organised convoys and mass escapes were by then virtually impossible; the Iraqis had started arresting people and taking them to installations.

On reflection, most members of the British community feel that no advice would at least have let them make their own minds up. It was the fact that the Foreign Office was giving the advice, not just the embassy, that carried such authority. People felt it must know something they didn't. In fact, it knew less. Should it have admitted its ignorance, decided to give no direction, and let people make up their own minds?

"We could have given no advice, but generally, whenever there's a crisis, people reckon that it's one of the duties of an embassy to give advice. It's not unreasonable that people should want advice. They don't have to follow it, and very often they don't. But the embassy's advice is normally something people take into account. We aren't all-seeing, we aren't omniscient. Sometimes people have better information than us. Those who knew the area well, who knew the desert tracks, who had confidence in their vehicles, were obviously in a better position to run for it."

Miriam Saleem was a British woman who had married a Kuwaiti. Her son was serving in the Kuwaiti armed forces, where he was guarding the main naval base at al-Jilaya. He was blond, blue-eyed, thirty-three years old and had received his military training in England. During the midnight hours of 2nd August, three Iraqi Atika class gunboats from al-Faw naval base sped down the straights between Bubiyan Island and the mainland and attacked the port at about three o'clock in the morning.

Jamail Sultan Saleem and the others on guard opened up with their heavy 30mm machine guns, taking out two of the boats and twenty Iraqi marines. The Iraqis managed to land about two hundred more men on the beach, but the Kuwaitis held up their attack for three hours. Finally, the invaders brought up heavy mortars and blasted Jamail and his comrades to pieces. But they had been delayed enough to allow the Kuwaitis to bring up several of their Saracen armoured vehicles. These now pounded the Iraqi positions and kept them pinned down near the beach and port.

His mother Miriam was not to know of his death until the summer of 1991. She prayed for his safe return every day until she heard the news.

Incredulity, Anger and Disbelief

"...for most of the relatives, the news came as if in a bad dream, enhanced by it arriving in the early hours. It spent days whizzing around their heads unable to get out. They struggled on in communal shock..."

For the relatives in Britain, and those on holiday across the world, the news of the invasion of Kuwait was nothing less than devastating. Whilst people trapped in Kuwait knew they were relatively safe if they stayed indoors, those out of the country had no idea where or in what state their loved ones were. It was not knowing, and not being with them in their hour of desperate need, which made the situation so impossible.

When Lynda Pickup rose from bed that Thursday morning and switched on the TV for the news, she "went bonkers". Her husband, Barry, was due home from Kuwait that very evening, and the whole family were going on to Spain for a holiday.

"I went mad. Just like a maniac. I threw everything up in the air, went running out of the house, round and round the garden screaming, over to the neighbours, screaming, screaming, 'They've invaded, they've invaded!'"

Her neighbour hadn't a clue what she was talking about. Once she had calmed Lynda down, she tried to reassure her. "He'll be all right. He'll come home tonight or tomorrow."

But, "Oh, my God! Oh, my God!" was all Lynda could say. She couldn't drink the tea offered her, she couldn't think about anything else or do anything else. Her mind was totally dominated by thoughts of Barry. Where was he? Had he gone to work? Had he been picked up? Would he get out? "Oh, my God, I'll have to cancel the holiday. They won't give us our money back. They won't. We've lost it all."

"Don't panic. It'll be all right. Don't do anything hasty. Don't cancel anything yet."

"We won't get our money back. They've got a get-out clause, in case of war. Well, this is war, isn't it!"

She suddenly thought Barry might be trying to phone. With one final, "Oh, my God!" she dashed back to her house. She didn't move from the living room all that day or night. She didn't stir from the settee, not even to open the curtains. She watched every single news broadcast, trying to glean every scrap of information, trying to find out whether the airport was closed or not, how far the Iraqis had entered and whether many people had been killed.

Would Barry make a dash for it? Foreign nationals were escaping across the border, and some Britons who had left Kuwait the day before were interviewed as they arrived at Gatwick. Lynda pulled the phone towards her, praying for a call. She lay on the settee, with her feet in the air, and didn't move. The shock paralysed her physically and emotionally. She wrote in her diary for that day, 'Iraq invaded Kuwait today. I... was devastated all day. Upset all day.'

"It's something I'll never get over, something I'll never, ever forget. It absolutely knocked me for six. It was absolutely terrible. I can't actually explain how I felt. I'd never wish that feeling on anybody."

At seven-thirty in the morning, Betty Stevenson's daughter phoned.

"Mum, have you heard the news?"

"No."

"Well, put it on. Iraq has invaded Kuwait."

"What?"

"Yeh. Go and watch it."

"Oh my God!"

As she flicked the set on and hovered in front of it, Betty's two grandchildren came downstairs. They and their mother were staying with her and her husband for part of their school holidays. Thomas was eight, Lucy ten. They came down to a spectacle of Iraqi tanks and soldiers swarming into Kuwait. Thomas gave out a high-pitched yelp.

"Mummy, there' tanks in Kuwait! They're going to get Uncle Andrew and Auntie Carolyn! Mummy! Mummy!" He was hysterical, screaming as he rushed to his mother in the kitchen. He idolised his uncle and appreciated the danger he was in, even more than the adults, who half felt that everything would be all right.

From then, the news was never off. Betty and her husband Andrew tried all day to phone their son and his wife, but all British Telecom would say was, "All lines into Kuwait are unavailable."

The same feeling of shock swept over Lesley Kerfoot as she waited in her new house near St Helens. Once she heard of the invasion she, too, watched the news constantly and phoned everyone she could think of for information. The news devastated her. Even a year later, she admits she is still coming to terms with it and feels it will take many more years before she has laid at least some of the ghosts to rest. As she sat in her armchair in the living room talking to me she was barely able to keep back the tears. Throughout the two hours she took to describe those awful months away from her husband Frank, her eyes glinted with water. Mine, too, at times, lost their self-control.

Her mind went wild; her imagination went out of control; her thoughts deepened, intensified and tossed her about. Where was he? What was he doing? He's all right, he can cope. What if the Iraqis capture him, or if he's trapped in a battle? What condition was he in? Because he had been in the army, Frank could look after himself, but that didn't stop her wondering repeatedly whether she would ever see him again. She knew how stupidly she was behaving, that she ought to remain calm, and she realised she was making things worse for herself. But it was like jamming on the brakes in a skidding car - she just went further out of control. Dozens of different scenarios flashed through her mind. For many relatives, that first day was like living a dream, because that was precisely what they were doing; their minds were dashing down one desperate day-dream after another.

After hours in front of the television, the phone by her side, she decided she must rush out and buy a newspaper. Not for the news, but for the TV programmes. She dashed to the car and sped through the housing estate. Once back from the corner shop, she took a highlighter pen and marked off every news broadcast on every channel, to ensure she didn't miss a single one. It was to become a routine for her - every morning, first thing - to get the newspaper and locate every broadcast and current affairs programme.

She didn't talk to anyone or eat anything that day. She watched the TV broadcasts until early in the morning, until she eventually fell asleep on the carpet in front of the screen, utterly exhausted.

Nicola Benwell had only been out in Kuwait for seven months when the invasion happened. She worked as a commodity broker on a two year contract with the Kuwait International Investment Company. But she became bored with it and had decided to return to England permanently on 9th August. She lived in Salmiya, in an apartment block just off the Gulf Road.

On the morning of 2nd August her husband, Andy Charles (he kept his maiden name when they married), was, in his own words, "Fast asleep, minding my own business". He was living in London where he worked as a press officer. At half six in the morning the phone rang. "Someone's pretty anti-social," he mumbled to himself as he pulled a pillow over his head. Someone else rang immediately afterwards. He didn't bother to answer it, just swore and turned over. It rang again. Still he didn't answer. When it rang for the fourth time, he grumpily climbed out of bed and staggered downstairs to find out what all the fuss was about. He switched on his answering machine to find all the calls had been people phoning to say Kuwait had been invaded.

Andy immediately decided to phone Nicola. He was eventually connected and, not being unduly concerned, they chatted away about the situation. He saw it as quite humorous, hardly taking it seriously at all. As they talked, Nicola peered out of a window of her apartment.

"That's strange," she told Andy. "Everyone seems to be looking up at this block."

"Why's that?"

"I don't know."

"Well, why don't you go out and see what's going on?"

She peered through the window, but couldn't see anything.

"Perhaps they're looking *beyond* your building," Andy suggested. "Go and have a look out of the kitchen."

She went off to see. The kitchen overlooked the road which ran along the coast. When she came back, she knew what was happening. "It's incredible. There' all these tanks rumbling down the Gulf road."

"Take some photos."

She rang off and did just that. Andy was not too worried, and neither was Nicola. As Andy explained, they both felt "It was just one of those odd things that happens, I suppose. We didn't think anything about it." He phoned her three or four more times that day to check on how she was, still not bothered. It was not until the next day, after the Iraqis had cut the international phone lines, that he began to take the crisis more seriously. It gradually caused him more grief as days without information turned into weeks and eventually into a month. He next spoke to her when she stepped off the plane at Gatwick in September and met him in the terminal.

You couldn't imagine a more pleasant and normal British family. Cynthia Hill and her three children live in a modern semi-detached house near Bolton. It is beautifully kept. The through living/dining room is full of ornaments from their travels. A Buddha and two green Chinese lions watch over them. Indonesian dancers and cases of mounted butterflies smile benignly. It is a cosy, homely, secure house, full of warmth and love. Yet the scars the family now bears might never heal.

Cynthia woke that first morning and heard the news of the invasion on her radio.

"Oh my God!" she swore. She pelted down the stairs and rushed into the living room to switch on the television.

The night before, Cynthia had heard the Iraqis were massing on the border. She had rung her husband Derek and told him. He had been totally unconcerned. He dismissed the threat of invasion. Even if they did come in, he certainly didn't believe it would affect him. He was staying at the SAS Hotel in Kuwait City whilst he completed a short-term contract which would soon have brought him home again. He was thirty-eight and a computer installation expert for a vibration monitoring firm. He was helping set up a computer for the Kuwaiti petrochemical company, PIC.

"Don't worry," he had told her. "Don't worry at all. I'll be perfectly OK."

Cynthia reluctantly went off to work that morning leaving her two daughters, Nyree and Rachel, and her son Jeremy at home. It was the school holidays. They were seventeen, twelve and thirteen respectively and well able to look after themselves. Before she went, Nyree reassured her mother that she would ring her father in Kuwait to hear how he was. Cynthia tried to play her own feelings down, but inside was praying that the Iraqis wouldn't be interested in him. She begged the heavens that it would soon all blow over and he would be home again. The last thing she wanted was to add to the children's tension. She smiled, kissed Nyree and told her not to worry.

"Phone me if you hear anything."

"I will Mum. I love you."

"I love you too."

The crisis preyed on Cynthia's mind all that day. Unlike the ex-pats, Derek had nowhere to hide. He had no friends in Kuwait. He knew no one. He was totally isolated. Nor did he have enough clothes with him for a long stay. He had gone out there on the Tuesday, two days before the invasion, with one suitcase and was due back ten days later. He was supposed to be attending a family wedding the day after his return. "That turned out to be an absolute nightmare because he was supposed to be back for it. That was pretty shattering."

Nyree was the last member of the family to hear from her father for nearly four months. She dialled and redialled, over and over again, constantly getting the engaged tone. But she wouldn't give up. For an hour she tried. For an hour and a half, for two hours, for two and a half hours, constantly redialling. Finally, at half past ten, she was connected. It was such a surprise, she almost forgot her father's name and room number. She fumbled around for it as the hotel receptionist waited. Once she found it, she was put straight through. Her father was surprised and delighted to hear from her.

As they talked, Nyree could hear gunfire and explosions in the background. Derek told her there were tanks rolling past the window and described something of what it was like. He assured her he was all right.

"I'll be fine."

"Come home Dad, please."

"I will, darling, just as soon as I can. We'll all be keeping our heads down, then we'll get out as soon...."

The line went dead. From that moment, Nyree carried with her an awful premonition that she would never, ever see him again.

Lollo Murthwaite is a Persian woman in her forties, married to Don Murthwaite. On 2nd August she was on holiday with her elderly mother-in-law at her house near Birkenhead. The first she heard about the crisis was when her phone rang at four in the morning. It was a friend calling from the United States.

"Have you heard?"

"No, what?"

"Kuwait has been invaded."

"Oh no, I don't believe it!"

"It's just been on the midnight news here."

Lollo couldn't believe her ears. Don, aged sixty-one and on the verge of retirement, was living in Fahaheel Towers, on the coast south of Kuwait City. Being so close to the beach and the coast road, the block was immediately surrounded by Iraqis digging in and tanks moving down the road to take up positions along the sea front.

Lollo immediately tried to phone Don in Kuwait but the lines were busy. She spent the rest of that night and the whole of the day worrying about him. She swung rapidly from deep fretting to reasoning, "Oh, don't be so stupid, he'll be fine." She phoned some friends. Whilst sympathetic, they couldn't understand what she was going through. Again, she tried to phone Don, but still with no success, and still she watched every news broadcast she could for information. There seemed so little of it, except for pictures of Iraqi tanks pouring across the desert. These she found extremely upsetting. Were the Kuwaitis resisting? Were there battles going on? Was Don caught up in the middle of it? Had he been captured, or killed? As the day grew, so did her anxiety. Her mother-in-law was getting increasingly worried and Lollo had to care for her as well. Those hours seemed to take an age to pass. Even minutes seemed to last for ever.

Eventually, Don managed to get through to his wife. By then, it was the next night, fifteen horrendously long hours after that first phone call from the USA. Lollo was already emotionally exhausted.

"Oh, don't worry," Don sparkled. "Everything's all right. I'll be fine. There's no shooting down here. Don't worry about me." He saw it as a joke, another of life's scrapes to build into a story for their grandchildren - nothing to worry about at all.

"Are there any soldiers where you are?"

"Some. But they're not bothering us." He deliberately played the danger down. "It's all quiet here. We're all fine. We're going to lie low for a few days. It'll all be over by then."

"I love you. Keep yourself safe."

"I will. Listen, I have to go now. Others are waiting to use the line. I'll keep in touch. You keep in touch as well."

"I will."

"I love you. Bye."

"Bye."

That was it. A very short call, with Don full of confidence and reassurance. It helped Lollo enormously. It was as if a great weight had been lifted from her shoulders. But that night she only slept fitfully.

Although they had both promised to keep in touch, the international lines had gone dead by the next day. Lollo wasn't to hear any news of Don until September, when some women brought letters from him when they were released, and nothing directly from him until late November.

As for Lollo, the news came to most of the relatives as if in a bad dream, enhanced by it arriving in the early hours of the morning. It spent days whizzing around their heads unable to get out. They struggled on in a communal shock which affected whole families, whole work places, whole groups of friends and relations. A crevasse split their subconscious in such a way their conscious blotted it out.

One woman was in a state of escalating shock: "The night before the invasion, I went to bed with the excitement of a schoolgirl. I had butterflies and finally fell asleep dreaming pleasantly. As I fell asleep, I listened to the weather outside, which seemed to be the biggest worry in my life at the time.

"The alarm went off at 6am and I enthusiastically jumped out of bed... As I began to dress, the radio news came on. I couldn't believe the news that Kuwait had been invaded... I remember lying on my bed in shock. I must have lain there for more than an hour trying to pretend the whole thing wasn't really happening. Then the heartache and the tears came. The pain and sorrow were to continue for a long time yet. Those immediate tears were only the beginning."

Her husband phoned her later from Kuwait.

"Are you going to try to get out?" she asked him anxiously.

"Oh, I don't know," he replied, casually. "I'll sort it out, don't worry. It's pretty quiet, not like a real war."

"You'd better get to the embassy."

"No, I'll have my lunch first."

For some, this unreality kept them cocooned in an almost light-hearted state. Many were able to continue in their normal frame of mind or even on a high for several days. Although most didn't realise it, they were in shock so deep their minds were cutting them off from the crisis as a way of surviving. It was telling them everyone would be all right, that it was a joke. Some even felt happy. Some even *laughed* about it.

The apparent nonchalance of many men phoning out of Kuwait that first day was the result of a mixture of factors. Firstly, they were anxious not to cause anxiety to their relatives. They realised they would be worried and wanted to reassure them that they were not in immediate danger. Secondly, they were getting very little information at the time and didn't realise the seriousness of their situation. Dubai TV was ignoring the invasion, Kuwaiti TV seemed, with only a few short breaks, to be pumping out its usual pap, and the British embassy staff had gone home for the weekend and left the answering machine on. Most thought it was only a comparatively minor incident which would blow over in a few days. There was very little fighting. What there was mostly took place in central Kuwait City, where few ex-pats lived, or in the desert. Gunfire was usually distant. They felt no need to panic. Those with holidays or weddings planned believed they would be out in plenty of time for them. Very few worried about money for their relatives or the children's schooling. Such problems were weeks away.

There was, however, a difference in response from people depending on where they lived. Those who *were* in central Kuwait and *had* witnessed the destruction of the Bayan and Dasman Palaces, the TV station and government buildings and who watched helplessly as Kuwaitis were being rounded up on the streets, were far more concerned than those in the remoter areas of Salwa, Fahaheel and Ahmadi where there was virtually no fighting. Later, this largely explained the differences in the depth people went into hiding. Those near Dasman, Shuwaikh, Bayan, or the central commercial district felt gravely threatened. Some had Iraqi barracks opposite them. Groups even had Iraqi units move into their blocks. Obviously, security was a matter of life and death to those people. But others in the quieter areas, often in villas surrounded by high security walls, tended to be so relaxed they astonished and angered those more desperately holed up.

Some British in Kuwait, in contrast to their anxious relatives, were so laid back, they were positively blasé. One, in the Plaza Hotel, central Kuwait City, recorded: "I woke somewhat earlier than normal to the sound of gunfire. Although I was sure there was the sound of bullets, my brain didn't register that an invasion was taking place by Iraqi military forces. It was only around seven o'clock, when I ventured downstairs to reception, that I began to realise the invasion was well advanced. I waited patiently for news of what we had to do. I tried to contact the embassy and my family by international call. The advice being given was to sit tight and stay indoors."

For Margaret Hanson, the realisation that something was wrong came immediately. She was asleep when the phone rang.

"Don't panic," the voice murmured calmly. It was her brother David Cunningham. "Iraq's just invaded Kuwait."

She woke from her sleepy daze with a start. "What?"

David explained what was happening, but that he was all right. He told her to switch the news on, then rang off.

Margaret clambered out of bed and, bleary eyed, staggered downstairs to turn on the TV. It was exactly 4am. The news headlines came on. The invasion was the top story - indeed, it virtually filled the entire news broadcast. However, it gave very few details about people in Kuwait and even news of the invasion was imprecise. Margaret sat with her mouth slowly opening wider and wider. Once the news was over, she made herself a strong cup of tea. Her husband came down and later her children. They sat watching news programme after news programme. Later that morning, emergency phone numbers came on screen and she phoned one of them. It was the Emergency Unit at the Foreign Office.

"Never in my life did I think I would have to ring an emergency number," she explained. Despite giving its number out for enquiries, the Foreign Office had no information. "They knew nothing. They knew no details - and weren't able to give me any hope either."

Margaret went on to explain how those first days felt. "We were due to go on holiday when we heard, just local mind. We still had to go, for the kids, but I had to phone the Foreign Office and other places I thought could help every day. It was an awful time. At first they weren't called hostages and we thought they would be released. We didn't think there was any real problem. We thought the foreigners would be allowed straight out."

One difficult task Margaret had was to tell David's mother the situation. She was an elderly and very frail lady who lived two hundred yards away. She was suffering badly from cancer, and the crisis was to do her a lot of emotional and physical damage. She worried constantly about David's health. She knew she was dying and every day prayed that her son would return to see her before she departed. It remains one of David's worst memories that he was unable to do so.

"When we heard they were going to be kept as hostages," Margaret continued, "well, that was terrible then. Especially as we had just found out David was diabetic. My Mum worried about his drugs all the time. The Foreign Office did say he would probably get his medication. I thought the Foreign Office was quite good really. I didn't want to hear rumours. The people I spoke to there tried to be as helpful as they could. We had a phone call from them that the Plaza Hotel, where David was Assistant Manager, was full of Iraqi soldiers, but that everything was still OK, there was no problem."

One of the many phone calls out of Kuwait on the 2nd August was made by Philip Long to his family. He was a member of a British Airways crew staying in Kuwait between flights. Phil told his family he would be all right, joked that he might be a bit late for the barbecue on Sunday, then rang off. One of the guests at the barbecue was to have been Rob Hayward MP. He was a long-standing friend of the family and knew Phil very well.

Another phone call from Phil five hours later was a different matter. Machine-gun fire and mortar explosions could be heard over his voice as he explained that there were Iraqi soldiers on his floor of the hotel, with tanks and army lorries outside. Although anxious, he still managed to treat it as a bit of a laugh. He thought it would blow over in a day or two, and that would be that. The reality of the situation was not to impress itself upon him, or his family, for several days. It took the developments over the weekend, with United States, British and French forces rushing to the area, and Saddam's equally belligerent response to make people realise the seriousness of their predicament.

Phil's family phoned Rob Hayward several times that weekend, asking what could be done, increasingly worried that no one seemed to have any information. By Sunday, four days had passed with very little news emerging. The television picked up on the few Britons in Kuwait who had risked running for the border, or who had been leaving anyway. It mentioned that the thirty-five British Liaison Team advisers arrested at the IBI camp had been taken to Baghdad, but offered nothing other than speculation about other British nationals, and was totally silent about the passengers of BA Flight 149.

On Monday night, Rob was driving home from his office at Westminster. He was listening to Radio 4 as he crossed the Chiswick flyover. The PM programme was interviewing Dorothy Croft from Matlock in Derbyshire on the problems facing the relatives of those trapped in Kuwait. Rob later found her number through the BBC and rang her that night. He discussed the problem with her and they agreed both to set up a helpline and that he would appear on the Today programme the next morning, if the BBC were interested.

The BBC agreed, keen on the cachet of having an MP. From the BBC's Bristol studios he described the position the relatives found themselves in and, taking his heart in his hands, gave out his home phone number as a contact point for an information line. That was at ten past eight in the morning. He went directly home, a journey of maybe half an hour, and there were already nineteen calls on the answer phone. Rob didn't manage to contact those first nineteen until he had unplugged his phone at quarter past eleven that night. "It was literally like that. Picking the phone up, putting it down, picking it up, putting it down, picking it up... It wasn't a case of waiting for the phone to ring, it just rang. The next day I received a delivered message from British Telecom which said they were installing a second line. They had been monitoring my phone line and had discovered I was losing thousands of phone calls an hour."

From that first day, people started volunteering their services. One had worked in Kuwait for several years and knew it well. Another couple had a daughter married to a Kuwaiti. Another was Sue Brownlow, who was due to play a major part in running the Bristol helpline throughout the crisis. Their aim at that time was simply to put each caller in contact with others facing similar problems or in the same geographical area. It was to help them to escape their isolation, their sense of being forgotten and feelings that their agonising was unique. It was to reassure them that many others shared their worries and to bring them into touch with those others. Of course, any information Rob received from British Airways, the Foreign Office or the government he would pass on, but at the time it was very difficult to get hold of any.

Rob used the phone to build a network. The vast majority of people wouldn't know other people in similar circumstances. Even the relatives of long-term British residents in Kuwait had frequently lost contact with them or didn't know other relatives here. In some instances, the husband's parents had never met or contacted the wife's parents. Such people were, in many cases, to build relationships out of the crisis where none had existed before.

Rob had no other intention than the very specific and limited one of building local networks of people in contact with each other, with a national centre to disseminate any information that came in. It was not a support group, nor even a helpline, simply a point of initial contact. It was to turn from this stuttering start into a massive operation.

Stephen Brookes came over, saw Josie's face as she listened on the phone, and wanted to know what was the matter. All his wife would say was, "My God, Wen; My God!" At the other end, Wen Li cried out the story of her efforts to get news of her husband, Eric Watson. Josie listened and tried to comfort her. Images of Eric's farewell flashed before her. His smile. A kiss and hug from his son, Tim. Tears. Regrets. Well-wishing.

She had thought about their flight as they had taken off, followed it in her mind and presumed they had arrived safely in Singapore. She remembered helping them pack, moving their furniture, loading their car. Upstairs they had a single bed Eric had given them. He had even given Stephen power of attorney to sell his flat.

Josie listened and tried to comfort her friend. British Airways had phoned Wen Li as she was about to leave for Singapore airport to meet him and told her Iraq had invaded Kuwait. At first, she hadn't understood. Only when she was told Eric's plane had been held up there as it refuelled and changed crews did she realise the implications.

Josie promised to do everything in her power to find out what was happening. Stephen, picking up clues from her eyes and words, was hopping about. As quickly as she could, Josie put the phone down and confirmed Stephen's fears to him. They were both overwhelmed by shock, stunned by the impertinence of Saddam, stung into an anger so frustrating it built into an explosion by the end of the day.

From the minute the call ended the couple started phoning frantically. They called everyone they could think of. Stephen turned on the TV for Ceefax. They tried every contact they knew. The local MP, Coventry Cathedral where Stephen was a volunteer, the BBC, British Airways, the Foreign and Commonwealth Office, friends, relatives, anyone.

When people suddenly find themselves victims of a major world event, who do they turn to? Who do they ask? Who is there to help them? **The fact that there was no one able to give reliable information is a fundamental criticism of the way the relatives and friends of the hostages were treated during the crisis.**

Stephen had bought *The Independent* that morning. When he had first glanced through it, the Gulf crisis had seemed but one story amongst many. Now he read every word intently.

"Iraq Warns West Trade Ban Puts Hostages in Peril," he muttered. The United Nations embargo on Iraqi goods had begun in earnest and the Iraqis were already using foreigners trapped as bargaining counters. He read the article to Josie.

"Thirty-five British servicemen taken by the Iraqis from Kuwait to Baghdad and thousands of Westerners living in Kuwait..."

"Thirty-five British servicemen? What will happen to them? They've just been captured and taken off. How could Saddam do such a thing?"

"It says here there are three thousand British nationals working in Kuwait."

"Three thousand? Oh my word! We have to do something for their relatives. What must they be going through?" Josie went over and read out an updated message on Ceefax. "The new government of Kuwait has said all foreigners and Kuwaiti nationals are free to leave for Iraq, for any reason whatsoever, using the land route. The airport has been closed."

"Then the flight must still be trapped there."

"Oh Stephen, those poor people. What on earth's going to happen to them?"

"Ah, it says here," Stephen read on from the newspaper. "Thirty-five British servicemen have been taken to a hotel in Baghdad. The British chargé d'affaires visited them yesterday and reports that they are OK... And down here they're called hostages..."

"That's exactly what they are. They're using them as hostages to break sanctions." Josie scanned the next page of Ceefax. "Oh, look. Ministers said Britain will continue to use diplomatic pressure to gain the release of the hostages. One minister said, 'There is very little we can do apart from keeping up the diplomatic pressure and hope they are released when things quieten down.' That doesn't sound very determined, does it. Er..." She read down the screen. "The Foreign Office has dismissed the threat of using British hostages as pawns. 'If this is the threat it appears to be, it is totally unacceptable.' Oh dear."

"This article says British frigates are going out. And they're sending missiles and jets."

"It's getting completely out of control. I can see this going on and on you know, Stephen. It'll just go on and on, building up and up into a terrible war. You mark my words."

"It's going to be a bloodbath. We've got to get Eric and Tim and all the others out of there, now! Now - before it's too late. Saddam's already threatening them. He's already using them as pawns. It says there on the television; he's using them to thwart economic sanctions. Look," Stephen added, "What's that? The new 'Foreign Minister' of 'Free Kuwait', Walid Saud Mohammed Abdulla, said on Iraqi radio, 'Countries which resort to primitive measures against the Provisional Government of Free Kuwait and fraternal Iraq should remember that they have interests and nationals in Kuwait'."

"Oh dear."

"If these countries insist on aggression against Kuwait and Iraq, the Kuwaiti government will reconsider the methods of dealing with these countries. These countries should not expect us to act honourably at a time when they are conspiring against us and our brothers in Iraq in an aggressive way."

"Look, there are three thousand British in Kuwait and two thousand in Iraq. Think of all their relatives!"

Further details of the thirty-five British military personnel taken to Baghdad emerged that day, splintered amidst other news. As part of its disinformation effort, Baghdad insisted it was only temporarily occupying the emirate. As Iraqi troops were actually digging in along the coast and the Saudi border, Baghdad announced it was beginning the withdrawal of its invasion force. In fact, Iraq now had a hundred thousand troops and three hundred tanks in the emirate. Its generals sent a few troops on ludicrous circling manoeuvres to persuade the rest of the world it was pulling out, whilst sending reinforcements in. They also set up the Kuwaiti Popular Army, which began recruiting amongst Palestinians and formed a ragged vigilante force, most of whom rapidly turned to looting. Meanwhile, American special operation and hostage rescue forces were said to be on their way to Saudi Arabia, along with three aircraft carrier battle groups.

The UN had responded very quickly to the invasion. On the first day, it had passed Resolution 660 condemning the invasion, demanding immediate and unconditional withdrawal and calling on Iraq and Kuwait to start intensive negotiations to resolve their 'differences'. Four days later, on Monday 6th August, it passed Resolution 661. This called for all member states to prevent the import or export of any products from Kuwait or Iraq, or the supplying to those countries with anything except foodstuffs on humanitarian grounds. Strict sanctions were imposed on supplying Iraq and Kuwait with any funds whatsoever, and a committee was set up to monitor the implementation of the resolution.

On that same Monday, Josie and Stephen decided to inform the local *Coventry Evening Telegraph* about Eric Watson. They explained who Eric was - a former musical director of the Belgrade Theatre in Coventry. The paper was very keen to cover the story and genuinely anxious to help in any way it could.

The reporter questioned them over the phone. He acquired their wedding photo and splashed 'Dad and His Boy in Iraq Ordeal' across the next day's front page. Underneath, the story concentrated on the BA flight. "The Foreign Office was today trying to discover the whereabouts of British passengers on the jumbo jet trapped in Kuwait since Thursday's invasion by Iraq. They were rounded up yesterday from hotels in Kuwait City by one invasion force and were reported to be being taken by bus to Baghdad." The report that the passengers had been taken to Baghdad turned out not to be true, but that in itself demonstrated the virtual news blanket which had descended.

Every local paper in the country carried stories of hostages in those first few days. Josie's local radio stations, Mercia Sound and CWR both wanted interviews and were anxious to help. She was very nervous of doing interviews at first, and Stephen handled the first dozen or so. But once she had grown in courage, she responded from her heart. She told them the crisis "made her so mad", that she was "stunned by the news", and that she "couldn't believe what was happening". Like other relatives and friends, she felt totally powerless. It was frustrating having nothing but rumours to feed on. This madman - as many began to call Saddam - had taken their husbands, sons, daughters and friends and was using them as pawns in a game of war. With so little news, her mind worked overtime. It made things up, imagined scenarios of Eric and Tim thrown into a cell, being beaten, or starved. All sorts of silly, irrational thoughts sped through her mind, chasing each other around and around, feeding on her fears, petrifying her.

"The Gulf crisis deepens. As the United Nations prepares to agree sanctions, Iraq rounds up hundreds of Westerners." Pictures of the fifteen members of the United Nation Security Council in full session are shown over the Channel 4 News headlines.

Josie and Stephen, like tens of thousands of other relatives and friends of Britons, not just in Kuwait and Iraq, but throughout the Gulf region, were glued to the screen. For many it was their tenth, or even twentieth, news bulletin of the day.

As the newscaster delved deeper into the story, his voice carried over pictures of an oil line. Iraq had cut one of its pipes through Turkey. Then, over a scene of the stock exchange, he explained its fear of oil prices going up. "Petrol here is rising ten pence a gallon."

"All the world's interested in's petrol prices," Josie complained. "Not in people. It's the people they should be worried about, not their stupid oil."

Under the title 'Upping the Ante', the report switched to the United Nations vote on sanctions, to pictures of the US fleet and to President Bush's hardening attitudes to the invasion. Over the weekend he had moved from a very defensive, non-committal stance of, "We're not discussing intervention, we're not discussing any military options", to a much more determined statement: "This will not stand, this aggression against Kuwait".

The United States Defence Secretary, Dick Cheney, was pictured flying to Saudi Arabia. He was followed by pictures of Saudi Arabian air bases, James Baker announcing a trip to Turkey and a whole list of top level military interventions and blockades. The broadcast then switched to Iraqi reactions, announcing civilian evacuation drills in Baghdad and doing an analysis of Saddam Hussein's motives and tactics.

As the Iraqi president's portrait lingered on the screen, Josie looked deeply at it. She concentrated on his eyes. They were so sparkling and even seemed kind. His face wore a smile as he looked up, doubtless to a glorious future for both himself and the Iraqi people. He was such a handsome man, she thought. A man whose face she would get to know so well, it would haunt her. From that very moment, Josie felt she was locked in struggle with that one man, and her own happiness would only return when he was defeated. "It felt like a personal battle between Saddam and me. I know it sounds silly, but that was what it was like."

The report moved on to a press conference with President Bush Margaret Thatcher. "The news from the United Nations and the strength of the vote... is very good," the British prime minister told the cameras. She emphasised her "condemnation of the action of Saddam Hussein in invading Kuwait. Japan also condemned it very strongly, and so did the Soviet Union." She used the word 'condemn' again and, in a very strong tone, refused to use Saddam's title of 'President'. Her anger over-rode such niceties.

Josie and Stephen watched every news bulletin that evening, even following them into the early hours of the morning, anxious for any fresh news. There was none. First thing the next morning they put the TV on and switched to Ceefax. To their amazement and joy, there was, after pages of news about the United Nations, a small piece on a national helpline for relatives of passengers on British Airways Flight 149. It was being run by a Conservative MP in Bristol called Rob Hayward. Stephen jumped to the phone and immediately rang him. It was engaged. He tried again. Then again. Still it was engaged. Finally, Stephen heard the ringing tone. Immediately, the phone was picked up.

"Hello, the Gulf Helpline. How can we help?"

"Oh hello. You must be very busy. I've been trying for ages to get through."

"It's mayhem here. Impossible. There are so many people phoning we've not enough time to breathe."

"Is that Mr Hayward?"

"It is."

"My name's Stephen Brookes. A friend of mine and his son are on Flight 149. I wondered if you had any information on it. No one seems to know anything. I've tried BA, I've tried the EPIC emergency number at Heathrow and the Foreign Office, but none of them knows anything."

"No, the Foreign Office knows less than we do."

"Do you have *any* information?"

"Very little at the moment. Some people escaping from Kuwait and a few of the resident community there have phoned us up with details. We know the passengers of the flight have been taken to hotels in Kuwait City and some might have been taken to Baghdad. Some might have been taken to a camp in Kuwait. But from all our reports they seem to be all right. We're trying to reassure people that they're not in any danger. Listen," He paused briefly before moving the conversation on. "Could you contact some people for me and act as liaison for the Midlands?"

"We'd be delighted to." He gave Rob Hayward his details and the MP in turn gave him a list of phone numbers to contact.

And so it started.

Josie phoned Wen Li back and gave her all the information they had and began phoning the names Rob Hayward had given them. Those few phone calls were to turn into thousands.

Let Our People Go !

"to comfort, console and inform"

"UN orders total trade ban against Iraq. Thatcher condemns Hussein for seizing Britons. Petrol prices soar as Gulf crisis deepens. The ANC ends its armed struggle against white rule."

"Good morning. The news from TVam on Tuesday 7th August. The United Nations has ordered a world-wide trade boycott of Iraq as President Hussein seizes nearly four hundred Westerners in Kuwait. They're the toughest economic sanctions ever imposed by the UN in its forty-five year history. Meanwhile, Mrs Thatcher, who has just arrived back at Heathrow from her talks in the United States, has strongly condemned Iraq for taking the Westerners, including two hundred Britons, to Baghdad. At home, the Gulf crisis has added up to ten pence to the price of petrol. Our first report is from Anthony Dworkin in Washington."

"As she prepared to leave Washington, the Prime Minister said she was making every effort to obtain the release of British citizens being held by Iraq."

[Margaret Thatcher] "Civilised nations will observe the rules with regard to citizens of other countries, and I hope that they will be observed in this case. The world will make its judgement on any country which does not act in accordance with international law and the rights of free peoples."

....

"In Baghdad, President Hussein is said to have warned an American diplomat that shutting off the oil to Iraq would provoke an attack on Saudi Arabia. And yesterday a new American battle group left harbour to join those in the Middle East. According to Mrs Thatcher, the growing fleet of international warships could be used to enforce a blockade of Iraq if sanctions aren't effective..."

"As the world waits to see how Iraq responds to the United Nations sanctions, teams of diplomats in Iraq and Kuwait are working towards the release of the four hundred Westerners seized by Iraq yesterday. Our Middle Eastern correspondent, Tony Birtley, reports."

"The fate of the four hundred Westerners, two hundred of them believed to be British passengers from the BA flight, now lies with Iraq's leader Saddam Hussein. They were rounded up yesterday and taken to Baghdad, [This turned out not to be the case, but a deliberate Iraqi ploy to deceive Western media and governments. It was the latest of many such disinformation schemes by the Iraqis.] raising fears that they could become hostages in this ever-worsening crisis. Meanwhile, the thirty-four [sic] British servicemen flown out of Kuwait to Baghdad on Sunday are still being held. There's new evidence to suggest Saddam is building up his forces rather than withdrawing them. According to American intelligence sources, Iraq now has ninety-five thousand troops and three hundred tanks dug in along the Kuwaiti border with Saudi Arabia, maintaining fears of a further offensive by Saddam. In response, America is to send more warships to the Gulf. France has also diverted a frigate from the Mediterranean to join the British and American warships already steaming towards the Kuwaiti coast."

....

"The sister of one of the British Airways passengers taken to Baghdad claims not enough is being done to secure their release. Cheryl Welsh now reports."

"Katharine Copley is thought to be one of the BA passengers now being held in Baghdad. Her sister Joanna in London, dependent on the Foreign Office and BA for news, is frightened at Saddam Hussein's motives."

[Joanna Copley] "I worry that she may be there for a very long time, because I think he'll use her and other people on that plane as pawns in a power game..."

"Well Joanna, I do hope you get some news soon. What are your plans for today?"

"I've given my telephone number to British Airways. I'd like to form some sort of support group or pressure group for the families of passengers on that flight, so if they'd like to contact me, my phone number's here and it's also with British Airways. The next thing I'm going to do is appeal to Kenneth Kaunda. He seems one of the few people whose opinion Saddam Hussein cares for and we'll probably go and see the Zambian embassy."

"Well Joanna, thank you very much for coming in and I do hope you hear some news soon."

When Josie Brookes' twenty-five year old son Richard walked into her house on Friday 10th August, he was not prepared for his reception. In the kitchen was a woman he only vaguely recognised, but who knew him immediately, making enough cups of tea for a regiment. In the lounge his step-father, Stephen, was sitting at the dining room table talking on the phone. Before him, on the beautifully dark-stained mahogany table top, was his mother's old portable TV beaming out Ceefax, another phone, several copies of the local evening paper and dozens of scraps of paper with scribbled notes all over them. Josie waved him in and smiled, then turned back to the reporter who was interviewing her and some man from local radio. The second phone rang.

"Answer that, will you Richard," Josie requested.

Though tired from his full day working on the counter at one of Coventry's Department of Social Security offices, he picked the receiver up. It was a Mrs Betty Stevenson. Richard had a relaxed phone manner from the start. Working at the DSS, he was used to irate, frustrated and desperate calls. But this one was none of those. The lady on the other end was calm and warm and was clearly suffering from shock.

"Is Mr or Mrs Brookes there?"

"They're both busy at the moment. Can I help? I'm Josie's son, Richard."

"Well, I saw in the paper they were setting up some sort of helpline for the relatives of people trapped in Kuwait."

Richard looked up at Stephen. Were they? He glanced at the Ceefax showing the latest news from the Gulf, at the scraps of paper on the table and the front page of the *Coventry Evening Telegraph* with Josie and Stephen displayed across it. "Is this a helpline?" he asked.

Stephen interrupted his own call, placing his hand over the mouthpiece. "We're now the Midlands Gulf Helpline."

Richard raised his eyebrows, smiled to himself and talked to the lady on the other end of the phone. "Yes, it seems we are." Stephen whispered to him to take her name and pushed a diary at him. Its pages were full of partially decipherable scribbles, crossings out and addresses. Richard turned over and started a new page. He wrote down Betty Stevenson's name, address and phone number and asked her what he could do.

"Well," Betty said, trying to remain calm, "my son and daughter-in-law are trapped in Kuwait and I haven't heard from them since Thursday. I wondered if you had any news."

"What're their names?"

"Andrew and Carolyn Stevenson."

"And where do they live?"

"In Kuwait City. I don't know exactly, but all the phones seem to be down. We can't get through at all. My husband and I are getting desperate. We don't know if they're still alive, or what. I thought you might know if they'd been picked up. We've heard that some British have been taken to Baghdad. We've tried Mr Hayward in Bristol, but he said he'd had that many calls, he couldn't cope. He gave us your number and told us to ring you. He told us a friend of yours was on the plane, you know, flight whatever it was."

Much of this went over Richard's head. Did Stephen and Josie have any information? Had they a friend in Kuwait on a plane? He looked at Josie, who was in full flow describing the work of the helpline to the reporter. Stephen glanced at him and saw his querulous expression. He nodded, hurriedly broke off his call to the Foreign Office and took up Richard's phone.

The door bell rang. Richard rose and answered it. It was a BBC camera crew, with presenter, director, cameraman and soundman.

"Yes?"

"The Midlands Gulf Helpline?"

"Yes..."

"We've come to interview Stephen and Josie Brookes." Richard looked at them amazed. "We phoned earlier. Are you Mr Brookes?" The presenter shook hands in that slightly over-friendly way reporters have when they want something and moved up onto the top step.

"No, he's inside. Listen, just wait here." He turned and went back into the lounge. Josie had finished answering the reporter's question and the man sitting next to her was now saying his bit. Richard quietly indicated to her. She rose silently and came through into the hall with him. The woman in the kitchen, whom he now recognised as Pauline Murphy, a friend of his mother's, slipped her a cup of tea and asked Richard if he would like one.

"Er, yes please... listen, Mum."

"Sugar?"

"Er, two please... listen, Mum..." But Josie had already seen the TV crew, who had slowly sidled their way in through the door and were now crammed in the front of the hallway. Josie let out a little giggle, her brown eyes sparkled and she squeezed her son's arm.

"Are you the BBC?" she asked.

"We are."

"Can you hold on for a few minutes. We've got Mercia Sound in here at the moment, but they'll be finished soon. Come on in. How many of you are there? Four. Right, well, watch the door, that's it. It's getting so crowded in here. Pauline, can you make some more teas and coffees." As Pauline came into the hall to ask the crew what they would like to drink, the radio soundman popped his head through the living room door and asked them politely to hush. Josie giggled again and waited silently in the hall. But not for long. Soon she was whispering to the presenter about the chaos their house was in. Richard decided to escape into the back garden, only to find the camera crew trailing through the kitchen after him and parking themselves and their equipment down on the patio chairs and table.

Stephen was still on the phone to Betty Stevenson. "All the information we've got so far is from the Foreign Office and some people who've recently returned from Kuwait."

"Have you not got any information at all?" Betty was finding it very hard to keep calm. For a week now she had been living on her nerves, growing more and more desperate for news. The pressure of trying to keep her worry from her two grandchildren, of putting on a show and hiding her tears away in the bathroom or bedroom, when all her thoughts were constantly turning to Kuwait, was causing her strain and anxiety. She was living in two worlds, the everyday world of getting by, and the dream world of Kuwait to which her mind constantly drifted. It was becoming too much. Although she tried to think of other things and keep herself occupied, the worry was far too great.

Friends had told her to turn her mind to other things and not to dwell on the situation, but attempting not to think about her son and daughter-in-law only made it worse. She was an elderly woman, in her late sixties, having cared for her children for more than half her life. She *couldn't* ignore them. She *had* to keep thinking about them, pray for them and keep them in her thoughts. By constantly holding on to memories of them she felt she was able to protect them, as though she was looking over them and helping them in some inexplicable, telepathic way through their ordeal. It was the only thing she *could* do for them.

As she spoke, her voice was breaking constantly, despite pulling on a cigarette to calm her nerves. She had smoked so many cigarettes that week, she had lost count. She coughed violently as Stephen tried to reassure her and as she talked about her grandson, Thomas.

"He idolises his Uncle Andrew. If he sees me crying, what's he going to think? What's going to go through his little mind? You never know how these things affect children, do you."

"No, you don't." Stephen knew enough about the relatives' needs by now to know he must say very little, just let Betty speak.

"Do you have any children?"

"No. Josie does, from a previous marriage, but I don't."

"Oh, well." She was slightly embarrassed at having pried, and went back to Thomas. "He thinks the world of me and my husband. We've been so worried about what he's thinking. Outwardly, we've had to keep calm, but it's been a great strain. We haven't slept, you know, not properly, not since Thursday night. Well, we didn't get *any* sleep that first night, but these last nights we've lain there in bed reading, then turning the light out for an hour or so, then one of us has had to get up and go downstairs. We can't sleep with worry. We go to bed thinking about it and we get up thinking about it. If only we could get some news. That's the worst part, not having any news at all. I know it might sound exaggerated; you might think I'm stupid, but I never doubt they'll come back. I'm sure they'll be all right. I will never say 'if they come back', always 'when they come back'. D'you know what I mean?"

Stephen offered a sympathetic grunt. "Give me their names and as many details as you can about where they live so, if we do get any information, we can piece it together for you." He waved to the TV crew outside the french windows. In the other end of the living room, the radio team had finished and were packing up their sound equipment. The TV cameraman began hovering around them, setting up his camera and tripod, measuring the light and rigging up a lamp.

"He's Andrew and my daughter-in-law's Carolyn. They've got no children. They live on a complex in... well, I'm not exactly sure where. I don't know exactly what Andrew does, but it's to do with an oil installation out there."

Stephen jotted down details in the diary which was making do as a notebook. Richard came back in, following the TV soundman, and avoided the exiting radio crew as Josie showed them to the door. He sat with his tea on one of the soft pink and beige settees. The living room was a through lounge and dining room, with an arch between them. It was decorated in pale pink and white. The whole decor of the room was calming and peaceful. The two settees were covered in cushions and each had white lace pillows on the seats. Gentle pictures of young women in floral dresses and rural scenes looked down from the walls. A glass coffee table had two ceramic cats curled sleepily up on it, some flowers and six half-finished cups of tea.

Richard sat and watched the camera crew prepare. Josie introduced him to the man she had done the interview with. His name was Alaistair Cameron. He was the agent for a Coventry MP, John Butcher, who had volunteered his services. They chatted briefly about the chaos the house was in before Alaistair remembered something he had left in his car. He excused himself, and ran down the short front garden into the road. He had to walk a fair way to his car, as the road was cluttered with media vehicles and cars belonging to helpline volunteers. He had brought Josie and Stephen a fax machine. He lifted it carefully out of the boot and carried it back to the house. As he did so, a transit van pulled up across the road and someone called out to him.

"Hello Alaistair, we've brought the table."

"Oh, that's marvellous. Hold on a minute. Let me take this in and I'll give you a hand." Alaistair carried the fax machine into the house and lowered it gently onto a newspaper on the dining table. Stephen stared in amazement. He was still on the phone to Betty. Alaistair asked the TV crew if they could give him a hand with the table.

Eventually, the table was lifted up the narrow, steep and twisting stairs into one of the front bedrooms. It had been Josie's escape room, her own space where she could read, relax and get away from the world. It had just contained the single bed Eric Watson had given them plus all her books and a small writing table. That had to be completely reorganised as the long table was squeezed in and as other equipment followed.

Richard, meanwhile, had had enough of the chaos downstairs and decided to buy a few essentials. Josie had told him previously about the phone calls they were getting, but he had no idea it was as hectic as this. What made it worse was that they had no office equipment at all. British Telecom had installed another phone line, but otherwise there was no structure to the helpline or equipment for it.

Richard knew they must buy some basics. The crisis would soon be over, so there was no point in going mad. By next week they wouldn't need it any more. All they required was a proper day book to record messages, along with the date and time, and a card index system to keep a record of everyone who phoned, with details of their addresses, emotional states, who their relatives were and what they were doing in Kuwait. He drove to his local shopping centre and bought some boxes of cards, felt pens, a large record book, paper clips, Blutack and drawing pins, then drove back again.

The helpline at this stage was *ad hoc* and spontaneous, evolving all the time. No one, especially not Josie or Stephen, had any idea it would last more than a few days. They believed the passengers on the BA flight would be allowed out very quickly, and everyone else in Kuwait would be let go. They weren't part of the war. They were nothing to do with oil or power politics. Surely, they would be allowed to cross the border and come home?

Nor did they have grandiose plans to set up a database of names and contacts, nor to develop a system of rotas for volunteers, nor to get essential office machinery. They didn't even have a photocopier. It was to be a small operation working from a dining room table for a few days until everyone was out who wanted to be out, and that was it.

By the time Richard returned, Pauline was sitting by Stephen, talking on the phone. Stephen was preparing to do an interview with the TV, whilst the cameraman was taking a shot of the equipment on the dining table. Josie was standing behind Pauline, staring at Ceefax, turning the pages with the remote control, looking for any new developments. She couldn't believe it when her son produced the packets of index cards and other assorted office items. She stood up. "Wow, Richard, we don't need all that."

"Look, this's got to be done properly. It's chaos at the moment. You can't move."

"I can't even think," Josie added, laughing.

"This helpline isn't going to work unless you get organised."

"Oh, I know, I'm exhausted. I don't know how we're going to cope. Thank heavens it won't be for long."

"Won't it?" a reporter interrupted. "It could go on for weeks."

"No!" Then "No?" Josie stared at her son, her eyes widening as a new truth began to dawn upon her. She looked around. Her living room had twelve people crammed into it, all talking, even arguing. Mugs, papers and TV equipment lay everywhere. A radio crew, a TV crew, volunteers, van driver, son, husband and herself were packed into it. She held her hands to her head and pulled them through her thick auburn hair, throwing a penetrating stare at her son. The outside world had invaded her peaceful, private sanctuary. She had let it take her over. She had been sucked into some maelstrom, pulling her down, drowning her and Stephen in a swirling vortex of press and volunteers and relatives and news and government departments. It had swallowed them down its twisting throat without them raising a hand against it. The enormity of it suddenly enveloped her.

Joanna Copley had seen her sister Katharine onto BA Flight 149 to Kuala Lumpur via Kuwait on the afternoon of Wednesday 1st August. The following morning she struggled off to work as an office manager for a computer consultancy firm. About midday she received an urgent phone call. It was Catherine's flat-mate Wendy. She had heard of the invasion and become anxious about the flight so had rung British Airways, but they had said everything was all right and assured her there were no problems. Relieved, but a little perplexed and worried all the same, Joanna then received another call. This time it was her brother.

"Oh, hi Jonathan, how're things?"

"Did you know Kat's flight's stranded in Kuwait?"

"No, I didn't. In fact, my flat-mate's just phoned me to say everything's OK. Does BA know what's happened to them?"

"No, that's all they would tell me."

"Isn't there an emergency centre, EPIC, or something, at Heathrow?"

"I'll find out."

"I'll phone the Foreign Office. It might know. Bye for now."

Another call came through for her on another line.

"It's your husband, Tony."

No sooner had she put the phone down from him than the first one rang again. It was Wendy again, this time in great distress, saying, "They gave me the wrong information. She's still out there. Oh my God, they might all still be on the runway!" She was crying, distraught and panicking. And by now Joanna was too. She had no idea what to do.

That day was a hectic, frantic one. There was nothing on the news at all about the flight. It had disappeared from the face of the earth. Joanna and Tony repeatedly phoned Heathrow, but no information came through. They phoned the television and radio networks, with no success. There was no information at all.

There was never any pussy-footing with Joanna. She wanted her sister and all the other foreign nationals out of Iraq and Kuwait, and was not prepared to let them rot there one moment longer than they had to. Her eyes would flare, her temper would rise, she would raise her voice and emphasise points in such a way that one dare not contradict her. But that was necessary at times. The press could have eaten her alive. The Foreign Office could have run circles around her. She had to be strong, both in self-defence, as a deflector shield, and to actually get anything done. Even so, it was very hard to get action taken, and impossible for it to influence the opinions of leaders in the conflict. All she could do was reflect the concerns of the relatives and hostages, try to improve their situation and keep them in the news.

Many relatives watching this demure looking woman in her navy blue and white chequered dress taking on everyone in authority responded warmly to her approach. She verbalised their total frustration at lack of news and action. They admired her sparring with world leaders. "Yes. That's what we wanted to say! That's how we feel, totally ignored, fobbed off with pleasantries, whilst nothing is done. Well, they're not going to let *our* relatives rot in Iraq for years, like they've let Terry Waite, John McCarthy and others in the Lebanon. No way!"

On Monday the sixth, British Airways finally rang her with some news but it proved to be inaccurate, and Joanna was very dissatisfied with what seemed to be its lack of urgency.

After the frustrating phone call from BA, Joanna admits that she blew a fuse. She rang the BBC, ITN and Channel 4, amongst others, whom time and anger has blurred. "I said to them, 'You do know there's a plane load of British people stuck out in Kuwait, don't you? And they said, 'Yes'. So

I said, 'Do you want a story?' They, of course, did. So straight away I told my boss I was nipping round the corner to ITN, and they interviewed me. Then Channel 4 wanted to interview me. Then I did an interview on TVam the following morning. At that final one, I boldly ventured where no one had ventured before and announced I was starting a support group. I left my telephone number with TVam and asked them to pass people on to me. The following day I was on TVam again. By that time, my brother Jonathan had come up to London from Somerset. In twenty-four hours I did seven TV and ten radio interviews. I pushed it for all it was worth because, by that stage, I was 'annoyed'." A girlish grin and charming lowering of her head accompanied the understatement.

"Tony and Jonathan spent Tuesday answering a non-stop stream of phone calls. I was still at work, but phoned around from there to find an office for the support group, because there was no way I wanted it to work from my home. On Wednesday, Tony again stayed at home answering calls - and there were hundreds of them. I had no idea the extent of it. People were desperate for information, and not just those with people on the flight. Everyone with relatives or friends out in Iraq and Kuwait seemed to be ringing us. It was incredible and overwhelming.

"Thursday was my birthday. I spent it doing more interviews and getting extra phone lines installed, whilst Tony and Jonathan answered the calls. I rang the darling BBC and said, 'Come on, you're not covering this; do something about it'. and they said, 'Well, have you got an operation going?' and I said, 'Yes, I'm getting one set up'. They agreed to come round, so I rang the chairman's office at British Telecom and told his PA I wanted four telephone lines put in that day. 'Look, we're desperate. We're getting more calls than we can cope with. Our phone is ringing off the hook. We put it down and it rings again, and again, and again, until two or three o'clock in the morning. We need help. We need it now! Today, not tomorrow or next week, but now! Can you please, please, please help us?'"

Whenever she did a television or radio interview, Joanna repeated that she needed an office, funds and volunteers. Helpers immediately began to respond. She, Tony and Jonathan started vetting them, sorted out rotas and briefed them on how to deal with people on the phones and what information they could give out. British Telecom came to her house that afternoon and had four lines installed by four o'clock, just ready for the BBC.

The next morning, she was back on TVam and able to tell them she had a support group up and running. This time, the programme gave her new home numbers out on the screen. As it did so, Tony, Jonathan and two volunteers were sitting by the phones, watching Joanna on their TV. As soon as the numbers came up, Tony raised his hand and started counting with his fingers. "One, two, three, four, five..." Dring, dring... dring, dring... dring, dring... dring, dring. All four lines erupted simultaneously.

Fortunately, Joanna was soon offered some offices in central London. They were at the New Connaught Rooms on Great Queen Street, Holborn, very close to Covent Garden and the BBC's World Service. There were two rooms, one large, the other no more than an office, but very well appointed. They were part of a hotel, with a plush carpet and full length, heavy curtains draped over the windows. Brother, sister and husband spent Friday, Saturday and Sunday with some of their helpers setting up the new system, getting everything ready to be transferred from their house. By Monday they were ready and the whole operation was moved into its new offices.

So, within a week of starting the helpline, Joanna had a fully staffed rota, four phone lines, a fax machine, photocopier and word processor. Her volunteers were able to put all the callers onto a database and cross-reference them with a detailed day book of every single call. The hotel staff were tremendously helpful. They treated them as if they were a permanent conference group, setting out cordials and mints on the tables, supplying white boards, writing pads, cups and saucers, even paper serviettes.

Joanna, Tony and Jonathan had taken a route very different from the Coventry operation. They had decided they needed to build an organisation, get proper offices and bring in equipment. They were positive they did not want it to remain in their home. It would give them the great advantage of being able to escape the helpline every evening and have some time to themselves, whereas Josie and Stephen Brookes were to find themselves totally immersed and unable to escape - unless they actually fled their own home. The disadvantage was that they began to lose control of the helpline to a certain extent. Some volunteers wanted more say and a more formal structure instigated. This tension was absent at the beginning, but later was to threaten the running of the London helpline at times.

Meanwhile, Joanna had told her boss she would be unable to go into work that week. He was extremely sympathetic and even helped her install a computer. He was very supportive and understood her need to do everything she could for her sister. Indeed, he was amazed at her energy and determination. He gave her indefinite, unpaid, compassionate leave.

Meanwhile, Sue Brownlow, who had been helping Rob Hayward in Bristol, saw her friend Joanna on the TV and contacted her. They told each other about their helplines and immediately the idea of liaison came to mind. Sue listened in amazement at the extent of what Joanna had taken on and told her that Rob Hayward was being inundated with calls as well. Sue offered to go up to London to help out, but there seemed to be so much work being done in Bristol that Joanna suggested she stay down there. Sue is an extremely able woman, a management consultant with a great deal of experience organising people and getting things going. She and the other Bristol volunteers were of invaluable help to Rob Hayward, working with him at his home.

By the end of that first week, Josie and Stephen had also contacted Joanna. Stephen phoned her home. Joanna was out organising the Connaught Rooms so he spoke to Jonathan. They built an immediate rapport and agreed to swop all information they had and work as closely together as they possibly could. Thus, within ten days of Iraq's invasion, a network of addresses and phone numbers had been built. Three major helplines were in full flow - at Bristol, Coventry and London - plus Dorothy Croft's one in Matlock. Each had moved swiftly into top gear with volunteers manning phone lines constantly, and, by the end of that period, they were all in contact with each other. The initial surge of emotion and anger had thrown up a nationwide organisation virtually overnight. It was now time to consolidate, co-ordinate and get as much information as they could. The long haul through to December had begun.

Guests of Saddam

"They were trapped within a four-walled skull, all their senses turned in upon themselves."

Dear Diary,
Thursday 2nd August, Ahmadi, Kuwait
Weekend. I was woken up at around 4am by bombs, but I didn't realise what it was at the time. Later on in the day, I was told that Iraq had invaded. We had to stay in the house all day. No contact out of the country... Fully stocked with food. Kuwait defenceless,

Love Jo

So began the diary of Joanna Mansell, aged twelve, living with her family in the town of Ahmadi, close to the main Kuwaiti oil terminal and southern oil field of al-Burgan.

Dear Diary,
Friday 3rd August
More bombs. The house has shaken so much because of bombs, it will probably fall! Boring. Nothing to do all day. Dad was told not to go into work because he could be taken hostage. Lots of troops passed our house in lorries which were towing guns. Once again, I was woken early. All the Iraqis wanted was money, even though Kuwait had already given ten billion to them,

Love Jo

Dear Diary,
Saturday 4th August
We went to the shops. They were very crowded. One shop was being looted by the army, but their officers told them off. Lots of artillery around, tanks and such like. Most shops are closed. Iraqi soldiers are walking round, being friendly. No harm is coming to us. No bomb explosions today,

Love Jo

Dear Diary,
Sunday 5th August
Didn't move from out of the house. Nothing much happened today. Had lots of telephone calls. Iraq is meant to be withdrawing its troops, but I don't see much of that happening. Atmosphere tense. Everybody is becoming anti-social. It's impossible to live with everyone. At least I got a good night's sleep last night...

Love Jo

Dear Diary,
Thursday 16th August
I shall briefly explain what happened on the days I missed.

We had three soldiers come to our house and we gave them food and drinks and for about an hour and a half they were teaching me Arabic. Stuart [her fifteen-year-old brother] and I received a watch each from Fahood. The other two soldiers' names were Khalid and Mahmood. They were polite and quite harmless, even though Mahmood did have a gun. The second day running, Fahood came, but he brought a different friend with him. His name was Sajeed. Sajeed had the gun. They were watching videos – Grease and Dirty Dancing. They recognised John Travolta and were particularly fond of Michael Jackson.

We moved out of our house and stayed in Eddie and Andrea Goodridge's house. The first day the air-conditioning went off, then there were cockroaches, then burst pipes. I could go on and on. The next day we travelled to where Dave and Keith were staying - in a German's massive villa. There were roughly fifteen people and babies staying there. They were going to take a convoy down to the Saudi border. It's a pity we can't go, but we don't have a four-wheel drive. Good luck to them. We went to the market. There is hardly any food left in it. We also went to the petrol station. We were waiting in the queue for fifteen minutes before we got any petrol...

Love Jo

Dear Diary,
Tuesday 21st August
We went to see Dave again. As we were about to leave there was a message from the embassy. Stay in your homes, the Iraqis are rounding up Brits! So we rushed home trying to take a safe route, but we took the worst route possible. There were soldiers everywhere! Anyway, we got home safely. Dave cancelled the escape attempt because the furthest he would get would be just down the road.

Boring as usual. Now we play darts and Scrabble. No Brits are venturing out. The only communication we have is the telephone. There is no food left in the country or Iraq. I don't see why the innocent Iraqis should suffer,

Love Jo

Dear Diary,
Saturday 25th August
We haven't been out of the house for days. The soldiers are looking for Brits, so every time there is a ring or knock at the door, Stuart, Steph [her four-year-old sister] and I run up to the bedroom. We keep as quiet as possible, but that is quite hard, because of Stephanie. We have made the house look as if it is not lived in. We have put the TV into a small room which is part of the lounge and we have cordoned the little area off,

Love Jo

Dear Diary,
Wednesday 29th August
Made a birthday cake for Dad - two days early. The cake was lovely. We also heard the women and children can leave the country. Yippee!

Love Jo

Dear Diary,
Thursday 30th August
We thought we would be leaving Dad, so we cooked and froze a lot of one-person meals for him, such as curry and stroganoff...

Love Jo

Dear Diary,
Saturday 1st September
We were captured by the Iraqi soldiers. They surrounded our house and had machine guns. At first, they took Dad away, but soon came back. They said if we all went we would get to England quicker. We were taken to the Iraqi administration building (the old Kuwaiti police station) and were taken from camp to camp. We wasted a lot of time sitting in a bus doing nothing. We arrived at the International Hotel at 2am, where we spent the rest of the day,

Love Jo

Dear Diary,
Sunday 2nd September
We were taken to the Regency Palace Hotel. Most of my friends were there. We had freedom within the hotel, which was good for the little children to move around in without getting lost. I did quite a lot of baby-sitting. Food? Well, we received quite a lot for hostages - sorry 'guests', as Saddam Hussein puts it,

Love Jo

The main concentrations of British in Kuwait were in the city, especially its south east part, in Jabriya, Bayan, Salwa, Mushrif and Salmiya. These districts also had concentrations of Palestinians, Egyptians and Indians, in low-rise tower blocks, either built in complexes with high surrounding walls, or standing alone. It is erroneous to imagine the British community lived in plush villas. True, a few did live in the wealthier areas such as Andalous and Shuwaikh, districts full of top-grade villas and mansions, but most lived in modest bungalows or apartments in mixed areas. It was fortunate. During the occupation, many British apartments were left alone because the Iraqis thought they were occupied by Arabs. Often, it was only if Palestinian neighbours knew who they were that they would be in trouble.

Outside the city, many British lived with other ex-pat groups in relatively modern developments down the coast at places like Fintas, Mahbola, Manqaf and Fahaheel. The old BP town of Ahmadi, set on a rise, and with its golf club and communications tower, had a much smaller British community than it once boasted. It had once held the largest concentration of ex-pats but the British population had shrunk considerably in the eighties as Kuwaitis and other Arabs had moved in. Now, like most other areas, it merely had British families interspersed amongst the local population. That helped them merge into the background and meant that many had friendly Kuwaiti neighbours who were able to help them.

Another extremely useful factor which saved many British was the chaotic road naming and numbering system. Streets in Kuwait have numbers rather than names, yet there is no apparent system about the numbering. It is so confusing at the best of times that people don't give addresses, but hand out little maps and hope their friends can find them. Everyone uses PO box numbers for mail. Between the villas and blocks of apartments, there are open spaces of sand, dotted with the occasional football pitch and very few trees. They have the look of oases of air-conditioned comfort within a harsh, barren desert landscape and it is frequently impossible to tell which street a villa or block belongs to. Thus, even if the Iraqis knew addresses of ex-pats, it was very hard to find them. The exception were the coastal developments, which were frequently exposed, close to the beach and clearly occupied by Westerners. The British in them either left for other districts very quickly after the invasion, escaped across the border, or were rounded up by the Iraqis.

Stephen Mansell worked for the Kuwait National Petroleum Company (KNPC) as a senior electrical engineer. His wife Anne ran a playgroup for two to five-year-olds. She taught them in preparation for entering the English School, an establishment for both Arabs and British people. It was run on the same lines as schools in England and the teaching language was English. By 2nd August it had been closed for the summer holidays and many of its pupils had left Kuwait on holiday, planning to return when the school term restarted in September. It was a considerable blessing as many families escaped being caught, but meant a lot of single men were trapped on their own. Their answer was to group together for safety and company.

They lived with their three children Joanna, Stuart and Stephanie on one of the main roads going into Ahmadi, some seven kilometres from the Gulf coast. In the dark of early morning on 2nd August, they were woken by a major air and ground battle. Iraqi aircraft were bombing the Kuwaiti military airport and missile base less than ten kilometres away at the international airport. An Iraqi column had skirted Kuwait City to the south and intercepted retreating Kuwaitis. But Anne had no idea what it was. In fact, she thought the noise was thunder from an electrical storm. She had been up most of the night with Stephanie, who wasn't sleeping very well, and had been very bad that night. She heard a series of loud bangs, opened the curtains and noticed some flashes on the horizon, but thought nothing more about it. It was not until her husband woke her at six o'clock, getting ready for work, that she learnt what had happened. Stephen had heard about the invasion on the radio.

Despite living on a main road, they didn't see a single Iraqi soldier for twenty-four hours and could have quickly slipped across the border. But they kept getting messages over the World Service from the Foreign Office warning them not to leave their homes. She now knows that, with better advice, they could have escaped. "We were so angry. I could have loaded up the car, driven down to Saudi and got straight out," she told me bitterly.

Incredibly, that first morning Stephen was called in to work at the refinery. Anne was left sitting at home with her three children. Outside, she could hear incessant explosions, gunfire and shells going off. Contrary to the view that the Iraqis met with very little opposition, a major battle developed north and west of Ahmadi. For several days the small Kuwaiti army put up stiff resistance, until it was driven back across the Saudi border. It was this battle the Mansells could hear.

The gunfire and explosions went on until nine o'clock at night, when there was a terrific bang. "The windows all bulged, the house shook, Stuart fell out of his chair. It took us all out of our seats, it was really that loud." The Iraqis had hit the communications tower to the east of Ahmadi, near Subahiya. Anne immediately phoned Stephen and ordered him back home, never mind what his boss said. So he left, and just missed the Iraqis occupying the oil terminal. There were British nationals still in it who were picked up and immediately taken into custody by the Iraqis.

At midnight, as the whole family sat awake in the lounge listening for more fighting, desperately worried in case Iraqis came into the house, they had a phone call. It was a Kuwaiti friend telling Stephen not to leave the house under any circumstances. Anne could go out, but not him, because the Iraqis were looking for British men. Immediately, they decided to move all the furniture out of their main bedroom and drag in the children's beds, so everyone was sleeping in one room. They were able to feel just a little safer that night by staying together. Their villa was very large, with four bedrooms, a large living area and maid's quarters. In those first nights its very size seemed threatening as they cowered nervously together in that one room.

The next day, Anne ventured out in her *abaya*, a black Arabic gown, with Joanna and Stephanie in tow, to get some food. She took every dinar they had. As she drove to the shops, she saw hundreds of lorries, tanks and other Iraqi army vehicles parked by the side of the road. She realised for the first time the extent of the take-over. It became apparent that this would last longer than a few days and it was obvious they would have to get in a large stock of food. She tried to get some money out, but the banks and cash points were closed, so she had to rely on what she had with her.

The shops were full of Iraqi soldiers, but they were suckers for children and Anne used little Stephanie for all she was worth. It was mainly Kuwaitis who were queuing and they were very anxious for the welfare of their European guests, so she was allowed to join the front of the queues. She went to one shop, returned home, then went off to another, hunting for as much food as she could get, until she had managed to fill the freezer. Always, the Iraqis and Kuwaitis were very pleasant and relaxed towards them. They even managed to sneak a video of tanks going by their bungalow, holding the curtain back a few inches to do it.

"That first week we were free, although there was a dusk-to-dawn curfew imposed from the very start. We had soldiers in and out of our house all the time. I even feed them a couple of times. Because it was so very hot that summer, they didn't want to stand in the street, so they used to come over and ask for a drink of water. We thought it best to be friendly, so we'd offer them Pepsi or squash. Then they would start showing us pictures of their family and bullet wounds from the war with Iran.

"They would talk about England and Mrs Thatcher. Oh yeh - everything and nothing. Their English wasn't very good, but they would come in and sit watching videos. Marilyn Monroe films and Olivia Newton-John. That was all they were interested in. But we began to worry about Joanna. She's only twelve, but is very tall and looks fifteen. We didn't know what the Iraqis might do to her if things got worse.

"They weren't very disciplined. In fact, they were a rabble. We called them farmers' boys. They were so scruffy; one would have his shirt hanging out and a pair of plimsolls on, whilst another was wearing carpet slippers. You know the plastic helmets kids use to play in? Well, they had equipment like that. They told us they didn't want to fight. They hadn't wanted to come into Kuwait, but if they hadn't've come they'd've been shot. If they deserted, their families back in Iraq wouldn't get fed. They told us that. They had no option. They didn't want to be there."

On Saturday the fourth, Saddam told the world his forces would begin to pull out of Kuwait. That evening, a soldier knocked on the Mansells' door and warned them that at two in the morning there would be an enormous bang, but not to worry; they were going back to Iraq and before they left they were going to blow up the oil refinery.

In fact, the soldiers were sent towards Saudi Arabia. Not only was Saddam conning the world, but even the Iraqi soldiers had thought they were going home, and even they were deceived as to their purpose in Kuwait and the length of their stay. Deception was endemic amongst the leaders of the Iraqi regime, the army, and especially in the *Mukhabarat*, the Iraqi state police.

The first Saturday after the invasion, Kuwaitis were still taking pot-shots at Iraqi soldiers. One patrol in Salwa noticed a sniper on the roof of an apartment block. An officer and three men came and checked the building. There were a number of Westerners in it, including a German woman and her husband. The soldiers searched the block thoroughly, but found nothing, except the terrified families staying there.

On the Sunday, one soldier returned to the building. He had seen the German woman and returned for her. He went to her flat and knocked. Her husband saw the soldier with the gun and opened it. He had no reason to fear the man, as the Iraqis were being very friendly at the time. However, when he came in, the Iraqi immediately pointed his AK47 at the husband, ordered him into the bathroom and tied him up. He then returned to the woman and pushed her into the bedroom. He threatened he would kill her husband unless she co-operated. She had no choice. As she verged on hysterics, the Iraqi raped her, then untied her husband and told them both to sit down at the dining room table. As he kept his rifle pointed at the man, he ordered the woman, who had tears streaming from her eyes, to make them a cup of tea and insisted they had a drink together. He even offered to pay them for their silence, but they refused to take his money.

Again, he offered them money, and again they refused. In another fit of sudden anger, the Iraqi soldier wrenched the gold chain and pendant the woman was wearing from her neck and left. She immediately burst into hysterics. Neighbours rushed in to see what was the matter. Within a few minutes, everybody in the building knew what had happened. Three families, including the German woman and her husband, immediately got into their cars with a few possessions and left for the border. The rest of the Westerners in that block and the one next to it spent that night in one flat for protection.

The British embassy was closed on the day of the invasion. It was a Thursday, the Arabic equivalent of our Saturday, and the start of the weekend. The answer phone service had been switched on the night before, as always, and all the staff had gone home. Incredibly, no one answered the phone all that first day. Hundreds of British citizens phoned in, but either met with the answer phone or no reply at all. Although there was an emergency contact number they could call, it was constantly engaged, so only a handful of people managed to get through.

At the time of the invasion, the British embassy staff numbered twenty-two, many of whom had their dependents with them. They included ten key personnel who stayed on in the embassy after 24th August, the Iraqi deadline for closing the embassies: Michael Weston, the ambassador, Larry Banks, his aide, Martin Roper (Vice Consul), Tony Millson, Donald Macaulay (Cultural Attaché), John Raine (Second Secretary), David McDonaugh (Immigration Officer), David Belgrove (Assistant Management Officer), Adam Perks (Registrar), and Brian MacKeith (Security Officer).

Because the embassy could not possibly keep contact with the whole community, it had appointed representatives to liaise with it. During the Iran-Iraq War, the British embassy in Kuwait had instigated a network of these wardens amongst the British community which had been kept in place since then. They were at the very heart of the way the community was organised and prepared for a crisis and were appointed from the community for precisely such an eventuality as war or invasion. They were meant to have local knowledge and experience and to be prepared to take responsibility when needed. Unfortunately, according to many in the British community, not all of them had that local knowledge nor that commitment. The warden system is used in virtually every British ex-pat community, but in Kuwait it was thrown into paroxysms by the Iraqi invasion. It quite simply collapsed and had to be rebuilt.

Wardens were not elected; they put themselves forward or were selected. They were not given training, nor were they chosen according to specific criteria which might be of use in a crisis, such as technical knowledge, length of stay in Kuwait, knowing Arabic, general experience, or leadership. They were not prepared in any significant way by the embassy for such an eventuality. Until they *are* selected along specific criteria, trained and provided with an adequate emergency back-up procedure, the system will time and again be found wanting.

Many wardens were dedicated to helping, or at least representing, their firm or locality, but a few took on the position for its fringe benefits and not out of a sense of duty. Most major firms either had a warden or a company representative registered with the embassy, to liaise with it and be responsible for company personnel. They were frequently senior managers, sometimes similarly lured by embassy social life. They hoped to gain entry to the embassy for garden parties and functions. They hoped to be invited to meet visiting dignitaries and the ambassador and his staff. They were invited to see the Prince and Princess of Wales when they visited Kuwait. In effect, since the Iran-Iraq War, the system had been let slip until it was virtually ineffectual. As soon as the Iraqis invaded, some of these erstwhile 'representatives' panicked and failed to carry out their responsibilities. Several, in that first week, made a run for the border or simply refused to answer their phones, leaving the community to look after itself. Others, on holiday, had an excuse.

Cliff Lindley was typically scathing: "Our warden system wasn't working at all. It was ridiculous. It could have killed the lot of us. The embassy and Foreign Office ought to sort that out. People were wardens because they loved the social life. They wanted to go to the embassy for the Queen's birthday party, so they said to themselves, 'We'll become wardens'. One warden, as soon as the first bullets started flying, hid under a stone and refused to answer the phone, nor would that person phone us, in case the Iraqis traced his calls. Yet there were good wardens. Mike Devey down in Salmiya. He was super. He had three phones put in. He had a team manning them all the time."

The Foreign Office and the embassy in Kuwait strenuously deny that any wardens either "put themselves forward", or sought "fringe benefits". "They were carefully selected. There are no fringe benefits of any sort attached to the task of being a warden, and the suggestion that there are is unfounded gossip. The idea that people may have agreed to be wardens in order to ingratiate themselves with the embassy is grotesque." It praised those wardens who remained as "behaving with immense courage". However, it also admitted that, with some wardens on holiday and others leaving, "at the start of the crisis, the warden system was ragged".

Another couple who were bitterly angry at the failure of the wardens system and the embassy were Bernice and Lawrence MacDonald. Lawrence elucidated his feelings during the first week, when the main issue was whether to make an escape bid, but the wardens were giving out conflicting information. "Some were saying, 'Yes, go', others were saying, 'No, definitely not', and yet others were saying, 'Well, it's up to you'." There seemed, to Lawrence, to be a complete lack of co-ordination and there was certainly no coherent, united policy or advice.

Like many other people, this couple found the behaviour of some members of the British community lacking during the crisis. "Basically, it brought out the strengths of some people and the weaknesses of others. We had expected the old wartime spirit we often hear of from our parents' generation, you know, the stiff upper lip. It was far from that. Some people were having parties and had plenty of food. How they could celebrate when people were getting butchered all around them, I don't know." Bernice and Lawrence were extremely short of provisions, even from the first few days, reduced to eating rice, lentils and flour riddled with weevils, ekeing out their food supply. Whilst they had to make a kilo of sugar last a month, others were using twenty-five kilo bags to brew beer and wine and some people had freezers stocked with food the entire time. This diversity of food stocks caused deep resentment amongst those worse off, who couldn't afford to party. However, those people who were lax on security tended to pay for it. Some were rounded up when, with a little more restraint, they could have remained undetected.

Mike Devey, an effective warden himself, tried to explain how those early days felt. Many people were very, very scared. Some went to pieces, They couldn't cope, and couldn't make decisions for themselves. They were so frightened that every coherent, logical and reasoned thought disappeared from their heads. They froze. "The whole thing revolves around people's fear," Mike explained. "You can't blame anybody for running away and you can't blame anybody for not doing their job, because, unless you were there, you wouldn't know what it was like. There was shooting going on every night. You didn't know if you were going to be shot. And some people just cracked up under that situation."

I asked Henry Hill, one of the few trapped in Ahmadi who survived the full four and a half months in hiding, "What about the warden system?"

"What warden system? There wasn't one. There was nothing effective at all. The wardens they had didn't know Kuwait or the people. First of all, you needed reliable people, but you needed people who'd been in Kuwait a few years, who knew where places were, so when you're talking about Rumaithiya, they knew where it was. But, mainly, you needed reliable people who had some sort of public conscience, rather than one local warden, who just flipped his lid in the first ten minutes. He was useless." He told me of another warden, seconded temporarily to the job, so with some excuse, who fled the country after a few days. "These guys were good for cucumber sandwiches and going to have a drink at the embassy, but that was all."

Several wardens who did stay on - some for just a few weeks - proved totally unsuitable. They did not do all they could to help the rest of the community and some of their actions actually endangered or worked against the community. One group kept information on escape routes to themselves, keeping maps of the routes from everyone else, then organising their own "ill-prepared and hair-brained escape attempts". Others panicked and saved their own skins whilst the community was left to fend for itself.

According to Lawrence and Bernice MacDonald, "there was actually one warden who stole another person's four-wheel drive vehicle and took off across the desert. He took off without telling any of the people in his charge. There were people ringing him up and getting no reply, wondering where he was, left without contacts, all their names and numbers in his villa for the Iraqis or any looters to find. He just took off and left all the people he was responsible for. Look, we were *all* frightened, but if you have a responsibility, if you take on the role of warden, damn well live up to it. Don't go running off at a time of crisis. The jollies are over. The bad guys are here with the guns. You don't go running away."

Dave Dorrington was equally frank. "Prior to the invasion, the warden system was a farce. Very few people knew who their warden was. The wardens only knew a percentage of the people they should have known. Obviously, a lot of that is not the wardens' fault, but that of people who didn't bother to register with the embassy. The wardens took the whole thing as a very good means of being in with the embassy, getting invited to embassy functions. That was all it was. There was no responsibility to it. None of them wanted the responsibility. A lot of them quite obviously dropped the responsibility the moment it became something more than just an invitation to the embassy."

I asked him how many wardens skedaddled in those first weeks. The answer came with still lingering anger and frustration. "I've no idea. I don't know who the wardens were. That's what I mean. Nobody seemed to know who the wardens were. I eventually found out who was warden for my area, I had never met him or spoken to him. I never did meet him either. I didn't know his phone number, his address or anything about him. I never made contact with him throughout the crisis." He went on, emphasising the point. "When it came down to the fact that they *had* got a job to do, the job they were originally asked to do against Iran in the Iran-Iraq War, some of them didn't want to know." In effect, the warden system in those first days "was falling apart."

Cliff Lindley also described his feelings of anger and frustration at some of the wardens, especially of the time, two weeks into the occupation, when their error in telling people not to escape dawned on them and they began to organise their own, disastrous, convoys. "This is where the warden system had failed miserably. They weren't operating. They were escaping, or trying to escape all the while. Organising these lemming runs, these convoys. They never got anywhere. What they were doing was total folly. Obviously, some people had to get caught, obviously some people had to get hurt. They were disorganised. 'We've got to meet at such-and-such a place', then off they went. It was absolute chaos out in the desert. There were vehicles everywhere. You lose the cars you're with and you follow somebody else, then you realise they've given up and turned back. People were all over the place. And some wardens were keeping all the maps and information on the desert routes very close to themselves. They were going to kill somebody sooner or later." Cliff was extremely cross that he hadn't been allowed to have a map to plan his own route and thus give his group a chance to get away if they had needed to. He had eventually been forced to get an ordnance survey map from Mike Devey in Salmiya.

"Several wardens left in a secret convoy," he went on, listing four names to me, then added, contemptuously, "God knows who else. Many of the people were supposed to be wardens. They all made off on a convoy, another lemming run, about the third or fourth they'd done; their own convoy. They got completely lost. Instead of heading south-west, they headed north-west and came straight onto a main Iraqi military base. The Iraqis came out and captured them all. The Iraqis took them to Jahra to be processed. There were six vehicles with wardens in. At Jahra, they took all their civil IDs from them, got all the information they needed, then drove them back towards Kuwait City. They put a soldier in each vehicle, except the one at the end. There was a lot of traffic, they got split up and the last vehicle managed to get away." Thus one warden managed to escape, but the others caught in the convoy were taken off to installations.

For those wardens who did stay, and who tried their hardest to help the community, including most of those mentioned as attending the embassy meeting, the first few days were demanding, frightening and exhausting. The warden system was the only organisation the community had. They *had* to make it work. Sandy MacMillan was very highly regarded by many people in his care. So were Stewart Dick, Mel Gage and Alan Jardine. These and all the others who risked their lives time and again for the community deserve nothing but the highest praise for their courage and selflessness, as do those members of the community who stepped in to fill the gaps left by absent wardens. Dave Dorrington was one who took over his warden's responsibilities and he described what it was like to be thrown in at the deep end.

When Iraq invaded, Dave had few worries. His wife, Sue and their children were in Cyprus on holiday and he knew they could cope without him. He just had his Filipino maid, Nellie, and her husband Jim to consider. He was very relaxed about the whole thing and felt the crisis wouldn't go into September. He did consider escaping, and half-seriously planned a route which would have taken him west past Jahra, across the desert along a line of pylons and into Saudi Arabia, turning north along the Saudi-Iraq border to Jordan, across to The Lebanon, and out from Beirut to Cyprus. "I would have done it as an adventure, as quite a lot of people did."

However, within a few days, his situation had dramatically changed.

Nellie and Jim's friends and family felt threatened by the Iraqi soldiers, who seemed to be raping Asian women indiscriminately, and had moved into Nellie's quarters in the villa. A number of Britons had also moved in because their apartment blocks had become surrounded or occupied by Iraqi units and were now unsafe. One of them was a warden who decided he had had enough and was going to escape across the desert. He left Dave with the responsibility of his names, handing him his list of people and asking him to look after them.

"Hello, is my warden, ..., there?"
"No, I'm sorry, he's left."
"Oh, can you give me his new number."
"No, I mean he's left, left the country. Gone across the desert."
"What the... ?"

It was very hard for Dave to have to tell people. "Within the next twenty-four hours, I think everybody on the list phoned me to speak to their warden... They weren't at all impressed."

Dave's responsibilities dramatically increased. Those people on the warden's list had no one to contact now he had left, a problem exaggerated both because people were very restricted in who they knew and because the wardens had become virtually the only source of information and linkage within the community.

"As I saw it, the job was keeping in touch with people, so at least they knew there was somebody around whom they could phone if they'd got a problem or weren't sure what was happening. And to pass information along from the embassy and back to it, in both directions." When people called him, they wanted reassurance that there were other people still in Kuwait, to say they were OK, had enough food, were in good spirits, and to get information. "Maybe fifty per cent called just for a chat."

By now, food was being distributed by both Kuwaitis and Filipinos to people who needed it. As Dave had three large freezers, he was contacted by Mike Devey and asked to take in large quantities of minced beef and chickens from a warehouse the Kuwaitis had emptied before the Iraqis could get to it.

Dave's villa became very crowded at one point. At its height, there were twenty-five people in it, with a family to every bedroom and two families sleeping in the lounge. Most of them eventually left, but later in August he agreed to take in another group of people, including teenagers who had been staying with Mike Devey, another warden. Mike proved to be an excellent warden and organised a great deal of support for the community. He had very close contacts with the Kuwaitis, including the Resistance. It was they who tipped him off about an Iraqi sweep of the area which was why some of his people moved to Dave's.

Despite the initial confusion of the first few days, many wardens did remain and others moved into the shoes of those who had left and performed a marvellous task. They phoned people to check they were all right, to gather names and details of who was in each group, and get contact addresses and numbers for relatives in the UK.

From the first day, most wardens realised the extent to which the registration system had deteriorated. Nearly all the people who had registered with Mike Devey had either moved out of Kuwait or into another area, or were on holiday. Most new people to the area hadn't bothered to register with him. That first day, he went through his old list and found that only two people on it still lived in Salmiya. It had been allowed to completely lapse. However, this was as much the ex-pats' fault as the embassy's. They simply hadn't bothered to register. Mike estimated that no more than twenty per cent of the British population in Kuwait had bothered to tell the embassy they were in the country. On the other hand, many people didn't know they had to register. Perhaps the embassy should have done more to encourage people. An advert in the local papers every month, for example.

Just as the invasion found some wardens wanting, it brought out the best in others. People stepped in to replace missing wardens, or just to help out. They received tremendous support from local Kuwaitis, many of whom risked their lives to get Britons out of dangerous neighbourhoods and into safe houses. Their names cannot be revealed because of the danger of reprisals, but every area had its Kuwaiti heroes.

On the whole, helping the community was left to those wardens still operating. They were thrown in at the deep end. They had no idea of how to operate under the conditions they faced, any more than anyone else. They had received no training, no briefing, and were getting very little guidance from the embassy. They had to sink or swim as best they could. Most of them did a fantastic job under extremely difficult circumstances. Many risked their own safety for others and should be saluted for the fine, self-sacrificing and dangerous work they undertook. Circumstances were extremely difficult for them. They had to cope not only with the Iraqis but with the generally lax attitude to the system taken by the community. A major difficulty facing the wardens in the first days was to gather together a comprehensive and accurate list of where people were and what state they were in. This problem was compounded by it being the middle of the summer holidays. Wardens were on holiday; thousands of people, mainly women and children, were out of the country. Whilst this was a blessing, the uncertainty of whether they were free in Britain or had been captured by the Iraqis made the wardens' task that much harder.

Even granted the surprise of the invasion and that some wardens proved inadequate, the embassy itself didn't seem to be much help. It had failed, in many of the community's eyes, even before the invasion. It neither prepared them for it, though it knew for days it was a possibility, nor did it give its wardens the support they deserved once the Iraqis arrived. It began to compile a more accurate list of those British in Kuwait a few days before the invasion, but nothing else, other than an aside to wardens at a meeting to stock up with tins and water.

One warden, very active throughout the hostage crisis, described the situation: "The embassy initially was running round like a chicken with a lost head." He went on, "But it couldn't do a lot because it didn't know where people were. The BBC was told about this, via the Foreign Office, which instructed it to inform people over the radio to phone the embassy and be allocated a warden. And so, through the network we had set up, through the World Service, and through seeing and speaking to friends, we eventually got into contact with most of the community."

Some people were able to visit their wardens in those first days to gather information and tell the wardens of their existence, some even to move in with them. Cliff Lindley drove over from his apartment to see Mike Devey, who had set up a large operation with two other wardens in Salmiya. Others visited them from the coastal towns, such as Abu-Hulifa and Fintas, because the telecommunications tower at Ahmadi had been destroyed and their phones were cut off from the city.

The lack of communication was not all the embassy's fault. Its whole telephone system was knocked out in the first few days and, later, it had only one line, which was undoubtedly being tapped by the Iraqis. On the third, Mike Devey took some mobile phones up for it to use but they didn't need them because, after a few days, their lines were restored. One very active warden argued in the embassy's defence that its staff should not be blamed for not responding immediately without first understanding their situation. It had to be remembered that they were as worried for their own families as every other member of the British community, or indeed, every other person in Kuwait. They had to get in food stocks and bottled water for them, retrieve what money they could, make sure they were all safe, and get petrol for their cars, as well as get to the embassy to try to provide some sort of service for the community. They were as unprepared as anyone else, and there were an awful lot of troops and shooting and bombing that day. Everyone with any sense stayed indoors.

Such an argument seems a very valid concern facing the embassy staff. However, the Foreign Office feels this should in no way be used to explain the constraints upon the embassy. "All diplomatic staff at the embassy worked immensely long hours in the days after the invasion. Maintaining contact with the British community was a very high priority, but not the only priority. One must not under-estimate the scale of the problem nor the confusion over who was where."

There were meetings of the wardens at the embassy every two or three days during the first two weeks, although the embassy took several days to get organised. It held its first wardens' meeting on the afternoon of Saturday the fourth. The wardens could still drive through the city, enter the embassy compound unhindered, and make their way up to the ambassador's residence. There were about thirty wardens in all who attended the first meeting. They included Sandy MacMillan, Dorothy

Goodwin from Fintas, Ed Simon from Lateefa, Mel Gage from the Masouk complex, Jeff Lugg for the Arab Bank, Dave Kirkpatrick from Ahmadi, Stewart Dick from Mushrif, Jeff French, Alan Jardine and Mike Devey from Salmiya. Donald Macaulay was the only embassy official who attended the meeting, as other staff had pressing problems to attend to. He had taken over an embassy telephone and had gradually been linking wardens up with each other. It was he who organised the meeting.

"We went in there and asked what we should do and what was going to happen. But the embassy admitted it didn't know itself." At that time, the embassy was simply recommending people to lie low and not attempt to escape. However, the wardens decided to take certain precautions and make certain checks, "mainly to make sure people had food and plenty of containers of water, in case the water went off." Fortunately, one warden worked for the water authority and gave an excellent report on the water situation. There were plenty of reserves up on Mutlaa Ridge, so there was no need to panic and the electricity system was still working, because the Iraqis needed it. Another warden had medical experience and told them he was establishing a surgery and medical centre in a safe house, in case it was needed. Unfortunately, he went across the border one day, before he had managed to set up the medical room. From then on, the rest of the wardens had to start building emergency medical supplies up again by scrounging them through their Kuwaiti network.

Mostly, the wardens reported on the situation in the country and built contacts with each other. Several described their early links with the emerging Kuwaiti Resistance and the cooler, more experienced and better organised ones raised points on security techniques, how to talk over the phones and how to keep a constant check on their people. Much of the discussion at this meeting, as at later ones, was about how to work as wardens, what to do, tactics, whether people should congregate in groups or disperse, phone codes, how to liaise with each other and the embassy, and what the embassy could do for them - which wasn't very much. They discussed chemical attacks and preparations against them. One warden described how they had developed a pyramid system in their area, of codes and group leaders, all with codenames.

Virtually every initiative came from the wardens. The embassy knew nothing about the situation outside its security wall and relied on them absolutely. It was the totally blind leading the partially-sighted. Any information it did have, it seemed reluctant to pass on even to the wardens. As one warden explained irately, "The embassy could have done much more than it did, passed on more information. It didn't pass on nearly enough information to the wardens."

For example, a meeting of the wardens was held in the city towards the end of August, shortly after the Iraqis had ordered the embassies to shut down. By then, Dave Dorrington's warden had left Kuwait and Dave had taken over his duties. Despite informing the embassy, it took no notice and he wasn't invited. As if he didn't have enough problems, he had to gather what information he could from other wardens. News of its decisions trickled through to him.

But they obviously hadn't decided anything radical. As a warden who did attend reported, the discussion didn't change anything. "We were just told the embassy had got to close, not to go out, stay low..." One thing they were trying to do was compile an accurate list of who was still in Kuwait, their phone numbers and addresses, so they could be allocated to the remaining wardens and so their families could be contacted in Britain. They had some success in that, but it was taking a long time. All that should have been done in July, when the embassy knew of the Iraqi build-up. It was all too late, and merely demonstrated the embassy's lack of preparedness.

In general, once the Iraqis had invaded, the wardens were left to fend for themselves. The embassy was never ahead of events, never able to offer new information or useful advice. It was out of touch with what was taking place in the country. It was always behind events, reactive to the community rather than taking a lead. It never seemed to really appreciate the danger its citizens were in nor take responsibility for them.

Dave Dorrington explained the embassy's stance. "Initially, we had been told by the embassy that the Iraqis wouldn't invade, and if they did, they would only come as far as Mutlaa Ridge. They were quite definite. They would just take the northern oilfield. This was disseminated by the warden system." However, this was not the whole story. There was a wardens' meeting shortly before the invasion, attended by some representatives of the embassy. From it, it seems clear that the embassy not only suspected the Iraqis might invade, but had warned the wardens to take some precautions - but **not**, according to one warden, **to volunteer this information to the rest of the British community** - "The embassy's advice was to get some dried goods, tinned food and bottles of water in, just in case. We do not believe the Iraqis will invade, but if they do, they will only take the Rumillah oil fields, down to Mutlaa Ridge. We don't need to worry."

Despite the embassy telling its wardens not to disseminate that crucial information, it did get around, especially the bit about the Iraqis only taking the northern oil field. It was one reason why, when some people, including Dave, heard there had been an invasion, they were initially unalarmed. It made sense. The Iraqis had repeatedly claimed that the Kuwaitis had illegally moved their border with Iraq seventy kilometres north from Mutlaa to Abdaly during the Iran-Iraq War, and stolen much of Iraq's oil. Compensation for the loss had been a major Iraqi demand at the Jeddah talks. So, many British workers thought it was just the northern part of the country the Iraqis wanted and most of them still went - or tried to go - to work. When they first heard and saw tanks and troops in the city they thought they were Kuwaiti. Later, they thought the

Iraqis would rapidly pull back again. If not, the British and American troops would be straight in.

Although Dave Dorrington is critical of the embassy - he described the embassy's advice to lie low as "another big mistake" - it is clear that many, if not the majority of the community, concurred with the view that the crisis would soon blow over and things would quickly return to normal.

Those people with Cliff Lindley were certainly relaxed about the invasion. Cliff remembers how they would prop up the bar in his apartment during the first days arguing about when the Iraqis would be out of Kuwait and when they would be able to get home. Some thought it was only a matter of a few days. But not all. Cliff wrote in his pocket computer diary, "Christmas Day". That was on the fifth of August.

In general, the embassy was not alone in its complacency, and some people may, on reflection, be transposing their own guilt into anger at the embassy. "The embassy and Foreign Office had a very difficult job," Dave Dorrington argued, balancing his previous comments, though still bitter over their advice not to try to escape. "They would have been far better off to have said nothing than to say 'Don't do it'. By saying 'Don't do it', a lot of people who could easily have got out, didn't." But the advice fell on willing ears, because everyone hoped - and hopes lead to expectations - that it would all soon be over. It was the firmness of the advice which confused people, because the embassy "had always given us the very best non-committal face. They didn't want to know the ex-pats in Kuwait. They were not there for us, but to deal with the Kuwaitis."

As a result, the consensus of ex-pat, embassy and Foreign Office in the first few days was that no one should try to make a run for it or be too concerned, just stay calm and wait for it to blow over. It was summer madness. It was taken light-heartedly. To some, the escape attempts of the first two weeks were "a bit of a game", nothing serious, merely giving it a go. Dave Dorrington was one. "If you get stopped by the Iraqis, well, no problem, they'll turn you round and you can try somewhere else. Nobody took any of it really seriously."

Symptomatic of the embassy's ignorance of the situation was the call to lie low, which increasingly looked like a major blunder. During one meeting of the wardens, on about the twelfth of August, the ambassador did stand up and apologise to everybody for that mistake. He admitted it was the wrong advice, and that it was his fault. He had thought the Iraqi occupation was going to be a very quick thing, a position in which he hadn't been alone; virtually everyone else had too. But most people weren't in the embassy's position with regard to military information or in its position of authority. It was terribly unfortunate that, had the advice been given to leave, most people would have escaped. Furthermore, the embassy refused to take any direct responsibility for individuals in the community or to give any firm advice. It told people who rang - when they could get through - that they must make their own minds up about trying to escape. Whilst this attitude clearly saved the embassy from being accused of wrong advice, it left people leaderless and floundering. The embassy had a duty to both lead and protect. It failed to do either.

Over the first two weeks of the occupation, the embassy staff had some freedom and did try to organise and protect some groups in the community. Unfortunately, many people in the community, and especially the BA passengers on Flight 149, complained that the visits were only after repeated requests, and were frequently unsatisfactory. The man the embassy often sent out was Donald Macaulay, the Cultural Attaché, but others went too.

Joe Wild was scathing of the meeting with an embassy official at Abu-Hulifa, condemning it as a waste of time, and Henry Hill was equally dismissive of the one in Ahmadi. "There is nothing to remember about it. The embassy guy was useless. He had no ideas, no plans, nothing even to give us confidence or to get us thinking about what to do, or to suggest that things were going to happen. There were, apparently, ideas in the pipeline, but he couldn't talk about them. Nor could he even name one, which suggests there were, in fact, none; no suggestions for getting the people out at all, no buses, no convoys, no boats, no escape routes. All he did was bring a bottle of whisky. In the situation we were in, when we were thinking of going over the desert or getting out of the place, the last thing we were thinking about was whisky. He was trying to find out about the situation, but didn't have a clue. We were having to tell him basic things. He didn't know his way around, nor even about the oil industry. He didn't even write it down because he didn't understand what I was telling him. They can muddle by in normal times, but when the chips are down, you need guys who can do things and know what they are talking about. It just was not there."

Another early call made by embassy staff was to the IBI camp, the collection of prefabricated huts which housed, at the time, half the British Liaison Team and their families. On the second, Mike Devey reached them by phone. The Iraqis had seemed OK at the time. They had been polite and drank coffee with them, but the next day a call from one of the wives was more desperate. "The men have been lined up and marched off to the mess, where they're under armed guard." They were subsequently ordered onto a coach and moved up to Baghdad, leaving the families were left on their own. Mike phoned the embassy straight away, which promised to send Donald Macaulay down with his own sons to the camp to stay with them.

The families immediately decided to move into several pairs of huts for safety. They knocked holes in the dividing wall of each pair of huts, so they could be of help to each other. It was very necessary. The Republican Guards who had taken the camp had been replaced, on the third, by a motley assortment of conscripts who had discovered the liquor stored in the mess room and proceeded to get blind drunk that night. Once well lubricated, they broke into the soldiers' cars and sand buggies and drove them madly all night long, skidding, revving, racing and crashing them until they ran out of petrol. Some ventured up to the huts to see if there was anything worth looting. A group broke into one of the huts. One began fondling the breasts of a women and put his hand up her skirt, whilst another held a knife to a five-year-old boy's throat and began to kiss him. Fortunately, it went no further.

After that night of drunken revelry, the women in the camp pleaded with Mike Devey to send someone down to them urgently. Donald Macaulay was despatched. As he drove through the refinery, he passed smashed-up cars where the Iraqis had discarded them. When he arrived at the camp, he saw the state of terror the families were in. The women were furious that it had taken the embassy that long to get to them. It was clear that they had to be removed to safety, so Donald arranged with the Iraqis for them to be put up in the International Hotel.

It was the Iraqis who escorted the BLT families to the International. They were forced to leave at very short notice and were unable to take more than a few clothes and personal possessions. Once they left, their chalets were ransacked by drunken conscripts out to destroy rather than loot. The damage they wreaked on the huts was bestial and mindless.

At the International, the women and children found themselves in desperate need of more clothes, baby things, toiletries and toys for the children. The hotel had no air-conditioning and no proper facilities for the children, amongst them those parentless children who had attended the disco party in the IBI camp the night the Iraqis had invaded. The phones in the hotel were still working and the women managed to contact Mike again and tell him of their plight. The warden system then sent out a general request for members of the community to give whatever they could, not only for these people, but also for the passengers from BA Flight 149, holed up at the Regency Palace and SAS hotels.

One of those who responded - and the response was marvellous considering how many of the community were now out of Kuwait, sharing someone else's apartment or in dire need themselves - was Gilly Colclough. She packed a suitcase from her own sparse belongings. There was hardly enough for herself, but Colin Eglington, in whose villa she was staying, told her to take whatever she needed from his wife's wardrobe. Margaret Eglington was on holiday in Britain, so hadn't been caught up in the invasion. Gilly packed a suitcase full of clothes, toiletries, dresses, games, magazines, anything she could think of. There had even been a request for a certain size of bra, which she managed to find.

All the suitcases donated were taken via Kuwaiti helpers and other nationals via the wardens and BA staff and arrived safely at the hotels. The embassy was not directly involved at all. When Gilly left with the other women and children and arrived at Baghdad, where the British Liaison Team families had by then been taken, she met some of them. One was actually wearing one of her tee-shirts. They were able to laugh about it and it showed just one example of the spirit of unity which developed amongst some of the community.

Some of the wardens admitted they tended to ignore the embassy and went ahead with their own ideas. They found safe houses where they could move people to in an emergency and organised food supplies and money to be distributed to people through the Kuwaitis. Towards the end of August, when the Iraqis ordered that people would be shot for harbouring Westerners, they had to 'encourage' certain Kuwaiti landlords and Palestinians not to disclose people in hiding. The Kuwaiti Resistance made it plain that, if they *did* give anyone away, they would be shot. However, as added insurance if trouble ever arose, the people in hiding were always moved on quickly. One group included Derek Wright and his family. They had to be moved from Sha'ab, near the centre of the city, out to the house of a British family in the southern suburb of Jabriya. Unfortunately, this precaution didn't stop him being held up by two Palestinians who came to the door with guns and robbed him of his money and valuables. The Resistance had to move him again, this time in with Mike Devey, who had himself been moved to Rawda, where he was staying with seven other men.

Mike Devey had been a warden for fifteen years. He lived with his wife, Lesley, in a villa in Salmiya. When the Iraqis invaded, his twenty-two-year-old daughter was also staying with him. She worked for Kuwait Airlines as an air hostess. Even from the first day, Mike and Lesley bore more than their share of responsibility for the British community. The first night, they had four people staying with them; within three days they had nineteen; and eventually they ended up housing twenty-six men, women and children. He and Lesley didn't turn anyone away who was desperate.

One of the first tasks was to gather information, both on who the British were and where they were staying, and on the Iraqis. That was difficult and dangerous. One of the few people who did risk driving through the city was Jeff French, one of Mike Devey's neighbours. He was a single man and would don a stethoscope as if he was a doctor, in order to scout around. It worked; the Iraqis waved him through their road blocks.

Another person who went out to reconnoitre was John Levins, an Australian. John was based in the Muthanna Complex at al-Qibla, central Kuwait City. It was the shopping and residential complex which led into the Plaza Hotel and where several groups of British, Irish and Americans were hiding. There were no active wardens for his area so he phoned Mike Devey, who suggested he come up to the embassy for a meeting of the wardens. In effect, he became warden for a large part of the city centre and did an excellent job. He was very laid back and didn't care a fig what the Iraqis thought of his activities. He was frequently picked up, but always let go again. It never seemed to bother him.

John's first task was to discover what had happened to the passengers from the BA flight. On the third day of the occupation, he found them.

From then on, Mike's wardens phoned every day to liaise with the BA staff and get things to them.

The same day that contact was made with the BA passengers, a Saturday, the Iraqis lifted everyone still in their apartments on Misila Beach - Tom and Gilly Colclough had escaped to a safe house that day, so managed to avoid capture, but not others. These latest captives had to be traced as well. The next day, the wardens discovered them in the Airport Hotel and made contact.

Mike and Lesley's villa was one of four in a group. Two of the others housed British people, and the fourth was safe, so the whole complex was an excellent place to organise a large operation from. The villas were in a square and set within their own compound. There was a doorway between Mike and Lesley's villa and one occupied by Jeff French, another warden. The villa behind, with Richard Bubbs in, had steps going over its wall so they didn't have to leave the compound to get between the three villas. They wired the three phones into Mike's house. Two were in-coming and one was for out-going calls.

The complex was affectionately known by the community as the 'command centre', and functioned like one. "We set up the HQ in our daughter's bedroom. We had the short-wave radio in there, the three telephones and a mobile phone. We used our house as a day house, for living and cooking in, but everyone went back to their own place to sleep." As well as Mike, there was Mel Gage and three other men acting as wardens. Alan Jardine, one warden, was picked up in late August. Chris Bell took some of his contact numbers over and helped them. He kept in almost daily contact with the embassy. Chris Bell was awarded an MBE for his efforts. Many others deserved them as well.

With three wardens in their complex, they were very busy on the phone. On the first day of the invasion, time was spent phoning the UK to tell people they were all right, but at half past eight in the evening the international lines went dead and they turned their attention to contacting everybody left in the country, collecting names, making sure people were stocking up with plenty of food and water, and had gas bottles for cooking, spare jerry cans of petrol, and cartons of cigarettes.

They initially phoned people every few hours to check they were all right, but this was cut to once a day as the situation stabilised. They received an awful lot of incoming calls as well, from people worried and anxious about the situation. "A lot of the women just wanted to talk. They wanted reassurance. We were like counsellors." Lesley then interrupted her husband. "Plus, there were British women married to foreign nationals, Kuwaitis, Iranians, even some Iraqis. They were terrified, so Mike would get me to talk to them, you know, chat to them about anything, their children, family, jobs, lives back in the UK, anything."

Mike Devey had a group of committed people with him and organised the other wardens as his assistants. He assembled people's contact numbers and kept a log of where they were. He had military training, and it showed. He had tape over his windows against bomb blast and a rota of people to do tasks and keep a lookout, especially first thing in the morning. People trying to escape would notify Mike. He would put them on a chart to 'do a run' and ask them to contact the British embassy in Riyadh, which would then contact the embassy in Kuwait, to then contact him, to confirm that they had made it. Otherwise, they would assume they had been taken prisoner, or had returned unsuccessfully. He organised an underground basement with food, for emergency or war. He had people sleeping everywhere, moved them to safe houses, had them sleeping on floors and knocked walls down between villas. Because of the very efficient and security-conscious way it became organised, other wardens looked to it as a central gathering point for information. A chain of command developed. There was nothing official about it; it arose naturally because of efficiency and commitment. Between them, they had perhaps four hundred people on their lists. Other wardens and ex-pats liaised with them rather than the embassy, as they seemed to have far more information, and be far more accessible. They would phone to get corroboration or denial of rumours and to pass on information. "Whatever was said by the embassy, he would relay it to the people," Cliff Lindley explained.

Dave Dorrington built close links with Mike Devey's 'command centre' in Salmiya. "Without that organisation, a lot of people would not have been as well looked after as they were," he told me. One key activity of the command centre was the organisation of food distribution. Dave Dorrington acted as a storehouse, rather than a supplier. He had a lot of food with him, but didn't use it. He kept it safe for distribution to others, as and when needed. In the main, he was supplied by Filipinos. "It was very difficult to get in contact with the embassy. That was why Mike Devey's command centre became so important. You couldn't get through to the embassy. There weren't enough phone lines in there, or people to answer them. A lot of the time you would find them engaged. We just thought, typical of the embassy. I only managed to get through to Larry Banks at his home on one occasion and to the embassy once in the early days." He paused. "But by October and November, it was a lot easier to phone the embassy."

"Why was that?" I asked, naively.

"Most people had given up."

Mike Devey and his group were never lifted, although they did have to leave their villas in Salmiya after a few weeks and split up into smaller groups. By then, their task had been complete. They had preserved the skeleton of a warden system, kept the community together and built supply lines for information, food and escape attempts. The work of Mike, who was awarded an MBE for his contribution, and of those around him, shone out like a beacon in the storm.

Every night in those first days there was shooting along the coast as the fledgling Kuwaiti Resistance attempted to keep the Iraqi soldiers awake and scared. It took the Iraqis about a week to establish themselves along the main routes and in the key buildings and to prepare their main defence along the border with Saudi Arabia and down the coast. In that time, Kuwaitis were fairly free to move about residential areas. However, rather than being organised or co-ordinated, the Resistance consisted of individuals who unilaterally launched sudden guerilla raids on Iraqi posts or isolated groups of soldiers. In response, the Iraqis rapidly set up roadblocks on side streets and systematically swept areas looking for arms. It then became much harder for the Resistance and its activities tended to be restricted to coastal and suburban areas.

Meanwhile, most Britons were facing increasing problems. Some had not ventured out for days, had no money and were rapidly eating through their meagre stocks of food. "People were running out of supplies," Mike Devey explained, "so we had to get food or medicines taken round to them." A Dutch woman, Lisa Lotti, helped many people in hiding with food, especially dairy products. A British woman, Rose Lambert, was employed at the Danish Dairies. She stayed at work throughout the crisis and was able to get milk products out to the community.

A Kuwaiti who owned several supermarkets threw open his stores and they were able to stock up with a mountain of tinned food. They kept going up to his warehouse and filling up their four-wheel drives with stuff. "Our house was chock-a-block with food," Mike told me. "All three houses were full of dairy products, bread, meat and tinned supplies. This we distributed to other people." The distribution network initially consisted of British couriers, including some wardens, but when Westerners began to be rounded up, it was a few daring people like Lisa Lotti and John Levins, friendly Kuwaitis and an Egyptian "who had an English wife and was marvellous" who took food round to Britons in need. "We got heart tablets for a woman called Rachel, we got doctors to go to one of the elderly couples, we got medicines for all sorts of things. It was knowing who to talk to, and getting them to give us the drugs." They had several contacts amongst the staff of the hospitals and amongst doctors. In general, the Kuwaiti professional class were very helpful to the British and many doctors helped Westerners whenever they could.

Almost immediately, the Kuwaitis were sending people into the desert to map out escape routes. The Kuwaitis supplied a copy to a German, Ottmar Lange, who passed it on to Mike Devey. Ottmar was a rally driver and his map was especially useful because it marked out all the varying types of sand - soft, hard, stony, dunes, stable, shifting. The Bedouin could read the desert like a book, but for Westerners it was vital to know these things if they weren't to get hopelessly stuck in the middle of nowhere. Ottmar actually drove out of Kuwait twice in the first week with people and returned to pick more up. The route he chose was to head south-west around the Fifth Ring Road to Jahra, past the town along the road leading to the military air base, then cut west across the desert, behind an enormous scrapyard of abandoned cars, then along one line of pylons until he reached another line, and headed along that west to Salmi. At Salmi he took a sharp left five kilometres from the border and sped straight across. That was the westerly route. The northerly route was along the Wadi al-Batin, but that was not used until later.

At first, routes due south or south-west across the al-Wafra oilfields were also open. Tom Colclough knew of one. It was to head south down the coast road, then off into the desert following a track beside a pipeline, then north of al-Wafra and south-west again across the border. In fact, there were almost as many routes across the desert as there were convoys trying to get out.

These routes were being used every day by escaping convoys until about the thirteenth or fourteenth of August, when the Iraqis suddenly became much more determined to close the border, more repressive against the Kuwaitis, and intent on capturing Westerners for their human shield. This inspired hordes of unprepared and badly organised people, of every nationality, to try to escape over the desert before it was too late. They went without proper maps or guides and frequently without four-wheel drives. The situation couldn't have been worse. At the very time the Iraqis shut the door, a great mass of people tried to escape. There was absolute chaos in the desert and a lot of people died as a result, one of whom was British. "The next day there must have been fifty thousand cars in the desert, all of different nationalities, going this way and that way, hopelessly lost. People actually died in the desert, it was so hot, fifty degrees." It was suicidal chaos, "lemming runs", as Cliff Lindley had described them.

It was not just the broadcast which caused the Iraqis to close the desert routes. Two greater factors were the increased military build-up in Saudi Arabia and the imposition of UN sanctions, backed up by the British and American navies. It was becoming increasingly obvious to the Iraqis that they weren't going to get away with the annexation of Kuwait. As a result, from about the thirteenth of August they became much tougher with people trying to escape across the desert. They no longer simply turned convoys back or waited for them to get low on petrol, but started systematically arresting people and taking them to the hotels. The wardens still managed to get people out after that, but in far fewer numbers and in absolute secrecy.

In the first few days after the invasion, the British not only phoned each other, but visited each other's villas and apartments to confer. The residences of those wardens who hadn't left became focal points for meetings. Such informal gatherings went on in the towns down the coast, in Fintas, Ahmadi, Abu-Hulifa and Fahaheel. If one complex of apartments had enough Westerners in it, they would hold meetings as well, to discuss security, escape, food and petrol stocks, how to get out messages, and similar issues. Or they would just gather for company and a party. In this way a strong community spirit rapidly developed.

Through all the fear of the Iraqis outside, through all the bitterness at the embassy, at ineffective wardens and at increasingly feeling abandoned, through the growing hardship they found a strength in unity and a resilience to help each other. In this sense, it was a similar closeness as developed during the Second World War. Just as during the Blitz, with homes being destroyed and families broken up, so in occupied Kuwait, all they had was each other. The self-sacrifice of many people during that time was a testimony to the undying spirit of hope and humanity which held the community in hiding together during that time.

One vital consideration in those early days was the safety of people who found themselves isolated. Many Britons knew of safe houses and the wardens began moving people out of central Kuwait City and the exposed coastal towns into the indistinct hotch-potch of nationalities and nondescript apartment blocks of the suburbs.

One such couple were Margaret and George Parkin. They lived in an apartment in the Muthanna Complex. It was a splendid, modern development comprising seven high-rise blocks linked by a three storey shopping and business complex which contained the luxurious Plaza Hotel. Being such a prestigious centre, just to the south of the main commercial district of the city, it became a prime target for looting Iraqis and Palestinians from the very first day. Shops were broken into and watches, jewellery, electronic goods, expensive shoes and clothes were all taken.

On the morning of the invasion, George woke at ten past five to go to work. As he shaved, he heard bombs exploding. Suddenly, there was a terrible noise. The whole building shook as if in an earthquake. When he looked out of the lounge window, George saw that a rocket had hit the Kuwaiti Television Centre across the road. Margaret joined him, fear straining her face. In the road below soldiers were milling about stopping traffic, ordering Kuwaitis out of their cars, telling them to kneel down with their hands on their heads or marching them off. They brought up some large guns and began pounding the television station from the ground. They also shelled the radio station next door to it. Soldiers were everywhere and the streets were full of abandoned and burning vehicles. The couple could hear bombs going off all around them and saw great palls of smoke rising over the city.

The phone rang. It was a work colleague, Brian Richardson, calling from a flat above theirs, asking whether George was going to work. He said no, not after seeing what was happening outside. Brian agreed. George then rang some other people to get their reactions. As he did so, he watched events unfold on the street below. There seemed to be very little resistance. He didn't see any tanks, as their complex was not on the main highway, but he certainly heard them.

Margaret tried to phone the British embassy. It was on answer phone. She and George never once saw anyone from the embassy, nor heard anything from the staff. In fact, they thought the embassy was deserted. It might as well have been. "We were very surprised when we heard there was anyone in there."

Their apartment was close to the Sheraton Hotel. The Iraqis rapidly took that building over and turned the Sheraton roundabout outside it into a central army depot. Iraqi troops were everywhere. There were lorry loads of them passing continuously. Even the Pizza Hut directly below the Parkins was taken over by soldiers. They virtually lived in it and hung their washing up outside. Other soldiers began looting the watch and jewellery shops in the luxury shopping complex. They were a scruffy bunch; many of them had no shoes. Those that had footwear didn't have boots. They wore flip-flops or plimsolls. But after a couple of days they all had brand new gold watches. Only the maroon-bereted ones had good uniforms. They were the élite troops, used to keep the rabble in line through fear and regular executions.

At first, the Iraqis didn't bother too much about foreigners, but house searches began after a few days. It was far more dangerous to venture onto the streets in the city centre than it was in, say, Ahmadi. There were far more troops around and they were a great deal more determined. Four Britons ran the gauntlet on the Saturday. They went out for cigarettes and never returned.

The Parkins lay low for four days before they decided they'd had enough. That day they had a narrow escape.

"Margaret was taking a bath and I was relaxing reading a book when suddenly there was a loud pounding on the door of the apartment. We heard Arab voices and one of them told us, in broken English, to open up. They were obviously Iraqi soldiers. One of them peered through the letter box, but I kept well back. I saw the barrel of a sten gun as the soldier stood up again. Once more, they rammed the door with their rifle butts. We didn't answer. After a few minutes, they went away.

"We were sure the soldiers would be back. It was getting far too hairy. We decided we had to move out." They had an address of some friends who were fortunate enough to be on holiday in England. Thinking the crisis would soon be over, the Parkins travelled lightly. They took a couple of suitcases and the car. The flat was in Bayan, near the Bayan Palace. It had been the site of a major battle and had been heavily bombed. They still did not feel safe. It was a Palestinian area and they didn't like any Westerners staying there. "They thought we would bring the Iraqis looking for us. And, of course, we were very aware they might turn us in at any time."

Margaret and George stayed there for two weeks. Another couple, Dorothy and George Robertson, moved in, as did a friend of George Parkin's, so there were five of them there in the end. "The Palestinians became more and more hostile, so we were given another address, this time in Mahbola. It's further down the coast, right out of the city. We stayed with Dave Gaskill and some other Brits. There were twenty-five of us in two apartment blocks. But within two days of us arriving, eight made an escape attempt early one morning, taking three Land Rovers with them."

The seventeen remaining had just one Land Rover left. They included ten women and children. The eldest child was eleven, the youngest two. They cleared one flat, covered the windows with curtains and turned it into a crêche with all the toys they could muster. They even tried to give lessons. Margaret taught English and someone else was good at maths and computer training. But the kids were reluctant to sit still and learn. Instead, they were content to do jigsaws and play games. Meanwhile, the adults busied themselves with household chores and making the block secure. Margaret spent her time doing a lot of the cooking. A night rota of three-hour shifts was drawn up to patrol the compound and guard the cars stored beneath the flats.

George Parkin was not very impressed with the warden system. Because so many had deserted, there had been no warden for them at the Muthanna Complex. They had no idea who he or she was and were never contacted by him or her. Nor was there a warden for them at Mahbola. They had only come into direct contact with the wardens at Bayan. Their warden there, Roy, had been very good to them. He brought them jump leads for their jeep and kept coming round to ensure they were all right. He kept a list of Britons in his area and asked George to help him keep track of them. Roy stayed in Kuwait until he was captured in December.

Thus, George, like a number of other Britons, took up the challenge facing them and became an unofficial assistant to his warden. He even attended a meeting of the wardens in the third week after the invasion. It was at Roy's flat. They were trying to compile a list of British people in Kuwait. Unfortunately, so many had left, were on holiday, or had failed to report their presence when they arrived that assembling an accurate list was proving virtually impossible. This, in turn, meant the embassy had only a rough idea of numbers in hiding, which explains the discrepancy between estimates of British in Kuwait and those who actually came out, by as many as a thousand.

By the sixth, the initially friendly attitude of the Iraqis to the British and Americans had dramatically changed. UN sanctions were met with a dramatic clampdown on both nationalities. A headline in *The Independent* of that day read, "Iraq Warns West Trade Ban Puts Hostages in Peril". Whilst the new Kuwaiti 'government' announced that foreigners were free to leave for Iraq overland, if they wished, this double-speak had the implied message that they were no longer allowed to leave for anywhere else, by any other means. The puppet Foreign Minister of the new Kuwaiti regime openly threatened to use Westerners in Kuwait as a bargaining chip if economic sanctions went ahead and announced that the international airport was closed. With it went any hope of BA Flight 149 ever leaving.

An article in *The Times* stated that "President Saddam yesterday threatened the well-being of British, American and other Western citizens in Kuwait in an attempt to thwart economic sanctions aimed at forcing Iraqi troops to withdraw from the Gulf state."

Again, *The Times:* "Last night, President Saddam's use of the British citizens of Kuwait as pawns was dismissed by the Foreign Office in London. 'If this is the threat it appears to be, it is totally unacceptable and not the way civilised countries behave.'"

Significantly, the sixth was the first day the press used the word "hostages". It was the day when it was learnt by the world's press that thirty-five of the British Liaison Team had been taken to Baghdad, and the day Gerald Kaufman, Labour Party spokesman, criticised the British government for allowing them to be "kidnapped". It was the day the first figures came out on British citizens in the countries affected. There were estimated to be three thousand trapped in Kuwait and a further two thousand in Iraq. The numbers were significantly less than the usual size of the communities because as many as two thousand, mainly women and children, were on holiday around the world at the time of the invasion. It was also the day Britain announced it was sending frigates to the Gulf and that it had frozen all Iraqi and Kuwaiti assets in the country.

After a week of nervously trying to accommodate the entire occupying army, the Mansells moved into the house of friends, the Goodridges, who were out of the country. It was better built than their villa and off the main road. The atmosphere was beginning to grow more tense as the Iraqis realised the British and Americans were not going to let them get away with the occupation and as world leaders started attacking Iraq. "Every time Mrs Thatcher kept saying things it was getting worse for us." Anne Mansell explained. "Don't get me wrong. I admire her and supported everything she was saying, but the Iraqis didn't. When they realised they would be fighting the Americans and the British, that was it, we were finished."

They waited until it was dark before they began to load one of their cars. Everything was packed ready, including every bit of food they had. Stephanie took her doll's house, Joanna and Stuart took their school books and brought every video they could find. Anne's husband Stephen packed two suitcases of clothes, photographs, documents and mementoes.

At their destination, they were careful not to disturb anything, so no one would realise the house had become occupied. They didn't touch anything outside, even things blown over, didn't park their car anywhere near the villa, and didn't water the plants wilting in the heat. "We went into a back room, put mattresses up against the window and put the one lamp we used on the floor, along with the television and video recorder, which we brought from our place. Other than using one of the bedrooms, where we had to be just as careful, and the kitchen, that was it. We never put any lights on. We kept the house really dark so it looked totally deserted."

The Mansells did everything they could to make life difficult for the Iraqis. Whilst in their own house, they cut an Iraqi communication cable which ran along the back of their garden, stealing out at night with a kitchen knife, peering round the back gate, sneaking over to the cable, then scampering back inside. And, in the morning, the Iraqis came along, cursed the Kuwaiti Resistance, and laid a new one.

The British community as a whole suspected their phones were being tapped and that the Iraqis were systematically going through phone books to find the addresses of English-speaking people, so the Mansells bought cans of spray paint and started to obliterate the names on the post boxes of the houses, ripped off their numbers, and pulled down or turned around as many road signs as they could find. Other people were doing the same, especially Kuwaitis. The idea was that, unless someone actually knew Ahmadi, they wouldn't be able to trace any particular address. They also removed the company markings from cars, so no one would know whether they were owned privately or by a Western company.

The situation was steadily becoming more acute for the British community. The phones were being tapped, the Iraqis were doing house-to-house searches, people were being picked up and the curfew was being strictly enforced. The Mansells, behind their closed curtains and mattresses, could hear gunfire and explosions every night. Stephen found a hammer and some nails and hung two thick duvets up across the alcove. He pushed the sofa up to them, so there was no light coming through from their makeshift room. The single lamp was always kept on the floor and the television's sound kept down low. Fortunately, the garden at the back had a six foot wall around it, which reduced the chance of anyone hearing or seeing anything.

The British were continuing to form into groups and the Mansells were asked to join one, but they decided against it. Stephanie was so young they felt they couldn't risk putting other people in jeopardy. Whilst the rest of them could be silent when Iraqis came snooping or knocking on the door, Stephanie was far too active and talkative to risk her with other families. That was why they never made any attempt to hide her father, Stephen, in a cubby hole or an air vent. She would very likely give him away if the Iraqis came, so why take the chance?

For three weeks, the five of them were stuck in one tiny room barely ten feet by eight, a mere alcove. They couldn't risk leaving the house at all. It was awful. Fortunately, they knew a Kuwaiti couple, Khalid and his wife, who regularly brought them fresh vegetables and other food. On the whole, those Kuwaitis who decided to remain in the country were extremely helpful to the British, often risking their own lives for them, especially when, at the end of August, it became an offence punishable by death to harbour foreigners. One Kuwaiti set about organising the British in Ahmadi, finding safe houses for them further north in Salwa, a suburb of the city. Once again, the Mansells refused to go, not wanting to put other people at risk.

Some of the British community were in desperate need of medication, but none dared go near any hospital or official building for fear of being picked up. The local hospital in Ahmadi had been turned into an Iraqi military hospital so, during the first week, British nurses went into it, at considerable risk, and brought out medicines for them. A local Kuwaiti doctor stayed in Ahmadi throughout the occupation, supplying Anne and many other people with vitamin tablets and medical advice. He too was acting under extreme personal risk as his sons had been threatened with being shot by the Iraqis for sheltering their mother, who happened to be British.

Although it seemed like a big game at times to the children, the strain soon began to tell. They couldn't go out, they couldn't play, they couldn't see any of their friends, they weren't getting any sunshine and for days at a time their food was lacking in fresh vegetables and fruit. They felt cramped, stuffy and bored out of their minds. It became tense and difficult for them. They soon worked their way through all the videos - they must has seen Mary Poppins fifty times. Stephanie would cry or make demands all the time and they had to give in to her. She was given anything she wanted, in order to keep her quiet.

"We were using the kitchen, but only during the day, because I daren't cook a meal at night with the lights on. If we had to walk from one room to another we had to use a torch, shining it along the floor and not up at all, trying to avoid the cockroaches as we went. We tried not to get too hysterical, to just be sensible. We put mattresses and beds against the window in the kids' bedroom to absorb any stray bullets."

The situation began to play on Stephen's mind. He was used to living such an active life, Anne often hadn't been able to pull him away from his work. But now, canned up like sardines, he was coping badly. Suddenly, he had no control over his life. He felt totally powerless. He couldn't escape his thoughts. There was nothing he could do, and yet he was desperate for his family's life to return to normal. Perhaps he blamed himself for getting his family into the situation. Perhaps all sorts of wild thoughts, emotions and schemes rattled about his brain.

They were trapped within a four-walled skull, all their senses turned in upon themselves. Their eyes looked inwards, their talking was inwards, their whole lives were contained within a tiny part of one room. It was an imprisonment where they were their own warders. They had to keep themselves indoors, they had to keep themselves quiet, they had to keep to a self-imposed routine and cook only one meal a day.

Being forced to impose these harsh conditions on themselves made their situation far harder to bear. The tension was claustrophobic. At times, they wanted to scream and pull their hair out, tearing at themselves to relieve their pent-up frustration. They would rip at themselves mentally as well, getting on each others nerves. They had no personal space whatsoever. The adults couldn't escape the kids, the kids couldn't be free to play without being told off, Stephen and Anne couldn't have time for themselves.

It was like serving a prison sentence, yet far worse. They had no idea when they would be released. They had no idea *if* they would be released. They were witnessing their children suffering every moment of the day. They couldn't relax for a moment. They didn't know whether the Iraqis would find them and they would be separated for months. Nor could they, like other prisoners, write home. No letters came in and they could send none out. It was hell.

Stephen coped by retiring to the darkened bedroom all day and night. He lay on the bed or sat in a chair, totally passive, unwilling to do anything, mentally escaping into his own world. Anne found it deeply worrying. She tried to motivate him, to get him making things, doing repairs or improving their security. She even had to force him to eat, cajoling him, encouraging him and, at times, losing her temper. Stephen was to lose over two stones in that first month. Again and again, he would blame himself for them being there. All through those sleepless nights he would tell her it was his fault, it was his fault. She couldn't cope with what he was going through. She would try to reassure him, but that didn't work; she tried to distract him, but that failed as well. It was as though he was intent on making himself suffer; it was as though he was loading all the guilt he could onto his shoulders to assuage the depth of his sorrow. But it made him worse. Anne saw her husband going down and down before her eyes.

The family had to conserve their food. It became very limited. The children soon became so used to onion soup and hard bread it became a joke amongst them. Joanna helped Anne with the cooking, which kept her busy. Two days before Stephen's birthday near the end of August, they made him a cake. It was barely two inches thick, covered in pink icing and hundreds and thousands, with one candle on it. That cheered them all up.

They made the best of their situation. Anne played Scrabble at least five times a day. "We had to force ourselves to do things and to keep the kids going. Perhaps that's why I feel so drained even now from that situation. But we did have many funny things happen as well. You can't go through a time like that and be morbid all the while."

Stephen and Anne sat around during the day wondering whether the Iraqis would find them. Invariably, one of them was on guard. They made a small slit in the top of a curtain and stood on a chair to see beyond the garden wall and into the road. Whenever they heard a lorry they quickly went silent, until they were sure it had passed. They only started to unwind after seven in the evening. The Iraqis tended to stop their activities about then and they felt relatively safe after nightfall.

None of them answered the telephone unless it obeyed a code the community had devised. It had to ring three times then stop and ring again. Some people went as far as to use codenames, so as not to give themselves away. Of course, there were those who took it to an extreme, or found it impossible to be serious. "Hello, this is Bo Peep. I've lost my sheep!" or "We're meeting round Miss Muffet's tonight. Bring your own tuffet."

At about seven, the tension would relax a little. The kids would jump in the bath in the dark whilst Anne threw their things into the washing machine and laid out their pyjamas. Once they were safely tucked up in bed, she and Stephen had some time to themselves. Things began to settle down. But then the gunfire and explosions would start and the kids would run in, and it would all start again. They tried to sleep, but the stress made it very difficult. Often, Stephen dozed fitfully in the bedroom as Anne lay awake in their little alcove. At about three in the morning, he would rise and she would try to get to sleep. They were taking it in turns to listen for trouble. This went on all night, every night.

Despite the tension, Anne found that she and Stephen argued far less than usual. They were emotionally and physically exhausted and anger requires energy. The kids were around all the time and they had to show a calm and co-operative face to them, so they wouldn't worry. They also needed each other far more intensely than ever before. It didn't mean there was no tension between them; in fact, there was more than usual, added to *because* they couldn't off-load it through anger or arguments. "The stress was awful. Our instincts took over. It didn't seem to matter how bad the stress got, we just had to live another day. We tried really hard not to let it show to the kids at all. In fact, I would say we argued *less* than we do normally, we were so intent on keeping outwardly calm."

As the days passed, the British steadily withdrew into hiding. They increasingly gathered into groups for safety and company. Barry Pickup ended up in one of these, but for the first two weeks of the Iraqi occupation he and others travelled about to different friends' houses, until the sixteenth, when they had to remain indoors. Just in case, he went out the first day and bought in as much food as he could. He was living in Andalous, to the west of Kuwait City. His wife Lynda and two children were in Greater Manchester on their regular summer holiday. He had been due to fly out to join them on the evening after the invasion.

Once it became obvious that the Iraqis were in Kuwait to stay and that the Western forces were massing for a major war to get them out, Barry realised he had better try to escape. He joined a convoy across the desert on the sixteenth of August, but was turned back near the border. The cars and vans had tried to get out south-westwards across the desert towards the Saudi Arabian border, but the track was completely blocked with hundreds of Egyptian, Jordanian and Indian families attempting to flee as well. They decided to turn back.

After that abortive expedition, Barry didn't go out of his villa for nearly four months. Some other British men and a Norwegian moved in with him. There was Yarl, Bill, Alex and John. They felt safer together.

Barry's flat was on the ground floor, which made it more dangerous. Whenever any Iraqi soldiers came snooping around, as they did on one occasion to steal their cars, they had to get down onto the floor and peer under the closed curtains to observe them. On that occasion, they had to lie still and watch them take the cars and not say or do anything. It was extremely frustrating for them all.

The Iraqis were around for about six hours, but didn't come into the flat. Barry had strewn old crates about outside and covered them in sand and rubbish, so it looked as though the flat had been empty for some time. They also locked and bolted every door into the flat. At night they would put some lights on to ward off looters.

Local Palestinians knew they were there. They would complain to Barry whenever they saw him, telling him he was causing them a lot of trouble by bringing the Iraqi soldiers round. Barry had to threaten them to ensure their silence. He told them that if they were caught, he would let the Kuwaiti Resistance know they had turned them in, and they knew what that would mean.

The men gradually began to settle into a routine. As time passed, they realised they may be holed up for months and decided to start rationing their food and make the best of their situation. They continued to make an effort and tried to laugh and lighten up. If it was someone's birthday or a special occasion, they would get dressed up, and someone would cook a really nice dinner. It gave them pride and kept them amused. However, the strain began to show. The two youngest men found the excruciating boredom hard to take. Cracks began to appear.

On the eighth, a large convoy of two hundred and fifty Westerners made a bid for the border. One member was Susan Breeze, a nineteen-year-old physical education teacher from Powys in Wales. Her group had been hiding in Mahbola, on the coast road. They had decided to leave because they heard gunfire for several days as the Resistance attacked Iraqi soldiers driving down the coast road and deploying along the beaches. It had become very dangerous to stay where they were. In Susan's words, "people started panicking and our food supplies started running out". They had felt they had no choice but to make a run for it.

Four of the cars were stopped by Iraqi soldiers near the border and escorted back to a local army headquarters. There, they were split into two groups of ten and taken straight to a strategic site. It was an extremely worrying journey. As they were driven along dusty desert tracks, they realised they had become some of the first members of the 'human shield', a phrase taken from the Iraqis themselves, who were describing the Westerners trapped in Kuwait as instruments of peace - in effect, pawns to prevent war. Those they joined at this early stage were mainly members of the British Liaison Team and a few others picked up on the first day, or on the streets subsequently. There were probably less than a hundred of them at the time, taken to a few key installations both in Iraq and Kuwait. But the policy had begun.

Very few of these people had many clothes or other possessions. Those picked up on the first few days, like Stewart Griffiths and Frank Kerfoot, had only what they stood up in. The BLT men only had hand luggage with them and those from the convoy had been travelling as lightly as possible.

There was never anything provided for them, no clothes or toiletries other than very basic stuff like bars of soap. The installations were usually filthy when the hostages arrived, and the first task was to clean them up. But their treatment was not harsh. They tended to be handled with respect and their guards usually tried to make their conditions tolerable. "The next day," Susan Breeze explained, "the Iraqis brought us sheets, towels, cigarettes, and blankets. Our warders were kind and respectful. We had no trouble from them."

However, the Iraqi leadership was intent on making life as difficult as possible for the hostages. After a few days, they were suddenly told to pack their meagre belongings and to board another bus for another installation. After a few more days, they were taken to a third. The Iraqis were attempting to fool any military attack by moving them at short notice around the sites. As they moved out, others moved in to take their place. A comprehensive strategy of moving the hostages, mainly British and American, but also French, German and Japanese, around the sites like pieces on a chess board was being evolved by the Iraqis by the middle of August. But they didn't have enough pieces. The systematic search for more was about to begin.

Thirteen days after the invasion, Carrie-Anne Dowsett carefully dressed herself in trousers, a shirt and heavy jacket to look like a boy. She pushed her hair up under a cap and slid down low in the back seat of her father's car. With her father Brian and step-mother Linda, she anxiously joined a convoy of cars heading for the border. Her disguise was in no way frivolous. She was only seventeen. They had heard of people being turned back from the border and reports of cars being stopped by Iraqis and women being raped whilst their men were held at gunpoint. They all knew the fate of the convoy including Susan Breeze.

It had taken three days to plan their escape. Tanks rolled by their apartment as they stocked up with tinned food and water canisters. Five other Britons went with them, and a Persian cat called Miso. The convoy consisted of every nationality. It was a motley collection of anyone who wanted to risk the three hour drive across the desert.

Despite their fears, the Iraqis they passed were friendly and made no attempt to stop them. Nor had the crossing been closed. The soldiers waved them through the border post without demanding to see passports or even stopping them.

The first thing she did when safely in Saudi Arabia was to phone her relatives in Rugby to tell them they were free. When she returned to England a few days later, the local press were there and covered her story extensively. Josie Brookes, of the Midlands helpline, had been in close contact with Carrie-Anne's family and gave them a ring to congratulate them. She was elated, but the situation Carrie-Anne described to her over the phone was worrying, very worrying indeed.

The Gilded Cage

"They had splendour without freedom; they were canaries in a gilded cage."

Foreign nationals continued to flee from Kuwait. At the time of the invasion, the tiny emirate had more foreign workers than Kuwaitis. There were an estimated 150,000 Egyptians, 300,000 Palestinians and 400,000 Asians from India, Pakistan, Sri Lanka, Bangladesh and The Philippines. Of the Western nationals, there were barely a hundred Australians, fifty from Ireland, less than a thousand from the Soviet Union, but up to 2,000 Americans and 3,000 Britons, if one deducts those away on holiday.

There were also thousands of foreign workers in Iraq who feared for their lives. It had 1,600,000 Egyptians living within its borders, as well as 170,000 Palestinians. Many of these poor souls piled everything they could on top of their cars and headed west towards the Jordanian border at al-Ruwashid. Huge queues formed both sides of the border and hasty refugee camps were built in the Jordanian wastelands. They were joined by thousands more who had fled from Kuwait up through Iraq or across the Saudi desert.

The problem rapidly overwhelmed the Jordan authorities. They had no means of dealing with so many homeless people. King Hussain pleaded for funds and supplies of food, tents and bedding for the refugees, bitterly complaining that the rich Western nations had ignored their plight.

Thousands of Indians, Filipinos, Pakistanis, Sri Lankans and Palestinians flooded into two large, makeshift camps at Shalaan and Ruwashid Bridge. They had no shelter, no toilets or washing facilities, very little food and barely enough water. As lorries arrived with bottles of water, they were inundated by desperate men and women who boarded them and indiscriminately hurled the precious cargo to the madly scrabbling, fighting, screaming crowd. Occasionally, they would be forced into huge queues by the Jordanian soldiers, where they would wait for hours in the fierce heat for a few unleavened loaves.

The refugees constructed makeshift shelters out of blankets, sheets and clothes to protect their children. A few doctors tried to heal injuries, some caused by violent scuffles for water, and to prevent an outbreak of typhoid. There was no sanitation and the camp rapidly degenerated into a huge cesspit. Within two weeks, Shalaan One had grown to over twenty thousand refugees and Ruwashid Bridge to nearly ten thousand.

A handful of doctors struggled to cope from their hospital tent and keep down the deaths as thirty a day collapsed from heat stroke and many more were weakened by days without adequate food. The situation was rapidly becoming explosive. Without proper supplies, there was a serious danger of rioting.

Thousands more Asian and Arabic refugees were pouring across the Saudi border every day. There were three main routes. The most direct was straight down the al-Safr Motorway, along the coastal marshes, to the border post at al-Nuwaish. After a few days, this was heavily guarded by Iraqi roadblocks. Although it was still possible to get through, it was a long and risky process, involving hours or days waiting in the searing desert heat. Then a second route became more popular. So many cars and trucks began to use it, it had the appearance of a motorway. Again, it was down the al-Safr motorway, but then the convoys turned off south-west into the desert along the oil pipeline through al-Gurain to al-Wafra. There was a well-used track running alongside the pipeline, but there were thousands of Iraqis at al-Wafra, so they had to turn off westwards across the as-Shaqeeq desert towards the Saudi border.

The third and final route to be closed was due west of Kuwait City. Convoys had to take the Jahra road then turn westwards across the Salmi desert almost to the Iraqi border, where they could drive down into the Wadi al-Batin. This wide, dried-out river bed was ideal for cover and ran south-westwards, with Iraq on one side and Kuwait on the other, up to the Saudi border. The wadi was so well used after a week or so, it had hundreds of vehicles going down it every day.

Whilst four-wheel drives could negotiate the desert routes fairly safely, many of the cars and trucks used by the Indians, Egyptians and other nationalities were virtually useless. The desert is not just one type of sand. There are hard, stony areas capable of taking tanks, but there are also regions of soft, shifting sand which wouldn't support a camel. The Bedouin could read these instantly, but most people fleeing from the towns of Kuwait found it beyond them. As a result, hundreds of vehicles became stuck along the routes, especially in the Wadi al-Batin. Their occupants had no choice but to try to help each other out, a task which was frequently impossible. Many cars overheated or ran out of petrol, so their passengers had to leave their vehicles and walk or hitch a lift with another group. Others put up shelters and stayed, especially as the Iraqis began to turn people back from the southern end of the wadi. A huge jam of cars built up in the old river bed. Some people waited for days to get across. They began to wilt in the heat which rose to 55°C (130°F) or more. As they ran out of food and water, many were to die. It became known as the Valley of Death and is one of the greatest tragedies of the Iraqi occupation. No one knows just how many did perish there.

On the third of August, rumours circulated the Airport Hotel that the BA passengers were going to be moved. The Chappells, Shattocks and

Watsons hurriedly packed their hand luggage, along with everyone else, then went down to the foyer to be told by the Captain Clark that they would be going by coach to another hotel in the city. It was a relief to Eric Watson. Conditions were rapidly deteriorating and he felt very unsafe near so many Iraqi troops. He was aware that the airport would be a key target for any counter strike by the Saudis or Americans.

Three coaches came for them in the early evening. As it was approaching the seven o'clock curfew, the Iraqis explained they couldn't take everyone. But the Chappells, Watsons, Shattocks and Dolwins were all shown on board. One coach went to the SAS Hotel whilst the other two were taken to the Regency Palace Hotel. Both hotels were on the Gulf road overlooking the beach and sea and both were high-class, plush establishments. They were no more than a kilometre or so apart. The Regency Palace was decked out in marble and chandeliers, and the SAS was nearly as grand. Although the Iraqis promised to bring the rest of the passengers out the next day, many of them had to stay in the Airport Hotel. Their conditions during August deteriorated severely and they had a very bad time. The food was appalling, Iraqis were everywhere and they were strictly confined to the hotel.

Amongst those left at the Airport Hotel was a young man, Gregor Shaltz. Of German origin, he had grown up in East Grinsted and gone to an English school, he was travelling alone to the Far East. After four days at the hotel, he was in a group of hostages bussed up to Basra, where they were held in another hotel. This, however, was merely a holding operation until they could be shipped out to military installations. Gregor was put in with some Germans and sent to Baghdad, where he was twice moved to different hotels. He and a group of other hostages were then taken towards the Jordan border and held for two days in a workers' camp, probably at al-Qaim. The journey was awful and the camp filthy. It consisted of old huts with no facilities, no proper toilets or kitchens and nowhere to relax. They were kept strictly guarded within a fenced compound and surrounded by hundreds of soldiers guarding a major installation nearby. They still had no clothes other than those they stood up in. The camp didn't have proper washing facilities and the few showers they had were filthy. They spent much of the time trying to clean the mess up.

This was not the end of his travels, although his surroundings greatly improved. His group, which included women, was taken to another camp, but this time they stayed in comfortable flats and had a swimming pool to relax in. Gregor stayed there ten days until the beginning of September when the women were returned to Baghdad to be released. He went with them, hoping to be included for release as a student. However, he and a number of late teenagers were forced to remain and he was soon driven off to yet another installation. Gregor's experience was typical of the nomadic, uncertain life many of the passengers of BA Flight 149 had to endure.

A Pakistani stewardess from the BA flight was with other stewards on board the coach taking Flight 149 passengers to the SAS Hotel. When the coach arrived, it was met by several Iraqi army conscripts without their officer. The passengers disembarked and entered the hotel, leaving the BA personnel to check the bus and help unload the passengers' meagre luggage. The stewardess climbed back aboard the bus to check for things left on or under the seats. Someone climbed aboard behind her. She thought it was another steward, until she noticed they were heading into the hotel. By now she was at the back of the coach. She turned to face a beaming Iraqi soldier who offered her a cigarette, his AK47 hanging over his shoulder. She said no and decided to get off quickly. As she tried to squeeze past, the soldier grabbed her and pushed her onto the back seat. She screamed and tried to thrust him off as his hands fondled her breasts. A steward outside heard her. He made for the door of the coach, but another armed soldier was guarding it and refused to let him on board. As the steward argued angrily, the woman went on screaming. She tried to force the Iraqi off as he thrust a hand up her skirt and ripped at her blouse.

Suddenly, the coach went quiet. A few seconds later, the Iraqi sauntered off the bus, a broad grin over his face, pushing arrogantly past the British man. The steward hastily climbed aboard to find the woman crying and trying her best to get her clothes back together. She had managed to force the Iraqi off, but was very badly shaken. The steward helped her from the coach and into the hotel, where other stewardesses took her off to wash and recover. Meanwhile, the steward complained bitterly to the Iraqi's commanding officer, who had appeared. The officer took the man's allegation very seriously. He questioned the woman and assured her the guilty soldier would be severely punished. Later, all his soldiers were ordered to line up and the stewardess was asked to identify the soldier, which she did. The soldier was taken away.

Nawal Bel Hadj, an air stewardess for Kuwait Airlines reported that six air stewardesses were raped during the first days of the Iraqi invasion. Two were allegedly British, two Egyptian, one a Filipino and the Pakistani woman described above. One worked for BA, the other five for Kuwait Airlines. She described the horror she and the other stewardesses underwent. "The Iraqi soldiers were like crazy, rabid dogs. They are savages. I will never forget these atrocities."[1]

[1]Although I came across no other no proof of these allegations, several British women, and a large number of Asian women, *were* raped and even more seriously assaulted. Dr Easton, co-author of a well-researched report on the trauma members of the human shield and their relatives endured, confirmed that a number of British women had admitted that they were raped and that many had suffered traumatic events at the hands of the Iraqis. See: *Detention of British Citizens as Hostages in the Gulf - Health, Psychological and Family Consequences,* by Dr J A Easton and Dr S W Turner, in the *British Medical Journal, November 1991.*

Those taken to the SAS Hotel included the Shattocks. They joined Britons already held in the hotel, mainly those who had been staying in it on short-term contracts, but also some picked up by the Iraqis from the streets or as a result of house searches. One was Derek Hill, husband of Cynthia Hill. He had gone to Kuwait two days before the invasion and was due out again the Thursday after it. He had only one suitcase of clothes with him and hardly knew Kuwait at all. It was his first trip there since his days in the Navy many years before. He had no friends or contacts to help him and after the first day had completely lost contact with his family in England.

When the people from the BA flight arrived, it was a relief for Derek. He was able to talk to them and build friendships out of what was a very difficult situation. After the first day, he had not been allowed out of the hotel complex. Once in that first week, he was permitted to go into the city. He and a Dutchman were escorted to a chemist's to get toiletries for the women and children staying in the hotel. They had been astounded by the state of the shops. They were being systematically looted. Steel grilles had been ripped away, windows had been smashed and the shops had been gutted by fire. Everywhere, cars had been stripped of their tyres, engines and seats. Even street signs were disappearing on the backs of lorries.

After that one trip, Derek had not been allowed out of the hotel again. He was to remain there until late August when the Iraqis moved the remaining men and some of the women in the hotel up to Baghdad to make way for women and children coming out of hiding. Several groups of people, including those from the flight, came and went during his stay.

Typical of the people taken to the SAS Hotel were Helen and Peter Habnett. They had just been married and had been flying out to Malaysia on BA 149 for their honeymoon. Their first days together were proving very traumatic. But it was to get much worse. After they were taken up to Baghdad on the same coach as Derek Hill, Helen was allowed to fly home with the other women and children, but Peter was forced to stay behind. Not only were the newly-weds cruelly separated, but Peter was led off to an installation in front of Helen, and alone. He was only freed in December.

The Shattocks, with their two children, were to remain at the SAS Hotel for about four weeks. The BA staff with them were excellent. They comforted the passengers in every way they could. They had a desk in the foyer for information and to answer questions. Some had cars. They knew Kuwait and were able to go around the city looking for supplies for the passengers, particularly for medication for those who were ill. They set up a library and even had toys for the children. There was a suite available with a television and video player, where the children could play. One of the ground crew, whose wife and family were, fortunately, in the UK, brought in his children's toys and clothes and the contents of his wife's wardrobe. They reassured the passengers, organised bingo evenings, held a Mastermind session and generally kept people going.

In all, there were five BA crews, plus some ground staff, trapped in Kuwait, totalling approximately eighty-five personnel. Some were resident in the country, but most were just stopping over in the hotels, notably the Regency Palace. Many ended up going to Baghdad with the bulk of the passengers, from where they were sent off to installations.

Conditions at the SAS were excellent. The Shattocks had a suite of rooms and the food for the first two weeks was superb. They were given a lot of freedom within the hotel, although they couldn't leave it. They were occasionally allowed to use the hotel pool and some men used the gym, though it was at the whim of the Iraqis on guard. There were Iraqis dug in all around and the officers used to come in to use the coffee bar, but they were always courteous and didn't interfere with the running of the hotel or daily life of the 'guests'.

The passengers in the Regency Palace, Airport and SAS hotels, plus those Britons staying in other Kuwaiti hotels, such as the Meridien, Plaza and International, were getting extremely annoyed that no one had visited them from the embassy. Virtually every other embassy had sent representatives. The Indian, Filipino and Pakistani delegations had made an appearance, as had the Americans, but there had still been no British officials. After repeated requests via the wardens, the embassy finally sent a couple of staff, including the ubiquitous Donald Macaulay, to the Regency Palace and SAS hotels. They came several time in mid-August. A senior member of the BA crew commented on one of these visits. He was less than impressed with a young embassy man who didn't seem to know what he was doing, or have anything intelligent to say about the situation. He seemed to know nothing and was completely unable to help them, apart from passing on messages to the UK to say they were safe. "Apart from that, the embassy was not in evidence. We certainly never saw anyone from it and I don't know anyone who did." This general view was backed up by Maureen Chappell, and Claire and David Shattock from BA Flight 149, and by a stewardess from one of the Tristar crews, who were all extremely disappointed in the lack of help from the embassy.

On one occasion at the SAS, the passengers were assembled in a large room and given "a stiff upper lip chat". They were not very impressed. "We didn't get a lot out of it. It was very much keep your pecker up, the stiff upper lip, and don't worry about anything, which didn't really do much for many people," one of the passengers told me. In fact, it was worse. The passengers were deeply worried whether they would ever leave on the plane and were looking for some reassurance. Instead, according to this passenger, the embassy official told them that, "If and when the aircraft was allowed to leave, there was no guarantee that the passengers would be those who went on it. It might well be used for other purposes." Not the most sensitive of comments. He went on, "And that did cause quite an uproar." The overriding impression gained by the passengers was that he simply did not understand the seriousness of their position. "A lot of people thought he seemed not to want to know."

They had come off the plane with nothing, not even that essential of travel, a toothbrush. Whilst the BA staff arranged to get these things from the city, the embassy did nothing. In fact, contact with the British embassy was so "extremely difficult", at times the BA staff had to go through the French embassy, which was far more accessible by phone, for *it* to contact the British embassy.

Let me introduce you to the Melia al-Mansour Hotel. It was a name which was to ring around the brains of the British community in Kuwait and Iraq until December. It was the holding and transportation point for those British coming up from Kuwait to be shipped out to the strategic sites. There, the five nationalities who were held hostage and formed the human shield, the British, Americans, French, Germans and Japanese, were kept on the top floors, usually in separate national groups, the men frequently separated from the women. Each floor had a stairwell with two corridors leading off it. There was only one way down. It was easy for the Iraqi state police, the *Mukhabarat*, to watch every room by setting up a table at the stairs and sitting there all day and night. They were always armed, and usually reading newspapers to hide their guns and walkie-talkies. They had the only telephone on each floor as all the phones in the rooms had been taken out. Whenever a 'guest' wanted to go anywhere, he had to ask permission. No one was allowed to go to another floor without an armed security guard and they could not cross the stairwell. They were only permitted to go from room to room on their corridor, and they might even be challenged if they stuck their heads out of their doors.

The 'guests' weren't allowed to go downstairs alone, only in escorted groups at meal times. Nor were any British embassy officials allowed up to the floors. It was impossible for the Baghdad embassy to effectively check on numbers or names, or to keep track of people as they came and went. The hotel was surrounded by armed guards and, for most of the time, the grounds of the hotel and facilities such as the swimming pool were out of bounds - except for occasional photo-opportunities to allow Western and Iraqi camera teams to take pictures of how well they were being treated. The first group to be taken to the Melia al-Mansour were the thirty-five British Liaison Team men taken from the IBI camp. Later, their families were to join them and be taken out to several strategic sites in Iraq.

Alma Pennington was one of those taken from her hotel in Kuwait up to Baghdad, put up in the Melia al-Mansour, then taken out to an installation. She and the hostages with her were kept in a windowless army hut in tiny bedrooms, each with fluorescent lights which were kept on all night. Although the treatment they received was basically civilised, they all suffered from headaches and migraines. They were kept in the hut for three days with inadequate food and poor toilet and washing facilities. Worst of all was their fear of the unknown. They had no idea whether they would be taken off again, nor where to, nor with whom, nor whether they would be split up and never see their families again.

Alma was later bussed in to Baghdad to meet Saddam Hussein for one of the bizarre "Guests' News" broadcasts. She became very depressed by his propaganda. The pretence that they were guests worried her in case the world believed him and they were kept in Iraq for months. "They wanted us to say we enjoyed being guests, we enjoyed being a pawn on a chessboard. But no one would say it, not in our group anyway."

The phone rang yet again.

"Hello, the London Gulf Support Group. Can I help you?"

"Oh, yes, I *do* hope so. It's about my son. He's trapped in Kuwait. I haven't heard from him for two weeks." It was a young woman's voice.

"What's your name?"

The woman gave it more readily than many relatives. "Jean Rollands. My brother Jeremy's out in Basra with his wife. He was working for the Kuwait Oil Company. I'm sure they're in desperate trouble. I have to get in touch with them. Do you have any information?"

"Where did you say he was?"

"Basra."

"In Kuwait?"

"Yes. I'm desperate to get in contact with Jeremy's wife's parents. I've lost contact with them. Can you help me?"

"What's her maiden name?"

"Jefferson."

That name rang a bell with the volunteer. She pressed the silence button on the phone and mentioned it to the shift supervisor. "Wasn't that the name of those relatives on the TV last night?"

"I think it was. They've phoned us to say they don't want to do any more interviews."

"Was their daughter married?"

The supervisor checked the index cards. She was, but not to a Rollands. Nor was she in Basra. The supervisor took over the call.

"Hello, who did you say your name was?"

"Jean Rollands."

"Did you know that Basra was in Iraq, not Kuwait?"

"Oh, is it?" The voice at the other end then went silent.

"Are you from the press?"

The silence went on for a few more seconds, then the phone went dead.

Although Sue Brownlow was still organising a small, local helpline in Bristol, Rob had finally closed down his Bristol helpline and merged it with the London operation. All the calls to his home phone were automatically switched to the Connaught Rooms, as were those to Joanna's home in south London.

Joanna had been cautious about merging with Rob Hayward as she was anxious to keep control of the London helpline and to keep it away from politics. Rob Hayward feels he did his utmost to be fair and balanced and not to let his position as a Conservative MP influence the helpline politically, but it did create some tensions within the helpline. Throughout the five months to the end of December, there was an undercurrent of debate and argument as to the extent the Gulf Support Group should be political and be active in events such as pickets or demonstrations. Joanna was very aware that people might try to move in on the support group to use it for their own purposes, whether from the right or left of the political spectrum, and she was not prepared to let that happen.

One of the most consistent volunteers at the London helpline was Corky McGuiness. Corky became involved with it from the very beginning, out of a strong sense of injustice against individual freedom. For her, it was a personal moral imperative. "When I saw what Saddam had done to Kuwait and its people, I felt, 'This is intolerable', and wasn't about to sit around doing nothing. It was such an aggressive thing to do and made me so very angry. I wanted to do something constructive. It was the only way I could deal with the anger I felt." She spotted the helpline number and phoned it.

A young woman answered. Corky explained who she was, in her American accent, and was invited along to the Connaught Rooms. She had received counselling experience before and settled into the system immediately. The atmosphere was electric - chaotic, hectic, exhausting, tremendously stimulating and very, very positive. The volunteers were a team, bonded immediately and tightly in their joint effort to help the relatives in whatever way they could. Joanna and Jonathan were cónstantly working with the press, doing interview after interview, as well as helping on the phones. The lines were busy from dawn to dusk. "I loved it there. There was a really good atmosphere because we were in a little room and there was a wonderful person co-ordinating the phone lines - Jocelyn. She was marvellous."

Jocelyn was a teacher. She had a lively sense of humour and a very buoyant personality. She exuded a relaxed atmosphere full of warm vibrations. She gave everyone a strong sense of team spirit. It was like a family who had all come together for one purpose and it is striking how similar it was to the atmosphere at the Coventry helpline. The operation at the Connaught Rooms was small enough to feel very personal, as if it was a home - their own home, comfortable, warm and friendly. "It was a wonderful atmosphere for taking the phone calls, perfectly relaxed."

They needed that ambience to cope with the calls. Corky knew her limitations. She knew she could cope with many difficulties, but not with deep personal trauma, and there was a great deal of that. Some people were extremely desperate, too much so for Corky to take on board. If someone rang up in a very bad state, she would pass them on to another counsellor. "If we had a distraught mother on the line, those people knew how to modulate their voices, remain tactful and say precisely the right thing."

The helpline occupied two rooms. Jonathan and Joanna were in the larger of them, along with a couple of people making up a database and gathering information, whilst the people answering the phones, ringing people with information, keeping the daybook and writing out index cards were in the smaller room. The first was used for interviews with the press, whilst the second, being more private, was known as the Operations (Ops) Room.

However, there were seeds developing of future difficulties. The helpline was growing bigger than anyone had anticipated. The number of people needing help or information and the demands of the press were beyond what anyone had foreseen. The original organisers were working hugely long hours, collapsing exhausted every night, barely knowing where they were, trying desperately to keep abreast of developments as they broke. The problem was the extraordinary explosion of need. The average support group might deal with a handful of anxious people a week. The London helpline was dealing with *thousands* a week. It was not a situation confined to the helpline. Even the Foreign Office was caught out by the scale of the need.

It was a credit to the volunteers that the helpline coped at all. Every morning Jonathan went through the Reuter faxes and Foreign Office situation reports (sitreps), pinning the relevant bits onto a noticeboard. He wrote points relatives or the press might raise on a whiteboard, updating it as news broke. These were very useful to the volunteers as any information was valuable for the relatives and gave the helpline something concrete with which to allay their fears. On one wall of the large room was a map of Kuwait and dozens of posters with phone numbers and contact addresses on. Every wall was covered with information scrawled in black felt-tip, giving lists of emergency organisations and latest news from the Foreign Office, Reuter or people who had escaped.

Most arresting were those pieces of paper giving details of conditions in Kuwait, on the looting, food situation, curfew, arrests and conditions in the hotels. The telephones rang regularly with escapees giving them information. According to Rob Hayward, "Most of our information at that time came from men and women who had managed to get out of Kuwait. About a third of all escapees were phoning us up with information, much of which we could pass on to other relatives. Often they would give us long lists of people they'd seen or knew were safe. We had to follow all of these up. By the end of two weeks, the helpline had dealt with over one thousand five hundred calls." It was primarily these first-hand reports which enabled the helplines to deal with anxious relatives who had read unconfirmed "horror" stories in the press.

Some of the volunteers were from the National Association of Bereavement Societies (NABS), which had strict guidelines on many issues and were able to give structure to the Ops Room. These guidelines were adopted by the helpline to the letter. Other volunteers were from the Samaritans, also highly trained. They too knew the procedures and, together with NABS, were able to offer at least one person at the helpline all the time, as shift supervisor. Even when Corky first went, there was a trained counsellor on every shift. "The people in the Ops Room were remarkable. They were amazing people. It was a revelation to me that there were such nice people around. They were very sensitive and very loving. Those who were counsellors knew what they were doing and that gave the rest of us a sense of security."

To make the volunteers' job harder, the press became so intrusive they seriously encroached on the running of the helpline. Reporters and photographers barged into the Ops Room unannounced, either to get an idea of how it worked, or to try to steal the names of relatives with 'juicy' stories. Many were only out for an angle and couldn't have cared less about what was going on at the helpline. In fact, they were frequently a menace. They descended on the helpline like vultures. "At times," Corky explained angrily, "they seemed to be running the show, rather than the other way around."

Meanwhile, the volunteers were trying to answer the phones and retain confidentiality. "There was one terrible time," Corky explained to me as we sat talking over tea and cake in her London house, "when the press got completely out of hand. They would ring up and pretend to be other people, just to get information from you. They were despicable." Another volunteer described how some reporters tried to play one helpline off against another. They would ring Coventry to say "London has given me this name. They say it's OK to contact them, and to get the phone number from you", when London had done no such thing. They tried every trick in the book, but the volunteers were instructed never to give out any names, ever, to anyone, without that person's permission.

Despite these intrusions by the press, the helplines were keen to get publicity and would gladly deal with reporters and television teams. Nor were the difficulties all due to the press. Part of the problem was no one trained to deal with such hordes of reporters, until Andy Charles took up the position of press agent. Even then, as Joanna Copley was anxious that the official position was consistently put across, it meant that either she or Rob Hayward tended to do interviews. This took up such an enormous part of Joanna's time, it meant less opportunity to work in the Ops Room. It seemed, to some of the volunteers, to be getting out of hand.

These are reflections made in the relaxed atmosphere of hindsight. At the time, the volume of work was incredible. It would have overwhelmed anyone. The miracle is that so much was done and so many relatives were helped. Volunteers might be on the phone for hours with just one traumatised mother or wife. The pain people were experiencing as they imagined what their relatives in Kuwait might be going through and read the gothic press stories was so intense it is a tremendous tribute to everyone involved. Those organisational problems which did arise were the result of this volume of work and the inexperience of the organisers. Perhaps what a support group should try to do is bring experienced management in at the top, not to make decisions, which must remain in the hands of those directly involved, but to ensure the smooth running of the organisation. But that is far easier said than done in the hectic atmosphere of coping with a crisis. It was a matter of simply coping. That was the prime task and greatest achievement of all the helplines.

David Cunningham was assistant manager at the Plaza Hotel in central Kuwait City. No Iraqis came into the hotel on the first day, but by the third an army unit turned up and posted guards in the foyer. They checked the hotel staff and residents' ID cards, but took no other measures. The Westerners in the hotel thought of making an escape bid, but decided against it. There were rumours of the border being closed and the Foreign Office was advising people to stay put and keep their heads down.

The hotel staff were in a terrible state. The maids had no idea whether they would be dragged off and raped. No one knew whether troops would occupy the hotel or where food would come from. David watched as the Palestinian manager of the hotel disappeared into his office, leaving David to sort out the mess. He managed to calm the staff down and reassure them. However, many were to slip away during the first few days, never to return.

With so many Westerners in the hotel, David tried to keep them separate from the Iraqis as much as possible. He didn't let on that there were British and Americans in the building when he was asked. He attempted to protect them as much as possible over the next few weeks.

As the days went by, the shooting died down. By the third day it had virtually stopped and people were allowed out of the hotel to walk around the shopping complex. They weren't stopped or questioned at all. Some of the more luxurious shops in the Muthanna Complex adjoining the Plaza had already been looted, especially the watch shops, perfumeries and jewellers', but most of the other shops were firmly shuttered up. The Plaza had a café which opened onto the shopping mall. It was a luxurious shopping area, the same one as Margaret and George Parkin had lived above and escaped from. It had a marble interior, with escalators, palms and fountains. The complex had over eleven hundred apartments in seven blocks, linked by the mall and by numerous walkways. "It's just like a maze with all the corridors, stairs, turnings and fire doors, it's an absolute maze. And a lot of apartments were empty where people had left in a rush."

By the end of the first week, many of the hotel's room were also empty as its foreign guests moved out to friends' or workmates' houses in the suburbs, or were moved into safe houses by sympathetic Kuwaitis. It was as well, because it was rapidly becoming unsafe to be a British or American national in the city centre. By the first Sunday and Monday, there were a lot more roadblocks around the city and the soldiers on them were being more stringent. Westerners had been removed from the

Meridien Hotel across the road and the nearby Sheraton Hotel had become the Iraqi military headquarters, surrounded by tanks and military vehicles. The Republican Guard had generally been replaced by ragtag conscripts - the Flip Flop Army - who were far less disciplined. "Some hadn't even got shoes on. Some had trainers, others hadn't. Some had one colour uniform, some another. Some had guns, some hadn't. There were lads of fifteen and blokes of sixty-five with guns. They looked like peasants straight from the fields," David graphically explained. "These people couldn't believe the wealth they found in Kuwait. They went wild. They were shooting locks off and kicking doors down everywhere. There was no law and order." Looting had begun in real earnest.

The manager of the Plaza arranged for steel plates to be welded to the doors of the hotel which entered onto the shopping mall, to stop people coming in that way. He also ordered all the side doors and emergency exits to be sealed. Meanwhile, the mall was being progressively stripped by soldiers, Palestinians and Iraqis from Basra and Baghdad. Lorries rolled up and were loaded to the top with goods.

David realised how difficult the situation was getting for Westerners. The Iraqi colonel who was keeping tabs on the hotel was pressing him for the names of all its guests and he feared soldiers might start room-to-room searches. Fortunately, there was a little-used and very private conference suite occupying the top floor of the hotel. It was very quiet and quite separate from the main hotel. He arranged for furniture and beds to be moved into it and all the British and Americans were moved up there. They made themselves a lounge with a TV and video player from one room. Another became their dining room, where hotel staff brought up their meals. They had a kitchen, a gymnasium and sauna, and they could get up onto the roof to sunbathe and watch what was going on below.

As the days passed, the non-appearance of any British embassy staff became a joke. "There was a lot of laughing and joking about it. There were probably a dozen British people in the hotel and every other embassy which came asked, 'Can we do anything for you chaps?' We gave them a list of every Briton, with our passport numbers and towns of birth. We couldn't get in touch with the embassy directly because the phone lines were down, though it was only just around the corner, and the phones came on again after a few days. The other embassies said they would pass the information on."

On the fourteenth, after twelve long days under the Iraqi occupation, the British embassy finally sent two of its staff to the hotel. Although the messages given to other embassies were certainly passed on, they didn't have a clue any British were in the Plaza. They were completely taken aback to find them there.

"That upset us a bit," one of the British residents in the hotel related. "We didn't expect them to get us out or perform any miracles for us, but we wanted some reassurance that they knew where we were and we needed some advice. Basically, they didn't want to tell us anything, but wanted *us* to tell *them* things. They seemed to hold back information. We could tell them more than they could tell us. In the end, we just said, 'Well, don't come to see us again, we're just not interested in you coming to see us'."

David Cunningham was equally scathing. He had in fact phoned the British embassy several times to inform it about events. "They seemed totally ignorant of what was going on. I wanted them to give me information, but found myself telling them what was happening. The embassy staff were totally out of touch. They didn't even know there were tanks down the coast road! I wondered whether they'd actually gone out of the embassy compound at all."

The following day, the Iraqis announced they wanted all British, Americans, French, Germans and Japanese to assemble at designated hotels. To help the Iraqis out, British embassy officials came back to the Plaza Hotel and asked them if they wanted to move to the International Hotel with other British and American nationals. As the hotel resident recalled, "We thought about it for two minutes and said, 'No, we're not going'. They were taken aback by this because they'd got a minibus laid on to take us. But we said, 'That's exactly what we *don't* want. We don't want to be in a place where there are so many other Westerners. That's the first place the Iraqis will come looking'."

There were twelve British people in the hotel at the time, two families and a couple of single men. The single men felt they were prime targets for the Iraqis, so collected some hand luggage and fled early one morning to another apartment in the Muthanna Complex, one which no one else knew about. The resident of the flat was a Swiss chef in the Plaza who had left Kuwait. David Cunningham had his key and instructions on where to find the place.

The hideaway was on the seventh floor of one of the blocks. They were soon contacted by the Australian, John Levins. The Iraqis weren't picking up Australians, New Zealanders or Irish so he was free to move around the city. John had been helping the Australian embassy and, since the crisis, had taken on the role of a warden for the British embassy, filling some of the gaps left by absent wardens who had fled. John introduced the two young men to some others hiding in their block, nine Americans, Irish and British. Two were women.

David Cunningham tried to hold off the Iraqis for as long as he could, but the Iraqi colonel was under increasing pressure to take him into custody. Eventually, he was told he would have to leave. He was asked to pack his things and go with an Iraqi squad. He expected to be taken up to Basra or even Baghdad and be put straight into a camp. Instead, to his amazement, they merely drove him across the road to the Meridien Hotel! David was virtually the only one there. Only two other British families were with him, the Liddles and the Bignels. All other Westerners had been taken to other hotels or to installations. He waited there quietly until it came to his turn to be sent to Baghdad.

The Regency Palace Hotel, where Eric and Tim Watson, Katharine Copley, sister of Joanna, and the Chappells ended up had every facility a 'guest' could wish for. Its own swimming pool, a gymnasium, several restaurants, a ball room, a conference room with conference suites, tennis courts and even its own running track. The basement had extensive health and beauty facilities with saunas, weight training rooms, manicurists, sun beds and massage rooms. The foyer was made of marble, with enormous chandeliers and fountains playing between luxurious sofas and tropical plants. It was plush and luxurious and the food was excellent. It was where British Airways put up its transit crews, so two Tristar crews were already there. One of them was Philip Long, friend of Rob Hayward MP.

Unfortunately, most of the hotel's facilities were not open to the flight passengers and other British people who had been rounded up. They had to watch as Iraqis used the swimming pool and could only use the sports hall when the Iraqis permitted, although the children could walk across the forecourt of the hotel to play squash or badminton.

The day after the BA passengers arrived, some more passengers turned up, including Erica Masters. What struck her more than anything else was the Kafkaesque situation of luxuriating in this wonderful hotel yet not being allowed out of the front door. They had splendour without freedom; they were canaries in a gilded cage.

The Iraqis were polite and courteous. There was a piano in the dining room and Eric Watson, a musical director, accompanied the 'guests' as they ate their meals. The BA crews helped people as much as they could and they were allowed to hold quizzes and entertainment evenings. At first, they were also allowed to watch the CNN broadcasts, until the Iraqis realised what they were doing. But the news simply depressed them. There was no mention of their plight and they stared incredulously at the huge Iraqi military build-up and the international response.

No matter how wonderful the surroundings, they become oppressive when one is staring at them all day, every day. Troops were everywhere, in lorries, jeeps, cars and pill-boxes. Tanks surrounded the hotel and columns of troops passed by all the time. The hotel was right on Arabian Gulf Street, facing the beach, which the Iraqis were busy turning into one long defensive line of barbed wire, tank emplacements and mine fields. There were even Iraqis posted inside the hotel who used its facilities and others in machine-gun nests on the roof. More ominously, there were Ba'athist Party members about. They controlled Iraq like a man with his fist about a child's neck. They were the instrument by which Saddam Hussein ruled his people and ensured absolute loyalty amongst his armed services. They enforced his power through obsequiousness inspired by propaganda, genuine fear of the West, and terror. Party members, in their green uniforms, kept a vigilant check on every military unit. Executions were frequent.

As the days went by, it became obvious to the 'guests' that they were being held for some purpose. The main fighting was over. They could have been allowed to cross the border at any time, or been put onto a plane to Baghdad and flown out. Clearly, the Iraqis had other plans for them. Tension rose as they began to wonder just how long they might be held. The phrase "kept as hostages" cropped up. They knew their relatives back home would be getting increasingly worried. *They* knew very little about their situation or how long they would be detained, so their relatives must be totally devoid of any information. Furthermore, there was no sign of any British embassy staff. Where were they? At least they could take their names and telex them to Britain to reassure their relatives.

An Iraqi soldier, his hands tied behind his back, was led from his company headquarters by two armed guards and marched to the beach in front of the SAS Hotel. There, he was ordered to squat and left all day. At nightfall, exhausted, on the point of fainting from the heat and dehydration, he was marched back, taken behind the HQ and shot. It was the Iraqi who had tried to rape the air stewardess.

The Fist Tightens

"It was like bereavement, like somebody's dead. I feel I've been to hell and back."

For Derek Hill's family, 2nd August was just the start of a very worrying period. His wife Cynthia tried repeatedly to get through to him again, but by then the international phone lines had been disconnected. They hoped the invasion was no more than a typical Third World coup, the sort which happened on a regular basis and which would soon be over. They lived with that comforting impression for three days. It was a typical way of dealing with the shock. Saying it would soon be over was a way their minds could blot out the worst scenarios and cope with the crisis. We all need such mental safety valves. They let us absorb one level of shock whilst holding back on more traumatic ones.

"On Sunday night," Cynthia recalled, "it hit us good and hard that it wasn't going to be over in five minutes. Over the weekend it developed really quickly from being a bit of a skirmish that we thought would be over in no time, to growing out of all proportion." By the news on Sunday night, with Bush and Thatcher saying they wouldn't allow the invasion to go unchallenged and with Saddam obviously strengthening his forces and threatening to invade Saudi Arabia if it cut Iraqi oil pipelines, Cynthia realised it would be a long time before she saw her husband again. She went from one extreme to the other. Now, she prepared herself for the worst. "I really thought they wouldn't be out before Christmas.

Lynda Pickup had no one to talk to at all in those first days, except her two children, Richard and Heather. She felt physically and mentally cold. There was no positive emotion, just a numbness, as though she was suffering long-term shock. The fact that Barry could have been safely out of Kuwait just twelve hours after the invasion was very hard to bear. It hit her like a sledgehammer.

Her first attempt to make contact with other relatives was with the Bristol support group, from a number she had seen on the TV. She spoke to Rob Hayward MP who put her in contact with Dorothy Croft in Matlock, Derbyshire. Dorothy's daughter had been caught in Kuwait and she had decided to organise a helpline in the first weeks, running it on her own. Lynda phoned her and was put on the list for information. Dorothy was extremely pleasant over the phone and gave her the number of a woman living nearby called Cynthia Hill.

Cynthia also phoned Dorothy, who similarly put her in touch with Lynda. Cynthia was the first to phone. They discovered they lived only ten minutes apart and Cynthia drove round immediately. That began a long and very important friendship which was to keep both of them sane during the next four months. Cynthia ended up virtually living at Lynda's, although she struggled into her employment as a legal secretary for a firm of solicitors every day. "I never lost a single day at work. I went in come what may. I amazed myself at that. I put myself in a rut and kept going along it. I knew it would be easier if I had a routine, a form to my day."

They spent their time together watching the news and talking. Lynda could tell Cynthia what Kuwait was like, as Cynthia had never been out there. She knew the SAS Hotel, where Derek was being held, could describe where it was and what it was like. Because she knew Kuwait so well, she could explain how life was led in the country. It helped Cynthia get a much clearer picture of what Derek might be doing and how he might be coping.

And Cynthia was a willing listener who could empathise with what Lynda was going through. "To be honest, we didn't need anybody else," Lynda told me. "Apart from ringing a few wives whose husbands were with my Barry, we just had each other. That was the only reason we survived. We would chat and talk and scream and listen to the radio and cry. If I wanted to cry, I'd go and cry in her house; if she wanted to cry, she would come and cry in mine. I've never had so many cups of coffee."

If one felt down, the other would cheer her up, tell her to get out of it, joke about things, make her forget her troubles for a while. They began to develop in-jokes and comments or phrases which would make them laugh.

Lynda especially would feel low. "We'll just send the kids away," she would say, as a standing joke, "Move the fridge into the bedroom and pull the curtains closed until it's all over." They both felt like that most of the time. They were enveloped in a fantasy. They wished they had a magic wand they could wave and it would all return to normal.

"Wouldn't it be great if we could just shut ourselves away, fall asleep like Rumplestiltskin and wake up to find it was all over."

They would sit in Lynda's front room, in the dark, with the curtains closed, not moving. The crisis paralysed them. All they did was watch every single news bulletin. Lynda describes it as searching. They were searching for any glimmer of hope, because all hope had been snatched away. Anything, just to know Barry and Derek were OK.

Often, Lynda would turn up on Cynthia's doorstep with *The Independent* tucked under her arm. Sometimes, the paper would give them a spark of hope. One of them would draw attention to a good piece of news and try to buck the other one up. More often, Cynthia would go round to Lynda's whilst her mother phone-sat for her. This sort of arrangement was common to many families. It is similar to baby-sitting, only instead of reading bedtime stories to little ones, the sitter would perch herself by the telephone ready to pounce should it ring. Calls were so rare and might have such vital information no relative could bear the thought of missing one. They might come from people who had been with their relatives but escaped, or from their husband's company, or from the Foreign Office or Gulf Support Group. People could only go out and feel relatively relaxed so long as someone was watching the phone. And for some it was *literally* watching it. One woman wouldn't let it out of her sight for weeks, taking it everywhere around the house with her, sitting staring at it, waiting for it to ring.

They seldom went out together. They simply sat comforting each other. The idea of going for a drink or to a show seemed like betraying their husbands. For them to enjoy themselves, even once or twice, seemed terrible when they were in such danger. They couldn't live with the guilt.

"We must have been the palest people in the country. It was such a lovely summer and we just sat in all the time. It was horrid," Lynda explained.

"Did you talk to other people about it?"

"Different people treated me differently. Some people, whom I thought I was quite friendly with, quite close to and would be able to depend upon, turned out not to be able to help. Perhaps it's because they were too close to me and it upset them too much. Certain people just couldn't handle it. Even now, a year afterwards, I still feel some people can't talk about it.

It was exactly the same for Cynthia. Many people simply didn't know what to say to her. She realised she had to get on with her life, develop an independence and come to terms with the situation as far as she could. She stopped telling people about it. People sympathised but weren't in the same position. She began to realise she couldn't impose it on them all the time. Their lives weren't dominated by the crisis in the Gulf, so she had to stop letting it dominate hers. "It's like a death. You're allowed to mourn for a week or two, during which time people will mourn with you, but after that you're left very much to carry on alone. They've got to go to work, they've got to laugh, they've got to go out and have birthdays and holidays and enjoy themselves. They can't stop their lives because yours has ground to a halt. You can't impose your grief on them."

Cynthia was too anxious to eat properly for nearly two months. She found it very difficult to swallow food. Although she managed to drink a lot of milk and fruit juice, she lost over a stone in weight during that time. The very thought of food put her off. Even at work she couldn't face any. Nor did she want to cook. She forced herself to prepare meals for her three children, Rachel, Jeremy, and Nyree, but no one was eating it - only the dog. They were off their food as well and wanted to eat when they felt like it, not at set times, so she left them to it. It became easier to fill them on snacks and nip down to the Chinese take-away. It did a roaring trade for the first three weeks. "At first, I felt that was the best way of coping with it, but after a few weeks I couldn't accept it. I knew we had to get back to normal and, with an effort, we did."

Meanwhile, Lynda was watching news stories of people who had escaped and was becoming increasingly angry at her husband for not doing the same. Why wasn't he doing his utmost to be back with her and the kids, to put them out of their misery? "I kept thinking, you idiot Barry, what are you doing there? You've got a Range Rover. Get in the car and go. I was really angry at him. Really, really angry."

She could imagine vividly what Barry was doing at any time of the day. Instead of this helping her, it made it worse. She could imagine him in his difficulty and debated whether to try to get back to him. She could visualise the route she could take, how to get to Saudi Arabia, across the border into Kuwait, up the al-Safr Motorway and through the streets of Kuwait city. If only they'd let her in! But there was no chance.

Such wild thoughts added immeasurably to her frustration. "I could see him putting the kettle on, cleaning, doing his chores, going to bed, cooking, everything. That was worse than anything." It became unbearable for her. On the ninth of August she wrote in her diary, "Crying again this morning."

However, Lynda never had any problem sleeping, simply because she was so exhausted when she went to bed, after watching every news programme of the evening, finishing with Newsnight. "I watched all the bulletins. When it was on all day, I watched it all day. The radio in the car was tuned to Radio Four all the time. Everywhere I went, I had the news on. In fact, when I was at home, I used to have the TV *and* the radio on, listening to the bulletin on ITV whilst recording something else on BBC... It's awful isn't it," she laughed, unable to believe the extent of her desperation.

Cynthia contacted the London Support Group to get more information. It passed her on to Josie and Stephen Brookes at Coventry. From then on she was in constant contact with them, to chat or gain information as and when she needed it. The reason she made contact was simply to find out what was going on. She felt the Foreign Office were so cagey about giving out inaccurate information that they were holding things back from her.

She is also critical of the information the Foreign Office gave out. "If the Foreign Office knew anything, they certainly weren't telling us. You'd got all these women who were desperate for information. Even before the women came out of Kuwait, you'd got their families. One lady I knew had her daughter, son-in-law and their three young children out there. They were an old couple in their sixties, retired. They were absolutely out of their minds with worry about their daughter and her children. The Foreign Office just weren't doing anything. When you consider the amount of intelligence information they've got, I believe they could have done more and kept people better informed." Cynthia's eyes glared as she remembered her frustration. "They gave me a lot of duff information actually. They told me that Derek had been seen somewhere or other when he hadn't been. The worst example was when the women and children came out. They had told people in the Foreign Office that my husband had been taken to the Melia al-Mansour Hotel in Baghdad, yet five days later the Foreign Office was still telling me he was in the SAS Hotel in Kuwait. I even telephoned them and said, 'Look, these people were with him'. And then I got a phone call. 'This is the Foreign and Commonwealth Office. We have news that your husband is in Baghdad.' It was about six days after I had told them. I said, 'I know that; I told *you.*' Again, in October they said Derek had been taken back to the Melia al-Mansour, yet Derek told me later he never went back. So their information wasn't all that good. I wasn't too impressed."

If Lynda Pickup felt upset at night, she would phone any of a small group of friends, sometimes Cynthia, sometimes other women. She found the late evenings worst, when the children were in bed and she was left alone with time to think. So she would call someone or someone would call her. They would talk for half an hour, then she would go to bed. On top of all her other problems, she had acute financial worries. Like many women, she attempted to get money from the banks to tide her over. One upsetting task was to try to get the money back from the holiday to Spain she had been forced to cancel. The travel firm refused to give her any refund. They said she had cancelled it due to war, for which they were not required to give her compensation. But, she argued, there was no war in Spain. It didn't matter. She lost eight hundred and ninety pounds. That really upset her. She felt that everywhere she turned, she received no help at all.

The emotional pressure on her was so great that Lynda frequently lost her temper with her kids and, if she ever did go out, found herself constantly crying. Whenever her mother came over, she found Lynda in a terrible state. "I couldn't go anywhere. If anybody spoke to me, I just cried. I was cross, I was sad." She wasn't helped by knowing so many British people in Kuwait. Every time she saw footage of women and children at the hotels, or men in the installations, she knew some of them and it would provoke the tears to flow again. She felt awfully upset when the women and children came out, not with anger but a mixture of joy and relief for them and anguish for Barry. Generally, Lynda wouldn't let her two children, Richard, aged ten and Heather, aged eight, watch the news, but there was once when a friend came out on a flight with her new baby that she let Richard watch that broadcast. She was in tears herself.

The children were very good to Lynda. They seemed to understand what she was going through. They tried to carry on like normal children. Although they didn't show it, their Dad not being there did have a deep effect on them. Richard started to sleepwalk and talk in his dreams. His worry would come out in frequent questions about his father.

"Do you think he's all right, Mum?"

"Yeh, I'm sure he's fine Richard. Your Daddy's not silly."

Whilst Richard tends to stand alone, Heather is a very cuddly child.

She would plonk herself on her Mum and they would have a good talk together. But she was too young to really understand. Much of it went over her head. Meanwhile, Richard had to be sent to a new school. He had been due back in Kuwait for the September term so it was the first time he'd been to a British school. Fortunately, he adapted very well. His teachers were very considerate and helped him to adjust and get on with the other children.

During the four months of the hostage crisis. Lynda felt awful. "You just can't believe what it was like. I've still got that feeling in my stomach. It's as though you're on a diet and are really hungry, and your stomach's in a big knot. It's like feeling that all the time." She lost a lot of weight and found herself coming out in boils, as her nerves and lack of sleep began affecting her body's chemical balance. Her mind was working overtime with worry. "To be honest, we never thought we would see Barry again. It doesn't pay to think good things all the time. If you think you won't see them again, at least it's good when they come back. It was like bereavement, like somebody's dead. I feel I've been to hell and back. As though somebody's kicked me. Everything goes through your mind. You've got your husband, but you don't know whether you've got him or not. You don't know whether you're ever going to see him again."

Lynda couldn't escape her worries - ever. She thought about them throughout the day and took them to bed with her every night. There, she mulled them over again and again, refusing to let herself rest. Even her dreams seemed to be dominated by them. "I would wake up really sweating and thinking, 'Oh, God!' then turn over and go back to sleep." By the time she went off, she was so jiggered she slept soundly and well. Sleep was a comfort. When she was really down she would crawl into bed and fall asleep praying that in the morning it would all be over.

After walking into the front bedroom with a mug of tea in her hand, still in her dressing gown and slippers, Josie flopped into a chair. It was seven in the morning yet, as she glanced through the shoe box of cards for Betty Stevenson's number, one of the two phones rang. She sighed deeply, breathed in, pushed her chest out and picked up the phone. "Hello, Midlands Gulf Support Group."

"Hello, this is the *Daily Express.*"

"Oh, hello."

"Can I have something for our grief column?"

"Your what?"

"You know, someone who's really up against it, really upset, a name of someone whose son or husband's in an installation. Anyone else who's been killed. A real sob story."

Josie was horrified. Was that all this reporter thought about the hostages - a grief column? She tried her best to be polite, but it was hard. Meanwhile, Stephen was having to deal with ITN news. It wanted the name of a relative to do an interview with. Stephen said he couldn't give out names over the phone, but would ask likely relatives to see if one was prepared to help him. That wasn't good enough for the reporter, who insisted on being given a name. Stephen politely refused again, but the reporter was insistent, even rude. Stephen put the phone down. That same reporter was to ring another half dozen times that hour, hassling for a story. Whilst the support group needed the media, it did not need some of its tactics or cynical, callous attitudes.

Still in her dressing gown, Josie decided to go upstairs. On the way, she bent over to pick up the mail by the front door. She grimaced as her back jarred. She had an abnormal curvature of her spine. The strain was clearly showing on her face as she slowly made her way up the stairs. Her eyes were tired, her skin sallow and forehead lined. She had begun to hate the phone ringing at times. She was terrified about what distress might come through. There had been very few moments of elation, but many times when she wished the day would just go away and she could sleep through it.

The latest problems of the relatives overwhelmingly concerned money. Families in Britain without their menfolk were finding it very hard to get by. They had managed to survive the first few weeks on their holiday money, or with help from grandparents, but things were getting tighter every day. Bank overdrafts were increasing. Building societies were hassling them for mortgage payments. Stephen and Josie, both financial advisers anyway, now had to phone these institutions and explain the relatives' circumstances. The London helpline had very similar calls. They actually brought in a financial adviser who was able to deal specifically with these problems, and his efforts were greatly appreciated by the relatives. They had successes, with building societies agreeing to allow people to just pay the interest on the loan and some banks taking a more lenient and understanding line.

The fax machine in Josie's front bedroom was printing out a sitrep from the Foreign Office on the Iraqi call for all British citizens to assemble at the Regency Palace Hotel. It gave a rundown on the situation in every country in the Gulf. Josie glanced at it wearily.

She opened one of the letters. It was from a woman she hadn't heard from before, Terri Hinksman. She had recently escaped from Kuwait and had sent the helpline details of some people still in hiding, who they worked for, their names, and, especially, who was at the Airport Hotel. She also gave details of the letters they had written, and had information on one of the installations, though she didn't name it. There was a British family of four, two Japanese, two Germans, two French and two Americans incarcerated at it. This was a typical distribution. The Iraqis put small groups of each of the five nationalities held hostage in most installations, so each government had someone to lose if they attacked. It was so carefully planned.

Josie put the letter by the index cards. Later, she would add the details in it to the cards, then set about phoning the Foreign Office and the relatives of those people mentioned in the letter with the information.

As she drifted into her bedroom to get dressed, the phone rang yet again. She went back, picked it up and forced herself to be cheerful.

"You bloody bitch, we're going to get you, you bloody bitch!"

Josie recoiled in shock at the Arabic voice.

"We hate you. We saw you calling our president Saddam Hussein a madman. You're the mad woman. We know where you live. We're going to get you. We're going to burn your bloody house down. Ha!"

The caller was gone.

Josie was left an absolute wreck. She fell into the chair and burst into nervous tears, the receiver still in her grasp. Stephen heard her crying and rushed upstairs. He joined her in the little room and threw his arms around her.

Josie's head fell onto his shoulder. "Oh, my God, Stephen, it was another crazy call."

"Don't worry, I've contacted the police. They're organising plain-clothes officers to watch the house. It's just some crank."

"It isn't. They're organised. It was a different voice this time. The paper should never have printed that headline."

"I know, I know."

"We'll have to stop the helpline Stephen."

"You know we can't."

"I'm so tired, Stephen. I don't know if I can go on. Is it worth it?"

"You know it is." He broke off, becoming irritated by her silliness, and glanced down at the Foreign Office fax. He switched on the word processor and began to print out a letter.

"I wrote this last thing last night," Stephen told his wife. "It's to Perez de Cuellar. Can you fax it to the UN this morning for me, please?"

"What does it say?"

"It's telling him about us and putting the point across that the relatives in this country are united behind the UN's efforts to find a solution to the crisis. We all want him to do everything he can to secure the release of those held in Iraq and Kuwait as soon as possible."

"OK then. Just leave it there and I'll send it."

"Right. Well, I'd best be off. See you tonight." He gave her a kiss and disappeared to work.

Josie stared down at the table covered with slips of paper, cards and the day book. She was exhausted. Her health hadn't been good for a while. She had colitis, which irritated her stomach. It was growing steadily worse, giving her regular and acute spasms of pain. Her wisdom tooth was playing her up and she looked drawn with tiredness. Her son Richard and her neighbours had commented on it. They were deeply worried about her. Neither she nor Stephen had slept properly since Wen Li had phoned. She had practically given her job up as a financial adviser, and the expense of the phone bill, electricity bill and of buying all the equipment and petrol to go and see people was causing her great financial worry. Where was the money going to come from to keep the helpline going?

People - friends - were telling her to give it up. It wasn't worth it. She would lose her health, her home, everything she had built and planned for. But she felt she had no choice. She had been called by God to serve and serve she had to. She couldn't turn away from these people. That was what everyone else had done. They needed someone; they had come to trust and rely upon her.

Josie found something deep within herself, a reserve of strength which was keeping her going. That day she wrote in her diary, "We must do what we can for all those relatives. They are so pleased for us to be doing what we have, yet to me it is natural to help them. I have a son and daughter... and I know how I would feel to have them held hostage. Words cannot say."

As she slowly dressed and combed her thick russet hair into shape. she heard two of the volunteers arriving. Maureen Evans came up first. She was the staunchest helper Josie had, staying with her virtually every day until the crisis was over, without pay or recompense. She was very businesslike and settled down by the phone straight away. Within seconds, it rang. She answered it warmly and efficiently, day book in front of her, pen in hand, the checklist of points to ask on the wall. It reminded her to request, not only the caller's name, address and number, but their relationship to the person in the Gulf, that person's details and employer, family details and passport number held. "Some callers may be distressed and less than articulate" the checklist added, "and a sympathetic, supportive but realistic approach should be taken. Second language speakers may have to be re-contacted through an interpreter."

The doorbell rang. Josie went downstairs to answer it. The other volunteer, Pauline MacIntosh, was making cups of tea in the kitchen. Josie opened the door. It was John Butcher, MP for Coventry South West. Immediately on his heels was a television crew. They turned out to be Dutch. Shortly after them the provost of Coventry Cathedral, John Petty, arrived. Josie invited them all in and drew her breath for another long, long day.

John Petty had come simply to see how they were, but agreed to do the interview with Dutch TV as well. He explained the role of the Church in supporting the helpline and in trying its best to get the hostages released. He did not tell Josie, but he was shocked by the physical state she was in. The helpline was taking an enormous amount out of her and Stephen, so he had decided to try to give them some spiritual support. After the interview, in a quieter moment, he suggested to Josie that he organise prayers for all the relatives and perhaps a special service, an idea which immediately brought a spark of enthusiasm back to her eyes.

That afternoon Doreen and Jimmy Paterson, parents of Carolyn Stevenson, who was trapped in Kuwait with her husband Andrew, called from the railway station. They had come down to see their son-in-law's parents, Betty and Andrew Stevenson, and to visit the helpline. It was typical of the way families of relatives came together to give each other support during the crisis and paid visits to all the helplines simply to thank the organisers for everything they were doing.

As they were talking and drinking a glass of wine, John Petty rang up. He had further considered his offer and suggested he held a special, private service for her and Stephen in the Chapel of Gethsemane of the Cathedral. Josie was overwhelmed. She turned to Betty Stevenson and explained her joy, then, on the spur of the moment, asked her and the Patersons if they would like to join them. They would, so that night, in the quiet of the Cathedral, a special service was held for them and for all those caught up in the crisis. In her diary, Josie describes it as "so unprepared but so perfect. We all departed close, our arms held. It was wonderful walking out into the night with the beautiful west screen glowing in the moonlight." It had given them all strength to go on. Josie's day had turned from despair to renewed hope.

Internationally, sanctions were beginning to take effect. On the thirteenth of August Saudi Arabia turned away an Iraqi tanker, the *al-Qadisiyah,* which tried to dock at the Yanbu oil terminal in an attempt to beat the UN blockade. The USA had sent more ships and aircraft to the region and Britain had despatched three mine hunters to strengthen its detachment. On the fourteenth, the Royal Navy began intercepting Gulf shipping to enforce the sanctions and US marines boarded an Iraqi freighter shipping arms to Basra.

The Iraqis responded harshly to these developments and, as if setting a pattern for the next four months, took out their anger on the Westerners in Kuwait and those already on installations. Throughout the hostage crisis, the Iraqis never merely used the Westerners as a human shield. They used them as a collective punchball. The Iraqis had no power over the British or Americans other than through the hostages. By treating them badly, they were 'getting their own back' on the alliance ranged against them, undoubtedly taking out their frustration on the hostages whenever international developments went against them.

On August 13th a car holding four people, including Douglas Crosgery, a middle-aged British man, tried to escape across the desert just north of Ruqi. Douglas was sitting on the back seat, keeping his head down. As they approached the border, they were suddenly ordered to stop by an Iraqi patrol. They refused. The driver panicked and tried to drive past, but the Iraqis opened fire and bullets smashed into the back of the vehicle, forcing the driver to stop. Douglas Crosgery lay motionless on the back seat, blood spattered across him.

The Iraqi patrol raced up and ordered them out. When they saw they were Westerners, there was consternation. They were very agitated. Ordering the other three to come with them, a couple of the soldiers took Douglas' body out of the car and drove into the desert where they hurriedly buried it in an unmarked grave.

All that day, the Foreign Office and embassy in Kuwait did everything it could to discover the facts behind Douglas Crosgery's death. An embassy official wanted to visit the area, but was turned back from the border region because he didn't have the correct papers. On the fourteenth, Michael Weston spent the whole day attempting to locate his body, with the co-operation of the Iraqi army. The British ambassador was accompanied by an Iraqi Lieutenant-Colonel as he and some units of Iraqi soldiers searched the barren desert north-east of Ruqi. The area was quartered off and thoroughly searched, but there was no sign either of a body or of shooting. Iraqi troops nearby in Salmi were questioned, but all denied even hearing shots in the last forty-eight hours. The ambassador was unsatisfied with this and demanded that the Iraqis urgently conduct a full enquiry into Douglas' death. The Iraqis ignored him.

On Monday 14th August, the Emergency Unit of the Foreign Office's Consular Department issued the following statement. In it, the different circumstance facing the British communities in Kuwait and Iraq were starkly portrayed:

Kuwait: General conditions appeared to be deteriorating; there were reports of wholesale looting; food and petrol is still available; banks remain closed. There has been no significant improvement in the internal telephone system and there are no civil police in evidence.

Iraq: Foreign residents in Iraq were able to travel normally both within Baghdad and Iraq. British nationals who have been removed from Kuwait remain in Baghdad hotels and were visited daily by consular staff.

Later that day, in a further twisting of the knife, the Iraqis issued an edict demanding the closure of all foreign embassies in Kuwait within ten days. They argued that the emirate no longer existed; it was now part of Iraq - the forty-ninth province. As such, all embassy staff had to be removed by 24th August or the embassies would be forcibly shut down.

The international community was furious. Mrs Thatcher boldly stated that the British embassy would remain there. She was backed up by most other Western governments. However, as a safety precaution, it was decided that all non-essential embassy personnel, plus all dependents, should be evacuated to Baghdad, where some would stay on to help that embassy, whilst others would fly home.

The embassy in Kuwait sent out a message to the British community that a convoy of cars would leave the embassy for Baghdad at eight in the morning of the fifteenth for Baghdad. It would be under Iraqi military escort and would convoy out wives and non-essential personnel from the embassy. Any British citizens wishing to accompany them could go as well.

It seemed a welcome initiative from the embassy. It would give people the opportunity to get to Baghdad and perhaps out of Iraq under the protection of the embassy. However, most British feared being picked up, either by Iraqi soldiers in Kuwait who didn't respect diplomatic immunity or, once they were in Baghdad, and so refused to come out.

Two of the few people who took the embassy at its word were the Reverend Michael Jones and his wife. They turned up at the Kuwait embassy, met the ambassador, who was very friendly, and drove up with the embassy staff to Baghdad. Once there, to their consternation, the Baghdad embassy told them it couldn't put them up, nor guarantee their safety. They would have to make their own hotel arrangements.

"It just goes to show how totally naive the embassy was," Dave Dorrington explained, commenting on this latest embassy fiasco. Most of the British in Kuwait felt their worst fears about the convoy had been realised and sighed with relief that they had stayed put.

Meanwhile, the embassy had persuaded the Iraqis to let the families of the British Liaison Team join them in Baghdad. Again, the embassy had no idea what would happen to them. They thought they would simply be kept at the hotels until the crisis blew over. Instead, they too were sent out to installations.

But it was to get worse. "By the fourteenth or fifteenth of August," Dave Dorrington told me, "it was pretty clear to us that the last thing you wanted to do was hand yourself over to the Iraqis yet, a few days later, the embassy gave out, through the warden system and over the World Service, the advice that all Westerners should report to hotels, the British to the Regency Palace, the Americans to the International, and so on." Dave was referring to a communiqué issued by the Foreign Office, in consultation with the embassy in Kuwait, on Wednesday 16th August:

"In a very grave and sinister development, the Iraqi authorities have instructed that the British community should assemble at a single point in Kuwait. The United States community has received a similar instruction...

"The Iraqi authorities have advised that, in order to better protect the British community, they want all British citizens located in one place in Kuwait. They have said that British citizens must move to the Regency Palace Hotel on 16th August. The Iraqis have stated that if the British community does not move voluntarily, it will face unspecified difficulties. The embassy takes this to mean that the Iraqis will take measures to ensure that British citizens are moved to one location. If you chose to move, please take all food from your residence with you to give to the hotel management to help their food stocks. We suggest that you take no more than one suitcase per person with you to the hotel."

The communiqué further instructed people not to travel to Saudi Arabia, Bahrain, Qatar or the United Arab Emirates. Non-essential workers in the Eastern Province of Saudi Arabia, closest to Kuwait, were advised not to return there unless it was essential. It went on:

"The border with Saudi Arabia is officially closed. The Iraqis have said that foreigners may travel to Baghdad but are not permitted to leave Iraq."

On the situation facing those in hotels in Baghdad, it stated that the embassy was doing all it could to be of help. "Items such as toiletries, books and games are being provided by the embassy and the British community in Baghdad. A doctor is on duty and the embassy is helping to provide any medicines required."

This communiqué was extremely misleading. The Iraqi authorities were rapidly building up pressure on the Western communities in Kuwait. Their grip was steadily tightening. People were being picked off the streets whenever they were found and being sent to installations. The call to the hotels was the first part of the Iraqi strategy to create a comprehensive human shield of hostages to deter attack. The Iraqi plan was to wire up the hotels with explosives and turn them into huge time bombs. Both a BA passenger and a stewardess noticed the Iraqis painting over the windows of the Regency Palace Hotel a few days before the edict for the British to report to it. The Iraqis also sealed all emergency exits and windows and filled the large sports centre nearby with hundreds of mattresses. Finally, they wired up the entire hotel with explosives. If the Western leaders did not give way, the British, American and other hostages would be blown up. That was clearly the plan.

Mike Devey explained what happened. "The official thing from London was to read out the Iraqi statement as supplied by the Iraqis, as if they were Iraqi radio. So I told the people with me, I don't have a short-wave radio, I didn't hear it, but I'm not going and don't recommend you to go, but you've got to make your own minds up." Fortunately, the British community ignored the call in their thousands. They realised the instruction was a ploy to gather them together as innocent victims of a massive Iraqi kidnap threat. They knew what had happened to those British who had been taken. Above all, they couldn't believe the recommendation to take their precious food stocks and hand them over to the Iraqis. The twenty people with the Deveys made a joke of it, especially the request to take their food stacks with them. To many of the ex-pats this episode was the biggest blunder the Kuwait embassy made. It demonstrated how completely out of touch the government was with the situation in Kuwait. It threatened to place the whole community in the greatest danger. The embassy, cut off and hopelessly out of touch had, in its naivety, actually abetted the Iraqis in one of the most appalling episodes of the hostage crisis. To the Foreign Office's credit, once it realised how the community felt and the true nature of the Iraqi demand, it rescinded its policy and told British citizens to ignore the ultimatum.

Four people went, and were turned away.

"We didn't go and so didn't fall for the trap," Mike Devey told me, "but we couldn't go up to the embassy from then on, otherwise the Iraqis would have picked us up." However, the wardens weren't unduly perturbed about that. As one told me, "I wasn't really worried. I felt it was good they were locked up and couldn't move out of the embassy, because we could do our own thing then, and keep the thing going." One thing they did, as they had been doing for some time, was to effectively ignore the embassy's instruction to people not to cross the border.

The embassy had no reason to know about the explosives in the hotels and perhaps it genuinely thought the food supplies of the people in hiding could be used to supplement their diets at the hotels, and not be confiscated by hungry Iraqi soldiers. One or two people did turn up, but were quickly turned away from the hotel by the Palestinian manager, who was able to warn them before the Iraqis realised they had arrived. The Americans also ignored the call. Just one couple arrived at the International Hotel. However, rather more of the Japanese turned up at their hotel, were arrested and subsequently taken off to installations.

The communiqué also inferred that the embassy in Baghdad was responsible for supplying the people in the hotels there with necessities. According to several people held in those hotels and the ambassador himself, it was people in the community who supplied these things, and the embassy had nothing whatsoever to do with it.

It was the death of Douglas Crosgery and the sudden Iraqi announcement that all British nationals should report to the Regency Palace Hotel which really sent shivers through the British community. Until then, they had felt relatively safe if they remained indoors. People were able to escape if they were determined to and Iraqi soldiers were not bothering particularly with house searches. People in the hotels were being well treated and there was no sign of any intention to move them. However, from then on, the situation rapidly deteriorated. By hoping to dupe the ex-pat communities into complying with what they had posed as a very reasonable request - to safeguard and protect the Westerners, not to corral them - the Iraqis had clearly shown their intentions. The people in the hotels were moved to installations, house-to-house searches began in earnest, including sweeps of whole areas, and those already at installations were moved closer into the strategic heart of the sites.

The Americans and British were continuously strengthening their forces in the Gulf, further escalating the situation. Both the US navy and the Royal Navy had begun intercepting shipping in the Gulf. The frigate Jupiter intercepted a Cypriot vessel off Dubai and questioned it about its cargo and destination. American marines boarded an Iraqi freighter which was trying to ship small arms to Saddam's troops. Once again, the Iraqis responded with their own tough measures, using the major weapon they had against the West - the hostages. For the first time, they openly admitted they would use Western citizens as a human shield at their vital military, chemical and industrial installations.

Since their hotel plan had failed, the Iraqis began to move their captives out of the hotels. In the second part of their hostage strategy, they started to systematically bus people out to installations. The intention was to keep the Western governments guessing as to where the hostages were. At that time, the British government knew the whereabouts of only sixty-six people held by the Iraqis. Even that paltry figure was to shrink as the hotels were cleared.

Some groups were moved up to the Melia al-Mansour Hotel in Baghdad, then out to Basra, Kirkuk, Mosul and other far-flung outposts of Saddam's domain. Those already held in Baghdad joined them. Two BA passengers, Don Fisher and his wife Suda, ended up at the Darbandikhan power station and dam in northern Iraq. They were forced to live right beside the turbines, Suda refusing to leave Don when the women and children were allowed home. He was so sure they would die he wrote a letter to his employers explaining how he wished his financial matters to be arranged - in effect a will. Many men wrote wills in the next few months. Many were able to send them out when the French, Japanese and Germans left. Some were extremely moving letters, asking friends and relatives for forgiveness, explaining how much they loved their families and how good life was with them, and detailing their financial future. Those men were torn apart by worry and the likelihood of death.

Others were kept at sites in Kuwait. Some were taken to Doha power station, others to the hydro-electric plant in Shuwaikh or the military airports at Jahra and at the international airport. Those who were still at the Airport Hotel were staying to shield the passenger terminal. Many were passengers from BA Flight 149, but others were British caught in the hotels at the time of the invasion. On the eighteenth, some were sent to the IBI camp in the centre of the Kuwaiti oil terminal, others to Shuwaikh Port, the University complex and Bayan Palace. One group, initially of about a dozen, were despatched from the Regency Palace Hotel to the Misila Palace on Misila Beach, just south of the city. They arrived on 19th August.

Misila Beach had been a scene of heavy fighting on the day of the invasion. There was a military club there, where some Kuwaitis had put up stiff resistance and there had been more heavy fighting around the palace itself. The Iraqis feared a seaborne counter-attack, so the beach was strongly defended with minefields, bladewire fences, machine-gun nests, tanks and gun emplacements. Kuwait was divided up into sectors by the Iraqi army, and one of the various headquarters was the large and luxurious Misila Palace, from where the beach defences of that sector were co-ordinated.

The group sent to the palace included a number of BA crew, including Phil Long, the close friend of Rob Hayward MP, passengers from the 747 trapped at the airport, and ex-pats rounded up from the streets of Kuwait. When they arrived, the palace had been thoroughly looted. Curtains had been ripped from windows, ornaments, clothes and broken furniture littered the floor, desks had been broken into, and carpets ripped and ruined by dirty boots and excrement. Every door had been smashed and none had locks on them any more. Obviously, the Iraqi soldiers had gone wild in the palace during the first days and wrecked everything they couldn't sell at the local markets.

The British hostages had to make the best they could of the mess. They drifted off in twos and threes to find rooms to sleep in and began tidying up the wanton destruction. It was eerie. The bedrooms were incredibly plush, with beautiful sheets on large double beds and sumptuous carpets, yet they were prisoners. They were guarded all the time. A stewardess remembers sitting on her bed with her Iraqi guard, watching the TV. He was no threat to her but had insisted she watch a lengthy, boring programme featuring Saddam Hussein. It had a long and splendid religious build-up, then Saddam came on. He was declaiming against the West and haranguing Western leaders. There were English sub-titles under much of it. Apparently, President Bush had made some comment about him, so in reply, he was telling the world he would return American troops in body bags. As he said that, the Iraqi soldier turned to the stewardess and said: "You understand? You understand what will happen? You will die if your armies invade us." He was obviously totally loyal to Saddam and convinced he could defeat the West.

The hostages were given a certain degree of freedom within their quarters, but kept separate from the main body of the palace, which was full of Iraqi troops, some very senior. The beach and palace enclosure was bristling with defences. The marbled corridors would clash with the sounds of army boots and Kalashnikovs coming to attention.

Soldiers were everywhere. Not only was it a headquarters for the Iraqi army, but a large building next to the palace was being used as a barracks. The hostages passed one room decked out with huge maps. The table was covered with another map, with pins and flags in it and telephones around the sides. It was clearly the control room. Soldiers were coming and going all the time. There was no privacy. There were no locks on any of the doors, so the soldiers would come into the hostages' rooms at any time of the day or night. The women especially felt very vulnerable and repeated complained to the Iraqi officers, until finally something was done about it and locks were put on.

The hostages tried to get into a routine as soon as possible. They could watch TV. CNN was on all the time and sometimes they could get Dubai TV, which occasionally had English programmes. They went for their meals in a luxurious dining room, where they sat under armed guard. But the food was sparse. The soldiers themselves had little. Whatever they did have, they seemed to share with the hostages. Whenever they managed to find something in the local shops, they would give some of it to the British. So they were eating tiny portions of rice and tomatoes, with perhaps a few chicken bones - and they *were* mainly bone - from Limoges china, using silver and gold cutlery and cruet sets.

The hostages tried their hardest to get more food and to ask the Iraqis for toiletries and other necessities. In the Regency Palace Hotel, they had initially been allowed out to get these things, but they were never permitted to leave the palace, even with armed guards. They weren't even allowed out to exercise. The stewardesses tried to build some sort of dialogue with the soldiers and officers, explaining what they needed, but with little success.

More groups of British arrived over the next two weeks, until by the end of August there were forty-four of them in the palace. They tended to congregate in little groups around the building. As more came in, so the food situation grew worse. Still, the Iraqis tried their best. They brought in a whole sheep one day and chopped it in half. The soldiers took the front half and gave the rear half to the hostages. They shared everything. Phil Long was something of a chef. He and some others cut the sheep up and devised recipes for them which broke the boredom of constant rice. Phil found some spices and did wonderful things with soups, to add variety to their meals. The Iraqis were always very polite and apologetic to them, and anxious to do things for them, but the food remained absolutely appalling. They all lost weight and some fell ill.

One of the ex-pats recalled what it was like: "We slept on camp beds surrounded by ornate vases and silk wall hangings. We were shaving in cold water with old, rusty razors in washbasins with gold taps. We were eating boiled rice and watermelon from gilded silver plates, drinking fetid water from hand-cut glass goblets. surrounded by priceless paintings and Arabic *objets d'art.* One painting hanging on the wall was in a catalogue, valued at $18m. We knew. We had the catalogue."

The British and American governments viewed the latest developments concerning the hostages with serious concern and persuaded the United Nations to pass Resolution 664 on 18th August. The Security Council demanded that Iraq facilitate the immediate departure from Kuwait and Iraq of the nationals of third countries. It further insisted that Iraq took no action to jeopardise the safety, security or health of such nationals, and called for the government of Iraq to rescind its orders for the closure of diplomatic missions in Kuwait and for the withdrawal of diplomatic immunity. Iraq merely replied with a torrent of rhetoric and abuse:

HOSTAGE BRITONS IN NEW TERROR

Iraq has said it will protect its military bases from attack by herding in British and American hostages. The country's official news agency said Westerners would be moved into key military and civil installations in Iraq and occupied Kuwait until the danger of war was over. And Saddam Hussein's government, which is known to have an arsenal of chemical weapons, today threatened the United Sates and its allies with "mass destruction". "We warn the forces of aggression of an incinerator that no one can get out of if they launch aggression," said the *al-Qadisiyah* newspaper, the organ of Iraq's Defence Ministry... "The weapons of mass destruction and strategic deterrence possessed by Iraq will be awaiting anyone contemplating aggression, to leave him in scattered fragments"... [and that they would] detain "citizens of aggressive nations"...

Coventry Evening Telegraph 18th August

That very day, the eighteenth, the remaining passengers of BA Flight 149 were sent out to the IBI camp in the heart of the huge Mina Ahmadi oil refinery, where the British Liaison Team had been living.

Mrs Thatcher was bitterly angry at the treatment of those held in Kuwait and Iraq. On the twenty-second she used the word "hostages" for the first time and accused Iraq of flouting fundamental human rights. She refused to contemplate negotiating with Saddam over them. "You do not bargain over hostages," she announced, her eyes blazing and her fist repeatedly hitting the table. "If you do that, in the end all you do is give those who use such tactics the idea that all they have to do is take more hostages. Human beings have their own rights as human beings and I will not sink to the level of using them as bargaining counters, *ever*."

In a fierce speech, marking her return from a visit to President Bush in the United States, she applauded the USA's strength and determination and called for the United Nations to renew its solidarity behind efforts to free Kuwait. Returning to the plight of the hostages, she added, "We are obviously very worried indeed, and gravely concerned about the callous way in which Iraq is treating British and other foreign nationals," then, in a phrase which was to haunt her, accused Saddam Hussein of "hiding behind women and children". It was an attempt to embarrass Saddam into releasing the hostages, but unfortunately served to anger the Iraqi leader and strengthen his resolve. There was a growing Iraqi resentment at this 'woman' daring to challenge them.

Mrs Thatcher further pledged to keep the British embassy open despite the Iraqi deadline of Friday the twenty-fourth for its closure, and insisted upon it retaining full diplomatic immunity for the officials inside.

SADDAM TROOPS AT EMBASSY DOORS

Iraqi troops surrounded seven embassies in Kuwait today - including the British mission - as Baghdad said the diplomatic posts were an anachronism in a state that no longer exists. Two lone Japanese diplomats waited for the soldiers to shut their defiant embassy, the first of nearly sixty ordered to close, as more troops patrolled outside the British, Norwegian, Hungarian, West German, Swedish and Romanian embassies.

Most foreign governments have ordered some envoys to stay on, ignoring uncertain deadlines for closure today, and to look after citizens trapped since Iraq invaded Kuwait.

Coventry Evening Telegraph, 24th August

A footnote to this article states that the United Nations Security Council had "now drafted a resolution which would permit the use of military power to enforce sanctions in the Gulf." The actual wording of the UN resolution, number 665, passed on the twenty-fifth, was for maritime forces "to use such measures as may be necessary" to halt shipping to and from Iraq and Kuwait. It marked a serious raising of the military stakes in the Gulf and further increased Iraqi hostility and anger. This, in turn, was taken out on the native population of Kuwait and on the hostages, as more were rounded up and placed in installations.

The Kuwaitis suffered even more harshly than the hostages as military conflict looked increasingly likely. From the first day, the Iraqis took over all Kuwaiti hospitals in preparation for an American and British counter-attack. As international pressure grew and more troops were moved in, the hospitals were surrounded with troops and security check-points. Some civilian patients were evacuated or sent home to prepare wards for troops injured in battle. As the Resistance grew in confidence and weaponry, it began to inflict serious losses on the Iraqis. These injured began to fill the hospitals, from which more Kuwaiti people were ejected. The al-Razi Hospital was ordered to evacuate its civilian patients in mid-August. At the al-Hadi Hospital doctors had to deal with emergency operations on Iraqi soldiers. Those staff who didn't turn up were 'visited' by the Iraqis and forced back. Others hid within the hospital complexes. They had quiet store rooms which the Iraqis hadn't discovered. Some Western staff in the hospitals were hidden in these rooms, fed and looked after by the hospital staff, until they could be found safe houses.

Once the British embassy was surrounded by Iraqi troops on the twenty-fourth, none of its staff were allowed out of the compound. Twelve of the twenty-two staff had been withdrawn, leaving just ten. They were ensconced behind the embassy walls, all essential services cut off, unable to do anything other than keeping the flag flying. It was to be the start of a very unnerving time for those men. Later, six more were escorted to Baghdad by the Iraqi army and on 8th October two more were sent up to Baghdad, to help preserve food stocks, leaving just Michael Weston and Larry Banks. Over those weeks, the embassy staff, especially the ambassador and his aide, showed resilience and determination not to be defeated. Their courageous stand gave strength to the rest of the British community, both in hiding and in the installations, to keep going, and sent a message to the Iraqis that state terrorism would not be tolerated.

Failed Escapes

"The whole British community was caged. They were trapped at the whim of the Iraqis and, just as one plays with a bird, so the Iraqis played with them."

During the first week after the invasion several 'organised' convoys tried to escape across the desert to Saudi Arabia. Jane and Jim McAlindin were on one. Jane was a teacher of French whilst Jim worked on a city roads project in Kuwait City. Their contracts were due to end in October, when they were hoping to return to Kirkcaldy in Scotland.

Unlike the stereotypical image of wealthy, money-grabbing ex-pats, which was the exception rather than the norm, they had gone out for two years simply because Jim wished to work abroad. They actually lived in a run down apartment block in Salwa, a suburb to the south of Kuwait City. It was one of six flats in a block owned by Mouchel, Jim's company. It was on the ground floor and was quite large, with two bedrooms. However, the concrete outside was starting to crumble and the block had the appearance of neglect. This was to save them. The Iraqis thought it too poor to house foreign nationals and left it alone.

None of the women in their group and few of the men were prepared to venture onto the streets after the first morning of the occupation. The whole group stayed together the first night and the following day. On the second night they received one call in particular. The caller told them the Iraqis were pulling out and taking their British hostages with them. That *really* terrified them. Jane was verging on hysteria. She was totally unprepared emotionally for what was happening to them all. As for many others, the shock of being plunged from peaceful happiness and joy into helicopter battles and friends being arrested on the streets in just six hours was unbearable. For days and even weeks some people were in a permanent state of shock. They couldn't believe what was happening to Kuwait. Their minds wouldn't accept it. They couldn't relate to it emotionally or intellectually. They tried to cut themselves off from it, ignore it and hope it would just go away - prove to be a bad dream. It didn't exist. The Iraqis weren't really there. There were no tanks, no soldiers, no guns. Just go away and leave us in peace.

For some, the whole period in hiding seemed a dream, not just the first few days. Even now, back in Britain a year afterwards, they still can't come to terms with the dreadfulness of that shock and the sudden powerlessness of having their lives torn away.

In sleep you have little willpower. The mind is led through scenes and flashes. It has no control nor sense of direction. That was exactly how those in hiding felt. Their will, their ability to act was denied them. And, just as in a dream you live in the confines of your head, so they had to survive in the confines of their four walled 'skulls', which rapidly began to feel very small and claustrophobic. Some still suffer from claustrophobia now, a year on. For months those in hiding wanted to get out. When they eventually did, many felt the opposite - agoraphobia, the fear of open spaces - because the confinement within their skulls had been so total.

From the first night, people from the other apartment blocks in their compound came over and stayed with them. There were plenty of empty apartments and they felt safer together. They scrounged around for food, tools and other useful supplies. Someone brought in a pool table, others had cards, videos, books and board games.

Always, people listened to the news and talked about the shifting situation. Hundreds of rumours flew about. They were the bane of everyone's life. On the first Saturday night the electricity was cut off and the air-conditioning stopped. Not only did the heat become unbearable because they had to keep the windows firmly shut, but they thought it was a prelude to a house-to-house search by the Iraqis. However, it came on again and that crisis passed.

So it went on. The one great crisis manifested itself into the constant onslaught of small crises, often over ridiculously simple things. But it was those little concerns which dominated their minds. How to get food? How to get a letter out? What should they do if the water was turned off, or polluted? How many lights should they leave on? Had they been spotted? Should they move their cars? Everything was discussed, often endlessly. Every option was explored in minute detail. It was necessary but oppressive. They were questions of survival.

The McAlindins decided they needed to become much more security conscious. They asked their Sri Lankan maid and her husband, another Sri Lankan, to move the cars away from the block to make it look deserted and at night they kept all the lights off. They drew the curtains and lived in virtual darkness day and night. Each evening they would put one small light on, but throw a cover over it to keep its glow dim. They were very careful of sounds as well, turning the television and radio volumes well down, not laughing loudly or arguing. Fortunately, they had a solid metal fence running around the block which acted as a security shield and hid the lower stories from the road. They ensured the gates were locked securely at all times, which helped them feel relatively safe behind them.

By the first Monday and Tuesday, there were still many reports of the border not being completely sealed and of people escaping across the desert. Jane and Jim, along with others in their group, decided to make an attempt, but none of them had a four-wheel drive vehicle, which was essential to get across the sand. Fortunately, a single, middle-aged man,

Mike Brown, who wouldn't accompany them, gave them his. He wouldn't go himself because of lack of space. One of the other two couples in the block had a little girl and he felt they should go instead. A quiet man, not a great socialite, Mike's was just one of many examples of generosity and self-sacrifice.

The embassy wardens were giving out conflicting evidence concerning escape attempts but most were telling people not to try because no one knew whether others had made it out safely or had been captured. Some escapees did phone once they reached Saudi Arabia, but not all.

Many people, including the McAlindins, didn't care for this advice, believing they should try to get out if they had the chance. They were fed up with the numerous rumours circulating that certain areas of the desert had become death traps and that the Iraqis were taking Western women and raping them. Whilst they knew it would be very risky - they had no idea where the Iraqi units were deployed, nor what would be the fate of the women if they were captured and separated from the men - they were aware of the increasing seriousness of their situation and felt they had to make a break from it. If they were stuck there when war broke out, or if the Iraqis captured them, it could turn very nasty.

The group which made the bid across the desert consisted of Jane and Jim McAlindin, Pete and Dawn O'Dowd and their little girl Samantha, and Steve and Sue Kelly. Dawn was seven months pregnant at the time. They spent several days preparing. Jim and Pete crossed to another block owned by Mouchel a few hundred yards away. A warden there had some maps of routes across the desert and gave them one. They sat and planned their journey then went back to load their solitary vehicle. They had extra petrol which they had stored in containers in a Land Rover, along with bottles of water. They also took plenty of apples to eat on the way. All these they packed the night before, to get an early start.

They set out at five in the morning. By going at dawn, not only were they avoiding the heat of the sun, but they hoped to avoid the roadblocks as well. Although the Iraqis didn't guard many posts at night, five o'clock was still within the curfew and there was a risk they would be shot at. They carefully passed through the gates of the metal fence, anxious not arouse any suspicion, then made their way to rendezvous with another car containing four men who had decided to tag along.

The Salwa roads were very quiet at that time of the morning and they reached the desert west of Jahra without once being stopped. Once out in the sandy scrub, they passed dozens of tanks, but the Iraqis simply ignored them. Every kilometre they passed more and more groups of tanks and bivouacked soldiers. None seemed to care, They were all asleep, their washing flapping in the faint breeze as they dozed.

The desert track led deep into the wilderness. Progress was rapid and they soon drove down into the Wadi al-Batin. They began to feel a little more confident of succeeding until suddenly they noticed the track had became clogged with an enormous traffic jam. There were still many kilometres to go before they reached the border, yet there were thousands of cars stopped alongside and across the track. Many were two-wheel drives which had become hopelessly bogged down in the sand. They looked ludicrously over-burdened with furniture, mattresses and open boots crammed with suitcases and plastic bags. They were full of families of every nationality - Indians, Sri Lankans, Jordanians, Egyptians, Filipinos... Some lounged in their overloaded cars, others had spread out on the desert and set up covers with sheets and blankets. Whole families were stranded, refugees trying to take what desperate possessions they possibly could as they fled for their lives. Some had been there for days without food and only a little water. Mothers tried to feed weakening babies by the side of the track. Small children dozed under makeshift awnings or in the cars. Others played amongst the dust and millions of flies. An old woman lazily flicked some from her face as she crouched in a patch of shade. Two men briefly argued then turned to watch the two Land Rovers pass. They were down to a crawl by now, trying to negotiate the stranded cars. A family lay asleep under a canopy without blankets, suitcases for pillows, sleeping in their clothes, huddled together against the cool of the early morning. There was no sanitation. The desert was their toilet and there was acute danger of disease breaking out, if they outlasted their hunger and thirst. Dozens of them had perished already. Their cars were stuck, out of petrol or overheated and damaged. They weren't able to return to Kuwait City. What would they be going back to? A war zone. They were hopelessly trapped, forgotten in their desert graveyard. The wadi was rapidly becoming a cemetery.

One of the Land Rovers, having to leave the track to get round an old lorry, became stuck in the sand. The driver revved it for a few seconds, then stopped. Immediately, a group of smiling children and young men ran over and offered to push them out. It was tremendous to see such companionship. Despite their enormous problems, despite having lost everything, they had the courage and energy to help others. Perhaps it was *because* they only had each other that they did it.

Even those Iraqi soldiers who had now appeared, in some strange, impossible game, began to help them and other stranded cars out of the sand and on their way. Impossible because, a few kilometres on, their comrades were turning these very people back.

Many convoys of British trying to flee across the desert in the second week were allowed to drive around the border region, run low on petrol and exhaust themselves, then turned back, rather than being arrested. The Iraqis didn't want a lot of prisoners at that stage. They simply wanted to slow down the process of them leaving so they could dig their troops in, stave off a quick counter-attack and give themselves time to strip Kuwait bare.

The two four-wheel drives finally left the track, realising they would get nowhere in this confusion. They struck off across the sand. It was getting very hot now. Samantha was beginning to suffer. As they neared the border, their hopes rising again, they drove straight into a huge Iraqi military camp full of tanks. They found themselves in their midst, gun barrels all around them.

These Iraqis were less *laissez-faire*. They began to pursue the two vehicles, giving chase in both tanks and a motley assortment of civilian vehicles they had 'requisitioned' from local Kuwaitis. One was a Hungry Bunny hamburger van. The Britons stopped and allowed the Iraqis to catch them up. When they did, they discovered that none of them could speak English. Only one of the British could speak Arabic. He tried hesitatingly to explain that they wanted to get to Saudi Arabia. The Iraqis wouldn't let them go on. They thought they might be Israelis. When they explained they were British, the soldiers warmly greeted them. "Welcome, welcome to Iraq!" one managed to spurt out. The Iraqis all smiled and shook hands, but still wouldn't allow the British to go on.

Eventually, an officer arrived who spoke passable English. He introduced himself very politely, then asked them why they were there.

"We want to get to Saudi Arabia."

"Ah!" he grinned and nodded. "But why you come these ways? Why come in the desert? It is very, very dangerous. There are many mines. Many mines, and many tanks."

"It's the quickest way."

"Oh, no, no, no." He shook his head and kept his grin. He was clearly a forceful man, used to having his way. Jane felt increasingly pessimistic about their chances. "Go Basra. Next you fly Baghdad and London. See Buckingham Palace, see Blackpool."

"We aren't allowed to leave that way. We'll be arrested."

"Oh, no, no, you go Baghdad. But why you want to leave? You guests of our country. But if you wish, you fly Baghdad and London. You go home like that. The desert, she no good."

"Why not?"

"Many mines."

The British didn't know whether to believe him or not. They felt sure he was bluffing, but what could they do? The officer pointed towards the desert and repeated, "Many, many mines. No good that way. You go Baghdad. You guests of Iraq now." He beamed again and they forced grins in return.

The group decided to agree to return to Salwa. The officer was satisfied with that, so they turned the Land Rovers around and drove back across the desert, hoping to skirt the camp and make another bid. But they found the Hungry Bunny van following them.

He was persistent, that Hungry Bunny driver. He pursued them across the desert and back onto the track. He even managed to keep up with them as they sped back towards the nearest highway. Only after a chase of ten kilometres did they manage to lose the little pest.

Almost immediately, they turned off into the desert again, trying to outflank the Iraqis. It was late morning by now. The sun was approaching its hottest and the vehicles were becoming unbearably stuffy. They couldn't turn the air-conditioning on because it used too much fuel. Samantha and her mother were both feeling the heat badly. They drank some of their water and refilled the petrol tank, then drove on. The Iraqis were up and about now and soon they found themselves back in their midst. They were stopped again and this time the Iraqi officer was less sympathetic. He confiscated their maps and compasses and ordered them to return immediately. His men looked rougher as well. They were conscripts without uniforms. One had an axe instead of a gun.

The Brits realised all hope of escape that day had gone. They had no choice but to return to their apartment blocks. It was to be the only time they really set out to escape. Soon afterwards, the Iraqis called for Westerners to report to the hotels and their situation rapidly deteriorated. "After our escape attempt we knew we couldn't even go out of the front door because we'd be taken away. That's when everybody started to get really frightened. We always expected someone to come to the door. We knew we were directly threatened. They were rounding us up to take us to the hotels. We kept hearing from the World Service or over the phones that so many people had been taken that day. We knew people who had been arrested trying to cross the desert and taken to the hotels straight away."

There was one other occasion when they planned to go. An Arab who had lived many years in Kuwait said he knew of a route across the desert. He had already taken some people out along it and could take them. They made their preparations and packed their things ready to go. Their wardens warned them against it - it was far too dangerous and they should forget it. But they were not to be put off. They went ahead with their plans.

It was only when one of the wardens, Sandy MacMillan, phoned them to say the route had been closed that they finally realised they were stuck in Kuwait. That was it, no more chances would come up. They had to stick it out. The McAlindins received a lot of help from Sandy throughout their time in Kuwait, for which they were extremely grateful.

They were still adjusting to this reality when they received some strange news. Their wardens had not been answering their phones for a day or so, which was very peculiar. Then they heard. They had taken advantage of the route, which *was* still open and had hightailed it themselves, leaving those people in their care like the McAlindins behind. And they *had* successfully escaped. Not only did the community feel left in the lurch, but people felt it was totally irresponsible for those wardens to leave maps, names and addresses behind where Iraqis or looters could find them.

The McAlindins, like others who discovered what had happened, felt this was perhaps the most irresponsible example of some wardens abdicating their responsibility. In their eyes, it was unforgivable. It made the selfless acts of the wardens who did stay, often when they had the chance to escape, even more worthy of praise and commendation.

Another group which tried to organise an escape in the first two weeks of the crisis included Barbara Griffiths. Her husband Stewart had been captured on Mutlaa Ridge and taken to Iraq the first day of the invasion and she had been left with no idea where or in what condition he was. That first night of the invasion she sat awake in a chair until the morning.

"I waited and waited. I really did get scared. I began singing to myself. Maybe that sounds irrational or stupid, but I sat there singing hymns. I was very cool and collected that night. At eight in the morning I rose and stood at our large balcony window, drinking a cup of tea. Everywhere on the road, going right around the corner below our apartment, there were columns and columns of lorries and tanks. At that point, I burst into tears."

The young soldiers in the street below, some of them barely sixteen, were waving and smiling at the few Kuwaitis braving the streets, as though they were great liberators. They were shouting up at people in their windows and on their balconies, obviously expecting to be hailed as noble saviours. Columns of military vehicles entered the grounds of the school across the road from Barbara and took up positions along the beach.

Manqaf is on the coast just north of Fahaheel and the oil terminal at Mina Ahmadi. It consists of five blocks with between four and ten floors each. Barbara knew a great many of the community there and had their phone numbers. She asked one of her neighbours and close friends, Don Majors, to help her. He was a grandfather and had two other generations of his family sharing his apartment. With him were his two daughters, Cindy and Wendy, Cindy's husband Tony, from the Lebanon, and her son Mario.

Meanwhile, outside the compound, the Iraqis were digging in. All along the beach and coast road they were filling sandbags, constructing bunkers for mortar and gun emplacements, building roadblocks and pillboxes and making trenches for their tanks. Dozens of soldiers were laying mines, and lorries, tanks and half-tracks were constantly rumbling past - in both directions.

Barbara found she couldn't go to bed for fear of what might happen to her if the Iraqis broke in. The wall of her apartment which faced the sea was all glass. So was the wall of her bedroom. And across from her apartment the Iraqis had set up a machine-gun nest which looked straight into her bedroom. She was petrified that they would spot her then break into the block, rush up the stairs and find her alone. She felt very scared and very isolated. The Iraqis were everywhere. She daren't open the front door of her flat in case they were on the landing, nor go down the stairs unless they were guarding the main entrance. There was no other way out except through the basement, so she stayed indoors and slept in an armchair for four nights, exhaustion finally allowing her some unsettled rest.

The safest place in her apartment was the bathroom, as long as she didn't let the light shine through the door. She would shut the bedroom door, switch on the light to the bathroom, which was on the outside the bathroom door, and quickly nip in. That was her windowless haven. She couldn't even put a light on to get to the kitchen, in case the Iraqis noticed it. "I had a little lamp in the corner, but I didn't dare put the big light on. I couldn't go to bed. If I wanted to have a bath, I would have to go into the cloakroom, change out of my clothes and creep into the bathroom."

Barbara's only company was her bird in its cage. It was trapped behind its bars and Barbara was trapped behind hers. She loved that bird, talked to it and used to let it fly about the apartment. But with the Iraqis watching she had to move it into the washroom and cover it with a cloth. It, too, lost what freedom it had. The whole British community was caged. They were trapped at the whim of the Iraqis and, just as one plays with a bird, so the Iraqis played with them.

By Sunday, Barbara had eaten nothing for four days. She had still heard nothing of Stewart and rumours were beginning to circulate. One was that a bridge north of Jahra had been blown up on the first day of the invasion. Knowing that was the route Stewart would have taken, her troubled imagination concocted pictures of him dead beneath the rubble. It was incredibly frustrating for her not to be able to see the bridge for herself and check the story out. It was the not knowing - one way or the other - which was so hard for her. Not only did she grieve for her husband but, without him, she felt a liability and drain on all the other British because they had a special responsibility to look after her, a woman on her own. She suffered a sense of guilt and inadequacy as well as loss.

In those first days, the men met together several times to make plans. "There was Ken Best, there was Lorie's husband, there was Don, a George, Peter, Chris and Eric." They decided to make the blocks more secure and to prepare a bolt hole, in case it was needed. Barbara contributed her medicines and bandages. She was a trained medical auxiliary. With these and other items, they organised a hideaway in part of the basement of one of the blocks. They carried their tins of food down, plus sewing materials, tools and toys for the children. Some of the men syphoned petrol from those cars they could get into, in order to have a good supply if they needed to make a run for it. They moved the vehicles well away from their secret room, sealed the doors on the stairs and sabotaged the lifts, so no Iraqi could get down to the basement. They rigged up a telephone down there and devised a phone alarm signal. When that code rang, everyone was to disappear to the basement, taking nothing and being extremely careful not to be seen on the glass stairwell.

Barbara began to spend the nights lying on the floor at Don's. She couldn't sleep very well, but would listen to the gunfire and watch the flashes of grenades and mortars against the walls of the living room. She would rise at five and go down to the basement, hoping that no Iraqis had entered the block during the night. From there, she would run across to her block and scamper up the stairs to her flat. Every morning she would approach her apartment with trepidation because she had no idea whether any Iraqis had occupied it during the night.

One day, staring mindlessly into the distance from one of her windows, her eye was caught by movement in the street below. A group of Iraqis banged on the doors of several Kuwaiti houses. After a few moments, the doors cautiously opened. The soldiers angrily pushed their way in, then appeared a few minutes later. "I witnessed Iraqi soldiers taking Kuwaiti boys off the street and tying their hands behind their backs. They took them across the road beside a school. They pushed them inside a large pipe waiting to be used as part of a new sewerage system, beat them up, tortured them, then shot them and dumped their bodies in the pipe."

Such atrocities made Barbara feel very alone. She longed desperately for her husband Stewart. Although she was now in with a group of friends, she still felt terribly isolated. The five women, two men and even the child Mario increasingly felt that the net was drawing tighter around them. They spotted Iraqi soldiers searching the compound between the blocks, asking resident Arabs and Filipinos where the British were. Their food was running low. They had none coming in from outside. They didn't know any Arabs willing or trustworthy enough to help them get supplies.

By the second week of the occupation, many British who had initially hoped things would rapidly get back to normal felt they had no choice but to make an attempt to escape. During that week, the wardens decided to organise a large convoy to cross the desert. The plan was for everybody who wanted to go to meet at the Lateefa complex in Mahbola and drive in a long column to Saudi Arabia. The wardens had concocted the plan, but Barbara was far from confident that it was well worked out. It seemed to her to be badly organised with no chance of success. In her rather direct words, "It was the most ridiculous thing ever."

The intention was to escape south west along a desert track, following an oil pipeline, turning northwest of al-Wafra and passing through the desert to Salmi and the Saudi border. It was one of the most popular escape routes and hundreds of cars were now taking it. Those going were told not to take any belongings, just food and water. Being a woman on her own, Barbara was advised to go.

Those going met as dawn was breaking. When Barbara arrived with a group from Manqaf there were already a lot of vehicles waiting. Only some were four-wheel drives. Many were normal cars and there were several groups containing families with very young children, prepared to take the risk of being stuck in the desert heat. It seemed chaotic, even suicidal. Some wardens were strolling about giving instructions, checking who was there, going through the drill for a desert crossing.

They were suddenly off. The convoy sped south along the Fahaheel Expressway, then southwest down the desert track to al-Wafra, the pipeline to their left. A few kilometres before al-Wafra, it turned off the desert track to cut north of al-Wafra to the Saudi border. The sun and temperature were starting to rise, but things went well. Many roadblocks were unguarded and those Iraqis they did see seemed unconcerned.

The convoy drove for two hours, trailing a great column of dust behind it. It grew hotter and hotter inside the vehicles as they turned west and entered the border area. They began to pass abandoned cars with their Asian and Arab families stranded in the desert, waking to yet another morning. With several kilometres still to go, this track, just like the Wadi al-Batin, was chock-a-block with cars and lorries. There was no way through. Even worse, Iraqi tanks overlooked the track from the crests of nearby sand dunes. Soldiers were turning thousands of people back. An Iraqi helicopter buzzed overhead. It had been tracking them for miles.

"There were cars and cars and cars. Again, we saw tanks and soldiers. There were helicopters up. They *knew* we were going. They just let us waste our petrol. It was an utter waste of time. We decided it was no use and turned back home."

After the failure of this warden-led convoy, morale took a sharp dive amongst the British community. Many were critical of the way it had been organised, though others felt it was a worthwhile effort, believing none of them would have known the difficulties of escaping unless they had tried. Everyone became much more aware of just how serious the situation was becoming and how determined the Iraqis now were to keep them in Kuwait. A lot of light-heartedness was knocked out of people that day. They returned to the dusk-to-dawn curfew, to the nightly gunfire and explosions, to the roadblocks and troop movements, to the house-to-house searches and looters, and to shrinking food stocks. People began to realise they might not get out at all. This was just a false truce between Iraq and the rest of the world, a phoney war as both sides built up their huge armies. The Allies were going to attack and Saddam was not going to pull out. Amongst some, a sense of desperation and even panic began to set in.

Don Majors had been seriously planning how to get his family out. Don increasingly felt the only option was for them to steal out in a small group and try to get across the desert far more surreptitiously. A couple of vehicles, tearing across the desert at dawn, could find a gap in the Iraqi border screen and get through. However, they didn't have a four-wheel drive.

It all happened so quickly. Chris Maloney phoned them. He'd been offered a lift with some people in the Lateefa complex. It was one of Don's maids who picked up the phone and answered it in Arabic, a standard safety procedure they had developed.

"Is Don there? It's Chris."

Don came to the phone.

"Hi Don. Listen, there' some friends of mine up where we all met before. They're organising another party to see our relatives. It's only a small do, but we have to be ready to go at any time. If I get the OK to go, by whatever means, I'll let you know immediately."

"Fine. We'll discuss what presents to bring and let you know our decision."

"How are you all feeling?" Chris suddenly changed the subject.

"Some of us are a bit down. Some don't want to go to any more parties. They've had enough. But I think most of us do, so keep us on your guest list."

At nine o'clock on the evening of Thursday 16th August Don's phone rang again, and again the maid answered it in Arabic. Again it was Chris and again it was for Don. He listened for a few seconds, said, "OK, thank you, we'll take it," and put the phone down.

All that night Don, Barbara and Wendy prepared. They stored as much water in as many plastic and tin containers as they could find. None of them took any bags or cases. The only possessions they had were a few documents and the clothes they stood up in. Again, they had to get to Lateefa before dawn but now, with the curfew being more strictly enforced, it was even riskier. If they were caught it could mean days in an Iraqi army centre, interrogation and separation from each other. This was especially worrying for the women, who feared being raped if they were arrested. However, they felt they had no choice. An Egyptian friend, Sama, agreed to take them in his car. He drove them at midnight, at great personal risk, past the lines of tanks parked along the expressway. Although Lateefa was only a few kilometres away, it seemed to take an age to get there as the Egyptian tried as far as possible to take side streets and avoid roadblocks.

"When there's a curfew on, you're terrified. It seemed an awful long way. Awful." Barbara pushed back her grey shoulder length hair as she spoke, her pale blue eyes betraying the emotions she had felt on that day, cramped between the seats of the car. "We got to this open piece of ground and hid under a wall by some buildings while Sama, Tony and Don tried to get into the grounds of the Lateefa complex, because it was all fenced off. Don and Tony went over the top and opened it up. Meanwhile, other groups began to arrive, mainly of people who worked for the Arab Bank and several other financial institutions. They decided to leave just before dawn.

At four, the small group of vehicles drove through the gate of the complex, turned north and proceeded for a few kilometres before meeting up with another group who planned to travel with them. They skirted south of the city along the Seventh Ring Road, past the sight of a heavy battle. Burnt out personnel carriers and tanks littered the sand and the side of the road. They joined the Sixth Ring Road which took them west past Jahra and drove through an enormous scrapyard of old cars and lorries - there was a terrible mortality rate amongst vehicles in Kuwait, even before the Iraqis added their special brand of vandalism to it.

Once past the scrapyard the main road headed north but their route was to turn off and continue west, using a line of pylons as a guide. As they drove, some of the cars became bogged down in the sand, forcing the others to stop and help them out, slowing everyone up. The sun rose and the heat intensified. Always, escape bids had to contend with the sun. It was their greatest enemy. They couldn't go at night for fear of losing the faint desert tracks and becoming lost. The routes were no more than wheel ruts, not metalled in any way, and it would be suicidal to travel in the dark unless one knew the desert extremely well.

That summer was one of the hottest on record. Temperatures in the desert could reach 55°C (130°F), a blistering, oppressive, wilting heat which was impossible to survive for long even with water. Barbara only had a tee-shirt, jeans and pair of shoes on, yet she was baking. She had no possessions apart from her key documents. She had left behind everything they had acquired over their years together, including photographs, mementoes, presents, ornaments, diaries, books and clothes. She was never to see them again. She was to lose everything.

They struggled through the sands for several hours until the reached the Wadi al-Batin. They were suddenly aware of being surrounded by Iraqis. "There were tanks with enormous guns pointing straight at us. Wherever we went they followed. Once again, there were hundreds of abandoned cars strewn about." Arabs and Indians whose cars had broken down climbed onto their bumpers to hitch lifts.

Eight hours after they had left they were still in the middle of the desert, going round and round in circles. They found themselves trapped. They couldn't go north, because the Iraqis would appear to the north of them. If they went south, there were more Iraqis. The soldiers were clearly playing with them, letting them drive around and run out of petrol as they watched and laughed. It was like a cat playing with a mouse. And the cat would even send up a jeep of soldiers to beg for water and food and tell them, "You're too early yet, come back later."

It became obvious to Barbara they weren't going to get out, but the group kept trying. "We'd go this way, we'd go that way, we'd go round and round in circles. We met up with other groups of cars, passing them on the desert tracks." It was like scared rats in a barrel. "We got out the shovels to dig each other out. We stopped for a bit. We tried to kid ourselves that if we waited until nightfall we could try again. But then, at one place, after we'd driven around it twice, we were told to halt. The soldiers demanded our passports. We tried to pretend we didn't have them, that we were just out for a run! In that heat! Who were we trying to fool?"

The Iraqis weren't entirely stupid. It was perfectly obvious they were trying to cross the border. They were ordered to remain where they were then told to follow a group of Iraqi vehicles. They were led back through Jahra, passing countless tanks, soldiers and military vehicles. They were driven to a large administrative building, a Kuwaiti police headquarters that the Iraqis had requisitioned. There, they were ordered out of their cars and led inside under armed guard.

Although questioned, they were treated well and given tea. There was no interrogation and they were not put into cells. They asked to be allowed back to their apartments, but were refused. The Iraqis, who included a doctor, told them not to worry, just drink their tea. By now it was four o'clock in the afternoon. They hadn't eaten for twenty-four hours and were starving. They asked the Iraqis for some food and were soon served with some goulash. Once they had finished, they were led back to their vehicles and told to follow their Iraqi escort, which took them to the Iraqi embassy, *en route* to the Regency Palace Hotel.

The phone rang yet again.

"Hello, this is Josie Brookes at the Midland Gulf Support Group. How can I help?"

"Hello. I got your number from a friend of mine. She's been in touch with you several times. She says you might have some information for me."

"Well, I hope so. I'm sure we'll tell you everything we know. Is your husband out in Kuwait?"

"No, it's my son. I think he's in Kuwait."

"Haven't you heard from him?"

"No, not since before August. He was on a ship in the Gulf. They were only stopping in Kuwait for one night. He phoned me from Dubai two days before Iraq invaded and that's the last I've heard." The effort to remain composed was too much for her. She suddenly began to cry. "I don't know where he is. I don't know if he's still in Kuwait, of if they've taken him to Iraq, or if he's on board his ship." She stopped and there was a long pause. Josie wondered about saying something, but decided to just sit and wait for the lady to speak again. They sat in silence for perhaps ten minutes before the woman managed to finish what she wanted to say. "I don't even know if he's alive. His ship's been taken by the Iraqis."

"What is the ship called?"

"I can't tell you."

"Can you tell me his name?"

"No I can't. I know I shouldn't've rung. You can't help me. No one can, no one can..." With that, the phone went dead.

Josie stared at Maureen. She didn't have the woman's phone number or any details to enable her to call her back. That woman had been in such distress, she felt beyond help. She was 'out there', on her own, in desperate need, crying for help, yet she couldn't be given any. Josie, tears in her eyes, had to go downstairs and walk in her garden. But even there she couldn't escape her thoughts and feelings and memories. She thought of Eric and Tim Watson. She remembered her and Stephen's marriage four years before. Eric had been Stephen's best man. Oh, it was all such an awful, awful mess.

At midnight on the nineteenth, the phone by Barbara's bed rang. She answered it and was asked to report to reception immediately. She struggled up and dressed in her only clothes - a pair of jeans and a tee-shirt. When she reached the foyer she saw dozens of British people, including the BA crews in their uniforms, standing around waiting. No one had anything more than a piece of hand-luggage which they had hastily packed before rushing downstairs. They had all been woken at the same time and given just half an hour to get their things together and board a coach.

An Iraqi officer spoke to them. They were leaving the Regency Palace Hotel for Baghdad!

The coaches had already arrived and they piled on, trying to keep together in family or friendship groups, Barbara sticking close to Don Majors, Maureen Chappell with her family, and Eric Watson with his son Tim. Many of them had formed into couples, as the Iraqis treated family groups with more consideration, or slightly less aggression. Barbara's group ended up on a mini-bus with a couple of Americans, but the rest were put on the coaches. It was to be the most terrifying journey of their incarceration.

The coaches and minibus were driven out in a convoy, westwards around the city and into the desert, ostensibly to Baghdad. It was pitch black. The coaches began to hive off and go different ways until Barbara's little minibus was alone. "The driver suddenly pulled off into the desert. One of the Americans said, 'You'd better start praying'. We honestly thought at this point they were going to shoot us." When Barbara told me this she spoke very slowly, with long pauses and sighs. It was obviously a deeply painful memory, one indelibly etched into her mind.

The desert track passed amongst hundreds of Iraqi tanks. Soldiers were sleeping under them, over them, between them, in them. Their washing was hanging between tank barrels. They were passing through the middle of a large army camp. The minibus became stuck in the sand. Instead of trying to dig it out, the Iraqis took their time. For some reason, they seemed to be dragging the journey out. After a while, they got free of the sand and left the military camp behind. Everyone in the back of the minibus heaved a sigh of relief.

The coach carrying Eric and Tim Watson endured the same uncertainty. It drove for hours across desert tracks. They were the only vehicle in sight. Suddenly, they stopped. Then it went on a bit further, then turned off, then stopped again. Images of mass graves and death camps went through many people's minds. Taken at night, with no witnesses, going no one knew where, was terrifying.

Eric Watson, explained his feelings as he and the rest of the British were driven into the midnight desert wilderness: "When I was taken out of the hotel where we had been kept for two and a half weeks, we were taken to a camp. In order to disorientate us, they took us at one-thirty in the morning. They took us out into the desert, then stopped suddenly. I thought we were going to be shot." It was the most terrifying time of his life.

Barbara Griffiths knew Kuwait. As the minibus rejoined a main road and sped along an expressway, she knew it wasn't towards Baghdad. In fact, they had gone twenty kilometres south, not north at all. They ended up at the back of Ahmadi, on one of the main desert roads, where they joined the other coaches.

The whole point of this ludicrous and petrifying ordeal was to try to fool the hostages that they were on their way to Baghdad. With most of them, it had worked. The BA passengers had no idea what was happening to them or where they were being taken. They had been driven for four or five hours and it was starting to get light. To keep up the farce, the Iraqis took everyone's passports, as though they had crossed the border into Iraq. Shortly afterwards, they drove on through a desert crammed full of soldiers. There were several hundred thousand billeted in Kuwait by then.

As the dawn strengthened, the coaches drove east towards the coast and, after half an hour, stopped at the gates of Mina Ahmadi oil terminal and refinery. They had travelled barely twenty-five kilometres from the hotel.

The hostages were driven through the barbed wire perimeter fence surrounding the refinery and into the IBI Camp, where they were eventually allowed to disembark. Forty-nine came off the coaches and walked into the growing heat of early morning. The refinery's barbed wire fence was barely fifty yards away from them. They were in the middle of a dozen huge liquid petroleum gas tanks, the nearest less than three hundred yards away. According to Barbara Griffiths, the Iraqis had already mined the tanks, so they were literally living in a time bomb. They had become part of the human shield, metaphorically strapped to a strategic pipeline.

The Iraqi officers still kept up the pretence of it being Baghdad, even though Barbara Griffiths could see her own apartment block from where they were standing. They began to laboriously allocate huts, firstly to families, then to couples. The hostages waited as the officers tried to sort out the accommodation, until they grew impatient in the heat and told the Iraqis not to bother - they'd all find their own.

When Maureen Chappell went to open the door of one hut, she could hardly move it. Her husband John tried to push it, putting all his weight to it. Slowly it moved, until he was able to squeeze inside. Behind the door, the hut was a complete mess. The Iraqis had been in and trashed everything. Cushions, papers, drawers, chairs, clothes and crockery were strewn across the floor. The wardrobes in the bedrooms had been broken open and pulled to the ground. Mattresses had been thrown from the beds, curtains torn down and carpets ripped up. All the electrical equipment had either been stolen or smashed.

Eric and Tim Watson moved into the hut adjoining the Chappells, along with Linda and Charlotte Dolwin. Their two huts had been ones the BLT families had taken refuge in and had a hole in the partition wall which the wives had created to give them added security. It proved useful. Whilst they all had their privacy, having the two huts knocked together gave more space for the children to play and for the adults to relax.

There was very little food in the huts. The freezers had been emptied, and the rest of the food strewn about. The children went off to those huts still empty to find more supplies, whilst their parents set about clearing up the mess. It would take them two weeks to finish.

Barbara Griffiths had to push her door hard to get in her hut as well. "Everything was a complete mess. It was like someone coming into my house now and smashing the whole place. The filth and smell was unbelievable." The bath was filthy with excrement, the toilets hadn't been flushed and the floor stank with dirt. There was excrement all over the floor. They had smashed up the freezer and all the meat had gone rotten and stank the whole hut out. "I don't know why they'd done it. It was utter, sheer destruction. Everything was smashed, everywhere. And every house was the same."

Like everyone else, they had to scrounge around for enough tins and packets of pasta to make a half-way decent meal. Fortunately, they had a washing machine and were able to clean some of the clothes they found strewn about the huts. They were a blessing. Although they had been left behind by the British soldiers and their wives, some fitted and it meant that, at last, they had proper changes of clothes.

Maureen Chappell and Linda Dolwin carefully collected all the clothes and stored them away neatly. They salvaged all they could, especially items like photographs and ornaments. Fortunately, the electricity and water supplies were both working, so they were able to cook and wash their clothes. Unfortunately, the water was warm and dirty, certainly not fit for drinking straight from the tap. They couldn't wash properly and constantly felt dirty and degraded. There wasn't enough soap and no shampoo or toothpaste. The consensus of opinion in their hut was that Eric Watson was the best cook. He prepared a rudimentary meal that first night out of what little he could find.

Don Majors' and Barbara Griffiths' group had to share three potatoes that first night. They found two pork chops in a fridge. Barbara cut them up with a pair of scissors. Wendy found some tomato ketchup, mustard and vinegar to make a sauce. They made a batter with some flour and fried the potatoes in slices in the batter. That was for seven of them. Over the next few days, food became the primary concern for many people in the camp. People kept scavenging through the other huts to find pasta, flour, sugar and other basics.

On the second day, the Iraqis brought in a lorry load of food. It contained some rice, some soap, tinned vegetables and potatoes. It was a hotch-potch of items, barely adequate for their needs. The rice was full of weevils and many items weren't in large enough quantities for everyone to share. Whether the lorry had been allocated to them or just been looted was hard to tell.

The Chappells were not to see any meat the whole time they were at the camp, but they did have milk. The Iraqis brought round packs of Carnation milk and gave them four, which lasted them until their release. They also brought tea and sugar to the huts, so that people didn't go completely without them, although both items were always in short supply and they had to use them sparingly. For the Chappells and Watsons, as for most in the camp, it was a matter of rationing their food and preparing meals carefully, with priority given to the children. During their ordeal, the hostages made soup out of anything. Barbara Griffiths lived on marmite and pitta bread. She had no orange squash or lemonade and survived on one meal a day. It would be either at lunchtime or in the evening and might consist of soup made from anything they could find or a couple of eggs. There were never enough eggs for one each, but sufficient to make some sandwiches. Her group might have one orange between them. Everyone lost a lot of weight the two weeks they were at the camp.

Once people had settled into a routine, a rapport and camp atmosphere built up. Many things were done as a group. When they couldn't supply butchered meat, the guards supplied live meat. A sheep turned up one day, courtesy of the Iraqis. Everyone stared at the pathetic creature, wondering precisely what to do with it. The children brought it some water and stroked it. No one had the faintest idea how to slaughter and prepare it. After much discussion, some members of the BA crew plucked up courage and slit its throat. Few people could watch. They hung the carcass on the refinery fence and cut it up. It was the only decent meat they were to get, though many of them decided not to eat any of it.

Thankfully, the hostages mucked in together a lot during those weeks, to make life more bearable for them all. Apart from three French lads, some Australians and two Americans, they were all British in the camp. Five of them were children. Some people discovered a couple of televisions and two video machines, together with a huge stock of videos. They gave one machine to the children for them to watch and kept the other in the mess. They also set up a bank of toys in the mess and established a school in one of the huts. There were plenty of books scattered around the camp. Eric could teach music and a woman called Denise taught English. She managed to find a copy of *The Lord of the Flies*, which was on the syllabus, and went through that with them. One of the French boys knew about computers and managed to find one the Iraqis had failed to smash up or steal. Someone else taught history and another taught geography.

The camp's mess room became the focal point of all social activity. During the drunken exploits of the Iraqi soldiers when the British Liaison Team families were there, it had been smashed up, but not too badly. Some of the women banded together and cleaned it through from the bar to the toilets. They found an undisturbed supply of wine and enough ethanol to keep the camp going for quite a while. Ethanol is the technical name for alcohol. It was imported into Kuwait in huge quantities for 'medicinal purposes' and used extensively by the British ex-patriot community to turn into an assortment of drinks and cocktails. Most lethally, three parts water and one part ethanol made a local brew called flash. That was indeed potent.

There was a large library of books and a good assortment of games, such as Monopoly, Scrabble, and dominoes. There was a billiard table and even a bingo set, which they made full use of during each evening's entertainment. It became an unstated rule that everyone would meet at the mess between four and six in the evening for a chat and to hear any news which affected the group as a whole. Whenever someone had a birthday, they made as big a celebration of it as they could. They would mock up some sort of cake, make banners reading 'Happy Birthday', play games and have a sing-song.

During the whole of their confinement in the camp, the hostages at the IBI camp didn't once hear from the British embassy at all. No one came to the camp, nor did they receive news from either the wardens or anyone outside. However, it is not simply a matter of blaming the embassy. Like the journalists who were reporting that the BA passengers as somewhere in Iraq, they had been deceived by the Iraqi ruse the night they left the hotel. As far as the embassy was concerned, they had disappeared from the face of the earth. Nor would it have made any difference if the embassy had known, because by now the Iraqis were consistently refusing to allow embassy officials to see British citizens, whether at installations or in hotels, and just six days after they arrived at the camp the Iraqis sealed off all foreign embassies in Kuwait.

Like many hostages in other installations, the lack of contact from either the Kuwait or Baghdad embassies and the conviction that the world had forgotten their plight left them feeling angry, alone and despairing. Nothing was being done to get them out. The deep sense of loss that isolation and feelings of unfairness brought on was the hardest to bear.

By now, Eric Watson was finding the total lack of communication with his wife, Wen Li, playing heavily on his mind. He hadn't heard from her for a month, didn't know where she was, what she was doing or how worried she had become. He longed to be able to spend a few seconds on a phone telling her he was all right. Just that would have eased his mind considerably. "The worst thing was the loss of communication, the utter isolation I felt. I could make no phone calls. I couldn't write a letter, nor did I ever receive a letter. I didn't know what had happened to my family. I didn't know where my wife was, whether she'd gone back to England or not."

It seemed so unfair. None of this crisis was their fault. None of it. Yet nothing was being done for them. They desperately wanted the Americans and British forces to invade and get it over with. Although they were stuck in the middle of a refinery and knew that, if it was hit, it would be death for them all, they wanted their trauma to be over. They were so desperate for an end to their appalling confinement they were prepared to risk being killed. The Iraqis were such a bunch of part-time squaddies, most of whom didn't know one end of their Kalashnikovs from the other, that they could be swept aside in a few days. They knew that. When war eventually did come, few of them were surprised at how easy the victory was. They knew the Iraqi conscripts were a waste of time as troops.

For all of them at the camp, those weeks were the most terrifying and debilitating of their lives. They became emotionally drained. Although they tried to make everything as normal as possible, they could never succeed when, down by the beach, they could see Iraqi tanks dug into the sand and signs for minefields running right up the coast. In every direction there were huge fuel tanks and missile batteries. They were surrounded by weaponry and danger, living over the barrel of a gun.

Yet some did build strong bonds between each other. It was as though they were the only people who existed in the world, a desert island where the rest of the planet had been decimated by war or plague. They were all that was left of humanity; they *were* the human race. They were in the clouds - or in some hell. It was a dream world, in which each of them constructed their own false reality. Barbara Griffiths explained this feeling. "The only way I can describe it to you is that I had actually died and was with strangers in some sort of pre-heavenly existence, a purgatory, if you like."

"Hello, the Midlands Gulf Support Group."

"Hello, this is Miriam."

"Hello Miriam. This is Maureen, can I help you."

"Is the other lady there?"

"Which one?"

"I spoke to her before."

"Was it Josie?"

"I think so. I spoke to her a few days ago. I rang off."

"Are you the lady with her son on the ship?"

"Yes."

"I'll get Josie for you. Can you hold on for a minute?" Maureen Evans put the receiver down and quickly rose from her chair. She ran to the top of the stairs and shouted down to Josie. There was no answer. The stairs were steep and she nearly tripped as she scampered down them.

"Josie!" She checked the living room, then went through the kitchen. "Josie!"

"Out here."

Maureen ran into the garden. Josie was sitting with a new volunteer, explaining to her what the helpline was trying to achieve and filling in the times she could man the phones. "It's that woman with her son on the ship. She's phoned back."

"Oh, thank God." Josie rushed past her and flew up the stairs.

"Her name's Miriam," Maureen shouted after her.

"I won't let her go this time," Josie promised herself. "Not till I've got all her details."

Miriam was waiting patiently. She was feeling calmer that day and the wait steadied her nerves. There she was, a woman who had coped with crises all her life, with work and bringing up her children. With death and schooling, with illnesses, adolescence and growing older herself. There she was, admitting defeat.

Yes, admitting defeat. That was exactly how it felt. Admitting that she was a failure, that she couldn't cope on her own any more, that she needed help. What a thing to have to come to terms with! Her self-respect had totally seeped away. Her life force was draining away from her. Her shell of calm capability was dissolving around her, leaving her emotionally stripped bare. Her son was missing!

"Oh Miriam, thanks for ringing me back. Now, give me your phone number." Josie fumbled for a biro and scribbled the London number down. "Don't do that to me again."

"Do what?"

"I was so worried about you. You mustn't just put the phone down. I had no idea what you might do."

"Oh, I'm feeling a bit better now."

"Are you?"

"No, not really."

"Tell me about him.What's his first name."

Miriam told her and then spoke for over an hour about her worries, her times with her son, what he was like, his whole life history. As the minutes passed Josie noticed her voice pick up, the silent pauses became shorter and less frequent, and that Miriam was even able to laugh at some things. But sometimes sudden awareness of her son's plight broke through her fragile giggle and she was catapulted back to the edge of tears. There was nothing she could do for him. She was so powerless. When he most needed her, she was totally unable to answer his call. Yet it was her duty to try. It was a mother's role. She had spent her life looking after him, she *had* to do something.

Her son's face haunted Miriam. She had a permanent vision of his great, pleading blue eyes drowned in tears, staring up at her from some vast ship's hold, his hands extended towards her. Oh God, help him, help him, somebody, please!

She lit candles for him. Every Sunday in the local church his eyes met hers, she saw his blond hair, his smile, his laugh, Every Sunday she drew faith that he could look after himself. He had a military past, he would be all right. She knew it. Every Sunday, for a few minutes, she knew it.

Into Hiding

"The silence was like death, ominous, haunting, dark."

By mid-August, those in hiding in Kuwait were bracing themselves for a long-term sentence. They were barricading themselves behind their villa and apartment doors against both Iraqi house searches and roaming bands of armed looters, rationing their food stocks for a long haul, and preparing themselves against chemical attack and the intensive air bombardment they felt sure would presage a war. The extent to which they prepared and took precautions depended both on the make-up of the group and the safety of the area.

Some groups took security very seriously, others were much more relaxed. Some areas were very quiet in terms of Iraqi searches, especially certain suburbs of the city, although, as a result, the Resistance tended to be more active there. The inner city was very hazardous. There were Iraqis everywhere. The coastal apartment blocks were virtually impossible to hide in, because the Iraqis took them over for bunkers for their beach-line defence. The small towns down the coast, such as Fintas, Manqaf, Abu-Hulifa and Fahaheel, as well as Ahmadi, were full of looters and indisciplined soldiers.

Bernice MacDonald set about disguising her house to make it look Kuwaiti. It had large plate glass windows, plainly visible from the road, and a glazed, spiral staircase. Passers-by could see in clearly. She and her husband Lawrence bought some prayer mats which they rolled out in the lounge and found some Arabic prayer scrolls for the walls. They began to walk about in Kuwaiti clothes; Bernice wore a black *abaya,* completely covering her head and body; Lawrence donned a *dishdasha* and put a white scarf and *gutra* headband over his head. He cut his hair very short, to mimic Arabs who had been on the *haj* and had the nose to carry off the disguise, strong and bold. Having retrieved some prayer beads, he carried them around the house, and even learnt the lazy Kuwaiti slouch which passes for walking. To disguise his green eyes, he wore very dark sunglasses whenever he ventured outside and taught himself a few Arabic phrases. His hope was that, if Iraqis came up to the gate of the garden, he could call out a few phrases, show a bit of *dishdasha,* and persuade them to go away.

To complete his disguise, he began to grow a beard and moustache. However, this only lasted a while. Late in August he heard that the Iraqis were making Kuwaitis shave off their beards, both because they were a sign of warriors going to war and because they were being used as disguises by Westerners. The penalty for having a beard was to be shot.

The MacDonalds' security was well-founded. After a few weeks, they learnt that a couple of streets away from them two schools had been turned into a barracks for an entire regiment of Iraqis. As a result, a host of machine-gun posts, roadblocks and patrols sprang up and hundreds of off-duty Iraqis began milling about. The area was swamped with them. After their ordeal was over, they learnt that a senior Iraqi officer had taken residence in a villa across from their back garden and could have spotted them at any time, if they had been less cautious.

The couple were very circumspect about answering the telephone, especially when an Arab voice spoke. "There were too many peculiar phone calls going on for it to be accidental. The general feeling was that the Iraqis were ringing round. We had one call at two o'clock in the morning. 'Ah! Brigia, Brigia!', meaning, 'British, British'. It was no longer safe to answer the telephone."

On the day of the invasion, Lawrence and Bernice had just moved house from Mushrif to Bayan. Whilst they had virtually no food in stock, on the plus side, their Arab neighbours didn't know for a month that any Britons were in the villa. They stayed low and their Arabic disguises worked extremely well. They kept the house in complete darkness at night, sitting in the blackness from about seven o'clock each evening. At the end of August, however, they started to go outside to water the bushes in the garden. If they died off, it would be far easier to see into the house and even at night time they wouldn't be safe. They also had a dog, Rastas, who they needed to let run around at night. That would have been impossible without the screen of greenery.

So Lawrence had to turn the hose on in the dark to preserve the bushes, risking being seen. On one of these nightly expeditions, he was spotted by a neighbour's manservant. It turned out to be a blessing. After initially being frightened in case the British brought the Iraqis down on the street, some Kuwaitis, especially two called Ahmad and Abdulla, began to help them. They advised the Britons to keep one light on at night to deter looters and generally looked after them. They were absolutely fantastic and ensured the Britons' survival. "By that time our food had virtually dried up and if it hadn't've been for the generosity of our Kuwaiti neighbours, we would have starved. Both of us had lost a lot of weight. We had a warden for our area who was supposed to distribute food to us and five other houses, but we didn't get very much from that source. In three weeks we received five mouldy, tiny cucumbers and three green peppers."

They had tinned food, but that was for absolutely the last, desperate resort. They didn't want to touch it except under the direst circumstances. Under the advice of the British embassy, they distributed this valuable supply around the house, so if they were looted, there was a chance not all their food would be taken.

Apart from that one piece of useful advice, the embassy proved a disappointment to the couple. "We phoned the British embassy in the first couple of days. With all due respect to those inside, they didn't have a clue as to what was going on. They just were not organised. I think the British embassy was absolutely abysmal. They were worse than useless, they were dangerous... Nobody could ever get information out of it." Lawrence was sitting with Bernice and his sister Cathy Willis in her home in Skelmersdale. "That was why people were going around to each other's houses in the first days. We had to use our own judgement of the situation all the time. Any information the embassy did give out tended to be contradictory."

Tom and Gilly Colclough lived in an isolated group of villas near Misila Beach, just down from Misila Palace, where a major skirmish had taken place on the day of the invasion. The families at the compound rapidly learned that the Iraqi Republican Guard were setting up a barracks only six hundred metres away. Wherever Tom and Gilly looked there were Iraqi gun emplacements and roadblocks going up. A whole defensive network was being constructed, with them in the middle. As troop convoys drove down the coast road, they were deploying anti-aircraft guns and digging trenches along the beach between the villas and the sea, and even right under their compound wall. Already, soldiers were patrolling around the perimeter. Thousands of troops began to dig themselves in. It would not be long before they came into the villas, both to loot and to turn them into a fortress.

The group with Tom decided they had to get out very quickly. They included Terry Slattery and Maureen and Mike Durnin. On the second day of the occupation, Tom called in on an old friend, Colin Eglington, who had a large villa in Mushrif. It was a quiet area, mainly Kuwaiti, and off the main roads. It had no police station nearby, for the Iraqis to use as an army headquarters. Colin agreed to let them move in, so the next day, Saturday, they hurriedly loaded their cars and drove the three kilometres to Colin's. Colin already had Pete Wakely and Simon Lloyd with him. Later Ted and Joyce Foreman joined them.

A few British families remained in the Marafi compound after the first few days, when most either headed for the Saudi border or to safe houses. On the first Saturday, one family, consisting of an English man, his Kuwaiti wife, and a newborn baby, were in hiding there. Their eldest son had managed to escape across the border before the Iraqi troops arrived. When they came and saw the wife, they held her husband at knife point whilst one soldier took the woman into the bedroom and attacked her. Her husband had to listen to her screams. The soldier pulled at her clothes and fondled her, but she managed to fight him off before he could rape her. The Iraqis thought better of it and hurriedly left. The Colclough's next-door neighbour, who had also been too slow to escape, was captured that day and taken to an hotel under armed guard.

The Colcloughs felt a lot safer at their new home. The area was much quieter, with far fewer Iraqis. Those they saw were friendly at first. And inside the villa it was a fairly relaxed atmosphere. They didn't really feel bored. There was plenty to do and enough of them to keep each other amused. They taught themselves morse code, watched videos, cleaned the villa until it was spotless, and at night watered the lawn and let the dogs out. They played computer games, one called 'Empire' which they adapted to the situation in Kuwait. It kept them busy many nights blowing up Iraqi tanks on the screen. Great fun!

Towards the end of August the atmosphere rapidly worsened. Whilst they still felt relatively safe within their villa, a war of attrition was going on outside. Kuwaitis were disappearing every day. Bodies would appear beside the road. Some days, dozens lay where they had been shot or dumped. The British in Mushrif suspected the area was a centre for the Resistance and that its leadership was in hiding nearby, because there was a lot of Iraqi activity and house searches. The back streets around them were constantly used by the Resistance to smuggle cars to prepare attacks against the Iraqis and then to escape. These cars drove without headlights, sometimes chased by Iraqi jeeps, machine-guns blazing away at them.

The Kuwaiti Resistance consisted of anybody. Some were soldiers and police who had gone underground, others were women or boys as young as fourteen. Their bravery was frequently suicidal as they drove cars full of explosives up to roadblocks or into groups of soldiers around tanks, killing themselves as well as Iraqis. One Kuwaiti woman drove her car, full of explosives, into an Iraqi ammunition truck. Her husband had been killed by the Iraqis. A *haji* truck was loaded with calor gas bottles and thermite charges hidden under crates of Coca-Cola bottles. This was driven up to an Iraqi position, where the soldiers rushed over to buy the drinks, and it blew up in their midst, glass cutting them to shreds and flames engulfing them.

During the day, the Iraqis were getting their own back on the Kuwaiti community, in a largely indiscriminate and sadistic way. Several times the group with Colin Eglington witnessed Kuwaiti civilians being shot right below their windows. On one occasion, a Kuwaiti *diwanyah*, a men's meeting place where everything under the sun is discussed, was infiltrated by an Iraqi intelligence officer. On his information, a group of Kuwaitis were taken away, including five relatives of the Kuwaiti helping them. They were a doctor, a mullah and three boys. They were all arrested in the house just beside Colin's, taken away to be interrogated and tortured, then brought back to the front gate of the house, where each one was summarily shot in the head by the Iraqis. Their bodies were left for their women to drag inside. In reply, the Kuwaitis discovered several Sudanese working as secret agents for the Iraqis. There was a large barren space behind Colin's villa. One morning, the bodies of the Sudanese could been seen lying on the waste ground where they had been dumped.

Within their walls, the British felt relatively safe. Colin had only just moved into the villa, so was confident no one knew where he was. They kept the lights low at night, at first turning them all off, but later leaving one on to deter looters. As the days passed and the situation steadily deteriorated, they became increasingly security conscious. They set up cameras to overlook the doors and roof and blacked out all the windows with tin foil. Houses all around were being broken into, so they set broken glass into the tops of the walls around the villa to deter the looters. They had little worry about sounds. The villa was double-glazed, with a garden around, a high wall and an alleyway up the side.

"There were a lot of times when it was a bit iffy, you know, the pressure got to some of us, but generally it was all right. We kept very busy." Stuart Dick was the warden for their area. He made a bid for the border, but was turned back three times. He had left his list of names and phone numbers with Tom for him to take on should he make it. In the event, he kept on doing the job of warden himself. He had a very dry sense of humour. Whenever he phoned up, his calls were very short. "Hello, how are you?"

"Fine."

"OK, bye."

No long conversations.

They built themselves a bolthole. There was a small anteroom and a bathroom in the middle of the villa which were completely surrounded by other rooms. They were protected from gunfire and easily lost within the overall lay out of the house. The occupants built a false wall across the hallway to block off the two small rooms and stored the bulk of their food in there, plus mattresses, a torch, water, books, valuables and anything else they might need in an emergency. They placed a bookcase across the bottom section of the wall which could be moved to reveal a hatch into the hideaway. They nailed up a trellis and screwed some plant pots to the wall just above the bookcase so, when the bookcase was in position, they appeared to rest on top of it, with the vines trailing up the trellis. This room was not only in case the Iraqis did a house search, but to prepare for war or a gas attack and to hide most of their food in case looters broke in.

Much of this activity and planning merely helped pass the time. If the Iraqis came, the Irishman with them would stay out of the bolthole and persuade the Iraqis that he was the only one living there. They even thought about spare cups lying about, or extra clothes around. No one was allowed to be untidy. Everyone had to wash their crockery up as soon as they had used them. No magazines were left about, or books or other possessions. Mattresses were always put away each morning and the beds made. They developed strict rules and a routine for security, which had the bonus of keeping the place tidy and making their cramped living space more bearable. The food situation was eased considerably with the aid of Mohammed, the Kuwaiti neighbour whose family had been decimated, who kept them supplied with provisions and information. On one occasion, he brought two lambs for them to butcher in their

Kuwait international airport

The Safat district of central Kuwait City, with the Muthanna Complex and Meridien Hotel in the background

The Bayan Palace, heavily attacked on the day of the invasion

The British Embassy in Kuwait

Josie and Stephen Brookes running their helpline from their dining room table in the first weeks of the crisis

Joanna Copley

Jonathan Copley

Joanna Copley and Stephen Brookes wait by the Reuter machine in Alexandra House

Jim McAlindin (on the far right) with three other men in hiding in Salwa

Kat Copley in hiding with John Collier (left) and John Heley in Dave Dorrington's

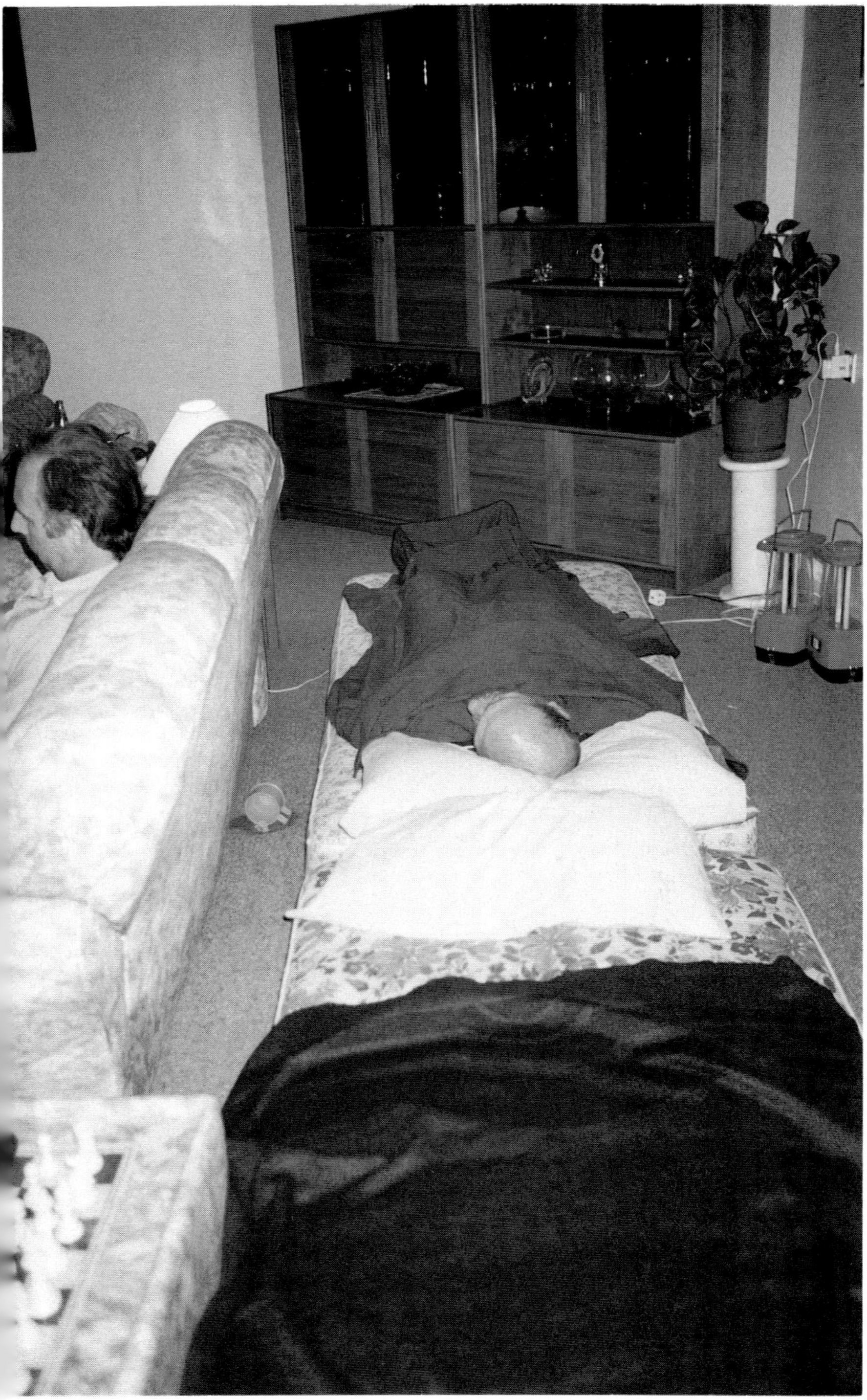

Tom Winston, an American, bedding down in Dave Dorrington's villa

The Regency Palace Hotel

A typical British villa in Kuwait City

The desert north of al-Wafra, typical of the flat expanse of southern Kuwait

HRH The Princess of Wales visiting the Emergency Unit at the Foreign Office
Christopher Denne is on the left, with Grant Lindsay and Duncan McDougall (far right)

Rt Hon Douglas Hurd MP, Secretary of State for Foreign and Commonwealth Affairs

Rt Hon William Waldegrave MP Minister of State at the Foreign Office

Margaret Thatcher, talking of Nuremberg-style trials on Frost on Sunday

Three of the volunteers in the Ops Room at the London helpline's suite in Alexandra House

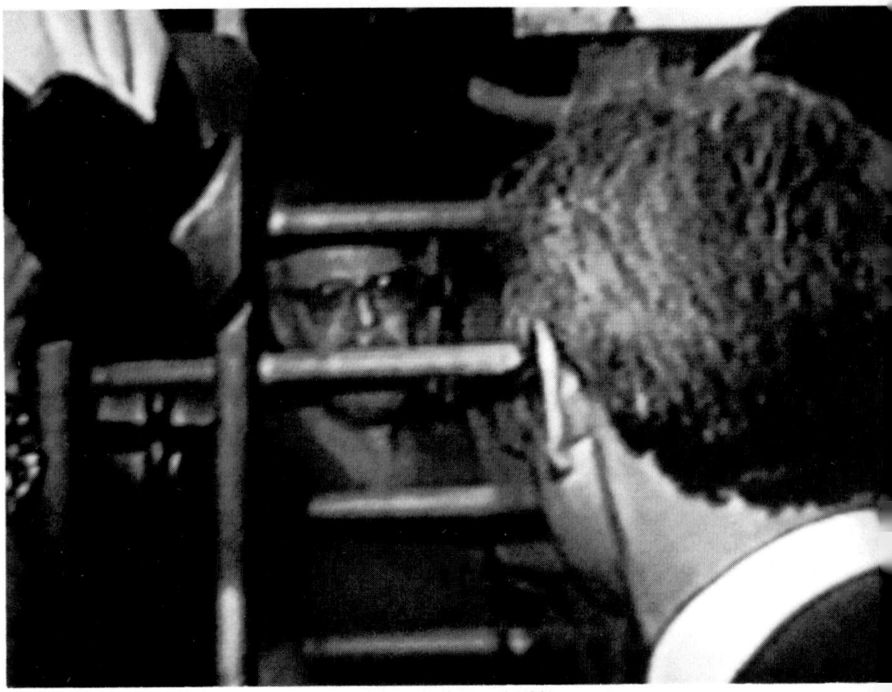

Jesse Jackson with the American ambassador at the entrance to the embass
Dr Joubaydi, Saddam Hussein's translator, watches

Jesse Jackson with Stuart Lockwood after leaving the plane bringing them back to

Saddam Hussein with Stuart Lockwood on the "Guests' News" broadcast

Saddam Hussein stares at the camera to deliver a speech concerning the hostages in which he calls them "Heroes of Peace"

The Sultan Centre

kitchen. It kept them in meat for weeks.The small group gathered in Henry Hill's villa in Ahmadi hardly ever used the phone, and then only locally, because they realised the Iraqis were probably tapping it and didn't went *anyone* to know that they existed.

In common with many groups, they made themselves a secret hiding place. Theirs was in the attic, made by breaking through the top of a linen cupboard into the roof space, which they fitted out with bedding, tinned food and an electric socket for a kettle, an electric fan and a light bulb. The hideaway was next to the water tank, so they would have a supply of water as well. They made a false ceiling and a new top to the cupboard and kept it full of sheets and bedding. They could drop a duvet down behind them, replace the top of the cupboard and slip the false ceiling back, which they could replace behind them. There were six in their group and it was too cramped for them all to sleep up there, although they could all have got in if they had to. It was for emergencies, that was all. The only time they slept up there was after the three women had left for Baghdad and home, when a group of Iraqis tried to break in. The dog barked at the prowlers and they cleared off immediately. "There was an awful lot of time and patience spent in doing that hideaway. But it was good for morale and for something to do. If you've played Find the Lady every day for four months, you don't ever want to play cards again."

They kept themselves going mentally by taking great pleasure in outsmarting the Iraqis and by a determination not to be taken to Baghdad. They considered what would happen in the event of a war. As Ahmadi was on a hill and fairly wind-swept, they felt that gas wouldn't be too much of a problem. If bombing started, they discussed where to hide and what to do. "I always felt very positive that we could survive in Ahmadi. We were very bullish for the war to get started. Certain guys were not happy about it, but over half of us were very strong for war to get started. Anyway, it was my house."

The group including Cliff Lindley had also been forced under cover. On the sixteenth, they lost all contact with the wardens. In his computer diary for that day, Cliff noted that they had to take a lower profile and stop Iraqi soldiers ambling into their block or giving them drinks. Fortunately, the units were constantly changing, so the new shambling bunches of conscripts didn't know they were there. They were moved to the beaches, or to the desert borders, then back to the city, keeping them on the move all the time. "They were digging trenches, filling them in; filling sandbags, emptying sandbags; digging tanks in, digging tanks out; moving up heavy artillery, then moving it out again. They were moving around all the time, as though they didn't really know what they were up to." It may have been a deliberate tactic, both to keep the indisciplined rabble occupied in the desert boredom, and to keep the allies guessing as to their deployment. There was to come a date when they did get serious, dug in well and permanently, and brought a lot more units into the area.

The empty apartment Mike and Ben[1] discovered in the Muthanna Complex was one among hundreds in a maze of corridors, lifts, stairwells, emergency exits, roofs and balconies linking the blocks of apartments with a three storey shopping mall. A lot of the apartments were empty in their block, as people had fled Kuwait or gone into hiding in the suburbs, most of them Kuwaitis.

Fairly soon, the two men contacted the Australian, John Levins. John introduced them to other groups sheltering in the same block. They included Americans, Irish and British, about nine or ten in all, living in five scattered apartments. Two were women.

Fortunately, all the occupied apartments were within three floors of each other in one block, so they needn't travel far to be together. They had two flights of stairs they could use, both tucked well away, so they made very little noise and drew no attention to themselves at all. Because a lot of the other flats were empty, there were few people to notice them or hear them. There was only one person on their level, an Egyptian, and downstairs a Syrian called Imad.

Imad was a blessing. He went to the market regularly and bought Ben and Mike fresh fruit and vegetables. They couldn't possibly have survived without him. He took their letters and passed them on to Arab friends leaving for Jordan or to wardens such as Sandy MacMillan who were running routes up to the British embassy in Baghdad. "He fitted locks on the doors, so we were more secure at night. He brought us gas cylinders. He welded doors up in the building. He took pieces out of the lifts to stop them working. He knocked lights out to make the corridors darker. He did anything to make the building more secure. He discouraged them from searching the block and even lied to the soldiers downstairs, saying he hadn't seen anyone upstairs. He would have been shot if he'd been caught."

Ben and Mike's apartment was quite large, modern and well-equipped. It had two bedrooms, two bathrooms, kitchen and large lounge. It was carpeted, fully furnished and had curtains on all the windows. It hadn't been touched by looters at all. In fact, even by the third week in August, none of the apartments in the block had been broken into.

The two young men stayed indoors much of the time. They kept the radio and television down low when they were on and were very quiet when in their flat. They would be extremely careful when they walked along the corridors between apartments as Iraqi soldiers were guarding the doors at ground level. They both gave letters to Imad in late August which did get through to their relatives, but never received any nor ever communicated with England by phone. Ben's letter was very matter-of-fact. He saw no point in worrying his wife unduly, so tried to sound as calm and unemotional as he possibly could.

The greatest problem they faced was coping with the boredom. They read more books in three months than they thought they'd ever read. They played cards, watched videos, listened to music and did the

[1]These names have been changed.

household chores. Highlights were visits to other apartments and listening to the World Service. They developed a coded knock for the door, to identify who they were. They used to softly rap out dit, dit-dit-dit, after which they gave their name. After a while, they dropped the name, so as not to speak any English in the corridors.

As the weeks went by, they had to become increasingly security conscious. The Iraqis began looting and searching the block, starting with the easily accessible lower floors, gradually working their way up. The stowaways became much more cautious walking about, venturing out at night rather than during the day. "We smashed knobs off the doors in the corridors and carried them in our pockets, so we could let ourselves in but nobody else could get by. We locked certain corridors off and had mirrors positioned at one end of our corridor. We had a spyhole in the door and a mirror opposite it at an angle, so we could see down the corridor and round the corner. We even had a coke tin by the main door. When someone opened it, the can clicked, so we could hear them down the corridor."

The phones were working within the block and within their locality of Safat, so they could phone before visiting another flat. The phone code was three rings, hang up and ring again. The person called would always wait for the caller to speak first. Some of them even put extensions on their phone lines to move the phone away from the hall and into a back room, so the ringing tone couldn't be heard from the corridor.

One of the Americans was a guy called Bob Morris who occupied an apartment above Mike and Ben. He did an interview for *Time* magazine and confirmed much of what Neil said. There were six British, an Irishman and an Australian in the flats around him, plus Mike and Ben. They kept their windows covered with heavy blankets and kept the lights off at night. The TV was turned down low and they had strict rules to cover everything they did. They were even careful of cooking smells reaching the corridor.

In the second week of their occupation, the Iraqis began to meet stiffer Kuwaiti Resistance attacks in the suburbs of the city and along the coast. Salmiya was no exception. Some nights it was ablaze with major skirmishes lasting for hours, with tracer fire and explosions going off in all directions. The area was becoming so unsafe Mike Devey and the twenty-six people with him in the 'command centre', including six young women and two lads, began to fear for their safety should the Iraqis break into their villas. They decided to move the women and lads out to the flat of Dave Dorrington in Salwa. Dave had taken up the reins of his warden after he had disappeared across the border.

No sooner had the women and lads gone when, on the nineteenth of August, a friend of Mike's phoned him and warned that the Iraqis were starting to move in on Salmiya. This purge of the area came just three days after the British had been asked to report to the hotels and coincided with people being moved from hotels to installations and with the sealing of the borders.

Mike hastily phoned a Kuwaiti contact, who found a place for the men in Rawda. All twenty-two were secreted across in *dishdashas*, glasses and headscarves, through countless roadblocks. Sweat was pouring off them as they kept their heads down and passed the Iraqi checkpoints. Mike and Lesley Devey, their dog, and Mel Gage, another warden with him, were the last to leave. They had a narrow escape through a road block on the Fourth Ring Road, but managed to arrive safely. He left a message on his answer phone telling people not to worry - *he* hadn't left the country - but would be in touch with them over the next few days.

At Rawda, Mike, Mel Gage and another warden, Jeff French, plus five other men, moved into a three storey villa. It wasn't particularly splendid. It looked run down, not the sort of place British would be living, and thus perfect for not being detected. Once ensconced, the three wardens phoned all their contacts up and gave them their new phone number. This time they were even more security conscious. They kept a close watch on who was coming and going and ensured the outside looked deserted. The number of people calling had to be curbed and most communication was done by phone.

In their first villa, they had taken elementary precautions. They had acquired some solid teak doors which they had placed across the top of the bar as a rudimentary bomb shelter. It had been big enough for all of them to get inside and had been equipped with cool jugs full of water, torches, reading materials and such things, so they would be safe for a few hours. However, it was not gas proof, mainly because Mike felt it was impossible to take any adequate precautions against such an attack and because they were not unduly worried about that prospect in the first weeks.

At Rawda, things were different. They taped the windows of the command centre immediately they arrived. They filled every bottle they had with water, hid food in the attic and around the villa, in case they were attacked and robbed, buried money and jewellery in the garden and built a secret hideaway. They closed all the curtains before they switched on any lights and blocked out the windows, but kept all the outside lights on to discourage looters. They had an early morning look-out for roadblocks, which were always erected first thing in the morning if the Iraqis were going to sweep an area. There was always one of them on casual watch.

Soldiers walked past every day. They could observe them and they even videoed them. They had an intercom between the floors of the villa to warn each other of danger or when meals were ready. What they didn't realise until later was that people on the street could hear it as well!

When Doug Crosgery was shot, it frightened a lot of people. Mike armed himself and carried a pistol all the time. He slept with it under his pillow. At first, he had a Magnum. He showed Lesley how to load it, but it was so heavy she could hardly aim it. Later, he acquired a Browning. Although it was for personal protection, he might have shot them both if the Iraqis had seriously attacked them. He continued helping the Resistance as he had done at the 'command centre', teaching them how to use explosives, where to position them, and how to operate a guerilla campaign. The Resistance even brought a load of rifles into their block at Rawda, which they kept hidden in the roof.

The villa had a cellar. It was slightly higher than ground level, so had windows all the way around. Each one was guarded with steel bars. It also had a kitchen in an annexe next to the villa. To get to it, they had to go out of the back door, which was above the cellar, and descend a flight of solid concrete steps between the villa and the annexe. These steps filled the space between the villa and the kitchen annexe, creating a sealed off area underneath them. One of the cellar windows happened to be underneath these steps, probably put in before the annexe was built.

The men blacked out all the cellar windows. They opened the one under the steps and sawed through the bars outside it. Once the bars were removed, they clambered through the window and crawled inside the small area under the steps - which was actually outside the house and cellar - and closed the blacked-out window behind them. Delighted with the cleverness of 'The Hole', they stored blankets, food, torches, a radio, bottles of water and anything else they would need in an emergency in it.

They gradually became more involved with the Kuwaiti Resistance. It had broken into an arms store and brought pieces of equipment around to them, to be shown how to use them. The Kuwaitis even took a video of the arms in the store, which they brought to Mike, who was able to tell them what they could use - a rocket launcher, grenades and fuses. They showed the Kuwaitis how to set up ambushes and make explosives. When they found a large supply of plastic explosives, Mike told them how to set the charges. The Resistance was very amateurish at the beginning. But there were a lot of ex-Kuwaiti soldiers in it who were able to use their experience and train others."We didn't do a lot, we just advised them," Mike told me, playing down his role.

Everyday, there seemed to be gunfire and a Resistance attack nearby. In response, the Iraqis were carrying out atrocities on Kuwaiti civilians. They regularly burned Kuwaitis out. The day after the women left, the Iraqis threw a group of Kuwaiti women out onto the street and set fire to their house. There were fires going on every day, some in villas, others just tyre dumps or skips. But some were major buildings. Mike's group witnessed the Kuwait Oil Company building going up in flames. They were playing a very dangerous game.

Andrew Stevenson worked for ABB Simcon Inc, part of a large international conglomerate acting as consultants to the Kuwait Oil Company (KOC) to modernise its refinery at Shuaiba to improve and enhance its process control. He and his wife Carolyn had been out there two years, and Andrew was negotiating for another year to finish the project. They lived in Abu-Hulifa, a modern town built on the coast a few kilometres north of the oil refinery. They had a two storey flat in a residential complex. It was quite large, with three bedrooms and a maid's room, as well as three bathrooms and large living rooms.

In the first few days after the invasion, they considered leaving, but felt relatively safe where they were. However, they did set up contact groups within the various complexes down their stretch of the coast, at Abu-Hulifa, Lateefa Towers, Manqaf, Mahbola, Subahiya and Fintas. Rumours began to circulate. Some people had made a dash for the border, where there was now a tented village for refugees. As some people had been turned back and their neighbours had two small children, as a group they decided not to risk trying to get out. They, like most others, thought the crisis would only last a few days, then be over. They certainly didn't expect the long drawn-out affair it became and they believed that, as British citizens, they would be safe from any problems.

The couple were bitterly disappointed in the warden system for their area. They felt it was very badly co-ordinated. "The communication chain was fragmented from the start and there wasn't any co-ordination. We were given the name of one guy who was supposed to be a warden, then the name of another guy, but we could never contact these people." They did have contact with one warden, who came down from Kuwait City and who, like many wardens, was telling people not to try to escape. This 'representative' even had maps of escape routes but refused to distribute them to people, to stop them escaping. To the surprise of many people in Abu-Hulifa this warden, after days of warning people not to try to cross the border, made an attempt along with a number of other wardens. They were unsuccessful and were turned back, but it undermined the confidence of a lot of people in those wardens. "All the Brits in our complex, about twenty-six of us, had a daily meeting. There was a very strong feeling we'd been let down." Apart from that, there was nothing they could do but sit back and wait. Their future was not in their hands. "We were all a bit bemused by the situation. We really were in a state of limbo. We were very isolated."

When the Iraqis ordered Westerners to gather at the Regency Palace Hotel and British people were being picked up off the streets, the mood quickly changed and their group realised they would have to go into hiding and take definite security measures to prevent being caught. They found two empty flats on the ground floor of their complex. They stored furniture, beds, linen and tinned food in there, to be used as a bolt hole in case of emergency and called it 'The Bunker'. It gave them something to do, as well as concentrated their minds on security.

The complex had no fence or walls around it, so the British organised a rota to guard the cars, day and night. Some Palestinians had been caught trying to hot-wire them. Andrew and Carolyn actually watched one group of looters break into their car and try, unsuccessfully, to drive it off. It was very frustrating not being able to rush out and give them a good seeing to. Soon, the Indians and some Arabs in the complex joined the rota as well. They kept all lights off at night and didn't use the rooms with large windows towards the road. There were Iraqi soldiers patrolling, but they didn't try to get into the flats.

Their routine soon became settled. Their greatest enemy was boredom. They rose early. Carolyn would do her aerobics; Andrew worked on his computer, writing up the minutes of staff meetings from work. He did an inventory of the contents of the house. He cleaned up the hard discs, and catalogued the floppy discs, working on one side of the table whilst Carolyn made a dress on the other.

On the twenty-first of August, a *haji* truck came round the complex with frozen meat, vegetables and coke. The next day some more came round and, as a group, they decided to go out and buy some food and give the children a breath of fresh air. As they walked across to one of the lorries, a car drew up and armed men in boiler suits climbed out and ordered them over. Surprisingly, they weren't arrested. The officer spoke English and said how he had children and sympathised with them. He told them to go back inside and stay hidden, then drove off.

The Iraqi was lying. He went back and reported to his commanding officer. The next morning the door to the complex was nearly broken down by hammering rifle butts. They had to open it. The Iraqis came straight in and gave them five minutes to gather some things together and go with them. Carolyn was only allowed to take a large handbag stuffed with a few clothes, nothing else. Apart from Andrew and Carolyn, there was Carol and John Gowland, Rosalind and Dave Buchan with their two children, and an American called Rocco Palazzolu.

The Iraqis had no idea how to get to their HQ. The street signs and road names had been taken down by the Kuwaitis, and they soon became hopelessly lost. The British had to give their captors directions. They drove towards Kuwait City and into the MEW Building in Andalous. It was a big guards barracks on the Fourth Ring Road which had been badly shot up and shelled on the day of the invasion. There were bullet and shell holes all over it, as though it had been a scene of major resistance. There were a lot of Iraqi tanks and troop lorries parked outside. At the end of the Fourth Ring Road the large roundabout where it meets the Jahra road had been turned into a bazaar by the Arabs. They'd set out their carpets and were selling everything they'd looted, plus a lot more, from car radios and fridges to rice and dates. After more driving around, still lost, they ended up at the Kuwaiti Police Training College behind the military barracks. The building was old and dilapidated, with crumbling plaster and old furniture. They were kept in a large, filthy room full of mattresses which the Iraqis were using to sleep in. The guards were very polite to them. There was no intimidation or interrogation. The colonel spoke excellent English and brought them some tins of chick peas and some water.

From there they were taken to the Meridien Hotel - the Iraqi soldiers following the British couple's directions. Within two hours of them arriving, the American consul was in the hotel talking to Rocco, but he was rapidly pushed out by the Iraqis. A day or two later Rocco disappeared, almost certainly removed by the Iraqis. Andrew, Carolyn and the others never saw him again.

Two British embassy officials, including the ambassador Michael Weston, rolled up four days later, as they were about to be taken away. The ambassador was very laid back. He told them how dangerous it was for him to venture outside, but that he had decided to visit them anyway. He wanted contact numbers for them in the UK, which they gave him, and Andrew's parents in Coventry, Betty and Andrew Stevenson, did receive a message.

The ambassador did not impress them. He didn't seem to know what was going on at all. Both embassy officials gave the impression that they had never been out of the embassy during the crisis. They were not able to give the British hostages any practical help and certainly not any information. "He was a waste of time and had no comprehension of what was going on." They found themselves giving *him* information. "He didn't know there were tanks all the way down the al-Safr Motorway south of Kuwait city. He was just so blasé about how well he'd done coming out to see us."

"Our hearing became very, very sharp," Ben explained. The block was very, very quiet. The silence was like death, ominous, haunting, dark. "We only ever wore soft-soled shoes like trainers, which wouldn't make any noise. We learnt to recognise people's footsteps."

Both Ben and Mike were very cool about their situation, but some of the others began to show signs of tension and depression. Two of those in hiding were shopped by their Arab neighbours one day and for a while they heard more Iraqis in the building, searching for others. They noticed Iraqis looking up at the flats at night to discover which lights were on, so they put heavy blankets over the windows. They even stuck tape over the spy hole in the door and made a pin-prick in it to see through, so it wouldn't show any light. They put blankets at the bottom of the door, with rugs leading up to it to muffle their footsteps as they approached it, with the telephone away from the door on a very low ring.

They established a set of rules to ensure survival. No one was to leave the building; no visitors were allowed in; they must never disclose their location, names or nationalities over the phone; they had to keep calls to a minimum and very short; everyone must ring ahead before visiting another apartment; no one was to loiter in the corridors; and no English was to be spoken in the corridors. Soon, they began to hear Iraqis moving about on their floor and several times they knocked on their door, but Ben and Mike simply ignored them. Robert Morris describes what it was like when they came to his flat. "To hear a sudden pounding on the door was terrifying... One day there was a banging on the door. I crept up and looked through the pinhole. Two heavy set men in dirty Arab dress stood there. One of the faces seemed to stare right at me. They were studying the nameplate on the door. I had posted up the name of an Egyptian friend... They muttered something to each other and left. I was elated."

As the days turned into weeks, Marie became more and more anxious. She was pregnant. She was in her Kuwaiti husband's house, away from her mother, with people she didn't understand, in a country she didn't know and under a regime which seemed brutal enough to drag her off to a camp if they found her. She had begun to bleed and was growing convinced that the foetus had died. They were the worst possible conditions to have a baby in. She had no milk or cheese and fresh vegetables were running out.

Marie was in a terrible state. She was positive she was losing the baby. She felt totally unprepared for it. She had no books or doctors to talk to; her mum was thousands of miles away; she felt completely unable to cope. It was all too much for her. The tension was tearing her apart. She screamed at her husband and his parents that she didn't want the baby. She couldn't cope with the thought of carrying it under such circumstances. It preyed on her mind constantly. She blamed everyone in the house, crying and ranting every night, storming out of the living room to the bedroom, slamming the door behind her. Nothing could placate her.

Nabil and his family tried their best to get food. Every day it was his job to join the queues and buy food. He and his sister would queue for hours, then queue again in an attempt to get a bit extra. Others in the family managed to get some chickens and some found more bread. It felt very peculiar. Their father had a Mercedes and yet the family was having to fill its boot with bread and chickens scrounged from a dozen stores in an effort to get enough to eat. And everywhere Iraqi soldiers were checking cars against people hoarding food, so they were running the risk of being caught, punished and losing the little food they had collected.

People were buying up old freezers to store meat in, paying inflated prices for decrepit machines. A large black market sprang up overnight. People were selling anything to get money, either for food or to leave the country. Most of the shops which weren't selling food had closed. Prices for everything rose rapidly. Washing-up liquid and washing powder became really expensive. Cans of food were much dearer than before. The one exception was melons. Iraq had thousands of them and they flooded into Kuwait. Yes, they always had melons.

By that time the soldiers were no longer the élite battalions of the Republican Guard, which had moved on to the Saudi border. Those who replaced them were a badly equipped rabble. It was then that the looting really began. "I couldn't believe they had invaded Kuwait. You could have killed them so easily. They were indisciplined and lazy. They would leave their guns lying about. They didn't care at all. And all of them were driving brand new cars. Tank transporters were coming in; they were unloading the tanks and loading them up with brand new cars. Everything that came in empty was going out full."

One of the first things the Iraqi soldiers started stealing were the tyres from vehicles. "My car was punctured in the Shuwaikh area and I got out to take the wheel off. I opened the boot and took out the spare. As I began to jack it up, I noticed the other side of the car coming up as well. I looked up and saw this Iraqi on the other side of my car. 'It's all right,' he said. 'You take the two that side, I'll have the two this.' I couldn't believe it."

I would describe it as a plague of locusts, only it slanders the locusts. A new verb should be coined, to 'Iraqise', meaning to plunder every conceivable thing and turn what's left into matchwood. Once they had stripped every tyre they could find, they began taking the seats. Once the seats had gone, they began to dismantle the engines. After the engines, they loaded the doors onto pick-up trucks. What anyone could do with four Mercedes doors in the back streets of Basra is anybody's guess.

People were leaving the country in droves. Huge convoys of foreign nationals were leaving every day, heading north to Iran or through Iraq, then south to the Jordanian border at al-Ruwashid. Mostly, they were Indians, Pakistanis, Egyptians and Iranians. None of them were British.

A few days later, every vehicle Nabil's father owned was collected together and the whole family packed its things to leave. It took them two days. They had a couple of small furniture vans and several cars which they loaded with most of their possessions. On the morning of the twenty-second, it came to leave. The family rose just after midnight and were ready by three o'clock. His father wanted Nabil's British wife, Marie, go with them, but she refused to leave her husband.

The goodbyes were very sad. Finally, amidst a great deal of crying, they said goodbye to Nabil and Marie[1] and drove to join the enormous gathering of vehicles in the centre of the city. They had only taken essentials. After they had gone, Nabil found all the children's toys and several of the women's handbags and purses left behind. They had taken so little time to prepare, one had left her diary. But, more significantly, the family had been forced to leave their home and all the furniture and possessions they had acquired over many years of hard work.

Once the family had left, Nabil and his wife had the apartment to themselves. From being overcrowded it now seemed deserted. Marie felt incredibly alone. She was totally dependent upon Nabil, who was now dependent on friends to help him because he couldn't go out. They did rally round. Some offered them money. Several brought them new gas cylinders for the cooker and supplied them with food. A couple of them said they had flats in other parts of the city, if they wanted to move out of the area. A Jordanian family asked them to move in with them. People he had never met before came up to Nabil and offered him help.

That first night they were alone seemed eerie. Marie and Nabil realised the depth of their fear as they lay in bed, holding each other and crying. They didn't know what would happen to them. They had the big short-wave radio, ready tuned to the World Service and they listened to that, but the reception was never good. They had to make the most of what was left of their life and hope they could soon escape the nightmare which had engulfed them. All they had left was each other.

[1]Their names have been changed.

'Heroes of Peace'

"Most sources were 'dodgy'; unconfirmed reports and vague sightings - rather similar to unidentified flying objects at times."

The Foreign and Commonwealth Office has contingency plans for international crises which can be brought into action at any time. It has an Emergency Unit located under the main building of the Foreign Office in King Charles Street, off Whitehall. There is a suite of rooms set underground behind security doors which is kept in a state of permanent readiness. Whenever a crisis blows up, the appropriate departments of the Foreign Office or Consular Department move in and set up operations.

The crisis was both political and consular, and the two aspects were closely related. The man who ran consular side of the Emergency Unit during the Gulf crisis was Christopher Denne, Head of the Consular Department. He worked closely with Rob Young, Head of the Middle East Department, who was responsible for manning the political team. On 3rd August he moved some of his staff into the Emergency Unit and from then on it was manned twenty-four hours a day until the following March. The crisis rapidly involved military strategy as well, so liaison developed with Downing Street and the military operational headquarters in High Wycombe. One of the rooms in the 'bunker' was given over to a military liaison team and another, a large conference room, to the discussion of major political and strategic issues.

From the first day, the running of the Consular Emergency Unit went smoothly. Christopher Denne, as Crisis Manager, and his deputy were drafted in, along with secretaries, political personnel and registry staff. The telephones were manned and support staff were at hand to operate fax machines, telex machines and photocopiers, to handle mail and internal messages and to provide refreshments. This was part of a routine the Foreign Office had perfected. Pat Terry, of the Non-Proliferation and Defence Department, was there permanently. She had opened the unit up immediately she realised there was a crisis, even before she was given the 'official' go-ahead.

The bunker is reached by a circuitous route. After passing along several corridors and through numerous sets of doors, you descend a narrow, dimly lit staircase to a reinforced concrete corridor under the main building. On the right is another door to an anteroom, where you must to phone in and identify yourself. The great steel door opens and you enter another dark corridor with rooms leading off. One is a large kitchen and rest room with table and chairs for people to take breaks and get themselves meals. Off that are two rooms used for sleeping quarters, one for men, one for women, with beds, wardrobes and washing facilities. Other rooms branching off are toilets and meeting rooms.

Passing these, you descend further, into the main operations suite. On your left is the large registry and communications room, where mail is sent and where the photocopier, telex and two fax machines - one classified, the other unclassified - are stored. The teleprinter receives reports from the BBC monitoring service. It has a tube link direct to the Foreign Office's Communication Centre. This would pass through reports on every country in the Middle East and every major speech or event which took place. During the crisis, a telegram could be despatched from this room and be in Baghdad within minutes - not to Kuwait, because all but links via the Iraqi military were cut very early on. The embassy there had its power cut off in late August and its generator was not sufficient to power the link to London, so it had to send messages via Dubai.

Next to the communications room on your left is the political and military room and in front of you are several conference rooms with private TV screens, clocks set to London, Kuwaiti and New York time, and sound-proof telephone booths. One is equipped with a number of scrambler telephone lines. On one wall is a closed-circuit television screen which gives the unit direct access to the Ministry of Defence. On your left is the main emergency operations room. On 3rd August, it was staffed with ten people answering telephones and giving out what little information the Foreign Office had to anxious relatives. It is about thirty feet square and filled with desks and phones. At one end is a TV monitor and a large whiteboard which had on it the latest information from the Gulf. The monitor had Ceefax on permanently, but could be switched over to cover all the major news bulletins as they occurred.

The bunker is a totally sealed unit, fitted with alarms as well as steel doors. During the Gulf crisis it had food delivered twice a day. Once a day, the cleaners came down, hoovering around the legs of the telephone operators. Pat Terry was the very efficient woman in charge of the administrative functioning of the unit. She organised the rotas, food and drinks, oversaw the installation of the computers, and was the linchpin who held the whole thing together. For her, it was a full-time and very exhausting job.

In those first days, neither officials nor Foreign Office ministers had any idea of the scale the crisis would develop into, nor of the extent of the human tragedy. The plight of the relatives and the demands placed upon the helplines astonished everyone. The Gulf Support Group was to become, in the words of Douglas Hurd, the Secretary of State for Foreign Affairs, "the largest independent humanitarian operation the Consular Division of the Foreign Office has ever dealt with".

In fact, the crisis rapidly overwhelmed the Emergency Unit. More staff had to be drafted in and a computer system had to be installed. That took time and until then the people on the telephones were having to fill in index cards for every call. Previously, this card system had been adequate to deal with an emergency, but the scale of this crisis dwarfed previous ones. One card per name soon became two, and in some cases three or four. They became dog-eared and difficult to keep in order. Each telephonist would have to scurry across to the boxes of cards and run back with the appropriate details in her hand. The telephone operators were out of their depth because of the sheer quantity of work. Because they were logged under the caller's name, different relatives of the same hostage were often given different cards and cross-referencing was inefficient.

Just as Rob Hayward found, and Joanna Copley found and Josie and Stephen Brookes found, there were thousands of people who wanted information. These people were so desperate for news that many phoned the Emergency Unit every day. Often, it had no new information, but it had to explain that to every caller. It tried to tell relatives they would be phoned as soon as there was any news. As call followed call, the pressure on these staff grew tremendously. None of the callers could appreciate the incredible volume of work they were labouring under, and each wanted to be treated as an individual, given time and respect. Most significantly, because the Emergency Unit was the only real contact relatives had with Whitehall - they couldn't get through to ministers direct - their anger and frustration was vented on it. They wanted something done to get their families out and when nothing seemed to be happening, their ire was directed at the Emergency Unit. The callers wanted action, and they wanted it immediately. They interpreted the lack of news as meaning lack of caring and would repeatedly demand that the Foreign Office do more.

The primary concern of the unit was to deal with the sheer volume of calls coming in. In the first few days, there were thousands a day as people wanted to register with it and ask for news. It tailed off after a while, as people realised it had little new information, but there were still hundreds calling every day. Anyone who was thinking of going anywhere in the Middle East seemed to be phoning them up to ask if it was safe to travel. The weight of numbers meant delays in people getting through and that meant further anxiety and anger. It caused difficulties, especially in the first few days. "If we'd had a hundred lines, it still wouldn't have been enough," Christopher Denne explained. Very early on, the unit contacted British Telecom for advice about the huge volume of calls. Its answer was to put the unit onto a recorded message machine. They opened it up and advertised a number to call for a message giving the latest news, although it was an 0898 number, for which the caller had to pay. The Foreign Office were not happy with this but concluded it was better than nothing. It gave all receipts to the Gulf Support Group. Thankfully, the emergency team didn't have to deal with the press as well. That side was handled by the Foreign Office News Department.

Towards the end of August, the unit finally went over to its computer system. Christopher Denne had called in a computer expert from the Foreign Office's Technical Department who formulated a programme for them and installed a whole computer network. Once the computers were installed, the information on the index cards had to be laboriously and meticulously transferred to them. Furthermore, the telephonists had to be trained in how to use them as they were handling calls. This took several nail-biting days of intense work and it was a nervous few hours one day early in September when it finally came to switching from the cards to the computers.

"Thank God we didn't have any hitch with it at all. It made a sensational difference to the service we were able to offer to the public. It meant that when people rang up, each telephone operator had a computer terminal on their desk. They could type in the name and all the details would immediately come up on the screen, with all the cross-references. They had details of the physical characteristics of each hostage, of his or her health and diet, where they were last reported, and so on. All the information was suddenly together in one place and immediately accessible. It immensely improved the confidence of the staff and of the public in the information the Foreign Office was disseminating."

By then, the staff working in the bunker had been permanently attached to the unit. In the first few weeks, when it seemed the crisis would only be of short duration, people had been pulled in from other departments on an *ad hoc* basis - whoever happened to be available. As the crisis drifted into its second month, this developed into a permanent core of people working on a rota basis. Each shift supervisor ensured everyone was updated as they came on shift. She or he would brief them on the latest developments and run down the latest news as it was written up on the white boards. They would show them telegrams received from the Gulf reporting conditions there. They saw statements by ministers, and the text of anything Douglas Hurd, the Foreign Secretary, had said. As important news broke, the shift supervisor would announce it to everyone. For example, if a flight of hostages had taken off from Baghdad, she or he would shout it out and a great hurrah would go up.

As well as making them more efficient and knowledgable about the situation, having a regular group of people allowed a warmth and camaraderie to develop. The staff began to share their emotions, increasingly empathising with their feelings. They would all be depressed together if there was bad news - a death, for example - and would all share the joy of a plane landing at Gatwick or Heathrow. A team spirit grew out of the sense of shared experience. By the end, they were as emotionally involved in the fate of the hostages as many of the people calling them and knew many of the relatives by their first names.

The unit divided the callers up between themselves, about a hundred families each, so that every relative would have a regular contact who would know the details of their case. Sometimes, callers would get to know their contact's shifts and would ask for them specifically. They began to develop a rapport, and that member of the unit would get to know the relatives, what jobs they had, how well they were coping, and even what the weather was like in their part of the country. In fact, it might be an idea for the Foreign Office to link up with the Weather Centre in future crises.

The staff drafted into the Emergency Unit were mainly people who had volunteered. Some had been to Kuwait or other Gulf states and their first-hand knowledge proved invaluable. But none of them were trained counsellors. Indeed, the Foreign Office had deliberately *not* set up a counselling operation. The unit was purely intended to gather and disseminate information. The staff were told to refer any caller they felt needed counselling to the Gulf Support Group, which, the unit felt, could provide a much better service. However, this was not a distinction the relatives could always appreciate. The calls which inundated the unit were from very distressed and, at times, irate and abusive people who needed emotional as well as factual help. The relatives and friends of the hostages were desperate emotionally, as well as for news. Many weren't sleeping and had become nervous wrecks. They would plead on the end of the phones, crying, sobbing with anxiety and worry. Some were on the point of nervous breakdowns. Some were suicidal. Callers could be frustrated and abusive. They weren't interested in being passed on to any other organisation, they wanted the government to do something for them, right there and then. Those answering the phones had been given no training in dealing with all this. Indeed, it proved too much for some of them, and for those who did try to cope, there was a real need for professional help.

Apart from dealing with relatives, the main task facing the Emergency Unit was overall strategy towards the hostage crisis. Together with ministers and staff from other departments and the armed services, it considered questions of policy and practice, and issues concerning the hostages as a whole, rather than individual cases. This side of the operation dealt with the evacuation of the women and children, with the flights in and out of Baghdad, with getting post and parcels to the hostages, and similar issues. It dealt with the Red Cross, with communications, with messages on the BBC's World Service. It negotiated with the BBC to set up a special Gulf Link programme as part of its overseas service, for which it paid the running costs, and acted as the contact point for that. It regularly briefed ministers on current situations and issued parliamentary briefings. This 'macro' side had a converted conference room all to itself, staffed with desk officers who manned telephones and compiled reports. Christopher Denne, who had a small office in the bunker, supervised both sides and merged them into one strategy.

Next door to the main operations room sat John Bryant, who was concerned solely with keeping track of hostages and people in hiding. He had a massive map of the Middle East on his wall with pins in it to mark every site at which he thought people were being held. He collated every scrap of information which came in about the hostages. Every day, and sometimes several times a day, he would try his best to calculate the numbers of hostages in each installation, attempting to keep up with the Iraqis' deliberate policy of blurring the overall picture and keeping the British, French, German, Japanese and American governments guessing. He was, inevitably, always behind the game. It was impossible to keep up with every manoeuvre Saddam instigated. It was a massive detective operation, a battle of wits, with Saddam using the hostages rather like pieces on a chess board. But in this game there were no rules. These pawns could be taken anywhere, at any time, and as quickly moved again, as part of the Iraqi's defensive strategy.

Sometimes, the information coming in on hostages or those in hiding was very patchy. Most sources were 'dodgy', unconfirmed reports and vague sightings - rather similar to unidentified flying objects at times - fleeting glimpses as people passed in transit to camps or hotels. A Japanese man might phone from Tokyo saying he had just been released from an installation and that there was a tall, red-haired Englishman with a beard there. An Australian from Adelaide might phone saying he saw a man called John at a camp, but couldn't get his last name. These snippets of news had to be pieced together with the physical characteristics of the hostages as given by their relatives, allowing for the fact that many men had grown beards, either because they had no razor blades, or to look more Arabic. Frequently, it was guesswork and, if the unit couldn't be sure, it might not be able to call the relatives to confirm a sighting until weeks later when another piece of information had been received. Occasionally, they did get sightings wrong, but far more often they were able to give the relatives reliable information. Generally, it found that people preferred even that dubious news to receiving nothing at all. But there was a very fine dividing line. As long as it qualified its news, it was all right. "But it was never enough for people. Constantly, they wanted more." Not infrequently, the relatives would say that the Gulf Support Group had beaten the unit to it, as it often received information directly from returnees or released foreigners before the Foreign Office. But when new information could be supplied by the Emergency Unit, it would come as an immense relief to the relatives.

As for other sources of information, the embassy in Kuwait was only operational for a short time before it was surrounded by Iraqi troops. From then onwards, it functioned as best it could, but was effectively cut off and facing an Iraqi threat to storm it with tanks. The Foreign Office admits that the embassy had no idea where many of the British nationals were in Kuwait. The system of registration, whereby everyone coming into the country should log their name and address with the embassy, was woefully incomplete and the FCO suffered greatly from the absence of a full list of expatriates. Although the wardens managed to get many people's names in the first two weeks, once a warden was picked up or left, the people he was responsible for would again be lost, unless another warden was able to pick up the strands.

The Foreign Office admitted it was disappointed when some decided to scamper across the border in the first two weeks. But the warden system recovered. "The embassy had to regroup as a matter of some urgency," Christopher Denne explained. Those wardens who stayed provided the greatest and most reliable information on the people in hiding to the embassy, and thus to the Foreign Office. They were the one link the Foreign Office had with the community.

The Emergency Unit co-ordinated with other organisations throughout the crisis. It worked with voluntary groups and other government departments, such as the Department of Social Security and the Housing Department. It also liaised with Richard Branson, who offered a Virgin Atlantic jumbo jet to be on hand for any hostages coming out. When Ted Heath and Tony Benn announced their flights to Baghdad, they were able to offer some help to them with names of hostages and other information, although this was severely limited by the government's determination not to be associated with either of their missions.

The unit really came into its own during early September when the women and children returned and in early December when the men were released. Before every flight, the operations room was pandemonium. It would be desperately trying to assemble reliable flight lists to inform the families, whilst dealing with hundreds of others who were phoning in to check whether their relatives were on the planes. Passenger lists would drift along in dribs and drabs from BA or the Iraqis or Reuter. In every case, the Iraqis refused to give detailed flight manifests, waiting until the last moment to issue partially completed lists, then changing them, then changing them again, all as part of an annoying cocktail of inefficiency, bureaucracy and deliberate bloody-mindedness. Even when the flights took off, they would be inaccurate. Not once did the Emergency Unit receive a one hundred per cent accurate passenger list from the Iraqis. Usually, they could only be absolutely certain of most of the people on the plane once it had actually taken off - and there were huge delays in the departures.

"We were absolutely torn between going down the provisional list, ringing people up and saying, 'Your husband is expected on the flight arriving at 5am tomorrow', and waiting until we were absolutely certain. It did happen sometimes that we got it wrong. People would be jubilant and would rush to the airport, only to find that their husbands weren't on the flight. Then, of course, they would suffer tremendous dejection. So we tried to hold on until we were reasonably certain, but at the same time we were under tremendous pressure to say who was on the flight, because their relatives were terribly anxious."

President Saddam Hussein walked cautiously into the compact room full of British men, women and children. He gently pulled on a sleeve of his smart grey suit before shaking hands with a nervous man wearing only a tee-shirt and shorts - the only clothes he had left. Behind the president trotted an interpreter and several senior Iraqi air force officers, armed and in uniforms.

Saddam smiled as he shook hands. The 'guestage' looked nervous and reluctant. The president moved on, past the TV cameras laboriously set up for this showpiece. They switched to four men and women sitting on a settee in a corner of the room.

"First, the small talk."

Perched, no, more like slumped, with his shoulders forward and hands together between his legs, as he sat on an upright chair, Saddam talked to a man sitting opposite him. Mr Lockwood had his young son Stuart fidgeting on his lap. The president's interpreter, Dr Saddun Joubaydi, stood beside Saddam and one of his officers stood behind him.

"You are British, all of you?" the interpreter asked.

"Yes," Mr Lockwood replied.

"Yes, this is a British family."

The camera panned across a group of three men, a woman and a boy, all in tee-shirts and slacks or shorts.

Saddam, sitting and smiling, waggled his fingers at Stuart Lockwood, impelling him to come towards him. Every movement of the president's body was precise, calm, and used the minimum of energy. Behind his smile stood the implied threat of two armed officers. The smile said, be nice for me, or I'll make it very difficult for you. How to smile and yet to threaten. It sent a chill down Josie and Stephen Brookes as they watched. It sent a chill down the world.

The president pulled Stuart towards him and stroked the back of his head, like one strokes a goat one's about to slaughter. He asked a question in Arabic to his interpreter.

"Does Stuart get his milk?" the interpreter asked, a microphone thrust between him and the president.

"Yes," his father replied.

Stuart, slim, fair haired, dressed in a white tee-shirt and blue shorts, tried to edge away, but the hand stroking his head was also pulling him in. He raised his hands out of the way, to avoid contact with Saddam's leg and looked away - to his father, to other hostages, anywhere but at an Iraqi. The rest of the room was silent.

Again, Saddam asked Stuart if he was getting his milk, his arm now around the boy's shoulder, holding him, lightly shaking him to answer as the smile broadened and his eyes tried to meet the boy's. Again, the interpreter asked the question, but now he moved closer to Stuart, hovering above him, his head leaning down towards him, smiling its threat. The two Iraqis were closing in to force an answer.

Stuart looked terrified, as though he was about to cry or break away. He refused to reply. Instead, his father, anxious but unable to approach and take him away, replied "Yes," again, and added, "on his cornflakes."

"Cornflakes too?" the interpreter asked.

"Yes," again.

The tension was steadily rising. This first confrontation was a draw. The Iraqis had been given answers, but very curt and reluctant ones. His young stage prop had come on, but refused to perform.

The cameras panned to another group. All held their hands in fists or tightly interwoven. Then came the political lecture. Speaking through Dr Joubaydi, Saddam leaned into the microphone as Stuart and Ian Martin, a taller and older boy who had been 'asked' across, stood next him, their backs against a table. The table kept them close to Saddam. A tall Iraqi officer behind them served as another warning.

"Your presence here and in other places is meant to prevent the scourge of war," the interpreter told them and the cameras as Saddam reached out for Stuart again. The boy tried to move away, his arms firmly folded, but the president kept pulling him towards him. He held the child's elbow as the lecture went on.

"Stuart will, I am sure, be happy to have, as part of his life, his personal history, that he played a role in maintaining peace."

One Iraqi officer walked around behind them, watching the other 'guestages' as another kept notes on a pad. Saddam let go of Stuart, who remained beside him, his arms still firmly folded.

"So when he, along with his friends and along with all those present here have played their role in preventing war, then they will all, as you, be heroes of peace."

Edward Stourton, the ITN news reporter, spoke over the images of the room full of British hostages. "For the Iraqi leader, the purpose of this was political, the events dutifully recorded by a note-taker behind him. But for those he'd gathered, it was an opportunity to ask at least some of the many practical questions troubling them."

The cameras focused in on another group. Three lads were crowded onto one armchair. A man and his two small children had to sit in another, with his wife perched on its arm. The room was hot and getting stuffier every moment with the press of people crammed in. Many had no seats and were forced to stand around the walls. People began to sweat. The young children, one little older than a baby, started to fret. They were hungry, tired and as anxious as their parents. A two-year-old and three-year-old crawled under a coffee table and nervously messed around. A woman spoke to the president.

"We appreciate that he has come in person, simply because nobody else has been able to answer our questions."

"I'm here to answer all your questions," the interpreter replied, smiling on behalf of Saddam who, incidentally, did not need the woman's arguments to be translated for him.

"We have school-going children here. I have myself got two sons. School begins in a week's time, on the first of September. Some of them are in the middle of important exams and that itself is going to cause immense problems."

But Saddam would not guarantee that they would be released before the school year began.

Twenty minutes had passed. Couples were holding hands, wondering when it would be over. For most of them, they had been prepared to be used, if just to provide a chance for their families in Britain to see them and know they were all right, but they felt very uneasy at the way the meeting was going.

"So the question that has to be posed by all of us," the interpreter continued, "to Mrs Thatcher, to Mr Bush is, what has Iraq taken away from them..."

Saddam now emphasised every point with a pen taken from his pocket. It was as though, having lost Stuart, he needed another plaything to roll around his fingers.

"....which has made them bring along their forces to the region, to threaten the people of the area and to threaten Iraq with an attack and destruction? All that happened was for this part... how would you say it? Kuwait?" The interpreter looked to Saddam. Was it safe for him to use the word 'Kuwait'?

"Kuwait," Saddam nodded.

"....called Kuwait has now come back to its motherland, in the same way as this little kid here which, God forbid, may be taken away and then brought back to her mother."

The threat was not lost on the world.

Nor Saddam's next point, that Arab opinion would turn against the USA if it remained in the Gulf for a lengthy period.

"Arab public opinion is against the presence of foreign forces on Arab territory. And if time drags on, with the presence of foreign forces on our territory, you'll find that the regimes under their foreign tutelage will fall one by one."

Patricia Moreton, with two of her sons sitting beside of her, was allowed to ask a question. The broken nature of Patricia's words, the pleading in her voice and hands, betrayed anxiety and deep worry. "We realise we're at an unknown destination, we realise that, but if only we knew that our families knew... we would like them to know that we are fit and well. Our parents are old, my husband and I are in ill health."

"Yes," the interpreter replied, "we shall make sure that your messages reach your families in England. So, as of now, you can write your letters, including photographs. If you want to take photographs, you can take them."

The air force officer behind Stuart Lockwood moved up to him as he fidgeted. He held the boy's head in his hands, stroking his hair, holding his chin up to him, tweaking his nose and patting him, as if to prove his power over the boy. So it went on. Forty minutes in all, originally broadcast live on the Cable News Network but then beamed around the world on every news channel. The Iraqi officers made notes; Saddam lectured; the children became more and more tired.

Glenda Lockwood later described her feelings when she walked into the room and saw her son with Saddam. "I was horrified, especially once I saw the response Saddam was getting. I didn't know what was going to happen afterwards. I didn't know we were going to be used as a propaganda weapon, but it didn't take long to realise that was what it was all about. We had been put in that room with him, with a lot of soldiers around. It was quite frightening. We had no warning Saddam would arrive. He came to the installation where we were being held. There was no notice that he was going to be there. On reflection, there *were* extensive preparations for him, pictures of him put up everywhere, modern amenities put in. We knew something was happening, but didn't know what it would be. The day he actually came in, it was a shock to everybody." Stuart himself remembered the event as "bad".

Saddam was with them for a couple of hours. He went through a lot of things whilst they sat together, going over most of their complaints. Many people asked him why they couldn't go home. They mentioned their young children, the appalling food they were receiving, the danger of disease and illness and that their children had to return to school. He sat and listened to it all, though he did keep putting over his political points. "Saddam eventually did leave." Glenda Lockwood explained. "He said he would have liked to have lunch with us - which I'm sure he wouldn't have - and left and said he would send in a woman's delegation that afternoon to see to our needs." That delegation did arrive, but the hostages felt their arguments had probably fallen on deaf ears.

The "Guests' News" incident deeply worried the helpline because it had shown Saddam to be a man completely unscrupulous in his means. But it also strengthened their resolve. Strangely, it was both depressing and yet a boost for morale. It demonstrated, out of Saddam's own mouth, that he was using Westerners as pawns in a game. He was playing them off against the forces ranged against him. They were clearly a human shield. And they were clearly in need of all the help they could get.

By now, late in August, the helplines were getting an increasing number of calls from people in serious financial and housing difficulties. At Coventry, it built to a peak of over forty a day, at London even more. Both the families of men trapped in Kuwait and those who had managed to escape the emirate, often with few personal possessions, were in a desperate state. Most of their money was frozen in Kuwaiti bank accounts, whilst British banks were refusing to give them loans and generally being extremely awkward. The DSS itself admitted it was making no special provision for victims of the Gulf crisis. Some were homeless and a few were not able to get emergency housing.

Those who had houses in Britain were finding building societies insisting on the mortgage being paid and threatening to repossess. They even began to receive Poll Tax demands, not only for when they were in Kuwait, but also for relatives still trapped there. It became so bad, and the helplines received so many pleading calls, that Rob Hayward MP felt he had no alternative but to relate the most acute problems to the press. In an interview with *The Times* on 20th August, he complained, "There is evidence that banks and building societies are treating people as if they have just driven up in their cars from their houses in the suburbs and not as hostages who have been imprisoned for two weeks, escaped across the desert and arrived home penniless, having left all their possessions behind. Most have no jobs to go to and no idea whether they would ever have anything to go back to in Kuwait. These people are facing financial ruin. Many of them were on fixed contracts and have not received any wages since the Iraqis occupied Kuwait. They have gone through considerable trauma, yet when they try to sort out their financial problems, they are treated unsympathetically."

Joanna Copley added, "There is a misapprehension that Britons working in Kuwait earn large amounts of money and are very rich. This is just not the case. Some have arrived with just £10 in their pockets and many are nurses and teachers earning ordinary wages."

Both Joanna and Rob were speaking from the Connaught Rooms. In an effort to deal with the financial problems callers were facing, the London helpline had brought in a financial adviser from Lloyds Bank and established a hardship fund. Joanna asked for donations from the public towards it. It was also looking at ways of raising finance for itself, to cover the enormous bills it was running up. Finance is always a key question for a support group, and one so large and active needed a lot of help, especially to pay off huge telephone bills. British Telecom remained unwilling to offer any help to any helpline towards any of their phone bills, a tragedy when one thinks of the company's huge profits and the excellent humanitarian work the helplines were doing. Perhaps in future British Telecom could review its attitude.

Meanwhile, in the United States, an organisation entitled Coming Home had been set up by Michael Saba, an Illinois businessman who escaped from Kuwait a few days after the invasion. It was created along similar lines to the British helplines, to aid in every way those with people still trapped in Kuwait and Iraq. It too was putting pressure on international bodies to get the detainees released, as well as trying to influence the United States administration.

On the same day as the "Guest's News", an Iraqi official announced chillingly, "Nationals of the relevant states will be accorded the status they deserve in proportion to their government's hostility to Iraq", plainly a further threat to use British and Americans in particular in defence of Iraq's strategic sites. But it also marked a subtle change in Iraqi strategy. It was no longer using them purely for defence. It was saying to the allies, "If you're good boys and girls, I will let your people go". They were now to become, not merely a deterrent against bombs, but central to a new Iraqi game, of trading them off against dropping sanctions, stopping the build-up of arms and getting the allies to the negotiating table. Every effort was directed towards using the hostages as bargaining counters, not merely deterrents, in a game of world strategy.

The Iraqis held more "Guests' News" programmes, mostly for the consumption of the Iraqi audience at home, but some of which were broadcast by CNN and British TV. In the second, Saddam faced another group of British men, women and children, but this time he had a much rougher ride. Several asked him directly why they were being kept against their will. Repeatedly, they were told it was to prevent a bloody war and that they were 'heroes of peace'. However, Saddam was clearly put off his stride by the points hitting him, especially that the children should be allowed to go to school, and was unprepared for the direct request from a British woman to be allowed home. He appeared briefly unsettled and began an embarrassed explanation for their continued stay. It must have troubled him, not because it pricked his conscience, but because these people were not proving as good propaganda weapons as he thought. He couldn't handle them. Furthermore, it was contrary to the Muslim code to keep them against their will - not that he cared for that, but other Iraqis and Arabs *did*, and their opinion mattered. It was not creating a good impression, hiding, as Margaret Thatcher had put it, "behind the skirts of women and children." He would gain more by letting them go. Within hours of that programme, it was announced that all the women and children could go home.

Stephen Brookes was now in regular contact with the London helpline and suggested both they and the Foreign Office met to discuss how they could be of help to each other. Both London and Coventry, together with Sue Brownlow at Bristol and Dorothy Croft in Derbyshire, felt it was time they formally organised themselves into a united Gulf Support Group and set up a trust to handle all monies they received. As a united group, they would have a far better chance of gaining financial support from the Foreign Office, especially for their enormous telephone bills. The Foreign Office to start feeding them far more information. The only way they could do that was to see its officials face to face. It would also be an excellent opportunity to visit the Emergency Unit and see how it was organised. Both Joanna Copley in London and Stephen Brookes in Coventry phoned Grant Lindsay, one of the shift managers in the Consular Emergency Unit. Grant Lindsay thought it a fine idea and said he would organise a meeting between everyone to be held at the Foreign Office. A date was set.

Josie and Stephen travelled to London by train to Euston, caught the tube to Westminster and walked over to the Foreign and Commonwealth Office on King Charles Street. It was a Tuesday, very sunny and very hot. They went through the security barrier and X-ray machine, before being shown over to a grand foyer furnished with large red leather settees set between marble columns rising twenty feet above them to an ornate ceiling. The room exuded Canning, Wellington and Palmerston.

Already there waiting were Joanna and Jonathan Copley with Dorothy Croft. They were extremely pleased to see each other. Jonathan was far younger than Josie had expected. He had such a mature and assured voice over the phone, he had seemed in his late twenties, full of life experiences. In fact, he was nineteen, with grey, mystic eyes, tall and slim. Josie shook his hand. The warmth from him was immediately visible. Joanna, in her sailor's dress, was full of charm, shaking hands, kissing Josie and laughing. Josie immediately noticed her eyes as well, intense and purposeful. She had obviously planned for this meeting and had established what she was going to say, whilst Josie was more relaxed. She hadn't prepared meticulously. She was someone who thought about things, went through them in her mind, then promptly forgot them and spoke from the heart. On the other hand, Joanna wanted to get things done. She was direct and businesslike, whereas Josie wanted get the emotional side across. As they settled into the enormous seats, Christopher Denne and Rob Hayward walked down the stairs and greeted them.

There were more introductions and laughter, after which they were ushered through the halls of the Foreign Office. The rapport between them all was immediate and tangible. The visitors were astounded by the great halls with their painted ceilings and stucco ornamentation, their pillars and pilasters, marble busts and tall, elegant windows. They passed through several sets of doors and a couple of foyers, until they found themselves descending a steep, dark staircase into the subterranean labyrinth of the Foreign Office.

They emerged into a well-lit concrete passage, wide enough for ten people to pass, before being taken into a small anteroom. Christopher Denne picked up a phone and dialled the number for the people inside the bunker. He told them who he was and the steel reinforced door clicked open. Inside was a narrow corridor with rooms leading off. On their right, people were relaxing in the kitchen. Sandwiches had been brought down and a man was pouring tea.

They pressed on, passed several closed doors and down another flight of stairs, into the heart of the bunker. Josie was amazed at the activity. The operations room was in full flow, with every telephone line being used. The TV was showing Ceefax and the white board was covered with up-to-date details of news broadcasts and the latest situation in Kuwait and Iraq. Pat Terry introduced herself. She showed them the operations room. To Josie's surprise, the telephonists were having to use index cards similar to those they had in Coventry. Coventry had two personal computers to store details and allow for cross-referencing. The computer system in the Emergency Unit had not been fully installed and the card system was at its most strained. Joanna was also amazed because, when she and Rob Hayward had merged their operations and had moved into the Connaught Rooms, they had immediately had the use of computers. It startled her that the helplines seemed ahead of the Foreign Office, at that time, in terms of organisation.

There were about twenty-five people sitting at desks, constantly answering the phones. As soon as one put the phone down, it rang again.

The shift supervisor had a word with one of them, who then left to have her lunch. A man took her place. The visitors were escorted across the corridor to the military and political room, then into Christopher Denne's office, and finally to the board room, filled by one enormous table surrounded by chairs. They nervously sat around it. Josie was taken aback by the whole place. Images of Churchill's bunker went through her mind. It brought the possibility of war sharply into focus. The place had a terribly ominous feel about it, an inevitability and a horror. Here was an operations centre equipped to deal with the most horrendous eventuality. On the door was a notice saying it could be locked from the inside and be made impregnable if the need arose. "That was when I realised how serious the situation was," Josie explained. "What frightened me most was when we went through this enormous hallway, down all these dark passages, into this war room and there was a great big, square table with all these phones and blotting pads all around. And I thought, oh no, war!"

Christopher Denne sat at the head of the table as the others settled around it. Next to him was Grant Lindsay. He had dealt a fair bit with the London organisation by then and was *au fait* with its set-up. Joanna remembers an embassy official from Qatar next to him who, she believes, was working from the military and political room. Starting with Stephen, everyone had an opportunity to introduce themselves and explain what they were doing.

The meeting was tense. Relations had not been harmonious between the helplines and the Foreign Office. Both sides were wary. There had been difficulties. The Foreign Office felt defensive. The discussion would be a chance for Christopher Denne to assess the groups' organisation, determination, support and motives and listen to what they wanted. For the helplines, it was both a chance to prove themselves to the Foreign Office and to get across their serious concern that the government seemed to be doing precious little to get the hostages out.

Josie was anxious to prove herself. Why should the Foreign Office trust them? Who were they? They had no official status. She explained the Coventry helpline's credentials and mentioned as many VIPs and Church people as she could who were supporting them. She wanted the Foreign Office to realise that they were professional, respectable and reputable people whom the relatives looked to and trusted. She tried to be as positive as she could about what they were doing, about the help the relatives needed and about the co-operation they required from the Foreign Office. She felt she had to win their trust and put on an official, professional manner because she wanted to continue to receive the situation reports the Foreign Office collated and faxed out to relevant organisations. In contrast, Stephen and Joanna felt that the Foreign Office had to prove *itself* to *them.* Rather than being grateful for the information the Foreign Office was giving them, they wanted to know why it wasn't giving them much more.

Certainly, for Joanna, who was furious at the lack of action by the government, it was a question of prompting the Foreign Office to buck its ideas up, get off its backside and at least be seen to be doing something. The young woman stated bluntly that people were unhappy about what the Emergency Unit was failing to do. She felt the Foreign Office was in danger of categorising the helplines either as politicos or as well-meaning amateurs who would not be able to sustain what they had taken on. So she explained that she had set up and got fully running an organisation within two weeks with no funds, emphasising through her manner and her points, just how serious she really was about it.

With the Bristol helpline now merged with hers and settled in the Connaught Rooms, she felt she had the organisation and authority to make demands. She listened patiently to the chit-chat, but obviously wanted to get across the needs of her group. Her nervous eyes switched from person to person. When she found the chance, she explained what she wanted as Jonathan sat quietly by her side.

"Look, I'd just like to make one thing clear to you. We are not a political group. I am not interested in politics. In fact, I find them exceptionally boring. We're not interested in being a pressure group. We're here because people need the help they are not getting from you, and we are going to provide it. That's what we're here for. We're a counselling organisation. We already have links with the Samaritans, with the people who ran the *Marchioness* help line after she was sunk in the Thames and links with other counselling organisations such as the Red Cross. We have trained counsellors manning our phone lines."

Rob Hayward also spoke bluntly. "I have set up my helpline and come to this meeting precisely because people have been saying to me, 'Look, the Foreign Office isn't doing anything, can you help?' It was set up in response to complaints about the Foreign Office as well as to try to put people in contact with each other. The support group is there, as far as I'm concerned, *because* of the failure of the Foreign Office. Whether you have failed or whether it just feels like that to us, because of what we want from you, I don't know. Nor do I particularly care. But what the relatives expect from the Foreign Office is not coming from you. Now, so far you have manifestly not trusted us and haven't used us."

"It's not that we haven't trusted you...." Christopher Denne tried to explain.

"It certainly appears that way to us," Joanna insisted. She wanted the Foreign Office to start doing far more for the relatives and those trapped in the Gulf. Putting to one side the many criticisms of the Foreign Office, and there were many, she wanted to link in with its organisation, at a people-to-people level, at the level of the telephone operators and shift supervisors. None of the helplines wanted to be dealing with the great, grinding wheels of bureaucracy, they wanted a short-cut through the red tape to co-ordinate their activities. They wanted to be able to phone anytime for information or to pass on issues of concern. They wanted to share lists of passengers on the BA flight and of people in hiding in Kuwait. They wanted the Foreign Office to fax them with regular updates and give them the latest news, before it broke in the press, so they would have the chance to prepare themselves and their telephone operators. They wanted details of people held as hostages as and when they came in. They wanted people referred to them who needed counselling. They wanted to be trusted.

William Waldegrave, who was a Minister of State at the Foreign Office at the time, arrived halfway through the meeting. He looked absolutely worn out. His hair was dishevelled and his suit was creased, as though he had been up all night. He sat next to Christopher Denne as Christopher finished explaining the role of the Emergency Unit. At once, Mr Waldegrave's sincerity came across. "How can we help you? Tell me what you need and I'll try and get it for you." He rapidly grasped the problem of trust and dealt with it swiftly. "I can see that you are operating in parallel with us, rather than in conflict," he said, leaning forward. "I can certainly see that you can do many things that we can't. I know, for example, that we have had some problems with the scale of need. We're getting in our computer system as soon as possible." He glanced at Christopher, who nodded. "And we all feel that it is far better that we work together than fall out over this. We shall endeavour to give you as much help as we can." His sympathy and co-operation were immediate. Everyone else around the table deeply appreciated it.

The meeting ended amicably and from that moment the support groups were given direct and immediate access to the Emergency Unit. They would phone each other several times a day and all information was shared as it came in. Both the London and the Coventry helplines were put at the top of the list for every situation report the Foreign Office released. From then on, because the Foreign Office immediately passed on news as it broke, they received it before it reached the papers. They were able to consider their responses before the television crews came round or the radio journalists ask for interviews. No one was able to spring news on them unexpectedly any more. If reporters phoned up and misquoted the facts, as they often did, they could put them right. They were able to correct their misrepresentation of events on numerous occasions and could calm relatives worried by press hysteria, simply because they had the same information the press had and knew what distortions the media were capable of.

Josie had kept in constant contact with Eric Watson's wife, Wen Li, since her first phone call. She had persuaded British Airways to give her a free ticket back to England so she could feel part of the efforts to get the hostages out.

Instead of helping her, being close to the helpline made Wen Li feel worse. By this time the Coventry operation was in full swing. There was a rota of volunteers, a photocopier, fax machine, computers and several televisions on full time. The press were constantly calling either by phone or coming round to do interviews. The house was chaos and it was impossible ever to escape. Every snippet of news, every alarming new development, every press scare came into those rooms. The phone would start ringing at five in the morning and go on until three at night. The walls weren't thick and she could hear every word on the phones. Every time the fax machine started it woke her up. She would head for the bathroom, only to find a volunteer in there, let alone Stephen or Josie. They were wonderfully welcoming, but she could never feel at ease. She felt she was imposing still further on them. She needed to escape her thoughts, to find release from her worry, whereas the atmosphere of the house was one which never let anyone forget. She tried answering the phone once, but found she couldn't deal with the difficult problems people were facing. She was not the only one. As Josie told me, "A lot of people found being here too emotional, too difficult."

Josie was continually on the point of exhaustion and felt the lack of privacy very intensely at times. Her house was no longer her own. It had been taken over. Volunteers would be everywhere, and even follow her out into the garden when she tried to find a bit of peace. The only way she could escape was by actually leaving the house, but there were only a few places she could go.

To add to her difficulties, Wen Li had no money and was forced to go down to the DSS and queue for income support. It is a humiliating process for anyone, even at the best of times. The waiting room was dirty, overcrowded and sweltering. She had to sit and wait and was made to go through the endless paperwork and questions the social security system imposes on everybody. It made her feel utterly ashamed at having to ask for money. She had never done it before. It was demeaning and depressing. She decided she had to get out. She packed her cases and took a train to London to enrol on a course studying law.

Once they had left the Foreign Office, the six members of the helplines, Rob Hayward, Josie and Stephen, Joanna, Jonathan, and Dorothy Croft made their way to the Connaught Rooms. It was extremely busy with people phoning for information, press reporters demanding interviews and groups of relatives sitting having a chat and requesting information.

They needed to get down to a serious discussion. After making themselves drinks, they withdrew into a small meeting room and set about establishing closer links between themselves. Out of this gathering the individual helplines merged into the Gulf Support Group. It was agreed that a trust should be established, with five trustees. They would be Joanna and her husband Tony from London, Rob Hayward and Sue Brownlow from Bristol and Stephen Brookes from Coventry.

This was to mark a considerable step forward for the helplines. They were now co-ordinated into a nationwide organisation. The London helpline had contacts especially in the south, though did have many nationwide as well, whilst the Coventry group had contacts throughout the Midlands, North and Scotland. One key element of the helplines strategy was to encourage relatives to get together locally, so encouragement could be given to a number of local support groups emerging regionally. There was one in Newcastle, and others in Manchester, Bournemouth and Edinburgh. These tended to be very informal. Relatives, perhaps put in touch initially by Rob Hayward, or whose husbands worked for the same firm in Kuwait, such as ICL or the Kuwait Oil Company, would phone each other for support and occasionally meet at each others' houses or a pub for a drink. Usually, one of them would keep regular, if not daily, contact with Coventry and London and pass on any news to the group.

In effect, there were now two main helplines, each differently organised and placing different emphasis on the balance of their work. From the beginning, the Coventry operation had been very much a family affair, kept strictly within the Brookes' house and firmly under their control. It had stressed intimacy and the personal approach. In contrast, the London operation had gone for offices, equipment, professional counsellors and a large number of ancillary helpers such as a press officer, a fund-raiser and a person to install a computer network. The experience of both have their lessons. Both had their advantages and both had their disadvantages.

THATCHER APPLAUDS RELATIVES' HELPLINE

"The work of the helpline for relatives of those trapped in Kuwait and Iraq received high praise from Margaret Thatcher when she visited volunteers working there yesterday..."
The Independent, Saturday 25th August

Margaret Thatcher's visit to the London helpline at the Connaught Rooms in Covent Garden lasted about half an hour. Josie remembers it well. She was there, along with Joanna, Jonathan and Rob Hayward. It was an excellent opportunity to open the Prime Minister's eyes to many of the problems the hostages and their relatives were enduring. Fifteen-year-old Alan Barnett was still the only detainee who had been allowed out by Saddam. He arrived home on the twenty-fifth after spending three weeks as a hostage, ending up in an Iraqi army block. The support group emphasised his case and that of the other children to the Prime Minister. Josie made the point that Tim Watson was out there with his father Eric, like many children caught in the crisis. Mrs Thatcher listened carefully, as her first interest did seem to be in the children trapped in Kuwait. They asked her to keep working for the hostages, even if it meant them coming out one at a time.

"There's one boy who's come out," Josie emphasised. "The door is slightly ajar. Can't we wedge it slightly more open, get a few more out, even if it's one or two at a time. Let's get them out slowly."

Mrs Thatcher was genuinely concerned. She went over to the computer with its lists of names and asked about the children held out there.

Josie told her about Tim, Eric's son and she promised to do what she could. The Prime Minister immediately understood what his mother must be going through, her worry and concern.

Joanna asked her to do something for the wives and families in Britain who had only come over for a holiday, but who now found themselves isolated and without money. She was very frank with her guest, especially about the DSS. She argued strongly for more to be done for the hostages and emphasised how petty the DSS were being towards their families. Its offices throughout the country were playing silly beggars, saying the wives should get money from their husbands, when most of them couldn't even talk to them over the phone and all their bank accounts were frozen. They were really totally out of touch with their situation. "Would you be able to do something about the DSS payments for some of these families?" Joanna asked finally. "A lot of women only came over here for a few weeks holiday, without their husbands. They're running out of money fast and need help."

"Oh, that shouldn't be. I'll look into that," Mrs Thatcher promised. She took note of their points and promised something would be done. A few weeks later DSS arrangements *were* changed, suggesting she had passed their concerns on to her ministers and followed them up.

Josie asked the Prime Minister about the contract workers in Saudi Arabia, and whether they could be allowed to break their contracts and come home. This time the Prime Minister was less sympathetic. "My dear," she replied, "if we allow them to come home, the whole economy would simply collapse."

"But they're human beings. If they want to come home and be with their wives, surely they should be allowed to do so?"

"I don't really think that is possible."

Josie didn't say any more. She felt she had blotted her copybook, and the mood seemed to change from then on. Mrs Thatcher again became the Prime Minister and her interest moved away. A formality crept in. It became more of a photo-opportunity for her. She congratulated the helpline on its organisation and the dedication of the volunteers, then had to leave.

The helpline was very pleased about the visit. It followed a similar tour by Douglas Hurd, so the government was clearly allying itself to the Gulf Support Group as well as giving it moral and practical support.

One very important result of the Gulf Support Group's meeting with the Foreign Office was a far better relationship between it and the government. Soon after the meeting, Douglas Hurd, the Foreign Secretary, visited the London helpline at the Connaught Rooms, where Rob Hayward MP and Joanna Copley were able to show him the great work they were doing. However, there was a significant threat to that work. The owners of the rooms were asking for them back. The helpline would only be able to use them for a little while longer. Could the Foreign Office find them more rooms in a government department somewhere?

It certainly could. Within days, a suite of rooms at Alexandra House, a large building housing the Inland Revenue on Kingsway, central London, was made available to them. The Foreign Office would pay for the rent and any electricity they used. It was a tremendous offer and demonstrated more than a thousand words the value the government placed on the work of the support group.

The rooms at Alexandra House were more spacious than the Connaught Rooms and gave the helpline greater flexibility. There were still just two, but they were appreciably larger. Immediately, Joanna and Jonathan Copley began to visualise how it would look. The computers could go in the far corner - but no, there were more sockets by the door, so they could go on the right, immediately beside it. They could get three or four volunteers working there, updating information, writing press releases, or searching for information.

"How about a sitting area over there in the corner?"

"I think in the middle would be better. We could have all the drink making facilities and food at the far end."

"Good idea."

"We'll make this into a large open area with easy chairs for doing interviews. It'll allow the press, volunteers and visitors to relax."

"We can get a television in here to watch you," Jonathan joked.

"Not a bad idea at all. And some tables where people can sit and have their drinks and sandwiches. At the far end we'll set more tables with coffee and tea making facilities. How long do you reckon it is?"

"About fifty feet," Jonathan replied. "And the smaller, private room is plenty long enough for six phone lines, a fax machine, our office supplies, Ceefax, whatever we need."

Joanna entered it. Although termed small, it was still quite sizable. There were plenty of sockets and they could use one corner for their direct wire from Reuter. It had been given only recently and after much persuasion, its rarity value enhanced by Reuter giving it freely. It proved invaluable as it churned reams of news out as it broke. It was always Jonathan's job first thing in the morning to lay it out on the floor in a long strip, cut out the relevant pieces and stick them together on a notice board, highlighting key information. "We received news before the press put a slant on it. Frequently, the press were asking us to comment, not on the precise Reuter's report, but on their interpretation of it, which was often exaggerated."

It didn't take the helpline long to transfer from the Connaught Rooms. Once they had completed the move, they noticed the difference immediately. There was more room for the people on the phones and they had better facilities for the media. Crews could wait in relative comfort as other interviews went on, and there was enough space to relax and talk.

By now, both Coventry and London had a much better idea of the press's needs and how to handle them. They were less anxious to please or go out of their way. It was too exhausting and too time consuming. If the press wanted a story, it had to fit in with their schedule, rather than the other way around. "I wouldn't have jumped through hoops for the press like we did," Jonathan told me. "We were naive at first, although we learned very fast. It wasn't worth all that effort for the coverage we got. We would have had as much with far less effort on our part. That was often the way with the press. They wanted their own way. It was very difficult; but we quickly learned."

Whilst the telephone part of the London helpline was working very well, they found they needed to move into other areas. Andy Charles joined as press officer. Steve King joined specifically to raise finance. Graham Clark became involved in order to get a fully integrated computer network established and enable the helpline to collate the information it was receiving.

Because it had a more relaxed and open attitude to the relatives than the Foreign Office, people were phoning the helplines with far more news. At times, it seemed to them that the Emergency Unit had no time for these details, nor to pass them on, although such snippets were very much what the relatives wanted to hear. The Foreign Office's reputation would have been greatly enhanced if it had taken just a little more time with people, even if it meant a few extra staff. It would have meant so much to anxious relatives desperate for even the tiniest piece of information.

"The Foreign Office wouldn't listen," Jonathan told me as he sat sipping coffee in his sister's house in south London. "In a lot of cases, it wasn't interested in people who phoned up and said they had heard rumours or heard of sightings of various people. It wasn't interested in anything except confirmed reports. That was the difference between us and them. It didn't mean we were perpetuating rumours, but that we often were able to piece things together far more quickly than the Foreign Office and at least give people an indication of what *might* be happening to their relatives."

Furthermore, when relatives phoned the Foreign Office, they might receive a rather curt service. Frequently in the beginning, they only had a recorded message to listen to, saying there was no further news. When they did get through to a living being, there was no attempt to allay fears or give anything but the barest details. At the helplines, the relatives could talk.

Whilst the Foreign Office insists its Emergency Unit was not intended as a counselling service, it still had a duty to provide more than an answering machine or a few seconds telling people they had no further information on their relatives, especially as they frequently *did* have news, even though it was often unconfirmed. Not only did it not provide a good enough service, it actually added to the relatives' anxiety. To be treated curtly when in distress greatly exacerbates that distress. That is why some relatives were still, a year later, bitterly angry at their treatment by the Foreign Office.

The support group worked on the assumption that every piece of information could potentially be of value. Even a vague rumour, if it was put with other rumours, could build up a picture. It could also be checked against Reuter's news line.

On 4th September, Shortly after the London helpline had moved into its new offices, Josie and Stephen received a cryptic phone call from Rob Hayward to tell them a VIP was due to visit, and could they catch a train down to London straight away. When they arrived at Alexandra House, they discovered the VIP was HRH Princess Diana. She came and spent forty minutes walking around the London office. As she went into each of the rooms she took a great interest in the phone lines, asking about the children of the hostages as she watched the frenetic activity of volunteers answering the calls. Afterwards, she went with the trustees into a small room for half an hour's intensive discussion on the helpline and about what they were doing. "A wonderful person," Josie enthused in her diary. "She spared so much time for us. The Princess was full of admiration for what we were doing and was particularly interested in the welfare of the children. It was very relaxed. It gave us the support and strength to go on."

When Stephen and Josie Brookes visited the Iraqi ambassador, Mr al-Salihi, late in August, they took the names of hostages with them, together with letters from relatives and details of both the installations they were in and the conditions they faced. They went well-armed. They raised their plight with the ambassador. Sitting in the plush reception room with the ambassador and his Cultural Attaché, under the gaze of security cameras, they debated whether the British were hostages or 'guests'. The British couple listened to their conditions being described as perfectly adequate and that they had no reason to complain. When they raised the case of someone who was sick or elderly and suffering particularly badly, arguing with the ambassador for their release, they were met with denials, bland assurances and waves of the hand. The ambassador was clearly an intelligent and cultured man, but he was not prepared to waver from his official government line.

"Keeping these people is against the United Nations; nearly every country in the world has condemned it, it is against humanity and all decency. You must let them go."

"No, no, no, Mr Brookes. These people are heroes. They will come back as heroes. They will have stopped a terrible, terrible war."

"But the tragedy of it is that they won't make any difference at all to whether there's a war. Mrs Thatcher has visited our helpline in London. There, she made it quite plain that she would send in the troops whether or not there were still hostages in the installations. They won't come back covered in glory, they'll come back covered in canvas. They will *not* stop the war."

Stephen was careful not to call the women, children and men 'hostages'. He had to keep up the farce of calling them 'guests'.

The ambassador insisted they were being very well treated, which was why they didn't want to come home. He was a pleasant enough man, polite and seeming to listen, but he never addressed his points to Josie, a woman. "Mr Brookes, please bear with me as I explain. Let me read to you the text of the peace initiative made by President Saddam on the twelfth of this month."

Josie passed to Stephen the letters smuggled out of Kuwait she was holding and crossed her legs as they both listened.

"As a contribution on our part to create an atmosphere of real peace in the region and to facilitate a state of stability and to expose the falsity of America and its disfigured ally Israel, as well as its small agents and their crimes against the nation, and affirming our right from a position of strength, we decided to present the following initiatives..."

Josie coughed impatiently as the ambassador read out the points made by Saddam. "...I propose that all issues of occupation, or those projected as occupation, in the whole area should be resolved on the same basis and principles as put forward by the Security Council.

"One..." And he went on to reiterate the demand for the "immediate and unconditional Israeli pull-out from the Arab occupied territories in Palestine, Syria and Lebanon, the withdrawal of Syria from Lebanon and withdrawal between Iraq and Iran, in addition to laying down arrangements for the case of Kuwait". The ambassador looked up. "You see Mr Brookes, we Iraqis want a solution to *all* the problems of the Middle East, not just one. We see them *all* as unbreakably linked."

"We're just concerned about the hostages."

"But Mrs Brookes..."

"Look, to us, all the other issues are essentially an irrelevance. It is simply wrong to take innocent civilians prisoner and use them as a shield for international policy. It is simply *wrong*. We *do* care very much whether there's a settlement in the Middle East. I very much hope there is. I very much hope the whole thing is settled peacefully and amicably. A war would be a disaster for the whole world. But we're here now to ask you specifically to release the hostages. They are not doing your cause any good whatsoever. They are making Iraq look very bad in the eyes of the world. You must release them if you want to portray yourselves as decent, law-abiding people. You must."

"Iraq has broken no laws. What laws has Iraq broken? Kuwait moved its borders seventy kilometres north without permission. It drilled oil from our oilfield, it stole our heritage, and it refused to listen when we asked it to negotiate. And now the Americans and British are stopping food from reaching our mothers and children. Who has broken the law? Not us, Mrs Brookes, not us."

"It is illegal to keep people of foreign nationalities against their will."

"We may if they are criminals."

"Are you saying they're criminals? What laws have they broken?"

"No, I am not saying that. All I am telling to you is that a country may request foreign guests to stay, in the interests of that country and of peace. It is wrong to say we are keeping them in Iraq. They are not detained at all."

"But they can't leave," Stephen insisted, leaning forward in his chair. A security camera gazed down at him and his wife. So did a picture of President Saddam. "They have bad food and conditions in some of the camps. There are old people, women and children suffering. For the sake of humanitarianism, you should let them leave."

"They can leave. They are all free to leave Iraq at any time they wish. They are our guests. We do not harm our guests, we treat them well. We are not like the Americans and British governments who deny food and medicine to the Iraqi people by their military blockade."

"It's the United Nations which sanctioned the blockade."

"Listen, my friend Mr Brookes, the United Nations is in the pocket of the United States. This blockade is denying many necessities to the Iraqi people. Our children are starving. It is a barbaric method of aggression to destroy Iraq. You say to me the British citizens in Iraq have bad food. Our people are starving, yet they share their food with all the foreigners. Every free and honourable human being is duty bound to deplore this crime of starving the entire population of Iraq and exposing them to diseases. It is the start of a new dark age for mankind." The ambassador hadn't liked the recent Amnesty International report on torture in Kuwait and Iraq. He was very angry at what he described as its 'lip-service' to the truth in Iraq.

Josie handed the ambassador a list of 'guests'. "Your excellency, these are names of people who are elderly or sick. We feel they should be let go on humanitarian grounds. We know the great history of the Arabs in protecting the weak and elderly. We beg you, let these people go." It made her cringe to have to fawn like this, but fawn she did - anything to play the game, give the Iraqis the attention they desired, stroke their egos, make them believe they were far more important than they were, if it meant more hostages would be released. They were both extremely careful never to raise any other issue apart from the hostages. They didn't mention the issues of peace or sanctions or war. They gave the ambassador no rhetoric, just stuck to the essential point of the men, women and children out there. They had no axe to grind against the Iraqis in general. They were no threat to them. That was why the ambassador respected their opinion and why Stephen was invited to the embassy on a number of subsequent occasions to explain their case. They were expressing British grassroots feelings on a central issue, which proved invaluable to the Iraqis in assessing the propaganda impact of the hostages. It was why their points *did* get through to the ambassador and was one reason the Iraqis began to realise holding women and children had become a serious miscalculation.

A Game of Cat and Mouse

"This is a cat and mouse game - now a little mercy, now some more ruthlessness." - Douglas Hurd, Foreign Secretary, on the Iraqi announcement that it would allow all women and children who wished, to leave Iraq and Kuwait.

20th August: The Foreign Office announces that eighty-two more British citizens have been rounded up in Kuwait, bringing the total to a hundred and twenty-three. [This was a gross underestimate. The Iraqis had in their clutches nearly two hundred from BA Flight 149; thirty-five from the British Liaison Team, plus their families, about seventy; those already in the hotels when they invaded, about thirty-forty; five BA crews and some ground staff, eighty-five; those picked up from the streets or taken from their homes, say thirty-forty; plus the eighty-two mentioned above (although this probably includes some of those already picked up). A precise total is impossible, but it is clear that the Iraqis had approximately five hundred British captives by now.] The State Department in Washington declares that the Iraqis are holding forty-seven Americans in Kuwait. Iraq orders foreign embassies in Kuwait to close within four days. For the first time President Bush calls those Westerners held by Iraq "hostages". He sends twenty 'stealth' bombers to Saudi Arabia.

21st August: Iraq moves Scud missiles into Kuwait. Egypt sends tanks into Saudi Arabia. Mrs Thatcher announces that there will be no deals over the hostages. President Saddam tells President Bush to seek peace or face global disaster.

22nd August: Washington rejects Iraqi calls for talks. Over two dozen countries defy Iraq's order to close their embassies in Kuwait. President Bush begins the call up of military reservists. Jordan closes her border with Iraq to allow the huge queues of refugees to be removed to refugee camps. Iraq threatens two UN envoys in Baghdad that the fate of thousands of foreigners will be decided by US military action.

23rd August: President Saddam appears on Cable Network News with detained British citizens, including Stewart Lockwood, saying they are not hostages but "heroes of peace". Baghdad says five million have joined its volunteer People's Army.

24th August: Iraqi troops surround all those embassies in Kuwait which refused to close and insist their staff have forfeited diplomatic immunity.

The Soviet Union evacuates all its nationals from Kuwait. Iraq begins to round up Saudis trapped in the emirate. Jordan reopens its borders to refugees. Sixteen thousand cross by six o'clock. Four Britons are rounded up, including a pregnant woman. Mrs Thatcher describes this as "totally contemptible".

25th August: The UN sanctions the use of force to back up sanctions. Austrian President Kurt Waldheim visits Saddam Hussein in Baghdad. Eight Britons are seized in the morning.

26th August: Iraq announces it wants a peaceful solution to the crisis, but that it will not leave Kuwait. UN Secretary Perez de Cuellar announces that he will visit Baghdad for talks. Late that evening eight more Britons are rounded up in Kuwait, bringing the estimated total held to one hundred and sixty-five, but the real total close to six hundred. These were regularly being bussed up to Iraq or to installations in Kuwait. The totally inaccurate estimates reflect how successful the Iraqis were in picking up Britons and how out of touch the outside world was with developments.

27th August: The United States evacuates fifty-two of its embassy personnel plus fifty-eight dependents through Iraq to the Turkish border. Iraq initially reneges on a promise to let them go and detains them in Baghdad, but finally lets them proceed. It allows nineteen Japanese businessmen to leave Baghdad, after being detained since the invasion. Iraqi soldiers bring machine guns and mortars up to the defiant embassies in Kuwait. Their electricity and water supplies are cut off. The Iraqis threaten anyone harbouring British or American citizens with hanging if they are caught. The vast majority of Kuwaitis ignore this threat, though some Palestinians start turning Westerners in. There are large rewards for doing so. Twelve British Tornados leave Germany for Bahrain. Mrs Thatcher brands President Saddam "a despot and a tyrant" and dismisses his calls for talks, saying sanctions must be strengthened to force Iraq out of Kuwait.

In a dramatic news broadcast on Iraqi television on 28th August, an edict issued by Saddam Hussein was read out. "President Saddam Hussein ordered that all foreign children and women in Iraq enjoy the freedom of either staying in Iraq or leaving whenever they wish, including the families hosted by Iraq, as of Wednesday 29th August."

The news was treated with cautious scepticism by both the Foreign Office and the Gulf Support Group. There had been too many similar announcements and dashed hopes. In an interview, Josie Brookes warned, "I feel we have got to wait and see. He has made promises before and not kept to them. We will have to see what he does tomorrow, because we do not know if we can trust him." She realised the immense emotional problem the families would face leaving their menfolk behind. "Some women might fear coming out of hiding in case they give away their loved ones. It's going to throw up a lot of problems because husbands are not being allowed to leave. We have been telling people not to let their spirits soar and then have to bring them down again if nothing happens."

Later in the same day, an official statement declared that Saddam had been "deeply affected" by meeting detained people, obviously referring to his experiences during the abortive "Guests' News" broadcasts. The statement repeated the Iraqi position that they had been detained for "humanitarian reasons, to prevent the outbreak of war". Meanwhile in Kuwait, the rounding up of Westerners went on. The Iraqis wanted men to replace the women and children on the installations and were doing their utmost to ensure they found them.

When the women and children were allowed to leave Kuwait and Iraq, there were several different groups of Britons, each of whom faced different problems. Firstly, there were those in Iraq, who had been comparatively free during the crisis anyway. They were in three groups. These were on contract with the Iraqis, such as the PARC nurses in the Ibn al-Bitar Hospital in Baghdad, were forced to remain, unless they could get replacements to come to Iraq for them. Those not under contract, such as the wives of men working there, women on holiday or on business, were allowed to leave once they had visas. Most were able to make their own arrangements and to leave on the first flights out. And, thirdly, there were a significant number on installations in Iraq. These included the families of the British Liaison Team, some from BA Flight 149 and others caught in Kuwait, some of whom had appeared on Guests' News and brought such pressure to bear on Saddam when he came to talk to them.

In Kuwait there were basically two groups. Firstly, there were those who had been caught by the Iraqis, such as the bulk of passengers from BA Flight 149, other British Airways crews, those caught at the hotels, or those taken from hiding. A few of those who had not already been taken up to installations in Iraq were still waiting in the hotels, but the bulk of them were on installations in Kuwait, such as the IBI camp, part of the University complex, Doha power station, and the Misila Palace. These were the first to leave the emirate. Most of them were bussed up to Baghdad rapidly by the Iraqis themselves in two convoys, a large one on the twenty-eighth of August and a smaller one of two coaches on the twenty-ninth. Secondly, there was the largest group of all, the hundreds of women and children in hiding. They were not to go up until a week later, in two more convoys on the 4th and 5th September.

In all, five major convoys of British women and children left Kuwait. The first two were organised by the Iraqis; one on 4th September was organised by the British themselves; and the final two came out on the fifth, one organised by the Iraqis, the other by the British. Each had a different story.

The people incarcerated at the IBI camp heard numerous rumours that they were about to leave. It was an Iraqi tactic to unnerve them. So when, on the morning of the twenty-eighth of August they were told they were being taken to Baghdad and allowed to fly home, they treated it with scepticism. All those women and children who wanted to leave were told to report to the guards' hut. Eric Watson was immediately in a dilemma. His ten year-old son Tim was with him, but not Tim's mother. It would mean the lad travelling to Baghdad and on to Britain without any other member of his family. He was very worried about what might happen to him, so went to the guards' hut and asked if he could go with Tim, because of the special circumstances.

At first the Iraqis agreed to let Eric go. He returned to his hut to pack his things as well as Tim's. But other men with children wanted to go as well, including John Chappell. Suddenly, the Iraqis completely changed their minds and said no men at all. Eric was shattered.

All those travelling had to fill in a form handed out by the Iraqis. It asked for their details and passport numbers, and had a space at the bottom to write, "I want to go to London". It was like being a piece of human baggage, parcelled up, labelled and ready to go.

They didn't have long to get ready; about twenty minutes - but then they had virtually nothing to pack. They had little time to dwell on the awful problem of saying goodbye to each other, but it was still a very emotional scene. Some women opted to stay, notably three air stewardesses and Wendy, who stayed with her father Don Majors. The rest of them decided to go. They each packed food and plenty of water to last the journey. It was as well.

The families had be given no warning, so had no time to prepare for separation. Many fathers were positive they would never see their families again. Children were screaming with agony at being torn away. Wives tried to put on brave faces, but it was impossible for many of them. Barbara Griffiths remembers the departure. "It was awful. It was the most terrible, horrible thing for grown men to have to turn away and cry at the wall. We knew we were leaving them, maybe to die." It certainly had a traumatic effect on her. She trembled on the verge of tears as she told me. The guilt she feels at leaving them is still strong. "Even now I feel I would have been better staying in Kuwait."

Andrew and Carolyn Stevenson were put into rooms on a top floor of the Meridien Hotel and had guards posted outside their door. Wherever they went, they were accompanied by an Iraqi soldier. But the hotel was deserted. Their little group were the only people there, so had the run of the place.

At eight o'clock on the morning of the twenty-eighth, they had a phone call to their room. It was reception. They were given ten minutes to pack and get onto a coach waiting outside. Thirty people were already on the coach. They had been picked up from other hotels, especially the Regency Palace.

Meanwhile, the coach containing the people from the IBI camp headed north into Kuwait City. It visited a couple of the hotels to pick up the women, children and men held in them, before joining the other buses and leaving the city. By now, it was late morning. The journey took eighteen horrendous hours. Some of the buses were not air-conditioned and, as the heat of the day rose into the fifties centigrade, they began to bake. There were a lot of women on board, some with small children and babies who were suffering badly in the unrelenting heat. Sweat poured off them.

John Chappell, only a boy, remembered the journey as absolutely appalling. The seats were cramped, they couldn't sleep, the children were tired and fidgeting, and babies were crying because of the heat and because there was nowhere for them to be changed. It was dreadful.

Some tried to sleep, others talked. People's experiences circulated the bus. Of couples hiding in cupboards, in water tanks, on roofs, under stairs, anywhere. Of people moving round to escape the Iraqis, sometimes five or six times from flat to flat, only to be finally picked up. Of women and children moved from installation to installation and the sometimes appalling food and living conditions they had endured.

They only had the bottles of water they had brought themselves and a little food. Someone passed round some cheese spread and crackers they had brought, but that was all. The Iraqis gave them no food, just hot, filthy water. It was full of dead flies floating in it, and they all had to share one glass, but they were so thirsty they drank it. They stopped at the old Kuwait-Iraq border town of Abdaly to get their passports checked, but weren't allowed to disembark. It amused them that, even as captives, they needed entry visas to get into Iraq - the Iraqis weren't going to let just anyone be their guest.

The passengers were allowed off the buses only once, near Basra, to relieve themselves in revolting toilets. "It was disgusting," Carolyn Stevenson recalled. "We had to roll up our trousers to get into the toilet. Oh, it was really disgusting." There, they could buy food, but it too was appalling. There was some goulash, which no one risked, and some bottles of beer at two Kuwaiti Dinars (£4) each. The alcohol helped them sleep for the rest of the journey.

There is no available record of the numbers on this convoy, but it was probably slightly fewer than the one hundred and thirty-nine names of British women and children in Baghdad hotels given to the British embassy in Baghdad after the convoy had arrived. When they did eventually arrive in Baghdad at two o'clock in the morning, they were driven to the Melia al-Mansour Hotel. To their surprise, they met some of the British Liaison Team families already there. They had been brought in from strategic installations where they and their menfolk had been held. The men on the convoy were allowed to remain with their women because the hotel was the staging post for them on their way out to the installations.

They were fed straight away, to give the Iraqis time to sort out their rooms. Everyone was put on the top four floors, which were securely sealed off from the rest of the hotel by armed guards. There were about three hundred Westerners there at that time. When they were eventually shown to their room, the Stevensons found the sheets were unchanged. They refused to go into the room until they had clean linen. The hotel staff quickly changed them, but the new sheets were still wet.

Conditions were very basic at the hotel. "Like everything, it was falling apart through lack of maintenance," Carolyn Stevenson explained. They were there seventeen days. Caroline had decided to stay with her husband and refused to leave with the other women and children. More convoys arrived, but gradually the numbers of women and children began to dwindle as the flights left Baghdad. At one point there were only about ten of them left in the hotel.

The food at the Melia al-Mansour was very poor. Both Andrew and Carolyn Stevenson caught dysentery there. And they were not alone. Nearly everyone who stayed at the hotel became ill, not fully recovering until they were home in Britain. The meals were frequently served cold, even meat such as pork. The bread was good and they occasionally had hot soup and side salads, but they were warned not to eat the latter for fear of picking up disease. The water appeared on the tables in jugs, from where no one was quite sure, and, after a while, they started buying bottled water instead.

When they were both down with diarrhoea, stomach cramps and sickness, all the Iraqi doctor would prescribe was valium - the second most common Iraqi cure-all, the first being an AK47. Later, they had to give Carolyn a drip-feed. When she came off it, she was violently sick and had to be put on another one. Their sickness continued for days, coming and going. As they weren't getting proper treatment, it lingered with them for long after they were taken from the hotel to an installation. They both lost a lot of weight, as did their friends Rosalind and Dave Buchan.

By Saturday, 1st September, four days after the announcement that they could all leave Iraq, still only a handful of women and children had actually been allowed out. A great deal of confusion surrounded who, when and how many would be leaving. All sorts of times and numbers and routes were bandied about. The Iraqis changed their minds and demands every few hours. They tried to segregate the men from the women and break up families. They lied about what would happen to the men and about whether some teenage lads would be allowed to go. Bureaucratic red tape required visas, passports, names and destinations to be sorted out. Western airlines were allowed to fly planes in, then they weren't. To add to the confusion, the Iraqis refused permission for British embassy staff to see those British at the Melia al-Mansour Hotel, so the embassy had to go ahead and charter what flights it could without knowing precise numbers. Things were made extremely difficult for the British embassy in Baghdad throughout the crisis.

The whole period of the release of the women and children was fraught with danger and changes of mind by the Iraqis. There were constant threats and bluffs from them as they responded to Western verbal attacks with rhetoric and abuse of their own. In response to the military build-up in Saudi Arabia they threatened to drop their "moral commitment" to safeguard the lives of Westerners in Iraq if the threat of military aggression continued. In an interview with *Le Figaro* Tariq Aziz, Iraqi Foreign Minister, even refused to rule out a return to international terrorism. He likened the taking of hostages by Iraq to a man who shields himself behind the wife of a man who is about to attack him. Meanwhile, in the peculiar Iraqi double-think, Naji al-Hadithi, an Iraqi government spokesman, admitted that foreign men were being kept at potential military targets. "Every place, every town that has a vital installation will host our guests." He went on, "We are relocating the foreign men all over the country, at airports, air bases, military bases, industrial plants, communications centres, power centres and oil refineries - wherever Iraq considers it has a vital installation, one exposed to the American threat."

Saturday the first was the earliest British embassy officials were allowed to visit the women in the Melia al-Mansour - though they were still not allowed to speak to the men on the top floors. At two o'clock in the afternoon they hostages were suddenly asked to assemble in the hotel lounge. The Japanese were very organised. Their embassy had chartered them a plane and they trooped in and departed as a well-drilled group to catch their flight to Amman whilst the British slouched around the foyer waiting for something to happen. Nothing did. The plane, due to leave the airport at 3pm, was not ready. As they waited, some children made paper airplanes and wrote "We are hostages" on them. They flew them out of the hotel windows onto people passing in the street below. At four o'clock they were asked to assemble once more. Again they waited and waited, until eventually a group of Iraqi officers came in and started calling out passport names and numbers.

Maureen Chappell heard her name called out. She went over and picked up her passport and Jennifer's, but couldn't find John's. She became very anxious and stood at the table, insisting the soldier find it. Other women were equally angry and frustrated. Finally, exasperated, the Iraqi turned out the whole box of passports onto the table and let them find their own. Maureen found John's and was then harshly ordered out by the soldiers onto a waiting coach. At first, the British embassy was told one hundred and thirty-nine had visas and would be flying out, but the number increased by the hour, and the flights may have been delayed to allow more people to get on them. By the time Maureen left for the airport, over a hundred and fifty visas had been processed. This later became one hundred and seventy-four.

When the Gulf Support Group heard the women and children were going to be released there was a lot of press speculation about who it would include, how many would risk coming out and when or where, and whether Saddam could be trusted. Hundreds of relatives phoned for details. The support group tried to calm everyone down. It insisted that no one in the media nor any relatives should say anything about Saddam or the Iraqi government until the hostages were out. Whilst most of the media and government respected that concern, Margaret Thatcher did not.

There was as much speculation over the numbers coming out amongst people in Britain as there was in Baghdad. No firm details emerged from Iraq until the flights were actually in the air. Relatives were having to gather any clues they could from TV pictures of the families arriving in Baghdad, staying in the hotels or being taken to the airport. The Foreign Office only ever had tentative lists of who was at the airport. They knew roughly what the numbers would be, but frequently not which flight they were on nor when the flight would actually arrive. They were given departure times and arrival times, but the Iraqis delayed the planes for so long they were totally unreliable. As a result, some people drove down to London only to discover that their relatives were not on the flight. They waited for the passengers to come through, only to be disappointed. For them it was heart-breaking. Those who could, made arrangements to stay in hotels and wait for the next flight to arrive, or the next, until their relatives did come out. Even then, some were still disappointed.

The Foreign Office had responsibility for phoning people to tell them their relatives were on a particular flight. This it did as promptly and efficiently as it could, phoning firstly to say it thought they might be on a flight, then again later, either to confirm it or say their previous information was inaccurate. It sent both the Coventry helpline and the London helpline their tentative flight manifests. It told people the Gulf Support Group would be at Heathrow and Gatwick to meet the flights and instructed them to follow the Foreign Office directives for relatives who wished to go to the airport. Only two were allowed per family and they had to be the closest relatives. This led to some anguishing confusion at times. Occasionally, the Foreign Office didn't accept relatives whose last name happened to be different to the family coming out, without proof and much shaking of fists.

Stephen Brookes was up very late every night, and sometimes all night, on the phone, sending and receiving faxes, writing letters, trying to get flight lists and contact people. As well as phoning people to confirm that their relatives would be coming out, the helplines dealt with personal problems surrounding the flights. If the nearest relatives of a family happened to be grandparents living in Scotland, or a sister living in the North of England, and they were unable to get down to meet the flight, they would phone up the helpline, often in a distressed state, to ask the support group to meet their people off the plane. The support group would find out the details: what were their names? would there be children coming out? how old were they? what help might they need? and would then meet the returnees as they came off the flights.

Josie, however, was suddenly crippled by a compacted wisdom tooth, which plunged her into great pain. It was undoubtedly brought on by the tremendous stress she had been living under. Stephen had to call out the emergency doctor. Coincidentally, he was an Arab, but he completely supported their efforts. He was later sent out to the Gulf as part of the medical team for the British army.

The doctor was astonished by Josie's condition. She was clearly exhausted. The worry and overwork had accelerated the problem with her teeth. They were so impacted, he insisted she take time off from the helpline and booked her into a local hospital. It took her out of the crisis for a couple of days, but when she came home, everything causing her the stress was still there. The house wasn't her own. She had no privacy. The toilet door was always open, no matter how often she would shut it, as reporters, photographers, television crews, good-will visitors and volunteers all tramped through the house and climbed the stairs to their little operations room. "I was so ill. My face and chest were so swollen. Yet I couldn't even be ill in my own house. There were people in it all the time, seeing me look like that."

One thing which did raise her spirits was when she discovered that Tim Watson, Eric's son, would be on the first flight. She was filled with elation, but couldn't help worrying that he was coming out on his own, having to leave his father Eric behind.

Tim Watson stood around in the departure lounge of Baghdad Airport, chatting with his friend John Chappell. They could see their Iraqi jet waiting on the runway, but had no idea what the long wait was for. By now it was evening of Saturday 1st September and they were anxious to be away. They had been ready since midday, and had missed lunch whilst waiting to leave for the airport. The atmosphere in the lounge was not one of elation, but of tension. There were over two hundred British, amongst them Glenda Lockwood and her two sons, Stuart and Craig, who had appeared on "Guests' News" with Saddam. The two boys had left their father Derek on an installation. There were also twenty or so French and large contingents of Germans and Japanese waiting for their flights, plus a handful of Australians, Canadians and New Zealanders. The Germans were waiting for a Lufthansa plane to arrive, whilst the Japanese embassy had chartered an Iraqi jet to Amman for its people. From there, the passengers would be transferred to Nippon Airways to travel on to Japan.

Eighteen of the Britons were British Airways stewardesses. A number were Arab women who had married British men, whilst others were British women who had married Kuwaitis and were wearing *abayas*. A lot had very young children on their arms. Many had babies, or three or four young children around them. These children were crying or fractious as the hours drained past. They had been incarcerated in camps or hotels for a month. They were bored, full of repressed energy and fears, and could feel their parents' worry. Everyone was tired. No one had slept properly for days. The journey to Baghdad had been awful and they still didn't know whether they would suddenly be stopped by Saddam and driven back to installations. A heightened, acrimonious and xenophobic atmosphere had surrounded them all their time in Baghdad. Even as they had left the Melia al-Mansour Hotel, yet another official demonstration of schoolchildren had honed in on the British embassy to protest against British and American aggression.

The month in Iraqi hands, being forced to leave their husbands and fathers, the final delays and the set-backs had all taken their toll of the families. Yvonne Washer described her feelings to a Channel 4 television crew whilst still in the airport waiting lounge. "We just had to walk away and leave our husbands there. That was the hardest part, knowing that they're somewhere in Kuwait and we are now on our way home; that is the hardest part."

At the airport, it became clear that about twenty French people would be flying with the Britons, and that it would stop at Paris *en route* to London. From there, it would pick up Iraqis who had been "stranded" in France and Britain by "brutal American sanctions" and return to Iraq. There were an estimated 5-6,000 Iraqi nationals in Britain, all perfectly free to leave the country whenever they wished. A few suspected of spying or of being a threat to national security were rounded up, and some were deported. Some of them argued at the time that they were enemies of the Iraqi regime and appealed to stay.

The Japanese heading for Amman were processed and their plane finally flew out. That came as an enormous relief. Once some had successfully departed, the rest felt more confident they would soon follow. They discovered that the reason for their delay was Jesse Jackson. Several seriously ill Americans were being flown up with him from Kuwait to catch the flight. He had secured the release of some ill and elderly American men from Baghdad as well, and they were being loaded onto the plane on stretchers.

Jackson had flown out to Iraq with his bodyguards on a 'mercy mission' to appeal to Saddam Hussein to release sick and elderly American hostages. He had visited Kuwait with the first foreign television crew allowed into the country. They had gone to the American embassy compound with Saddam's own interpreter, Dr Saddun Joubaydi, who read out a list of those people holed up in the embassy who would be allowed out. It was a very short list and was extremely humiliating for everyone as the embassy staff haggled through a plate glass screen for more to be taken. I shall never forget the scene when the American ambassador shook Jesse Jackson's hand through the metal bars across the entrance of the embassy, nor of the girl in her cowboy hat trying to hold back the tears as she said goodbye to her father, nor of her pushing her way through the steel turnstile to get out of the prison the embassy had become.

This initiative by Jesse Jackson and its success proved significant in hindsight. It inspired other world leaders and the Gulf Support Group to pick up on special cases and press for their release on humanitarian grounds, a ball which was to really start rolling in October. As the first visit by a world 'opposition' leader and key supporter of the anti-war lobby in the West, it also marked the initial step in the Iraqi strategy to encourage and abet peace movements in the countries of the alliance, of the UN Security Council, and of those Arab states opposing them.

Late in the evening, Jesse Jackson's entourage finally arrived. Altogether, he had with him twenty-nine American women and children and fifteen sick American men. Nine had come with him from the US embassy in Kuwait. Together with a hundred and ninety-nine British and twenty-two French passengers, they passed through customs and walked across the tarmac to the Iraqi 747 jet. With weary legs and clutching children to tired bodies with exhausted arms, they climbed up the steps and collapsed into their seats, thankful to be finally on their way. There was no cheering, no elation. They were all very subdued. Were they leaving? Would they be turned back? Could their ordeal be finally over? Would they ever see their menfolk again? These thoughts overawed them and made any attempt at celebration impossible.

Maureen Chappell explained how she couldn't quite believe it. "It was unreal. I just switched off from what was going on." It was an emotion which lasted well after the family were back home. She would take every day as it came. "I used to repeat to myself, 'It'll be over soon, it'll be over soon'." Even now, things will trigger memories, as though she has been permanently scarred by her experience. That has been the hardest of all to come to terms with; the permanent mental damage it has done to them all.

The flight took off shortly before midnight, after a total delay of over eight hours. During the journey, they received a poor chicken meal which many found impossible to eat. Then Jesse Jackson appeared, trailing his minders down one side of the plane whilst reporters and a TV crew came down the other. He talked to a few women and stroked a few young heads for the cameras. His bodyguards were pleasant enough. They chatted and had beers with the passengers. Having the American preacher on the plane reassured them. They felt his presence was a strong guarantee that they would arrive safely.

The plane landed at Orly Airport at 3am to let twenty-two French passengers disembark. The Iraqi security men on board refused to let either British or French government representatives onto the plane. Instead, Jesse Jackson descended with the passengers, walked along the red carpet laid out and gave his "window of hope" speech, virtually identical to the one he later gave at Heathrow. He then climbed back aboard. It was a whistle-stop tour for the US presidential candidate. He was in his element.

The French ex-hostages were far more reticent than he. They refused to speak to the cameras, for fear of putting their men in danger. They were tired, very relieved to be finally safe, and anxious to get home as quickly as possible.

At Heathrow, the plane touched down shortly before 5am on Sunday morning, after a journey of seven hours. It taxied past the terminals and away from the concourse where the press were corralled. Once more, Jesse Jackson descended, this time clutching Stewart Lockwood. It was his finest hour, his most photogenic moment, and he found tears to suit the occasion. What we didn't see were the women pushing him out because he was blocking the doorway.

The British women were anxious to be firmly on British soil. Such was the fear and distrust these women had built up for the Iraqis, they wouldn't believe they were safe until they were off the plane.

The passengers slowly disembarked, clearly relieved, passing Jackson as he gave his speech for the cameras, and boarded British Airways transit coaches which whisked them away to a private arrival lounge. Dozens of police, airport security guards and stewardesses surrounded the plane and helped the passengers off. Among them were many who had been on Saddam's "Guest News", including the Lockwoods, Jane Liddle, who, like many other families, carried with her a photograph album of Saddam with her and other hostages, and Jacqueline Joyce, who had courageously demanded of Saddam why he was using children for propaganda purposes.

William Waldegrave carried a young, photogenic blonde girl, clutching her doll, down the steps of the plane. Immediately behind him came Maureen, John and Jenny Chappell, looking tired and subdued. Behind them came the BA stewardesses and many of the passengers who had been on Flight 149. British Airways took especial care of them as it felt a direct responsibility for their plight and went out of its way to provide them with everything they needed. There were also representatives from the army there, including trained army counsellors, to care for the families of the British Liaison Team.

The returnees walked from the coaches through a series of rooms, where the BA stewardesses were taken aside, then entered the arrival lounge. They were not debriefed, because of their physical and emotional state and the early morning hour, although the MoD took everyone's names and addresses. However, many of the women were anxious to part with the information they had on people still held hostage as quickly as possible. Feeling the government was not interested, most turned to the Gulf Support Group, which handled their information rapidly and efficiently. That disappointment in the government was to linger on in the minds of some women for a long time.

The arrival lounge was full of relatives. It erupted when they saw the first passengers walking wearily in. They were the British Liaison Team families, being quickly ushered through by MoD staff. There was a tremendous, spontaneous surge of cheering and clapping as they came through, but also a lot of crying and numb emotion. As the other passengers followed, the room filled with people hugging each other for minutes, bouquets of flowers hanging limply from exhausted hands. Grandparents lifted up their small grandchildren and simply held them. They were cold, having stepped off the plane into a chilly September night, they were tired, and they were totally bewildered. All they wanted to do was go home and sleep.

The Gulf Support Group was there with a table and leaflets giving information about its role and services. So were the DSS, the Housing Department, the Red Cross, and the Salvation Army, with a great pile of brand new children's clothes donated by Woolworths and Marks and Spencer. William Waldegrave and Grant Lindsay were there from the Foreign Office, as well as Joanna and Jonathan Copley. Food and drinks had been provided, both for waiting relatives and for returnees. Some of them partook, having not eaten properly since the previous morning, but others were too tired and too anxious to be on their way home.

Neither Josie nor Stephen went to the first flight. Josie had enough pressures to deal with due to her illness and painful tooth. She knew she couldn't have coped with the sight of poor, bedraggled people coming home with tiny babies, their older children looking exhausted and bewildered. In fact, her friends were sure she was having a nervous breakdown and were pressing her to pack the helpline up. One warned her, "I'm telling you girl, you're going to crack up. You've got to pack it up. You're going to be in a mental hospital. What are people going to care about you? If you go in, you'll be there a long time - and who's going to care about you?" They watched as she deteriorated, steadily losing weight, not sleeping, growing more and more pale and exhausted, and repeatedly complaining of tiredness and pain.

Rob and Sylvia Brown were the only people she could let her feelings out to. She would pop around to their house for a few hours, simply to escape. "It was my little haven, my little cocoon, my refuge." Rob is sixty and Sylvia fifty, so were like parents to her. She had no father and her mother was being cared for in a home, so they took their place. She felt at home at their house. It was the one place she felt secure.

The atmosphere in the house even effected Wen Li. She arrived in England from Singapore on the sixth. Josie had arranged a free ticket for her on a British Airways flight and for her to live with them in Coventry. It was a very joyous reunion and they had a month of stories to swop. However, Wen Li couldn't settle. She was a young woman, not used to such activity. She was racked by her own personal trauma and found the crisis impossible to handle. She couldn't cope with a house full of people and press constantly talking about the Gulf, and with a fax machine, two computers, three phones, Ceefax and Teletext going all the time, never being able to get away from it. The house was in a constant state of chaos. "The press were ringing up all the time. The locals, the free papers, as well as the nationals and TV and radio." Wen Li cooked a couple of Malayan meals and tried to answer the phone a few times, but couldn't do it for long. She went down to face the humiliation of signing-on at the local Employment Office, then applied for a course at London University, in an effort to build some stability and purpose into her life and escape the constant reminders of her husband's situation.

Tim Watson's mother Janet was at the airport waiting for him. He was healthy and fit, although the long journey had taken a lot out of him and he was very tired. He had virtually no luggage, only what he stood up in. Barbara Griffiths had no one to meet her. Her only relative was languishing in an Iraqi installation, she knew not where. Maureen Chappell and her two children had no one to meet them either. The Foreign Office laid on taxis for all those who weren't met or who had no transport, so they were driven back to Stafford whilst Barbara was driven up to Cheshire. Nearly all the passengers were reluctant to talk to the press and hurried away from the media scrum. Those who did consent to do interviews refused to give names of their relatives still in Kuwait and talked only in general terms. Glenda, mother of Stuart Lockwood said a few words. "We are all very tired, but we are relieved to be home. We hope my husband will be back soon. My heart is still with him. I had no choice but to leave him, for the children's sake."

Some waiting relatives were disappointed. Their loved ones were not on the plane, so they had to either return home or go to a hotel to wait for the next flight. Amongst those who had not returned were twenty-four British Muslims on *haj* to Iraq. The father of one of the pilgrims, Murtaza Bandali, described his feelings. "I will have to keep on hoping... Waiting was a cruel uncertainty; it was very depressing finding that she wasn't on the flight. Maybe she will be on the next one..."

Meanwhile, the Jesse Jackson Show had re-embarked and taken off with the American passengers for Washington.

In the packed press conference held at the airport after the flight, William Waldegrave was emphatic about the government's determination to act for the hostages. "We've got a lot more women and children [to get out]. Let's not forget that. This is a hundred and ninety-nine. We've got another eighteen out through Frankfurt on a Lufthansa flight, but we had maybe a thousand plus women and children in Kuwait to begin with, so that's the next target. But we must get them all out - men, women, and children." He added, in reply to a question, "We are getting our people who had a right to come out, out. It's not really a matter of gratitude, it's a matter of the law being obeyed. That is a good thing. But this is not a bargaining situation. This is a matter of the law, the Geneva Convention, being obeyed... It's not a matter of bargaining."

In all, nearly seven hundred women and children, mainly Japanese, American, French, German and British, flew to freedom that day. There were two hundred and sixty-five on the Paris-Heathrow-Washington flight. Three hundred and eleven escaped to Frankfurt. Over a hundred, including seventy Japanese, flew to Amman, having left one hundred and forty-three of their menfolk in installations. Every passenger had endured hours of unbearable tension at Baghdad airport and on their flights and all were bitterly upset at leaving their men behind.

Meanwhile, 60,000 Arabs and Asians were now suffering terrible deprivation in the Jordanian refugee camps, in the most appalling conditions, and a further 100,000 we trying to flee to Iran.

That very morning, Margaret Thatcher was interviewed live by David Frost. With determined eyes, she made it quite clear that the hostages would not stand in the way of military action to free Kuwait. In the final analysis, she would not let them interfere with those military options open to the allied forces.

"If you allow the taking of hostages, terrible as it is, to determine your own action against a dictator, he has won, and all he will ever do, or anyone else with similar ambitions will do, is to take hostages, knowing that other people will never take the requisite action to stop such a dictator. So I'm afraid we would have to take the necessary action we feel vital to stop a dictator, even though he still held hostages."

She went on, "If anything happened to those hostages then, sooner or later, when any hostilities were over, we could do what we did at Nuremburg and prosecute the requisite people for their totally uncivilised and brutal behaviour. We are all making due note of the people who do it, because these days they cannot say, 'We were only acting under orders'. If they are doing something which is totally cold and cruel and brutal then they could, in fact, be prosecuted later. I don't want them to think they are going to get away with it, because they *won't*." She added: "I do not regard [Saddam Hussein] as mad. I regard him as totally calculating and brutal and having no regard whatsoever for the dignity or rights of the individual. None whatsoever."

Later in the interview, she reinforced this sentiment. "We do know that a person who has taken hostages cruelly, brutally, and a person who has hidden behind the skirts of women and children, is now manipulating them and using them, and although he has let some of them go - and they should never have been taken - he is obviously using their husbands and sons and not letting them go. That sort of person really would have to be brought before the court of public opinion internationally."

No matter how much one might sympathise with those comments - and many hostages and relatives did - for them to be uttered slap in the middle of the women and children coming out was, to say the least, foolhardy. Later that day, Saddam banned any further foreign airlines sending aircraft to Baghdad on 'mercy flights', both in response to Margaret Thatcher's outspoken views and to a UN ban on Iraqi Airways. The Iraqis had agreed to let a Virgin Atlantic plane and an Air France plane land, but now withdrew permission, unless the UN ban was lifted, The authorities in Baghdad stated that every flight from then on would have to be Iraqi and direct to Europe. As the ban wasn't lifted, the British embassy had to hurriedly charter Iraqi jets to fly the women and children out as and when they arrived in Baghdad. Even when Iraqi jets had been chartered, the Iraqi authorities refused to say when they could take off. The Iraqis condemned Thatcher as "a grey-haired old woman" who was "mentally unbalanced". It responded to her accusation that they were hiding behind the skirts of women by accusing her of having a "canine, harsh voice", and being "a circus buffoon... vomiting poison like a spotted serpent". "The old hag Thatcher seems to have been upset by the permission given women and children to leave Iraq, as she had wanted to make an issue of them in her electoral campaign."

All this sparring put the women and children still in Iraq and Kuwait in further jeopardy. They felt even more vulnerable as the storm broke around their heads. Those in hiding in Kuwait panicked about coming out and exposing themselves to this international slanging match. It provoked renewed and angry demonstrations outside the British and American embassies and brought to a sharp end the negotiations being held in Jordan between Perez de Cuellar and Tariq Aziz, the Iraqi Foreign Minister. The UN Secretary General was in an impossible position and was clearly a disappointed man. He plainly had no power over the build-up of military forces in the Gulf and every time President Bush, and especially Mrs Thatcher, uttered off-the-cuff remarks, his position was further undermined. Did the British Prime Minister ever hold out any belief in the UN being able to solve the crisis? Her remarks suggest she didn't.

Josie was astounded by what was going on. Nor could Stephen believe it. Joanna Copley was furious. Her sister Kat was amongst those in hiding in Kuwait waiting for a convoy to be arranged to take them up to Baghdad. Everything the Gulf Support Group and international pressure had achieved was hanging in the balance. Hundreds of innocent people's lives were in the palms of Saddam's hands. She expressed her bitter anger at the Prime Minister's comments: "I feel total despair that anyone can say that. Some years ago I remember a woman whose son was lost in the desert and she was utterly desperate. Her name was Mrs Thatcher. Today, there are many mothers whose sons are effectively lost in the desert. Does Mrs Thatcher not feel for them?"

That day and the next, the helplines received hundreds of very distressed calls from relatives. They overwhelmingly believed the Prime Minister didn't care for their relatives trapped in the Gulf and were desperate for someone to stand up and put their point of view across. They were desolate.

Meanwhile, the military confrontation sharply escalated. That weekend wasn't just part of a gradual build-up of forces. It was chosen to really turn the screw on the Iraqis and a further twenty F1-11s were flown to Saudi Arabia. In response, Iraq continued to call up its reservists as part of the continued war of words and show. As always, the Iraqis also took their anger out on those Westerners they held. Dozens more were rounded up for the installations and the women and children waiting in Baghdad began to be treated really appallingly.

This new air of fear and war-mongering petrified large numbers of other foreign nationals. Hardly noticed by the Western allies, Jordan now had a hundred thousand refugees in its grossly overcrowded camps after a surge of panic-stricken Asians fled across its border that Sunday, forcing the Jordanian government to introduce food rationing.

In the Middle of a Fire

"We have felt abandoned and expendable. We have been in the middle of a fire. And it has seemed to us that Mrs Thatcher has been rushing to chuck kerosene over us. We want our families negotiated out."

The first flight out of Baghdad had been mainly women and children held in Iraqi hands - those from installations in Iraq and Kuwait, and under detention in hotels in Kuwait and Baghdad. The journey of those from Kuwait had been organised by the Iraqis: the coaches, the arrangements for picking people up from the hotels and installations, the journey itself and the hotel accommodation in Baghdad. For those in installations in Iraq the same had been true.

The British community in hiding in Kuwait was not so fortunate. The Iraqis weren't going to organise anything for them and the community weren't going to hand themselves over. They couldn't be sure it wasn't another Iraqi ploy to get them out of hiding and round them up. So several days passed before anyone really believed they were free to leave. The wardens wanted confirmation of announcements made over the World Service. They waited for news from the embassy and for other signs. Rumours came through that women and children had indeed been moved from installations in Kuwait and there was confirmation that men, women and children had been taken from the hotels up to Baghdad. But they might still be going out to installations.

One event that helped was when Jesse Jackson flew down to Kuwait on Saturday 1st September with his entourage, including a camera team, to bring out the first pictures from Kuwait since the invasion and visit the American embassy compound.

The difficulty of safeguarding the women and of negotiating Iraqi red tape was made much worse because Iraq no longer recognised the British embassy in Kuwait and refused to have dealings with it. The embassy was under siege, with its water and electricity cut off and only one working phone line, tapped by the Iraqis. The four staff remaining inside had enough problems trying to brew a pot of tea, let alone deal with the hostages. So it had to be left to several wardens to rustle up some coaches and get a convoy organised. It was extremely difficult for the wardens because they faced arrest if they ventured onto the streets. All contacts within the community had to be made over the phone, through a few Kuwaiti friends or via one or two other nationals free to move about, such as an Australian, John Levins.

It is clear that, despite it being called the 'British Embassy Convoy', it wasn't organised by the embassy at all. In the first few days after the announcement that the women and children could go, its position was, according to one warden, "'You are free to leave, but you must organise your own transport.' The embassy quite specifically said, 'You must organise your own transport'."

This stance was impossible. Many British had had their vehicles stolen, and those who had cars certainly didn't have enough petrol to get all the way through Baghdad to Jordan or Turkey. Many had no money. Some women couldn't drive, or had small children and babies to take with them. That was impossible in a car without their husbands. If they travelled alone, they could be picked up by Iraqis and robbed or raped. It was simply out of the question to let these women and children make their own way up.

It was left to a few wardens and John Levins to organise the convoy themselves. A warden explained John's role: "He's the man who embarrassed the embassy. He organised the coaches. When it was said the women could go, he organised buses to take the Australian women to Baghdad. He found a Kuwaiti with a bus. He had less than a coach load, so said he would take anyone else, starting with elderly or sick women, then women with sick or very young children. He found he had so many, he had to organise a second bus. He got nurses on the buses - I think a doctor as well - to deal with the sick. Meanwhile, a friend of John's said he'd got some British women wanting to go. John then organised another two buses. Suddenly, the two of them had organised four buses. The British embassy was still doing nothing about getting the women and children out."

Another warden, Mike Devey, confirmed this. "The Australians were organising coaches and so were the French and Irish. It was through those systems that coaches were organised. It took the other embassies to get detailed plans in operation before the British embassy would do anything. When the Australians did it, we thought, 'Why can't our embassy do it?'"

Tom and Gilly Colclough, both actively involved in helping people and with the warden system also confirmed that the convoy was not organised by the embassy. "They say it was a British embassy organised convoy, but it wasn't."

Meanwhile, the Americans were organising aircraft to fly into Kuwait. It would take longer, but the journey would be luxurious compared to what the British women and children would have to endure. The Foreign Office did consider using aircraft, but the Iraqis at that time refused to allow planes to land in Kuwait. Whilst it was very aware of the problems a road convoy would face, with countless roadblocks and possible delays, it seemed the only viable alternative. In response to criticism of not organising a plane in time, a British embassy official in Baghdad said it had thought bussing the women and children out would be easier than organising a flight and that speed was a priority.

The embassy in Kuwait finally decided to take over the organisation of the coaches. Donald Macaulay began phoning people to tell them that coaches had been organised and when they would be leaving. According to Dave Dorrington, "It's 'organisation' was to say, 'Turn up at the Sultan Centre at seven o'clock in the morning and there will be buses waiting for you'." **According to several wardens, that was virtually all the British embassy in Kuwait did to help the British women and children leave Kuwait.** "No names, no numbers, no idea of who was coming and who wasn't." Because it *had* no idea.

In fact, symptomatic of the general lack of organisation, there seems to be a great deal of confusion amongst people as to the time they were asked to report to the Sultan Centre in Salmiya. Times range between five and eight o'clock in the morning, with several people confirming that the time was changed at least once. Mike Devey remembered the time as six o'clock, but his wife Lesley thought it was five. Others said half six or half seven. Dave Dorrington thought it was seven. The World Service was instructing people to arrive at the shopping centre at five-thirty, to leave at six. This confusion led to a lot of unnecessary worry for some women. "Several people turned up at the time they'd been told and the buses had been filled up and gone. Luckily, the Australian bus was still at one of the hotels and was able to take these women. They were far better organised, with details of the numbers coming, their names and seats allocated for each person."

Donald Macaulay phoned Mike Devey and other wardens to inform them of the convoy of buses, and for the women and children to meet at the Sultan Centre - at six o'clock - in the morning of 4th September. But Mike was emphatic that it was not the embassy who organised the convoy. "The coaches were organised between John Levins and Donald Macaulay. It was definitely through the Australians. They already had two of their own coaches going later the same day from the Misila Beach Hotel."

The one thing John Levins couldn't do was persuade the Iraqi soldiers not to arrest any women or children trying to reach the rendezvous. This was something only the British embassies in Baghdad and Kuwait could do. When asked whether they had sought Iraqi permission for the convoy, the British embassy in Baghdad informed British journalists that there was no need. Unfortunately, there was.

A correspondent for *The Independent* wrote: "The 'opportunity' is, however, fraught with problems. There is no guarantee that the Iraqis will allow such a convoy to leave; the journey normally takes between ten and twelve hours, but a convoy of cars took twenty-six hours through the scorching desert; and there are no British officials to see the convoy off or escort it because the four members of the British embassy in Kuwait have been confined to their embassy. They have, however, been able to assist in organising the convoy." And in the *Guardian:* "Britain last night [the third] urged hundreds of women and children trapped in Kuwait to gather in the centre of Kuwait city to join a convoy of buses waiting to take them to Baghdad - a journey which the Iraqi authorities have not cleared. The six hundred mile trip to Baghdad was being undertaken without seeking Iraq's permission because this was not necessary [!], although the authorities had been informed." This incredible admission was to cause great problems for the women and children trying to leave.

Those in hiding also had more general fears that they may well be refused permission to leave Baghdad once they arrived there, or be whisked off to installations. The Iraqi government was continuing its war of threats. It issued an ominous warning to countries with trapped nationals to ensure that food was allowed through the UN blockade, otherwise it could not be responsible for what happened to them as a result of shortages.

There was also worry that the women, either inadvertently or under force, would give their menfolk away when they emerged. On the second, ten men had been picked up, seven of them British, when their wives went to apply for exit visas.

The wardens decided the women had to risk it. Sandy MacMillan, Chris Bell, Mel Gage and the others phoned around the women. The recommendation was not to go with any men, otherwise they could all be picked up: get a Kuwaiti friend to lead the way from a car in front. Another suggestion was to leave their cars a little way from the Sultan Centre, and maybe the wardens could get some Kuwaitis to pick them up later.

There were hundreds of enquiries and difficulties. Several families phoned their wardens to ask about their grown-up children, lads between sixteen and twenty-one. Would the Iraqis allow them out, or would they haul them off to strategic sites? Several families decided to take the risk, but two teenagers who didn't go were Rory and Alex Duncan, sons of Colonel Bruce Duncan. Their mother left, but they decided to remain in hiding in Salmiya with their father. Another enquiry was from an elderly couple, the Wrights, who didn't want to be separated. Should they both go or both stay? The advice to all of them was to risk it. It seemed a better option than remaining trapped in Kuwait.

Most people were phoned with final details of the convoy on Monday the third, the night before it was due to leave. The World Service kept broadcasting details over the air and gave brief instructions. "Those wishing to travel should be at the Sultan Centre at least thirty minutes before departure. They should have with them no more than one suitcase per person and hand luggage. They should be prepared for a long journey - which means just that - taking food and water accordingly. The Foreign and Commonwealth Office hopes that all those women and children who are able to do so will be able to take advantage of this opportunity."

Jim McAlindin, trapped with his wife Jane, described how that night felt. "At 6pm that evening the British embassy warden phoned to tell us that a convoy for the women and children was leaving the Sultan Centre at 8am the next morning. All the women and children were to be there by seven." He mentioned how the departure time was later brought forward half an hour. "The next morning, after a sleepless night, all the women in our block got together to drive to the rendezvous point. The only one who didn't go was a Canadian woman. At the last moment, she was told she couldn't go. It was just for British woman and children and she wouldn't get on. They left at 5.30am and us men went back to one of the flats to sit and wait. We were worried for the women's safety, so we phoned an Arab friend of ours. He went to the Sultan Centre, but didn't see our women arrive. We presumed something had gone very wrong and anxiously rang our warden. All we could do was sit helplessly and wait."

Lesley Devey and thirteen other women and children with her left their compound at half past four. They didn't feel the curfew was a particular problem. Most Iraqis were asleep and Lesley didn't see an Iraqi soldier until she reached the Sultan Centre. However, the only time she felt really frightened during her month under Iraqi occupation was on that journey, in the dark morning hours, tracing their way cautiously through the back streets of Rawda, Hawalli and Salmiya to reach the Sultan Centre. It is a large shopping and residential complex with an extensive car park overlooking the shore in Salmiya, to the south-west of Kuwait City. Even when they reached the rendezvous, they didn't feel safe. "We stood there for an hour and a half waiting for the buses. I didn't want to go. I only went because Mike had insisted and because, if I'd stayed, other wives would have stayed as well, and Mike wanted them all out."

Gilly Colclough was with another group of women and children who left that morning. They had been sharing Colin Eglington's villa in Mushrif, just down the coast from Salmiya. It felt awful to leave her husband, Tom, behind. She believed she would never see him again. But the men were insistent all the women went. It would be a load off their minds and would help the food situation enormously. The men would feel a lot happier knowing that at least their wives and families were safe.

The night before they left, Gilly went to sleep crying and woke up crying. They spent much of the night packing. In the morning, Tom had to get her showered and dressed, whilst she cried the whole time, but once the time came to leave and they were finally on their way, the tears quickly dried and she became more businesslike.

Gilly went with Joyce Foreman and Maureen Durnin. They left at five-thirty for the rendezvous which they had been told was at six-thirty. They carefully emerged from the villa, after checking all was quiet outside, climbed into a car and drove to the Sultan Centre along countless side roads. The Kuwaiti Resistance had supplied them with a map of the back streets to circumvent the checkpoints. It proved invaluable. None of them took their ID cards with their addresses on in case an Iraqi patrol stopped them and demanded to know where their men were hiding.

They managed to reach the car park safely and, following the advice of the wardens, left their car with its keys in it a little distance away, for someone to pick up. No one did.

Gilly's group had been told to take only one bag plus hand luggage so Gilly took her suitcase and a cool box she had filled with water and some food. She carried them out of the car and waited for the coaches to arrive with Joyce and Maureen. They met some old friends they hadn't been in contact with for a month. In fact, there were many reunions in that car park.

When the coaches arrived, they were clearly not in very good condition. They had been told they would be modern, with drinks machines and toilets, but they were old, cramped and some had no air-conditioning. Gilly's group climbed aboard one of them and found some seats. "There were kids there and babies. Quite a few Muslim women with British passports had come along. They tended to sit together at the rear of the bus. One had a Down's Syndrome baby who was really sick. The mother was very worried because she was certain the baby wouldn't survive the juddering journey and the sweltering heat. She told us that the poor child had a hole in its heart as well."

Julie al-Enezi was brought to the Sultan Centre by her Kuwaiti husband, Faisal. She was an air stewardess with Kuwait Airways and was two months pregnant. She was very upset at having to leave Faisal behind. As he helped her onto the coach and watched her settle into a seat, a group of Iraqi soldiers approached him. The coaches had attracted the attention of several patrols by now, who were watching and questioning people, especially Arabs. They began to demand answers from Faisal. Julie watched anxiously from the coach as more Iraqis drifted over. The group began to hassle Faisal. They pushed him backwards several times. One shouted at him. Guns came from shoulders to point at him. Julie heard them demand to see his ID card and heard them accuse him of harbouring a Briton in contravention of the new edicts. He faced summary trial and execution.

Faisal protested that Julie was his wife, but they didn't listen. Instead, they pushed him harder. One raised the butt of his Kalashnikov and rammed it into his stomach. He doubled over in pain. Julie stood up in the coach and shouted at them to stop. The soldiers hit him again. As he fell, they began to kick him in the head and kidneys. Julie screamed and rushed off the coach, yelling at them to stop. She bent over Faisal, forcing the Iraqis to halt. Her protests caught the attention of an Iraqi officer who ordered his men over to him. They obeyed.

Julie realised she couldn't leave Faisal now. She helped him back into their car and watched as the coaches slowly drove out of the car park. With them went her best hope of leaving. Although there was a later convoy, she knew she would have to stay with her husband, come what may. She drove him home and stayed with him throughout, not only the hostage crisis, but the war as well. She gave birth to her baby in February, whilst bombs were dropping around her.

Another Kuwaiti man taking his English wife to the centre met with trouble. Nabil decided to drive his wife Marie to the rendezvous but at one of the checkpoints he met with trouble. The Iraqi soldiers, saw him and ordered them both out of the car. They began to question Nabil. He tried to reassure them, to tell them his wife was allowed to leave and he was just taking her to the coaches. Marie was pinned against the car as Nabil was forced a little way away. He could see what some of the soldiers were thinking. One began to touch Marie's clothes, then ran his fingers over her hair and neck. Another smiled at her and touched her necklace, then her blouse. Nabil shouted at them to stop. He threatened them and pleaded with them. He even told them that if they took his wife, he would take one of theirs.

Finally, the soldiers laughed and let them go on. Nabil hurriedly opened the door of the car, then climbed in himself. He quickly drove off, leaving the soldiers laughing behind them.

There were about eighty women and children who failed to reach the Sultan Centre. As many Britons had feared, because the convoy had not been cleared with the Iraqis, the officers at the roadblocks arrested whole groups of people trying to get through.

Jane McAlindin left with Janet Somerford and her three boys, one of whom was aged seventeen and another eighteen. It was a risk taking these eldest two as the Iraqis might not class them as children, but they decided to take the chance.

There were two other women with them, plus a boy of nine and a little girl. They decided it would be safer to travel together rather than in separate cars, so the nine of them piled into a pick-up truck in the early hours just before dawn. They made their way carefully through the darkened streets of the curfew, but as they approached the Sultan Centre they had to join a main road, where they were stopped at a roadblock. There were two cars at it already and another five soon drew up behind them, all with British women and children in. "They wouldn't let us go," Jane recalled. "They couldn't speak English and we couldn't speak Arabic. An Indian did all the translating for us. He told us they were not going to let us go. They didn't know we had been allowed to leave. They took all our passports away and threw them into the back of a truck. They drove us to a school where they left us until seven o'clock, when their commander came on duty."

The Iraqis had turned many Kuwaiti schools into barracks and area headquarters. At the beginning, they had tried to induce the school children back into them, to keep the schools going as 'normal', but few children attended. From being an advantage to live near your child's school, it had become a distinct disadvantage.

When the commander arrived he was very apologetic. He told them their arrest should not have happened and that they would be taken to the Meridien Hotel, as by now it was too late to catch the convoy. They were driven around the city in a group of Iraqi military vehicles with soldiers guarding them with AK47s and machine guns. It was an unnerving experience. "It was quite frightening because we hadn't been out for such a long time. For the first time we could see what was really happening - all the soldiers about, all the road signs destroyed. It was very emotional because we'd left our husbands behind, hadn't slept the night before, and had left our apartment, our possessions and the people we knew. We had thought we were going to get out, but now we didn't know what was going to happen, where we were going to be taken."

Margaret Parkin was another Briton arrested that dark morning as she attempted to reach the rendezvous, but under far more ominous circumstances. She and the other British women and children with her tried to steal out of their apartment block and get to their cars without being seen. The men had carefully removed the barricade from behind an entrance to their block of apartments and had checked that there was enough petrol in the cars. They said goodbye, gave each other a few last hugs and wiped away the tears as they slipped into the courtyard and along the wall towards the cars.

Suddenly, the women and children were caught in several searchlights. A voice over a megaphone ordered them, in broken English, to stand still. The shock stunned them. The children began to cry, terrified of what was happening.

"Do not move. You are all arrested."

Soldiers clambered over the perimeter wall and broke through the gateway. Several vehicles drove up in the dark and uniformed officers jumped out. One counted the women and the petrified children clinging to them. "Where are your husbands?"

The women, dazzled by the lights, were too paralysed to reply.

"Where are your husbands?" he shouted, unfastening the holster for his pistol. He waved at some of his soldiers to guard the doorway they had emerged from. It had been locked again and the men inside had run back upstairs to hide. More soldiers closed in on the women and children, pointing their rifles at them.

"Where are your husbands?"

"They are not here," one woman replied, her voice barely audible.

"What?"

"They've gone."

"Gone? Where, eh? Who locked the doors if they are gone, eh?" He approached, his face evil in the sharp shadows of the night. "You tell me where they are or I will tell my men to shoot your children." There was a quiet sadism in his voice, a hint of pleasure at being able to say it. And there was no doubt he meant it. "And then we shall blow the house down, eh?" He turned to his second in command and laughed. "Just like the little pigs, eh? Ha." The soldiers behind him laughed, ignorant of English, but pleased to further intimidate the captives.

The women glanced at each other. It was obvious they were lying. Either they co-operated, or the Iraqis would blast their way through the block. There was no point in resisting or antagonising them further.

"They are inside," one woman told the officer.

"What numbers?"

"Are you going to hurt them?"

"Not if you tell me the truth. I promise." Another smile flashing a perfect row of white teeth.

The women, left with absolutely no other choice, reluctantly gave the Iraqis the numbers of the apartments their men were in. Two soldiers had already broken through the door to the entrance hall and now the rest ran up to the selected flats and demanded the men come out. They didn't resist. They had seen and heard the commotion below and knew what must have happened. Somehow, someone, probably a neighbouring Palestinian, had tipped the Iraqis off. Once they knew of the convoy arrangements, the Iraqi army had been warned to watch for emerging British and so had been ready and waiting.

The men were given a few minutes to grab their passports and one bag each, then were bundled downstairs into waiting trucks and cars with the women and children. From there they were driven to an old Kuwaiti police station which had become a local interrogation centre. However, they were treated civilly there and not unduly questioned. After all, the Iraqis had their prize. Their passports were confiscated and, a few hours later, they were escorted to the Regency Palace Hotel.

Joe Wild estimated that there were about a hundred road blocks between his complex in Abu-Hulifa and the Sultan Centre. The soldiers at these checkpoints had been fired on virtually every night by the Resistance, which used one tactic very frequently - driving up in cars and opening fire, then speeding off again. It was extremely worrying to think that car loads of British women and children would be travelling during the curfew hours into a very dangerous situation, and may be shot at.

The group of women from Joe's complex packed their things for the journey the night before, including some food, water, nappies and baby things. As the embassy had told them to only take one bag of hand luggage with them, it was very difficult to pack enough for babies and small children. They left from Abu-Hulifa at four-thirty in the morning, setting off in the dark. There were ninety-odd in their convoy, once they had been joined by others from Fahaheel, Fintas, Manqaf and Shuaiba. The Iraqis were suspicious of so many people travelling together and they were soon stopped at a roadblock. The officer in command refused to let them go on. Instead, he arrested them and took them to the Abu-Hulifa police station. There, they were not treated well. They were threatened with guns and interrogated by Iraqis who wanted to know where all the men were hiding. Some, especially teenage girls, were so pressured they were forced to tell the Iraqis, for fear of being beaten or raped.

Amongst those given away were the group with Joe Wild. "At quarter past nine, the Iraqis surrounded the building and began shooting off the locks and smashing their way into the blocks, through the barricades we had erected behind them. They stormed the buildings, kicking in every door and breaking every lock to every flat." Joe was lying in bed asleep when they came into his apartment. Like many in hiding, he had prepared an emergency bag in case he was suddenly taken. Because he suffered from a heart complaint, he had packed his medicines, X-rays and some clothes ready for such an eventuality.

The Iraqis ordered him to come with them, but he is an obstinate man. He swore at them and refused to go. He told them he was too sick to go with them and showed them his X-rays. They contemptuously flung them across the floor. He showed them his tablets, but they scattered them across the floor as well. One picked up his TV in contemptuous anger and hurled it against the wall. Another smashed his photographs and ornaments. "They were extremely aggressive. They turned on me. They tore my clothes off and beat me to the floor, then picked my arms up and dragged me round my flat, twisting them up behind my back, wrenching my shoulder, from which I'm still suffering. They went on smashing the place up, then put a gun to my head and pulled the trigger twice. They dragged me out of my flat on my knees."

Joe wasn't the only Briton to be assaulted. One man had his face smashed in with a rifle butt as he stood at the top of his stairs.

When he was dragged into the hallway, an Iraqi officer saw that Joe was clearly ill and treated him with more respect. He ordered Joe's bag to be brought with him, took him downstairs and brought him a chair. The Iraqis then drove him and the other captured men off to Abu-Hulifa police station, where they met up with the women and children who had left that morning and were still being held there. From there, they were all taken to the Regency Palace Hotel, where they were allowed to stay, so long as they didn't venture outside.

After Joe repeatedly complained of chest pains, an officer agreed to escort him back to his flat to recover his medicines and X-rays. He found his home completely desecrated, smashed up senselessly. It was wrecked, a total mess, looted, completely destroyed. The floor was littered with things which didn't belong to him, scattered jewellery boxes, bags, empty wallets and suitcases. The Iraqis had obviously used it to divide up their loot from all the other flats. All his wife's jewellery had gone, as well as nine hundred Kuwaiti dinars (eighteen hundred pounds).

The Canadian woman who had stayed behind began to regret not catching the coaches. The Australian coach was due to leave later that morning, well after the curfew and with the permission of the Iraqis. She was offered a seat, but had to be at the Misila Beach Hotel for eleven o'clock. She decided to grab her chance, rushed down, took Jim McAlindin's car, and just made it. There were twenty-three woman and twelve children on board when it left, from Britain, Canada, Ireland and Australia. Lesley Bell, wife of Chris Bell, who had taken on the role of warden, was amongst them. They reached Baghdad shortly after the British convoy. Their journey was as awful as everyone else's.

At the Meridien, Jane McAlindin and the people with her were met by a senior Iraqi officer who apologised and assured them they would be taken to Baghdad as soon as possible. He suggested they return home until coaches could be arranged for them. His soldiers could take them. The women realised this was a ploy to discover where their husbands were, so refused. The officer did not pursue the point. Instead, he smiled and accepted it. They were brought some tea and allowed to make phone calls. Jane rang her husband Jim.

As their families were driven around scenic Kuwait City and dumped in the Meridien, Jim and the other men had chewed their fingernails. "We sat and waited. At 4pm Jane called to say she had been picked up and taken to the Meridien. It was a relief to know she was safe and hadn't been involved in an accident. My main worry was whether she had fallen into the hands of indisciplined soldiers." Jane rang him again that evening and several more times the next day, until she and about a hundred and eighty other British women and children were taken up to Baghdad by the Iraqis.

Soon after Marie and her Kuwaiti husband reached the Sultan Centre, she climbed aboard one of the buses, full of trepidation. Whilst she was very glad to be going home to be with her mother and receive proper medical attention for the baby she was carrying, she was desperately upset at leaving her husband behind.

As Nabil watched her settle into a seat and mouthed final messages to her through the window, tears ran down their cheeks. A car drew up behind the Kuwaiti. It held two English women in a brand new TransAm, Jean and Jenny Haig-Prothero with their cat Mittens. They had left Jean's husband John behind in their villa in Andalous, to sweat it out in hiding. Their plan was to take their four-wheel drive all the way through Turkey and Eastern Europe, across the Channel and home. Apart from one other car, theirs was the only private vehicle to accompany the convoy.

There were no embassy officials nor wardens at the Sultan Centre to see them off, nor on any of the coaches up to Baghdad. There was only the wife of an embassy official on board one of the buses. Nor were there any Iraqi guards with them, as it was not an Iraqi-organised convoy. In effect, they were left to the mercies of the coach drivers and any bunch of soldiers or looters who happened to stop them. They felt very vulnerable.

Not as many people turned up at the rendezvous as the wardens had hoped. They estimated that about five hundred women and children were trapped in the country, but only two hundred and seventy-one turned up. Of course, the eighty who had been arrested at the roadblocks would have brought the total to three hundred and fifty. In one sense, it was as well those extra people didn't make it. There were only seven coaches available, perhaps just enough to squeeze them all on. As it was, they were packed and it became so incredibly hot and stuffy that the people inside felt they were suffocating.

Lesley Devey described her experience of that journey. "It was horrendous. We were kept waiting an hour and a half before the buses arrived. Because there were fourteen of us from our group, we wanted to stay together. We all managed to get onto one bus. I think there were seven coaches in all. We then drove around Kuwait City for another hour. Then we stopped on the Fourth Ring Road and the driver said 'Toilets' and pointed to a house. It was some Kuwaiti's house they had probably hijacked. We were still no more than four hundred yards from where we had started. They threw us back on the buses and off we went. We went through Jahra and up the Mutlaa Ridge. It was full of burnt-out cars and Iraqi trucks which had come down to Kuwait to fill up with anything they could find and were driving back with their loot piled high on the back. There were Kuwaiti cars full of Iraqi soldiers, being taken up to Iraq for sale, and trucks going by with brand new machinery taken from the ships in the ports, or stripped from the factories, all going up to Iraq."

The driver refused to put the air-conditioning on, even with babies on board who were being sick all the time, crying, sweating and unable to sleep on the bumpy roads as they jolted along. At Abdaly, close to the old border with Iraq, the coaches were stopped at a sort of taverna. Everyone wanted a cold drink, but there were none available, just beers.

The driver of Lesley's bus bought a great container of beer for himself which, to the women's alarm, he started drinking. He steadily became more and more drunk, until he was weaving the coach across the road. Suddenly, he left the convoy and headed out across the desert along a series of side roads. He was a Jordanian, and had a friend with him. This man now made his way down the bus ordering the women to give him all their Kuwaiti money.

"Give me your money. You cannot spend in Iraq. No possible. No good. No good. We keep it safe for you."

Not likely, the women thought and denied they had any.

"Give me your watch and jewels."

"Certainly not."

"It is for pay to take you in Iraq. For petrol and wages. If you no pay us, we no take you."

Again, the women refused, to the man's anger.

"We have no been paid," the man insisted.

None of the British women believed him. "You must speak to the British embassy."

The Jordanian was very angry by now and tried to grab a woman's bag, but she held onto it. He gave another tug, then angrily let it go. Once he realised he couldn't take them all on, he retreated, only to report his failure to the driver, who started to drive as if he wanted to make the journey as difficult as he could. He still refused to turn on the air-conditioning and began to drive very fast. He braked hard and flew crashing over potholes and cracks in the appalling roads, bouncing against the curbs and refusing to stop unless he wanted to. When he did stop, he refused to go on until he was ready. As dark descended, the women had no idea where they were going, whether they would end up at a camp, or ever be seen again.

Several women were pregnant and others had periods, yet the driver refused to stop for them. Some children and babies began vomiting with the heat and rough ride. Once the sun was down, the driver turned the air-conditioning on full in spite, so everyone froze. When the children tried to sleep, the driver turned the music up full blast and switched all the lights on, to wake them up again, laughing as he did so. The driver went on drinking from his container of beer.

The women had brought bottles of water, but that soon ran out. Although the coach owners had provided a cool box full of water, it was filthy. "At the bottom of it was a sludge, but we had to drink it. There was nothing else. How we didn't all get a stomach bug, I don't know." The truth is, that many women *did* become ill as a result of both the journey and their few days stay in the Baghdad hotels, where the food was not always prepared hygienically.

Things grew worse. The coach suddenly lurched to a stop and an Iraqi officer armed with a machine gun boarded the bus whilst the driver refilled his beer container with more alcohol. As the driver pulled away, the officer stood at the front, waving his gun, petrifying the women and children. One elderly lad, about twenty-one, rose and told the Iraqis to stop frightening them. After this, the driver angrily pulled into the side of the road again, turned off all his lights and sat there, refusing to move. They were completely at the Iraqis' mercy.

"We thought, oh God, what are they going to do now? They could have ordered us off the bus and anything could have happened. We could have all been shot and buried out in the desert. Nobody would have been any the wiser."

In the end, the driver irritably moved off again. To their relief, they eventually reached Baghdad some time after midnight, eighteen hours after they set off.

Gilly Colclough had a similarly exhausting experience. As Lesley Devey had recalled, the coaches didn't get very far once they left the Sultan Centre. Just outside the city centre they stopped. The driver of the bus carrying Gilly Colclough began to argue with some of the passengers around him, but they couldn't understand what he was saying. Then nothing seemed to happen for a while. They just waited. A Kuwaiti woman with a sick baby became very agitated. People were already sweltering in the coach and her baby was in a very bad way. She rose angrily, stomped up to the front and began to argue with the driver in ferocious Arabic. She eventually returned to the back of the bus to inform the rest of the passengers he was holding out for more money. She began to open her purse, but the other women said there was no way they would let her pay him.

The driver descended from the bus to have a cigarette and the drivers of the other buses joined him, refusing to budge. Gilly remembers one of them going down her bus demanding money and jewellery from the women on board. "Basically, the drivers were holding us to ransom."

By now, the Arab woman with the baby was hysterical, screaming that her infant was going to die and that she would rather risk Kuwait than the journey to Baghdad. Suddenly, and apparently from nowhere, although they must have been contacted by someone, some Kuwaitis appeared, had a short discussion with the drivers and then led them over to a nearby house. A few minutes later the drivers emerged with enough money to satisfy them, lazily clambered aboard the coaches and pulled out towards Jahra.

Marie was aboard another of the coaches in the convoy. "The journey was horrendous. The coach was old and without air-conditioning. I sat beside a young woman from Blackpool who was pregnant. All we had to eat were tins of tuna, red hot from the sun. It was so hot the sweat was dripping off my chin. My hair was soaking. Everybody was a mess, smelly and horrible. Because the driver wouldn't let us stop to use a toilet, they were passing round a plastic mineral bottle to wee in. I wouldn't use it, but some people had to, especially the children."

Gilly Colclough remembers the first part of the journey vividly. "We reached the border, where we waited a long time. It was funny, because Kuwait was supposed to be part of Iraq by then, but we still had to be cleared through. We handed over all our passports and started on our way again, but then became very worried because we were driven off the main road onto a dirt track. It was supposed to be a short cut."

Because of the rising tension and not being allowed to stop for the toilet, the children were growing desperate. One boy of about six began to cry. His mother had fitted him with a nappy in case of an emergency, but he was so ashamed of using it, he refused and cried repeatedly for the bus to stop.

The women, too, were at the end of their nerves. Finally, a lad who spoke Arabic persuaded the driver to pull up. There were no facilities. It was the middle of the desert and they had to use the side of the road. The little six-year-old boy was so proud of having lasted without using the nappy he informed everybody on the bus.

Marie takes up the story again. "Towards six o'clock in the evening, after we'd been driving all day, they stopped us at a sort of inn at the side of the road. We went in to try the toilet, but there was a long queue and the Iraqis were pushing in front of us. When I reached the head of the queue, I discovered that the toilet was just a hole in the ground. It stank and was filthy. It hadn't been cleaned for weeks, if ever. I was desperate, so had to use it, but I held my breath as I did so."

"Some Iraqis were eating in the inn," Gilly Colclough recalled. "A few women went up to ask them if their children could have some salad. In response, the Iraqis threw some onto the ground, spat on it and told them to eat that." She squirmed at the memory. "So the children had nothing to eat. They were selling cans of coke, but they were the equivalent of six pounds a can." Instead, Gilly bought herself some beers, to help her sleep.

The coaches only stopped once more, to take on petrol. Those women who wanted to relieve themselves were once again forced to squat by the roadside. Once they had climbed back on board, the coaches drove off. It was getting dark and cooler by now as the night descended, but it was impossible to sleep. All that was possible in the narrow, cramped seats was to doze fitfully. The road was too bumpy and the air too stuffy for more than a catnap.

The children suffered the most. There was no room to move and nowhere to change or feed the babies. Their mothers had brought bottles and nappies, but they were running out. The babies were crying and the older children were growing restless with tiredness. They were clinging to their mothers or lying across them, hungry, thirsty, crying with exhaustion. It was survival, trying to last out those awful hours, counting every minute as it passed, desperate for their ordeal to be finally over. What little food they had brought with them was gone and their water was running out.

The British embassy in Baghdad planned to meet the convoy as it neared the Iraqi capital, but was refused permission. It had arranged for accommodation in several Baghdad hotels, notably the Melia al-Mansour, the ar-Rashid, Novotel and Sheraton. It had also agreed to pay for their hotel bills and had chartered their flights out of Iraq, so had not been idle and had done much to ease the passage of its citizens.

When the convoy arrived at Baghdad in the morning dark of Wednesday the fifth, the coaches first drove to the Sheraton. So far, the journey had taken eighteen horrendous hours. Dozens of television crews and reporters were waiting for them, as well as staff from the embassy.

The Sheraton is a very plush establishment. The exhausted passengers slowly clambered off and drifted into the reception area, where they waited patiently. However, once the reporters and Iraqi television crews had taken pictures of how well the women and children were being looked after in that luxurious establishment, the Iraqis ordered the families, to their astonishment and consternation, back onto the buses. They were too exhausted to argue or offer more than token protests. They reboarded and were driven off, this time to the Melia al-Mansour. Even more camera crews and reporters were waiting for them there, to film the weary women and children as they flopped off the coaches and struggled into the second hotel foyer.

But this was still not the end of their ordeal. As the women in the buses began to unload their things, all the suitcases and pushchairs and carrycots and bags of nappies and baby things, they noticed a man from the embassy, looking very concerned. He had been waiting for them for hours. He tried to talk to them, find out who they were, what the journey had been like and whether they needed anything. Suddenly, a senior Iraqi officer armed with a pistol approached him and ordered him to leave. They exchanged some sharp words in Arabic as they argued the point. After a few minutes, the Iraqi pulled out his gun and pushed it under the embassy official's chin and started to scream at him. There was clearly no point in arguing any further, so the man turned to the women and told them he would have to leave.

It was a prelude to the next stage in the farce. The women and children were ordered back onto the buses. They were told they were not going to be staying at the Melia al-Mansour but had to reload all their baby stuff, all their pushchairs and carrycots and bags of nappies and toiletries and suitcases, and clamber back onto the buses. Some women were leading three or four children and were totally exhausted by now. The buses drove them across the city to the British embassy. Near to it, the buses were flagged down and Brent Sadler from ITN boarded one of them with a TV crew.

"Are you part of the convoy?"

"Yes," came a tired chorus back.

Meanwhile, the drivers effectively went on strike. They took out the keys, sat by the side of the road and smoked cigarettes, saying they weren't going to drive any further.

The ITN crew filmed and talked with the passengers as they waited, until the embassy officials caught up with the coaches and persuaded the drivers to re-enter their vehicles. They continued filming and interviewing as the buses drove back through Baghdad to the Sheraton. Those pictures, when they were broadcast on the news in Britain that night, were the first sight many people had had of their relatives since the invasion. It was of people with eyes bleary from lack of sleep and from being moved from pillar to post, their hair and clothes damp from sweat, their children too tired to complain any more. A baby sucked on the teat of an empty bottle; a young boy stood forlornly in the gangway with his mum; a one-year-old in a nappy sat on a seat nibbling a piece of unleavened bread as his mother struggled with a new-born baby; others blinked away from the bright camera light.

This TV crew were the first Britons these passengers had spoken to since the invasion of Kuwait. As Brent Sadler described them, "They were weary, disorientated and hopelessly out of touch with the evacuation plans." A woman explained to him that the journey had been the first time she had been outside for a month. She had always moved from hiding place to hiding place at night. "This is the first time we've been outside and seen the sky since August the second... It's been quite bad. Everybody was scared. We were very frightened. This is really the first we've seen of the world since then."

Another woman, again with no name, for fear of reprisals against her husband in Kuwait, said, "Today has been almost going along with blinkers, never knowing."

"Are you happy to be out?"

"Extremely. But very sad to leave my husband behind." She barely fought back the tears as she spoke.

Another woman, clutching a baby to her body, tried to rock it to sleep.

"I've had no chance to leave before; I was too scared to go out. I've been in the house for a month, as soon as it happened, too scared to go out, waiting for the Iraqis to bang on the door." She could hardly keep her eyes open.

Finally, one woman spoke. She was extremely distressed at the government's role in their plight. "We have felt abandoned and expendable. We have been in the middle of a fire. And it has seemed to us that Mrs Thatcher has been rushing to chuck kerosene over us. We want our families negotiated out."

As they filmed, two embassy officials boarded the bus and tried their best to explain about exit visas and flights out. Meanwhile, the women continued to talk to the camera crew about the terrible conditions they had left behind in Kuwait and their worries for the men still trapped there. Kat Copley was on board the bus. She spoke to the camera, to the absolute delight of Joanna and her family back in England when they watched the news that night.

The buses eventually arrived at the Sheraton, but were nearly turned away from there again. The hotel already had seventy French citizens and initially insisted it had no room, but was eventually persuaded to take at least some of them. Others were driven on again - this time to the Novotel, where they finally booked in. They disembarked and carried their luggage into the foyer, where they sat exhausted, waiting. The hotel slowly signed them in, but refused to give them any food. "The embassy staff had to go to different hotels and get food parcels for us. Some of these staff were very, very good in those hectic early morning hours, trying to get food and accommodation for us." The passengers were all finally accommodated by three o'clock in the morning.

The Australian coach arrived soon afterwards, with about twenty-five more British women on board, amongst Australians and Canadians. In all, three hundred and six British people made the journey up that day, approximately half women and half children.

The British-organised convoy left an estimated two hundred British woman and children in Kuwait (in fact, if one includes the eighty arrested by the Iraqis, there were about two hundred and seventy) and plans were made to organise a further convoy to bring these women up. Meanwhile, on the fourth, another two planes, carrying two hundred Westerners, half of them Germans, had been allowed to fly out to Jordan. They were both Iraqi Airways jets, one a Boeing 727 chartered by the United States which included forty Britons on board. A Virgin Atlantic jumbo jet flew to Amman to pick them up, carrying thirty tonnes of food and medicines for the Jordanian refugee camps on its outward journey. Richard Branson had hoped to pick up two hundred and fifty Egyptians as well, dropping them off in Cairo, but the Egyptian government refused him permission.

As they left, so Iraqi intimidation of foreigners went on. Another eighteen British men were seized in Kuwait and, at the Turkish border, Iraqi guards were turning back Western women and children in Kuwaiti cars They were demanding they return to Baghdad to get Iraqi number plates before leaving the country. Some Westerners simply abandoned their vehicles in protest. The Iraqi authorities announced that foreign 'guests' would be made to suffer the same food shortages as the rest of the Iraqi population. If they had, the conditions for some would actually have *improved*, as their food was *worse* than their Iraqi guards, who were creaming off the best for themselves.

On the fifth, twenty-four more British women and children were flown out to Amman with a group of French hostages, where they waited for an Air France jet to take them on to Paris. Meanwhile, the Virgin Atlantic jet arrived back from Amman with just a hundred and five passengers, only fifty-seven of whom were British. The plane was two-thirds empty, a fact that led Richard Branson to repeat his criticisms of Egyptian and French diplomats in Jordan for not allowing their citizens to use his aircraft.

The women and children from the British-organised convoy remained at the hotels whilst the British embassy and the Iraqis sorted out their visas. Whilst the food at the Sheraton was good, that at the Novotel was sporadic and poor. One day cornflakes without milk, the next milk without cornflakes. The Iraqis were not sympathetic to complaints. They told the British to be grateful as the average Iraqi family was suffering starvation.

Posters and pictures of Saddam Hussein were everywhere in the hotel and in every room. These rooms were not secure. Many people were sharing with people they didn't know and some were having to sleep on the floor. The hotel was also crawling with the *Mukhabarat*. Gilly Colclough lost her suitcase on the second night. When it was eventually returned to her, the Iraqis had clearly gone through it. Several times, women returned to their rooms to find an Arab cleaner or plumber in them. They could tell they had been going through their things, trying to find information on their husbands. When asked to leave, they would hang around the rooms, acting as plain clothes security police would act. It was scary for all the families. Whilst some tried to remain calm, others found the tension unbearable.

It was eerie at the Melia al-Mansour. Whilst the women and children at the other hotels had a large degree of freedom, those in that hotel were treated like prisoners, yet the 'true' guests of the hotel were allowed to come and go as if nothing had happened. Irish, American and British businessmen, doing deals or on contract with the Iraqis were perfectly free to move around. Whilst they continued to eat well, go to the bars, and move about Baghdad freely, the women were restricted to the hotel and denied any drinks.

The women in all the hotels were continually perturbed and distressed, spent most of the time sitting in reception waiting to be called to the airport. Certainly, their experience was totally divorced from the scenes of carefully selected hostages swimming in hotel pools and relaxing in gardens that were beamed back to Britain.

The *Mukhabarat* were constantly swanning around the hotels. Soldiers came and went too. At one point, on the sixth, some marched in and ordered four lads over sixteen to leave with them. This came as a complete shock. They had been assured they would be allowed out of Iraq. It was especially upsetting because those lads had not needed to come out of hiding, but could have stayed with their fathers in their apartments. Now, they wouldn't even have their fathers for company, but would be removed to an installation. Their mothers were very upset. One was refusing to leave without her son. Other women stood around and supported her as a major row blew up, but the Iraqis insisted on taking them and they were eventually led away to the Ministry of the Interior, *en route* to strategic sites. The embassy immediately stepped in to get them the necessary papers to leave and argued vociferously for their release. Fortunately, the pressure worked and the four lads were eventually allowed to leave.

Such were the constant pressures on people in the hotels. The Iraqis continuously hassled them, denied them their rights and baited them psychologically. Spies and microphones were everywhere. The phones were bugged, the hotel staff couldn't be trusted. Every so often they would spot a gun concealed in a holster inside a suit jacket, or a walkie-talkie wrapped in a newspaper.

Rumours were flying about. They didn't know whether they would be flown out or have to go on another coach journey - this time estimated at twenty-nine hours - to Jordan. They had only a couple of radios between them, so couldn't get news of the outside world, or of what plans there were for them. On the sixth, they were repeatedly told they would be going to the airport, only for it to be called off after they had hung around for several hours with their bags. "You're going, you're not going; your visas have come, your visas haven't come; if one on the list has no visa, none of you can go..." A woman with a South African passport was summarily refused permission to leave. Two women travelling on Belgian passports were denied visas without explanation. Yet a Japanese woman was waved on her way. So it went on, a stupid, puerile game, a sadistic cocktail of bureaucracy, hatefulness and lies. "For that forty-eight hours plus that we were there, we didn't know what was happening."

Two of the people who went out on that first British convoy were Mr and Mrs Wright, an elderly couple who had been visiting their son Derek Wright and his family. The elderly couple and Derek's wife and children reached Baghdad. There, the Iraqis refused to let Mr Wright leave and were going to send him out to an installation. His wife refused to leave him. They hurriedly informed the British embassy and the ambassador agreed to let them stay at his house for as long as they needed to and they were whisked off in a diplomatic car. The Iraqis had no choice but to agree to let them stay in Baghdad. They remained there until they were let out with the other men in December.

The British embassy continued to be severely restricted in its access to its citizens, especially at the Melia al-Mansour, where the men were held. So cunningly was this done that the embassy staff had no idea when groups of men were moved in and out of the hotel on their way to the installations. It was going on all the time, yet very rarely did the embassy get access to them, or even know they were there. They were allowed to see the women and children, however, as there was no point in hiding them, and their husbands, so long as their families were with them. They were permitted to process the women's passports and visas and were even allowed to organise a large meeting at the Melia al-Mansour for them. But not for the men secretly held on the top floors of the hotel.

Families from the ar-Rashid, Novotel and Sheraton were brought to the Melia al-Mansour by coach for the meeting and assembled in the crowded dining room. Television crews were permitted to film it. Unfortunately, the women were too exhausted to appreciate it.

BRITISH HOSTAGES ARRIVE HOME WORRIED ABOUT THOSE LEFT BEHIND

Fifty-seven British hostages, mostly women and children, arrived home from Jordan yesterday on board a Virgin Atlantic jet which flew into Gatwick Airport less than one-third full... The freed hostages were rushed through immigration and customs to waiting friends and relatives. Those who spoke to journalists said they had been treated well by the Iraqis, though they were anxious over the fate of husbands, boyfriends and fathers they had left behind in the Gulf...

Another of those on board was Ann Ibrahim, her nine-year-old daughter, seven-year-old son and baby Yasmin, born in Iraq two weeks ago. Mrs Ibrahim was forced to leave hospital only hours after giving birth and had to leave her husband behind. She said Western rhetoric was worrying people held in Iraq. "We thought [Mrs Thatcher's statements] would put the whole exodus in jeopardy. People are very worried, not knowing what will happen to them next." ...

Bhuvan Joshi arrived with his wife Bimali and told how he was smuggled to freedom by two journalists after hiding for weeks inside a Kuwaiti hospital...

The Independent, Thursday 6th September

The regular Iraqi announcement that they would be going to the airport finally proved accurate on the afternoon of the sixth. Those who had exit visas were told to pack and be ready for five o'clock. Most turned up early, to be sure not to miss the coaches, then had to sit in them for three to four hours as they waited for more paperwork to be finalised. It was a very anxious time. Another nasty Iraqi trick.

Even as they were sitting in the coaches, they were told several times that they wouldn't be going, then that they would. By now, many of them were ill with diarrhoea. Much of it was due to fright and general upset, but the food at the Novotel and Melia al-Mansour had been badly prepared, unhygienic and frequently cold. As Marie sat in the coach, her stomach went through spasms. Her temperature was rising. She felt ill and faint in the heat. When they eventually moved off, over roads broken up by tanks, the bumps added further to her discomfort.

Even at the airport there was no let-up in the tension. Every woman had to collect her family's passports once again, after having been given them and had them taken away four times since leaving Kuwait. This time, the office was the floor. The Iraqis casually threw all the passports onto the ground and made the women sort through and collect them as they stood by watching. It was another example of the Iraqis degrading these women, making them suffer for wanting to leave. "It was frightening. We still didn't know if we were going to get out. The Iraqis were trying to search everybody's bags." Lesley Devey had to slap one Iraqi's hand as he grabbed her handbag. She had a videotape in it which she was smuggling out. They also tried to take her daughter's walkman from her.

Two planes had been chartered by the Foreign Office to fly them to Amman, where they would catch a British Airways flight to Gatwick. There were between two and three hundred British people altogether who had visas. The airport was further crowded with over a hundred Canadians and some Americans and Irish. These latter were flying out via Ankara to Toronto. There were also a large number of Arabs who wished to leave, so the concourse was heaving. As they waited, many became anxious about whether they would get seats on the planes. No seat numbers had been allocated, so there would be a mad rush to get on board. No one was looking forward to that.

After sorting through and eventually finding her battered passport, Emilie made her way to passport control and the departure lounge, only to be stunned by the news that there were no planes ready to go. They would have to return to the hotel!

Harold Walker was there with other Western ambassadors. They angrily and forcefully intervened. pleading with the Iraqi officials to find aircraft for them. After much shaking of heads and waving of hands, the airport staff managed to find a single plane in one of the hangars. The Iraqis must have known about it all the time, but simply wanted to further upset the women and children.

The passengers had to sit and wait for the plane to be prepared. It took a few more hours. During this wait, they were further humiliated by being taken into a room to be body searched, as if these women, stripped of all their possessions, might be slipping something through customs - or want to blow themselves up with a bomb. What on earth were they supposed to be smuggling out? Their own clothes, perhaps? A few remaining photographs, diaries of their time as hostages, or the odd watch the Iraqis had missed in their looting spree of Kuwait or whilst rifling through their rooms at the hotels? It was purely to degrade and rob these defenceless women one final time.

Once the plane was ready, people were allowed to board it. However, it was not big enough for them all, so some people had to wait behind. Marie was allowed through to it. So were Tess Clark and Joyce Foreman, friends of Gilly Colclough. But Gilly herself missed it. She had stayed behind in the concourse to help a woman with two young children. By the time she reached passport control, it was too late. She was given a different ticket and had to wait another hour and a half whilst a second aircraft was made ready.

Both planes were elderly Iraqi jets with skeleton Iraqi crews. On the first plane there were just four crew to look after all the passengers. Of course, they weren't looked after at all. Even boarding was chaos. It was the mad scramble for seats everyone had feared. Some Iraqi passengers tried to push their way up the steps, causing consternation amongst women queueing on the tarmac who thought they would be left behind. Even inside the plane the passengers' fears were not allayed. It was an old aircraft. They were given no help with seat belts or to store away their luggage. Women with young children and babies had to manage as best they could. None were helped up the steps or to find seats. Children were crying with the pressure of bodies and with the struggling. Mothers were fraught, tired and desperate. The mood was as tense as a bow string.

Marie had the fortune to find herself sitting next to a Seventh Day Adventist who chose that moment to try to convert her. As they strapped themselves into their seats, the plane taxied over to the runway. The woman warned her about the coming apocalypse and warned her to turn to the Bible before it was too late. Did she know something about the pilot the others didn't?

"We're leaving from Babylon Airport. Have you heard of Babylon ?"

"Oh, yeh, yeh." Marie was not overly interested. She was trying to be brave for the take-off.

"And you know Saddam's King of Babylon."

"Yeh." 'Oh, shut up,' Marie thought.

To her horror, as she closed her eyes and prayed they would be safe, the woman began to quote Revelations from memory. "And I stood upon the sand of the sea and saw a beast rise out of the sea, having seven heads and ten horns and upon his horns ten crowns, and upon his heads the name of blasphemy. And the beast I saw was like unto a leopard and his feet were as feet of a bear and his mouth as the mouth of a lion; and the dragon gave him his power..." The Day of Judgement was upon them!

As the plane sped along the runway, its engines screaming, a rumour suddenly flew around that a bomb had been planted on board. Some women were verging on panic. The plane began to weave and wobble as it tried to lift off. Children began to scream as one wing tipped right over towards the ground, then flipped back again. More started crying. Marie was gripping her arm rests desperately. This was sheer terror. Everyone thought the plane was going to crash.

The woman sitting next to Marie suddenly undid her seat belt and stood up. She told everyone to listen as she opened her bible and began to read from it. The plane went absolutely silent as she quoted a passage.

"Be not afraid of the King of Babylon of whom you are afraid. Be not afraid of him sayeth the Lord, for I am with you, to save you, to deliver you from his hands. And I will grant you mercy that he will have mercy upon you and cause you to return to your own land."

The passage had a calming effect upon those listening. People realised the meaning in the words and their panic dissolved. From then on calm reigned and the plane seemed to sigh with relief as it climbed into the sky and banked southwards towards Amman. When they landed and disembarked they were met by British Airways and embassy staff, who cheered them and welcomed them to freedom. As soon as they stepped off the plane they were met with smiling, friendly, warm faces. It was another world.

The airport was buzzing with press and TV crews. They were desperate for interviews but the passengers had no time to stop. They were ushered along one tunnel from the Iraqi plane, through the arrival lounge and into another tunnel to the British Airways flight, without having to be cleared through customs. A number of people were on hand to offer help. There was a priest, a social worker, psychologists, doctors, Foreign Office officials and plenty of BA staff on hand. The reception in Amman was overwhelming. It was a victorious homecoming.

The passengers from the first flight had to wait several hours on board the British Airways plane until the second flight from Baghdad arrived. The atmosphere was different to any other returning flight of women and children as it was not an Iraqi plane. They were served champagne and an excellent in-flight meal and the children had ice-creams and Mars Bars. By the time the second flight landed much of their tension had been replaced with relief.

The second flight was much more relaxed than the first but was still tense. It was also an old plane, but there was no pushing for seats, no hysteria and no problem with the take-off. Once on their way, they were served tea and sandwiches by very civil stewardesses, without any guards being present. At first, people were subdued, but once they were flying and had left Iraqi airspace, Gilly Colclough and those around her began to feel far more confident. They managed to laugh and crack a few jokes. The mood visibly lightened as peoples' faces relaxed, as children slept and as smiles replaced frowns. They soon landed in Amman and taxied alongside the waiting British Airways jumbo jet. The passengers already on board waved at them through the windows, and held glasses of champagne up in salute. They were obviously having a whale of a time.

The new arrivals were quickly and quietly transferred to the British plane. It now had two hundred and fifty-two passengers on board, including twenty babies, plus dozens of ancillary crew and medicos. The jet took off to cheers and immediate relief that they were finally on the last leg of their journey. They were given more champagne and served with plenty of food. The children received more sweets, ice-creams and lollipops than they could cope with and there were proper facilities for babies and toddlers. It was the largest single group of British women and children to leave Iraq.

The BA crew at Amman were exceptional. They had all volunteered to go out to meet the women and children, expecting at the time to be flying into Iraq, and not a hundred per cent certain of returning. Together with the medical and support staff, they had been on stand-by and short-haul flights for days waiting for the go-ahead.

There were also MoD officials on the flight who wanted to gather as much information on the people still left in Kuwait as they could. But some women were still very cautious about giving any information. Marie refused to tell them anything about Nabil. Instead, she told them to leave her alone and let her read a newspaper she had found. It was the first English paper she had seen in six weeks. Before she read it, she felt certain the women and children would be front page news. After all, they were the people at the heart of the crisis. But the headline shocked her. The price of oil! Other women saw other papers, all with the same story. They became very upset. Was that all they and their husbands were worth? A few barrels of oil?

Their reception was overwhelming. There were a lot of tears. The rapidity of change from fear, panic and rough, ill-mannered treatment by armed Iraqis to a glorious party - and being free! - was, perhaps, as shocking to them psychologically as the invasion had been. They had no time to adjust. Suddenly, it was bright lights and the media.

For many of them, it was too much. Their reception was wonderful, but they had left their husbands and fathers behind and many of them were going back to no home, no money and the most difficult months of their lives. Lesley Devey remembers the dilemma they all felt. "The BA flight back was absolutely marvellous, brilliant. It was the relief of finally being out. But it also wasn't relief, because the men were still in hiding." For many, the months awaiting them were to be far worse than the four weeks of captivity they were leaving behind.

Other countries tried their best to get their nationals home as well. A plane load of a hundred and seventy-one Americans followed the British into Amman as they left. In the Jordanian refugee camps, a major airlift had begun to repatriate tens of thousands of Bangladeshis, Pakistanis, Indians, Sri Lankans and Filipinos. Huge Russian Antonov cargo air-ships were used to carry up to four hundred and fifty at a time, sitting on mattresses rather than seats. There were still a hundred thousand left stranded but, by the middle of September, over a hundred flights had taken thirty thousand of them home. Many more waited in Turkey, Iran and Saudi Arabia.

The purge of those in hiding went on. In Iraq, the Justice Minister Akram Abdul-Kadeer, ordered prosecutors to enforce a 1987 law carrying a possible life sentence for any "foreigner violating the entry and exit procedures". He ordered that everyone had to report any change of address within forty-eight hours or face up to three years in jail.

One Briton trapped in Kuwait, Adrian Clark, managed to make a phone call out in which he was able to give some indication of the plight of the people still trapped. He reached the BBC:

"Conditions are very difficult. Food is difficult to get because we can't get it ourselves - we were being picked up by the soldiers. Every night we heard gunfire; whether it's coming from Iraqis or the Kuwaiti Resistance Movement, we don't know at the moment. We also live in fear that maybe one day the Iraqi soldiers will knock on our door and take us to Baghdad. It is very dangerous. Literally, all we can do is just sit tight and hope nothing happens to us."

Clem Prothero waited patiently for confirmation from the Foreign Office that her niece was on the second flight out of Baghdad. Jenny Haig-Prothero had been in a car with the British convoy up from Kuwait, with her mother Jean and their tabby cat, Mittens.

Although the Iraqis had let them cross the Kuwaiti border in their car and drive up to Baghdad without any trouble, once at the Melia al-Mansour Hotel they were told they had to take it back down to the Kuwaiti border to change its Kuwaiti number plates. Jean would have to return to Abdaly then come back again, twice repeating her horrendous journey. Fortunately, she was a friend of Jane Walker, the wife of the ambassador. Through her, the embassy provided one of its staff to accompany her whilst Jenny stayed in Baghdad with Mittens. Unfortunately, before her mother returned, the Iraqis called Jenny away to the airport for her flight out. She had to call Jane Walker and ask her to look after Mittens. She agreed and was told the cat would be in a particular wardrobe in a particular room on a particular floor, with some water and food. Then Jenny hurriedly left to catch the coach. Her mother arrived back in Baghdad later and picked Mittens up. The next day she set out again, this time north-west towards the Turkish border.

Clem and her other niece, nineteen-year-old Heather Haig-Prothero, waited all the evening of Thurday 6th September as they watched news bulletins of women and children from the first convoy leaving the hotels and going to the airport, staring anxiously at the screen for any sign of Jean or Jenny. The next morning, they watched the first flight as it landed at Heathrow, praying that they were on board, but didn't hear any news of their arrival. They even checked with the Foreign Office about the flight which landed in via Frankfurt and the fifty-seven who came from Amman with Richard Branson.

Then came pictures of the second convoy arriving. Again, they hovered in front of the television as the ITN newsreel of the passengers on the coach were shown, for a glimpse of the two women. Two days later, they heard that more people were leaving on two more flights.

Once again, they scanned pictures of the departure lounge as the British passengers prepared to leave and heard that the two planes had taken off from Baghdad and landed at Amman. They even heard that they had been transferred to a BA flight at Amman, which was due into Gatwick at 4.15 the next morning. But there was still no confirmation from the Foreign Office of Jean and Jenny being on board.

Clem and Heather both had a strong premonition that the two women would be on the flight. In fact, Clem was certain. She calculated that, by the time the Foreign Office had the flight list and had begun to ring the relatives, it would be about ten at night, so they waited up. But no call came. At eleven they decided to get some sleep and retired to bed. They were just dozing off when the phone rang. It was twenty to twelve and it was the Foreign Office. It said it thought Jenny was on the flight. Clem asked about Jean, but the woman on the other end told her there was only one name. This caused Clem some worry. However, the woman at the Emergency Unit gave her a special number at British Airways to phone. Clem dialled it. Whilst they had no information about Jean, they did give her precise instructions about meeting the flight. Only two relatives were allowed per family. They had to take their passports, both for identification and because they would be meeting the passengers air-side. Clem had to give her and Heather's names and addresses and ages. They had to be at the Sir Winston Churchill Suite at Gatwick by 3am.

It was not a lot of time. By now it was midnight and the journey from Worcestershire was a good three hours. It was panic stations as they dressed and searched for their passports. They still weren't certain Jenny was actually on the flight, but if they waited until they were sure, it would be too late to meet it. They drove across country to the M1 and picked up a friend in Northampton, then drove down to the Watford Gap services and phoned the Emergency Unit from there. It seemed like an age as the Unit checked the flight manifest. Clem stood anxiously in the phone box, watching her money being guzzled. Finally, they came back to her and confirmed that Jenny was on the flight, but they still had no news of her mother, Jean.

The three of them drove down an empty M1 and M25 and arrived at Gatwick just before 3am. Their friend parked the car and waited as Clem and Heather made their way to the Sir Winston Churchill Suite. They had all to be issued with passes. By now, hundreds of relatives had arrived and they had to join a queue which stretched along two corridors, through a waiting room to the outside. As it was moving at a snail's pace, they began to freeze in the cold, autumnal night air.

"When we got there, we were in a general state of panic. Was she going to be there? Was she going to be all right? We'd seen pictures of the first flight arriving and it had looked absolutely terrible, those people coming off the plane weeping, so relieved to be out. I think I was getting a bit apprehensive as to what it was going to be like."

The queue did not help Clem's state of mind. "I was taken aback because there were at least five hundred coming to meet this flight, people of all ages - young ones, old ones, pensioners, babies, Grandma, Grandad, all sorts. The queues went from the suite right round, almost to the other side of the airport."

Eventually armed with their passes, Clem and Heather walked through to the Sir Winston Churchill Suite. It was a large room, full of comfortable seats. At that time it wasn't very full and they were able to get a cup of coffee and some biscuits provided free by the airport staff. At last they could relax, go to the loo and sit down, perhaps even to catch a little sleep. They sat and waited for the rest of the relatives to come through and for the plane to land.

After half an hour, the suite was getting full. Josie and Stephen Brookes arrived, as did Joanna and Jonathan Copley and Andy Charles from the London helpline. They were there both as members of the support group and because Kat Copley was on the flight list. They had set up a table and were standing near it, giving out information and chatting to relatives, many of whom they had spoken to over the phone. Foreign Office representatives, plus all the familiar organisations were present. People were having to stand by now and the humidity was rising. It was half past four. They heard that the plane had arrived, though no one saw it come down. There was no cheering. In fact there was rising tension. Some people were anxiously thinking they were not going to get to the arrival lounge in time and were going to miss seeing their relatives off the plane.

Eventually, coaches arrived to transfer them over to the arrival lounge. They were herded on and driven across the airport, leaving behind the press, who were not allowed over with them. Both Clem and Heather were hoping Jenny was all right after her ordeal. They wondered what her flight had been like. Once they were reunited, they planned to get away immediately from the noise and crush.

The arrival lounge was far too small for the numbers of people there. As many as five hundred relatives were pressed into a room barely large enough for two hundred. Then there were a large number of airport staff and people from a variety of care organisations and official departments, such as the MoD, all with their own tables. "It was absolutely teeming, absolutely packed. There was every organisation there. There were Red Cross workers, the Salvation Army, the support group, DSS, financial advisers, the Housing Department. Each had its own trestle table set up. There were even Church of England people and priests there."

At the far end, British Airways had set up a canteen providing free sandwiches and drinks. The demands was so great it soon ran out. There were doctors and the St John's Ambulance Brigade. A pile of blankets, clothes and baby things such as nappies and baby powder was waiting on tables along a wall. The airport staff were much better prepared for the people coming off this plane than off the first flight. Far more thought had gone into their needs. They had the experiences of the first arrival to guide them. MoD staff were also there.

The Gulf Support Group had set up its own table and was distributing its leaflets amongst the waiting relatives. Earlier that evening, the London and Coventry helplines had received faxes from the Foreign Office giving the flight list of passengers on the plane. It was just a long alphabetical list of names and their passport numbers, with no indication of addresses, when the plane would arrive, or other details. Once they had received the list, they, along with the Foreign Office, had to identify and match it with names on their computers in order to phone the relatives of every person on it. It was a major detective job tracking down the names, barely two or three hours before the flight was due in. The Iraqis gave the British precious little co-operation and what they did give was almost too late to be of use.

It had been just after 4am when the plane landed. The relatives had to wait another three quarters of an hour before the first passengers started to come through. By then, the crowded arrival lounge had become very hot and sticky. People were sweating so profusely there was perspiration running down the walls. At five, as the passengers started coming through in numbers, there was a sudden surge of people anxious to see their relatives. Officials were trying to get them to stand back, but it was a hopeless task.

It wasn't a joyous occasion. There weren't any cheers or hurrahs or songs or laughter. There was just a lot of relief and love and tears and holding.

One of the first to come through was a woman in her fifties. She appeared dazed by the whole experience. As she reached the top of the stairs, she collapsed and had to be helped to a chair. She was verging on hysteria. She was emotionally drained and overwrought by the reception. Seeing all those people waiting was too much for her.

Gilly Colclough's sister was there to meet her and they fell into each other's arms. Marie was tremendously relieved to see her mother and father there to meet her. She cried all over them. Tess Clark and Joyce Foreman had their relatives anxiously waiting and were overjoyed to be reunited.

Clem Prothero stood waiting by the rail holding back the relatives. People behind her were pushing forward. She is only a small woman and the press of people was quite frightening. She suddenly saw Jenny walking towards her and shouted to her. Her first impression was one of relief. She seemed fine. She looked healthy, though was clearly very tired. They hugged and kissed in sad reunion, then forced their way through the crowd to Heather, who was sitting by a wall. They hugged each other for a long time before sitting down and trying to talk. Jenny told them what had happened to her mother but, after all that waiting, there seemed little to say. They were so relieved to see each other that it took the words away. Pleasantries seemed inadequate; it was such a relief to be together again.

It took the passengers nearly an hour to come through, entering the lounge in dribs and drabs. There were a lot of children, many very young, quite a few babies. They were in a terrible state. They were all very, very tired. It had been seventy-two hours since they had cautiously emerged from hiding to join the convoy from Kuwait. It had all been very emotional, very sad and desperately upsetting. Clem found herself caught up in the emotion just like everyone else. "I like to think I'm fairly well controlled, but all that went out of the window. Everyone else felt the same."

Joanna Copley described it in a similar way. "It wasn't a joyful occasion at all, because they'd all left their husbands, fathers and sons behind. It was absolutely traumatic. One woman was in a hell of a state. She was very heavily pregnant and hadn't been able to feel the baby moving since she had left Kuwait, worrying throughout that dreadful journey up to Baghdad and on the flight home that she had lost it. She hadn't been able to get any medical treatment, check-ups or medication. She was desperate because she didn't know whether she was carrying a live baby or not."

The whole room was full of very emotional people. Everyone coming off the plane was crying. So was every relative. "It was really awful," Clem Prothero told me sadly. "I found it quite upsetting. You can't begin to imagine the emotion. A lot of people who came off were in a pretty bad way. Not ill, but obviously very strung up and upset. As they came out, they were falling into each other's arms. Everyone was crying. It was very emotionally charged."

It had all been too much for them.

After twenty minutes of hugging and crying, Clem, Heather and Jenny rose to leave. Jenny is a tiny woman with long, fair hair and a slim face. Her eyes were sore from crying as they made their way onto a coach which took them back to the Sir Winston Churchill Suite. It was seeing Jenny is such a state which most concerned Clem. Jenny had always been such a great optimist, a happy-go-lucky woman seemingly without a care in the world. Nothing would ever get her down. She was carefree, full of energy, very outward going. But not that night. It was a most dramatic and fundamental change in her. It was the first time Clem had seen her in such a state. Not only had the flight taken its toll, but the car journey to the convoy, up from Kuwait, and around Baghdad, when she had driven for nearly twenty-four hours, had severely drained her. She would take weeks to fully recover.

Joanna and Jonathan's sister Kat suddenly showed herself. Her parents were there to meet her as well. When she saw her face peering up from the stairwell, Joanna squeaked with joy. Everything Joanna and Jonathan had been fighting for on a personal level suddenly seemed worth it. All the sleepless nights, financial loss, worry and exhaustion, the hassle and the interviews paled into insignificance beside the pure joy of having their sister safely home once more. But neither could forget the other passengers. They stayed and helped other relatives and passengers with problems and questions, handing out their leaflets as they talked. So did Josie and Stephen. "A lot of people were totally disorientated when they came back," Josie explained. "They were hyped-up because they'd got out and were under the constant glare of television cameras." They helped with directing people to other agencies, such as Housing or the clothes stalls and informed them that the Foreign Office had laid on free taxis for every family that needed them, to any address in the country.

One family waiting were Julie al-Enezi's parents, Mr and Mrs Price. They had been told Julie was on the flight and had come down from the Midlands to meet her. They waited and waited, becoming more and more anxious and distressed. Josie went over to them to provide comfort and wait with them. They had no idea she had jumped off the bus at the Sultan Centre in Kuwait to save her husband from being killed by the Iraqis. After an hour, there was still no sign of her. Josie took them over to Grant Lindsay at the Foreign Office table to explain their dilemma. He was extremely sympathetic. He rechecked the flight manifest and asked a BA stewardess to check both the corridors and the plane. When she returned, shaking her head, they finally knew Julie had not come out. But had she been taken by the Iraqis? Had she been killed? Her parents were distraught. They had no idea whether she had been in an accident, or was in prison or at an installation. Was she in Iraq or still in Kuwait? Was she in danger or safe? What of her husband? Where was he? Was he with her? They had to return to the Midlands empty-handed and empty-hearted.

The Final Flights

"The Melia al-Mansour Hotel was the holding point, the processing plant, the prison ship, storing the men in its hold for a few nights before shipping them off again."

When the Iraqis came, they surrounded the house. Six heavy machine guns pointed towards them as the Iraqi officer knocked on their door and demanded they come out. There was no point in resisting or trying to hide; they knew the game was up. Stephen Mansell answered the door and spoke to the officer, who tried to reassure him that they would not be hurt. It was just after eight o'clock in the evening. The children had to get out of their bath and run dripping into their bedroom to get their clothes on. The villa was in a right mess. All the washing was lying about and they hadn't tidied up from the children's day of games.

They were taken totally by surprise. It was Saturday 1st September, four days after the announcement of the release of the women and children. They were on a high, discussing when to poke their heads out, where to go, would they be safe, was the release an Iraqi trick, would Stephen be all right on his own?

To their surprise, the Iraqis didn't enter the house. Anne had heard of other villas where they had burst in and manhandled the British they discovered. But these were very civil, patient and apologetic. They wanted to take just Stephen and assured Anne he would be brought back within half an hour.

It was a very emotional time. They had no idea whether they would ever see him again. Anne told the children to say goodbye to him. They were crying, trying to be brave and not let him see how upset they were. Their family was being ripped apart.

Stephen was driven off in a requisitioned car, typical of the Kuwaiti vehicles Iraqi officers now used. Anne tried her best to get organised. They were all in a state of shock. She chivvied the children to get ready, packed some suitcases and collected together what possessions they could carry. All they had left of their home, of years of life in Kuwait, was now reduced to two suitcases and a few odds and ends. A few days before, the Iraqis had offered a substantial reward for every Westerner handed in, and threatened the death sentence for anyone found harbouring a Westerner. They were sure a Palestinian had told the Iraqis where they were, to collect his blood money. And, after they were taken away, they were sure it was another Palestinian who stripped their house bare.

The Iraqi officer was intelligent, polite and spoke excellent English. Apparently, he had studied for his PhD in England. But the rest were a rabble, poorly dressed and hardly soldiers at all, except for their Kalashnikovs. The jeeps and cars they were using were old and tatty. Some of the soldiers were grandparents and talked about their grandchildren as they waited, terribly apologetic about the inconvenience they were putting the British through. They didn't want to be there, they wanted to be back home with their own families. Anne described their indiscipline: "They were a joke. They kept giving the children sweets and Pepsis, telling them not to worry, showing off their photographs. They just didn't want to be there."

Stephen was taken to Ahmadi police station, which the Iraqis were using as a collection and interrogation point for captured foreigners. He was asked questions about himself and his family, though the officer was polite and it was not an interrogation. He was asked his name, where he worked and how long he had been in Kuwait, that was all.

Eventually, the Iraqi officer brought Stephen back to his family. He had been very anxious about Anne and the children. He managed to persuade the Iraqis to take them with him. If they were together and safe in a hotel, even though under armed guard, there was a much better chance of them getting out with the other wives and children. After a delay, the Iraqis took them off in a coach. More people had been rounded up in the operation. The driver drove around for a while, but didn't seem to know where he was going. They went around Ahmadi, across the desert, and around in a long, tedious circle. It was the middle of the night by now and they were getting very tired. At two o'clock in the morning, they reached the International Hotel, where they stayed for one night. The next day, they ended up at the Regency Palace Hotel, where they were put into a room to await their next move.

More raids went on as the Iraqis searched for men to replace the women and children released from the installations. They launched a major sweep and search campaign through certain areas of Kuwait City and the outlying towns. As always, they gave with one hand only to take with the other. In Kuwait, the decree to execute anyone harbouring foreigners was rigorously enforced, resulting in panic amongst some Arabs and quite a few arrests of Westerners. It was part of the steadily increasing terror the Iraqis were now imposing upon the population of Kuwait. They had failed to win the local population over, so were starting to kill them, replace them with Palestinians, or terrorise them into submission - in other words, fully integrate them into Iraqi democracy.

In one instance, an Iraqi patrol burst into an apartment hiding a group of Americans. Despite it being during the curfew, one of them made a dash for the window, jumped through it and tried to make a run for it. An Iraqi soldier ran to the window and fired after him. Shots peppered the ground around him and one bullet smashed through his forearm, shattering a bone. He grabbed it in pain and screamed. He stopped and held his bleeding arm as several other Iraqis ran up and arrested him. He was rapidly taken to a local hospital and given first-class medical treatment. The last thing the Iraqis wanted was another dead hostage.

News of the incident spread down the phone lines like a fireball. All Westerners in hiding were deeply alarmed. The use by soldiers of live ammunition when rounding them up was terrifying. The Iraqis speedily admitted the incident and the American embassy was allowed to see the man, but it still provoked a virulent attack from the US State Department. Partly in response to this incident, but also to generally increase the pressure on the Iraqi regime, it decided to expel a number of Iraqi diplomats from their embassy in Washington and severely restrict the movements of the remainder. Britain soon followed suit.

The 'guests' at the Meridien were well fed during their brief stay. Jane McAlindin and Janet Somerford and her three boys received a three-course meal with steak the single night they were kept there. Their rooms were very pleasant, each with a shower and bathroom and they were allowed to use the hotel's facilities, including the swimming pool. However, they couldn't leave the hotel. Plain clothes *Mukhabarat* kept a vigilant eye on them and the phones were tapped. Although they were allowed to make local calls, they kept their phone conversations to a minimum in case they could be traced. To the women's surprise, no attempt was made to get them to say where their menfolk were hiding.

In all, an estimated eighty British women and children were arrested the morning of the first convoy organised by the wardens. Many were taken to the Meridien but others, like Margaret and George Parkin, were in the Regency Palace. There were also a large number of men picked up following tip-offs and interrogations as a result of the women coming out, a key reason the Iraqis had allowed the women to go. There were also those families, like the Mansells, who had been picked up in the last few days as a result of information or house searches. They posed the Iraqis a problem. It was their fault the women and children had been detained, so they felt obliged to escort them up to Iraq. As the men would be useful to replace those women coming off the sites, they had to go up as well. The Iraqis decided to organise another convoy.

At precisely 5pm on Wednesday 5th September, the British held at the Regency Palace and Meridien hotels were ordered down to the foyers, and given five minutes to gather their belongings and climb into the waiting coaches. Jane McAlindin, Joe Wild, the Somerfords, Parkins and Mansells were all amongst those who went. There were about a hundred and eighty altogether, on six coaches. The two eldest Somerford boys, aged seventeen and eighteen were repeatedly assured by the Iraqis that they would be allowed out as 'students', as they were still at school. It turned out that this was merely to keep them happy until they reached Baghdad, when a different story was to unexpectedly emerge.

The Iraqis, for reasons best known to themselves, chose to split families by putting the men on some of the buses and the women on others. It was a cruel tactic. Once again, Anne Mansell and her three children were split up from Stephen, not knowing whether they could trust the Iraqis, or whether at Basra or some other point the men's coaches would suddenly veer off, never to be seen again. Once again, they had to say goodbye, not knowing whether they would *ever* be reunited. That was very nearly what happened.

Joe Wild recalled boarding the coach. "All our bags had to go in the back of the bus, because all the baggage space underneath was packed with the driver's loot, like televisions, videos, radios and clothes."

It was hell. They were on the coaches for fifteen hours in all. They soon became unbearably hot and sweaty. It was even worse for the men because their coaches had no air-conditioning. They were given virtually no food on the journey and only had what water they had brought with them. As they drove up the Mutlaa Ridge and along the Basra Road, they passed hundreds of cars and lorries laden with looted goods. A lot of the cars had Kuwaiti number plates, part of the loot as well, but most of the lorries were down from Baghdad and Basra, returning to the shops and market stalls of Iraq. They were piled high with household furniture, office equipment, parts of cars - from doors and engines to tyres and bumpers - machinery, clothing, shoes, and street signs. Several times Anne Mansell thought she spotted her three-piece suite going past the window.

They had Iraqi guards with them the whole journey, but this proved an advantage. The soldiers were relaxed and civil. They didn't threaten the passengers at all. Rather the reverse, as they would leave their guns lying about for anyone to pick up. In fact, they were able to speed through the roadblocks far quicker than the British-organised convoys, which took, on average, three to five hours longer to reach Baghdad. It was a very strange experience. The soldiers would walk up and down the aisles of the coaches offering passengers cigarettes and smiling, but they all had Kalashnikovs strapped over their shoulders. Smiling and apologising as they did so, they stopped the passengers listening to the World Service or Voice of America on their short-wave radios.

There were about seven coaches on the convoy. They stopped only twice to allow the passengers some relief. On neither occasion were there any toilets. The men had to use one half of the desert, the women the other, with the Iraqi soldiers watching as they tried to hide themselves behind pieces of scrub. The women with trousers on were in a particularly embarrassing position, but they couldn't do anything about it. They had to just laugh it off.

Joe Wild graphically explained their plight. "It was terribly degrading. The women had to go to the toilet in front of the guards. They had an air-conditioned bus with all the babies, but by then it was starting to smell."

By the second stop, the night had drawn in. The coaches were cooler and the women and children could settle down to get some sleep. However, the roads were badly worn and repeated jolting made sleeping impossible. The coaches were still very stuffy, starting to smell with used nappies and stale sweat. Few could get more than fitful bursts of sleep in the cramped conditions. On Margaret Parkin's coach they had no food other than twelve sandwiches for the whole bus. They hadn't been fed before they had left, so were famished by the time the coach approached Baghdad in the early morning. One woman sitting near to her was in a desperate state. She had a new-born baby with her, barely a week old. She had given birth whilst under detention by the Iraqis. It had been a caesarian and the wound was opening with all the bumps. The baby too was suffering. It was underweight and had diarrhoea, possibly dysentery. It cried with pain throughout the journey.

As it turned out, the men's coaches followed them all the way to Baghdad but, outside the Melia al-Mansour Hotel, the men were let off their coaches whilst the women and children were ordered to stay in theirs. By now it was eight in the morning. Anne immediately realised that the men were being taken away and she wouldn't see Stephen again. The Iraqis were refusing to let their families off even to say farewell. There was so much Anne had to say. All their luggage was mixed up with the men's. She couldn't understand why their captors had suddenly become far harsher towards them, but of course, the whole mood of the Iraqis changed in Baghdad, right under the noses of the state police and Ba'athist Party apparatchiks.

Jane McAlindin described the sudden change in the Iraqis' demeanour. "The Melia al-Mansour was the worst place for being treated. They weren't nice to us at all. They were quite harsh, giving us sharp orders and shouting. They weren't going to let us off the coaches." Margaret Parkin remembers the argument which developed as well. "They wouldn't let the women off their buses, but the women refused to be separated from the men." Her husband George was amongst those who had been taken into the Melia al-Mansour. She wasn't about to leave him without a proper goodbye. "The women decided they needed to do something. They all simply rose and climbed off the coaches. There was nothing the Iraqis could do about it."

Presented with this sudden surge, the Iraqis caved in. They were completely unprepared for women and children to disobey them. By the time they overcame their shock, the passengers were past them and into the hotel. As the soldiers went off to ask their officers what to do, the women were reunited with their men. They were to have just one more hour together.

Most of the women had left their husbands in Kuwait. They grabbed something to eat and drink and used the toilets whilst the others spent the time saying their farewells and discussing last-minute financial and personal arrangements. It was an extremely emotional time. Finally parting from their husbands and fathers was sickeningly heart-rending. They felt positively ill. For days, they had been building up to this, trying their best to prepare, to be strong. But when those final moments came, even the bravest broke down.

Stephen Mansell was one who was deeply upset. Living in hiding had been very difficult for him and the days in the Regency Palace hadn't seen a great improvement. Anne had to constantly keep his spirits up, as well as her own and the children's. None of them could keep back the tears.

But Anne didn't cry for long. No, that was not how she wanted Stephen to remember them. She was determined that their final memory of being together would not be a scene of great wailing and tearing of hair but up-beat and optimistic. She tried to pass the occasion off, to tell them it would all be over soon, Dad would manage very well on his own and he'd be back with them, sniff... in a few weeks.

As they waited, they were given a peculiar floor show. A couple of Iraqis came into the foyer to distribute their passports, but neither could read them properly and they mispronounced their names so badly they were unintelligible. "It ended up a complete farce. Nobody could get their passports. It took them two hours to take all our names and details."

All too soon the Iraqis received their instructions from the mountain top and ordered the women and children back onto the coaches. By now, the women had sorted their luggage from the men's. They only had time for a few hasty words before they were wrenched from each other. The bags separated, the families separated.

"The Iraqis didn't even help us with our bags," Jane McAlindin explained. "And some women had babies and pushchairs to cope with. There was no system on the buses. It was just everyone clambering on. The Iraqis were totally unhelpful. They wouldn't even help a woman who was pregnant. They couldn't've cared less."

Perhaps the Iraqis enjoyed seeing the British women struggling. Perhaps it was beneath their dignity as men to help women. Perhaps it gave them a peculiar sense of superiority. Or was it simple revenge? "And all the time they refused to let the British embassy people come into the Melia al-Mansour Hotel. We hadn't seen anybody from our embassy in that time. The Iraqis wouldn't let any of them in."

In one final act of cruelty, the Iraqis suddenly refused to allow the eldest Somerford boy to travel with the coach. After having promised all the way that he would be allowed out, and being permitted to travel up from Kuwait on a coach with the women and children, and even allowed back on the coach as the women were about to leave, he was curtly ordered to join the men. Janet Somerford argued ferociously with the guards, pleading with them to let her son travel with them.

"I was promised he could go."

"We have men of sixteen in our army. Your son is a man."

"He's not. He's still at school. I was promised he could come out with us."

"No, he must come off the coach. Now. No, now. Perhaps he can come with you tomorrow, but today he must stay." The Iraqi was deliberately lying to placate Mrs Somerford, but she would have none of it. She kept on at the Iraqi, until it was clear his temper was about to go. The eldest son couldn't watch his mother being intimidated and getting so upset.

He suddenly turned to the other passengers and told them he would have to leave. He walked off the bus to spend three lonely months at Basra power station.

There were also problems with the second brother, who was coming up to his seventeenth birthday in a few days. The British embassy had to rush his visa through as rapidly as possible and get him on the very first flight they could. He did just get out.

The women left the men at the Melia al-Mansour and were taken to the ar-Rashid. They arrived there at midday. By now, they hadn't eaten for twenty-eight hours, nor slept properly for thirty. They were exhausted and very emotional.

The ar-Rashid is a plush and comfortable hotel. It has a spacious, cool, marbled entrance hall and large foyer. The menu is *à la carte* and the bedrooms are very pleasant, all with private bathrooms. The women were allowed to visit the local *souk* and the hotel was clearly making an effort for its British 'guests', including those resident businessmen unable to leave.

At the Melia al-Mansour a whole floor was sealed off under armed guard and used to accommodate the British men. Americans were on another floor. The hotel was the holding point, the processing plant, the prison ship, storing them in its hold for a few nights before shipping them off again.

After one night, Stephen Mansell and George Parkin were whisked away to an installation at Basra. Joe Wild went to al-Muldane a few days later, and the other men were rapidly farmed out to sites all over the country.

On the day of the second Iraqi convoy, a second British convoy was also organised. It was for those who had missed the first one and was broadcast as their last chance to leave Kuwait in an organised way, though others did drift out over the following months and there was a late, abortive attempt to fly some out of Kuwait.

Only fifty-one Britons turned up for the buses, plus eight Americans and a German. Once again, the wardens had expected far more, up to two hundred, but part of their miscalculation may have been the large number captured on the morning of the first convoy, who were thus unaccounted for. They left at dawn. Once again, although there were Iraqis around the buses as they loaded they had no Iraqi guards, no embassy official, nor any wardens on board other than Dorothy Goodwin. Incredibly, her husband Peter was travelling with her. He had shaved his arms and legs, put on make-up, a dress and covered his hair. He boarded the bus as Jennifer Price, but his disguise was so hopelessly ineffectual, it failed to fool the Iraqis standing around the rendezvous point. They contacted their officer and refused to let the coaches go. They kept calling for Mrs Price to get off, until he was forced to go. He was very nervous as he climbed down, petrified of being taken away and shot. He was removed from the bus and taken to one of the installations at Basra.

Dorothy didn't see him again until November, when she returned to Baghdad with a group of women to plead for their menfolk's release.

When the buses arrived in Baghdad, after familiar hassles they were put up at the Melia al-Mansour. Their accommodation was paid for by the British embassy. Whilst this was essential to ensure the British citizens escaped safely, it still rankles with the government that it was billed for what amounted to costs of kidnapping its citizens and holding them to ransom. As usual, the Iraqis denied the British embassy access to the hotel. With the arrival of the convoy, some seven hundred Britons, the vast majority women and children, had now been bussed up from Kuwait. Perhaps another hundred and fifty had come in from installations in Iraq. All had arrived safely, though many were in far from good health.

By now, it was shortly after the first flights out of two hundred and twenty-one British citizens. The British embassy estimated there were four hundred Britons "in transit" in Kuwait and Iraq, *ie* in hotels waiting to be flown out or shipped to installations. It believed that another two hundred were actually at the installations and one thousand eight hundred were in hiding in Kuwait - this figure was about a thousand too high - whilst four hundred were living in relative freedom in Iraq.

With the benefit of hindsight and a much clearer idea of the numbers involved, it is possible to estimate these figures far more accurately. However, those figures with ? are 'guestimates', and all figures have been rounded off.

Britons Taken Hostage by The Iraqis
August 1990

	Total Hostages	Women and Children out	Men Left
BA Flight 149	200	130?	70?
British Liaison Team	100	65?	35
Caught in hotels	30?	10?	20?
4 BA crews	70	30	40
Arrested 1st-19th	50?	15?	35?
Arrested 20th-28th	120	70?	50?
First British convoy	80	80	0
After first convoy	100	0?	100?
Totals	750	400	350

Although some of these figures are very tentative, it is clear that the numbers of British involved were far higher than anyone suspected at the time. This is not surprising. The Iraqis were much more successful than believed in rounding Britons up and were very adept at keeping them hidden from the embassies and the media.

Of the seven hundred Britons bussed up from Kuwait, 271 had come on the first British convoy and 81 on the second. About 25 had followed on an Australian convoy, and a few more made their way up later, making perhaps 400 who came up independently of the Iraqis.

The first Iraqi convoy brought out an estimated 130, the second 180, totalling 310. Thus, over 700 British people, overwhelmingly women and children, made the journey up to Baghdad and were processed through its hotels, either on their way to the airport or to strategic sites.

Of the estimated 3,000 Britons in Kuwait on 2nd August, over a 1,200 had escaped, leaving under 1,800 in the emirate. Of these, the Iraqis had lifted 750 and 350 women and children had journeyed up on the British convoys, on the Australian convoy, or by car, and had left on the flights. Thus, less than 700 remained in hiding, nearer a third of the number estimated at the time.

The last two convoys arrived on the sixth, as three hundred and six women and children from the first British convoy were leaving for the airport and home. The new arrivals were too late to journey out with them. They had to get visas, a process which would take another three days.

Within the ar-Rashid the women had a great deal more freedom than at the Melia al-Mansour. The whole atmosphere was more relaxed. Anne Mansell was able to use the squash courts and go swimming. There were large gardens with a pond, shaded areas to sit and wander in, a coffee shop and various dining rooms. It had been built to accommodate state dignitaries and so had bullet-proof plate-glass windows to protect them and electronic bugs everywhere to listen in on them.

A further difference to the Melia al-Mansour was that the embassy staff were allowed access to it. The ones who tended to visit were actually Kuwaiti embassy staff who had been relocated to the Baghdad embassy. They talked to the women in small groups, never as a whole, and handed them forms to fill in which asked for their basic details. They told them that two flights had already reached England without any major hiccups, which reassured them. "But we were all aware we were still in Iraq and they could change their minds at any time," Jane McAlindin emphasised. The women also had visits from several people from the Baghdad community, notably 'Tug' Wilson, who had gathered money together to buy the people from Kuwait clothes, toiletries, cigarettes and any other necessity they were short of. These supplies were very welcome indeed.

When the time came on Sunday the ninth for them to leave for the airport, seven coaches came to pick them up. There was an embassy person on each one. The airport was chaotic. It was a mad scramble to get their luggage out of the coaches and into the airport. There were a lot of Irish and Americans already there, waiting for their flights. The Americans had been flown up from Kuwait that day and had only a few hours stop-over before their flight, a totally different experience to the British. With so many people trying to get onto the planes, the concourse was packed. No one was given a seat number for their flight, so had no certainty of getting on the plane at all. Nor did the airport staff check the luggage. "Everyone was scared there weren't going to be enough seats on the plane. There was that sort of tension at the time."

Once they had checked through, the British passengers sat in the departure lounge for several hours until their flight was ready. The tension stayed with them throughout this time. No one knew whether they would be taken back to the hotels at the last moment, a very real worry as planes were announced as cancelled or delayed, then reinstated.

In the end, they did not have very long to wait. The flight was only three hours late - almost on time, Iraqi-style. It left in the early evening. They were well treated on the plane, an Iraqi Airways jumbo jet. Two meals were served and they watched a film, although there was no sound. There was no duty-free, but otherwise it seemed like a perfectly normal flight. After they had landed at Gatwick and were taxiing towards the terminal building, the stewardesses actually asked them if they had enjoyed their stay in Iraq and hoped they would visit their country again.

There had been a muted cheer when the plane had taken off and more exuberant celebration when it landed at ten o'clock at night, British time, but nothing like a party atmosphere. It was relief rather than elation. Jane McAlindin summed up their feelings: "Everyone was happy to be back, but it was very subdued."

Despite the throbbing pain from her operation to remove a wisdom tooth, Josie made the journey to Gatwick with Stephen to meet the third flight. They made their way down in the afternoon and were ushered through the security room where they were given lapel badges. They were then directed to the Sir Winston Churchill Suite. It was quite familiar to them now. There were none of the problems with long queues waiting for security clearance and the room was already filling up with relatives waiting for the flight to land. Once it did, they were bussed over to the arrival lounge at the side of the airport reserved for relatives and voluntary organisations. Members of the London helpline, notably Andy Charles, who met every flight, were already there with their stall and information leaflets.

By now, the Foreign Office and the airport had got their act together. On Saturday the eighth, as soon as they knew a flight was due to arrive on the Sunday, the wheels rapidly turned. Gatwick's Airport Duty Manager was phoned by the Consular Emergency Unit. He in turn called the Red Cross which organised forty-five volunteers to be on hand. He then phoned Travelcare, volunteers who are trained to help people arriving at Britain's airports, and Gatwick's chaplain, the Reverend Stuart Wilson was alerted. He in turn contacted the Salvation Army, Roman Catholic priests, the Methodists and five local Church of England vicars.

Meanwhile, the Foreign Office phoned the relatives of those it believed were on the flight, as well as the MoD, Social Services, the Housing Department, coach operators, taxi firms and caterers. Ten times the normal compliment of airport staff detailed to a flight, some one hundred and thirty, were on hand.

First figures on the number on board came through. A hundred and seventy-six Britons, over a hundred Americans and forty-five others. The staff were called together and their specific responsibilities explained. Some would be on the aircraft, some on the runway, some on the coaches, others at various points inside the terminals, either with the relatives or waiting for the returnees. Immigration was told to process people as speedily as possible and the MoD had forms for the passengers which asked for details on themselves and on those they had left in Kuwait or Iraq. Foreign Office personnel were on hand to offer advice and help. Other voluntary organisations were there, as they had been for every flight and table lined one wall with coats and clothing donated by several large department stores.

Again, there was confusion over precisely who the passengers were. The Iraqis hadn't supplied a manifest and their first figures proved incorrect. There were actually a hundred and ninety British, including ninety-six children, plus a hundred and seventy-five Americans and seventy-two others, of fourteen different nationalities - four hundred and thirty-seven in all. One of the Americans had died of a heart attack in Iraq and his body was being flown home.

Relatives were sitting about in small groups unsure whether their loved ones were on the plane or not. Even when the plane landed at 10pm, they didn't know for certain. When the passengers eventually came through at about eleven o'clock, some relatives were disappointed. They waited until after one in the morning, when the very last people drifted through, still with no joy, and had to return home alone. It was very hard for them. As Josie Brookes explained, "How awful to be built up and smashed down again."

But for most it was a time of incredible relief and tension. Jane McAlindin was overwhelmed by the reception they received when they walked into the arrival lounge. "I for one didn't expect there to be anyone to meet me, because my family are all from Scotland. The British Airways stewardesses had asked me if anyone would be there to meet me and I'd said, no, I don't think so. I had no idea what the situation was going to be like. When I saw the number of people there waiting, I was shocked. I had no idea it would be so big, or that there would be so many people. I think none of us realised how much our plight had affected people back in Britain. We didn't know what they were being told or what they were thinking. I suppose we were fearing the worst when we were over there. None of us had any idea of the concern people had for us over here. I was completely unprepared for all the clapping and cheering. It was overwhelming, really. Then I heard the voice of my Mum. That was it for me. I was very emotional. I burst into tears with relief and joy."

There was as much cheering, as much crying and hugging, as for all the other flights, if not more. Josie too was overcome. "What an experience and, oh, it was horrendous to see people coming through with little children, their relatives just waiting, fathers and mothers crying altogether. That was a most difficult time for both Stephen and me. I hoped we could find the strength to hang on. It got to us both."

The first children to come through were Chinese. They were lovely children, but had a fixed, glazed expression on their faces and huddled in bedraggled blankets wrapped around their little bodies. They were very upset as they met their relatives. "How they put on such a brave face! They were shivering, so I picked up an armful of jumpers and slowly approached a group of them. They didn't object as I walked slowly up to them and knelt beside them. I attempted to talk to them and put the jumpers on. They were too big for the little ones, but their parents didn't mind. They had a long, cold and tiring journey ahead of them."

Everyone coming off was in tears. One slim young woman had a baby in a carry holster on her front. The baby was asleep, but she was crying. She was in a flimsy cotton shirt, brown culottes and boots. She looked very pale and exhausted. Four more small children followed her, wrapped in blue blankets. Two were three-year-old twins. All were in light summer clothing, gaunt, with staring expressions. They looked forlorn, their eyes full of bewilderment and wonder. They didn't know where they were, or even who they were any more.

The mother was breaking her heart. Her parents were so tense themselves before she came into the arrival lounge, but their daughter was absolutely distraught at leaving her husband. She didn't know whether she would ever see him again. The flight had been awful for her children. None of them had eaten or had much to drink. The baby had been hungry the whole time, but she had been too exhausted and thirsty to provide him with milk. They had endured the hell of that baking journey up from Kuwait, the confusion and worry at Baghdad, the hours of waiting in the plane on the runway in temperatures in the forties centigrade, and now stood in temperatures around zero in the middle of a cold September night. For security reasons, they had all been made to disembark away from the terminal and walk across the windy, freezing runway. Her five children were pale and shivering with the cold. They had left Kuwait with nothing. Josie and the other members of the support group approached them with more jumpers. The girls, aged seven and five, and the twins, were fitted with some, but the baby boy was too tiny.

The mother explained to her parents the awfulness of their month in Kuwait and their journey home. She had been given only five minutes to pack her bags and gather the children onto the bus for Baghdad. The children had been forced to use a bowl for a toilet on the bus and at Baghdad airport she had been made to carry and lead her children across the tarmac to the plane and struggle up the steps into the crowded seats without help. One of her children cried throughout the whole flight. They were desolate. She had no idea what she would do now, no idea how she would get money or manage with the children by herself, even with her parents by her side.

Stephen Brookes wasn't immune to the very special human tragedy unravelling before his eyes that night. He was about to experience his worst moment of the entire crisis. He still recalls it amidst tears. "I went up to one lad. He was maybe seven or eight. I'd found an anorak just the right size for him. I went over to him but made the mistake of trying to put the anorak round him. I surrounded him. I was a man surrounding him. He was terrified. I'd never seen terror in a child's eyes before. The only men he'd seen for the last month had been Iraqi soldiers killing his friends and he couldn't cope with it. Neither could I." He paused briefly. "But I made a joke of it. We couldn't get his arm through the sleeve of this anorak. We laughed. Eventually, his hand came through and took mine and wouldn't let it go. He just wouldn't let it go." It was a pivotal experience for Stephen. He recalled that boy's eyes. They brought home to him precisely what those people had been going through. "How could that man Saddam, how could the Iraqis do that? How could they? That was the worst form of brutality and torture you could do to anybody, to make a child fearful of other people. They set my mind firmly that we would do whatever we could. At that moment, we decided we would do everything we could for those people. We would go and beat the Iraqi ambassador's door down, we would fight people as determinedly as we could, to make something happen."

Myra Wetherspoon was also on that flight, with her five children. Janet Somerford met her parents and described to them why her eldest son was not with her. She went home in great distress. Anne Mansell was met by her mother and father and by the local press. They had actually interviewed her in Baghdad because Thames TV were following the story of her parents every week, as a personalised attempt to keep up with developments. When she returned, she found the TV cameras following her back to her house and filming the welcome home party. There were a lot of them. But it was too overwhelming for Anne and her three children.

Stephen and Josie slept overnight at the Hilton Hotel by the airport. They were up again at seven to return to Coventry. They had breakfast on the motorway and, before returning home, visited a local radio station to record an interview on the sick and elderly, requesting people send in information. When they eventually arrived back at their house, their volunteers were waiting for them. They had been staffing the phones all the time they had been away, taking hundreds of calls from relatives and wives just released. It was two o'clock in the afternoon. Josie was so exhausted she slipped straight into bed and immediately fell asleep.

In a final act to this drama, James Tansley, a Baghdad embassy official, flew down to Kuwait to persuade any lingering women and children out of Kuwait. The embassy had jointly chartered a plane to fly from Kuwait up to Baghdad with the Americans. About a hundred women, mainly without children, were believed to still be in Kuwait. They were asked to assemble at a Safeways car park, to be taken to the military airport north-west of Jahra. The World Service broadcast the arrangements and exhortations to leave over the airwaves.

Mr Tansley also tried to get access to meet Michael Weston and the three other officials trapped inside the Kuwait embassy, but without any luck. The Iraqis refused point-blank to let him near the compound. Meanwhile, the Bangladeshi, Swiss, Greek and Austrian governments announced they were withdrawing their missions from the emirate. There were now fourteen hanging out, all with dwindling supplies of food and water and no electricity apart from that provided by private generators.

Despite James Tansley's and the embassy's efforts, most of the remaining women refused to come out. The flight, which would have been a godsend a week earlier, was too late.

Heroines for a Day

"At first, when I got home, I didn't cry or anything, I didn't cry in front of people. I think it was still too much for me to take in. A lot of the time, even when I was in Kuwait, I used to think it was a dream - you know, it wasn't really happening. It was too much to comprehend."

Fatima cautiously climbed down the slippery, cold steps from the Boeing, letting her nine-year-old son Ishak lead her and her two-year-old daughter to the waiting British Airways staff. She was a Kuwaiti married to an Englishman. She had never been to England before, spoke no English and had no address to go to. Her black *abaya* blew in the wind, causing her to lose her balance on the bottom steps. She tripped and fell, but was caught by a steward. She was heavily pregnant and felt the baby kick her violently as she landed on the man. She apologised in Arabic as he steadied her and pointed his hand in the direction of the waiting bus. She shivered as she crossed the tarmac in the cold September night and as the chill cut through her thin cotton clothes. Another steward wrapped her daughter and son in blue blankets as they climbed aboard the bus.

The vehicle took the women and children across to the arrival suite, where they passed through several rooms and corridors to meet their relatives. Fatima blinked in the harsh light of the lounge and cringed at the cheers and shouting. As women rushed passed her to greet their relatives, she crept away to a side wall with her two charges and waited, completely lost. After a few minutes, a Salvation Army volunteer came up to her and tried to communicate. He couldn't see her face beneath her purdah veil. She shook her head at him as he spoke, petrified as to who he was or what he might do. The man went away, only to come back with a helper from the support group and an Arab man who was able to speak with her. The Arab discovered she had no one to meet her and nowhere to go, so told her to come with him. She followed, her children close beside, fear staring from their exhausted eyes. They were taken to the DSS stall, where the man explained the woman's situation and several forms were filled in. She needed money and help to buy essentials for her children and also needed immediate accommodation.

As others were leaving in their cars or Foreign Office supplied taxies, the man took Fatima to the Housing Department stall where they arranged somewhere for her to stay. It would not be salubrious. That first night was all right. She was put up in a hotel at the airport, in a large room, with a cot for her little girl and beds for her and her son. But the next day she was driven into London and moved into a double-room in a bed and breakfast guest house.

Fatima was visited once or twice by social workers, concerned as much about her children as anything else. She received an emergency payment and help with buying clothes and food. She was taken to a doctor, who prescribed vitamins and plenty of rest. After she had settled in she was left to fend for herself at the shops, existing in her single room with her two children as best she could, until her husband was released from hiding in Kuwait three months later. He tried to look after her but was severely hampered by having lost his money, job and house.

"The Salvation Army was superb," Joanna Copley beamed, describing the scenes at the airport and the desperate need of some families as they arrived. "It was very, *very* good. It had a big operation and helped us get housing for people. It made its hostels available to us, looked after people and made sure they were all right through regular checks. In fact, its visiting officers kept a close eye on families who were moved into rented accommodation or guest houses. We would get calls from them telling us if someone had acute problems and asking us to help as much as we could. It referred people to us if it thought they needed counselling. We also referred families to it. It worked both ways."

There were ambulances at both Heathrow and Gatwick to meet every flight. A substantial number of the young women returning were pregnant, some in the later stages. For them the coach and plane journey had been even more traumatic. Several had to contend with high blood pressure and excessive emotional and physical strain. Many, including children, were suffering from diarrhoea. Any suspected cases of dysentery had to be deal with immediately. Others had the worry of babies only a few days old. They were exhausted. The ambulances, medics and doctors were on hand to help them, give them check-ups and prescribe medication for them.

The Gulf Support Group had hurriedly prepared an information sheet for the flights. Virtually everyone who came off them received a copy, so they could contact the support group should they wish to. It explained who they were, what the support group was for, and the help it could give... "You may want to talk about your experiences" ... "there may be people you are still concerned about" ... "finding accommodation" ... "financial problems" ... "intermediary with the press" ... "complete confidentiality" ... "we accept reverse charge calls". It gave guidelines for social security, income support, resettlement grants, travel grants and signing on. It mentioned the Poll Tax, which became the bane of many families in the succeeding months. It told them about Citizen's Advice Bureaux and local government offices. A whole page was devoted to job-hunting, giving addresses and suggestions. It discussed how people could get their mortgages deferred, surrender their insurance policies and cash in their investments. These were the basic financial facts many returning women needed to know in order to survive. Some had not been to Britain for years; a few had never been here before. In their joint paper for the *British Medical Journal*, Dr Easton and Dr Turner found that a significant number of people who replied to their questionnaire had returned to face "serious accommodation problems".

Two pages of the news-sheet was devoted to health. The support group had anticipated that the returnees would suffer from stress, fatigue, under-nourishment, depression and sickness. It was not proved wrong. The anxiety of the families was scrawled across their faces in indelible ink. Those home-comings were not joyous occasions. Many felt they couldn't cope; those who felt they could had no idea of the problems which lay ahead. Of course, their relations were glad they were home, but it was a time of crying and of relief.

Stress came out in physical symptoms. Families suffered a lot of illnesses during the first weeks back. Some women found they were suffering so badly from tension they didn't eat properly until their husbands came home in December, even after that. Some had nightmares, others suffered from attacks of vomiting, poor concentration, inability to hold down even the simplest of jobs, difficulty in talking, withdrawal, and repeated flashbacks to Kuwait and Iraq. One woman said she coped by thinking of her husband as dead.

According to the report by Dr Easton and Dr Turner mentioned above, a number of families returning suffered from post-traumatic stress disorder, which is associated with flash-backs, bad dreams, lack of concentration and depression, as well as severe functional impairment, avoidance behaviour and changes in attitudes. The study covered both returning families and the men who came back and found that 55% of the people it surveyed had "lost their livelihood as a result of the invasion and, a year after they came back, 123 [31%] were still unemployed... 47% reported that their physical health deteriorated in the Gulf. Some reported serious problems, including untreated bacillary and amoebic dysentery, giardiasis [which causes diarrhoea and nausea] and absent medication. A pregnant woman lost ten kilos and had repeated untreated blood loss." 83% of the survey reported weight loss, "often very considerable, many losing eighteen to twenty-five kilos". 81% thought they might be killed. Several men were forced to watch their wives being raped.

The report also highlighted psychological problems the families and men had endured. 54% felt guilty at being safely home whilst their husbands were still trapped and 55% suffered from "abnormal" health and psychological problems.

The support group recommended all returnees see a sympathetic doctor. It also recommended counselling and suggested how they might be reacting. "Many people feel intense guilt about Kuwait and other friends they have left behind. If you have lost your home and business in Kuwait, it is difficult immediately to find the courage to start again."

Revealingly, it pointed out to the returnees that "relatives here have also faced crises. Many have been near to nervous breakdown and, now that you are back, need to talk as well... You may find that parental or marital relationships have changed as a result of stress and that you need a period of adjustment. Children in particular can find it difficult..." Clearly, the support group was *extremely* anxious about the emotional state the women and children and their relatives would be in after they were reunited. Unfortunately, its fears were to prove well-founded.

Especially on flights later in September and early October, but also on the first ones, there were a significant number of women who had been living in Kuwait or Iraq for many years. Quite a few were married to Kuwaitis or Iraqis. Quite a few were Arab women married to British men. Often they were young, with three or four children to cope with, and sometimes pregnant as well. They had been out of the country for years, or never been here. Many women said how much Britain had changed and how depressed the place looked. Most suffered from culture shock, having been thrown from a blisteringly hot desert with a rich Arab culture to a cold, damp, urban environment of economic depression. The weather was different, the language was different, the religion was different, the laws were different, and financially they had fallen from being well-off to being pauperised. Their children arrived in blankets because they had no warm clothing and those without British or EEC passports had to apply to the Home Office for refugee status.

Many women hadn't seen their parents for years, or had never met their parents-in-law, with whom they now had to share a home with. Some had become estranged from their parents who had, perhaps, disapproved of them marrying a Kuwaiti or Iraqi, or from their parents-in-law, who objected to their son marrying an Arab woman, and had simply broken off all relations. They didn't know how much a pint of milk or loaf of bread cost. They didn't know about the transport system, about family allowances, or their DSS entitlements. They had come from the family life of the Arabs where women were more restricted, but also more protected, to being lone adults with all the responsibilities of caring for a family and having to make every decision completely by themselves. They were totally displaced emotionally, culturally, economically and geographically.

At their most vulnerable and most in need, these women were most isolated. They had no idea how to survive in this country. For some, their children couldn't speak English or understand British society. They had never been to British schools. It was a complete culture shock for them too. In a few situations, where mothers had no room or were otherwise unable to cope, families were split up as children went to stay with grandparents or aunts. These families were totally displaced. They were refugees in all but name.

But *were* they refugees? Should they have had precisely what everyone else had, or did they deserve extra resources? It is very hard to argue that the returnees *didn't* deserve special treatment. True, most of them were not refugees and would be horrified to be called that. They had lived in

Kuwait and Iraq whilst their husbands were on relatively short-term contracts. A lot had homes here and plenty of relatives who could look after them. They had money here and knew the country well. A few had simply been on holiday in Kuwait when Iraq invaded. But there was a small number to whom none of the above criteria applied. They had no relatives, or were estranged from them. They had no home and many couldn't speak English. They had nothing. No furniture, clothes, money or possessions.

These families were housed in very poor accommodation; bed and breakfast rooms, hostels or hard-to-let council properties. Contrary to the belief at the time, they weren't depriving British families of housing because these were properties people in Britain didn't want to live in. They were cold, frequently old or jerry-built, often damp, occasionally vandalised. Norma was typical. She was a British woman married to an Irishman. He was badly ill and, as the Irish were able to leave, he came out with her. They returned to Coventry to live temporarily with friends. They were offered some appalling accommodation by the council, which they refused, until they were eventually given a pokey flat on an estate. They had to beg for money to buy secondhand carpets, a cheap suite, a bed, curtains and a few second-hand pieces of furniture from their DSS furnishings grant. They had only a few pounds a week to live on, from which they had to buy clothes, pay heating bills and eat. Josie Brookes even went a the local radio station to beg for furniture, bedding and cooking utensils for them. It was not just hard, it was dire.

Other women were in as bad a way. One, who had been interviewed by ITN in Baghdad on a coach when it arrived from Kuwait, had been very strident and confident at the time. She had wanted an action group set up and other things done for the men. By the time she arrived at Gatwick the trauma had exhausted her. She was bitter at the government for not doing more to get them released. She was hyped-up about it and very resentful. She had left her husband in Kuwait and moved in with his parents, whom she found difficult to get along with. She began to suffer badly from health problems and became very nervous. Over the next few weeks, she descended into a state of emotional and physical collapse.

The Foreign Office had predicted that some families would not be met by relatives. Some were put up in bed and breakfast accommodation in London until they could sort themselves out, in some cases for several months. Others had to find rented accommodation or move in with parents or parents-in-law. The initial relief at being finally safe and basking in the glow of media attention - although many wished the media would just go away - rapidly changed to depression, the feeling that the world had forgotten their plight, and that their whole world had collapsed around them. It had.

It was a similar feeling to post-natal depression, a sudden let-down mingled with trauma and a feeling of abandonment. They felt bitter that they had lost everything and yet so little was being done to help them by the government. In many ways, their real problems had only just begun.

When Barbara Griffiths arrived home to her house in Cheshire, she had no clothes, no money, nothing. She was dominated by the loss of Stewart, her husband, who was on an installation in Iraq. She felt so alone, making a cup of tea for herself, trying to make a meal, forcing herself to eat. She just wanted to be back in Kuwait. She wished she hadn't come out. She wished she was still there with her friends and her husband. It was all such a horrible waste, a dreadful nightmare. She spent all that first night crying.

Barbara wished she was back in Kuwait for many days and weeks to come. A year later, she still wished she hadn't come out. She was racked with guilt both at what she had gone through herself and at not being with her husband, as though both were her fault. She feels her capture by the Iraqis and detention in the IBI camp were punishment for trying to escape. She couldn't sleep, even though she had managed only three full nights of sleep since the second of August, and had eventually to visit her doctor because of sheer exhaustion.

The attitude of people around her didn't make it any easier. At times it was frankly abrasive and rude. "Their attitude was: OK, you've been out there, you've had a good time, you must've had a good life, so you'll have to get on with it."

Rachel[1], from Newcastle, had been a bubbly, extrovert character but the month in hiding, then the journey up to Baghdad and the flight home had destroyed much in her. She was insecure, unsure of herself and other people, and shook physically with trauma. The ordeal of saying goodbye to her husband, Bill, in Kuwait had been too much for her to bear but when she arrived in England she found her problems had only just begun. She was used to dressing smartly and well, but arrived with no clothes or shoes apart from the ones she was wearing. Whilst on the outside she appeared strong enough to offer help to others, inside she was an emotional wreck, crumbling into little pieces.

Rachel came back to her grown daughter and, fortunately, had a property in Newcastle she could move into, but it was so cold and lonely without her husband. All the things which had brought them together, all their memories, now seemed to pull at her heart, reminding her of her loss. Her great sense of humour had been worn down by difficulty after difficulty. Tiny incidents blew out of all proportion. She had one pair of boots which she lovingly cared for during the financial hardship of those months on her own. But when a heel broke, it was the last straw. It seemed as though all her attempts to keep her life together and retain some semblance of respectability had been defeated. She felt totally emotionally and physically drained. Everything was such an effort. Just keeping going was so hard to do. She felt so tired, so tired.

"Why do I feel so tired? Why can't I do things as I used to? Why is everything such an effort? Why do I cry and cry and cry?" She stared at

[1]Her name has been changed.

the broken heel and held it in place, as if by some miracle it would bond together again. She wept more than she had ever wept in her life. Rather than diminishing now they were out of Kuwait and Iraq, the emotional stress suffered by many families grew as the weeks went by. Rather than their trauma being over once they landed at Heathrow or Gatwick, the worst was just beginning. Some children underwent great psychological hardship. They were missing their fathers desperately and finding it hard to adjust to new schools. Some families could no longer afford to send their children to the boarding schools they had been in, perhaps having to change schools in the final years before exams.

Simultaneously, the threat of war was rising and the feeling that their menfolk would be trapped in Kuwait and Iraq was gripping whole families. Their tension, sleepless nights, headaches and medical problems were worsening. Women were ill with overwork, worry and stress. It was impossible for some of them to cope even with daily chores or cooking meals for the children. Sons and daughters were constant reminders of missing fathers, especially when they would ask twenty times a day, "Mummy, when is Daddy coming home?". Many were living on the edge of their nerves, verging on a nervous breakdown. And some went over the edge.

Decisions were so difficult to make. They wanted someone to talk to about them, to share things with, to take the burden of responsibility from their shoulders and give them a break from constant anxiety. At times, life seemed too unbearable. They had to search for jobs whilst trying to find schools for their children and buy them clothes for the winter. It was horrendous.

It is difficult to imagine the extent to which financial worries dominated many women, but they became paramount. No matter how much they missed their husbands, they still had to find a roof for their children, buy them warm clothes and pay the gas bill. With winter approaching, this became desperate. So they greatly appreciated financial advice from the helplines, especially from Stephen and Josie at Coventry, both of whom were financial consultants, and from a financial expert brought in by the London helpline.

The families needed help and, in practice, only the Gulf Support Group was offering it. Certainly, government departments such as the DSS weren't. It will be a permanent black mark again the DSS that it left many of these families to flounder in those months; often unsympathetic, frequently forcing them to beg and wait, seldom giving them the help they were crying out for. These families were not only forgotten; when they tried to be heard, they were ignored.

When Anne arrived back with her three children, they were all ill. They had managed to contain their stress and worry on the journey back but once safely home, it all came out. They were emotionally drained. The two eldest were both joining new schools, but started them a month late. Joanna, aged twelve, was very ill. It wasn't with a disease, but because she was totally run down. During her first term, she was constantly in the sick bay. It was a similar story with her elder brother, Stuart, aged fifteen.

"My youngest, Stephanie, who's four now, has been to four different schools in the last nine months. She doesn't know whether she's coming or going. For us it's not ending, you see." The family had no money so Anne's father and mother-in-law gave her some to tide her over. She went to the Social Services, but had little joy from them. They told her she couldn't be classed as a single parent because **her husband could work**!

At first, it was virtually impossible to get DSS offices to pay out any money because of the blinkered and penny-pinching ethos they were dominated by. Where did the returning families fit in? What category? Which forms ought to be filled in? Some were told **their husbands had given up work voluntarily**, so weren't entitled to payment, others that **their husbands weren't looking for new jobs**, so weren't eligible, others that **their husbands should leave Kuwait and return to look after their families**! Some offices simply had no idea what the situation was like in Kuwait and Iraq - and didn't try to understand.

Meanwhile, the families were plunging into ever more dire straights. One of the trustees of the Gulf Support Group summed up the consensus of opinion: "As far as I'm concerned, you might as well burn down every social services office in the country. They were a total and utter waste of time, space and money. They were absolutely useless."

All Anne received was fifty pounds a week for herself and her three children. "I had to go to the children's boarding schools and tell them I had no money for their fees. They were very good and told me to send the children in and they would sort the fees out later." Other women received just thirty-five or thirty-six pounds a week.

During those first weeks in her Hampshire home, Anne visited her building society to stop the mortgage and the bank to get a loan to tide them over. They had a large house with a relatively small mortgage, so there was no problem borrowing against it. However, their savings they had spent half a lifetime working for were steadily being eaten up. There were essential expenditures. She had to buy clothes and uniforms. She was stuck in the countryside so had to get herself a car just to get to the shops. All she could afford was an old banger. Fortunately, her family were very good to her. With their support, she began to pull her life together. But there was still the problem of getting Stephen and the other hostages out.

Jill was extremely surprised to find her mother and aunt at the airport to meet her. She had no idea what news they had been getting, imagining coverage of the hostages' plight had been minimal and that they had been forgotten. She didn't expect her mother to know which flight she was on and certainly not for her to come down from Scotland to meet it. She was surprised and overwhelmed by the reception at the airport.

They caught a flight back to Scotland the next day and Jill stayed with her parents for a few weeks. "At first, when I got home, I didn't cry or anything, I didn't cry in front of people. I think it was still too much for me to take in." She had been forced to repress her feelings when in Kuwait, otherwise she would have gone crazy. "A lot of the time, even when I was in Kuwait, I used to think it was a dream - you know, it wasn't really happening. It was too much to comprehend. There had been times of terrible fear, when I was really, really scared, but at others when I tried to forget what was going on. I couldn't live with that fear in my mind all the time. I tried to put it out of my mind, otherwise I would have cracked up. I think that, when I got back home, people wanted me to be more emotional than I was. But I was trying to block so much of the fear out, I think. It took me quite a long time to talk about it. I could talk about experiences, what had happened generally, but not to talk about what had happened to my husband, or the fear I had felt - it took me a long time to be able to talk about that. That was too deep inside me." The longer she had been in hiding in Kuwait, the more the immense tension she was living under and her desire to break out of it was reflected in her desperation for something to be done diplomatically. Either the international situation had to break or she would break. Fortunately, Saddam gave way first. But it had been close.

One of the first things to strike her on her return was the news coverage. She hadn't realised there would be so much, but what there was appalled her with its constant talk of war and armaments. When the Iraqis had invaded she had wanted a quick war to clear them out. But once she returned, her attitude completely changed. She feared that her husband would be killed if there was a conflict. It was such a dilemma.

There were many emotional problems lying unresolved in Jill's head. Should her husband give himself up, or stay in hiding? She knew the Iraqis had mined many of the buildings in the city, so the whole place could be destroyed before they left. Where was it safest for him to be? Should there be a war or not? Iraq was pouring men into Kuwait, so where was safer - in hiding in Kuwait or in an installation in Iraq? She could resolve none of these questions. She was powerless and at the mercy of world strategy. She phoned the Foreign Office to discover what advice it was giving to people in hiding as she became more and more convinced there was going to be a war and that Kuwait was going to be the centre of it. With each escalation, her heart sank lower. Other wives were more optimistic, but she feared the worst. That was a terrible emotional burden for her to carry. She tried to put a on brave face around her local village and not let it dominate her, because most people couldn't really understand what she was going through. She only had one friend to whom she could reveal her deepest fears to and who proved sympathetic and understanding.

"I didn't cope very well at the beginning. People told me I should go back to work to take my mind off it, but I couldn't. Teaching's a demanding job and I didn't think I could cope with going into the classroom. I stayed at home with Mum and Dad for about eight weeks, constantly watching the news and speaking to people on the telephone about it. People would ring up all the time and I would ring them. And anyway, I didn't *want* to forget it. That would have been giving up on my husband, deserting him. People encouraged me to stop thinking about it, saying it wasn't doing me any good, but I didn't want to." She felt a strong surge of guilt at having left her husband in Kuwait, that "I had deserted him", despite knowing that he had wanted her to go and was much happier with her being safe.

Unfortunately, families did not always come together. There were so many emotions and so much family history to deal with that, occasionally, returning families didn't realise that it wasn't just they who needed help. Some women from Kuwait had no idea what their relatives had gone through. They thought it was just they who were traumatised, whereas frequently their parents or brothers and sisters had gone through a far worse experience. It was very hard for these relatives to be expected to help the returnees over their shock whilst nothing was done for them. Some felt pushed aside and taken for granted.

One woman who did realise this problem and tried her best to help her relatives was Mary[1]. She returned from Kuwait to find her parents emotionally exhausted, ill with worry and in need of tender care. Her mother had met her at the airport, but been in a very upset state. Her father had been so distressed he hadn't been able to come down. Mary had to lead her mother away and look after her on the long journey back north. When they arrived home, her father, an emotional man anyway, broke down. The trauma he and his wife had suffered throughout August had been terrible. They had been desperately upset in case their children and grandchildren were killed. The relief at seeing Mary safe was too much for both of them.

Thus, rather than Mary getting emotional support from her parents, she found herself giving them support. Just as for Mary, their worry was not over. They were frail and far less resilient than their daughter. She found her own emotional needs suppressed whilst she listened to and coped with her parents' experiences and helped them through by reassuring them, keeping them going and looking after them. But who was there to reassure Mary, to keep her going, or look after her? Several times that first month back she phoned the Samaritans, usually late at night when her feelings of loneliness were at their worst and she was so very close to ending it all.

Mary stayed with her parents for several weeks, trying her best to look after them. She had to keep her deep fears for her husband to herself. Sharing them with her parents would only have made them deteriorate more rapidly. But it finally became too much. She was no longer able to cope with repressing the pain within her. Her heart felt like bursting; her head felt like exploding with memories and guilt. Every few minutes she would collapse into floods of tears as a flashback paralysed her. She had to return to her own home to gain some personal space.

[1]Her name has been changed.

It was a similar story for many returning wives. When Gilly returned and was taken in by her parents' at their house, she was shocked to hear of the worry they had been through. From the first day of the invasion they had been living on their nerves. Fortunately, they had received a lot of support from ICL, their son-in-law's company, which had phoned them and other families regularly to offer solace, advice and practical help. The company had brought families into contact with each other, and provided support for the wives when they were released.

ICL, like British Telecom, Mouchel, Bechtel, British Airways and most other large British and American companies, continued to pay the men's basic salaries, which was an enormous weight off the women's shoulders. Like some other large companies, such as BA, ICL ran their equivalent of a helpline. It kept in continual contact with the families and passed on news from ICL in Iraq. Its office in Baghdad was open throughout the hostage period and sent faxes from employees still out there. Gilly's husband, Tom, was able to send one as late as his release in December. It passed on letters and messages through Tony Lavery, the Managing Director out there. Tony was very active in his support for ICL employees held hostage. He managed to get into the Melia al-Mansour Hotel as part of the British embassy team to liaise with Tom. He even brought him a fax from Gilly, as well as faxes for the other hostages with Tom, because Gilly had phoned round all their wives and arranged for them to send messages to their husbands. For some of these men, it was the first contact they had made with their families since 2nd August. It meant such a lot.

Rachel queued patiently in the foyer of the DSS office. Beside her, an unmarried mother, heavily pregnant and with twins in a worn-out buggy, was waiting to change the details on her child benefit claim form. A young man was applying for social security. Dozens of men and women were queuing for benefits or with queries. The room stank of urine.

Rachel had never been in a DSS office before and the experience was humiliating. She was made to feel like a beggar, someone forced to crawl for the right to live. It had been absolute desperation which had brought her there. Several times she had turned away from the building, only to turn back again, but she hadn't expected it to be as bad as it was. A girl had overdosed and was lying on a bench, moaning.

Rachel had to wait nearly two hours in the packed, sweaty, smoky room. Every five minutes or so, another person would be called up to one of the booths at the end of the hall. These booths had a panel of high-security, shatter-proof glass between the Social Services officers and their 'clients', with a wire mesh barrier reaching up to the ceiling. Each appplicant had to shout through a grille in the plate glass, so everyone else in the room could hear every word they were saying.

Finally, her name was called out. Rachel rose and sat in one of the booths, on a hard, formica chair bolted to the floor. The woman in the next booth had had her benefit cut and wanted to know why. She was in tears.

Rachel had to wait whilst two officers talked about another claim. After ten minutes, a young, harassed-looking woman in glasses asked her what she wanted. Rachel leaned forward towards the grille and explained that she had just returned from Kuwait...

"Speak up, I can't hear you."

Rachel didn't want the whole room to know her private affairs. She quietly repeated herself. Still the woman couldn't hear, so she was forced to speak as loudly as everyone else. The woman screaming abuse next to her wasn't helping.

"I've just arrived back from Kuwait. I've got no money to pay my mortgage or buy food. I understand you can give me a loan or a resettlement grant to help me get back on my feet."

"I don't know about that."

"I understood..."

"Give me your details," the woman interrupted, pulling a form from a drawer. "Name? Age? Address?" The questions rained down, until it came to husband's occupation.

"Why isn't he working?"

"He's in occupied Kuwait. He's in hiding."

"But why isn't he working? He's got a job, he should be at it."

"How can he when he's surrounded by Iraqis who'd take him off to an installation if they caught him?"

"Did he give up work voluntarily? If he gave up work voluntarily, we can't pay you anything."

"Of course he didn't. He'd've been shot."

The woman was not sympathetic. "What about bank accounts? You must have money saved."

"We have, but it's all tied up in Kuwait. We can't get at it."

"Why can't your husband send money to you?"

"He can't even send me a letter."

"Why not? He's financial responsible for you, not us."

"How can he? He's got no money himself. He can't even buy food for himself. Kuwaitis have to bring him food."

"What's his address?"

"I can't tell you."

"Why not?"

"Because he's in hiding."

"We have to know."

"Why?"

"So why can write to him and ask him to support you."

"You're kidding?"

"We are not financially responsible for you, your husband is."

"But all our money's frozen. He has nothing. He can't even phone me."

"Why did you leave him then?"

"What?" Rachel was finding it very hard to keep her temper by now.

"Why did you leave Kuwait? Why did you escape? You're not divorced are you?"

"No, I am not. I escaped because we were down to one meal a day and because I thought the Iraqis would burst into our apartment at any time and rape me. Do you want me to go back to Kuwait?" Her voice rose as her eyes glared at the woman. Her stupidity was making Rachel angry. The woman sat back, worried in case Rachel tried to attack her.

"Let me go and sort this out with my supervisor." The woman rose. She disappeared for about quarter of an hour, before returning. "We've phoned the London office. Apparently, there *are* special regulations for people from Kuwait, but we haven't been sent them yet. Let me take the rest of your circumstances. You have no income coming in?"

"None at all."

"No savings?"

"None I can use."

"What are your outgoings? How much is your mortgage? Do you have children? How much do you spend on heating? Do you have central heating?" And on and on and on. Eventually, Rachel was told she would receive an emergency payment until the office had sorted out her requirements. With that, and a barely-felt smile, the poor woman, further broken-hearted and demoralised, turned and tried to walk out of the room without her tears showing to too many people.

The women also went through the mill of the media. For a day or two the press sought good horror stories. Headlines like "If You Harbour Britons You Die" (*Evening Standard*, 10th September) fed off stories the women brought out of Kuwait: "Others spoke of fears for their men who were in hiding, as death threats were issued to Kuwaitis who harboured British men. Bhavna Trivedi, 32, sobbed as she told at Gatwick last night how she had fled with sons Nishant, five, and eighteen-month-old Adarsh, but left husband Naresh behind. 'My husband is still there. I haven't seen him for ten days.'" It was all good, heart-rending stuff, aimed to pull at the emotions of their readers rather than to show concern for the returnees. And within a week the articles and 'concern' had dried up. They were heroines for a day.

So disgusting were the efforts of some national media to get 'a good story', Rob Hayward MP felt obliged to bring the matter up in Parliament during the debate on the Gulf crisis on 7th September. He accused newspapers and broadcasters of setting out to "hype up the pain" and suffering of the relatives and hostages. "When ITN ring one family thirty times in one evening, until 1am, because they are relatives of a hostage, they ought to be ashamed. When London Weekend Television ring us three times within an hour to ask whether we can provide the names of families 'to show the distress and agony that families are going through', they ought to be ashamed."

The television presenter mentioned here by Rob Hayward at first denied the charge, but the MP simply played back his answering machine. It was full of calls the man had made during just one day.

The same young 'journalist' from the *Daily Express* who had asked "for something for the nine o'clock grief column", decided to pester Josie Brookes for Eric Watson's mother's phone number. He didn't just ring two or three times, he rang *fifteen* times in a *hour*. Josie tired to deal with him quietly and patiently. "I felt that if I couldn't handle one obnoxious little journalist, what chance did I have with Saddam Hussein? There had to be a way of quietly succeeding. I felt we had to talk, talk, talk, until we achieved the right result." The reporter didn't hound just Josie. He rang Rob Hayward until his answer phone was full. Stephen became so cross with his badgering and rudeness to Josie, he pulled the telephone line out of its wall socket with anger.

On 18th September there is an entry in the Coventry helpline's daybook recording a call from someone claiming to be from the Glasgow helpline, asking for some names and addresses. Stephen promised to call back and phoned the number the next day. He was put straight through, not to the helpline, but to the newsdesk of the Glasgow *Daily Record*. That was enough for him and he immediately put the phone down.

Like many of the relatives, Josie and Stephen were anxious to keep the hostages in the news and regularly contacted the media with press releases and phone calls. There was a constant stream of genuine calls from papers, TV and radio stations to both London and Coventry. Joanna Copley was never out of the news. The helplines also gave advice to relatives who wanted to contact the media themselves, telling them what to say and what to be wary of, and contacted those willing to appear on television or radio about discussion programmes such as *Kilroy* and *The Time, The Place,* or to raise specific issues such as the families' enormous phone bills with British Telecom.

When the hostage issue began to slip to the inside pages, tucked away in a few column inches and nearly forgotten, it annoyed and frustrated the relatives as much as over-intrusion. Armed now with the energy and determination of the wives from Kuwait, they were not going to allow the media to forget that their people were a central concern. As the front pages became dominated by the military build-up and diplomatic manoeuvres, wives, especially, began to apply more pressure. Many were quiet about it, writing to their MP or the government, but others were much more vociferous.

Within hours rather than days of the women and children getting back to this country they began to phone the Gulf Support Group. They wanted to put their names on its list of contacts and discover if it had any more information. They called to discuss how to get their men out and gave the support group a tremendous amount of detail about life in Kuwait and Iraq, where the men were living, what their conditions were like and how it was to live under the Iraqi occupation. Some of this information was highly sensitive. It contained names of Iraqi strategic sites, military bases and chemical weapons plants.

Josie and Stephen felt the problem of security acutely because information was stored in their house. They knew where many of the were and what their conditions were like. Josie became more and more fearful that their house might be attacked, or that Iraqis would come into the house. She began to have nightmares about Iraqis entering the back garden, breaking through the french windows, creeping up the stairs and murdering her and Stephen before destroying all the evidence they had amassed.

But much of the news was more general. Many women had brought out letters from men they had been grouped with which they posted onto their families. Others had lists of phone messages to send. For the first time, news of what happened on 2nd August emerged. In just one of hundreds of examples, the Coventry helpline daybook records a call from New Zealand by someone who had been in hiding with a group of Britons. They were still living in three flats and had scanty, but adequate food stocks: "Seventeen tins of tuna, six tins of corned beef, two and a half kilos of rice, Black Label, and Johnny Walker; an Arab friend brings food from Basra; Iraqis shifting everything back to Baghdad."

Maureen Evans, a helper at the Coventry line, remembers what it was like. "They would ring up and say, 'We were out there with Joe and Jeff and John'. Their relatives might not have heard anything about them at all, so we'd go through our index cards, find their relatives and phone them up. We'd tell them we'd just spoken to a lady who'd come out and was with their son or husband a few days ago, and maybe that there's a letter on the way to them. That gave them a tremendous lift." Sightings were frequently no more than names, which the helplines had to trace back to relatives. It became more and more like a detective puzzle as they tried to piece together the reports and was an enormous task. They had an awful lot of information to assimilate and disseminate.

As financial pressures rose, many of the calls turned to money. The helplines began to receive pleas for help from distressed women in very similar circumstances to Rachel, described above. In many cases, they were experiencing little sympathy from the DSS, despite national policy changes. Many returning families either didn't know they could get resettlement grants or failed to receive them. They spent weeks trying to work their way through the complex, disheartening red tape to get enough money to survive.

Both the London and Coventry helplines passed these concerns on to the Foreign Office and the government did realise the problem. It acted quickly. On 17th September, William Waldegrave and Mark Lennox-Boyd of the Foreign Office and Norman Scott of the Department of Social Security held a joint press conference to launch the Gulf Families Support Centre. William Waldegrave opened the meeting.

"It's perfectly clear that the Gulf crisis is affecting a large number of families...[and] there are a number of cases where people are facing quite acute difficulties. So the government has decided to set up a new unit... to bring together the resources of the various departments... we have a steering group... [and] will designate some of our telephone lines here in the Foreign Office for this service. All this represents the fact that we face really an unprecedented situation... We're now dealing with literally hundreds of families and we have to show that... we in Britain are going to do the best to look after our people."

In reply to a question from a journalist, he covered many of the problems the returned families faced: "...when people arrive back here, some have families to go to, others have employers in this country who take care of them... Each case in a sense is different. Some people have property in this country which they may not have access to immediately, others may need housing and, in those cases, the local authority housing departments can provide a roof over their heads in the interim and we can provide cash. Help with advice on education, on health provision and a whole range of social policies will be available." He described the returnees as "this particular group who I think ought to have a very high priority", although not enough to warrant additional financing. All the money for them was to come out of existing budgets. The major concern was to get people home, for which free transport was laid on, and to provide shelter for those with no destination, "to make sure they are housed or accommodated on a temporary basis and then, in the longer term, our local Social Services offices have been asked to address these cases in the most expeditious and compassionate way possible."

Emergency accommodation was clearly seen as the most essential provision, but Mr Waldegrave also promised people help with unfreezing their bank accounts and emphasised the Foreign Office's close work with the Gulf Support Group, especially Rob Haywood MP. "Their special brand of mutual support will continue to be an absolutely vital ingredient of the overall support for families."

To a certain extent, the ministers were out of touch with reality. Whilst clearly very concerned with the problems faced by the families, this concern was not getting through to the local Social Services offices or to the banks and building societies. The support group had as much trouble with banks foreclosing on mortgages and overdrafts as it had with Social Services offices. Eventually, the special payments and "extra statutory" requirements for the Kuwaiti returnees did filter down, but not until much hardship had been gone through.

It was also emphasised by ministers that only a minority of families faced hardship. Where they got that information from is uncertain. Certainly, those in *desperate* need were a minority, but a majority of the families were in financial hardship of one sort or another, some having lost enormous sums of money and property.[1] The press conference unfortunately tended to understate the problem and overstate the effect of the government's response. In fact, as members of the Gulf Support

[1]In their survey, Drs Easton and Turner found that 45% of respondents had serious financial problems, 55% had lost their job or livelihood and 73% had suffered "serious loss of property".

Group later admitted, the Gulf Families Support Centre was largely ineffectual. It was a damp squib, with no extra funding, no special personnel and no real expertise. It could only pass people on to other departments. It faded into oblivion after a few weeks. The one lasting achievement was to produce a leaflet covering employment, education, social security, housing, finances, immigration and voluntary organisations, though it notably failed to mention the Gulf Support Group and was criticised by some families for being insensitive to their real needs.

Cathy Willis had not been idle. After getting nowhere with her MP, she contacted the Foreign Office's Emergency Unit several times. On the first occasion, she gave her details and those of her brother and sister-in-law. She was not enamoured of the unit. Whilst she empathised with it's position, trying to cope as best it could with thousands calls, she felt they were too abrupt at saying they had no more news and at putting the phone down. Like most relatives, she found the support group far more sympathetic. She phoned the London helpline and received a much warmer response. "Someone was always there to talk. It was never a case of, 'Oh we don't know', and putting the phone down. As time went on, the helpline became even more supportive and even the Foreign Office was as helpful as it could be. But it didn't comfort us. *No one could come up with positive answers. It wasn't possible.*"

That last point was a key remark. The relatives were desperate for answers. When no one could give them any, it merely fed on their frustration. At times, the Foreign Office and even the government became the target for anger and bitterness, no matter how sympathetic, helpful and understanding they tried to be. Although many people criticised the Foreign Office for its lack of information and sympathy, much of it may be down to the high emotions generated by knowing their relatives and friends were trapped in a terrifying predicament and not necessarily to the Foreign Office's performance.

"I'll tell you how I felt," Cathy went on. "I felt like a hostage myself. I felt I was a prisoner in my own home, because I couldn't do anything to help. I wanted to do something positive, but I couldn't. It was the most horrible feeling. I didn't sleep very well. I was obsessed with taping the news so Lawrence and Bernice could see it when they returned." Watching the news was her way of coping. It was doing *something,* even if it was essentially passive. She was looking out for them, garnering every scrap of information, overcoming her terrible, crushing sense of powerlessness. "I would watch discussion programmes, Brian Walden, everyone. The meals in this house were arranged around news broadcasts. I just wanted to be able to get up and do something - anything - to help. I don't think those weeks will ever, ever be far from my memory. It will always stay with me, it was so awful an experience."

Cathy kept a diary. Much of it contains very emotional comments, like "Please God, help us!" It was her husband and children who kept her going. They rallied round marvellously and gave her a lot of support.

Whenever they heard any news, they would ring her at work to tell her. "There was no information we missed."

The first real news she heard of Lawrence and Bernice was not good. Following on from a contact she had made, she received a call from the wife of someone in Kuwait telling her that Lawrence and Bernice had completely cut themselves off. They wouldn't answer the telephone, or have anything to do with anyone else. This information had a devastating effect on her and the rest of the family. Cathy wondered what state of mind they were in. "I had visions of them being suicidal, or dead, all kinds of crazy thoughts." In fact, the couple were keeping, not only their own spirits up, but also those of others who would phone for a chat. Such was the danger of rumour.

The day she received the first letter from Bernice was unbelievable. It had been sent to Bernice's mother, by a returnee who had photocopied it and sent it on to all the other relatives. Above all, it told them that she and Lawrence were all right and relatively safe in their villa, but that she had decided to remain with her husband. They seemed well, especially as Bernice tried to make the letter funny and played down a lot of the worst parts of their life under the Iraqis, not mentioning the fighting and gunfire or their diminishing food supply.

Thereafter, letters came fairly regularly. Cathy received one about every two weeks. However, they began to change in tone as time went on. The humour faded and they contained a lot of anger at what was going on in Kuwait, especially at wardens running away and leaving others in trouble.

It didn't take long before it dawned on Cathy that, if letters were coming out, there *must* be a way of getting letters back in. She rang the Foreign Office. It was sceptical, but she insisted that if they could get letters to Baghdad in the diplomatic bag, then 'Kiwi runners', New Zealanders and other nationals who were visiting Baghdad and returning to Kuwait, could take them back down with them. Surely they could deliver letters as they pick others up?

The Consular Emergency Unit agreed to try for her, so Cathy wrote a letter - a crazy letter, trying not to sound depressed, but to find humorous things to write about - exactly the same consideration as went through Bernice's mind in Kuwait. Everyone felt they had to protect their loved ones from their own hurt. Everyone was aware how terrible a burden others were carrying and didn't want to load any more onto their shoulders. It is a very touching example of how much people *did* care and do for each other during the crisis.

Cathy sent the letter to the Foreign Office. The most serious problem she faced was how to address it. She couldn't put the street or area on, nor their last names, so just wrote LAWRENCE AND BERNICE, KUWAIT on the envelope. It is an amazing testimony to the unofficial mail system which had evolved and to the intimacy of the British community by that time that it actually arrived. Imagine the delight of the couple in hiding when it was handed to them. What a coup! Virtually no one else in had received mail at the time.

Cathy couldn't be sure her brother and sister-in-law had received the letter, but she rang up the Foreign Office and asked if she could send some more, including birthday cards and Christmas cards. The Emergency Unit was as helpful as it could be and passed them all on through the diplomatic bags. On one occasion, shortly after receiving another letter from Bernice which confirmed that her letters were getting through, Cathy had a specific request of the Foreign Office.

"I've had a letter from my sister-in-law," Cathy explained to the woman at the Emergency Unit. "She says she's got no cigarettes left. How can they survive in hiding without cigarettes? They've got no money to buy any, so I want to send them some."

"Oh no, you can't do that."

"Why not?"

"That would be breaking sanctions."

!!!!

Cathy was undeterred by the threat of undermining Western strategy and decided to buy an ounce of tobacco. She flattened it with a rolling pin, laid it into a little polythene bag and slipped it inside her next letter. She did it for the next one as well. Lawrence and Bernice received both of them. What joy!

Next, she started to send long, thin, brown cigarettes in the letters. She rolled them flat and scattered cigarette papers in between the pages. What with the Christmas cards she was sending, the letters had turned into little packages. She duly posted them off to the PO Box number the Foreign Office had set up. They all got through.

When the first one arrived, Bernice's eyes popped out: "Other Britons in hiding couldn't believe it. They asked us, 'How come you've got a letter?'" The effect was electrifying. It gave a tremendous boost to Lawrence and Bernice's morale. They had put one over on the Iraqis. Soldiers might be outside patrolling the streets, arresting and shooting people, but they couldn't stop them getting birthday cards and tobacco.

The Pain of Separation

"Each day brought joy and grief, often within minutes of each other, as families' emotions were tossed around like playthings."

The Scene: A small, converted bedroom. A table is set in front of a window. On it are a daybook, open, two shoe boxes full of index cards, a black plastic container for pens, a willow-weave basket for felt-tips, paper clips, in and out trays, card files, telephone directories, a stapler and a small white lamp. To the right is a bookcase full of books with Edd the Duck perched on top. There is a single bed covered with fax messages, boxes and files. Along another wall is a long table with a fax machine, photocopier and word processor on it. Underneath are an electric typewriter, reams of paper and ink refills for the photocopier. An old filing cabinet donated by Owen Owen's is in one corner. There are two phones.

The room still has many of the trappings of a bedroom. There is an embroidered Home Sweet Home. Ornaments line the mantlepiece and window ledge. There is a yellow teddy bear, a pink elephant and glass paper weights. Several rag dolls peer down from the bookcase.

One wall has a notice board covered with messages and letters from people such as Douglas Hurd, Buckingham Palace and the Kuwaiti Embassy, plus UN resolutions, photographs and newspaper clippings. Another wall is covered with a large map of the Arabian Peninsula, a map of Kuwait, a map of the Middle East and an embroidered picture of the countryside with a farm gate, fields and a winding lane. All spare space on the walls is taken up with sheets of paper bearing phone numbers written in bold, red felt-tip. There are military helplines listed, British companies in the Gulf, a Finance and Unemployed Advice Centre, a blood transfusion centre, Sky News, the London helpline, Rob Hayward MP, Foreign Office numbers, the Grampian helpline, the Glasgow support group, interpreters, the Samaritans, the police, army wives' support groups, and many more.

There were still the routine calls. The Coventry and London daybooks were full of them. Page after page after page. At Coventry, someone enquired about getting an exit visa for a relative. A number of Kuwaiti citizens trapped in Britain phoned, asking for asylum or extensions on their visas, and desperately worried about their relatives. Several Indian and Arab families enquired about their relatives in Jordan, Saudi Arabia and Bahrain, anxious to get them out before a war started. An Indian caller from Birmingham with relatives in Kuwait wanted to know how to set up a helpline for other Indians and Arabs with families in the Gulf. One woman was phoning frequently about getting an Irish passport for her fiancé, who was in hiding in Kuwait. Returnees were phoning to get in contact with relatives they had lost touch with after years of living in Kuwait and by wives who wanted to contact their in-laws. Clem Prothero called to say her sister-in-law Jenny Haig-Prothero had arrived safely in Turkey with her cat Mittens. The London helpline phoned, which it did several times a day, to tell them a man who had tried to escape had been caught. He had 'flipped' and tried to run down some Iraqi troops on the border. He had then been taken prisoner, and was now in a very bad way psychologically, in desperate need to come home.

With all the health problems the returnees were facing, the helplines advised women who called to take their families to their GPs because, in the insanitary conditions of some of the camps, they could have picked up hepatitis, dysentery, and all sorts of other diseases. Perhaps their doctors could also help them with their psychological problems. Many women who came out, especially those with no children, felt very guilty about leaving their husbands. Whilst they had to cope with their own practical problems of finding somewhere to live and paying the bills and Poll Tax demands, they were also very guilt-laden. Some were worried that the Iraqis had deliberately let the women go so they could lay into their men - round them up, march them off to camps and torture them. They were aware that the Iraqis might be far less gentle to men on their own than men with families. It turned out to be a largely unjustified fear, but nonetheless was very real for the relatives at the time. Typically, one caller, in tears, cried: "I should never have come out. I should have stayed with him. I'm his wife. He shouldn't be out there on his own. No one should have to face that on their own."

Quite a few women asked if they could contact other wives, although quite a few had continued to remain in contact with friends they had known in Kuwait, thus establishing their own informal support group. There were calls about the plight of the PARC nurses in Baghdad, and a woman upset by the BBC's One O'clock News which reported the flushing out of more Westerners, asking whether they had any information about her husband. References for all these calls had to be written onto the appropriate index cards for each family. When action had been taken and the cards made up, each entry in the daybook was ticked off. The cards were constantly kept up-to-date by the volunteers as they sat by the phones, between waiting for calls, cross-referencing, following up, calling the Emergency Unit and London helpline, and phoning back those people who needed checking on.

Some families had two or three cards, recording every call they made, what information they had requested and what emotional state they were in. This system was duplicated on a computer list of Britons known to be in Kuwait and Iraq. Each had a code for whether, for example, they were in hiding, held hostage, or a contract worker. These codes were put onto the cards for cross-reference with relatives who had phoned them. By September there were over two hundred families which had contacted them about their relatives or friends in Kuwait and Iraq. All were kept on cards in two shoe boxes. Far more were held on computer, all exchanged with the London helpline and the Foreign Office. By the end of September there were over five hundred and, by the outbreak of war in January, they had over eight hundred families on their lists.

Amongst the cards were ones for the volunteers. Their details were kept on file for staffing the rota. Not only did Josie have to organise that rota, but she had to brief the volunteers and be with them until they were confident enough to answer the phone on their own. On the whole, they weren't professional counsellors, but people who wanted to give their time, so they needed to be looked after and helped to deal with what were often very traumatic calls. "I'd be briefing one volunteer, say at nine in the morning, then be briefing another one at eleven, then others in the afternoon," Josie explained. "So I wasn't able to pull myself away from it at all."

The rota was divided into hours, but some volunteers did stretches as long as five hours. In one two-week period over the end of August and beginning of September, thirty-one different people put their name down on the rota, starting from nine in the morning until ten at night. Some came for just one or two sessions, others, like Maureen Evans, came nearly every day. Every hour was covered, usually with two people on plus Josie. She was there nearly all the time and she and Stephen dealt with those calls which came early in the morning and late at night.

The calls never stopped. The wealth of problems continued to pile up. Josie rang one woman just out of Kuwait who was desperately worried about her and her husband having to start their lives again at their ages, nearing retirement. Eunice Smith, who had left Iraq on the first flight out after being held on an installation in the Rumillah oilfield near Basra, called. Her husband was still being held at the camp. She was able to give details on the conditions there and on several of the men with him at the site. She had returned with her two children to stay with their grandmother in Grantham. Eunice soon began to set up a helpline in her area, keeping in touch with other wives, especially of two men held with her husband.

Barbara Griffiths also contacted the helpline several times a week once she was home. She was in a very emotional state and the helpline had to keep a close eye on her. At one point, it called her nearly every day, until she began to climb out of her sadness and cope with life again. The daybook records calls to her in September, on the twelfth, twenty-sixth and twenty-eighth; in October, on the second, fifth, eighth, twelfth, nineteenth and twenty-second; in November, on the sixth and ninth; and into December and the new year. These do not present the whole picture, because many of the calls to her were not recorded, as they became routine.

Remarkably, Barbara still found the strength to help others. She built a little circle of other relatives of hostages in the Cheshire and Lancashire area and kept them informed of any news. They bolstered each other through the long weeks of September, October and November.

October was particularly bad for Barbara. During the call on the second, her deep anxiety finally began to emerge, especially her guilt at being safe whilst her husband, Stewart, was at an installation. She was in such a state that a few days later a friend rang the helpline, expressing her concern. The helpline decided to call Barbara back and, on the fifth, she was contacted. She was feeling slightly better. The daybook records her state of mind: "I spoke to her at length and, considering her difficulties, I felt she was coping quite well." On 19th October, Josie Brookes had contact with her twice again. This time, the index cards record the gist of the conversations: "Mrs Griffiths rang me today. Very angry, but she kept saying, no disrespect to me, but no one was doing anything. I felt I had let her down - Josie." And again in the afternoon: "I phoned Barbara back and managed to persuade her that we were doing all we could for the hostages. Today she believed me, but who knows how she will feel tomorrow?" Barbara's crisis went on throughout October and into the next month. On 11th November, when Josie called her, she found her in a very anxious state: "Rang in the morning. Is crying and worried about it. Told her to continue to cry and not to suppress it, as it is a 'safety valve'. Pleased to hear from me. Husband phoned last night. Is well. Getting no mail. Has sent out ten letters (not arrived)." On 14th December there was better news: "Husband home. All appears to be well with them so far." But within a week, her emotional problems had re-emerged and it became a hard fight for both Barbara and Stewart to cope. Only by the last entry, in February 1991, did they seem "generally better".

Another group of cards reveal the unravelling story of a hostage as snippets of information came out. We'll call him John and his wife Jane. John had been taken on the first day of the invasion in Kuwait City and transferred immediately to the Melia al-Mansour Hotel in Baghdad. His wife was at home in northern England. She received some letters from John in the first few days via other nationals leaving Iraq, but then heard nothing. She contacted the helpline at the end of August. From then on, it kept a close eye on her:

14.9.90 Phoned. Left message on answering machine.

17.9.90 Contacted. Finding it difficult to cope with the tension. No news at all.

18.9.90 Rang about government sheet. [This was the leaflet sent out by the government's Gulf Families Support Centre. The daybook: "The last thing relatives want to see is impersonal telephone numbers, and to deal with tax problems just would be too much. A lot of relatives would be upset by the circular. You could not even read the print."]

Thought it might confuse and worry people. Not complimentary about the Foreign Office.

3.10.90 Jane received a letter from her husband. He had been held at the al-Taji armaments factory, north-east of Baghdad, since the 4th September.

[This letter graphically described the conditions in this camp. He had first of all been taken to a uranium plant, where no news had come in or filtered out, then been transferred to the chemical plant at al-Qaim, near the Jordanian border. Their conditions were apparently appalling. The food was cold lamb gristle and bone, fit only for the packs of wild dogs roaming the site. They had to walk a mile to the canteen for each meal and by the time they arrived, the food was cold. They were usually served with greasy lentil soup and dirty, stale rolls covered with straw from the market roof. They were all big men at the plant and were losing a lot of weight. They had soon had enough. One day, something sparked a riot and they began hurling chairs through the windows of the canteen to protest for better food. The camp commander was petrified in case they threw him through the window as well and promised them an improvement. Things did get better from then on, although they were still sleeping in old huts with old beds, had inadequate washing and toilet facilities and were provided with very little in the way of entertainment, except for a bit of volleyball. Above all, life in the camp was incredibly boring.]

29.10.90 Needs call back.

1.11.90 [More details of John's capture and how he was kidnapped and taken away.] Held at al-Qaim... John got mail via three MPs [who visited the site].

4.11.90 Spoke to Jane for fifty-five minutes. John rang yesterday and today; sounded in good form, has lost two and a half stone (needed to!), being fed, playing volleyball, weight training, keeping morale up, listening to Gulf Link [the BBC's World Service programme for the Gulf hostages]. She sounded in very good spirits. Spoke at length about her family and going on boats with her husband. She may refer her husband's friend's wife to us if she can persuade her.

8.11.90 Now has a London address for mail to her husband - PO Box 1370. He had phoned her this morning as is now very angry about remarks by Sir John Stokes MP. Says they are all angry. She has also contacted the Red Cross about sending a parcel, but the Red Cross was not very pleased she knew about them. They said it was a possibility but had to be cleared by the Red Crescent.

23.11.90 Rang in the morning. Answer phone in operation. Told her we will ring again if she doesn't ring us first.

12.12.90 John phoned. He was back home and feeling fine. Grateful for the help given to his wife.

3.1.91 [About claims for compensation.]

12.4.91 [The final call, about family trauma, is too personal to record here.]

These are typical entries on the cards for just one family. Their case took up seven cards in all, covering twelve recorded conversations and calls.

By mid-September, the acute financial problems of some families become clearly reflected in the daybook and on the cards:

"A man called worried about his next-door neighbour who has a husband in Baghdad. She has three children and is only receiving £60 a week from the DSS. Can't manage. Can anyone help?"

"Rachel called. Worried about her husband and about their bank account held in joint names, and about payment of bills."

An Arab doctor called, "offering counselling help to wives and their children who may have returned without their husbands and who have no financial support or have to rely on relatives for accommodation. She has in the past experienced such difficulties and would like to help. Could travel to Coventry for counselling or meetings. Telephone after 4pm."

"Worried sick about phone bill. Will send information about petition [to British Telecom to get their phone bills reduced]."

There were intense housing problems. One family who had recently returned was staying with the woman's step-mother, but were desperate for alternative accommodation as the house was overcrowded. And another: "Mrs..., homeless with three children, phoned from Perth for information. Requires a phone call."

Many callers were getting increasingly desperate. One caller's sister had died. The aged mother of a hostage had also passed away. Another had "Bad. Ring regularly," beside her name. Another: "She is in bed. Bad way, but they are getting a counsellor to talk to her." Another: "Counselling necessary." Another: "Daughter in distress. Living in Folkestone." People with particular problems tended to call frequently for a few days, then not be heard of again. This is probably a good sign. It means those relatives received close support when they needed it, until they felt strong enough to carry on alone. The building of relationships during this period, which both the Coventry and London helplines did more and more, was essential for people to unload many of their problems.

There were many worrying calls about sick and elderly men trapped in Iraq and Kuwait. One caller told Josie about his twin brother held in a Baghdad hospital with a bad heart condition and wanted any information the helpline could give to enable them to get him home. Another was more specific: "Dad moved to Baghdad. High blood pressure. Trying to get him out. Heard reports on the news that elderly, sick men may be airlifted out..." The card went on to give details of his medical requirements, stating that the family were "not sure whether medication there".

Both helplines began to collate a database of the sick and elderly, which they co-ordinated between each other. The Foreign Office added to it by passing on any information it received. Josie wrote to the Iraqi ambassador in London, pleading with him to ask Saddam to let them go and both helplines began to put systematic pressure on the Iraqis, targeting this especially vulnerable group as a 'special case'.

Another major concern of the relatives was to get letters back to the people in Kuwait and Iraq. Like Cathy Willis, they couldn't understand why, if mail was coming out, it couldn't get in. One caller asked whether a postal system could be arranged through the FCO via Jordan and Iraq, into Kuwait. Others wanted to know how to get mail to Iraq. The Foreign Office received an awful lot of phone calls on this subject and tried to get a PO Box number working properly, but without any real success. The problem was compounded by post offices refusing to take mail to either Iraq or Kuwait and telling relatives that all mail to those countries had to be sent through the Foreign Office. The Royal Mail appeared to make no special effort to help the relatives of the hostages. Many relatives received their letters back with NO NORMAL DELIVERY TO IRAQ scrawled across them.

Many of the volunteers had experienced voluntary work of some sort, but not done any telephone counselling before. Quite a few were general nurses. A number volunteered through the churches, which were very supportive. Maureen Evans found it strange at first. "It's quite different talking to people over the phone. You can't hold their hand or make eye contact or see how they're reacting. If you're calling them, you don't know who's with them, whether they've got a house full of people or have been on their own for days. You can't see their expression, their demeanour, how well or ill they look, what physical state they are in, what the house is like - are they keeping it and themselves tidy? Are they coping, or are they letting things slip? And you wonder as you dial - is she going to feel the same today as she did yesterday? Do you continue from the day before, or do they want to forget what they said yesterday? You have to be very careful about how you open the conversation. It's trial and error." From the beginning, each volunteer built a relationship with certain families. They would promise callers they would phone them back, if they wished. People were always glad to hear from the helpline again. Maureen didn't make a single call where she felt the call was not welcome. "It is something you can sense very quickly. People were delighted that someone was taking an interest and cared about them. And, if we called, they didn't have to pay for it. That was a big consideration. For a lot of people, money had simply stopped and the phone company still wanted their bills paid...

"They invited you, albeit over the phone, into their family and home. Often, it was not just one person in the family we were supporting. There may be three or four people in the family who needed support. It may be three generations who needed help. The grandparents who made the first contact, then the brothers, sisters and friends of the people out there, then, when the wives came back, they needed support, and, of course, the children. Often they were extremely upset and, if they were teenagers, we would try to talk to them about their fathers. That could be extremely distressing."

It was Maureen and another counsellor, Josie Howie, who worked out a set of guidelines for the volunteers. Everyone who came in had to read them carefully before they were allowed onto the phones. They classified possible calls into two groups: the press; and relatives/friends. Regarding the press, instructions were simple - take their phone number and Stephen or Josie would ring back. For relatives and friends it was more detailed: "Some callers may be distressed and less than articulate," the guidelines explained, "and a sympathetic and supportive, but realistic, approach should be taken. Second language speakers may have to be recontacted through an interpreter."

The guidelines warned volunteers not to be too directional, just to give commonsense advice, and try to be yourself. They were general and intended to instill confidence over the phone. They were rather more giving and generous than the strict don't talk, don't make suggestions, just listen, of the London helpline. "Some volunteers were very frightened to pick the phone up, in case they couldn't handle what they heard from the other end. In the end, no one really couldn't handle it. Some were happy to make the coffee and tidy, and were reticent to pick up the phone. But for most, confidence came after a few calls and it was enough for callers just to get things off their chest."

By now, an excellent relationship, based on mutual trust and co-operation, had been built between the support group and the Emergency Unit. Whenever Stephen phoned up, he was put straight in contact with Grant Lindsay or Christopher Denne. On just one of the frequent occasions the Emergency Unit called, it informed them it had been sent a telegram from the Melia al-Mansour Hotel from a man "Suffering hyper-tension. Moved with a group of women." The helpline then liaised with this man's wife over what his medical history was and what they could do for him.

The support group began to build a detailed list of installations where the men were kept. The strategic value of the information they were gathering began to dawn on them. They were assembling, by chance, a list of Iraq's secret weapons plants, chemical establishments and key military and industrial sites. This was vital intelligence information which the support group passed on to the Foreign Office. The Iraqis were inadvertently helping the British and Americans create a comprehensive list of their strategic sites, with eye witnesses who could describe them and their defences, which building housed which type of machinery or equipment, and so on. When the men came out, this intelligence was dramatically increased. They included soldiers, ex-soldiers, engineers, computer experts, managers and technicians. As they were debriefed by government officials, they were able to give precise details of the geographical position of the sites, their accessibility from the air, and even the products they were making. They were to prove of enormous value to the bombing missions at the start of the war.

Because of this sensitive information, the both helplines began to take more security measures. The Coventry one, being a private house, was particularly vulnerable. There were reports of Iraqis threatening to poison the water supply. Newcastle had a bomb scare. Iraqi nationals were being rounded up and some were being deported. The atmosphere in the country at the time was growing tense. Iraqi embassy officials were banned from travelling beyond London. They couldn't even go as far as Heathrow or Gatwick. Iraqi students in England were under suspicion. There was a bomb scare as close as Leicester Polytechnic. People feared the Iraqis might use chemical weapons against Britain. It was a time of worry and fear. People felt they had to be careful.

Several times volunteers had reported strange cars parked across the road with the drivers apparently watching the house. Whether they were working for the Iraqis or were part of the British security services was uncertain. "One of the volunteers was leaving the house at four o'clock one the afternoon. There was a car parked across the road. As she got into her own car, the other car did a U-turn in the road until he was parallel with her and took a photograph of her."

On the other hand, security was no problem at all. Despite dozens, no hundreds of people traipsing in and out of the house, volunteers, journalists, television crews, local VIPs, nothing was ever stolen or went missing. Furthermore, there was always at least one person in the house all the time. It was *never* empty.

The strain of constantly answering the phone continued to tell on Josie's physical and mental health. She was perpetually run-down and emotionally exhausted. The phone calls were so unnerving at times. She had no idea whether the next phone call would be yet another private grief invading her own, nor whether she would yet again be up all night dealing with someone at the end of their tether, nor whether it would bring back some long-forgotten personal memory of her own past. It was a very traumatic time for her.

"It had taken over their lives," Maureen Evans told me. "Josie hadn't gone into work since the crisis began and Stephen was struggling to find time for his job because the helpline was so time-consuming. I don't think there was one of the volunteers who weren't worried for them. They've suffered more than anyone. I mean, they lost their privacy, people were phoning all day and into the early hours of the morning. They put in an enormous number of hours. They were *never* off duty. Their lives have been turned completely upside down. I doubt they will ever be the same people again.

"They had journalists ringing them at four in the morning and faxes coming through at all hours of the night in the next bedroom. They would hear them, wonder what new developments were coming over the machine and get up to have a look. Josie was not trained to keep herself distanced from the problems of the callers. We had many, many discussions about the need everyone has to put perimeters around what they're prepared to do without harming themselves. I would warn her that if she ended up breaking down, that wasn't going to help anybody. She had to learn to put a limit on how much she was prepared to give. We all have too. She would promise to cut down but that night would still be on the phone at four in the morning. She never really managed to cut her work load at all. Not only was she pinned in those four walls but suddenly it wasn't her house, it was someone else's office as well. If she wanted to lie down, she was lying down with a total stranger answering the phone and talking to people. She didn't have any privacy for a year. She couldn't even get to the loo at times. The kitchen wasn't their own. People were drifting in and drifting out again. They were so long suffering, they really were."

"Should the Coventry helpline have been more structured or professional?" I asked. "Should it have moved into an office and had a more organisational approach?"

"From Stephen and Josie's point of view, it might have been better if it had moved out, but it would have changed the nature of the whole thing. It was a very friendly, good-natured place and we had a lot of laughs and made the best of the situation. If one of us had endured a heavy session with a couple of families that were very upset, she could go downstairs, make a cup of coffee and have a laugh for half an hour, and then get back to it. The informality and ability to have a bit of a giggle certainly kept Josie's sanity." Crucially, this informality meant people could debrief each other, at any time, and for as long as they wanted. That is really all debriefing had to be, letting a volunteer get some trauma off her chest. There is no mystique about it.

Paid co-ordinators, experienced counsellors and professional structures don't work. They are not necessarily the answer to a support group's problems. Throwing money, resources, equipment and offices at them may do more harm than good. Whilst it may give greater opportunities and take some of the pressures off the central core of people who set the group up, control, intimacy and close contact with the people the group it is supporting can be lost.

Different pressures, of management, organisation, policy-making and size, can cause greater problems than those the office and extra staff were designed to relieve. A lot of the goodwill can be lost, people start wanting to be paid or to receive expenses, and the social cohesion of the group can be lost. There was a tremendous amount of goodwill in the Brookes' house, everyone trying their best to get on with everyone else. "We shared so much," Maureen enthused. "We shared the downs and the tremendous euphoria when the men were released. That was terrific. We wouldn't've got the camaraderie if we'd gone into a social services office or community centre and had everything nicely organised. It wouldn't've been the same Gulf Support Group. I'm a great fan of these amateur organisations of people with a bit of goodwill and a bit of time. I think you get a lot done. But if you start making rules, people having to be in for nine o'clock, or whatever, they won't want to do it as volunteers. But for us, people would always be giving because they saw so much giving around them. They would turn up with a jar of coffee and bottle of milk, or a fruitcake, to help us all out."

The London helpline took a different route. Joanna Copley was quite critical of the Coventry approach, feeling it was too amateurish and low key. She constantly asked them to get proper offices and be more organised. She felt that by keeping it in their house, Josie and Stephen were making a big mistake. And in one particular sense, Joanna had a great advantage. She could walk out of the office at night, turn off the light, switch on the answering machine, and escape to her home. There, she could relax, sleep and have time for both herself and her husband, Tony. She went for size and numbers in an effort to cope with the incredible demands put on the helpline from relatives, press and government departments.

In effect, the different approaches were the result of different circumstances. London is the capital and the requirements on a helpline there are bound to be different. It is far too big, there are far too many press and television people, too many VIPs and government departments, for a small operation to work efficiently. A private house would have been inadequate and it is unrealistic to imagine that a small operation could have coped. It had to grow to accommodate the huge media interest and enormous number of calls coming in from relatives. It had a much higher profile, with articles in the London papers and items on the regional news every night. They had a whole string of dignitaries visiting them, including Margaret Thatcher, Douglas Hurd and Princess Diana. London required a large organisation simply to cope.

However, the London helpline was beginning to find difficulties arising out of its size. It had grown considerably. Not only had it moved into a suite of rooms at Alexandra House, but it now had a fully staffed Operations [Ops] Room to handle the phones, faxes and Reuter reports, a press officer, a fund-raiser, someone struggling to install a computer system, and an advertiser. It had dozens of volunteers organised into three shifts to operate the telephones, write up the index cards and update the database.

Despite this growth, there was no management structure. Whilst, on policy matters, her consultation would always spread to the Coventry helpline, mainly to Stephen, on other matters she was determined to retain her authority. The two main helplines phoned each other at least twice a day, mainly on questions of policy and reactions to events. There was a great deal of co-ordination between the helplines, but not always between the management and volunteers within the London helpline.

There was no official policy-making or management body at London. The Gulf Support Trust only dealt with financial matters and not policy. Joanna was adamant that none of the other trustees should have a say in the running of the London operation. She had frequent arguments with Rob Hayward over this.

Several volunteers at the London helpline spoke of the problems they had as a result of its growth. There was increasing pressure to set up a committee to make decisions. Some people wanted a greater say and felt that Joanna should share policy-making. Under duress, she agreed to set up such a committee, but was not about to hand control over to it. Energy began to be wasted over a power struggle. Those answering the phones thought of it all as a bit silly, and kept away from it, but it was a source of friction within the London helpline.

As one volunteer revealed, "There was a great feeling amongst people in the Ops Room once we had moved to Alexandra House that there were communication and physical difficulties. We went from a small, cosy place to a tremendously big room with a television, a printer, a coffee area with seating, tables with brand new clothing, and with the trustees' room to one side and the new Ops Room down the far end. There was a physical barrier between the trustees' room and the Ops Room and there was also a communications barrier. The volunteers felt strongly that there was a lack of communication."

It is important to put these difficulties into perspective. There were also many positive developments in London. People were working extremely hard and under considerable emotional and physical pressure. The volunteers on the phones knitted together well, despite different backgrounds and sometimes widely divergent political attitudes to the crisis. They worked as a unit. If one of them was clearly upset by a call, the others would tell him or her to go off and have a coffee, and that they would cope. They used their commonsense, refusing to overdo things. That way, they spread the load and prevented anyone becoming too depressed or emotionally exhausted, an area in which they were better equipped than Coventry.

Whilst people coming off the telephones after, perhaps, a three or four hour session were not given a formal debriefing, there were often other counsellors sitting in the coffee area whom they could chat to about the calls, and go through any particularly harrowing ones. Occasionally, Jonathan would also sit with them, talking about how the callers were feeling. "Some days, with some news developments, it was very tough," Jonathan explained. "It was murder. I'll never forget the time of the CNN broadcast of Saddam with the hostages. It caused no end of problems."

The Gulf Support Group was a completely voluntary organisation. Its volunteers worked tremendously long hours and were under a lot of strain, especially as some had the added burden of relatives trapped in Iraq and Kuwait. As Joanna explained, "My volunteers put in an incredible amount of effort. They gave up their time, took time off work, spent their own money on petrol, convenience foods and on the phone from home to help the effort. Young people would give up several evenings a week to help." The work they performed, under the glare of the media, for the hostages and their families over those months was a testimony to their dedication and self-sacrifice. It was something truly noble to emerge from a very tragic and inhuman world event.

Pawns in a Game of War

"MY HUSBAND IS NOT EXPENDABLE!"

Virtually the entire Kuwaiti population remaining in the emirate were passively resisting the Iraqis. The Resistance itself was full of young man and women, and even old men took part in attacks. Many more helped Westerners get food and letters, or simply harboured them and kept the Iraqis away.

The clearest and most powerful demonstration of their total opposition to the Iraqis came on 2nd September, exactly a month after the invasion. At precisely midnight, the Kuwaitis went up onto their rooftops and began chanting, "Saddam Hussein adou'Allah! Saddam Hussein adou'Allah! Saddam Hussein adou'Allah!" - Saddam Hussein, enemy of God! It began with the mullahs in the minarets of the mosques calling through loudspeakers over the rooftops, then came over the city in waves as thousands of Kuwaitis stood on their roofs and chanted.

Tom Colclough remembers it well. "It really freaked the Iraqis out and they began firing up at the rooftops with machine guns, tracer bullets and thunder-flashes, although they couldn't see any of the people. They were firing wildly to try to shut the Kuwaitis up and calm their nerves." Mike Devey described his feelings as the waves of calls swept over the city. "They were all on the roofs chanting. All these guns were going off. It was unbelievable. All these people staying on the roofs. We were on the roof as well. There were bullets flying everywhere. They were shouting all sorts of things." Perhaps for the first time, the Iraqi soldiers realised just how bitter the Kuwaitis were and how desperately they wanted them to leave. Many of them were petrified. Reprisals were inevitable.

By the end of September, the Foreign Office estimate of the number of Britons in Kuwait was reduced to eight hundred. Whilst this was a far more accurate assessment, it was still too high. The wardens had done an excellent job that month in collating information on nearly everyone in hiding, so the better information was entirely down to them. Those in Iraq were thought to number some six hundred and thirty, of whom two hundred and thirty were thought to be on strategic installations. These figures, too, were much more accurate. The Iraqis had not taken many more during September, once they had rounded up enough to replace the women and children. There were still about 350 who had been taken, with about 100 held in Kuwait and the rest, about 250 - maybe slighty more - in Iraq. Despite worries by the community, there were no major house-to-house searches. The Iraqis were quite happy to let Westerners stay in Kuwait, where they had to feed themselves and were, of necessity, protecting the emirate from attack.

British women and children were still leaving Baghdad until the end of September. Thirty-seven arrived on a jumbo jet carrying nearly four hundred Americans on Wednesday the nineteenth. On the twenty-sixth, another group arrived which included three British Airways stewardesses from the IBI camp. They brought with them letters, including ones from Eric Watson to his wife Wen Li and to Stephen and Josie Brookes, from Don Majors to his wife and from John Chappell to his family. They also brought news of conditions in the camp. The men were being fairly well treated and had adequate supplies of food. This news put many families' minds at rest.

Of the other nationalities trapped in Kuwait at the time of the invasion, there were estimated to be between 1,300 and 1,800 Americans, with eighty-four being held at the sites. Half a million Indians, Palestinians, Egyptians, Filipinos and Sri Lankans had made it across the borders of Saudi Arabia and Jordan by now, where their governments were organising flights to get them out of the squalid refugee camps. A million still remained in Kuwait. The Indian government estimated that 126,000 of its nationals were still there; a further 300,000 were Egyptian, though this was in both Iraq and Kuwait. Stories continued to come through of terrible conditions and starvation. In desperation at accounts of them running out of food, the Indian government sent three ships laden with supplies to Kuwait. The first arrived about the twenty-third, the others shortly afterwards. They all took refugees with them when they left.

The British government was quick to offer help to these people. At the end of August it contributed £500,000 to the appeal launched by the International Committee of the Red Cross to help refugees stranded on the Iraqi/Jordanian border. Subsequently, it donated funds for supplies to the refugees and gave financial help to Virgin Atlantic to fly in two hundred tonnes of relief supplies. A further two million pounds were given for the evacuation costs of Third World nationals under a scheme organised by the International Organisation for Migration (IOM). The European Community granted twenty-one miliion pounds for the evacuation of refugees and for relief supplies to the refugee camps. With Britain's share of this sum, the total donated by the government came to about ten million pounds.

As the international airlift 'took off', the pressure on the camps rapidly eased. 100,000 refugees in Jordan at the beginning of September rapidly fell to 30,000 by the twentieth. The worst camp was closed and conditions in the others were improving. British Airways donated one of its Tristar fleet, capable of holding four hundred people, to the IOM for its evacuation plan. Furthermore, Lynda Chalker, the minister responsible for co-ordinating Britain's relief effort, was in constant contact with the

UN Secretary General's special envoy, Prince Sadruddin Aga Khan, to co-ordinate funding and supplies for international relief.

During September, the United Nations steadily stepped up its pressure on Iraq. On the thirteenth it passed Resolution 666, which promised to continuously review food aid to Kuwait and Iraq in the event of sanctions causing unnecessary distress to civilians. Just three days later, in response to the Iraqis surrounding foreign embassies in Kuwait, and even seizing them, as in the case of the French, it passed Resolution 667 strongly condemning the aggressive acts perpetrated by Iraq against diplomatic premises and personnel. It demanded the immediate release of all foreign embassy staff as well as all other foreign nationals detained. It further demanded that Iraq immediately move to protect the safety and well-being of diplomatic and consular staff and premises in Kuwait and Iraq and to no longer hinder their work. Within eight days, Resolution 669 on economic aid to countries suffering as a result of the UN sanctions was passed. The very next day, September the twenty-fifth, Resolution 670 on implementing an air blockade of Iraq was passed. It requested all member states to refuse permission to any aircraft to take off with a cargo for either Iraq or Kuwait, other than food or medical supplies for humanitarian purposes. It also asked member states to refuse to allow any planes *en route* from or to Iraq or Kuwait to overfly its territory, unless the flight had been approved by the UN's special committee on sanctions.

For Kuwaitis, the war didn't start in January, it started in August and went on right the way through to liberation. The tiny country had become a battleground, with a vicious underground war of attrition going on. Every British person in hiding knew of a Kuwaiti who had been murdered. Every one of them could hear the daily and nightly gunfire and see the bloody remains in the morning. It the UK, many women and children who had been in Kuwait at the time of the invasion could remember similar scenes. They had nightmares about it, and many sleepless nights. All of them became increasingly anxious - some terrified - of what might be happening to the men still trapped in the middle.

Not surprisingly, the Free Kuwait organisation emphasised the looting and shooting. It was *their* families who were bearing the brunt of the repression, *their* houses which were being blown up or set on fire, *their* sons who were being taken away and shot. There were atrocities being perpetrated against them every single day and the tabloid press was building each little incident out of proportion. The whole atmosphere in Britain was growing increasingly tense and worrying. Many British families had close Kuwaiti friends and Sri Lankan or Filipino maids, and had no idea how safe they were. Whilst those actually in hiding knew they were relatively safe, their relatives in Britain were terrified of what was going on. No news was bad news.

Meanwhile, reports continued to drift out of Kuwait from the Kuwaiti Resistance or in letters carried by foreign nationals able to move about

Kuwait. A picture of the systematic stripping of the country began to emerge, petrifying those relatives with men in hiding. On the twenty-first, Robert Fisk of *The Independent* sent in the following report:

KUWAITIS TELL 'BLOODY' TALES OF OCCUPIERS

> ... A young woman with a narrow, lined face holding the hand of a small, very pale skinned boy sat on the stone seat of the Khafji customs hall [northern Saudi Arabia]. 'The Iraqis took five young men from our area,' she said. 'They didn't say why. Maybe they thought the boys were in the Resistance. I saw them later. The Iraqis executed them. They threw their bodies on a rubbish tip in the street.'
>
> ... One man described how two special teams of Iraqi soldiers were used for executions. He had seen the corpse of a young man who had been burned alive in an unfinished building. Another refugee told how young men living close to the scene of the killing of Iraqi soldiers were routinely taken to vacant building sites and shot. The two Iraqi execution groups, according to a Kuwaiti engineer who arrived here [Khafji] on Sunday, wore shoulder flashes which identified them as 'Squad 65' and 'Squad 68', the Iraqi 'special forces'.
>
> *The Independent, 21st September*

The article went on to list a whole series of alleged atrocities. A boy grabbed in the street, taken to a basement, made to lie on the ground, doused with petrol and set on fire. A Kuwaiti ex-policeman shot in the neck in his house, then the house set on fire as his family watched. Hundreds of young men taken away to prison camps. Kuwaitis refused hospital treatment. A supermarket owner shot dead because he refused to stop home deliveries of food. And so on. Whether these particular stories were true or not - and they were appearing nearly every day now - they created a very striking image of a city under siege, wilting from the most intense repression and state terrorism. How were Westerners faring in such a situation? How long would it be before some of them were killed or tortured? Each story to come out of Kuwait further fuelled the anxiety of the relatives and added to the climate of deep fear and intense worry. Each caused some relative a sleepless night.

Jonathan Copley described the situation the families were in. "They became very despairing. It didn't look as though the men were going to come out. Many were at installations. An awful lot of them were British women married to Kuwaiti men. Not only were the Kuwaitis being randomly killed and tortured by the Iraqis, but these families often had no one here to look after them."

Meanwhile, on the diplomatic front, nothing much seemed to be happening. Very little news came out of Kuwait. No access was allowed for journalists to the men at the Melia al-Mansour Hotel in Baghdad, nor to the installations. Instead, the pictures sent back tended to be of the men lazing contentedly beside swimming pools or playing snooker in company clubs. These were the contractors and businessmen who, whilst denied the freedom to leave Iraq, mostly had a very easy time of it. The media soon tired of these sanitised shots and news focused more and more on the huge military build-up as it went boldly ahead. September marked the decisive shift, in terms of military build-up and American rhetoric, from Operation Desert Shield, defending Saudi Arabia, to Operation Desert Storm, the recapture of Kuwait and humbling of Iraq. There is evidence to suggest that President Bush and Mrs Thatcher had planned Desert Storm from the beginning, but that is a side issue here. Certainly, the headlines which dominated the papers either tended to be about the military escalation: "UK Will Send 6,000 Men and 120 Tanks to Gulf" (*The Independent*, 15th September), or sent shivers down the spines of the relatives:

BUSH OFFERS NO COMFORT TO HOSTAGE FAMILIES

[Relatives of the 1,800 American hostages] showed signs of unusual strain yesterday. They listened to Mr Bush's speech to Congress as closely as anyone, but he could not provide them with any more hope that their loved ones would be home soon. In fact, quite to the contrary. The president prepared the nation for the prospect of bloodshed, or for a long haul with an uncertain ending. Neither was comforting.
The Independent, 13th September

Whilst paying lip-service to the hostage issue, both President Bush and Margaret Thatcher did not change their policy. Indeed, many relatives of the human shield believed the British and United States governments should *not* change their policy. They believed they were *right* to insist that the general interests of freeing Kuwait, defeating the Iraqi threat and securing oil supplies must be fundamental, and that hostage-taking must *not* be allowed to succeed. The majority of relatives wanted Kuwait freed, and supported a war to do it as quickly as possible. Where most disagreed with the government was over whether the hostages should be an issue *at all*.

Diplomatic manoeuvres also dominated the headlines. Iraq issued its first full justification for annexing Kuwait on the thirteenth of September. It made it quite clear it would not withdraw from the emirate. On Friday the fourteenth, it sent troops into the French, Belgian and Dutch embassies in Kuwait and arrested the personnel inside. Four Frenchmen were taken. The military attaché was later released, but the other three were driven off. In response, on the seventeenth, European Community countries expelled a large number of Iraqi embassy officials from their countries. All Iraqi military attachés were expelled, plus some support staff, in direct retaliation for the Iraqi intrusion into the embassies. In all, eight were thrown out of Britain. A further twenty-three non-embassy Iraqis were also served with notice, as their presence in Britain, according to David Waddington, the Home Secretary, "was not conducive to the public good, for reasons of national security".

All this tit-for-tat activity sent shudders through the relatives. The more it went on, the less chance there seemed for a diplomatic solution to the hostage problem. Rather than negotiating, the whole atmosphere seemed to be one of deliberate escalation and a total breakdown in talks. In fact, neither the British nor the American governments were prepared to enter into any 'talks' whatsoever, one of the most scandalous aspects of the whole thing, in many relatives' eyes. It was preparation for war, not for diplomacy.

The Gulf Support Group continued to work for the hostages despite this deteriorating climate. It began to concentrate on the release of special cases. If the old and sick could be brought out, it might soften the Iraqi attitude to letting everyone go. In this, it was supporting an initiative by Perez de Cuellar of the UN to persuade Iraq to release the elderly, sick and those still students.

The approach met with some encouraging signs. On the fifteenth, the Iraqis let all sick and elderly Frenchmen leave, despite France expelling forty of its diplomats. By the seventeenth, the first four of these men had arrived in Amman, straight from some of the installations where about fifty-six Frenchmen were still being held. At that time, a further three hundred Frenchmen were estimated to be in Iraq and a hundred more to be in hiding in Kuwait.

In the Iraqis' peculiarly contradictory way, three Irishmen who had been captured in mid-August by Iraqi soldiers as they tried to escape across the border to Saudi Arabia were now sent for trial. Two had been contract workers on a German-built petro-chemical plant 120 miles from Baghdad. Despite protests from the Irish government, the three prisoners were moved to a Baghdad jail. (Or should we call it a hotel?)

Every trustee of the support group, as well as many of the relatives, fought hard to keep the hostages in the news and to keep the pressure up on both the British government and the Iraqis. Rob Hayward MP raised their plight in Parliament, Joanna was constantly in the news, giving the Gulf Support Group's views, and Josie Brookes went on the BBC's World Service to plead with Saddam to let the human shield go. Josie argued that releasing them would give him more public acclaim and show him as a man of peace. The hostages were a weapon against him, an excuse for the USA and Britain to continue their build-up. Rather than a deterrent to war, they were stimulating it by turning the world against

Iraq and giving a wonderfully emotive propaganda weapon to the West. Whilst they were an extremely useful propaganda weapon for Iraq, they were hugely more so for the allies.

The support group constantly hammered home the point that the hostages would not stop a war. The Iraqis believed they would, that the public outcry in the USA and Britain would be so great the troops would have to stay out. But it seemed quite evident to the Gulf Support Group that President Bush and Mrs Thatcher, when it came down to it, did not care about the hostages. They would bomb the installations whether there were British and American people in them or not. Indeed, the hostages themselves realised that. Many of them were making plans to escape immediately war was declared and those in hiding were preparing rooms against gas and chemical weapons and creating bolt-holes where they could hide until the fighting was over.

During September, some groups of relatives became more vociferous and began to press for more action. They had used the initial publicity surrounding their release to highlight the plight of their husbands but, once that forty-eight hour interest had evaporated, felt very strongly that a constant stream of activities had to be organised to keep the hostages before the media. These relatives would phone the helplines with suggestions about events or complaints about lack of activity. Those living near enough would call in to discuss activities and to get involved. Many felt useless sitting at home all day.

Whilst virtually none of the families wanted to get embroiled in party politics, some wanted to be political in a general, non-party sense. Party politics were universally seen as dangerous and counter-productive. They would alienate the government and a lot of the relatives. However, frustration, anger and a determination not to be forgotten pushed many otherwise very moderate and quiet women into becoming much more positively active campaigners for the release of the men.

As a result, a number of divisions opened up between the relatives. A strong current wanted to be more aggressive towards the government, whilst a large, silent majority felt they should support the government's stance and not criticise it. Some wanted marches, vigils and pickets; others wanted no activities at all. One or two even suggested jumping naked off Westminster Bridge to draw attention to their plight, they were so desperate.

Perhaps the greatest difference of views was over whether to press for an immediate war or to delay war for as long as possible. For most of the relatives of people in hiding, the only answer seemed to be an invasion to release them before it was too late. For those with people in the installations, war meant the immediate extermination of their menfolk. Most of them wanted talks with the Iraqis to begin - not negotiations, not concessions, but *talks*, to put across their feelings and arguments and to pressurise the Iraqis through force of argument, as well as force of arms. It is not surprising the arguments became bitter even between the relatives themselves. It was a matter of life and death of their loved ones. The Gulf Support Group tried to stay neutral on this issue. It stuck fervently to its commitment to remain non-political and refused to comment on general government policy or international strategy. For the support group to have embroiled itself in such matters would have been fatal.

However, the support group did criticise the government, mainly for not doing enough to help the hostages, or for doing and saying things which actually put them in increased danger. Jonathan Copley explained its position. "If we felt not enough was being done, for example by the DSS to help families out financially, we would criticise in order to improve the situation. But always, we were careful to voice the opinions of the people who were ringing us." As a result, they found themselves supported by some relatives and criticised, sometimes severely, by others.

One active group of wives which did emerge comprised Anne Mansell, Marcia Griffiths, Lollo Murthwaite and Anne Hill, whose husbands had all worked for the Kuwait Oil Company. Three were in hiding in Ahmadi, whilst Stephen Mansell was somewhere in Iraq.

These women pulled around them a wide network of other wives and relatives who had grown to know each other either in Kuwait, on the journey to Baghdad, or through friends. The four central organisers continued that relationship over the phone and by visiting each others' homes. They supported each other and began to think of ways to keep the hostages in the news. They began to plan a campaign of contacting the media and organising high-profile events. Anne Mansell converted a room of her house into an office and had letterheads printed with Gulf Support Campaign, the title of their informal group.

From her office, Anne Mansell phoned everyone she knew would be interested in a march. She sent out eighty envelopes with five letters in each, asking people to circulate whomsoever they knew. The paper work and activity took her and the house over completely. It kept her mind away from dwelling on her husband Steven. By now, she knew he had been taken to the oil refinery at Basra, where he was having a very rough time.

Organising her group gave Anne a way to burn off the tremendous nervous energy pent up within her. She was receiving phone calls from one o'clock in the morning as she built a helpline around her and prepared for the march. She visited the Metropolitan Police in London to tell them about it and gave them the route. From there it snowballed. Her friends phoned her regularly to keep in touch with developments. In turn, many of them were setting up little groups of people in their own areas, to give each other support. Anne contacted the helplines in Coventry and London and went on television to promote the march and generally talk about what they were doing. By mid-September, she was appearing everywhere, on televison and in the press, purely to make people aware of what was going on.

"We wanted to get it onto the news and onto the World Service," Anne Mansell explained, "because we knew that all the guys out there were listening to the radio and, if they heard the women were doing this, that and the other, they would realise someone was doing something for them. Because, believe you me, when you're in hiding in a small, small room and you've only got the radio and you put it on every hour to listen to what's happening, it's wonderful. If there was no news when we were listening, we'd go flat for days, thinking they'd all forgotten about us."

The march was held on Sunday 28th October. Whilst there was a tremendous amount of support for the idea, a lot of relatives couldn't make it because they had no transport. Many were pauperised and couldn't find the fare to get to London. Groups had to get together to pool petrol costs or hire a minibus. One woman went as far as arranging with a car hire firm to get a picture of one of their cars in the local paper if she could have it free for the day.

Yet the march was very well supported. There were about three hundred on it, including two hostages who had been released. It started in King Charles Street and wended its way quietly along Whitehall, past the end of Downing Street, and down Horse Guards Avenue to Victoria Embankment. It was a short and slow march because they had a lot of children with them. Whilst some Kuwaitis did turn up from Free Kuwait, and many women wore Free Kuwait badges because of their overwhelming sympathy for what the Kuwaitis were going through and gratitude for the help they were giving their men in hiding, the organisers were determined to keep the issue of the hostages completely separate from that of freeing the country. There was no shouting, no sloganising nor calls for the government to resign. It was a peaceful, quiet and solemn walk through a small part of Whitehall. The women were careful not to attack Saddam Hussein or the Iraqi government. Most called for their daddies or husbands to be allowed home.

Many women had made their own posters or banners. Anne Hill's read MY HUSBAND IS NOT EXPENDABLE and appeared on the front of *The Independent*.

They stopped at Downing Street to present a letter to Mrs Thatcher, to which they are still awaiting a reply. Anne and a few other women were allowed in to present it. It was written in general terms, asking her to please not forget the men in Iraq and Kuwait and to try to do something to get them out. It wasn't asking her to go to war or not to go to war. It said it was from the friends, relations and families of the hostages who just wanted them home and the crisis resolved quickly.

Lollo Murthwaite told me why she went on the march. "I think the press were trying to keep the march and things like that down. I don't think it was in the news much. But we thought, at least we were doing something, instead of doing nothing for them. Maybe it was for our own satisfaction rather than for its effectiveness. I don't know. It made us feel a little bit better. At least we were trying to do something, so the men wouldn't think they were being left and forgotten. It was to boost morale, that's all." It succeeded. After the demonstration, Anne Hill, Anne Mansell and other wives did interviews for the World Service, which the men heard and welcomed with great enthusiasm in their dark apartments and security camps.

The march was just the start of the campaign. The next event was to organise families to write letters to President Saddam which they would present to the Iraqi ambassador in London. Anne Mansell phoned the Iraqi embassy to ask if she could have an appointment to see him on that day. The embassy agreed that someone would receive them.

Anne Mansell and ten other women and children, including Lollo Murthwaite, were allowed to enter the embassy to deliver a hundred and fifty letters from relatives, including children, asking for their husbands and fathers back. The ambassador, Dr al-Salihi, refused to see them, but they did meet the Cultural Attaché, Mr Allousi.

After passing through security gates and having their bags searched, they were shown into a large reception room. It was very bare, with couches around the walls and security cameras staring down on them. They didn't receive a very positive response from the Cultural Attaché. "It was pure propaganda. He was saying how the men were well looked after, being well cared for and were guests of the Iraqi people. According to him, they were being well fed and had good medical facilities. Stories of bad conditions were all American propaganda. The real people suffering were the Iraqi people. All Iraq wanted was peace. The men still in Kuwait and Iraq were not hostages but guests of the Iraqi government. They were ambassadors of peace. And they were still in Iraq because they didn't want to leave. They were being so well looked after that they were happy there."

Anne Mansell was furious. She sat and listened to the diatribe, then turned to the embassy official and told him of a tape she had been given by a Frenchman recently let out of Iraq. In it her husband, Stephen Mansell, had graphically and bitterly described his conditions.

After hearing her points, the Cultural Attaché had had enough. He interrupted her and insisted she was wrong. He then rose to leave. But the women still had to present him with the letters and a petition on which they had collected hundreds of names of relatives who wanted their menfolk to be let go. Once again, the petition was not critical of Iraq, nor political in any way. It simply asked for those held to be released. It didn't even call them hostages. They asked the attaché if the ambassador could send them to Saddam Hussein, and were assured they would reach him. They also asked for lines of communication between the hostages and their families in the UK to be improved, and suggested they be allowed to send letters to the installations and the men be permitted to make phone calls out.

The following week, on the second of November, the group of wives organised a picket of the Iraqi embassy, to mark three months since the invasion. Anne and Jackie Hurley from London organised the picket between them. Once again, Anne phoned the police and asked them what they should do, telling them what they wanted. She organised it for the day many of them had been invited down to London for a *Kilroy Programme* to participate in a live debate on the plight of the hostages and people in hiding.

The *Kilroy Programme* turned out to be a fiasco. It was hijacked by the impending leadership crisis in the Conservative Party. To the intense frustration of all those who went down, it was hardly about the Gulf crisis at all, but a discussion on Margaret Thatcher's future.

The Conservative Party leadership crisis panicked the relatives. They weren't sure whether the British government's policy on the hostages would change. It completely pushed the Gulf crisis off the front page and meant the hostages and men in hiding were virtually forgotten.

After *Kilroy*, the wives made their way across London where they joined other wives and children in the protest outside the Iraqi embassy. There were about sixty women altogether. Once again, there would have been many more, but people were constrained by lack of money and by having to look after their children. Many actually brought their off-spring, who had to be periodically taken off - to the toilet, to get something to eat, or for a rest. It was very deliberate to include them. Indeed, they included children in every event they organised because they found Arab people very quick to respond to them.

To the women's surprise and disgust, the police refused to let them near the embassy. They had erected barriers across the road and the women were forced to stand on the opposite side to the embassy, penned in like sheep. They were a hundred yards down the road from the embassy and surrounded by dozens of police, making their protest ineffective. They were nearer the Kuwaiti embassy than the Iraqi one.

Someone likened the high barriers to a cage. "Isn't it great. Our men are out there as hostages and we're stuck here behind a cage."

"I know. They're trapped and we're trapped."

There seemed to be no reason for the barriers nor the large police presence. Perhaps the police had in mind the shooting of a policewoman outside the Iranian embassy a few years before and believed it was for their own good. However, the women felt the way the police treated them was insulting and unnecessary. As they held placards proclaiming, 'WE WANT OUR FATHERS HOME!', 'I WANT MY DADDY BACK!' 'LET OUR MEN COME HOME!' and 'FREE THE HOSTAGES!', they felt that they too were being denied their rights. Joanna, Anne Mansell's thirteen year-old daughter, carried one saying, "ALL I WANT FOR CHRISTMAS IS MY DADDY". None of the slogans were political or anti-Iraq. In fact, Anne had warned those coming on the picket that they must not put anything controversial on their placards or shout out either against the Iraqis or for or against war. Nor were the women heckling or shouting through megaphones. It was very peaceful and well-behaved. It was aimed solely at getting their men out of Kuwait and Iraq.

As the day drew on, the picketers grew increasingly frustrated by not being allowed near the embassy. So, at half-past two the families began to pack up and told the police they wanted to go home, coincidentally past the Iraqi embassy. They also wanted to cross the road, but the police wouldn't let them. The ensuing tussle with the police was ideal for the news. An ITN cameraman filmed the women and children behind the cage, shouting at the police inspector as he tried to stop them crossing the road, then making their way up to the Iraqi embassy and kicking up a fuss as they were held back. This time, they did shout slogans and wave their placards. Marcia Griffiths was near the camera. She turned to it and told the news reporter precisely what she thought about the Iraqis, the police, and their treatment behind the cage. It was broadcast in full on the national news.

It is important not to forget that the great majority of relatives were not active at all in this campaign. They didn't want to become involved in marches, petitions or pickets, but stayed at home the whole time. They wanted to remain completely anonymous. Some felt that if their names were quoted in the media, it would endanger their husbands in Iraq or Kuwait. Many were simply trying their best to get on with their lives. After all, they had enough problems as it was. Some were positively against the activists. They were worried in case such street actions either angered the Iraqis and made them more determined to hold onto the hostages, or encourage them in their strategy of using protest movements to undermine Western governments.

On 2nd October, Margaret Atack received a letter from the Foreign Office informing her of the death of her husband William. He had died in hiding, they suspected of a burst ulcer. They had few details of how it happened, only that there appeared to be no suspicious circumstances and that he was dead on arrival at a Kuwaiti hospital.

Sadly, the reality was grimmer, as facts around William's death emerged. He was on his own, in hiding, and had become severely depressed. Other Britons in his block kept an eye on him, but he kept himself to himself much of the time. He had a serious ulcer, but hadn't told anyone. Instead, it grew worse until, one day, it burst and he choked on his own blood, alone in his apartment. William was the third Briton to die during the crisis. If he had been free to go to hospital and receive proper medical treatment, he would have been alive to celebrate his freedom.

"I don't know what you're complaining about."

"You what?"

"You and Barry chose to go out there. All you wanted was the money."

"You what?"

"You wanted to make a fast buck. You took the risk. You deserve all you get. Good riddance."

"You what?" Lynda was, in her own words, gob-smacked. She was so angry she could hardly get the words out. "Barry worked damned hard out there to earn what he earned. He worked eleven hours a day, sometimes in 40°C or 50°C. Some weekends he worked all Saturday and Sunday. He didn't get any overtime or time off in lieu."

"He still got a fortune. I wish I could earn that money. Now all you do is whinge and complain because you can't get the government to pay your bills. I'm sick of it. You've all got more money than I've ever had. I don't give a damn about your husband. I hope he rots out there. I wish the Americans would go in and flatten the lot of 'em, Iraqis, Kuwaitis, everyone."

Lynda Pickup was so distraught she dropped her carrier basket and ran out of the shop.

On Monday 1st October, three Britons, Ivan Manning, Michael Teasdale and Keith Barkworth, plus two Frenchmen, Amadée du Paty and Gamel du Burean, launched a ten-foot fibreglass boat they had carefully repaired and fitted with a diesel engine.

They were all at Khor Abdulla, near Basra and barely sixty kilometres from the Gulf. Ivan Manning was a process engineer running a processing plant for a marine loading terminal. He had been there for three months working on refurbishing one of the jetties.

Although not in Kuwait, they were still held on their site as part of the human shield from day one, because it was regarded as a strategic installation. At the gas storage terminal just up the road, the Germans working there were moved out to another site.

Initially, their conditions were not bad. Their movements were slightly restricted, but not much. However, as time passed the controls became tighter, which made them feel more and more threatened. Officially, they were not supposed to leave the site but unofficially, Ivan and the others could venture along the pipeline for about six kilometres to a swimming pool. They could even get permission to go into Basra, where they were escorted on shopping trips.

Their accommodation was in portacabins by the side of the waterway, but otherwise surrounded by desert. There were armed guards around them all the time, and they had no entertainment, only alcohol to drink, in a camp predominantly Italian and Filipino. No letters were allowed out nor did they receive any in. They were three Britons and two Frenchmen on their own. At night, the site became the preserve of packs of wild dogs, so they had to keep inside.

The food was never good at the site, but steadily deteriorated during the crisis. By October, they were running short. Fortunately, some Germans at the camp were allowed into Baghdad where they bought food and distributed it amongst everyone when they returned. They had plenty of cigarettes, alcohol and food, and fished for prawns. Some hostages came up from Kuwait and were dispersed across the site, but kept well away from the contract workers.

The five of them received direct moral support from French and German government officials and help to plan an escape. They had military satellite pictures of their region of the Gulf smuggled in, money brought in, and a radio link established. They managed to steal a marine radio set, so could regularly phone London and their wives via a ground link in France. They also stole a lifeboat and an Iraqi flag and went to scout around the area to check for possible escape routes.

It was mid-afternoon when they ventured into the boat. They chose that Monday because everything was going for them. The tide, the moon, the Muslim calendar. They had some cheese, bread and water for provisions, plus a good stock of vodka and whisky. They steered their way through the marshes surrounding the workers' camp where they had been held hostage for two months and headed down the Shatt al-Arab waterway to enter the mouth of the river at nightfall, as planned. They had to quieten the engine with insulation material and fix a silencer to the exhaust.

They hit the river mouth at dusk to use the darkness to get past the Iraqi pilot boat which carried a gun on deck. The descending night and a mist over the sea hid them from Iraqi patrol boats and coastguards. But it also disorientated them. They went round and round in circles in the wide river mouth, watching the lights of the pilot boat in the distance, before finding their way down into the Gulf. There, they made a major error. They had a detailed navigation map of the waterways, but they headed south instead of south east. It took them too close to the coastline of Kuwait. As they chugged along the coast past Bubiyan Island, they were still screened by the mist, but Iraqis were no longer the main danger. The Gulf had turned rough. Whilst the swell had been only three or four feet at the start of their voyage, it rapidly rose to over ten feet. One of them had to work the bilge-pump constantly to keep them afloat.

As the night wore on, the swell became too great to use the diesel engine, so they turned it off and let themselves drift at the mercy of the currents, the waves washing over the gunwales. They rapidly lost their bearings. The map they had managed to steal had been drawn up prior to the Iran-Iraq War and many of the landmarks, such as oil terminals, had been destroyed or moved. They had a compass and a rough idea of where to head as they zigzagged to avoid an Iranian naval ship which seemed to be trying to catch them. (They later discovered that it was actually trying to rescue them.)

Instead of circumventing the Iraqi shoreline and landing in Saudi Arabia, they found themselves steadily drifting towards the heavily defended Kuwaiti coast and unable to use their engine to steer away. Fortunately, the current was strong enough to push them southwards and, after twenty-five dreadful hours, they were found drifting in a shipping lane by a Saudi coastguard vessel off Khafji. The five men were extremely relieved to be picked up. They realised their escape could so easily have ended in disaster.

Mission of Mercy

"They are letting out a few dozen from one end, but pumping in the same number from the other. It has become almost industrial... The Iraqis had instigated a conveyor belt of hostages; a production line of human sacrifices."

Edward Heath MP, previously Conservative prime minister and now elder statesman of the House of Commons, began to receive a large number of letters from relatives of hostages asking him to please do something to help them. There were hundreds of them, from relatives all over the country, pleading with him to do all he could to get the hostages out, including visiting Iraq. Many of the letters expressed frustration at the government's perceived lack of action and saw Mr Heath as someone who favoured dialogue with the Iraqis. "The relatives who talked to me asked me to do my utmost to secure the release of the hostages."

Virtually every MP had been inundated with letters, phone calls and attendances at their surgeries, particularly the leaders of the parties - several relatives in Paddy Ashdown's constituency said how marvellous his office was in giving them help and support. Niel Kinnock and Margaret Thatcher were similarly approached by a large number of people. However, it struck the relatives that the people most likely to have influence were those elder statesmen who had expressed a stronger desire to enter dialogue with the Iraqi leadership than the government, such as Mr Heath, or who had openly attacked the government's position, such as ex-premier James Callaghan and the anti-war campaigner Tony Benn. Accordingly, these three MPs were the focus of a huge, unco-ordinated and spontaneous campaign by relatives, trying everything they could to get the hostages back.

When he received this deluge of letters, Mr Heath passed them on to his private secretary, Robert Vaudry and decided to investigate the possibility of going on a trip to Baghdad. Mr Heath asked him to approach the Foreign Office to give its blessing for such an expedition. Now confusion arises. Mr Heath's office is certain that the Foreign Office not only okayed the mission, but even suggested it, and told me categorically, and somewhat bitterly, that it had kept in close contact with the Foreign Office as plans developed. Certainly, Douglas Hurd initially welcomed the trip, telling Mr Heath he would receive "all the facilities which the embassy in Baghdad would normally give to a former prime minister." He did mention a "point of difference" over Mr Heath's call for the Iraqis to be offered a peace settlement, but still gave his basic support because "his purpose in going is primarily to get some of the hostages out."

Under the impression that it had been cleared with the government, Mr Heath's office went ahead with its plans. It approached the Iraqi embassy and asked for visas and audiences with Iraqi leaders in Baghdad, including Saddam Hussein and the Foreign Minister Tariq Aziz. It explained that Mr Heath would request the release of elderly and sick hostages as an act of mercy and would be bringing a list with him. It contacted both the Foreign Office and the Gulf Support Group in London and Coventry for lists of people they considered at risk from illness or old age. The helplines contacted the relatives and asked them to write in with letters giving full details of why they felt their particular hostage should be considered, with a medical history where applicable. These letters and lists came in rapidly and it was a major task sorting through them and getting them into order. They were not prioritised in any way. No one person was put before another, so long as they were obviously ill or old. There was no pecking order, no order of merit presented to the Iraqis. All cases were presented equally.

Those put forward included Tony Wilbraham, who had severe heart trouble, Mr and Mrs Wright, the elderly couple staying at the ambassador's house in Baghdad, Joe Wild, in his sixties and also with a bad heart, and David Cunningham, a middle-aged man with diabetes. Even relatives who didn't have sick or elderly men involved wrote to Mr Heath expressing their gratitude for his efforts and wishing him every success. Meanwhile, Mr Heath informed his personal doctor, Dr Jeffrey Easton, of his intention and asked him to help sort through the letters and lists and collate the details.

Lollo Murthwaite was amongst the relatives who wrote to him. Her husband, Don, was sixty and so clearly qualified as being elderly. However, he was not a hostage, but in hiding, and it was uncertain whether he would risk coming out even if the Iraqis allowed him to leave. The London helpline worked closely with her and all the other relatives anxious to give Mr Heath their men's details.

The support group helped relatives get forms and information. For example, they informed Lollo that she had to get a copy of Don's birth certificate for Mr Heath to take. To save time, the London group offered to get it for her, if she sent them the money for it. She readily agreed and they arranged a copy for her. Along with the certificate, she had to write a letter fully explaining Don's situation and giving the reasons why she felt he should be let out. This she sent to the support group, which passed it on to Mr Heath.

When Margaret Thatcher heard about the trip and that the Foreign Office had given Mr Heath its blessing, she, by all accounts, blew a fuse. One report had her "furious", another stated that she "hit the roof". She demanded the Foreign Office withdraw any support from Mr Heath. From then on, instead of co-operation, he met with constant obstacles. He was refused security protection and had to finance the trip himself.

It had to be a purely personal expedition, humanitarian and not political, and not sanctioned in any way by the government. Nor, once in Baghdad, did he receive the diplomatic service or help he needed, despite Douglas Hurd assuring him that he would "receive all the courtesies from our ambassadors, particularly in Amman and Baghdad, which were due to a former prime minister."

As this major row burst around his head, Mr Heath explained to David Frost on his television programme that it had been Douglas Hurd who had approached him initially with a suggestion to visit Iraq, adding that "I think, in fairness to Douglas Hurd, one must say that relatives of some of these people in Iraq and in Kuwait who are very ill, and in one case dying, approached him and said 'Look, can't something be arranged?'" Mr Heath had considered the risks of going, "but I finally said, 'Yes, if I was required, I was prepared to go'."

Conservative ranks began a systematic campaign of vilification and scorn against him. Douglas Hurd tried to paper over the cracks by rejecting any suggestion of a rift between the Foreign Office and the Prime Minister. He denied asking Mr Heath to go to Iraq, saying that they had merely discussed the matter. "I neither encouraged nor discouraged him from the enterprise." Thus a former Conservative Party leader and prime minister was left completely isolated by his party, after believing he had its full blessing. He could scarcely contain his anger.

The organisation of the trip moved ahead rapidly and the date for Mr Heath's departure was announced as 12th October. However, as that date approached, it became clear that some arrangements wouldn't be ready, so it was postponed for a week. It was as well. It gave more time to make ready the files on the hostages and to prepare the case Mr Heath would present to the Iraqi leadership. But it also gave the press and certain Conservative MPs the chance to continue their campaign against his trip. They accused him of splitting the government and breaking the solidarity of the alliance ranged against Iraq. Other government ministers criticised Douglas Hurd for his initial support for Mr Heath. One said "It's a disaster. He [Mr Heath] is a meddler. The Foreign Office should have blocked him." The Defence Secretary Tom King strongly attacked him for laying himself open to be used by Saddam for propaganda purposes. "There is a very great danger in it and a very great danger in appearing to give respectability, aid and comfort to a regime as totally unacceptable as Saddam has become in international terms."

Mr Heath had previously angered some Conservatives by calling for Saddam Hussein to be given a face-saving way out of the crisis. Now, they sensed blood and went for the kill. They thought his and other missions only gave Saddam more publicity and diverted attention from the central issue - getting Iraq out of Kuwait. They merely served as a propaganda weapon against the United Nations. The drip-feed of hostages undermined the military alternative by making war far less politically acceptable.

In reply, Mr Heath emphasised that he was not going to Baghdad to do any secret deal with Saddam, nor to offer concessions, nor to sympathise with his invasion of Kuwait in any way. "I am not going to discuss politics and if people get angry about that, I am sorry." He added, "I have thought long and seriously about this. I cannot tell what good it will do but I felt, after discussions I have had with the relatives, that I could not go on living with myself if I refused to try to help those who are sick and dying and get them back to our own country. That is the purpose of my visit... It is humanitarian." On Tom King, he merely told him to "talk to the Foreign Secretary and get his view". He denied he was giving validity to the Iraqi regime. "Look at all the other regimes we deal with which do things we don't approve of. Really, this is what very often makes other people, especially in Europe, think the British are somewhat hypocritical."

Furthermore, during that week's delay, Mr Heath was able to present an alternative to the official gung-ho position presented by the unholy alliance of tabloids and ministers. He wanted Saddam Hussein to be given the opportunity to withdraw from Kuwait peacefully and still save face. He was strongly against what seemed a one-track, high-speed drive towards conflict.

The negative attitude of the government angered most of the relatives and they told the Foreign Office and their MPs so. Mail bags full of hundreds of letters of support continued to flood into Mr Heath's office, wishing his mission every success. It helped tremendously to soften the criticism. Mr Heath had overwhelming public support for his mission.

Even as the government accused Mr Heath of undermining their policy, it announced that the British 7th Armoured Brigade was due to land in Saudi Arabia almost to the day Mr Heath was flying out, bringing British Army strength up to 8,000. Personnel, equipment and supplies were pouring into the country as allied might rose well above the minimum necessary to defend Saudi Arabia. There were now 175,000 American troops, 100,000 Saudis and Egyptians, 10,000 from the Gulf Co-operation Council and small groups from France, Syria and Pakistan. British and American special forces units had been active behind Iraqi lines for weeks, surveying the Iraqi defensive strategy. An offensive capability was clearly being prepared.

The Gulf Support Group gave Mr Heath its full co-operation all the way along. It was even pleased the mission had been delayed, because it felt it had been too hurried. It issued a press statement saying: "We are delighted that Mr Heath is going out on this humanitarian mission and wish him every success in his undertaking", adding elsewhere that "our hope is that his statesmanship and the respect he engendered as prime minister on the international scene will give a base for his humanitarian visit to succeed..."

Other people gave their moral support to Mr Heath and worked for him in other ways. One of the seriously ill men Mr Heath was hoping to bring back, Tony Wilbraham, was interviewed in Baghdad. He was clearly desperate for Mr Heath to come out, seeing it as his last chance for a life-saving operation on his heart. Other hostages interviewed in Iraq supported his initiative as well. Behind the scenes, Stephen Brookes met the Iraqi ambassador again, this time to present a list of the sick and elderly to him and to plead for the early release of *all* the hostages. Stephen wanted them all out, but was prepared to hassle for the release of even one, if it meant that he one could be brought out safely. And, on the quiet, Mr Heath received support from other Conservative MPs and certainly from members of other parties. Whilst the official government line rapidly hardened to oppose his and all other 'mercy missions' as divisive and diversionary, its voting fodder would sidle up to him in the corridors of the House and metaphorically pat him on the shoulder.

There *were* some criticisms of Mr Heath from relatives, especially from relatives with people in hiding, who thus couldn't come out with Mr Heath. One woman stated that whilst "a great admirer of the GSG [Gulf Support Group]", she was "strongly opposed to the concept of categorisation [*ie* of breaking the human shield into groups with special problems]... the driving force must be for the release of *all* hostages in Kuwait and Iraq. Otherwise, who is to play God and determine the value of one life beyond another? Such an attempt would produce division and bitterness amongst relatives in the UK. I am the mother of a son hiding in Kuwait."

Anne Hill opposed not only Mr Heath's visit, but other visits by politicians and wives to Baghdad because she felt they were encouraging Saddam to draw out the release of hostages and denying the alliance their 'window of opportunity' to recapture Kuwait before the intense heat of March. She felt that every time Saddam was persuaded to let a few more go the publicity and world attention actually underlined the advantage to him of keeping the others. He had a forum, a world stage. The attention of the world was upon him and it encouraged him to draw the releases out. From his letters, Anne knew that Henry, her husband who was in hiding in Kuwait, was very much against them as well. "He was vehemently against the mercy missions, and told me that 'If one goes, we all go'." Henry Hill was not alone. A great many hostages and a majority of those in hiding were against them, sometimes bitterly so. They saw them as divisive and working *against* their final release, not for it. Whilst some thought dialogue was valuable, others felt that the way the Iraqis simply replaced people released with new hostages from Kuwait made them a waste of time. There was considerable support for the government's tough stance as being the only real alternative.

In one interesting development, Yusuf Islam, formerly the pop singer Cat Stevens, flew out to Baghdad on a peace mission. He met a few people, was courted for press coverage by the Iraqis, and was allowed to take four Britons home with him. They arrived in Britain a few days before Mr Heath flew out. It was a good omen. Hostages *were* being released to people who wished to talk.

However, other developments in Iraq suggested the mission was very risky. Even as Mr Heath was organising his trip and emphasising his policy of dialogue, Iraq was using Soviet nationals as pawns. It was threatening to stop them leaving Iraq unless Moscow agreed not to give Iraqi military secrets to the United States. The Soviet Union had nearly five thousand nationals still in the country. Many of these were military advisors working closely with the Iraqi armed forces. Whilst not officially prevented from leaving, their visas had been repeatedly delayed.

Furthermore, in another petty act against British diplomats, Iraq withdrew diplomatic accreditation from the eight members of the Kuwait embassy who had moved up to Baghdad to help with the work load there. Meanwhile, the British embassy in Kuwait remained one of only six foreign embassies in the emirate. The situation was becoming increasingly difficult for them. After two of the four remaining British staff were withdrawn on 8th October, only the ambassador Michael Weston and his aide Larry Banks remained. The constant intimidation they faced was condemned by the British government as "a further example of the Iraqis' flagrant disregard for international law". Dr Azmi al-Salihi, the Iraqi ambassador in London was summoned to Whitehall and "told of Britain's displeasure".

Iraq also distributed highly controversial new maps of Kuwait to its diplomatic missions abroad. The map showed the northern third of Kuwait - down to the Mutlaa Ridge and including the islands of Warbah and Bubiyan - incorporated into the old Iraqi province of Basra, now renamed Saddamiyat al-Mutlaa. The rest of Kuwait became a new province, Iraq's nineteenth. Mr Heath was venturing into a very uncertain climate. He wasn't even sure whether *he* would be allowed out of Iraq, let alone permitted to take some hostages with him.

Mr Heath finally flew out of Heathrow on 19th October. The day before, he had contacted Dr Easton and asked him to come as well. Together with his private secretary Robert Vaudry, they first landed at Amman. In the Jordanian capital they were entertained in King Hussain's palace and Mr Heath was given dinner. Mr Heath clearly had a great deal of sympathy for the position Jordan found itself in.

The next day, Saturday the twentieth, they flew on to Baghdad. Mr Heath was in a confident mood. He was hoping to bring back up to seventy British hostages and had put the controversy about his visit behind him. He had several journalists with him and took the chance to reiterate his stance. He told them he had little fear of being used as a propaganda weapon by the Iraqis. *En route* they heard more encouraging news. The Reuter news agency announced that four Japanese hostages were to be set free, though no reasons were given.

Gilly Battersby, from Lincoln, was also on that flight. She was on her way to see her husband, without knowing whether she would be successful or be arrested and sent to an installation herself. Becoming increasing frustrated with the lack of diplomatic action on the hostages and increasingly anxious about her husband, she had resolved to apply to the Iraqi embassy for a visa to go back to Iraq. Not only was she granted one, but the Iraqi embassy announced that it would welcome requests from other British women to return. Furthermore, it promised her she would be allowed to see her husband and to return home afterwards.

The Foreign Office called this move by Iraq a "cynical manoeuvre" and the Gulf Support Group also advised relatives not to go. They both felt the relatives would be used as propaganda weapons and be further split into two camps - relatives with men in installations and relatives with men in hiding. However, the support group could also understand the enormous emotional pressure on those women who wanted to go.

Gilly had hoped just to see her husband and she *was* successful. Not only was her husband brought to her Baghdad hotel from his chemical installation, but they spent ten very happy days together, holding on to every precious second. Although her husband was not allowed to return to England with her, it gave them both a tremendous psychological boost. More significantly, when the news of her success reached the UK, a lot more women decided they had to try as well. Almost overnight, there was a flood of calls to the Iraqi embassy, the support group, the Emergency Unit and to British Airways for information about visas, flights, and the addresses of others who wanted to go.

Diplomatically, the flak was still flying. Proposals were being met with counter-proposals and outright denials. Yevgeny Primakov, the Soviet envoy sent to Iraq to get his nationals out, let slip that he thought Iraq might withdraw from Kuwait if it could keep the Rumillah oilfield and the islands of Bubiyan and Warbah in the north of the country. The official Iraqi news agency immediately condemned such a suggestion: "Those disseminating such baseless reports are well known and so are their aims. Kuwait was and will continue to be Iraqi land for ever." That very day Iran and Iraq reopened diplomatic relations and announced the reopening of their embassies.

Thus the international name-calling and hurling of abuse went on. Saddam attacked Bush for spending millions of dollars to "invade" Saudi Arabia whilst Iraqi children were dying through lack of food and medicine caused by the blockade. In a message on Children's Day, Saddam announced, "Those who shed crocodile tears on World Children's Day for children dying all over the world are themselves, together with their regimes, responsible for those tragedies." He was shown kissing several young children as an announcer read out his message. Western leaders were to blame for "the tragedy of any Iraqi child who dies from the shortage of food and medicine caused by their unjust blockade". He described Bush as "shameless and impudent" and championed the Palestinian cause as he denounced the West for "oppression and crimes against the children of Palestine in particular."

In their turn, the United States complained of Iraq's "sinister manipulation of innocent lives [which] again demonstrated its willingness to disregard every recognised standard of humanitarian conduct". And James Baker, US Secretary of State, referred to the unacceptibility of Iraq's "rape of Kuwait". Meanwhile, a resolution was going through the United Nations criticising Israel and hectic behind-the-scenes pressure was being applied by the USA to get it amended or even dropped.

As all these diplomatic squabbles thundered over their heads, more ex-hostages were attempting to leave Iraq. A group of three hundred and six Americans tried to fly out of Baghdad. The American press described them as being treated like animals by the Iraqi authorities as they were caught in the middle of this war of vitriol. Three Britons made a dash for freedom across the desert from Iraq to Saudi Arabia. They arrived in the northern Saudi town of Arar late on Monday 15th October after spending two days crossing the desert. One was a businessman, but two of them were nurses, part of the PARC organisation's contingent at the Ibn al-Bitar Hospital in Baghdad. It was the second escape attempt by members of PARC. The first, by three Irishmen, had resulted in them being caught at the border and being thrown into an Iraqi jail. They, like two hundred Irish and another forty-one British nurses and hospital staff, had been on contract in Iraq and had been denied exit visas until their contracts ended, and only then if other Irish and British replaced them. They were feeling increasingly isolated and vulnerable. Whilst their conditions were good and they were mostly relaxed about their situation, they were anxious to be allowed home. The PARC organisation immediately condemned the escape attempts as endangering the rest of the hospital team. It feared that the remaining staff would have more restrictions placed upon them as a result.

Mr Heath's party was not met at the airport by anyone from the British embassy, nor was an official car provided for them. Instead, it was the Iraqis who brought two limousines, one for Mr Heath, the other for his companions. Dr Easton was rather reticent about letting Mr Heath go into a car on his own. Images of Terry Waite's abduction went through his mind and he was seriously worried that he might not see him again.

They were taken straight to a large, secure house on the outskirts of Baghdad. It was very well furnished and extremely comfortable. They each had separate bedrooms and there was plenty of room for relaxing and working, with a study and several reception rooms. Surrounded by high walls and barbed wire, and in an extensive concrete compound, it was reminiscent of a Russian *dacha*, an exclusive private residence for some very senior minister. At no time were they offered accommodation or a diplomatic car by the British embassy. Robert Vaudry certainly thought its treatment of their party, virtually ignoring it, was appalling.

Dr Easton noticed certain striking aspects of Iraq and the regime very early on. He characterised Saddam and his regime as a collective psychopathy. Saddam came to power by killing people, and had remained in power by killing people. "He is extremely suspicious of people and therefore uses terror to impose discipline and dissuade opposition. He greatly admires Stalin's methods. He manipulates people, especially children, who are encouraged to criticise their parents and inform on them, and encourages a huge, omnipresent cult of hero-worship which totally dominates the media, the streets, public buildings and the private houses of the population. All over the country, there are minders. Everywhere Mr Heath went there were minders and microphones. I hadn't understood before, but now I really do understand, what a totalitarian government is like. Writers from Iraq describe the country as having been dehumanised. Saddam greatly fears a coup against him. He fears his relatives and other people plotting against him. He has instigated many purges of the Ba'ath Party and uses power sadistically. He requires hysterical, contagious peer support. He combines hatred and adulation in a cult of personality. That is how he succeeds in his reign of terror." Dr Easton paused for a second, before going on. "I think he's come to believe he *is* Iraq. He believes he *is* a second Saladin and even claims descent from the Prophet Mohammed. He's engaged in a massive, crude reconstruction of Babylon and in putting up enormous follies to himself everywhere, on every highway and every square. But I don't think he's mad. I think he's paranoid, but also very pragmatic. He can change his posture to suit circumstances."

That first day and the next, Mr Heath met groups of hostages in a number of hotels, including the Melia al-Mansour and ar-Rashid, the PARC nurses at the Ibn al-Bitar Hospital and those Bechtel workers stranded in the embassy compound. It also came to his attention that the contracts of thirty workers employed on Saddam's own palace were due to expire in a few weeks and that they were worried in case they weren't allowed to leave.

During Mr Heath's visit to the Ibn al-Batir Hospital on his first day in Baghdad, his party were followed by a bevy of British and Iraqi journalists and TV crews. The PARC nurses were being kept very busy. They were in good spirits, but some were very anxious to get out of Baghdad as soon as possible. One, Mary Kerrins, a twenty-four-year-old from County Sligo, was worried about her family and her boyfriend. "By the time I get back he will probably be married," she laughed. They were being well treated and carrying on their usual duties as nurses. The only change was that they wouldn't be allowed to leave Baghdad when their contracts were up unless more nurses came out to replace them.

That evening, Mr Heath and his party had dinner with Tariq Aziz, the Iraqi Deputy Prime Minister and Foreign Minister. Mr Heath and Mr Aziz sat and talked at length about the situation in the Gulf, about the need for peace and about Mr Heath's mission to free some of the hostages. Both men put their respective positions clearly and politely. Mr Aziz could speak very good English. He knew a great deal about the UK and was pleased to show off his knowledge. He was very well briefed and knew about the Poll Tax. (The Iraqi press made great play of the anti-Poll Tax riot at Hyde Park that day, saying how Mrs Thatcher was due to be toppled.) He joked about cricket, but seemed to have only a superficial knowledge of British culture. He was obviously very intelligent, yet was clearly in fear of Saddam and unwilling to step out of line. He was not prepared to negotiate or offer anything but the official position. He plainly had no power to make major decisions, and was very careful to preserve his privileges by not taking any initiative. He gave the impression of being polite, but not a man to persuade. He would agree politely, but do nothing.

The dinner went on for five hours. Mr Aziz, as all the Iraqis, refused to regard the hostages as anything other than 'guests'. Mr Heath fell in with the terminology, as all the emissaries had to, simply to 'play the game'. As demonstrated by Mr Aziz's arguments, the Iraqi regime had clearly calculated that the allies would be less likely to attack Iraq if they kept the human shield in place. "It was clear from that dinner with Tariq Aziz that they had underestimated the allied reaction to the invasion of Kuwait." Dr Easton explained. "They had expected something like sanctions and speeches only. That was undoubtedly how they felt. They couldn't understand why there had been such a reaction and kept saying to Ted that they couldn't understand why the UN had passed resolutions against Israel and done nothing, then passed a resolution against Iraq and was using force to implement it. They just couldn't understand that."

Another impression he received was that it was more acceptable in Iraqi society to take 'guests' to prevent people attacking you. It was an acceptable means of defence. "They certainly couldn't understand the *increased* British resolve, why the British public was much *more* angry and concerned *emotionally* about the hostages than about the invasion of Kuwait, why it greatly increased the public's resolve behind the British government, why it enraged the British public."

That night, Dr Easton was up late with Robert Vaudry trying to sort out the names of people to present to the Iraqis. They did not prioritise them at all. They assembled all the people who were elderly or with any medical condition whatsoever and gave them to the Iraqis. There were several hundred. Robert went to bed while Jeffrey worked on. At three in the morning, he took a couple of hours sleep, then rose again at five.

The man Dr Easton had most dealings with in Baghdad was Dr Saddun Joubaydi. He was Saddam Hussein's personal interpreter and had appeared at his side during the "Guests' News" with Stuart Lockwood and other hostage families in late August. Dr Easton was to get to know him quite well. He was not a medical doctor, but attached to the Ministry of Foreign Affairs. He was married with a family and had studied Shakespeare at Birmingham University. "It was clear that he had tremendous resentment about the English class structure, as he saw it." His first child had been born in England, but there had been some problem with the treatment for him. Perhaps he experienced prejudice, perhaps he felt his wife had been badly treated because she was an Arab, but the ill-feeling had lingered. Of such little things are attitudes formed. "I thought he hated the British."

There was a meeting between Mr Heath, Dr Easton, Robert Vaudry and Dr Joubaydi at the 'secure house', as it became known. Throughout, they were aware they were being bugged. "Saddun and Ted were talking politics and pleasantries. Saddun was saying we couldn't take very many with us. Robert was sitting in another corner. I took my shoes off and sat down on the floor. In front of me, I had the names of people with serious illnesses, or of people we'd met in Baghdad, plus letters from relatives and doctors documenting that people had a substantial problem. These letters were all in medical terms. They proved of no interest to the Iraqis whatsoever. I never once talked to an Iraqi medical doctor. The cases for these people had to be given in lay terms. So I used a separate sheet of paper for each person and wrote down the man's name on it and his age and diagnosis. As the pleasantries were going on, I would say, 'He's having chest pain at night and I'm told his medication is running out. He's frightened. His angina's getting worse. He may have had a heart attack. His wife has told me he's getting breathless at night. Please let us take him home.' And I would hand the piece of paper to Saddun, and he would look at it and take it. There would be no discussion, just pleasantries. And this went on and on and on and on." They weren't presented in any order of need and there was certainly no bartering or 'haggling' going on.

Two of the people he was especially concerned about were Alex and Rory Duncan. They were the teenage sons of Colonel Bruce Duncan, commanding officer of the British Liaison Team. They had decided not to risk coming out with the women and children, for fear of being taken to an installation, so were still in hiding in Kuwait City. Mr Heath had received letters from Alex's tutor and his family, which he had passed on to Dr Easton. In trying to get a good case together for them, he felt he had grown to know them like old friends.

Of course, there were general discussions. All three members of the British team emphasised that the more hostages let out with them, the more the principle of negotiation would be seen to be working, so it was in Iraq's interests to release as many as possible. All the time, arguments had to be presented in such a way. "It's in *your* interests to release them, not just ours. It will strengthen *your* arguments. It will enhance the chance of a peaceful solution. It will encourage negotiation." Similarly, it was argued that, if very few were let out, it would strengthen the case for those who simply wanted a military solution without negotiation.

Never on any occasion did Mr Heath or anyone in his party suggest that allowances might be made to the Iraqis. It was never argued that the release of hostages could help them win any territory, financial compensation, or concessions on any other grievance. Nor did he ever attempt to carry out negotiations on wider issues, which would have undermined the allied front against Saddam Hussein. In no way did he link the release of the hostages to any concessions, bargain or deal. Mr Heath was quite frank. The hostages were a completely separate issue. Keeping them was doing tremendous damage to Iraq's image abroad. Both the men and their families were suffering enormously. They should never have been taken and should be released immediately.

Yet at home, the attacks against him went on. One Conservative MP described Mr Heath and Saddam Hussein as a "couple of rogues together". The negative headlines continued, as did the dismissive leader articles. One article in *The Times* carried on the general media hype that such visits threatened to split the alliance against Iraq. Even as Mr Heath was discussing his hostages, the Iraqi government announced that all French citizens, plus a dozen Americans, would be allowed home in what the paper described as "a tactic calculated to drive a wedge into the Western alliance".

On Sunday, Mr Heath visited the British embassy and spoke to the fifty-nine Bechtel men who had been camped in its gardens since the beginning of August. Mr Heath stated that "they had accommodated themselves very well and organised themselves satisfactorily. They were worried about the onset of cold weather and what would happen to them then. There were some of them who were seriously ill, but who hadn't told their colleagues in the compound. They were living in tents at the time, but were not distressed. They had very good food supplies. They had very large stocks to last through the winter if they remained there during the winter months. It was mainly the question of the weather which was worrying them."

Mr Heath's office was not pleased with the lack of help from the embassy in Baghdad. It was polite but gave little practical help to his mission. His companions both felt it was shabby treatment to deny him access to embassy facilities and to refuse him the help of embassy staff. It is clear from talking to diplomats who were in the Baghdad embassy at the time that all the staff, including the very highest, at the embassy wished to give Mr Heath far more help than they were allowed to by the British government. In fact, they *did* give more support than they were instructed to by Downing Street, including inviting his party to dinner at the embassy one evening.

It was similar for the press. The reporters in Baghdad gave their overwhelming support to Mr Heath. They were extremely helpful. They knew what was going on in Baghdad and the situation in the hotels and installations. Yet the leader writers and copy editors back in Britain gave their articles negative titles, such as "Heath Haggles Over Hostages" (*The Times*, 23rd October) when the last thing he ever did was 'haggle', or "Heath Mission to Baghdad Hits Problems" (*The Independent*, 23rd October). The first of these articles went on: "The fate of British hostages was being negotiated in an atmosphere better suited to the Baghdad *souk* [marketplace] than the presidential palace, as Mr Heath's aides haggled with Iraqi officials..." Interestingly enough, the source of these two stories was Whitehall. I wonder why? When Mr Heath came out with the hostages, and received tremendous support from the British people, the press quickly changed its tune, but those articles were symptomatic of the concerted attempt to pour scorn on his visit.

The Foreign Office continued to tread a very careful path throughout Mr Heath's visit. It was worried in case his mission undermined the government's 'no negotiation' stance. Was Mr Heath suggesting concessions the West could make to Saddam? What *was* he saying? Was he undermining the British position? Douglas Hurd reiterated than any concessions to the Iraqi leader would be "very dangerous for the future". He stressed how important it was for the alliance to "stand firm" on Iraq's unconditional withdrawal from Kuwait. "Anything which blurs that is clearly a mistake." The Foreign Office couldn't be seen as condoning the trip, yet couldn't criticise it outright. When Mr Heath returned, Douglas Hurd continued walking his tightrope when he stated that the release of the hostages was wonderful for the individuals concerned and their families, but Mr Heath's mission must not give any signals of a reduction in Britain's resolve to defeat President Saddam.

Meanwhile, Mr Heath's team continued to work in increasingly difficult circumstances. The Iraqis were up to their old tricks. They used Mr Heath for extensive propaganda purposes in their own country and throughout the Arab world, despite Mr Heath's wishes. Saddam was able to pose as an international statesman, as the leader of the Arab world, negotiating with world leaders, fighting for the rights of Arabs and especially the Palestinians. There were dozens of photo opportunities with television crews, radio and newspaper photographers. Although Mr Heath did not say anything in support of Saddam, he couldn't help being used as he was.

On Sunday morning, Mr Heath went to meet Saddam Hussein. The President was dressed informally in a tie and leather jacket, not his usual military uniform. They sat in the plush surroundings of the Presidential Palace and talked for some three hours.

It became clear to Mr Heath that President Saddam was anxious for a peaceful solution to the crisis, but not prepared to give any ground on leaving Kuwait. He was not prepared to alter his position at all. Mr Heath raised the question of the hostages with him, arguing that they were doing terrible harm to Iraq's image abroad. "Retaining them in Iraq created ill-feeling in Britain and did not help to reach a diplomatic solution." Although Saddam was "sympathetic" to that argument, he remained convinced that his 'guests' were a protection against a sudden American attack.

Mr Heath did not raise specific names of hostages with Saddam. Most of the conversation was on general political matters, the issue of sanctions, of negotiations and the positions of the British and Iraqi governments. Only 'categories' of hostages were discussed, such as the sick, the elderly, the PARC nurses, the contract workers at Saddam's palace, the Bechtel workers in the embassy compound, several young men still students, and the British passengers on BA Flight 149. "These particular groups of people ought to be returned to their homes, as they have a particular reason for being released." When he argued for the release of the thirty contract workers employed on Saddam's own palace, whose contracts were due to end, the Iraqi president agreed they would be allowed to leave when their contracts were up.

Mr Heath avoided any outright criticism of the Iraqi regime, nor did he criticise it for its invasion of Kuwait, nor for its alleged atrocities in the emirate. In the conversation, Saddam's knowledge of world affairs was extensive and impressive. He was clearly not a madman. He knew what he was doing and why, and had weighed up every possible course of action. He very much knew what he was doing. Mr Heath emphasised the need for dialogue and diplomacy to counter the threat of war. He hoped that if the Iraqi leader showed willingness to compromise, by letting the hostages go, but also in other ways, it would encourage the British and American governments to try harder to find a diplomatic solution. He pressed the President on the taking of the hostages. They should never have been arrested and certainly never been taken to the strategic sites. In very careful and diplomatic language, which yet managed to be quite frank, he told Saddam that he must release *all* the hostages without delay.

The Iraqi President did agree to let some hostages go, though he refused to say how many. When asked whether he would want anything in return, he said no, they would be released without strings.

That night, Mr Heath and his team talked far into the night with Dr Joubaydi about the hostages, arguing for each in turn. It was becoming clear that they *would* be allowed to take some of the sick and elderly home with them, and that more would follow later. They would also be allowed to take some teenage boys back with them. Two of these would be Alex and Rory Duncan, sons of Colonel Bruce Duncan. When the Kuwait embassy passed on the good news to them they hurriedly packed and arranged to meet an Iraqi car which would whisk them up to Baghdad.

By Monday the twenty-second, Mr Heath's team was approaching the end of its mission. They were still unsure precisely who would be flying out with them and spent that day reiterating the urgency of some of the cases and trying to persuade the Iraqis to release as many as possible. The Iraqis gave no indication of their response other than to serve up several vague figures. In fact, they had already contacted the installations for the top thirty or so on Mr Heath's list and ordered them to be despatched to Baghdad on Sunday night for Mr Heath's flight out on Wednesday. All Mr Heath could do was meet a few more of the British trapped in Baghdad and await developments.

One of the men who flew out with Mr Heath was David Cunningham, aged forty-four but with diabetes. David had been assistant manager at the Plaza Hotel in Kuwait City when the Iraqis invaded. After about a month, he was arrested and taken up to Baghdad, where he was held at the Melia al-Mansour Hotel. There, he met the ambassador, Harold Walker, by the hotel pool one day and asked him what the embassy was going to do for the British community. The ambassador was not able to offer much help and David was not very impressed. "Basically, the embassy was only gathering names and telephone numbers to contact relatives in Britain. There was no other help really. We were all anxious to get messages back home. Our main concern was to tell our families that we were safe and well."

When David was taken from the Melia al-Mansour, he was escorted by four Iraqi security guards. They drove for half an hour or so to a house on the outskirts of Baghdad. There were five Westerners already there, an American, two Englishmen and two Irishmen. They were kept in the house for ten days. "The house was all right. It had three or four bedrooms, a lounge, kitchen, dining room, and was quite big and comfortable. It was the house of a factory manager." At the time, they were told the factory, thirty-five kilometres north of Baghdad on the Mosul road, made spare parts for tractors. In fact, it manufactured T72 tanks. Close by was a gas-bomb plant.

The factory manager's house was just outside the gate of the plant, right by the perimeter fence. At two o'clock one Saturday morning, Iraqi soldiers suddenly entered their bedrooms and ordered them to pack. They were given five minutes to get ready. As they made their way out with their meagre suitcases and bags, the Iraqis stripped their rooms of beds, furniture and electrical equipment - even the kitchen sink - and piled it onto the backs of some trucks. The six men and all the household possessions were taken inside the factory gate to a converted computer office in the very heart of the factory. As they walked in, still in the middle of the night, Iraqis were spraying all the windows white to prevent them seeing what was going on in the factory. The windows were welded closed.

Their conditions in this office block were significantly worse than at the manager's house. They had but two large rooms. One they used for a bedroom, the other for a lounge. The guards had three smaller bedrooms, and another small bedroom was turned into a kitchen. There were two shower rooms. Fortunately, it was a brand new block so, although dusty, it was full of new equipment - new showers, new toilets, new lighting.

The toilets were simply holes in the ground. David refused to use them, but was told that was all there was. "I was standing there with a toilet roll in my hand, demanding to be taken back to the manager's house to go to the toilet, arguing with the Iraqi guards. They eventually brought up a four-wheel drive. I climbed in with several security guards and was driven back up to the house, where I relieved myself and was driven back."

The men set up their single beds and sorted themselves out. "Conditions were OK. We had some reasonable furniture; we had a television; we had a dining table and a bookcase; I had my stereo with me, so we had music; and we had a short wave radio, so we could pick up the BBC's World Service."

They were not allowed outside for the first few days, until the Iraqis had constructed an eight-foot high corrugated steel fence around the block to prevent them seeing what was going on in the factory. "Once that was up, we were allowed to go into the exercise yard."

The hostages couldn't sleep. On their first night they had demanded a proper toilet, which the Iraqis agreed to, but all that night there were drills and hammers going as they installed it. Whilst they were building the fence, the noise was impossible. On top of that, the factory was in full production, working all night as well as all day. Drills, lathes, hammers, trucks, crashing sheets of steel, and oxyacetylene torches clattered through the darkness. There were also floodlights blazing through the windows, both to watch them and to light up the factory. The men complained, and the work on the fence stopped at night. Once the fence was completed, the noise of the factory seemed to be deadened and they could sleep.

The men had already built a relationship with the factory manager. They asked for the paint to be stripped off the windows and the bolts on them to be removed so they could let in fresh air. He was amenable and things improved. They were given chairs to sit outside, and also a garden swing - supplied by the workers in the factory. They sorted out the showers and kitchen and fell into a routine.

The biggest problem was boredom. "You couldn't go anywhere. You had no idea what was happening or how long you were going to be kept. At least, if you're a prisoner in a jail, you know exactly what your sentence is. You're allowed visitors, you're allowed mail. We were denied all those things. We had no access to the embassy people; we were allowed to write out, but weren't allowed any mail coming in. The only link we had was by shortwave radio, where we could pick up messages from our families."

They gradually built a rapport with their minders. They were like plain clothes security men and wore neither uniforms nor guns inside the compound. They were undoubtedly reporting back to their officers and had a file on each of them, but they were very friendly. "The people that looked after us became part of the family. We discussed our families. It came down to that level." It was a conscious strategy by David to build this relationship, both to ease their conditions and to win the guards over to their point of view. It's harder to shoot someone you know. The guards would sit with them and talk and listen to the radio. "They were as happy for you when you received a message as you were. They would come over and clasp your hand when you'd heard from your family. They were just as bored as we were. They were stuck there six days a week. They had one day off each." In many camps, the guards shared the hostages living conditions, their food, rooms, and showers, and were confined most of the time to the same few rooms and the small compounds. They would talk and laugh, and occasionally they would empathise with their prisoners.

In some camps, the guards became more sympathetic to the plight of the Westerners than the Iraqi leadership. They grew more attached to them and more friendly. In many ways, they were won over to the views and ways of thought of the hostages, although the constant propaganda and their position as minders ensured their discipline. Some of them were definitely developing divided loyalties. Just some - and in some camps more than others. But the image of hard-nosed Iraqi soldiers was not generally true. There were some camps where the Iraqis were nasty, often where they were Ba'ath Party members or secret police, but the average guard was a simple soldier, warm, sympathetic, even apologetic. It was that guilt which played on many of their minds and made them want to establish friendships rather than enmities. They wanted peace whereas the hostages overwhelmingly wanted war - immediately. They supported Mrs Thatcher and President Bush's tough stance and often took great pleasure in goading their guards with the threat of cruise missiles and carpet bombing.

The secret police were a different matter. They were much more formal and intimidatory. They visited David Cunningham's installation once a week and questioned the hostages on their political attitudes, what they thought of Saddam Hussein or the Americans or the British government, trying to draw them into a political conversation. The hostages told them to get lost.

Similarly, the hostages developed a certain sympathy for their immediate captors, but definitely *not* the Stockholm Syndrome. The so-called Stockholm Syndrome arose from an incident when a group of terrorists kidnapped an aircraft and held the passengers prisoner in a coach in Stockholm. They were held at gunpoint, staring at grenades ready to go off. The passengers began to fear a police or army assault on the kidnappers as much as the kidnappers themselves. They began to share a common interest in a peaceful outcome. Their attitudes began to coincide with the kidnappers as they felt they shared a common fate. Whilst all the hostages in the human shield were acutely aware that, once the war started, it would be only a matter of hours before the installations were bombed and that both they and their guards would be exterminated, there was certainly no Stockholm Syndrome developing amongst them.

In fact, amongst the ordinary soldiers guarding them, the opposite seems to have been developing - a sympathy for their captives' situation, a guilt and apologetic stance. The hostages felt the Iraqis were totally morally unjustified in keeping them and constantly told their guards so. Some camps were characterised by anger and bitterness, a constant battle between hostages and guards. In others, a rapport developed and life was fairly civilised.

The overwhelming feeling amongst those held hostage at the installations was for a war to start as soon as possible. They didn't focus on their personal safety but on the treatment meted out to them and their families, on the rape of Kuwait and on the threat to a whole geographical region. No, this time, it tended to be the guards who sympathised with their captives, rather than vice versa. In some installations, the hostages would constantly bait the guards with taunts of "They can see you light a cigarette from their satellites. They know everything you're doing. There's a missile with your name on it. You're all going to be blown to pieces." On the whole, the hostages remained aggressive, angry and bitter. They would constantly test the guards, question them, disobey them and see how far they could be pushed. Some became very depressed and withdrawn, but not out of sympathy for their captors. Rather the opposite - out of hatred.

They were constantly bombarded with propaganda. The television was full of it every day. There was a special "Guest's News" [sic] programme, which started with a picture of Saddam and had stars shooting past his head. Then came male singers praising him, then film of him sitting on a throne with children dancing around him, then speeches and declarations of Iraq's might against the infidel, then declamations against American and British imperialism and the harmful effects of sanctions on innocent women and children, then more speeches and Saddam touring the city shaking hands with people.

Every street was decked in huge portraits of Saddam and slogans supporting him. Everywhere, there were posters of Saddam, even in the installation and their compound. Whenever the guards put them up, they disappeared, only for the guards to put more up the next morning.

The rank and file soldiers would praise Saddam, but in private they would express their fears. "There was a lot of fear." The soldiers would bring videos for them, nearly all British and American movies, and sit and watch with them. Their anti-American sentiments would disappear as they and the hostages sat as a family around the television to watch Rambo, Top Gun or The Green Berets. The hostages would tease the guards whenever the American hero blew some poor Asian soldier to oblivion. "Look, that's what'll happen to you!" The guards would just laugh.

The security around the plant made it perfectly obvious to the men held with David that it produced more than spare parts for tractors. There were machine guns on the main gate and the towers on each corner of the compound also had machine guns. They were in a sealed prison camp. Not a concentration camp, but certainly a prisoner-of-war camp. If any of them tried to walk out the gate, as they did, they were stopped.

Three were kept in the office block until late October, including David. The rest were moved around, with new hostages coming every few weeks. The three stalwarts continued to build a good relationship with the guards, especially the factory manager. David realised they had to get organised and develop a routine if they were to survive. With his managerial experience, he became a middle man, negotiating with the manager. Every few days, David would get a visit from him and be asked what they needed. The manager was tall and intelligent. He had a very pleasant manner and spoke excellent English and German.

"The main points we discussed were the conditions in the house, especially the food, because it was so very limited. We had no dairy produce whatsoever, no minerals, tinned coffee, hardly any sugar, and only flat, unleavened Arabic bread for breakfast. We had rice, cucumber and tomatoes as our staple diet for lunch and dinner the whole time we were there. Occasionally, we were given tiny chunks of gristle which was intended to be meat. We could barely eat it. We would down what was there because we were so hungry. I pleaded with him to let us have some fruit or something different, but he told me those things were limited within Baghdad; no one was getting them. The guards ate the same food as we did, so we knew there wasn't anything special laid on for them. If there was ever any shortage of food, they would ensure that we ate first."

Every letter was censored, but every one David sent to his family made it to Newcastle. They are like a diary of what happened to him. He was allowed to take photographs of the guards, and managed to hold on to the film and bring it home. They held a birthday party for Sid, one of the Irishmen, making him a cake with 'Sid' written in icing sugar and handing him a bouquet of plastic flowers. "We sat around the table to eat the cake and took photographs of the security guards. The Iraqis loved having their photographs taken."

David had worked with chefs, so trained the two Iraqi 'cooks' in basic hygiene and cooking methods. He showed them how to use spices to vary the rice as much as they could. The cooks were also the cleaners and David would inspect their cleaning and call them back if it wasn't good enough. Saturday became washing day. Everything was taken to a laundry, except for daily things like underclothes, for which they had a small tub. He even organised the guards to strip their beds. They accepted his organisation and played at calling him the manager. It all helped build a relationship.

"Were there any difficult moments?"

"Only one for me personally. At two or three o'clock one morning, I was woken up by soldiers in green uniforms and was told to get dressed."

"Where are you taking me?"

"You're going to a hospital for a check-up."

David was a diabetic, but he couldn't understand why they were taking him in the middle of the night. "It's two o'clock in the morning."

"Do as you're told. Get dressed. You're coming with us."

By this time, the whole room had woken up and everyone was anxiously asking him where he was going.

"I don't know," was all David could reply. He took his address book from his bag and gave it to one of the guys. "If I don't come back, this has got details of my family in it. If you ever get back to England, please contact them." Neither David nor any of the other hostages knew whether they would see each other again, or even whether David would see that morning's sunrise.

Once dressed, the hostage followed the soldiers outside to two vehicles - a brand new Range Rover and a car. He was told to get into the Range Rover, along with the driver and two armed guards. There were four more soldiers in the car behind.

It seemed far too many guards just to escort him to a hospital. He felt increasingly nervous, trying to make his peace with the world, silently praying, remembering his aged mother at home in Newcastle, his sister and her family, his life, his hopes and achievements, reconciling himself to what was about to happen.

They drove through the desert, but kept to the main Baghdad road. After half an hour, they entered the city and approached its centre, where he *was* taken to a hospital. He was led into a small room where he was seen by a specialist in diabetes, who gave him a thorough examination and then told him he could go.

When he arrived back at the factory in time for breakfast, the others were extremely relieved to see him. It was suddenly all jokes and laughter: "The whole house was in uproar when I got back." But David could tell that they had been as anxious as him about his fate. Even the guards had been concerned about him.

Although nothing did happen, it was symptomatic of the tension, uncertainty and powerlessness the hostages constantly endured. With hindsight, none of the people held on installations was murdered, but at the time, none of them knew whether the next morning would be his last. Everything was done in the middle of the night, when the hostages were disorientated, sleepy and at their most vulnerable.

Later, David was told that the seven soldiers who went with him to the hospital were not intended to intimidate him, but to protect him. They were worried in case anything should happen to him. Many Iraqis had been built into a frenzy of hatred for Westerners by Saddam's propaganda and might have dragged him out of the car and butchered him. This was part of the peculiar double-think the Iraqi authorities engaged in. They deliberately moved hostages in the middle of the night, with only a few minutes notice, yet said they were concerned about their safety.

In fact, they were only concerned about the hostages' safety insofar as their necks were on the line. So long as they were safe, so long as their food was adequate to survive, so long as they received just enough medical attention so they didn't die, enough furniture and facilities - such as a pack of cards, a volley ball or a few square yards of compound to walk around in - they didn't care. So long as the hostages survived and didn't kick up too much of a fuss, they were treated as badly as they could get away with. So long as they didn't actually die, they could be treated like animals.

David developed a routine whereby he rose at seven, had an early morning shower, then sat outside in the gentle morning sun until breakfast time. That was usually a very simple meal of unleavened Arabic bread, but it was always fresh, baked that morning in the factory. After breakfast, he would read or spend time in prayer and meditation, asking for help, guidance and strength. "I don't think I could have coped without the strength my faith gave me. I'm not a physically strong person. It was this inner strength which kept me going and I was able to pass it on to one or two of the others who weren't coping very well." A couple of the other hostages were also religious. Discussions between them happened automatically over their weeks together. They would sit

The Meridien Hotel in the centre of Kuwait City, after the Iraqis exploded a bomb in it

An apartment block in Fintas overlooking the Gulf, typical of the way the Iraqis fortified the whole coast

A deserted Iraqi checkpoint in al-Sharq, central Kuwait City

A deserted Iraqi command bunker in Shuwaikh Port

Apartment blocks fortified by the Iraqis and surrounded by burnt-out cars

The SAS Hotel, burnt out by the Iraqis as they left

A group of British hostages relax upstairs in the Melia al-Mansour Hotel, Bagho

A group of hostages at the T72 tank factory just north of Baghdad with David Cunningham celebrate a birthday with their Iraqi minders

The group of hostages kept with Frank Kerfoot at Baiji, a photograph taken by another hostage and smuggled out

The Gulf Link team in their studio at Bush House

A group of men in hiding show their appreciation of the Gulf Link programme

HE KUWAIT INVASION TIMES

2nd November 1990 DAY 93

22 YEARS

he big news today the 22nd wedding iniversary of *Mel Carol Gage*. As is ;ual, in this ırrent situation, el & Carol will ıld separate lebrations.

ɔwever, we all ɔpe that Mel will t a message on ılf Link tonight, herwise it will be *VORCE* time in e old town night. The editor staff of the VASION TIMES wish th of them best shes and we hope u will be together ain soon.

sex sex sex sex

an Heley Bares All to the SUN

Pictures on PAGE 3

MONEY

Have YOU heard the news about money ?? It would seem that the Kuwaiti Government has sent ID 200 for each ex-pat in the country. Full details of where and how to get it on *Page 2*

NEW CARS FOR OLD

The latest offer from the Iraqi Government is that if you give them your old car, you will get a new one (From the Kuwaiti Government).

Anyone wishing to take advantage of this offer should drive into the City.

uwait Invasion Times, one of two occasional underground publications, the other the Hostage Herald. They were both produced on word-processors then a few ous copies were photocopied and circulated amongst the community via couriers

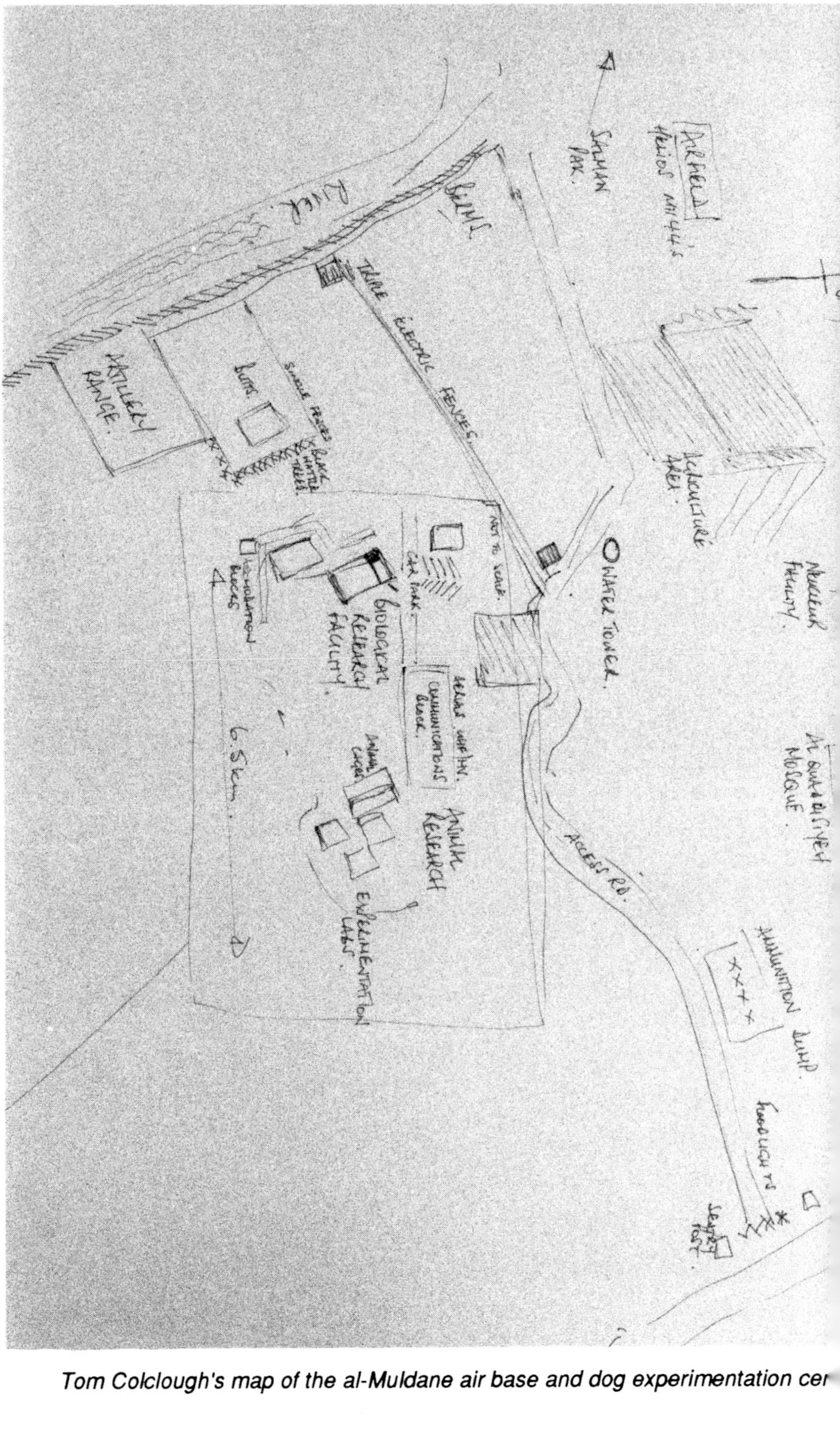

Tom Colclough's map of the al-Muldane air base and dog experimentation cer

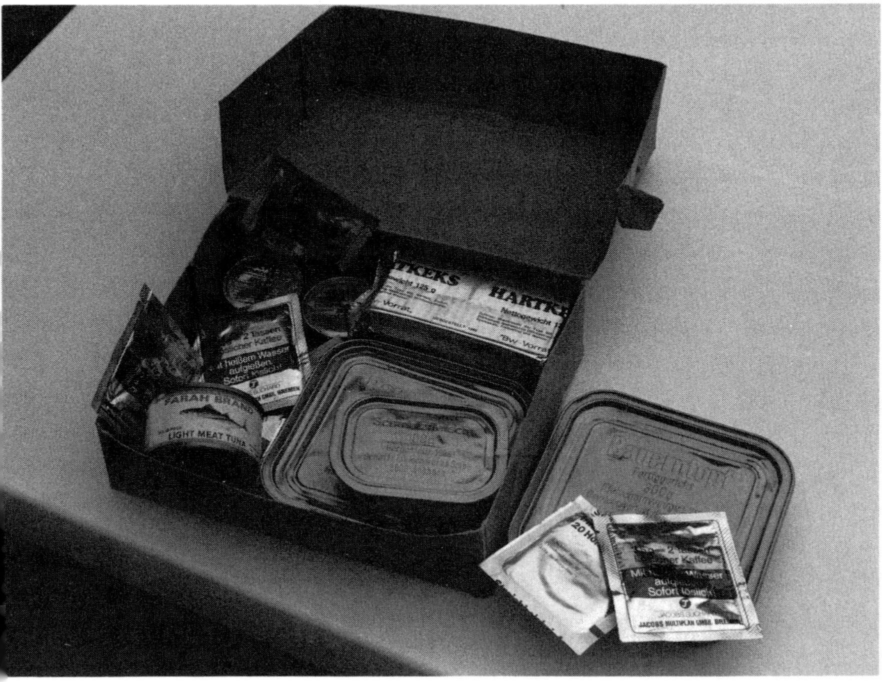

One of the ration packs supplied to German hostages on the sites

The three lines of electrified fences and barbed wire which surrounded the IBI camp, typical of the fencing surrounding many installations

Rt Hon Tony Benn MP

The reception area of the Regency Palace Hotel, after the Iraqis destroyed it

The devastation on Mutlaa Ridge after allied planes bombed escaping Iraqis

and Palestinian destruction of the computers rooms at Shuwaikh Port Authority

Kuwaitis clamber over a deserted Iraqi tank in a suburb of the city

The trophies of war outside a British villa in Salwa, including part of the tail section of BA Flight 149

Two Iraqi street signs 'liberated' by some British. Note the Iraqi name for northern Kuwait - Saddamiat Al Mutlaa

A firefighting team move in to cap an oil well fire in the Rumillah oil field in northern Kuwait

One of the many oil wells burning fiercely in the al-Burgan oil field after the Iraqis set fire to them

outside in the morning and have a prayer and quiet chat together.

The feeling of being close to God helped him come to terms with what was happening to him now. David would say the Lord's Prayer and recite prayers of his own. He had a copy of the Koran, which had been given to him, and which, because it runs so closely to the Bible, was a great comfort. He would discuss it with the guards, intermingled with conversations about their families, the situation, their hopes, and Islam. "They hoped we would be allowed to go soon. They were tired. They had been involved in an eight-year war with Iran. They wanted to be with their families. They didn't want all this, but they had to obey orders. They would be pleased when the whole thing was over."

Then it was lunchtime.

Thus David found purpose to life in the compound. Unlike other hostages, he didn't see captivity as a huge hole in his life, as a waste, as existence put on hold until he could begin it again. He wasn't full of negative emotions, of frustrations, anger and futility. He wasn't constantly looking to it to end, living for tomorrow rather than today. He wasn't fuelled with bitterness, but with calm acceptance. As with Tom Colclough, who found purpose through nightly stalking his installation and gathering information on the Iraqis, or Cliff Lindley, who wrote a book whilst in hiding, or Dave Dorrington who compiled news-sheets such as the *Hostage Herald*, or others who worked on computer games, he kept himself going by feeling that incarceration was actually a positive experience, something which was forming his life and him as a human being. That positive sense of purpose and acceptance of imprisonment as a valuable part of life proved essential to David's survival and mental well-being.

In hindsight, whilst a positive mental attitude was vital, it was essential to recognise the trauma in that experience as well. There was a great deal of hardship, uncertainty, fear and appalling treatment. Failure to accept that it was a terribly stressful time and that there are bound to be psychological scars can lead to retention of that anger and bitterness for a very long and self-destructive period. The human shield had to both think positively to survive then, and be realistic about the long-term effects on them if they are to survive now.

David became closer to himself. "You discover your limitations. You find out who you are and what your capabilities are. I found that I had the strength, not only to support myself, but to support the people around me and to be a friend to the Iraqis. It was pointless trying to be an enemy of someone who didn't want to be your enemy but was just there under orders."

At the beginning of October, David's group heard over the World Service that Edward Heath was flying to Iraq to try to secure the release of the sick and elderly. On the Sunday he met Saddam, the twenty-first, the radio announced that a number of hostages would be released with him, but not how many or their details. At six o'clock that evening the telephone at the compound rang and David began to sense that something was going to happen. "I remember it well. It was the first time we had ever had potatoes. I was in the kitchen getting the chips ready for the guys. A guard walked in and said, 'Get packed, you're going.' I went ice cold. I started shivering. He said, 'You've got half an hour. Please get ready and go quickly.' I was running around. Nobody could believe it. Everybody was happy for me and helped me pack and get things ready. Then the emotional side just fell apart. All eight of the guys and the security guards were wound up. I shook hands with them all and then the Arabs hugged me and kissed me on the cheeks, saying how happy they were for me." It was a very genuine feeling and a very emotional parting.

David thought he would be taken straight to the airport, but instead ended up at the Melia al-Mansour Hotel. There, he recognised two guys he had met previously at the installation, but who had been moved on some time ago. More people drifted in in ones and twos, until there were thirty-three of them assembled. "We were kept at the hotel for three days. No one knew what was happening. No one would tell us anything." So they fell into the hotel routine of meals interspersed with hours by the pool or in the lounge as they waited.

One passenger waiting in the hotel was Joe Wild. He had been captured by the Iraqis late in August and taken up to Baghdad in a convoy of women and children. On September the seventh, he and two Frenchmen were bundled into the back of a truck and driven to a chemical weapons plant forty-seven kilometres south-west of Baghdad. Joe was never to discover the name of it, symptomatic of the intense secrecy the Iraqis kept about the locations and names of their sites. It may have been Karbala, where there was a large chemical weapons installation sited on a tributary of the Euphrates, but was almost certainly further down the river at al-Muldane.

There were already a number of hostages held at the installation. Amongst them were Roy Willatt, Chris Hughes and his girlfriend, Caroline [now also named Hughes!], several other Britons and a group of Japanese. Chris and Caroline had endured a remarkable series of events. They had been hiding in Kuwait when Chris was arrested one morning whilst out on the streets, and Caroline never saw him again. She was terrified he had been shot, tortured or buried in some unmarked grave because she received no news whatsoever about him. Eventually, she ended up in the hands of the Iraqis as well and was taken up to the Melia al-Mansour Hotel in Baghdad. As she came down to breakfast in the hotel one morning, she noticed Chris. They flew into each other's arms and refused to be separated when the rest of the women left for the UK.

After a few days, the couple were brought to the al-Muldane camp, where they remained for a while with Joe and the others. They were soon moved on to what was no more than a ship's container in an installation in Basra, where they lived in appalling conditions with atrocious food.

On one occasion their rice was prepared in a dustbin lid and stirred with the cook's boot! They asked for water to drink, but were given water from the drum the guards had used to wash in.

Meanwhile, Joe soon fell ill. Since the start of his ordeal in Kuwait, his daily intake of tablets had risen from two to ten, as a result of the hardship and stress he was enduring. The installation didn't have the necessary tablets to care for his heart problem so he was driven to a hospital in Baghdad. The hospital was in an appalling state. "When I say Dickensian, I mean *Dickensian*. It was the filthiest, dirtiest dump I could ever imagine. You never saw anything like it in your life. It was attrocious."

During his visit to the hospital, he was guarded by a soldier with a rifle, as though he was going to run all the way to Turkey in his condition - his diarrhoea was so bad he couldn't run the length of the corridor. He was X-rayed and saw a doctor, then was allowed to go to the toilet. "It was a hole in the floor with a pile of shit in a great big cone. I couldn't have used it."

He was returned to the camp then, four days later, taken away again to be "assessed". By now, Joe was in a bad way, complaining of stomach cramps, groaning all night and hardly able to move. They took him back to the hospital and this time put him in an intensive care unit to monitor his heart. "I laid on a bed which was the filthiest, dirtiest bed I've ever seen in my life. An air-conditioning unit was spraying black dust onto it all day and night. It was covered in blood. Underneath it was a bucket full of pink swabs and dirty needles. And I'm worried about getting AIDS, you see."

He paused to let the full impact of the conditions sink in as I listened. "So, I took my shoes off and put them on the floor. They were immediately filled with great, black cockroaches."

The hospital staff removed the patient next to him, who was in a near-terminal state, and put the guard in it with his gun. He slept alongside Joe the whole time he was in the hospital. "I was in there for thirty-six hours. The only meal I had was a piece of bread as big as a walnut and half a glass of water - the water was to soften the bread so I could eat it!"

The hospital was so bad Joe pleaded with the doctors to let him go back to the camp. "At least at the camp we did get rice with cucumbers." So they discharged him and Joe and his guard were driven back to the camp in the rear of a pick-up truck.

Dysentery was rife at the camp. There was one toilet that worked and one which spewed its contents over the hostages' feet. There had been a lot of men in the camp at one time, but their numbers had dwindled as some had been moved to other installations. There were still fourteen of them, any combination with dysentery at any one time - all desperate for the single toilet. The only way to get clean was to use the shower and wash the excrement down their legs and, in Joe's words, "poke it down the drainage hole".

What suggests it was al-Muldane was the presence of a dog experimentation laboratory. Wild dogs arrived in lorry loads to be gassed, injected, or whatever, then their corpses were removed the next morning in trucks to be incinerated or buried in the desert. The howls, turning to cries, gradually descending to whimpers, then to nothing, kept the hostages awake all night. It was impossible to get used to the sounds of such cruelty.

There were about half a dozen guards at the camp, headed by a major. At first, they were allowed to walk around during the day, although they were not allowed to approach the laboratory area. There were neither fences around them nor a compound, but they were constantly guarded by armed soldiers. Later, they were only allowed out of their living quarters in the evening, when the light was fading. However, the site was low-lying, close to the marshes surrounding the Euphrates. There were millions of mosquitos which were most active in the cool hours of evening. They became so covered in bites it was a waste of time venturing out, unless they wanted to be eaten alive.

Joe became close friends with Roy Willatt and Chris Hughes. The three of them used to think of any ploy to annoy the guards, including putting frogs in their rooms, asking them for cigarettes at all hours of the night, marching up and down singing *God Save The Queen* and *Rule Britannia* and, perhaps even worse than Joe's singing, slipping mouse droppings into the guards' soup. They had found the dropping in their cornflakes, sifted them out and kept them for the guards. They were so hungry, they still ate the cornflakes.

Their accommodation, a few rooms in an administration block, was overrun with mice and rats. "The grub was terrible. It was just rice and cucumbers. We had a woman who used to look after us and cook for us. She had a big bandage on her finger which was black and used to pick her nose whilst she cooked the rice. The guards were stealing our food. There were twelve inmates by then, and only six guards. We had four cups of rice for the inmates and fourteen cups for the guards. They also kept other food to themselves. Of one consignment of a hundred and sixty eggs, the inmates saw just two each. The rest went to the guards and their families."

The Japanese with Joe had been receiving food parcels and letters from their embassy every week. The British heard nothing and received nothing during their entire internment. "The Japanese and Germans looked after their people beautifully. You never saw anything like it in your life. As far as the British were concerned, we received nothing. We were considered to be the bad people. We were the last to be released. It was the way their whole attitude was towards us." The Japanese parcels were not delivered by the Red Crescent or the Iraqi government, but directly by the Japanese embassy staff. The German hostages had a similar system.

The Iraqi guards allowed their hostages to keep well informed. They were permitted short wave radios and even had a TV. The programmes were virtually all about Saddam Hussein, making speeches or visiting some school or hospital or military base, interspersed with rousing music and songs hailing him as a demi-god. The guards used to kiss his image when it came on, stroking the screen in admiration and tell the hostages, "This is our great leader".

"Every night there was a special programme the Iraqis called "The Peace Broadcast", but which we called "Traitors' Half Hour". They used to get all these Brits and Americans and French to appear on it and give a peace message: 'We think President Bush should not be doing this', and all that."

Iraqi interrogators visited the camps frequently. They had a dossier on every hostage, some quite thick, and would ask each person in turn if they wanted to give a peace message over the TV. It was moral blackmail, because most of the men hadn't seen their families for months and were desperate to let them know they were all right. At least their families would be able to see them, even if they were being used for propaganda. The interrogators even 'suggested' things they might say. Joe was asked, but refused point-blank.

"Oh, but Mr Wild, we move you to a better camp if you say Mr Bush and Mrs Thatcher is wrong. There will be better food, more freedom, a phone call."

Joe's reply isn't printable. But his attitude to Margaret Thatcher is, just. "We had a lot of problems with Margaret Thatcher. She came out with a lot of rhetoric. Whenever she did, we would get hardly any dinner that day, you know. She never helped our cause. I can understand her attitude, but it didn't help us any. We simply received less dinner that day, and sometimes didn't get any. She might be quite brave in England, gobbing off, but it affected our conditions every time."

However, when it came to arguing about the effectiveness of the human shield policy with the guards, which was often, Margaret Thatcher's resilience was a key point of strength for the hostages. It gave them strength and pride to know she wouldn't be deterred from her course and would sort Saddam out. Unfortunately, her strength seemed to them to rest upon the belief that the hostages were merely chaff on the wind of her voice.

"The Iraqi major would tell us we were preventing a war. We told him, 'You don't think we're going to stop our war effort just because you've got a few of us? You're wasting your breath. You're wasting your time. Margaret Thatcher will no more think of us when it comes to war than she has up till now."

Whenever the war was mentioned, the hostages would taunt the Iraqis with the weaponry and power of the Americans, but the Iraqis would reply that they, as hostages, would be the first to die if there was a conflict. Taunts went on about the satellites watching them, telling them the Americans even knew their names. It was not at all jovial. The hostages felt a deep bitterness towards their captors and it was a deliberate policy to attack them, be aggressive towards them, and give them as hard a time as they possibly could.

There was little love lost between Joe and the guards. One threatened to take him out and beat him up, but received a torrent of abuse, such as only Joe could come up with, in reply. He was not intimidated by them. It was too easy to let the whole situation get you down. Joe didn't have religion to fall back on, but he had his army career, including time spent in Korea. It was his aggression, anger and strong sense of humour which kept him going. He used to complain virtually every day about something, whereas others would never complain at all.

In the middle of October, the men learnt from the BBC World Service of Mr Heath's visit. Joe was immediately hopeful that he would be one of the hostages released, as he was both elderly and very sick. He wasn't disappointed. Similarly to David Cunningham, the Iraqis came for him on Sunday night, gave him just a few minutes to pack, and ordered him into an army vehicle. He was not told his destination, but arrived an hour later at the Melia al-Mansour Hotel, where he was given a room on a top floor and told to await further developments.

On the Tuesday night, the twenty-third, Joe Wild, David Cunningham and the others were finally told they were going. The next morning, the twenty-fourth, they collected their bags and assembled downstairs in the foyer where a number of British and foreign camera crews were waiting to interview them. A short while late, they were bussed over to the airport.

It was early Tuesday morning, still dark in the streets of Kuwait City. The Kuwait to Basra road was crowded with military vehicles and trucks loaded with loot plundered from the city. The Iraqi driver had to get his two passengers to the airport at Baghdad for them to catch Mr Heath's flight. He was nipping in and out of the traffic, driving suicidally to get them there on time. He overtook on a junction. As he came round the outside of a truck, another lorry was bearing down on him from the right. He had no time to stop or think. He swerved and veered, but the lorry smashed into them, hurling them across the road, through a barrier and into a ditch. The car came to rest upside down. The driver was badly injured. An Iraqi escort from the foreign ministry was dead. So was Alex Duncan. Rory was still alive - just. He and the driver were rushed back to Kuwait's Sabah Hospital.

Harold Walker, British ambassador to Iraq, had to break the news to waiting journalists. "These young men were on Ted Heath's list and the Iraqis were really doing their best to get them to Baghdad to catch the Branson flight with the other freed hostages. The embassy is trying to organise a visit to Rory and is requesting that his father be allowed out of Kuwait on compassionate grounds. We are also trying to repatriate Alex Duncan's body." He was obviously deeply upset about the whole affair.

Mr Heath and his party were waiting at the ar-Rashid Hotel to be taken to the airport. Their schedule had been so rushed that Dr Easton had eaten nothing all day. Mr Heath had been offered a snack, and was sitting waiting for it. Dr Easton was sitting fuming. He was enraged at the number of hostages who were actually to be allowed out, and was furious that a young man with cancer in the embassy compound would not be coming with them. Neither would a British Muslim at the ar-Rashid who had suffered a nervous breakdown. The official excuse was, "It was too late for them to get visas". It seemed petty, heartless, and to be reneging on the agreement they had come to. Mr Heath's party was experiencing the same deliberate obstructionism, bureaucracy and outright deceits the hostages had endured for nearly three months.

Dr Joubaydi was with them. "He opened up to me for the first and only time," Dr Easton recalled. "I thought that, in many of the places we went, our conversations were being bugged. But now, either he was in charge of the bugging, or he knew we were somewhere we could speak freely. Mr Heath was sitting across from us tackling a very large open sandwich, his first food of the day. Despite my rage about those not coming home with us, I had kept my mouth shut. But as we were waiting, I gave S J a very small list of names, including the man with cancer and the man who had suffered the breakdown... Totally unexpectedly, he said to me, 'Things aren't good in Iraq. We've become dehumanised here.'"

HOSTAGES' RELEASE HIGHLIGHTS PLIGHT OF TRAPPED BRITONS

It should have been a day of celebration on the tenth floor of the Melia al-Mansour, the five-star hotel that has served as a makeshift prison for the British hostages held in Baghdad for nearly [three] months. But there was little jubilation as Edward Heath concluded his four day mission, taking with him some of the 1,350 Britons trapped in Iraq [and Kuwait].

"They are simply giving with one hand and taking away with the other," said one disgusted diplomat after visiting twenty-six Britons recently caught in Kuwait and destined to replace those who left yesterday as the latest deterrents in President Saddam Hussein's human defences. "They are letting out a few dozen from one end, but pumping in the same number from the other. It has become almost industrial," he said. The trauma of being left behind was particularly acute for one British mother who was brought into Baghdad with her nineteen-year-old son on Monday night. They were told that he had been selected to go home because he was a student and only visiting his parents in Kuwait at the time of the Iraqi invasion.

"The Iraqis then said they had made a mistake and took

> them both back to the installation, said Mrs Gilly Battersby, aged 43, of Lincoln, the wife of a British hostage whose relative youth and fitness make it unlikely that he will be looked on favourably for release. "Morale is the lowest I have ever seen it, everyone is very sad they are not going," said Mrs Battersby, whose husband Peter is restricted to one floor of the hotel and watched day and night by armed guards...
> *The Times, 24th October*

A further fifty-seven British men were under arrest at hotels in Kuwait, waiting to be moved up to Iraq. They included seven taken the weekend Mr Heath was in Baghdad. The Iraqis had instigated a conveyor belt of hostages; a production line of human sacrifices.

No one in Mr Heath's party had any idea more men would be moved onto the installations as a result of their mission. When they heard, they were extremely upset. "What was very demoralising to me," Dr Easton explained, "was that a similar number of people were brought up from Kuwait that same day, taken to the Melia al-Mansour and put onto strategic sites. That made me feel very bad."

Until the very last minute, Dr Easton was making applications for the release of more men, without knowing precisely who would be coming out. Mr Heath *was* assured that the thirty contractors from Liverpool working on Saddam's palace would be allowed to return home once their contract expired in a few weeks' time.

At the very last minute before they had to depart for the airport, they were given a list of names in Arabic of who was coming home. Dr Joubaydi was there to translate them to the waiting hostages, but couldn't read some of the names, causing confusion and heart-break. It was another very distressing scene. It meant that even then, they couldn't be sure the names were definite. There was suspense all the way to the airport. It wasn't until they were actually on the plane that they knew who would be going with them - and who not.

David Cunningham described the flight and their reception in Britain. "We were put onto a bus, taken to the airport, went through the routine of checking in, and made our way across the tarmac to the plane. As we climbed the steps into it, Richard Branson was standing in the doorway to greet us. Once inside the plane, we were passed over to a medical team, which gave each of us a thorough examination. Everything about us was documented before the plane was allowed to take off at about nine at night. We were all labelled with our names." Here he broke into tears with the memory of his feelings at that time. "It was very emotional. Everyone was very excited at being released, but full of regrets about the people we had left behind. We were looking forward to being with our families and friends, and we wanted to just get on with it." Dr Easton checked their names as they came aboard against the list he had been given. Two nurses from the PARC organisation turned up at the airport and Dr Easton and Robert Vaudry tried to smuggled them aboard. They got them through the checkpoint in the departure lounge, but they were stopped at an armed checkpoint by the plane and turned back. In all, thirty-three hostages finally managed to board the plane.

There were seven nurses and four doctors on board. All the flight stewardesses were trained nurses as well. Joe Wild had collapsed and was laid out on a stretcher with a drip-feed and oxygen mask. He needed intensive therapy the whole flight. Forty stretchers had been brought from Britain, as well as a lot of hi-tech equipment. Fortunately, most of it wasn't needed. "The hostages were very relieved when they entered the plane," Dr Easton explained. "They broke down in tears or cried with joy." The atmosphere was one of relief, but subdued by the thought of all those they had left behind, plus worries that they might still be turned back, or the plane shot down. They had just heard about Alex Duncan's tragic accident and that Rory Duncan had been badly hurt. None of them trusted the Iraqis at all.

"Then we were handed a glass of champagne," David Cunningham went on. "The 747 was just for the few of us. The atmosphere was tremendous as we all celebrated. There was a TV crew on board, which interviewed some of us as well as Mr Branson and Mr Heath. Richard Branson was on the phone to the pilot and announced when they were out of Iraqi airspace. The whole plane erupted, because we were free then. For the next four hours, we had a party, just drinking and eating. Ted Heath came downstairs from the lounge and talked to us for a while and we had our photographs taken with him. We were all so happy. Mr Heath was very friendly. He was obviously tired. It had been an exhausted period for him. The young crew were just as excited as we were. It was an historic moment. We were the first hostage flight and we were part of that period of history. It was an incredible, incredible situation. The thought of being free and returning home!"

Dr Easton confirmed what the atmosphere was like. "They were very delighted that they were going home. They were very excited about the thought of seeing their relatives at the airport." Like Mr Heath and Robert Vaudry, he was exhausted. Every night he had been up very late. The flight was something of a blur to him as he reflected on the experience. He just remembered that the talk was not about what they had gone through, but what they were heading towards. "They didn't want to go back into the past. They were thinking about the future."

David Cunningham sobered himself up as the plane crossed over Europe and approached Gatwick. "We landed at three in the morning, after a four or five hour flight, got off the plane and were taken into a reception room. I rang my sister, but she wasn't there, so I spoke to an official. He told me she was in the next room! I went to get my luggage, then went through to meet her. It was very emotional. My sister grabbed hold of me and said she'd thought she would never see me again. Jim, her husband, was there, and her son David, aged sixteen, who had demanded to be brought to Gatwick to meet me. There was a barrage of press outside, hundred of photographers with cameras flashing away. I did an interview. Everybody was asking questions. We tried to think clearly. I hadn't slept properly. I was told my dear mother had died a few weeks before. Then we drove up here to Newcastle. There were press calling the whole of the next day and they wanted me to appear on live TV. It didn't cease until ten o'clock at night. It was exhausting."

Joe Wild's experience when the plane landed was somewhat different. He had collapsed on the airplane and so arrived at Gatwick on a stretcher - the only British hostage to do so. He has nothing but praise for the doctors and nurses aboard the flight and deep admiration for Richard Branson and his crew, who were wonderful to all the passengers.

But, unfortunately for Joe, his trauma did not end at the airport terminal. He was so weak from his ordeal that he had to be taken immediately by ambulance to hospital. He was rushed to an intensive care unit, where his twin brother, daughter and some friends met him. Reporters and camera crews had picked up on his plight - it was a good bit for the 'grief column', a good bit of pain and gore for their readers - and followed the ambulance. As he was stretchered out, they rushed up to photograph him. There were so many reporters crowding around him, Joe's family had to push its way through the mêlée to reach him.

Joe spent three days in intensive care, after which he was discharged onto the pavement. He had none of his clothes with him, nor even a pair of decent shoes or socks. He was discharged in his dressing gown and a pair of open sandals, and had to get himself a taxi. Despite DSS and government assurances that resettlement grants of up to £2,500 and travel grants of up to £500 were available to returnees, Joe was neither offered any nor received any such grants. (Indeed, very few returnees ever received any of the grants available to them. It would seem that the vast majority of people didn't know about the grants until too late and never received a penny.) He had neither psychiatric help to overcome his trauma, nor visits from health workers or the local DSS to ask him what he needed or to explain his rights to him. He was ignored and left to fend for himself.

As well as the thirty-three hostages who came out with Mr Heath, others were allowed to follow in later planes. Ten more sick and elderly, including the young man with cancer and the Muslim who had suffered a breakdown, came out in the next few days. When their contracts were up, the thirty workers on Saddam's palace were allowed to go home. So, in all, about seventy were released, Mr Heath's original target. However, they were not all sick and elderly and some of these were 'claimed' by later missions.

On the value of his mission, Mr Heath stated, "I did what I thought was right. The value it had was that... British subjects came back to this country instead of being in Iraq."

Dr Easton was convinced that Mr Heath's mission actually did more for the hostages left behind than for those they had brought out. Some people in the installations noticed a distinct improvement in their conditions after Mr Heath's visit and some began to receive food and clothing parcels. In early November they were suddenly allowed to make phone calls home, a surprising and significant development for men who hadn't spoken to their families for three months. Some of the credit for this has been put down to the Iraqi response to the release of the French hostages at about the same time, with their stories of how they were treated at the camps, but Mr Heath's mission highlighted the plight of the hostages and undoubtedly embarrassed the Iraqis into improving the conditions.

In retrospect, Dr Easton firmly believes the mission contributed, within the overall context of other missions and pressures, to the eventual release of all the hostages. "It undoubtedly greatly increased awareness in this country of the hostages' plight and made their plight more important to the British government and British public. I thought that was very valuable. They stopped being people stuck in Baghdad who couldn't get home and became human stories of real people, as they hobbled or were carried off the plane at Gatwick, some very ill. It made a lot of people think it was disgraceful they had been held against their wishes." Certainly, the mission put the hostages firmly on the front pages again after nearly two months off them, and put their plight into the sharpest focus it had *ever* been during the crisis. For two weeks, it dominated the British scene, vying with gung-ho pictures of the Desert Rats, giving at least an alternative to constant war-mongering.

Gulf Link

"Grown men would burst into floods of tears over a few seconds of message. Two words could send them into a spiral of uncontrollable sobbing. Yet, for all, those few words were absolute godsends."

Throughout August, the BBC World Service[1] provided its regular news service to the Gulf but, increasingly, relatives were contacting it to send messages to their families trapped in Kuwait and Iraq. The Gulf Support Group raised the possibility with both the Foreign Office and the BBC of sending messages in a special programme. By the end of August, when the women and children were released, the BBC realised that, once they were home, the need for messages would dramatically increase. Events moved rapidly. At the beginning of September, the Foreign Office agreed to finance a special programme to people trapped in the Gulf who were unable to contact their families in the UK. It was to start immediately.

The very first programme had to be rushed together. Genevieve Eckenstein, Head of Topical Tapes, was only given a couple of days notice that the programme would be going out. She was informed on the evening of Wednesday 5th September of the idea and it was agreed that the Topical Tapes department would mount the operation. She asked Brian Jarman to be the editor and told him the first broadcast would be on the Friday. It would be quarter of an hour, twice a day, every weekday. They had less than forty-eight hours to prepare a format, do interviews, arrange a series of frequencies to use which didn't conflict with other World Service outputs, and get the equipment and staff sorted out. They didn't even have a name for the programme at that stage. Nor a single telephone. They had to hurriedly move into Genevieve's office, clearing out her desk and files, to provide room. They had to move desks in, pick the presenters, find a signature tune and format and get an answer phone. They had to publicise the service and encourage people to send in their messages by doing interviews with other radio stations and with newspapers and by announcing it on the BBC channels.

Because of the hurry, it was decided to send Chris Loosemore, one of the programme's presenters, down to record a feature about the London helpline at Alexandra House, which was just up the road from the BBC World Service at Bush House. The Gulf Support Group had already built

[1] All the names used in the Gulf Link messages in this chapter have been changed.

strong links with the World Service, passing on messages and doing interviews for it. This first broadcast immediately strengthened that rapport.

"This is the first edition of Gulf Link from the BBC World Service, broadcasting on 11.76, 15.245 and 17.185 Megahertz in the twenty-five, nineteen and sixteen metre bands." [These wave lengths varied slightly over the months of broadcasting.] Then came the first playing of a theme tune which was to bring joy and hope to so many in the human shield, followed by the warm, enthusiastic voice of the presenter.

"Hello, and welcome to Gulf Link from the BBC in London. I'm Chris Loosemore bringing listeners in Iraq and Kuwait news and messages from Britain. We'll be with you at this time [16.45 GMT] every weekday and at 04.45 Greenwich Mean Time. More details at the end of the programme.

"We're hoping to set up a personal link with those of you who cannot leave the region. As well as the voices and messages of your relatives in Britain, we'll be keeping you up-to-date with all that's being done by way of support groups and advice. We're going to use first names only, for reasons you'll understand, and there'll be no clues as to your whereabouts. The messages are already coming in thick and fast and we'll begin sending them out on Monday evening. But, to set the scene today, we've been to the first Gulf Support Group to be organised, just a few doors away from us here at Bush House...

Brian Jarman left the answer phone on over the weekend, in case there were one or two messages for the first week. When he came back on the Monday, it was full, his desk was covered with messages, and hundreds more flooded onto his in-tray that day. By Tuesday the programme had received over six hundred messages! They were inundated.

Once relatives heard on their network that messages could be sent, they began ringing every number they could at Bush House. As a result, the programme's equipment proved inadequate and they had to rapidly pull more in. They brought in answering machines, more telephones and a tape recorder to take down phoned messages. The programme had first one, then two, of its own direct outside lines, plus use of a fax machine to relieve the switchboard, which was inundated with calls. The two lines in operation were in use without respite.

Genevieve's office, about twenty feet by fifteen, was very hectic. It had to accommodate all the staff, all the equipment to record messages, and the telephones. "There were three desks, all the telephones and recording equipment, a board full of items to go into the programme, charts and lists of numbers all over the walls, and piles of files, folders and letters."

The fifteen minute programme went out live in the evening and was repeated in the morning, from Friday 7th September until shortly before Christmas. There was never any let-up in the number of messages coming through. Day upon day they flooded in and the backlog grew steadily worse, rather than better. They decided during the first week to broadcast on Saturday and Sunday as well. Again, they had to check frequencies and transmitters and call for more staff to do the overtime. By the second week, it was obvious that quarter of an hour was not going to be enough, even with the weekends. "It was a slow realisation," Brian Jarman explained. "We had got an initial rush of messages, but couldn't tell whether they would fall right away once everyone had got at least one message out. We couldn't tell at what rate they would want to come back, so we left it a while."

It soon become clear that the number of messages was going to remain very high. Furthermore, they began to get telexes from relatives who had received letters or phone calls from people in Kuwait and Iraq to say they were all listening to it avidly. That in turn encouraged the relatives to send more messages. And in their letters, the hostages and those in hiding were asking questions of their relatives, which were prompting even more responses. They wanted to know how the kids were doing at school, what the finances were like, how Grandma was, whether Manchester United had beaten Liverpool and how the budgie was doing. "The messages kept coming thick and fast." It was then that the decisions were made to expand the programme, firstly to half-an-hour a day, and finally to three quarters of an hour.

The Foreign Office, having supplied the money to set up the service, continued to give it encouragement throughout the crisis. "They were enormously supportive and were very grateful for our work. We interviewed one or two ministers. We had William Waldegrave, Mark Lennox-Boyd and Douglas Hogg on, and others."

Whenever the programme format was changed Brian Jarman consulted with the Gulf Support Group about the relatives' needs because "the support group was getting a lot of feed-back from the families and also from the hostages who came out". That was invaluable. People in the Gulf were ecstatic about the programme and emphasised the importance of the messages. It proved crucial in getting the programme extended.

Gulf Link in turn kept the Foreign Office informed of developments, so it was a shared service all round. The programme interviewed key support group members, including Joanna and Jonathan Copley, Rob Hayward MP and Josie Brookes. "It was a wonderful four months. It was a very special programme. It was very intense, there was a wonderful team spirit, with a lot of sharing and communicating."

Gulf Link refrained from doing more than the occasional news item. It was essentially a service linking the hostages and people in hiding, providing messages from their relatives and useful information to help them survive. It broadcast a number of recipes and had an expert talk about nutrition and the need to get a balanced diet. It had puzzles, brain teasers and word games, plus a psychologist on to talk about surviving on your own and the problems of isolation.

Whilst there was not an official limit on how many messages people could send, a guideline of about ten days between messages was set. This was based on the number of messages coming into them and how quickly they could be transmitted. As that fluctuated, so the length of time allowed between messages changed, and it came down sharply in November when the men in the installations were allowed to make phone calls. Provision was made for particularly urgent messages, such as the death of a close relative, without sticking to the ten day period rigidly, and special cases were made for birthday and anniversary messages, to ensure they were broadcast on the correct date. "It was the fairest way to give everyone their fair whack."

The team would prioritise those who hadn't sent messages for a while over those who had, but would always try to send every message they received. When the programme was extended to three-quarters of an hour and the men in installations could make phone calls, those in Kuwait were given preferential treatment. From then on, they could get a message sent every few days, whilst those in Iraq could have about one a week. At its height, they were sending out a hundred a day, seven hundred a week, three thousand a month - eight thousand or so in all from September to mid-December. That is an enormous workload for such a small programme, unlike anything the World Service had experienced before, dwarfing every other specialist message service they had ever run.

It was a very impressive, slick, yet low-key and beautifully simple presentation which served the purpose perfectly. It was the hostages' life-line. It kept many people sane. They lived for those two broadcasts each day, hanging onto every word, recording them and replaying messages they received over and over again. Grown men would burst into floods of tears over a few seconds of message. Two words could send them into a spiral of uncontrollable sobbing. Yet, for all, those few words were absolute godsends. None would have missed them for the world. Only freedom was more important than the messages, even over food. In fact, meals were arranged around Gulf Link broadcasts. In recognition of this invaluable service, the programme won the bronze medal at the New York Radio Awards in 1991 for service to the community.

Some of the letters sent from Kuwait demonstrate the immense value the programme had for the people trapped out in the Gulf. "You're doing a fantastic job", "Keep up the good work", "The programme has taken on an almost religious status as we all huddle in hopeful anticipation around the radio twice a day. It is the most thoughtfully put together of all the various stations. The changes of voice and pace help the concentration, as does the phone ring punctuating the calls. Well done!" "To all the wonderful people at, or working hard for Gulf Link, just to let you know that your daily broadcasts are heard loud and clear by us all here and to let you know that we think you are doing a fantastic job. Thank you." "Life-line" is the most frequently mentioned word in the letters to describe the service.

"You're listening to the BBC World Service from London. Hello, I'm Chris Loosemore, and welcome to Gulf Link. First today, a message to Mark. Vicky called to say 'I've just returned from staying with Sarah and Co and had a lovely time. Everyone's well and sending messages for you. BA are flying June and Paul from Florida on the twenty-first. Ken, Alan and Graham won't let me pay for any drinks. They say they're running up the bar bill for you. I love and miss you and I'm constantly thinking of you. Bundles of love, Vicky.' A message from Margaret. 'Hello Nigel', she says. 'Valerie and James came over with Ruth for the carnival and we had a great evening. It was Bill and Louise's anniversary on the twentieth, so Dean had a drink for you. I'm going to see Rex and May this week. Keep smiling Nigel. Everyone sends much love and hugs, Margaret and Dean.' Barry, your dad Charles says 'Myself and Shirley are well. Hope you are safe and well. The best of luck and love from us all.' Shukri, Anne from Illinois loves and misses you. All the family is fine and waiting for you. Love from Susie and all of them. Now, over to the Gulf Link phone line, and a birthday greeting."

"Hello Steve, this is Carol calling to say happy birthday and lots of love from me, the BBs and Bournemouth tribes. I won't sing happy birthday or doh-ray-me; that would be too embarrassing, wouldn't it. Eileen had a baby girl, Rachel, last Wednesday. Mother and child are fine. All my love for ever. Kisses, cuddles and hugs, as always. Happy birthday. I love you."

Dring, dring...

A man's voice. "Hello, this is Colin and I have a message to Pierre, Ron, Phil, John, Bill, Steve, Dick, John, Alec and Dave. The first message starts for Steve. The embassy has received your letter and has replied positively. There is absolutely no problem with your wife. And Pierre, Jean and Michel are still in the hotel and send their regards. I had a call from Australia and Kamal. DF is still in jail, under circumstances concerning the vehicle. I will contact all the families today and I will also follow up on items that we discussed previously. Take care of yourselves. We'll keep going."

Dring, dring...

"Dear Brian, I was so sorry to hear about Mike and Jim. I hope you are safe. Lots of love to you from everybody here. A little about the children in this week, October the fifteenth. Sally has started to be herself again. She's missing you terribly. I've saved her models and paintings from school and she now knows the days of the week. Timothy has just started to sleep through the night and is so much like you it hurts. He's sitting up now and starting to roll over. He has a gorgeous laugh which far outweighs his horrible smile. He's down to four feeds a day and gets very grizzly in the evening. Take very special care of yourself, darling. We all miss you so much and wish you were here. Yours, Sarah."

Cliff Lindley hadn't been in contact with a warden since 16th August, when the Iraqis demanded Western 'guests' assemble at the hotels. His group of twenty to thirty Westerners had built a wall across the entrance to their apartment block and barricaded and wired up all the doors, so any soldiers or looters would have to force their way in. It was as well because, by the end of August, house searches had begun in earnest. It was when the women came to leave on 4th September that their luck ran out.

Between Cliff's group and the Sultan Centre, a distance of fifteen kilometres, were thirteen Iraqi roadblocks. September is dark until six-thirty in the morning and there was a curfew from seven to seven. The Arabs who were supplying them with food warned them it would be madness to drive through the curfew, but the women in the group decided to risk it. A Filipino woman drove several of them, another women drove her own car with some more women and children in, and Abdulla, a Palestinian, drove a car full as well.

The women were all stopped at the first road check, where they were kept and questioned, until it was too late to catch the coaches. They were taken to an Iraqi intelligence unit, where they were interrogated and had their civil IDs confiscated. These had their addresses on. Eventually, they were taken off to a hotel, where they went up to Baghdad on the second Iraqi convoy. Abdulla was not treated as lightly as the women, He was threatened with torture and forced to tell the Iraqis where the men were.

Cliff was fortunate. The others had gone to bed, having been awake all the previous night, nervously packing or saying last goodbyes. Even once the women had left, Cliff couldn't rest. He was worried about them being captured and being forced to give the men away. He made himself a coffee and stood by his lounge window, looking down into the street below and across at the other three blocks in the complex. By now, it was eight in the morning.

Without any warning, Cliff noticed some soldiers enter one of the blocks waving AK47s, with armed vehicles in support. They were Republican Guards, in their red berets. He ran down to his friend Dave and told him what was happening. Within two hours, the Iraqis had searched the block, removed all the British men in hiding and grouped in the square, as the remaining British in hiding watched them. Suddenly, the soldiers stormed the other three blocks. Thirty-six entered Cliff's block alone.

Cliff and Dave immediately fled to a hideaway they had constructed. It was in an empty flat just below Cliff's, in a cupboard which they could lock. They had kitted it out with blankets, pillows and bottles of water. It was the size of a normal fitted wardrobe. The flat had been empty for a long time; the curtains were broken, the floor was thick with dust. Careful not to leave footprints, they dived into the cupboard with just seconds to spare. "The Iraqis came in. They smashed every door down. They smashed the glass, putting their boots through every door. They captured everybody except Dave and me."

The Iraqis came into the flat and even wrenched at the cupboard door several times. That was very frightening, waiting for the door to be smashed through or for bullets to be fired into it. The two of them sat there for four hours, their backsides going numb, then heard noises of people going through the flats and thought the Iraqis were back. As the voices approached, they realised it was Abdulla and his wife, going round, looting food and electrical equipment from the flats.

The two Britons emerged, to Abdulla's immense surprise.

"Where you been? The soldiers, they look for you. They know you here. They want you. You can't stay here."

"We're not going to."

The two men grabbed a couple of escape bags with their essential documents in and a bag of food each and pelted downstairs. With a careful glance around at the entrance, they ducked through a half-built mosque, through some bushes and round the back of the block into another complex. It was broad daylight, about three in the afternoon.

About sixteen men were taken in all from the four blocks. They were all processed, taken to a hotel in Kuwait, then up to the Melia al-Mansour, from where they were put onto Iraqi sites.

"... My arms are waiting to give you a gigantic cuddle. They're very lonely without you to grab hold of. Be careful chuck. Forever in my thoughts, love you, Sarah."

"... We all miss you very much. Bye for now, and we hope it won't be long before we see you. Be strong and take care till then. Mum."

"Hi Brian, this is Julie here. Everyone is well here. I hope you all are there as well. I've seen just about all the relatives and friends up here now and they're all thinking of you and asking about you. Keep cheerful. Missing you. I love you. Julie." The last few words were barely audible as she struggled to keep back the tears. It was like that for many of the callers.

Christine Pedley, 31, was eight months pregnant. She was arrested by Iraqis at gunpoint as she drove home from an ante-natal clinic on Saturday 25th August. Her husband, Trevor, a teacher of computer science for four years in Kuwait, was also taken hostage.

"... All our love to you. We are thinking of you..."

"... Stephen and Michelle are missing you and send their love. They are being very good and making endless surprises for you. I hope you come home soon. All my love, Jean." Again, the voice just finished the message before it broke into a thousand parts.

The Iraqis denuded the airport of everything. They took out every piece of machinery. They stripped down the conveyor belts and removed them bit by bit. Things they couldn't move, they destroyed in a mindless orgy of violence. At a printer's, they stripped out the enormous Heidelburg presses in their entirety, taking everything from ceiling tiles to wall sockets. At Shuwaikh Port they stripped the computer room of every piece of equipment. Road signs were going. Street lights were going. Telephone boxes were going. Lorries were queueing up in open spaces to load up with household goods and loot from the shops. Everything removable was being transported up to Iraq.

Lawrence McDonald spent a lot of time preparing for war, although most of his efforts were simply to keep himself occupied. He investigated the air-conditioning vents because he had heard that some people were using them to hide in, and the one in his villa were certainly big enough. The hole in the ceiling of the bedroom was about ten feet by eight. He and his wife Bernice considered fitting it with a rope ladder which they could pull up behind them, but it would be the first place the Iraqis would look and would be no protection in a war. They needed somewhere which could withstand shelling and was sealed against chemical attack.

Lawrence's first engineering feat was to dig some foxholes in the garden, about ten feet from the house. But they were not a good idea. In the event of a gas scare they would have to run into the garden, where the Iraqis might well see them, and they were no protection against the gas. So he filled those in.

Next was the basement. The plan was to bang away at its floor with a hammer and six inch nail, trying to get through twelve inches of marble and concrete. Unfortunately, that too proved abortive.

The third project was also on the floor of the basement but this time with the help of a cold chisel brought to him by an Australian. As he banged, the noise echoed in the chamber and threatened to alert the Iraqis. He wrapped a towel around the chisel, which did the trick and he was able to penetrate the thick marble floor tiles and begin on the eight inches of solid concrete underneath them. He managed to break through that to the sand below and began to dig out a hideaway. By the end of his efforts, he had worked a pit six foot square and three feet deep, big enough for him, Bernice and their dog Rastas to scurry into should the need arise. As the days passed, he worked on it some more, making it a little bigger each day, storing the soil and rubble in plastic bags and tipping them into the garden at night.

The fourth plan involved the garden. It had a large, round water tank which measured ten foot by eight, by six foot high. He and Bernice pumped and hauled the water out of it so that, if they were caught outside when shooting or a gas attack started, they could dive into it. However, this was risky because the Iraqis were looking under manhole covers and in water tanks for weapons hidden by the Kuwaitis, who were storing them anywhere, including drains, sewers, water tanks and holes in the ground. Lawrence did plan to knock his way through from the basement into the tank, but found the banging was making far too much noise. Instead, he decided to use the tank to take the waste sand and rubble from the growing dugout in the basement. Meanwhile, his wife Bernice would sit on the front step in her *abaya* keeping watch.

Bernice's main job was cooking and learning what to do with endless supplies of rice and flour. They hardly ever saw meat but she made plenty of cakes and biscuits. "Bernice's baking is what kept us going," Lawrence beamed. Like many other people, she had to compromise constantly on ingredients. A whole new way of cooking emerged within the British community. New recipes were like gold dust. A thousand and one ways to boil pasta. Cucumber fritters, cucumber soup, cucumber sandwiches, cucumber scones, cucumber flans, cucumber pies, cucumber salads... She did manage to get hold of spices and once a month the Kuwaitis brought them a scrawny chicken they had put out of its misery. She would make sauces or "would delve into our precious supply of tins and maybe get a small can of sardines out. I would use the oil separately to flavour some rice for a later meal. On the few occasions we did have meat, I would save all the bones and the chicken carcass and make soup out of them the next day. That soup would be the main meal. All the things we usually throw away or take for granted we kept and used. Even coffee we used very sparingly. If we didn't finish a cup, we would keep it, reheat it and have it later. Nothing was wasted."

They smuggled letters out, usually to Bernice's mother, who photocopied them and sent them on to all the other relatives, including Lawrence's sister, Cathy Willis. Brave Australians, New Zealanders, Canadians, Danes or Irishmen would go around the villas and apartments and collect the mail. It was then taken to several wardens who were acting as collecting points, including Dave Dorrington, Mike Devey and Sandy MacMillan. From there, the letters were despatched to various points in Baghdad, including a private house (Mike Devey's route) and the embassy (Sandy MacMillan's route), to be sent out to Amman by courier.

Their one regular contact was with Dave Harran, who lived a quarter of a mile away. He put on a *dishdasha* at night, made up bags of food and slipped through the back streets to their villa with them. These were a matter of life or death as their food supply had virtually dried up. Dave was eventually picked up. His villa was next to the Cuban embassy. It was being regularly attacked by the Kuwaiti Resistance, so the Iraqis moved soldiers into all the nearby houses to protect it. That was how they found him. He was taken to an installation in Iraq where the food and conditions were as bad as in most of the camps. He spent his time suffering from vomiting and severe diarrhoea, the classic signs of dysentery.

"... keep safe. Love and best wishes from Ruth."
"... Take care my darling. Love you, June."
"... Longing to have you home, love, Kathy."
"... All our love. We're thinking of you always, love Sue."
"... We got the eighty pounds back. Everything you noted down has been sorted out. The items are all paid and will be for a long time. No need to worry. The bond and policies will be honoured... All my love, Sugar."

One day in late September, Dave Dorrington's phone suddenly went dead. He immediately suspected an Iraqi sweep of the area. If the phones were cut off, people couldn't warn each other. As they fervently discussed what to do, there was a rap on the door, scaring the life out of them. Should they ignore it? Yes. Complete silence.

But the knock came again, and an Arab voice spoke English. One of them thought they recognised it. It might be a friend, in trouble. He decided to take a peek over the curtain. At first he couldn't be certain. The man knocked again, then turned. It was a Kuwaiti they knew. With relief, they let him in.

The man informed the group that three British servicemen hiding in Salwa needed to get out quickly. The Iraqis had been knocking on their doors, but gone away. They were sure they would be back and so wanted to move out immediately. Could Dave take them temporarily? Without hesitation, he said yes.

The Kuwaiti drove back from their house to Salwa, noting all the roadblocks on the way. He picked the British Liaison Team men up, loaded the car with as much food as he could, told the men to put on *dishdashas* and drove back via the side streets. They spent half-an-hour on what was normally a five minute drive, turning down the back of apartment blocks and driving across waste land to avoid the Iraqis, scared out of their lives. When they arrived, they were dripping with sweat from the heat and fear.

They were two RAF guys, Dave Walls and Brian Redland, and an army technician, David Duttson. They were just a few of the thirty-five or so BLT who had not been at the IBI camp and who had gone into hiding. They knew Colonel Duncan's two boys, Alex and Rory. Brian Redland had worked directly for the colonel and knew them well. He was badly upset when Alex was killed. They had no idea what had happened to the BLT members at the IBI camp or to their families. Several other members of the BLT in hiding in Salmiya remained in regular contact with Dave until one day they stopped phoning and he learnt that they had been arrested.

Dave also had two BA crew staying with him, John Collier and John Healey. "They were really angry about the whole thing because they hadn't been due into Kuwait until the day after the invasion, as part of the BA relief crew. They had been flown in a few days early. Neither had their luggage or spare sets of clothes except for a second pair of shorts and shirt to keep them going. Otherwise, they just had their uniforms."

Dave's group tried to take security sensibly, and not over-react. Theirs was a quieter area than most so they felt relatively safe. They didn't bother keeping the lights off or noise down particularly low but they did drape blankets over the tops of the curtains to cut out light at night.

However, a nearby group went to the opposite extreme. They were three guys, one of whom was sixty-four years old. He would take ten minutes to close the curtains and would sit with just one lamp on, a cushion set behind it so there was no light shining towards the window, and the TV down very low with its screen dimmed. The two with him were much more relaxed. They were driven crazy by what they saw as ludicrous security measures and would rather take the chance of nipping out at night to Dave's to sample his home-made beer, than stay in their own place.

Dave Dorrington did introduce various security measures which he and other groups had discussed over the phone. The basic ones were not to go outside, stand near the windows, or do anything which could be seen or heard by people passing by. None of them trusted their neighbours unless they knew them well. When Dave's group were arrested, their neighbours were very surprised to see them there. They thought the villa had been empty for months.

Dave admits he was perhaps a little bit too laid back at times. "I was very relaxed about the whole thing. I was brewing beer and distributing it to all and sundry. I was producing an underground newspaper, the *Hostage Herald*, just to keep people amused. It was certainly no game, but I had no intention of letting it get me down." He couldn't see the point of imagining the worst possible scenario, of intense bombardment or a chemical attack. "I reckoned that, if the situation started to change, we would probably be warned and we'd deal with it when it happened. I couldn't see any point in sealing the house against chemical attack. If you seal the place up, it becomes unlivable in. If it came to it, it came to it. There was nothing we could do. We made provision. We had a study with no outside windows. We made sure there was water and food stashed in there and had spare mattresses stored in there as well. So, if it came to a ground offensive, which we were convinced was going to happen by the end of September at the latest, we would be protected, not from a direct hit, but from broken glass and flying bullets."

"... God bless you. I know how much you must be missing the kids. Kieran, Emilie and Elena send their love. I keep praying all the time, love T."

"... Anyway my love, you take care. I miss you loads. Hope to see you soon, Julie."

"... We've got you in our prayers and hope you'll be home soon. Remember, we love you very much. Take care, Lots of love always, from me, the kids, Grandma and Grandpa."

"Hi Dad, this is Jonathan. I'm working *really* hard. I don't know what's wrong with me. (That was a joke, Dad.) Anyway, keep well and look after yourself. I miss you. Bye."

"Hi Dad, it's Louise. I miss you so much. Can't wait till you're back here... Hi Dad, it's Clara... I miss you a lot and it's not the same here without you. Well, I have to go now. Bye... Hello Dad, this is Anne. I dreamt about you last night and I thought about you all day. I miss you very much. Goodbye."

"The twins talk about you every day and will miss you on their birthday..."

Dozens of Kuwaitis were being tortured and killed every day by the Iraqis. In one torture centre, the helpless victims were lowered into a bath of acid and their bodies allowed to burn away until they died in searing agony. At another, the Iraqis used a soldier's helmet which they put on each victim's head and plugged into the mains, blowing his brains out. Others were hanged on meat hooks until they died.

Many Kuwaiti families suffered fatalities. Dave Dorrington's landlord told him about his relatives. His immediate family survived, but one young cousin was taken for being in the Resistance. The Iraqis phoned the family, saying they were bringing him back at six in the morning. The family were all waiting. At six, the Iraqi soldiers turned up with the teenage lad. The family rushed out to greet him. As they did so, an Iraqi put a gun to his head and shot him, right in front of them. Three other cousins are still missing.

After their narrow escape from the Iraqis, Cliff Lindley and Dave reached the Union Centre. There were already three British hiding in one apartment and above them were two Americans and five Filipinos. All the other Westerners in the block had either been caught or had escaped. Cliff and Dave were given a key to the apartment next to the British trio and stayed there for a while. There were other residents in the block, such as Palestinians and Egyptians, from whom they kept well hidden.

During the next two weeks, the two men turned their apartment into a gas-proof chamber, sealing rooms, air-ducts, windows, doors, and even the electric sockets up with tape. They broke through the heavy front doors of other apartments with screwdrivers to take food, toiletries and any useful tools they could find. They either carried the food back to their flat or hid it in other flats. A favourite place was behind gas cooker hoods. But there was not a great deal of food about and they weren't getting supplies coming in. On the fourteenth of September, Cliff wrote in his diary, "Today we are running low on food. Going to try 702 and 602A with spare keys. Tried 506 and 502. They all had gig locks. Just managed to hide in the fire escape when two kids came running along the balcony."

They began to build a hidey-hole in an apartment on the tenth floor. They took the doorframe from a doorway and slid a wardrobe into the space. They sealed it in place with trim they had removed from the skirting board, then cut a hole in the bottom of the wardrobe. They stocked the hideaway, which consisted of a double bedroom and en suite bathroom, with food and equipment, including a microwave. They made it completely self-contained.

On the eighteenth, Cliff and Dave were upstairs working on this false partition when Don, one of the other Britons, phoned and announced that soldiers were on their landing. He had managed to get away, but the two with him had been given no chance to escape. Cliff and Dave managed to get into their hideaway and seal it behind them before the Iraqis came in. A Palestinian doctor who had just moved in had fingered them. They saw him come up the stairs with the Iraqis, pointing to their apartments.

This time, they couldn't leave their refuge after a few hours. The Iraqi soldiers had decided to conduct a major flat-to-flat search and seemed to be around all the time. They remained in their two rooms for three days. They had lost all their clothes and possessions and rapidly exhausted their tiny supply of food. It was obvious that they couldn't survive for long where they were so decided to risk moving into another apartment they had discovered - 802. At two o'clock in the morning of September the twenty-first they left their hideaway to slip back to their old flat and pick up their possessions and documents. They crept along the balcony and corridors and silently traced their way back to the fourth floor. As they peered through a window on the stairwell they noticed a soldier asleep in the corridor on their floor, waiting for them to return. They couldn't get to the flat, so had to make their way to 802 empty-handed.

However, the guard turned out not to be for them. He was keeping an eye on the complex because the next day an Iraqi unit moved in and stated to use the block as a barracks! They were really Dad's Army types, wearing anything they could lay their hands on: plimsolls, stolen trainers, sandals, or no shoes at all. Some were in khaki, others in old camouflage jackets dating from the war with Iran, and some in boiler suits. They had no respect for their AK47s, which were old, tatty, battered, and dented, but which could fire six hundred rounds a minute. One soldier carved his name in a wall with the sights of his.

Cliff watched them take over the building and carefully peered from the windows of his latest apartment as they lazed about in the courtyard below. He gave them nicknames. Pinocchio, because he walked like the wooden puppet with someone operating his strings and would never have been allowed into a good army; Wooden Legs, whose knee joints didn't seem to work and who walked with a stiff shuffle; Hey Ho Silver; Baldy, a middle-aged soldier with very little hair; Mouthy, about the same age as Baldy, but always shouting - maybe he was a low-ranking officer, a corporal or suchlike; Hyperman, who could never sit still or stay in one place - on one occasion he put his rifle down, walked off, then forgot where he had put it; Titch, a very short guy; Quackers, who always accompanied Titch and did strange things such as wear tea towels on his head. Watching them was Cliff's prime occupation, a major source of entertainment.

The only other man to escape detection when the Iraqis raided was Don. He came up to join them after a few days. By then, the Iraqis had stolen all the cars from the courtyard and basement. Soon after, they were kitted out with new equipment. The incident is still recorded on Cliff's computer diary. "On the twenty-second of September, they were issued with new battledress and new guns." Cliff recalled that day. "They were all fitted out with dark green. I wondered why, in a desert, they weren't in light brown, but it was so they couldn't be seen at night, when the Resistance was attacking them." A lot of the later entries in his diary describe how the Iraqis started trying the front door of their apartment with keys, then screwdrivers, then rifle butts, but never managed to break in.

"Hello, Andrew Dunn here with Gulf Link... First, happy birthday Garry, from Debbie in Dubai, who says 'the balloons, cake and sweets are awaiting your safe return to Dubai, which I hope is really soon. God bless, Love from Debbie'. And happy birthday too to Adrian, from Damian and Joan. They say, 'Happy birthday, our thoughts are with you, love from Damian and Joan, and hugs and kisses as well from Steven and Alan'. And Adrian, here's June."

June's voice took over. "Hello there Adrian, it's June and Sally again. All our family and friends at home want to join us in wishing you a happy birthday for the first of December. Hope you're making the best of a bad job and that some of your cards made it through. We've been busy writing letters, as you have. Sally sends you not one, but forty big kisses. All our love, and happy birthday, June and Sally."

Dring-dring...

On the fifteenth of October, Cliff Lindley wrote, "Big brass military inspection on beach positions. Looked like Hussein's brother [who was in command of Kuwait]. Running low on writing paper." He was trying to write a book to keep himself occupied.

The Iraqis were digging in far more seriously now. The allied armies were massing in Saudi Arabia and Desert Shield was increasingly looking like Desert Storm as they practised seaborne landings off the Saudi coast. Hundreds of new Iraqi units were moved into Kuwait, especially along the beaches. Cliff could see the Iraqis driving in. On the sixteenth, he wrote, "The Iraqis were placing rolls of barbed wire along the beach and digging in along it."

Immediately they entered this latest flat, the British men decided to barricade the front door and fit it with a security lock. But they had to do it very quietly. They couldn't make any noise at all now, and had to be extremely careful if they ventured out.

Unfortunately, there was very little in the apartment. Their food rapidly ran out and Cliff's diary records their constant efforts to search other flats to find enough to live on. On the sixteenth of October, they had some good fortune. "Flats 501B and 401B have food for ten weeks. Have to plan how to get it." The problem was how to slip past the soldiers to get to it, then drag it back with them, crawling along the balcony so they couldn't be spotted from the courtyard below. On the seventeenth: "Went to 402B and got some food to last for another two weeks." They had to go back to 402B several times to get this food, right past the soldiers. "That was the terrifying part of it."

They didn't have any spare clothes either, so decided to try the flat they were originally in once again to get some clothes and personal possessions. They made the run in the early hours of the morning, at about two o'clock. They managed to avoid the soldiers this time and stole back with a large quantity of food which kept them going for some time.

After a month of this type of existence they didn't bother going out any more. There was no need. They stayed in their apartment, without any lights, living in total darkness in the evenings, keeping sounds to a minimum as their existence closed in upon them. It became a waiting game. Waiting for either release or for the Iraqis to finally break down the front door of their apartment. They were completely cut off from the wardens or other members of the community. They had no way of getting letters out. They had a short wave radio, so their only link with the outside world was the World Service, especially Gulf Link. "We never failed to listen to Gulf Link and looked on that as a life-preserver. We really looked forward to it and listened to it every day. Even when we had to take an extremely low profile we would listen to it with headphones on. I used to listen to it in the evening and tape it. The other two listened to it in the morning and taped it, so we always had it. If the reception was bad at night, we got it the next day." Unfortunately, his wife Wendy wasn't aware of the service, so didn't send any messages, which was demoralising for Cliff. It became very frustrating for him, day after day without a message, when others were getting them every few weeks.

Throughout hiding, they kept to the routine of one and a half meals a day, always having something cooked. The main meal was at about six or seven o'clock at night and they would have a snack at midday. In the end, it was just pasta with some sort of sauce. "The dog bones ran out a good month before we were caught," he half joked, then added, "We *did* eat the meat off dog bones one day. We were becoming increasingly concerned about our diet. The cat and dog food we had found in the flat was definitely going on the menu."

Increasingly, they heard news over the radio of possible places the allies might attack, especially from the sea. As it turned out, it was a massive disinformation plan by the allies to divert attention from the planned desert sweep north and eastwards. But all the talk of a seaborne invasion petrified Cliff and Dave. "I saw what the situation was along the beach. I could see all the soldiers, as well as the tanks and heavy artillery. There were dozens and dozens of soldiers in each complex. We counted fourteen in our block alone. When we were captured, we counted dozens and dozens throughout the complexes, right along the beach. There were tens of thousands of soldiers in these apartment blocks, all with AK47s, right along the coast road, just waiting for an invasion."

"Hello Nazeem, this is Carol here. I just want to tell you that we're thinking of you on this special day. Geoff and Margaret, and Rose and Eddie are asking for you. And Ken and Sam have been in close touch with me. Hopefully, *inchala*, we'll see you soon. Bye-bye now, take care, and God bless."

Dring, dring...

"Hello Alan, everyone OK. Received your messages. Doing all we can this end. No, I didn't go to Blackpool, but I'm going to London soon. Some family news. My nephew's having a baby. Keep your chin up, darling. Hope it won't be too long now. All our love, Jill."

Dring, dring...

"Hello Mark, it's Dorothy. I've spoken to Jane and John recently and they send their love. They're just back from a nice, restful holiday in Tenerife. John's fine and he's off back to the Middle East soon. Linda and I are planing a Yellow Ribbon Day here on Sunday the second. Hopefully, they'll have them in lots of areas all over the country. Here, we'll have ribbons all around the town and at ten forty-five outside Trinity Church there'll be prayers and letting free some yellow balloons, so do all of you join us in thought. Bye for now."

Dring, dring...

One woman was barely able to hold back the tears, the next was almost brazen in her jolliness. "Britain will be yellow on Sunday, plus a big yellow ribbon round Gray's Monument. The Christmas cake is here for you and Marg and Lee and I will not stop until you are here to eat it. Keep as you are. All our love and prayers for you and all the men trapped."

Dring, dring...

A community spirit had developed over the weeks in hiding as people discussed escape plans with each other and kept a check on who needed food or other supplies. Most people would chat over the phone, cheering each other up, laughing, passing on recipes, gossiping about the Iraqis and discussing the countless rumours which circulated. Dave Dorrington's home was known as the 'Salwa Arms', he did so much brewing. He was producing beer up until he was captured late in November, labelling it *Kuwaiti Survival Ale* and distributing it either by bottle or gullet. A number of people living locally would sneak out at night for a quick bevvy or two - or ten. Several late night sessions went on until well into the morning, in which case the visitors would simply kip down and sleep it off.

"Dear Ralph, Colin's going to grow up with a nice suntan. He's a great help to us. Poor chap. Must be glad to be on a flight, away from this married life-style. Christopher can now say, 'apple', 'hi', and every photograph he sees, he says 'Daddy'. Paul is arriving on the fourth. Mum and the rest of the family are OK and send their love. Regards to the maids. We could do with them now. I miss you, Misha and Christopher. Not forgetting our friends, love and God bless."

Dring, dring...

"To Richard. I am so frustrated I could not get through to you again, despite trying constantly. Dad had the same problem, but I'm so thankful you spoke to Mum. Be reassured, I love you very much, my darling, and want to be with you. Love always, Barbara."

Cliff, Don and Dave were finally picked up late in November. It was inevitable. There were sixty-two apartments in the complex and, by now, the Iraqis had burst into sixty-one. For six weeks they tried the final door. "They kept coming up, pushing at it and rattling it. Sometimes they came up with screwdrivers and prised at it. They almost got in once. The door was just hanging on by a thread." But the three men had built a barricade behind it with a large, thick plank of wood, which they nailed and screwed to the floor and door. "I put chains around the wood and door, as well as strips of metal around the door. It made it difficult to get out for food, but it made it difficult to get in."

Finally, the Iraqis came at eleven-thirty on the night of 27th November. Don woke Cliff and Dave to tell them they were smashing the door down. They were obviously serious this time and had come with spikes, levers, sledgehammers, blowtorches and drills. After two and a half hours, they still they hadn't got in. They had burnt a hole all the way around the door, but it still wouldn't give way. The Iraqis were perplexed and went away to find their officer.

As the door hung by the chains and plates behind it, the three stowaways decided to dismantle the barricade and let the Iraqis in. They knew the game was finally up and there was no point in antagonising the soldiers any further.

When the Iraqis came up with their officer, the three men had removed the barricade, taken off the chains and plates, switched on the lights, packed their bags and were waiting in full sets of clothes they had scavenged from other flats. "We sat back and pulled the dining table out, poured ourselves gin and tonics and waited. The soldiers came back and one came bursting through the door. It gave way and he flew halfway up the corridor. The officer walked in after him. He turned back to his men to tell them off for being so feeble, then looked round to see the three of us sitting calmly at the table, sipping our G and Ts. It was beautiful." The officer was astonished to see them, and horrified when they told him they had been there since September. He sat down at the table and put his head in his hands. "Oh. my God! You've been here since September? Since we've been here? Oh, my God! What are we going to do with you?"

"Let us go?" Cliff ventured.

"Oh, I wish we had never found you. Perhaps we can seal you back in. Can we do that? Will you be good and quiet if we close the door again?" He put his hands back into his head, wiping them down his face. He was clearly petrified. He had been harbouring three British people right under his nose. He was sure to be severely reprimanded, if not shot. "Oh my God," he murmured, "Oh, my God!" He stared at each of them in turn. "Perhaps we can drive you to the desert and let you go."

"No, you'll have to turn us in," they insisted, anxious not to be taken out into the wilderness.

He finally agreed to turn them in, after much persuasion from the British and his own men. "OK, we will come back for you in the morning, but first you have a good night's sleep." By now, it was three o'clock in the morning of the twenty-eighth. The officer explained that they were a Kurdish unit and would have to get an Iraqi officer, otherwise they would be in big trouble. He apologised, then left them, still murmuring that he wished he had never entered the apartment.

A few hours later, several Iraqis turned up, including an intelligence officer. These fellows were very different to the ordinary soldiers. They were pushy and sharp. One in particular was nasty.

"What cars you have?"

"None. You've taken all our cars."

"Where your cars?"

"You've stolen them."

"No cars? Where your cars?"

"Iraqis taken them."

"You show me."

They led the Iraqis down to the basement. Every car had gone apart from Cliff's Jaguar XJS, much to his surprise. It was even still there when Cliff returned to Kuwait a year later.

The three of them were taken outside and driven to the local intelligence headquarters, but weren't interrogated. They were seated in an office in a medical centre, before being taken to the Regency Palace Hotel. They later discovered that the officer who had found them had been taken away and probably shot.

The next afternoon, the twenty-ninth, the Iraqis drove them at 180kph to the military air base at Jahra then flew them to Baghdad. They stayed for a week at the Melia al-Mansour.

The hotel food was bland, but adequate and there was plenty of it. Like virtually everyone else, they suffered from a severe attack of dysentery whilst there, but the Iraqis had good medical centres in Baghdad. They were well cared for and their illnesses cleared up fairly soon.

They were put in rooms on the ninth floor. Wherever they went, they had to have a 'minder' with them, usually a member of the *Mukhabarat*. There were minders sitting at a table where the two corridors met at the stairwell. A minder always went down in the lift with them to the dining room, where another minder would take over. At first, they were not allowed outside at all but, after a lot of complaining, they were permitted to go for walks around the gardens of the hotel - with a minder.

"John, your sister Paula called to let you know that they haven't forgotten about you. 'We love you and miss you,' she says. 'The children are fine and we're looking after your family. Joanne and the baby are doing well. And Colette says to tell you she got nine GCSEs. Susan, meanwhile, has managed to get another trophy for her trumpet. Hope to see you soon, love Paula, Gary and the girls.' ...

'We all miss you and think about you. Greg, when asked what he'd like for Christmas said, 'Daddy home!', which is how we all feel. They're both fine and glad to be home. Let's hope it won't be long before they see you in person. Keep your spirits up, love Pat, Charlotte and Greg.'

When arrested, the six men in Dave Dorrington's group - Dave, the three BLT men and two BA crew - were taken to an Iraqi command post. There, they weren't interrogated or questioned but were ignored. It was lunchtime. The Iraqis did nothing with them until after they'd eaten, when they were taken to the Regency Palace Hotel and told to settle into their rooms and wait. The Iraqis were very polite, let them eat a meal and then gave them room keys. That evening they met five East Germans and three British boys who had been allowed to return home to go to university.

It was Thursday 22nd November. The Germans had booked places on a charter flight out of Baghdad on the Sunday. The Britons were told they would be taken up to Baghdad with them on the Saturday by plane from the military airport near Jahra. So the Germans, three British lads and six hostages flew up to Baghdad together. At the airport, there were no Iraqi guards to pick them up. Obviously, there had been some confusion and the whole party were regarded as free to leave Iraq. Whilst the six 'hostages' were waiting around to be arrested, some East German embassy officials arrived to take care of their nationals. The British men joked about their situation, until the Germans suddenly offered to take them to their embassy in their diplomatic cars. In the general confusion, the six men slipped outside and were smuggled into the waiting vehicles. They were calmly driven to the East German embassy, where they managed to remain until the general release two weeks later.

Puppets on a String

"I can see what's going to happen. Saddam's twisting your emotions all the time, dangling you on strings, just like puppets."

SADDAM OFFER TO FRANCE FAILS TO CHIP AWAY UNITY

The French government has again slammed the door on any possibility that its citizens held hostage in Iraq could be released in a special gesture from President Saddam Hussein. In response to yesterday's news that the Iraqi leader "suggested" [the Iraqi] parliament debates this, a French foreign ministry official repeated that Paris is interested only in "the liberation of all foreign nationals being held against all the principles of international law"...

Against growing evidence, the Iraqi leader appears to believe that his government's once close ties with Paris could be used to split France away from the Western alliance now confronting him. Even with five thousand French troops against him, President Saddam believed the prospect of more releases... might tempt the government to break ranks.

The Times, 23rd October

Early in October, Saddam unexpectedly released some Germans, all Finns and Spaniards, and nine French hostages in an attempt to reduce Iraq's diplomatic isolation. During Edward Heath's mission, he announced the release of all the remaining French in Iraq and Kuwait. There were about three hundred of them, including approximately fifty-six on strategic sites.

The French government, especially President Mitterand, had seemed more willing to negotiate with Iraq than either Britain or the USA. The French President had suggested a four-point plan which included a wider Middle East settlement and incorporated Iraq's demands for the Palestinian question to be discussed alongside that of Kuwait. It was part of the long diplomatic struggle over 'linkage' of the two issues, a concept the British and American governments firmly rejected. However, since then, the Iraqis had invaded the French embassy in Kuwait, ransacked it and despatched a number of its staff to Iraq. That had enraged the French government and transformed its position. Shortly afterwards, it took the lead in extending the Security Council embargo against Iraq to include most air traffic.

It is important to analyse why the Iraqis released the French hostages so unexpectedly. The announcement came on 22nd October. Two days later, Iraq suggested that all hostages from countries with no hostile intent against Baghdad could be freed. That same day, Mr Heath flew home with thirty-three British hostages and with a promise of about thirty-seven more to follow.

Throughout the hostage crisis and up to the war, Iraq held to one central tactic. It wanted to delay any military operations against it until it could either split the alliance or force America and Britain to the negotiating table. The hostages were originally taken to gain them time to build their defences in Kuwait whilst diplomatic manoeuvres went on to wean the Arab states from America, and to divide the United Nations and Security Council. France, as a member of both bodies, was a key player, especially as President Mitterand had initially sent a relatively small force to the Gulf and had repeatedly attempted to put forward his own initiatives to prevent war. The release of the French hostages was one of a series of attempts to persuade France to withdraw its troops from Saudi Arabia and drop its support for force in the UN Security Council.

By releasing the French hostages, Iraq hoped to encourage the French peace movement and persuade the French to call for a peaceful solution. But it also hoped it would give ammunition to the peace movements in other countries. It was to isolate America and Britain diplomatically and to so encourage the development of the peace movements in those countries that President Bush and Mrs Thatcher would be forced to climb down. The release of hostages was a huge gamble by the Iraqis, for they might lose their best card, which is perhaps why they started with the relatively small group of French (and soon afterwards German) hostages.

The announcement of the release coincided with a diplomatic offensive by the Iraqi ambassador in Paris and by clear signals from Iraq that it was re-evaluating its hostage policy. France had, in fact, earlier announced that its forces in Saudi Arabia would not be used in an offensive operation against Iraq or Kuwait. In response, Latif Jassim, Iraqi Information Minister, and a member of the ruling Revolutionary Council Committee, announced that "We will monitor the situation and watch how this country behaves and that country behaves, and on the basis of that, we will make our decisions", thus raising the prospect of a general release of American and British hostages if their governments showed signs of not attacking Iraq. He went on, "We want to give the French people, the French government, a signal that we are satisfied with their behaviour over the crisis. They said they will not enter the war. They will not take part in aggression against Iraq. They will take a defensive position towards Iraq. This is very important to us." In a telling speech a few days before, Saddam himself had mentioned "the refusal by France to adopt the hostile tactics of Bush or to use arms against Iraq, as expressed in popular demonstrations, messages and meetings." This later may have been a specific reference to an anti-war march held through Paris a few days before. It was carrot and stick. If you are good children, we will let your people go.

The other member of the Security Council Saddam targeted was the Soviet Union. He was keeping thousands of Soviet advisers and contract workers trapped in Iraq under the guise of getting them visas They were only allowed to leave very slowly, as he attempted to bring pressure to bear on President Gorbachev. It backfired on him badly when the Soviet Union made its displeasure known. It seems that the Iraqi leader was unprepared for the new role the Soviet Union, its old ally and arms supplier, was now playing in a world of disarmament and superpower co-operation.

In response to British and American concern, the French government had hastily announced that its policy in the Gulf would not change, especially on enforcing the UN resolution on Iraq leaving Kuwait. It wanted "the liberation of *all* foreign nationals, unconditionally and in conformity with the resolutions of the United Nations." A spokesman for the French government stated this unchanged position clearly. "The taking of hostages is odious. Their liberation is merely an atonement for that inadmissible act. France cannot lend itself to any negotiations whatsoever on this issue." He also emphasised that the release was not part of any secret deal France had done with Baghdad, but Iraq's unilateral decision. He strongly emphasised that he had "engaged in absolutely no negotiations", and insisted on the united stand behind the UN resolutions. Later, it was to emerge that an envoy of the French government, Claude Cheysson, *had* been sent to negotiate the release of the hostages, involving clandestine meetings in Tunis and, reports at the time suggested, even involving the Palestine Liberation Organisation.

Presidents Mitterand and Gorbachev were due to meet together a few days after the announcement of the release of the French hostages. Saddam hoped to influence that meeting and persuade both leaders to call for peaceful negotiations. Tariq Aziz confirmed this when he said, "The meeting of President Gorbachev and President Mitterand in Paris should be an opportunity for them to demonstrate the great interest which their two states have in all aspects of this region's problems". The Iraqi parliament, a mere puppet of Saddam and his mouthpiece, dutifully announced the release of all remaining French hostages and expressed its hope that the French would echo Mr Gorbachev's view that war in the Gulf was "unacceptable". The release was timed to coincide with that meeting, even to the extent that the French hostages were only allowed to fly back to France on the very day of the summit. It put maximum pressure on Mitterand and gained maximum publicity. It was a blatant attempt to force the French president to acquiesce with the call for a peaceful solution to the crisis. It failed. After five hours of talks with Gorbachev, Mitterand emphasised that the release had changed nothing. In fact, the Quay d'Orsay called the Iraqi ambassador to its premises to complain vociferously about the privations imposed upon the French embassy in Kuwait.

Over the evening of Sunday 28th October to the night of Monday 29th, two thousand relatives of French hostages released from Iraq and Kuwait converged on Charles de Gaulle Airport to meet two hundred and eighty-two returnees. They were reunited with their menfolk amongst the most incredible scenes of joy and relief: husbands and wives, mothers and sons, fathers and children hugging and kissing each other amidst flashing cameras and television crews. They were exhausted, but each returnee received a substantial resettlement grant from the French government to help with readjusting to life until they had found new jobs.

After the release of the French hostages, the Gulf Support Group contacted the French hostage support group to get as much information as possible about where British people were being held and what conditions they were in. Many British relatives received letters and phone calls from France in the next few days as the French hostages ran down their lists of British - and American and German - relatives to contact.

Meanwhile, Saddam kept up the propaganda war to persuade Arab leaders, such as President Mubarak of Egypt and President Assad of Syria, to break away from the alliance. He played the pan-Arab card, then the card of a war against British and American imperialism. He called himself the second Saladin, come to unite the Arab world, and he even came close to declaring his struggle a *jihad*. He used television and radio to whip his people into a frenzy of support and those pictures of a defiant Arab people struggling against imperialism were beamed across the Arab world. There was tremendous popular support for Iraq in every other Middle Eastern country. Large demonstrations were held throughout the Arab world in support of its position. Furthermore, Saddam linked his struggle with the fight to expel the Jews from Israel and to win a homeland for the Palestinians. He clearly wanted to extend the war to Israel. Whilst it helped bring many Arabs behind him, it was a tactic which worked against him as well, for some Arab leaders feared his growing power, especially when the Americans told them how close he was to having a nuclear bomb.

As diplomatic pressure seemed to be failing, the other key element of Iraqi strategy played a growing role. This was not so much to split the alliance, as to encourage popular movements, even revolutions, in the countries of the alliance, which would force them to pull out of the Gulf. Everywhere, the Iraqis fomented popular unrest. They called for Egyptians, Saudi Arabians, Tunisians and Syrians to overthrow their governments. In Britain and America, they concentrated on the peace movements in an effort to force their governments to the negotiating table.

Every little action was glorified and praised out of all proportion on Iraqi television. The Japanese movement received large coverage, especially whenever it organised a demonstration. The German government, which refused to send troops - under its constitution it couldn't, but it gave money - was praised, and a demonstration outside the Chancellery for peace was followed with great interest. The hostages were described as ambassadors of peace. All the time, the Iraqis said how they simply wanted peace and talked of the justice of their cause.

In this light, the Iraqi people's jubilation when Margaret Thatcher resigned is not surprising. It was presented to them, not as the result of the European question, or the Poll Tax, but because the British people wanted peace in the Gulf. It explains Tariq Aziz's close interest in the violent anti-Poll Tax demonstration in London in October. Any opposition to either Margaret Thatcher or George Bush gave the Iraqis encouragement.

NAKASONE PLEADS FOR HOSTAGES

Yasuriho Nakasone, the former Japanese prime minister, is joining the band of foreign statesmen making hostage mercy missions to Iraq. He plans to leave for Baghdad in early November to talk to President Saddam Hussein, to request the release of all the hostages being held in Iraq and Kuwait.

"I would like to go as soon as possible to see President Saddam Hussein and talk about the possibility of resolving the situation peacefully, and of arranging for all the hostages of the world, not just the Japanese, to return to their home countries with me," Mr Nakasone said yesterday..."

The Times, 27th October

The British government was becoming increasingly anxious that so-called 'mercy missions' by leading politicians did not split the anti-Iraq alliance. An important part of that alliance was the united stance taken by the European Community to the crisis. The Community was just beginning to emerge with a unified voice on foreign matters. Social, political and monetary union were rapidly moving forward. Most of its leaders were aware of Iraq's attempt to split the forces ranged against it and felt a common interest in remaining firm and rejecting any unilateral deals with Iraq, especially over hostages.

On 28th October, during a summit in Rome, the leaders of the EC strongly condemned Iraq's annexation of Kuwait and the holding of Western hostages. They were equally firmly opposed to 'mercy missions'. They pledged "not to send representatives of their governments in any capacity to negotiate with Iraq over the release of foreign hostages and to discourage others from doing so". It further suggested the United Nations should intervene on behalf of the hostages, urged the Security Council to continue to press for their release, and encouraged the "Secretary-General to send a special representative to Iraq to this end".

This sentiment was reinforced the next day at the United Nations when it passed Resolution 674. This demanded that Iraq cease and desist from taking third-state nationals hostage, from mistreating and oppressing Kuwaiti and third-state nationals, and from any other actions that violated the decisions of the Security Council, the UN Charter, the Fourth Geneva Convention, the Vienna Conventions on Diplomatic and Consular Relations and international law; it invited member states to collate information on any grave breaches of those laws and conventions by Iraq; and it demanded that Iraq ensure access to food, water and basic services to Kuwaiti nationals and nationals of third states in Kuwait and Iraq (partially a reference to the state of siege of the embassies in Kuwait). The Security Council further reminded Iraq that it was liable for any loss, damage or injury arising in regard to Kuwait and third states as a result of the invasion and occupation of Kuwait - a fundamentally important principle which not only allowed nations to claim reparations, but the hostages and those in hiding to claim for their losses as well. It invited member states to collect information relevant to claims for compensation against Iraq and finally called upon the Security Council to make every possible effort to ensure a peaceful outcome to the crisis.

The Iraqis continued to release small groups of hostages. On 2nd November, seven PARC medical staff from the Ibn al-Bitar Hospital in Baghdad were allowed home. Over two hundred and thirty remained, including sixty who had by now finished their contracts. Twenty of these were refusing to go on working. In response, the Iraqis threatened them with eviction from their flats. The following day, four sick and elderly Americans flew out.

The British embassy in Baghdad made constant representations to the Iraqi government over the treatment of British citizens and the ambassador, Harold Walker, repeatedly tried to ensure better treatment for them. It is interesting how he perceived Iraqi actions over the hostages: "Representations to the Foreign Ministry went on all the time. Politically, the hostage story is a complicated one because the Iraqis were very skilful. They put different nations in different boxes and let it be known, in private to the diplomatic missions, that they were not only going to treat each country differently but that its position would change according to how it behaved, meaning how it behaved in relation to, a, sanctions, and b, the provision of military force in the Arabian Peninsula. So, for example, some 'neutral' nations like Sweden were on a sort of quota system. They were told 'We are now going to let out ten per cent of your citizens and, if your country behaves, then you'll get another ten per cent'. The system was so sophisticated that in one area it seemed to become over-sophisticated, because the Japanese seemed to be on two lists. On the one hand, they were on the list of baddies, with people being sent to installations like us, and yet they were allocated a quota and the Japanese ambassador was allowed - I forget - ten, fifteen or twenty per cent of his community to leave."

Iraq was hoping to draw out the hostage crisis as much as possible, using releases as *hors d'oeuvres*, whetting the appetite of Western governments. It was, on the one hand, an attempt to draw foreign leaders into a dialogue which, once under way, would make it harder to go to war and, on the other, trying to make a nonsense of its diplomatic isolation. Simultaneously, it was threatening that any war would be drawn out and very bloody, using bluster and sabre-rattling to scare foreign leaders to the conference table. "The last bullet will surely be a merciful Iraqi bullet fired at the dying American cowboys."

The Iraqi leadership's main tool was the media. Both Iraqi television and foreign crews covered each of the peace delegations flying out to Baghdad and every release. 'Mercy' and 'compassion' were aimed at counter-acting the bad coverage Iraq was getting over holding hostages in the first place. Such was Baghdad's developing dilemma. Much of the propaganda surrounding the release of the hostages was to nullify the appalling world press it was getting as a result of its hostage policy. The Iraqis began to wonder which was worse - keeping the hostages and enduring united world condemnation, or releasing them and hoping that would encourage the peace movements sufficiently to bring the USA and Britain to the negotiating table.

Foreign politicians were literally queuing up to visit Iraq. Before Willy Brandt's mission, a delegation of three Irish TDs arrived to secure the release of the rest of the PARC medical staff, plus sixty other Irish trapped in Iraq and Kuwait. Then Willy Brandt was due and, after him, Saddam was to receive the Chinese Foreign Minister, Qian Qichen. It was wonderful publicity and kept Saddam blissfully in the limelight. He was a man of mercy, a great and compassionate world leader, a powerful figure on the international stage.

Every release was calculated. Only a tiny handful were ever released on purely compassionate grounds. They all served an over-riding purpose for the Iraqi regime. The British ambassador in Baghdad, Harold Walker, saw that at close quarters, for he was constantly arguing with the Iraqi ministers. "We were dealing with a very tough regime... People were only allowed out as part of a political package, *ie*, when there was a visit by Ted Heath or Tony Benn or whoever. In all those cases, to my knowledge, the visitors might produce lists of who they would like to see, but it was always the Iraqis who decided who would be released. And in all those cases, except one, the lists of people the Iraqis allowed to go was different from what the visitors put forward. There might be an overlapping, but they were *Iraqi* lists. The exception, as far as I know, was that the Greek embassy put forward a list of people it would like to see released when there was a visit from a delegation from PASOK and the Iraqis let precisely those same eleven people go.

One could spot in the Iraqi lists of people they allowed to go a bias in favour of employees of big, international companies that the Iraqis might like to do business with again in the future, like Bechtel.

So long as it had the hostages, Iraq believed they were a powerful weapon against war. But Iraq's position was not simply to stave off conflict. It had to start peace negotiations if it was to get a satisfactory settlement. This was why it encouraged King Hussain of Jordan to act as a peace broker, touring the Middle East and Europe, where he spoke to Mrs Thatcher and President Mitterand in late October-early November, touting Saddam's peace proposals around with him. If Iraq was to win the race between war or negotiations, it had to present its case to the rest of the world as effectively as it could. Whilst the human shield gave Iraq some breathing space to build its defences, settle with Iran and move hundreds of thousands of troops into Kuwait, it was becoming increasingly clear that, in terms of public relations, they were a huge mistake. The hostages were giving the alliance their strongest moral card. More than anything else, taking hundreds of hostages and using them as a human shield disgusted and appalled world opinion. If Iraq was to encourage the peace movements in both the Arab world and the West and present itself internationally as having a just and honourable cause, it had to solve the hostage problem.

Even whilst he was encouraging them, the 'mercy missions' were clearly backfiring on Saddam. The tactic of allowing senior world leaders, usually opposition figures and ones inclined to the view that discussion was preferable to war, to confer with him had a double edge. Yes, it brought the Iraqi leadership, as intended, an immense amount of world coverage. It allowed Saddam to portray himself as a caring man who was merciful enough to let these people go. At every opportunity, he used his meetings with Heath, Brandt, Benn, Nakasone, Mohammed Ali, etc, to portray himself as a man of peace, who had a just cause and wanted to talk. They were huge propaganda coups and he milked them for all they were worth.

However, these world leaders, rather than condemning their own governments and saying what a wonderful man Saddam was, that he *had* a case and that their governments *should* negotiate, unanimously told him he was wrong, that *all* the hostages should be released immediately, and that he should get out of Kuwait unconditionally. They emphasised to him what a disaster holding the hostages was for Iraq's case, and how it was enormously strengthening world resolve and the unity of the United Nations against him. These leaders brought home to him, in no uncertain terms, the folly of his ways.

A very similar line was taken by the British ambassador in his many representations to the Iraqi regime. "I argued that holding hostages is against numerous international laws and conventions, some of which the Iraqis were party to and had signed, that taking hostages was obviously very damaging to the Iraqi image in the world, and that it would not affect a government like Mrs Thatcher's, whose policy on not negotiating over hostages was well known."

The ambassador took a similar position on not negotiating as Mr Heath and the other delegations, even over the question of 'categorising' the hostages. "We had to be very careful over this. Since the posture of Her Majesty's Government was not to negotiate about the hostages, we didn't want to get into the position of offering anything in return for letting certain categories [of hostages] go. But we did say, 'If the policy of your government is to break all these international agreements and to hold hostages, at least you ought to let out categories in respect of whom there are particular reasons'. And we were ready for a positive response at any time; we had lists of hostages we believed had medical conditions that might require treatment not available in Iraq or who required regular medication that might not be available in Iraq. We did, in effect, make special cases for full-time students, regardless of whether they were over or under eighteen.

"The 'elderly' came in a bit later. The Iraqis asked the Irish embassy for a list of all the members of the Irish community over, I think it was, fifty-five. So then we prepared lists of British citizens we knew to be over fifty-five, in case it should be helpful. We made sure the consular side of the [Iraqi] Foreign Ministry had our lists. If I was asked by anybody, Ted Heath, Tony Benn or anybody else, either for advice on their lists or for information about the hostages, we had our lists of the sick, the elderly, and full-time students for them to use as they saw fit... When Ted Heath came, the embassy offered him all the facilities and help it would afford to any ex-prime minister. It helped him with names and with setting up meetings with Iraqi ministers. On his first night, Mr Heath met Tariq Aziz and myself and on the second night I met Mr Heath alone."

Thus the British government's position, as faithfully reported in *The Times* and most other papers, that the mercy missions were undermining the alliance and that the release of the French hostages was "a tactic to drive a wedge into the Western Alliance" was not only a crude and emotive response, but in flat contradiction to its actual policy in Iraq. Unfortunately, it played on people's fears. By denigrating the release of hostages and, by implication, attacking Mr Heath's mission, Willy Brandt's mission, Tony Benn's mission and all the others, it was both undermining sympathy for the hostages and instilling unnecessary anxiety in their relatives.

The official government position undoubtedly placed restrictions on the operation of the British embassy in Baghdad. Key members of staff would have liked to have done more for the hostages and to support the missions by Mr Heath, Mr Benn and the handful of other, less successful, British political delegations.

Through all these peace missions and peace initiatives, Iraq continued to prepare for war in Kuwait. It strengthened its defences and had an estimated 350,000 troops in the emirate by November. Its soldiers still surrounded all foreign embassies and all their vital services were still cut off. Its bluster and propaganda war went on. In Baghdad, the official government daily, *al-Jumhouriya* declared that war would turn the region into a barren wasteland. "The Gulf region will return half a century back. The Americans and other warmongers will be preoccupied with nothing but searching for remnants of their dead bodies in the desert and the Gulf."

Similarly, the alliance went on building its strength as before. Following the UN resolution calling for services to be restored to the embassies, the Americans considered dropping supplies into their embassy by plane. President Bush adopted a new, hard line. The plight of the embassy staff and the hostages infuriated him. "I am more determined than ever. This aggression will not stand... The brutality against innocent civilians will not be tolerated and will not stand."

This period marked a major new offensive aimed at intimidating Iraq into submission, in which the plight of the hostages began to play a key role. The detention of the hostages was central to the moral justification for this belligerence. The Americans too, were using the hostages for propaganda purposes. The primary concern of President Bush and James Baker, his Secretary of State, was emphasised as being the plight of American and other Western hostages. Their suffering was used to rally public opinion and to turn any sympathy away from the Iraqis. The hostages were, from the beginning of November, being used as the strongest, most emotive justification for intervention. By doing so, they rapidly turned the hostages from a weapon for Saddam into a millstone around his neck.

Despite the united stand taken by EC leaders at the Rome summit, by the first of November it was clear that Willy Brandt, socialist ex-Chancellor of West Germany, would be going out to Baghdad. To the consternation of the British government, it seemed he would be leading a delegation which would include an Italian and a Belgian, who together would represent socialists, conservatives and liberals from Europe. Furthermore, the initiative at first had the backing of Chancellor Kohl, who, it was reported at the time, began phoning around Europe and the UN to firm up the idea.

The German government, which officially backed the visit, said it was in line with UN resolution 674, in so far as it called for a special commission by the Secretary-General to strengthen efforts for the release of all hostages. And, indeed, there was support for Herr Brandt from the Christian Social Union Party in Germany, which welcomed the trip as purely humanitarian and of special importance in a time of growing threat of war; from the Social Democratic Party leader, Hans-Jochen Vogel; and from the German Foreign Minister, Hans-Dietrich Genscher, who believed that the best way to help the hostages was for missions to go to Iraq.

In response, Douglas Hurd protested strongly to the German and Italian governments about the Brandt mission. He complained about the lack of consultation and stated that it was in breach of the Rome declaration not to send representatives to Baghdad to negotiate. When Perez de Cuellar declined to sanction the visit, it further added to the British government's indignation.

In response, the Germans and Italians denied it was to negotiate. They insisted it was merely to argue for the release of hostages and rejected what they saw as the British stance that only a military solution to the Gulf crisis was possible. The German government was particularly adamant, although the Italian position soon crumbled. However, Willy Brandt brushed aside objections to his visit and continued to press other European politicians to join him. Brandt's office insisted he would not be going just to plead for the release of the estimated four hundred German hostages, but for *all* hostages being held. Nor would it be one country going it alone but an international mission representing at least three countries.

Before he went, Herr Brandt secured support from the Belgian government to raise the question of thirty-eight Belgian hostages being held and had agreed to act on behalf of Swiss and Scandinavian hostages as well. He also had the blessing of the Socialist International, significant because Saddam Hussein regarded himself as a socialist, and responded positively to foreign socialists who visited. Edward Heath supported him as well, at the same time accusing the British government of "abdicating responsibility" for both the hostages and a peaceful solution. Furthermore, David Lange, former prime minister of New Zealand, announced he was going to Iraq to plead for twenty of his countrymen held there, and Anker Joergenson, Denmark's former Social Democratic prime minister, confirmed he would visit Baghdad to try to release Denmark's seventy-five hostages. His visit was in response to a direct appeal from Danish hostages.

This sudden proliferation of missions alarmed several EC countries. Anker Joergenson did not have the support of his government and the Dutch government called for a special meeting of EC foreign ministers to try to prevent any further missions by prominent individuals. Neither the Italian politician nor the Belgian who were originally going with Herr Brandt eventually went. Nor did the United Nations ever sanction the visit.

The British hostages in hiding and on the installations were as divided as the European Community leaders. Many were firmly against these visits. They regarded them as divisive and as not addressing the real problem of getting *everybody* back home. They were simply propaganda tools for the Iraqis - "arse-licking" as one hostage graphically put it - similar to the manufactured pictures of contented hostages playing pool or having Thanksgiving Dinner in a 'show installation'. Others were for them. At least someone was doing something and the hostage issue was being kept in the news. Every hostage out was a gain. Any pressure on the Iraqi leadership was useful and would eventually lead to the release of all the hostages. They were opening the first cracks in the Iraqi policy, and perhaps forcing the flood gates.

It was a dilemma too for their relatives and for the Gulf Support Group. Both were split over the value of the 'mercy missions'. The Gulf Support Group's official position was to welcome the missions, but that hid serious debate within its ranks. It had fully supported Ted Heath's mission and supported the Brandt expedition for similar humanitarian reasons, whilst continuing to put pressure on the British government to do more and calling for the release of all hostages and people in hiding. In fact, in a letter to the Iraqi ambassador in London, it suggested that a 'peace plane' be organised to carry relatives and close friends of the hostages to Iraq "to talk with members of your government and to discuss the possibility of a peaceful solution to the crisis". Unfortunately, nothing came of it, mainly because other events overtook it.

BRANDT SETS OFF WITH BONN'S BLESSING

> Willy Brandt, the former West German Chancellor, flies to Baghdad today on board a Lufthansa Airbus, taking with him £300,000 worth of medical supplies and children's food. He has the best wishes of the German government for his mission to free as many hostages as possible... The German government... is ready to risk EC condemnation rather than allow Herr Brandt, a Social Democrat, to win all the glory for what is domestically a very popular mission. Relatives of hostages have demonstrated outside the Chancellery in Bonn and opinion polls show that there is wide backing for negotiations to win their release...
>
> [Herr Brandt stated that] his mission... would be both humanitarian and political. "It is obvious what humanitarian means. Political efforts will mean finding out if there is any alternative to war."
>
> ...The fact that the former chancellor asked Lufthansa for the use of a wide-bodied Airbus capable of carrying up to 375 passengers suggests he must hope to come back with more than the thirty-three Britons handed over to Edward Heath, the former British prime minister. Within government circles here some scorn has been poured on Mr Heath for trying to win the release of only British hostages. The fact that Herr Brandt is going to try on behalf of hostages from all nations is seen as further evidence that his mission is not one included in the terms of the EC summit declaration...
>
> *The Times, Monday 5th November*

The next few days were to further confuse the hostage picture. Clearly, the Iraqis had come to realise the harm the hostages were doing to its cause, yet they still tried to play them for all they were worth. If only they could win over international opinion by a steady stream of releases which would allow them to hold on until the crucial spring months of 1991, when Ramadan and the desert heat would make war impossible. To do this they had to make large concessions, especially to those powerful and influential governments which had not sent troops to the Gulf, most notably Germany and Japan. It was no coincidence that both Yasuhiro Nakasone and Willy Brandt were invited to Baghdad at virtually the same time.

The Japanese politician was rewarded with the release of a hundred and eight hostages on 6th November. Seventy-seven were to be Japanese - about a fifth of the four hundred held - the rest being twenty Italians, five Swedes, two Germans, two Portuguese and two Australians. Most of the Japanese were businessmen under house arrest or restricted to remaining in Iraq, and not those on the installations. The other nationalities were mainly in response to other, minor delegations, including one from Arab trade unionists.

These releases came the day before Willy Brandt was due to meet Saddam Hussein in face-to-face talks. Yasser Arafat was also in Baghdad. He and Herr Brandt gave a joint press conference on the sixth. They both expressed guarded optimism about a peaceful outcome. Herr Brandt urged the USA and Britain to start talks. "I believe all parties involved in the Gulf crisis should resort to dialogue, including America, to save the area from the danger of war." He was more critical of the British position: "I hate to say it, but perhaps at the moment there is a little bit more flexibility on the side of the United States than on the side of the United Kingdom", and reiterated that peace was possible "if a certain amount of flexibility could be discovered on the part of the partners dealing with the Gulf crisis." It was a clear appeal to allow Saddam to safe face and withdraw peacefully from Kuwait.

The German ex-Chancellor held his talks with Saddam Hussein on the seventh, That same day came the stunning announcement that he would be allowed to return with a hundred and seventy-seven hostages. This was a major triumph for the German politician. Within two days, nearly three hundred hostages had been released, a significant proportion of the total being held. In his talks, Herr Brandt had discussed ways to achieve a durable settlement in the Middle East and shared with President Saddam the view that linking the Kuwait crisis with the Palestinian question should be taken more seriously. Whilst clearly wanting a peaceful solution, Herr Brandt didn't enter into any negotiations, merely dialogue. In no way did he threaten to split the massive military alliance ranged against Iraq. Yet he came away with a plane load of hostages, more than the belligerence of the British and American governments had achieved. Perhaps it was because they gave the impression that the hostages were essentially a side issue to them, useful for propaganda purposes but little else.

The Japanese flew out on the seventh, with a final total of seventy-four

Japanese plus others, and the mainly German contingent flew to Frankfurt on the ninth. In the end, Willy Brandt took out one hundred and ninety-three. There were a hundred and forty Germans on board, plus seventeen Italians, twelve Britons, three Americans, and an assortment of other nationalities. The German government congratulated Herr Brandt on the success of his "humanitarian mission", stating that it shared the joy and relief of the hostages and their families. Two hundred Germans still remained in Iraq and Kuwait.

The Iraqis' attempts to persuade Japan and Germany to withdraw from the alliance and demand peace negotiations were faint hopes. The Japanese government had pledged $4 billion to help pay for the war, a gesture the Iraqis felt was *worse* than a direct military contribution, and Germany had also pledged a large contribution. However, the release announcement did come the same day as Japan's government scrapped plans to send two thousand non-combatant troops to the Gulf. Whilst both Mr Nakasone and Herr Brandt clearly wanted a peaceful solution - and by giving them a world platform, Iraq was encouraging a diplomatic solution - neither politician entered into negotiations. How could they? They had nothing to give in exchange. They did no deals.

The Iraqis released hostages to them because they could gain more by that gesture than by holding them. The release of the French hostages resulted, a week or so later, in a public opinion poll which showed a dramatic fall in support for French military involvement in the Gulf. On the ninth, Iraq finally capitulated to Soviet pressure and announced that all two thousand Soviet citizens detained in Iraq would be free to leave from the eleventh. The Soviet Union had consistently refused to send troops to the Gulf and was still attempting, through diplomatic initiatives by President Gorbachev and his Foreign minister Yevgeny Primakov, to find a peaceful solution. If Iraq could keep this stream of releases up into the new year, war weariness would set in and its occupation of Kuwait would more and more take on the appearance of a *fait accompli*. It was a race. A race between the growing peace lobby and the United States and British governments' commitment to war.

As if to confirm this, the White House launched another salvo against the peace missions on the seventh. Mr Heath was specifically named by Martin Fitzwater, the White House Press Secretary, claiming that he and others were being exploited for propaganda purposes by the Iraqis, who were bent on splitting the international alliance against them. He warned the visiting statesmen that they "walk a very fine line between trying to help their countrymen and being used by Saddam Hussein for inhuman treatment of the hostage families and the hostages themselves." Fine words from someone who had done comparatively little, if anything, to help the hostages himself.

In the UK frustration grew. The mercy missions and release of the French and German hostages only added to it. The British government seemed to be doing nothing. The hostages were rotting away, waiting to become war fodder. It simply wasn't good enough and they phoned the Emergency Unit to tell it so.

Whilst much anger was directed at general government policy, the perceived attitude of some Foreign Office staff didn't help. Relatives complained that, at times, some reacted as though they were being a complete nuisance calling them Others complained that they were dismissive, simply cut callers off or didn't ring them back enough. Some relatives felt increasingly frustrated that the Foreign Office was keeping the information it did have to itself. They would have liked it to have phoned with a lot more news, not just sightings or details of flights. Others suspected that it was keeping a lot of the information it was given for its own records, whilst failing to tell them. One relative compared calling the Emergency Unit to phoning directory enquiries. "You were given no sympathy, they were short with you and would just cut you off. There were never any explanations, as though they had no time for you, but wanted to get you off the line as fast as they could."

As a result of these protests, the relationship between the Foreign Office and the Gulf Support Group had degenerated in August as complaints streamed in about the Emergency Unit, but this had improved once they pooled information and once the Emergency Unit had its computer system up and running.

Much of the frustration was not the Foreign Office's fault. The Emergency Unit had a limited and overworked staff. They cared, but were overworked. People expected the Foreign Office to have the most up-to-date knowledge, but its hands were tied in Baghdad and Kuwait and it had inadequate resources to keep track of people. Throughout the crisis the Foreign Office had no independent means of gathering information. It relied on precisely the same sources as the relatives. The Iraqis were deliberately concealing hostages from embassy officials, denying they were in the hotels, refusing to let the officials see them, and giving wrong or out-of-date information. The embassy had to cope with a systematic programme of disinformation from them which made keeping track of people very much harder than it otherwise would have been.

Perhaps in future, both the public and the government should recognise each other's limitations and strengths. As it turned out, the gathering of information rested virtually entirely with the people in the crisis, with eye witnesses, and not with the government. However, its *dissemination* should rest with the government department in liaison with any support group set up.

Far more information should be divulged by the government and a far greater effort should be made by people caught up in a crisis to inform the government. A mutual and equal relationship is required, where all unnecessary procedures and processes are dispensed with and information becomes a joint resource rather than a source of power.

In response to the growing anger at various government departments and to developing events, the Gulf Support Group organised a series of meetings between the Foreign Office and relatives of the hostages. The first was held in the Connaught Rooms in London on Saturday 20th October. Josie Brookes travelled down to it by train.

About a hundred and fifty relatives, mainly wives, attended, helped by the provision of a crêche. They came, from all over the country and were clearly angry and frustrated at what they felt was a total lack of effort by the government to get the hostages back. Extreme emotions were bubbling just under the surface as people tried to keep calm. One little thing could cause them to explode.

Both the Foreign Office and the DSS were invited to send a speaker. Both agreed. Rosemary Spencer came for the Foreign Office and Donald Wildie represented the DSS. Joanna Copley chaired it and also on the platform were Josie Brookes, Rob Hayward MP and Tony Morley. The bulk of the meeting was taken up with the situation in Iraq and Kuwait and the role of the Foreign Office, so Rosemary Spencer was the first to speak. It was difficult for her as she stood in front of so many people. From the moment she had taken her seat on the platform she had sensed the hostile atmosphere and had even mentioned it to Joanna, who was sitting next to her. She began her speech by giving an outline of the current situation in Kuwait and Iraq.

"There are now three hundred and four people, mainly men, but including a handful of women, who are held hostage in Iraq. There are also seventy-two at strategic sites in Kuwait, notably in the Mina Ahmadi oil terminal, at the Kuwaiti port of Shuwaikh, at the university, at Doha power station, at military bases, and at some palaces in Kuwait City. These are on top of eighty-three at present being held at the Regency Palace Hotel in Kuwait who are expected to be moved to Baghdad soon." The audience listened quietly, some there just to listen, others ready to explode with months of pent-up frustration.

"We estimate there are some six hundred and fifty still in hiding in Kuwait. That brings the total to about one thousand one hundred in the human shield. There are also five hundred British in Iraq who are not free to leave, but are otherwise completely at liberty within the country. Many are in their own homes, doing their normal jobs. Forty-one of these are British nurses working for the PARC organisation in Baghdad. The embassy has been asked to give as much help to these people as possible." There was unkind laughter from the floor. She went on. "A lot of our work is behind the scenes." A man shouted out "What work?".

Undetered, but increasingly nervous, Rosemary continued to describe the work the embassies were doing. "Britain is now one of only five countries with embassies in Kuwait, the others being the United States, Oman, Bahrain and France. The Canadians withdrew their diplomats at the weekend. Our ambassador, Michael Weston, and his assistant, Larry Banks, are virtually cut off from the country, although they do have a phone line working and are able to get some information in and out. They also have a link with Abu Dhabi. It was they who told us about the latest round-up of hostages. I can assure you the government is trying everything in its power to gain the release of the hostages."

"Listen," a man rose from the floor, unable to control his anger any longer. "I escaped from Kuwait at the end of August with my wife and two children. We spent over a day crossing the desert, avoiding Iraqi tanks and helicopters. When we arrived in Saudi Arabia and got to the British embassy in Riyadh, they didn't want to know. They wouldn't give us any money to get home, they wouldn't give us any help at all. And I know of other people who say the same thing. The embassies in Qatar and Bahrain are just the same." He was visibly shaking as his finger emphasised every point he made. Rosemary sat down.

A woman rose. Joanna let her speak. "My husband was taken prisoner by the Iraqis in the first week. I haven't heard anything from him except one letter which came out with one of the women in September. Since then I've heard nothing. Now, the Foreign Office must be getting *some* information. It must have some news of him or of the situation out there. We know nothing. We're stuck in our homes without any information at all. We have to keep phoning up the Foreign Office, it never phones us. I'm dreading my phone bill. Why can't the Foreign Office keep us more informed? Why does it keep all its information to itself?"

Rosemary rose again to tell the people that the situation in Iraq and Kuwait was not nearly as bad as the press were making out. "As far as we know at this time, there is no evidence of ill-treatment by the Iraqis of people held, although everyone in Kuwait is obviously under considerable strain." There were more cynical laughs. "The conditions in Kuwait are uncomfortable but not dangerous, with water, electricity and phones still working. In Iraq things are still relatively normal. I must say again that the Foreign Office is doing all in its power to help people out there, especially the sick and elderly. The embassy in Baghdad is organising comfort parcels for those held on installations, although we are having difficulties organising them from this end, but we are still looking at the possibility."

"How long's it going to take you?" a heckler demanded. "Until one of them dies?"

"Seven more hostages were rounded up on Saturday," a woman rose. "I left my husband in hiding in Kuwait. I've had letters; I've been lucky in that respect. But I wish I hadn't sometimes because he's getting so depressed I can't bear to read them. It's nonsense to say things are 'comfortable' in Kuwait. How out of touch can you be? My husband says they're running out of food. There' looters coming round every night and Iraqi patrols every day. The Iraqis are shooting Kuwaiti women and children right outside their apartment. What are you doing about it? There' over three hundred out on the installations now. How many more do there have to be before the government gets off its backside and decides to help these people? Why have we been left to do everything ourselves?"

An elderly man from the back of the room wanted to speak. Joanna indicated to him. He rose slowly on his walking stick as the room hushed.

"I want to know why the Foreign Office isn't doing anything to get our letters through to the people in Kuwait. I sent several to a post box number, but I know for a fact they haven't got through. My son and his wife have been held as hostages at an airfield in northern Iraq. I had a phone call from an Australian who was at the same camp. He tells me the conditions are appalling - absolutely appalling. They've only got rice and a few vegetables to eat. The toilets are filthy. They've got stomach complaints, diarrhoea and have lost a lot of weight.

"Now... wait until I've finished. Now, I sent a food parcel and some clothes to you and asked you to send it out to them in a diplomatic bag. I put a letter with it to explain my son's and daughter-in-law's plight. But you sent it me back, with a letter saying you weren't allowed to send food parcels out in the diplomatic bag because it was contrary to the Vienna Convention, or something. Yes, well, you can nod your head, but I know for a fact that other nationals are getting food parcels, so why aren't ours? This Saddam bloke doesn't respect diplomatic niceties. Look what he's done to our embassy in Kuwait. And you're telling me you can't send them a packet of chocolate and a woolly jumper? Grow up."

Rosemary rose to answer the points. She was in a very difficult position, taking flak for a wide variety of problems, many of which she felt were beyond the Foreign Office's control. The hostility was washing over her in waves as she emphasised that no one in Iraq was in danger of going hungry and those in Kuwait mostly had adequate food because they had stocked up at an early stage.

"How could the Foreign Office possibly know that?" someone demanded.

"Will you please just listen," Joanna rose. "You will have plenty of opportunity to reply."

"The seven arrested on Saturday have joined others held in hotels in Kuwait and may soon be moved up to Baghdad. The British embassy in Iraq has done all it can for them and others. It has settled the bills in the hotels for those who couldn't afford to pay. It has spent a total of one point three million pounds so far, including other costs. We *have* received a lot of mail from relatives and it *has* arrived in Baghdad. We are in the process of sending it down to Kuwait, though the route is tortuous and I obviously can't give away any details. But it *is* getting there. Mail for people in the installations is much harder to get through because the Iraqis are stopping us sending it. They are collecting it and we have to hope they pass it on, but I'm afraid I have strong reservations about whether it is getting through. The embassy is also making up food and clothing parcels in Baghdad and sending them to the Red Crescent, but again we have no way of knowing whether they are reaching the men on the installations. We have no way of checking that. I personally doubt whether any are getting through. The Iraqis seem to be deliberately favouring some nationals in the camps, such as the Japanese and Germans, but not the British, in an effort to divide them against each other."

The next speaker from the floor complained about the way they were treated over the phone. "We're not animals you know. We do have feelings. How would you like it if you phoned up and someone said to you, 'Sorry, we've no more information today,' and put the phone down? I mean, it's rude more than anything else. I mean, I know the Emergency Unit's got to deal with a lot of calls, but you should put on more staff. It wouldn't take much to just listen to us for a bit. I'm sure the people on the phones *do* care, but it sounds as though they don't. The phones just go straight down. And they never phone us with any information. I heard that my husband had been moved to the Melia al-Mansour Hotel a week before you lot did. I got a phone call from a German. A few days later I had a phone call from my husband from the hotel to tell me they were taking him to an installation. He didn't know which one. When I phoned you up, this girl said, 'Oh yes, hang on a minute, we have information on your husband. He's perfectly safe. He's been taken to the Melia al-Mansour Hotel.' I had to tell her, 'No he hasn't. That news is a week old. He's in an installation now'. Why aren't we getting the information when we need it?"

"The Foreign Office is doing everything it can," Rosemary replied. "And you should be grateful for what we have been doing for you."

That hit a nerve. Grateful? For being left to struggle on alone? Grateful, whilst their husbands rotted? Oh no. Relatives shouted back at her in absolute fury. There was uproar for three or four minutes as Joanna tried to calm them down.

A lot of the frustration was aimed at the government, but the poor Foreign Office official was the one standing in the way. The meeting was screaming, angry, and bitter. The relatives really let their frustration loose. Joanna tried to chair it, but at times it threatened to get out of hand and she had to repeatedly stop the meeting to calm people down.

Josie Brookes felt the criticisms were constructive, although "it was a difficult meeting to chair, and was very angry". She was genuinely shocked by the depth of animosity towards the Foreign Office and DSS. She described the meeting as "a real slating for the government and Foreign Office. I just had to sit and listen."

Not all of this frustration was aimed at officialdom. Some of the anger was directed between relatives who had differing points of view. Two people nearly had a stand-up fight and Joanna had to rush from the platform and tell them to sit down. The dispute concerned the most fundamental division over policy developing in the Gulf Support Group. "The meeting clearly showed the polarisation of the war faction and the peace faction. This is a generalisation," Joanna explained, "but those with relatives in installations didn't want war, whilst those with relatives in hiding in Kuwait did want war." There were also divisions between relatives of those in installations and of those in hiding over food parcels and phone calls, as those in hiding could get neither. Joanna later reiterated to me the point she had tried to make to the meeting. "There is no point in arguing about whether it's peace or whether it's war. If we don't act together and we are not seen to be united, we don't stand a chance of persuading the Iraqis that they should be released."

The final part of the meeting was taken up with DSS issues. Donald Wildie, the DSS representative, spoke on what his department was trying to do and the difficulties it was facing. He was onto a no-hoper. People were angry with the Foreign Office, but they were bitterly furious at their treatment by DSS officials, about lack of money, about uncaring, insensitive treatment and about countless bureaucratic forms. There was a veritable explosion of people vehemently detailing their financial and personal difficulties and demanding to know what the DSS was going to do about them. Story after story came out about hardship. One woman and her two children had moved in with her mother-in-law, but her mother had never approved of her son's marriage and after a few days had ordered them out of her house. She had been forced into bedsitter accommodation with her two children, where she was still living. The social fund, from which they could claim a loan to cover resettlement costs, was not being run smoothly at local level. Many people were finding it very difficult to get the money. Local DSS branches had not received directives or didn't know how the fund was operated.

As with the feeling towards the Foreign Office, a lot of this was simply bitterness. People who had a Mercedes and swimming pool in sunny Kuwait were now on £30 a week in rain-sodden Britain. It was very hard trying to adjust, and they were just angry, full stop. There was very little order to their feelings. People were simply standing up and saying what they thought, one after the other, getting months of frustration off their chests. It was barely constructive, and it proved very hard to direct people positively towards the future.

Josie tried. When her turn came, she spoke about the work she and Stephen were doing in Coventry, listing the calls they were getting and the counselling they were undertaking. She sat down to applause. A following speaker from the London helpline mentioned a demonstration and Joanna spoke about a date. Josie remembered the preparations for a National Day of Prayer, so stood up again and announced that it would be on 24th October, United Nations Day. Services would be held in Britain and in the Gulf to remember all the people caught up in the crisis, not just the hostages. The reaction to the news of these events was wonderful. They seemed to be positive things to have arisen from a very negative, acrimonious meeting. It uplifted people. Many spoke from the floor to give their support and Joanna took their names.

The only other constructive aspect of the meeting were the ideas put forward for further activities. Local groups were encouraged to continue using their local media to keep the plight of the hostages in the public eye. A list of relatives willing to talk to the media would be compiled. The Bishop of Cyprus, planning a visit to Iraq, would be asked to intervene on behalf of the hostages. Gulf Link, the World Service and CNN should all be used to get news back to those held by the Iraqis. And finally, more efforts should be made to press British Telecom into helping with the telephone bills of the relatives.

The meeting enabled a lot of anger to be released, but its achievements were limited. Rosemary Spencer, as Assistant Under-Secretary at the Foreign Office, was a very able woman, intimately involved with organising help for the hostages, but she hadn't realised the degree of anger towards the Foreign Office. The meeting was at least useful for getting that point across.

There were several immediate improvements for the relatives. The Foreign Office set up a PO Box number for sending mail to Iraq, though it was not well thought out. There could be no parcels, and all letters and postcards should have "British Guest in Iraq" written after the name and address! On 31st October - three months into the crisis - the DSS announced that it was making a maximum of £500 available as a travel grant to any returning hostage, and that people could also apply for a loan of up to £2,500 to help with resettlement. This loan was not repayable during the period of the present crisis. Unfortunately, the travel grant had to be claimed at the airport, or within twenty-four hours of arriving and very few people returning either knew about it or sought out the DSS table to claim it. Even fewer people, virtually none, seemed to have received it. Of the loan, there was a similarly very low take-up, partly because the news of it took a long while to filter down to local DSS branches and the relatives who applied had to go through so much red tape to claim it, it was not worthwhile. It was a humiliating experience to beg for money through the DSS system, and many people were very wary of falling into debt.

The next day, British Telecom announced a concession to the relatives. All telephone calls to Iraq and Kuwait would be charged at half rate for the duration of the crisis. As the company was taking two hundred calls a day to those countries, this represented a massive saving for the relatives. A five minutes call, which had cost £13.23p, now cost £6.76p. Unfortunately, British Telecom did nothing to help relatives who had run up huge phone bills through contacting each other, the Foreign Office, the Gulf Support Group and other officials for help. Some of these bills were huge. £169, £189, and £147 for households where they were usually £40 are three examples.

During November, the Gulf Support Group took several major steps forward organisationally. Its local branches began to develop, helped by a series of regional meetings. Events seemed to be moving faster again. October had been a long haul, with relatives desperate for news and developments. However, with the military build-up and the peace missions in late October and early November, this atmosphere changed to one of hectic activity, where every day brought a new development. The Gulf Support Group had to respond to each one immediately, often fielding press questions and speculation at all hours of the day and night.

One local group was set up by Ivan Manning, who had escaped by boat with four other British and French early in October. When Ivan flew back into Britain on Friday 5th October he met Andy Charles at the airport, who was meeting every flight, and who gave him a leaflet about the support group. Just a week later he went to the London meeting between the relatives and government officials.

From the meeting, Ivan became deeply involved in the support group. Relatives began to phone him with questions, mainly because he was virtually unique in having been in an installation and knowing the conditions on the sites. He spoke to a lot of the wives and families. Most of the names were passed on to him by other helplines. He talked with Pauline Stringer in Cornwall, and women as far afield as Scotland and Cyprus. In the end, he was in contact with about two hundred relatives. He set up a local helpline for Sussex, but it soon stretched beyond there. He was given all the names of relatives around him. He asked for a copy of the London database, and although he was not allowed it for security reasons, he was given a print out of the addresses and names. He was as anxious as people from other areas to set up support groups locally. "It looked like it would be very much an on-going thing. It was a chat-up line. When they used to feel down in they dumps, they used to phone up, have a word, and let go of their sorrows." Whilst doing all that, Ivan found time to visit London frequently and was invited to several TV and radio debates and interviews. He ran up a phone bill of £1,500. He received £600 from the support group's trust fund towards it.

The other thing Ivan did from his dining room table was to keep the hostages in the news. He wanted to publicise their plight as much as possible. But also the plight of the relatives. He came across dozens of families facing acute financial hardship, desperate for help. He found the DSS frequently unsympathetic and obstreperous. Housing was an acute issue for families who grandparents were running out of patience, or who had been in bed and breakfast or poor quality council housing for a month. Children were suffering emotional problems from missing their fathers and from the huge upset and uncertainty in their lives. Ivan and his helpers had to argue with the DSS to get people financial help and with the local housing authorities to get people accommodation, threatening them with going to the press. Eventually, they did manage to get people housing and financial help and, once the departments realised the value of the helpline and its support, they began to co-operate. By the time the men were released, they had even built up a rapport.

The crisis was seriously affecting the health of those running the helplines. Joanna Copley was losing weight and looked pale and exhausted and Josie Brookes noticed how thin Stephen was looking. "I was so worried about Stephen. He had taken so much of it. He really had been the buffer for everybody, I wondered how much more he could take. He put on this 'I'm coping' manner, but I didn't know how he managed to absorb it all. Right in the middle of it, he was keeping everybody calm. Even I was giving him a hard time." When showing me a photograph taken of him then, she commented quietly, "How thin he looked."

Josie too was showing the strain of overwork and sleepless nights. One week, she estimated that a hundred people had come into her house, volunteers on the rota, press, friends and acquaintances. Theirs was an open house. "We allowed our house to be used for humanitarian reasons. The little bedroom had been my hideaway. Now it had become a war room. We would have five people in there. Steve and I would be answering the phones, then others would be filling in cards or typing information onto the computer. We would do press interviews from there all the time."

Josie records her state of mind in her diary at the time:

"I keep mixing the past with what's happening now. I can't put things in their proper timescale. My mind's not as active; it's as though I've lost something. My memory. I suppose it'll come back when I've had a rest. It'll come back, my concentration and memory. I think it's because I'm so tired. Every few hours, more volunteers arrive and I have to be with them all the time, helping them, being nice to them, making them coffees, talking to them, informing them. Where I went wrong, instead of having just a couple of people a day, I had eight or ten, so I was briefing someone every one or two hours. Those briefings might take half an hour. Then there were interviews for the press and phone calls only I could deal with, or people calling round. It was as though I got out of bed in the morning. took a deep breath in and didn't breathe out again until night-time. In fact, I don't think we've breathed out for months.

"I'm just walking around in a trance, rushing, the feeling of hurrying to catch a train. If there's ever a really bad incident, I go downstairs and wash the kitchen floor. Aggressively wash the kitchen floor. If I'm terribly upset. That floor must have been washed as much in four months as in the whole of its previous existence. Things get on top of me and I get so annoyed, I scrub that floor spotless. Otherwise, I would hit someone, anyone, or smash a window or throw something, I'm so pent up and frustrated with tiredness. I have never felt like this in my life before and it really upsets me."

Another entry in her diary records how even her beloved house was turning into a prison for her:

"I used to be glad to get out of this house. The tension, the people, the lack of privacy, arguments, distress, everything. I could get into my car, put the radio on, go down to the Tech and escape. But never for one moment did I think it wasn't worth it. I had no time for those - many - people, including close friends, telling me to give it up. I just wanted to have the strength to cope until it was all over, without ending up in an asylum. That was my main fear; that I hadn't got the strength to cope with what was coming - ie death."

Josie was racked far more than Stephen by the fear of all the hostages being killed. She would dream of their bodies coming home in canvas bags, have nightmares about what they were suffering and the horrors of war. No one knew when war would start. Throughout October and November, the military build-up was such that the conflict could commence any day - and that would be the end for the hostages in the installations. Her diary reflects this growing concern, even from as early as the twenty-eighth of September: *"The Iraqis are threatening to stop feeding foreigners from Monday. Things are hotting up. I'm sure there's going to be a war. I hope not."* She was very ill for about a week with her wisdom tooth and colitis, both aggravated by the sheer strain she was under. On 2nd October, *"Very weary. Exhausted."* She was fearful of losing her job. On the eleventh, *"Felt down and depressed about money problems - where are we going? I am so worried about losing my job. What will I do?"* On the fifteenth, *"Worry over mounting bills, especially the phone. British Telecom is less than co-operative. Although I try to have hope and faith, there are times when I'm listening to the rhetoric of Saddam and I think, with this man, I don't know whether I'll ever seem them again. There are times when the news is so bad, I just don't know if they'll come out."*

A few days later she had a very good and relaxing meeting with three other relatives at Rackhams in Birmingham. David Barnes, from the local DSS, visited her and let her get a lot off her chest. But by the eighteenth she felt ill again. Tensions were constantly growing at home with the pressure of work and the lack of any privacy or time to themselves. Arguments seemed to grow more and more frequent. *"Felt very ill. Lying on the floor with discomfort. I felt that poorly, almost as though I wanted an injection to put me out. I don't want to appear weak, but I feel ill."* She couldn't face sitting an exam for her beauty course that night. *"It's all the calls from relatives getting me."*

And the next day, *"Woke up feeling grotty after a horrid dream."* She hoped Eric Watson might be coming out with Edward Heath, but heard of the twenty-third that he wasn't. *"Pure despair when I was told there was no Eric. I am glad for so many other families but sad for Wen Li and family and no Eric... I broke up when I rang Eric's mum. She sounded so despairing."* She then went down to London for the relatives' meeting with the government officials. That was *"a screaming, angry, bitter meeting, with frustration really let loose"*, and she felt exhausted after it.

By the end of November the tension had become unbearable as the prospect of war and its casualties were made starkly clear by the media. Army doctors in the Gulf were interviewed about body bags and reports appeared on projected casualties if there was a war. British hospitals were being prepared for thousands of casualties, and an article stated that "British hospitals might be unable to cope with large numbers of seriously injured casualties from a conflict in the Gulf, a leading plastic surgeon said today." (*The Times, 27th November*)

On the thirtieth, when Saddam invited relatives to visit their 'guests' over Christmas, Josie wrote: *"Feeling war coming nearer. The government said negotiations are failing. Everybody is just waiting for it to happen. Oh dear, all those lives being lost."* And on 1st December, when Saddam announced he would release all the hostages if the UN decided on a peaceful solution: *"Feet hurt all last week. Colitis dreadful; cold; losing weight. My body is crying out for a rest. Steve has faxed all the embassies with a press release. We hope they publicise this to avert war."*

At times, she felt like ripping the posters and maps down from the walls of the room and throwing out all the computers, phones and cardfiles because of the pressure it was putting on her and her marriage. It was putting her relationship with Stephen under severe strain.

Josie had an old duffel coat, which was like a life-long friend. It gave her warmth and comfort. She would put it on, even in the house, and it kept her emotion intact. Within it, she felt safe, enclosed, comfortable and warm. She had all the pain and distress from the relatives, but she could put on that coat and feel safe and intact. She would go into churches in it and pray. "If ever I could get out of the house for a couple of hours, I would get into the car, put a Cliff Richard tape on and head for Birmingham Cathedral." There, she would find a quiet spot, kneel and pray. As she left, she would write in the visitors book, asking people to pray for the hostages and their relatives. And the cathedral did pray - every day - for them and for all those people trapped in the refugee camps.

Josie had to consciously conquer all her fears, of driving, of unknown cities, of finding her way about. She would seek out coffee shops to relax and get away from things. One in Coventry donated as much coffee to the helpline as it needed, and put up a poster in its window requesting volunteers to get in contact with Josie.

It was as though her empathy with all the other relatives, friends and hostages overrode her other needs, her ingrained fears, and even her personality at times. She became intimately, totally immersed in their feelings and moods. She found it impossible to separate herself from them. Rather than keeping her distance, it seemed essential to her to become at one with the people who called her, to be of them completely.

It never seemed to stop. In fact, things were growing more intense as developments began to unravel. At the end of October, the Iraqis played their last major card. On the thirty-first, the Iraqi ambassador to Washington, Mohamad Sadiq al-Mashat, told a press conference that Western 'guests' were being well-treated, whilst in Baghdad it was announced that "The families of those who are staying as our guests can come to visit them during their Christmas and New Year. They can call at our embassies to get visas."

The response from relatives, especially women with families, to this emotional blackmail was immediate. Some instinctively and spontaneously determined to go. Nothing would stop them. Wen Li was one. She was going out to see her husband Eric and to bring him home with her. Many phoned the helplines in great distress. The enormous moral pressure being put on them to go was made unbearable for those who had no money and were living on social security or with their parents. Their children were desperate to see their fathers and grandparents were also wanting to go, yet many wives knew their husbands would not want them to take that risk. They didn't know whether they would ever be allowed back.

Josie remembers the feelings of the wives. She was deeply saddened by it. "They really believed Saddam would let them out, but he was using the wives for propaganda. He was using them as puppets again. I could see it. I said to them, if only they could stay here and fight with us together. Don't do this. We're going to achieve more by holding back than by going over in dribs and drabs. I can see what's going to happen. Saddam's twisting your emotions all the time, dangling you on strings, just like puppets."

The Gulf Support Group reacted angrily to the news. "The offer must be seen in its true context of both fudging the issue of the fact that the people held should be issued with the visas to return home and being a totally cynical and divisive tactic aimed at the most vulnerable part of society, young mothers with distressed children...[We] reject it in the most forceful manner available..."

On 4th November, perhaps the most cynical manoeuvre yet was unveiled by the Iraqis. Suddenly, wives with husbands held in installations started to receive phone calls from them. The men had been told - some ordered - by their Iraqi guards to call their wives and invite them to Iraq over Christmas. It was portrayed by the Iraqis as a humanitarian move, but the calls were made under armed guard and only lasted a few minutes before they were abruptly, and without warning, cut off. They were told to say how well they were being treated and to invite their wives to come over. Many of the men refused point-blank to place such emotional stress on their relatives. Others saw it as at least a chance to contact them and tell them they were all right. Most of these men tried their best to make it plain to their wives that they did *not* want them to come.

The calls were a tremendous relief to relatives, who were hearing from their menfolk for the first time in many months, but were also very distressing. Some men were clearly suffering. Some broke down over the phone. Some pleaded for their wives to come out and take them back with them. Others were calm, unemotional, then suddenly cut off.

One woman described her first call. "It came at 9.30 in the morning. I was amazed to hear my husband's voice. It was the first time we had spoken since the end of July. He said I could go out and join him for Christmas, but it should be entirely my decision and he said I was not to bring our daughters." It was great to know he was safe, but it threw her into inner turmoil. "I couldn't understand him asking me to go out to join him. That was not my husband talking, I was sure about that. In his last letter [received on 6th September] he said 'Thank God you're out of it'. The telephone call lasted ten minutes. I said I didn't know what to do and he repeated that it was entirely up to me... The call confused me at first, but I'm not going. I can't go. I don't believe what my husband said and I don't believe he really wants me to go... I can't see what it would achieve. How could anyone, particularly an Arab who is the president of his country, use women in such a way?"

The helplines were deluged with more calls. Ivan Manning running his line in Sussex commented in a television interview that "some of these wives are very upset. Saddam Hussein is once again using women and children as a propaganda weapon." However, not all shared that view. All were glad to hear from their menfolk at long last and anger or worry at whether to go was tempered by absolute delight at knowing their men were safe. One relative described her first call as "a source of joy and relief to hear his voice after three month's separation... for a few brief minutes we forgot the acute anxiety and anguish with which we now have to live. The rest of our family were equally delighted with the call." Perhaps such raised hope and joy was the real reason why it *was* so cynical a tactic. These relatives were being given renewed hope, only for it to be shattered as the world continued to prepare for war.

The Foreign Office, which had denounced the offer to visit over Christmas, condemned the calls as another cynical ploy. It urged relatives not to take up Saddam's invitation to visit Iraq. Tom King, the Defence Secretary, asked relatives to "think very carefully" before going. "We can well understand the emotions, the longing to see your husband, your father. It is quite significant the Iraqis are ordering [hostages] to ring up. These floods of telephone calls that have been coming in are quite clearly being made at the request of their captors and they are required to include the invitation that their wives should come for Christmas." The government was clearly very concerned that the spectacle of hundreds of relatives flying out to Baghdad for Christmas and the New Year would give Saddam Hussein a perfect defence against war. They might be being enticed over there only to become a far more numerous human shield.

The phone calls undoubtedly *were* a ploy by Saddam, but there was more to it than that. The hostages and their relatives were very pleased to finally have some contact with each other and it relieved a great deal of anxiety. It had an humanitarian element. The Iraqis simultaneously announced that the men in the installations would be able to send and receive mail from 15th November and several men held in the camps reported noticeable improvements in their food and conditions around this time. By the middle of November the Red Cross finally managed to arrange with the Red Crescent for food parcels and mail to get through to the camps and, by the end of the month, the first food and clothing parcels released by the Iraqi government *did* begin to arrive for British and American hostages. Some were moved to better camps. The Iraqis were responding to international condemnation of the camps and to repeated demands and protests from the hostages themselves about their, at times, appalling conditions.

Every day, Stephen and Josie updated their volunteers on the news and recent developments relatives and the press may be interested in. The one for Friday 9th November shows how events were bursting at breakneck speed around them:

Political

Cardinal Basil Hume says limited military action is morally justified;
Iraq threatens to reduce the Arabian Peninsula to ashes if attacked, but it will spare Muslim holy places;
Tony Benn is to visit Iraq on a personal peace mission;
Iraq will allow Britons to set up 'peace camps' in Kuwait to act as a buffer between Iraq's army and the US-dominated multinational force;
Shevardnadze [Soviet Foreign Minister] says force undesirable - priority must be given to economic sanctions;
Brandt extends his visit to Baghdad; may stay until Saturday;
Unofficial visit by Swiss MPs planned to negotiate the release of Swiss hostages;
Germans held as human shields threaten to sue Chancellor Kohl for inactivity.

Hostages

Nakasone arrives back with 74 Japanese;
8 British construction workers and a nineteen-year-old Scottish student are given permission to leave;
243 Poles freed on Thurday - 150 others refused exit visas.

Military

Saddam Hussein sacks his Army Chief of Staff - replaced with Lieutenant-General Hussein Rashid;
US told NATO allies to send 100,000 more troops to the Gulf, but sanctions should be given time to work.

The work load and pressure continued to mount. The organisers of the Gulf Support Group sent yet more letters and faxes to the Iraqi ambassador, to Margaret Thatcher and to other politicians and Church leaders, trying to keep the hostage issue foremost in their minds. Both London and Coventry had headed notepaper by now, for both their own circulars or letters and for formal items from the group as a whole. In fact, the London helpline had invested in T-shirts, badges and support group logos.

The second support group newsletter appeared early in November. It dramatically showed the changes in needs and issues facing the relatives. It mentioned the key points arising from the London meeting with government officials, without going into the bitterness and anger which dominated it. Whilst trying to persuade relatives not to return to Iraq, the support group did all it could to help those who wanted to go. The newsletter gave them details of visas and how to get them. "If you still wish to go, we will help in any way we can... We are receiving letters from people advising us that, in the main, the men [in the installations] do not wish families who have returned to the safety of the UK to be put back into a dangerous situation."

It also reiterated details of the Gulf Link service, giving a phone number to contact it. With Christmas approaching, Gulf Link was considering putting on special arrangements, including a pre-recorded, non-denominational service for Christmas Day, with one message from each hostage's family to go out over Christmas week.

Financial considerations were clearly still paramount. The newsletter mentioned that the FCO was collating a list of people who wanted to register claims against the Iraqi government, as called for under UN Resolution 674, and asked people to send for a claim form to the Nationality, Treaty and Claims Department of the Foreign Office. Many relatives had phoned the support group complaining of the claim form's inadequacy, but it was still an important initial step in registering a claim. Discussions were going on with the US support group and with lawyers about establishing an action group to pursue the claims privately.

Another significant financial point was that the Bank of England had finally unfrozen bank accounts and assets of former residents of Kuwait now living outside the emirate - it had taken the bank three months to realise the hardship its freeze had been inflicting on those people. However, they still had to write a letter to the bank informing it that they had no intention of returning to Iraq or Kuwait until the crisis was over! Doubtless, some petty bureaucrat's idea of a joke.

There was also a concerned item about those British pensioners, former KOC and BP employees, who had been living in Kuwait. What was happening to their pensions? Were they still being sent to Kuwaiti bank accounts, or being held in Britain for them? Were their pensions still being paid at all?

The beginning of November marked a further decisive escalation of the conflict:

> "Amid heightened martial war rhetoric from the American administration, James Baker is to visit Saudi Arabia next week... Colin Powell, the Chairman of the Joint Chiefs of Staff, called for reinforcements of up to 100,000 troops so that the US and its allies should be able to retake Kuwait. It coincides with tough speeches from Richard Cheney, the Defence Secretary, and William Webster, Central Intelligence Agency Director... the Saudis were encouraging the US into war, rather than *vice versa...*"
> *The Times, 27th October*

Britain was supporting the Americans all the way. On 1st November, the British press reported that nearly all 8,000 members of the British 7th Armoured Brigade were now in Saudi Arabia. In response, facing them and the rest of the alliance, Iraq had ten divisions in Kuwait: 400,000 men,

4,000 tanks and 2,000 pieces of heavy artillery, in a twenty-mile deep defensive line of minefields, trenches, berms, ditches filled with oil, and dug-in positions.

In response to that response, which was in response to a previous response, President Bush decisively changed his response. His speeches were now full of belligerent rhetoric:

> President Bush did his best to quash growing talk of a compromise solution in the Gulf yesterday, accusing President Saddam Hussein of "crimes against humanity"...
> Using uncharacteristically forceful language, Mr Bush spoke of the "rape and dismantling" of Kuwait... He continued: "Good God, this is 1990... these are crimes against humanity. There can never be compromise with this kind of aggression."
> He recalled how "Hitler rolled his tanks into Poland..."
> *The Times, 24th October*

President Bush clearly upped the ante as he prepared the world for war in his most significant and memorable speech of the crisis:

> President Bush said last night he had 'had it' with the brutal treatment of Americans by President Saddam Hussein. He voiced his exasperation as President Mubarak of Egypt gave a warning that the confrontation in the Gulf could explode at any time. The British commander, Douglas Hurd, and a former Saudi minister also indicated that war was increasingly likely. Iraq said that it was prepared for a 'major confrontation' and that 'war may break out at any moment'."
> *The Times, 1st November*

Bush's whole demeanour, his firm hand movements, his fists, his angry expression, his hard words and impatience, all sent signals that war was now firmly on the agenda. And he had an election to win. The mid-term Senate elections were coming round and he wanted to appear as firm and decisive a leader as possible. Domestic bluster was papering over a severe economic mess in the United States. He was playing his trump card to its full effect.

The Human Shield

"This, I thought, I could survive."

KURDS PINPOINT HOSTAGE SITES

The wall of secrecy surrounding Western hostages in Iraq cracked yesterday when Kurdish rebels said four groups, mainly British and Americans, were held at three dams, an air base and an oil field in northern Iraq (Reuter reports).

The first report pinpointing the location of hostages at possible war targets said hostages, including women and children, had been moved on 24th August to the Eski Mosul, Dukan and Darbandikhan dams and to a military air base at Kirkuk...

The hostage groups were moved to these locations: the Eski Mosul Dam on the Tigris; the Dukan Dam on the Lesser Zab River; the Darbandikhan Dam, also on the Lesser Zab, which, like the Durkan, supplies Baghdad and Kirkuk with power; Kirkuk, where they are located at an air base and an oil installation...

The Dukan and Darbandikhan Dams were frequently attacked by Iranian planes during the 1980-88 Gulf War.

The Times, 1st September

After being captured by the Iraqis on the first day of the invasion and witnessing their advance into Kuwait from behind their lines, Stewart Griffiths was taken off to an army camp, where he joined several other prisoners.

The next day, an Iraqi officer interrogated them about basic concerns such as who they were, where they were from and how much money they had. Afterwards, they were given a meal in the canteen. As they walked back across the compound to their box rooms, they passed a number of stolen Kuwaiti vehicles. There was a Kuwaiti police wagon, a Kuwait Airlines bus, a *haji* truck used by small shopkeepers and craftsmen in Kuwait to sell their wares and a number of Kuwaiti cars. "They were full of food from Kuwait. All these Iraqi soldiers were drinking cans of condensed milk as though it was pop. They were unloading plastic bin bags of radios, cassette players, tapes, telephones and car radios which they had stripped out of vehicles. The bags were so heavy they were splitting and spewing their contents over the ground."

One Kuwaiti vehicle was a covered wagon, a metal truck with bars over its tiny windows. There were screams coming from it. An Arab voice was crying out for water, pleading to be let out. Stewart approached it, wondering who could be trapped inside, but an Iraqi stopped him and told him not to go any closer. Stewart had to turn his back on the tortured pleas and sobs and return to the little hut he shared with two other men.

Stewart was eventually driven up to Baghdad and dumped in the Melia al-Mansour Hotel, where he was held for two weeks. At the hotel were a number of British and other Western nationals taken from Kuwait. The embassy officials came round to see how they were. Stewart met them and they arranged to get some clothes for him and the other British captives. They also took a message for Stewart's wife Barbara, which did get through to her and informed him that the British community in Baghdad had held a collection for them to buy such basic necessities as clothes, shoes, razors, books and toothbrushes.

Harold Walker recalled his first attempt to see the men in the Melia al-Mansour Hotel. "The first I remember of hostages, properly so called, was a convoy of mixed men and women and they were diverted to the famous hotel, the Melia al-Mansour. Then we found out that the men were not being allowed to leave and you had the extraordinary sight of the French, American, German, Japanese and British heads of mission arguing on the pavement outside the hotel, not being allowed in to see their own subjects, demonstrating and making a scene on the pavement, trying to get into the hotel. We were arguing with the security man on the gate but, in the last resort, we were facing people with Kalashnikovs who said we were not allowed into the hotel. We couldn't win; we couldn't force our way in. All the diplomats had to go to the Foreign Ministry and start making regular diplomatic representations."

Even from those early days of August, captive Westerners were being taken off to installations. They included the men taken in the first few days, such as the thirty-five members of the British Liaison Team, and those subsequently caught and despatched to Baghdad. The Iraqis were preparing their human shield tactic even in the first week, whilst denying it to the rest of the world.

Stewart was amongst a group of six men left at the hotel after virtually all the other captives had been escorted to installations. For days, he had watched short-term acquaintances being taken off and was waiting for the dreaded knock on the door telling him it was his turn. It came. An Iraqi walked upstairs to his floor and pointed to six men. "You, you, you, you, you and you. Pack your bags. Be ready in the hotel lobby in twenty minutes."

They packed, went downstairs and were ordered into two army

vehicles with armed guards in each. The guards wouldn't tell them where they were going until they were virtually there. They headed north through Mosul, the third largest city in Iraq, to a site thirty-five kilometres north-east of it. It was a large hydro-electric complex called, not surprisingly, Saddam Dam. It was newly constructed and they were ordered out by some German contract workers' huts which overlooked it. They had been unused for two years.

Stewart had heard rumours about some sort of human shield, but not realised what it was all about. It didn't seem to be anything particularly threatening. The accommodation was fairly decent, although they were guarded by soldiers with AK47s and surrounded by a barbed wire fence and enormous arc lights which shone down onto the compound all night. Things weren't bad. The food was basic, but adequate and not unhygienic.

The dam was heavily guarded. They could see its wall and lake clearly from where they were, as well as the surrounding hills. Those heights were covered with anti-aircraft batteries, ground-to-air missile sites, machine-gun nests and observation posts. They were on the Tigris, in the middle of Kurdistan, and could see Duhok and the mountains bordering Turkey and northern Syria in the distance.

At first, there were just six of them but the next day some Japanese were brought in. At the beginning of September two Americans rolled up. They had good news for Stewart. They had seen his wife Barbara in Baghdad and told him she had left on the flight with Jesse Jackson. It was the first news he'd had of her for a month and proved a considerable relief. Maybe two weeks later some Germans came, then another group of Americans. It peaked at twenty-six.

Conditions were still not that bad. There were between two and five men per hut. They had a canteen where a Kurd cooked their food. The meals were reasonable. They were mainly rice, with okhra, aubergines and cucumbers. The food did become very repetitive, the same thing every day and Stewart and the others did become sick of the sight of it, but Stewart was relatively satisfied with their treatment: "This, I thought, I could survive."

However, after three weeks, he began to suffer bouts of severe migraine. The pain was terrible. The arc lights must have been one reason for the attacks, as well as the change of diet. Also, they couldn't get much exercise. The compound was off limits, except for the walk across to the canteen for meals. He saw an Iraqi doctor, but all he gave him was valium and some injections to help him sleep. They didn't do much good.

Stewart shared his hut with two other men, George Chinchala and Dick Hearns. They were very comforting to Stewart and helped him settle into the camp. They were deeply religious people and drew strength from their faith. They developed a warmth of trust and friendship over the months they were together. Stewart spent much of the time thinking about his situation and the future and worrying about his wife Barbara. He couldn't believe what had happened to him or to Kuwait. In his state of prolonged shock he couldn't understand how the Americans and British, seeing the huge build-up of Iraqi troops on the border, had let the invasion happen. He was certain they could have sent troops there before the invasion and prevented it. He felt they must have known for days what was going to occur.

Stewart's migraines grew steadily worse, until they became unbearable for him. "They knocked me sick. I couldn't stand it and was screaming with every attack." He had been ill with gout about a month before the invasion, so was run-down anyway. He'd been on crutches for two weeks, with pain killers and injections.

The Iraqis took him to a clinic built by the Germans, but the doctor there simply injected him with valium and stocked him up with pills. Stewart tried this 'treatment' for a few days, then demanded to see a neurologist. He was taken to one in Mosul, who recommended he wore glasses. They procured him two pairs, but they were useless.

At the end of August, to balance the 'humanitarian' gesture of releasing the women and children, and to prove to themselves they still had power over the remaining hostages, the Iraqis moved the men at the strategic sites inside the installations. In many cases, the hostages had been held in decent accommodation some distance from the sites, but now nearly all of them were moved closer, usually right inside or adjacent to the key area of the installation, whether it was a liquid petroleum tank, a chemical laboratory, an army barracks or a plastic explosives store.

Those held at Saddam Dam were ignominiously shunted out of their workers' compound down the hill into the second floor of an administration block beside the dam wall. It was immediately next to the generating plant. They were packed in six or seven men per room, all on camp beds, with only one toilet and shower between twenty-six of them. They couldn't go out. They were locked into their floor day and night.

Curiously, the guards were still civil. They certainly never hit or interrogated the men. They even told their 'guests' that they were there merely to protect them from the civilian population, who were angry at British and American aggression. Their guns, they said, were to shoot any snakes, lizards and wild dogs which came into the area. Meanwhile, the 'guests' could hear military exercises and shooting practices in the hills around them as the Iraqis prepared for war.

The situation rapidly became more stressful for all the men. Now, the food had to be brought to the block from the compound five kilometres down the road, it immediately deteriorated. "It was totally disgusting. It was cold and had been sloshed around on the way. The plates and cooking utensils were filthy."

The Iraqis brought them a television to break the boredom but it was useless, with bad reception and programmes they couldn't understand and didn't want to watch. There was no intelligent news on it. Apart from one pack of cards, they had absolutely nothing to do.

The Iraqis were full of Saddam Hussein and most of them deeply admired him. They adulated him and were convinced their glorious leader would lead them to victory in any war. They had brought the men the TV so they could sit around and watch the fifteen minutes a day of English-speaking news. It was constant propaganda: "Down with Bush and Thatcher!", with crowds denouncing the USA and Britain for imposing sanctions and demonstrators chanting, "Down, down, Bush!". There were scenes of babies screaming for food, of starving mothers and hospitals without supplies, and then Big Brother Saddam, comforting, offering words of solace and denouncing the heartless, murderous aggressors in words of fire. A constant psychological battle went on at the camp, more so than at other installations. There was no love lost between the hostages and their captors. Stewart never felt any sympathy for the Iraqis at all, merely contempt.

The strain began to tell. Men, angry and frustrated at the Iraqis, had no one to take it out on but each other. Tempers became short, arguments flared, some became withdrawn and depressed. It became unbearably claustrophobic. They needed fresh air and exercise. Eventually, it grew so bad, they snapped and made a commotion about their conditions. They told the Iraqis plainly that, if they didn't want more trouble than they could handle, they better let them spend some time outside. Faced with a revolt, the Iraqis allowed them one hour a day for exercising - that was all.

At the beginning of November they were moved again. It was in response to President Bush's clear change from the defensive posture of Desert Shield to the more aggressive stance of Desert Storm, with his belligerent, election speechifying and America's huge military build-up.

The men had thought the office block bad enough, but were completely unprepared for what was about to happen. They were moved into steel ship containers dumped right on top of the sluice gates of the dam. If the dam was bombed, they would be bang in the centre of the target. There were three men to a container, with no windows, just the large metal swing doors at the back end. Each was eighteen feet long by seven feet high. Stewart's had three beds around the sides, a fridge and four plastic chairs. They had managed to salvage an old cupboard for their meagre clothes. The bedding was old, tatty and smelly, the sheets had all been used many times before, the chairs were old and the floor was covered in dust and cockroaches.

The Iraqis occasionally took their bed linen away to be laundered, but it always came back as filthy as it went, covered in stains and dirt. So the men began to wash the sheets themselves in buckets and rigged up a washing line. The lone Japanese asked to do some fishing over the side of the dam, to supplement their diet. He was not very successful, but it kept him sane. The Iraqis also tried to construct a recreation room for them by joining two containers together, but it was leaky in the rain.

One of the men had a small short-wave radio which could intermittently pick up the BBC World Service, though the reception was bad. He had to be very careful with the batteries as well, so as not to use them up.

Stewart and the other British men had been receiving messages over Gulf Link from Barbara and other wives and families since October. It was a tremendous morale boost for them. Stewart described the broadcasts as "magic".

There were six containers perched on the wall of the dam, the lake to one side, an enormous drop to the other. The toilet was another container fitted with a makeshift shower and a toilet straight over the side of the dam. The containers were like ovens during the day. They were burning to the touch and it would have been death to remain inside them. The soldiers rigged up a portable air-conditioner in one of the containers, but it was useless. Outside, they were confined to a small work area, surrounded by guards and a wire fence. In practice, it was a prison camp, a stalag.

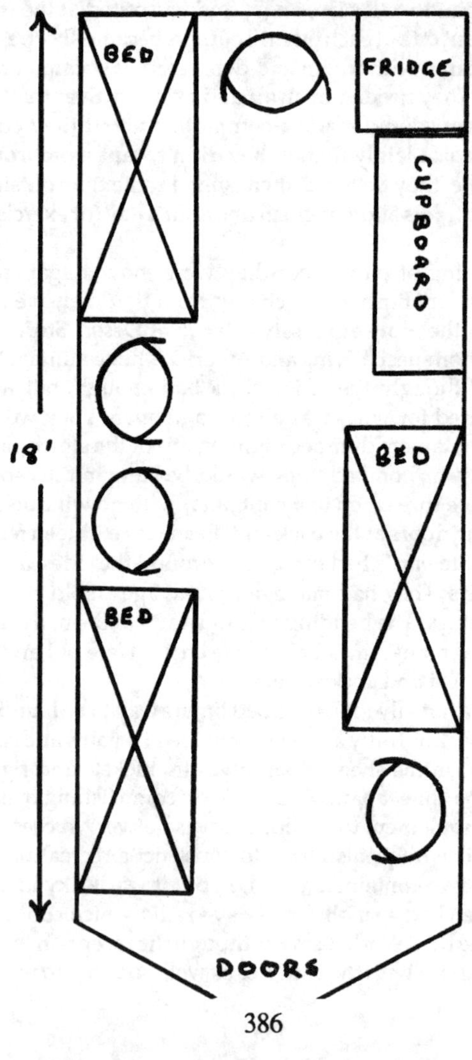

Another container was used for a canteen. Once, it had been occupied by Egyptian labourers working on the dam. It was heaving with cockroaches, flies, beetles, weevils and maggots. It was unfit for dogs. The food had to come yet further and deteriorated even more. They were being made to pay for the imposition of sanctions, for more intense UN resolutions and for the refusal of the Western nations to join discussions. All the way through, the only way the Iraqi authorities had of getting back at the allies was through the hostages. They couldn't punish America or Britain directly, so they punished the men and rare woman they held captive. It was simply a way of getting back at the alliance, in frustration at their general impotence and fear of what was being lined up for them in Saudi Arabia.

In Stewart's case, this tit-for-tat became petty and barbaric. The attitude of their captors changed noticeably over the weeks. At first, the hostages had been treated with respect and even sympathy, but then contempt crept in, with deliberate mental and physical cruelty. Stewart used the word 'cruelty' himself, as he sat in his armchair in his house in Cheshire, still shaking with the trauma of those days, nearly a year after they had happened. His eyes were still scared, his movement nervous and jerky. Those days will never leave him.

During this time, he only had one set of clothes, those he had been captured in. A shirt, a pair of trousers and a pair of boots. He and all the others realised that if there was war, the dam would be a key target and they would be killed. Stewart felt sure it would come by February. He made a calendar from the second of August to the end of January. He called it his count-down calendar, crossing off what he felt may be the last days of his life, waiting for the bombers to strike.

The men spent a lot of time chatting. They discussed plans of all sorts, including several escape plans in the eventuality of war, which seemed imminent the whole time they were at the camp. Several of the men made contingency plans, though Stewart felt escape would be impossible. They were surrounded by barren hills, each with hundreds of Iraqi soldiers hiding in a maze of trenches, dug-outs and emplacements. They would have to make their way through kilometres of defences, then over the high, snow-capped mountains if they were to get to Turkey. It would be suicidal. There were packs of wild dogs which roamed the desert and came up to the fences of the camp every night. These dogs were a serious hazard. They were big, ferocious and hunted in packs. They were extremely dangerous and would have torn a person caught in the desert to pieces. But even if they managed to avoid them, the mountains were inhabited by wolves.

Frank Kerfoot was also taken prisoner on the second of August. He was mistaken for a Kuwaiti soldier and spent two hours in a military barracks in Basra, in cells with a group of captured soldiers. It was only after explaining at length during questioning that he was a British citizen that he was escorted, firstly to the Basra Sheraton for a night, then up to the

Melia al-Mansour Hotel. He was there twelve days, along with Stewart Griffiths, during which time he began to suffer, like everyone else, from diarrhoea. As he waited patiently in the hotel, he watched the television news of Margaret Thatcher's speeches and listened to them on the World Service. Every time she opened her mouth, the Iraqis responded with rhetoric of their own and by increasing the hardship he and the other hostages were suffering. He noticed a direct correlation between her attacks on Saddam Hussein and a worsening of their treatment. It culminated in them all being taken off to installations. On the fourteenth he, nine other British, a German and an American were told to pack their meagre possessions and were driven two hundred and twenty kilometres north to a 'fertiliser plant' at Baiji. In fact, the 'fertiliser plant' was manufacturing chemical weapons.

Their treatment at the plant was reasonable. In fact, the food, mainly rice and chicken was, Frank felt, better than in Baghdad. But they were only there two weeks. About the time the women and children left, three of them were moved into Baiji power station, resting on a bank of the Tigris River approximately halfway from Baghdad to Mosul. Just as with Stewart Griffiths about this time, the Iraqis imposed worse conditions on the hostages whilst they were portraying themselves as 'humanitarian' to the rest of the world. As many of the women had feared, once the men were on their own their situation deteriorated. The Iraqis felt more justified in putting men within the installations rather than women and children, so moved many into the heart of the plants.

Baiji power station was rough. The hostages were forced to live in one long, run-down, decayed, prefabricated hut separated into a number of rooms. The whole building was on the point of collapse. Their beds were thin mattresses and all the furniture they had was a table and few chairs. The two showers barely worked and were inadequate for a proper wash. The toilets were disgusting. The food was passable. It was brought in from a local café and shared by their guards. However, hygiene was non-existent and they had to boil all their water. Despite taking every precaution he could, and not eating a lot of the revolting scraps he was served with, Frank became seriously ill. He thought he had caught hepatitis or dysentery. He was so badly dehydrated the Iraqis had to rush him to a local clinic for treatment, where he was put onto a plasma and glucose drip for an hour.

The clinic was in Salalsikat Hospital. When he had recovered sufficiently to walk around, he was horrified by the general state of the place. Local Iraqis had to put up with dirty walls, dusty surfaces and filthy floors. There was virtually no hygiene. The corridors were crowded with people on stretchers or sitting aimlessly on the floor. Reception was teaming with people. He walked past an open door to an operating theatre as an operation was going on, with hundreds of flies able to come and go. He was appalled by what those people were having to suffer.

Frank returned to the same festering conditions he had left. There were still flies over everything, including his food, and it was still rice and chicken with monotonous regularity. For a while, they were given a luxury - eggs. On rare occasions they had a really special treat - meat, on the bone, no less. In fact, *all* bone. But they did get some fresh fruit, some cheese and some bread. Frank believed that the central Iraqi authorities probably wanted and expected them to be treated better than they were, but not much.

The power station was situated beside the main railway line from Mosul to Baghdad. Every day, staring through the wire fence, Frank witnessed train loads of tanks going south. In effect, it was a prison camp. It was surrounded by wire fences and razor wire. There were armed guards and searchlights around the perimeter and they weren't allowed out at all. Their conditions grew so bad that the men couldn't take it any longer. They began to protest strongly against their treatment. Above all, they wanted somewhere to wash and get exercise. They knew there was a swimming pool locally and demanded to be allowed to use it. The Iraqis refused, but the men kicked up such a fuss they had to give in.

Frank spent much of his time planning how to escape in the event of war. The railway line and power station would be prime targets for American bombers so he knew he would have to make a run for it as soon as war was declared. They were given a radio by the Iraqis, which was a blessing, but it only worked intermittently. However, it did allow Frank to monitor the crisis as it grew and the UN resolutions as they were passed. He could sense the build-up of tension as the weeks went by.

His plans were brought to an abrupt end when, on about the twenty-third of September, he and two other British hostages were suddenly ordered to gather their skimpy possessions and board an army vehicle. They were driven south to another power station on the Tigris at Daura, a suburb of Baghdad, and housed in a two-storey office block rebuilt after the Iranians had hit it during their war with Iraq. Their accommodation was very makeshift, being just a few beds scattered around a room.

There wasn't a fence surrounding the block, so they were allowed to exercise in the compound around the power station. However, there was a formidable barrier protecting the plant. There was a line of barbed wire, then a six foot wire-mesh fence, then a passageway for patrols, then another six foot wire fence and finally another line of barbed wire. The wire-mesh fences were probably electrified.

Frank spent a lot of time staring through the fences towards Iran. It was a hundred and thirty kilometres away, but still the closest frontier. Once more, he passed his days planning how to escape if war occurred, but rapidly realised it was a sick joke. Although he had received army training and knew how to survive off the countryside and how to avoid detection, he probably wouldn't get beyond the first perimeter fence, let alone across Iraq. But such daydreams kept him sane.

He also thought a lot about his wife Lesley, at home in Lancashire, wondering how she was coping. He knew she would be doing what she could to get him out. But what was the British government doing? It seemed to be doing nothing. All the men with Frank felt the same. They felt abandoned, neglected, totally forgotten, the footnote to what promised to be the greatest holocaust since the Second World War. He and all the others in the camp wanted the American and British troops in as soon as possible. They loathed what the Iraqis had done and felt they should be made to pay for it. Despite being a target, they felt their best chance of getting out of the camp was for the allies to invade. They could see what a shambles the Iraqi army was and knew it would be over rapidly. Every day, Frank prayed for them to come in.

Apart from the luxury of those few thoughts, he tried to shut everything else away, not to dwell on things, but to think positively and hopefully. He felt he coped well with his internment, far better than some. It became too much for one or two and they cracked under the strain.

The food at Daura was far worse than at Baiji. It was disgusting. "We felt a lot of our supplies were being syphoned off by this manager, who was a strong Ba'ath Party member. He *detested* us." The Iraqis reluctantly provided them with a cook, but he was just a worker off the power station's shop floor. He was hopeless. He had no idea about hygiene, either personal or for the food. Flies were everywhere in the kitchen. The meat was fetid or gristle. Frank thought it was probably camel and had to leave a lot of it. There were no potatoes, and it was always rice, rice, rice - and camel.

This Ba'athist member took it into his head to take Frank and several other hostages into the desert one night. They weren't told their destination, just ordered into a truck and driven out into the wilderness. They stopped near an excavator which was digging out a trench. Suddenly, the men realised what was going to happen. They were pushed out of the truck and told to line up alongside the trench. They all started to pray. Some Iraqi soldiers lined up in front of them, their rifles at the ready. It was the end. Of that they were certain. They bagan to whisper goodbye to each other and take their last glimpses of the world, when suddenly a car sped up and a more senior officer climbed out. He was furious with the camp commander and ordered the hostages back into the truck. If he had been a minute later, they would all have been shot. The camp commander was *not* playing a game.

In early November, Frank was allowed to make some phone calls to Lesley, so long as he asked her to visit him for Christmas. It was the first time they had been in direct contact since 2nd August, and the first time Frank had heard anything from his wife, because none of her letters had got through. He said the words to her, but made it plain he didn't want her anywhere near Iraq. It was a tremendous relief for both of them to here each other's voice. Towards the end of November they finally began to receive British Council parcels containing food, winter clothing and other supplies. They were very welcome, but arrived too late to be of much use. It was only two or three weeks before their final release. The

Iraqis were already relaxing their position towards the hostages. Frank was at Daura until the beginning of December, when he and the others were finally allowed home.

Someone else at Daura for part of his holiday trip to Iraq was David Shattock, from BA Flight 149. He had travelled up to the Melia al-Mansour at the end of August with his wife and two children. They had caught a flight out in the first two days of September. From then on, the men were kept to the top floors, under armed guard, and only allowed downstairs for meals. They constantly challenged this restriction, until they were permitted slightly more freedom to wander the hotel and visit the bar, so long as they remained within the hotel. They were allowed to drink alcohol in their rooms as well and there was nearly always some gathering in honour of the beer god.

On the third, David, two Americans, two Germans and three other British men were driven up to Daura, but not to the power station. They were billeted in the oil refinery there. David was given ten minutes to pack his meagre possessions and be escorted to the foyer. "We left the hotel after eleven at night, in the dark, and were taken on a deliberately round-about route, crossing the Tigris at least three times, in the hope that we wouldn't know where we were. In actual fact, we ended up not very far from where we had started.

"Given the circumstances, the camp was quite pleasant. The refinery had probably been built by a Western oil company in the Fifties. There was a residential compound of five parallel roads, each with little bungalows and even gardens. There were eucalyptus trees around and it was not an unpleasant little environment. The eight of us were put in two bungalows about a hundred yards apart. We had a large lounge-dining room, a kitchen, three bedrooms and a shower-room. The toilets were flushable, we had fresh running water and rudimentary air-conditioning. There was a flat roof we could get onto if we felt like sunbathing, but it was extremely hot, so we didn't do a great deal out of doors.

"Within the compound we were free to do as we wanted and I used to walk around the roads every day. The two guards lived in a portacabin at the end of our road. They didn't bother us very much. They'd drop in once or twice a day and we used to take letters down to them. That was all we ever saw of them."

Some of those letters did get to Claire and the kids back in England. Nothing ever arrived from them at any stage in his detention, despite the many that were written.

The hostages were given a television and video recorder and were provided with a couple of films a week. Every other day each house received a case of beer and they had a fridge to keep them in. The chief engineer of the refinery, who had been trained in the UK, gave them a supply of books to read. They had a short-wave radio to listen to the World Service and Gulf Link. The guards were *Mukhabarat* but in plain clothes and were pleasant enough, in so far as they saw each other. They had side arms hidden discretely. They spoke some basic English but, being state police, they didn't fraternise much and didn't sympathise with the hostages at all.

The men had the choice of having prepared meals from the refinery canteen, or of cooking their own. As they had a couple of guys who enjoyed cooking, they went for that option. "The food was quite reasonable. Beautiful unleavened bread, hot out of the ovens. We had fresh vegetables and fruit, as well as milk and cheese. We had potatoes, melons and fresh dates. We got on very well as a group. True, we were a bit pissed off, but that was because our families weren't there. That was a pain. There were a lot of things I wanted to do but couldn't."

David did *not* want the allies to attack Iraq as soon as possible. "I thought the waiting game was probably best for us. Some of the others thought the best thing to do was 'come in and slam'em'. There were various theories about what would happen if things did turn nasty. The guards assured us - both here and at our next installation - that they had strict orders to push Iraqis aside in order to get us into the shelters, which surprised me. The other theories were that they'd shoot us, or that they'd just run. That seemed quite feasible." They made some contingency plans for escape, but nothing definite. It was a long way to the border, there was little cover and they would clearly stand out as Westerners.

On 24th September, all eight of them were taken up to Kirkuk, two hundred and twenty kilometres north of Baghdad, leaving at nine in the morning. It was unusual as it was a daylight journey and they were allowed to look at whatever they wanted. Once at Kirkuk, their guards had no idea where to go and had to ask at a police station in the city centre. From there they were driven to a gas refinery south-east of the city, only to be told by the guards at the gate there was no room for them. "We ended up being driven to a compound near a canal which had no strategic site beside it. It was several kilometres from the refinery. There was another group of hostages in the process of leaving. They were part British Liaison Team and part Air France, with various others. They were getting into buses and waiting for us to arrive. As far as we could gather, they were taken down to Daura to replace us." They had only fifteen minutes to chat before the two groups were separated again.

Once more, the accommodation was good. The prefabricated huts were air-conditioned, each with two bedrooms, a shower and toilet, a kitchen and a lounge. They were put two to a hut. One hut had been turned into a common room and another into a dining room. They had been used previously by Eastern European construction workers on some local building site. "It was fairly primitive in terms of dirt roads around, but the little huts were quite well made." They felt good about the place. There was no installation nearby, and they felt relatively safe. They began to draw a map from an atlas left behind by the previous hostages, in case they needed it. But they were only there two days.

"We'd been for a walk in mid-morning and came back around the corner of our prefabs to find they were moving our bookcase and television and so on out into a lorry. We asked them, 'What the hell are you taking that away for? That's ours. Leave it.' 'Oh no, you move.' That was how we discovered we were moving again."

Once more, they were moved in daylight. They were taken back to the gas refinery from where they had been turned away. They were ordered into the canteen, where they were kept hanging around for some Iraqi photographer, who never arrived. "At about one, they gave us lunch. At two-thirty they took us over to our accommodation, a bungalow which used to be the transport office for the refinery. There, we had three bedrooms, a lounge and a bathroom with only a hole in the ground for a toilet. Later, they put in a flushing loo and gave us a washing machine. We had a tiny kitchen and they put some portacabins alongside for the guards." That evening two more Germans joined them, bringing their number up to ten.

The bungalow was not actually in the refinery compound but within a large perimeter fence surrounding the refinery and adjacent land. The refinery itself was fenced off, but it gates were always open and it wasn't guarded at all. However, the outside perimeter fence was heavily guarded. "It comprised several lines of barbed-wire fencing and there was a little control tower every couple of hundred metres. It was floodlit at night and every control tower was occupied."

The perimeter contained extensive areas of bamboo groves, a frog pool, scrubland and large dumps of old chemicals, sulphur and industrial refuse. There was an old contractors' camp nearby which had been totally destroyed. It was a very mucky place.

The hostages were relatively free to wander about within the perimeter, but it was too hot to do much. They would wander off a few times a day. "We were playing at *Last of The Summer Wine*. We all acquired a piece of bamboo and wandered around poking at this, prodding at that, telling jokes, nattering away, generally enjoying life as best we could. We gradually became more and more adventurous until we were wandering over much of the guarded area." This exploration and camaraderie helped them retain a positive mental attitude, especially as most of them felt their lives were on hold for the duration of their time as hostages. "There was no point sitting moping about it. No, better to enjoy it as best you could."

There was no serious illness at the camp. Whilst David lost some weight, he felt it was to his advantage, and he certainly wasn't over-thin by the end of his incarceration. However, one man who had suffered a serious abdominal injury some years previously, did find it become serious again. One night, he started vomiting up blood at three o'clock in the morning one night. The Iraqis initially refused to summon a doctor. One only arrived seven hours later. By then, he needed hospital and an emergency operation.

The food, in the circumstances, was quite good. The meat was awful - "a third fat, a third bone and a third gristle" - and the bread was not as good as before. "There was a time when the bread became so bad that I took the bread container and tipped it over the floor on the far side of the canteen and told the Iraqis it was only fit for nailing onto shoes." The guards sent away for some more, and it was better, but not a lot. Although the cooking was done mainly by an Iraqi, they were able to cook some meals themselves, to provide variety. Breakfast was basic. Lunch and supper were mainly salads consisting of chopped tomatoes, peppers, cucumbers, onions and chillies in great big bowlfuls, alongside rice, cracked wheat or pasta. They were never short of food and always had more than enough. They had more fruit than they needed, and would take some back to their rooms with them. "It was seasonal. We had melons in the early stages. Watermelons sometimes, cantaloupes sometimes. As time went on, we were having pomegranates, grapes, dates, apples and oranges, both for lunch and for supper. Our only complaint was we didn't get as much beer as in other places. We only had two or three cases the whole time we were in Kirkuk."

Other passengers from BA Flight 149 were taken to Shu'aiba air base at Basra. Amongst them were Eric Watson and Don Majors. Both had lost weight and Don especially looked paler and older. The two men went jogging every morning to keep themselves fit. The food and accommodation at the site were basic but adequate. They were not as rough as some hostages endured. Being a musical director, Eric, half jokingly, asked his Iraqi minders for a piano. Amazingly, they brought him one, but the next day he knew why. An Iraqi television camera crew arrived to film him playing for propaganda purposes. He refused. I wonder what tune he would have played if they *had* televised him?

The cameras came again sometime later and this time Eric *was* filmed. He appeared on British television a few nights later, indulging in his other *forte*, cooking. The cameras went into the kitchen, where Eric was standing stirring the daily pot of rice. He had grown a beard, which he was stroking, as if to say, 'Don't take any notice of this film, it's all garbage'.

The worst aspect of the installation was the total isolation. In this sense, it was *worse* than being a prisoner of war. They received no mail, no phone calls, no relief parcels, no news of their families. All they had was the World Service and Gulf Link programmes. Eric and Don listened to them intently for any messages. Eric was missing his son Tim and wife Wen Li badly and was delighted when he had several messages from the Coventry helpline. He heard over it that his son Tim had arrived safely in England and that Wen Li was there as well, waiting for his return.

Hamish Ross was one of the most unfortunate people to end up on an installation. He worked on a ship which had called into Kuwait for a few days. On the day the Iraqis invaded he was staying at the Continental Hotel. His wife had phoned him the night before to warn him that the Iraqis were massing on the border and to get out quickly, but he thought she was panicking.

The hotel was by the al-Khalji roundabout in central Kuwait, where there was a great deal of shooting that first morning. He woke at seven to hear gunfire nearby. Outside a lorry was going around firing into the air, but he was unsure whether it was the Iraqis or Kuwaitis. Later, there was heavier firing as tanks moved up to shell the Emir's palace at Dasman and a ministry building close to the three Kuwaiti towers. At about ten in the morning, twenty to thirty helicopters went over and landed men by the palace. Simultaneously, artillery was brought up to blast away at the palace and ministry. The ministry building had its roof spectacularly blown off by a rocket.

Hamish stayed at the Continental for a few days. On the first day, he phoned the embassy. Its line was on answer phone, but it gave another number for emergencies. He phoned it, but the voice at the other end told him the staff were busy. Hamish insisted on speaking to someone and was only reluctantly put through to an embassy official. He was anxious for them to get his details because he wasn't registered with the embassy. Being on his own, he was thinking of leaving Kuwait, so asked the embassy whether he should go, but they told him to stay put and not risk the border.

The fighting went on south of Kuwait city centre and down the coast that day and night, and into the next day. Hamish was able to go out in those first days and went as far south as Fahaheel without trouble. When some friends of his moved into the International, he joined them. All the Iraqi government officials were there, so the hotel was doubly guarded. In the first two weeks, they had relative freedom to move about. A warden visited them every two days and Donald Macaulay came in several times to keep an eye on the BLT families who were staying there. However, he only spoke with them and not with the rest of the British. Frustratingly, the embassy man said he knew nothing about Hamish, so his first day message hadn't been processed. Hamish can't remember him ever passing on any information to them, whilst other embassies, notably the Indian embassy, kept them much more informed. He had no time for the Kuwait embassy at all.

The British in the International ignored the call to assemble at the Regency Palace Hotel on the sixteenth, and only one American couple turned up at their hotel, which was where the Americans were asked to go. On the afternoon of August the twenty-second, the Iraqis suddenly demanded their passports. After they had been taken, an embassy official came, but he was told to leave, which he did. The American embassy man came to protest as well, and he too was told to leave, but he only departed when a gun was produced on him.

Immediately afterwards, a group of twenty-eight, including Hamish, were taken in an old, shot-up bus to a military camp at Jahra, where they were put up in a large room filled with camp beds which served as a dorm. All twenty-three of them were in one room, including four air stewardesses from the BA relief crew and their co-pilot. The toilets were disgusting, a filthy hole in the ground, and the British had to stand guard over the door to keep the Iraqis out when the women were using it.

Later, the Iraqis ordered the women to be separated, to their consternation, as they had no idea what might happen to them. The co-pilot intervened and said there was no way he would let them take them, and the Iraqis backed down. They were there one night before they were split up into three groups. Nine were taken to an electricity sub-station, the four women were taken to another installation, and the other ten, including Hamish, ended up in the military air base north of Jahra. They stayed in the old airfield buildings for one night before they were moved up to an army camp near Abdaly, where they all came together again.

This time, they were put in Nissan huts, four or five to a room. They were there a night before they were moved up to the Melia al-Mansour Hotel, where they stayed a couple of nights until the women and children were moved up from Kuwait to be released. The four stewardesses remained whilst the twenty-four men were driven to Hadithah Dam, two hundred kilometres north-west of Baghdad. They stayed there for a few nights, in an old Yugoslav workers' camp. Although they were warned not to wander too far, they were given relative freedom.

Hamish and the others had obviously been assigned to the Iraqi Water Authority, because, although they were frequently moved around sites, they were always taken to dams. Other hostages were always in power stations, others always at chemical plants, others always at refineries. Whilst not true for all hostages, it seems most were allocated to specific Iraqi ministries, for them to deploy their pawns at will.

From Hadithah, their group was split up and Hamish was moved to Darbandikhan Dam near the Iran border. A few weeks later, he was moved again, this time to Hemrim Dam, a hundred and sixty kilometres north of Baghdad. At Hemrim, they were put in a caravan right on top of the dam. Although they had a fence around them, the Iraqi captain opened it and said they were free to walk around. The Iraqis were very lax about security, as they had faith that the hostages would not risk heading for Iran, with its reputation towards Westerners. The captain would even drink gin with them, especially before telling them they were about to be moved.

Over the next months he was moved backwards and forwards between these locations. At one time, he was with a group actually in the generator room of the dam, sleeping right next to the machinery. Hamish found the average guard to be fine, whereas the secret police were extremely nasty. Their food was reasonable, although there was a shortage of rice, because the guards were creaming a lot off for themselves, but Hamish felt he needed to lose some weight anyway. In all, Hamish was moved fourteen times.

Derek Hill only spent one night at the Melia al-Mansour Hotel in Baghdad. The day after he arrived, he was taken up to the al-Qaim chemical installation near the Jordanian border in north-western Iraq.

Along with a group of others he was kept in a compound just outside the plant. The food was passable, but not good, and had little variety. Early in October, after nearly five weeks as a hostage, he was suddenly ordered to pack his things and told to get on a bus. He was full of high hopes and threw his few possessions together with a smile across his lips. He thought he was being taken to Baghdad and possible freedom. However, the pointless and infuriating journey lasted less than half an hour. They drove around a few desert roads until they saw the plant again, and promptly entered it. This was typical of the psychological games and intimidation the Iraqi authorities perpetrated against members of the human shield. They deliberately sought to disorientate and confuse the hostages by waking them up at night, taking them off in coaches, then bringing them back to another part of the same site, just a few hundred yards away.

Derek spent the rest of his time as a hostage, until December, in a shed inside the chemical complex, surrounded by equipment manufacturing phosphates and extracting low-grade uranium for dubious purposes.

Conditions in the shed were appalling. It was nothing more than a large portacabin and was cramped and spartan. There were about a dozen of them, including four British, some Americans and some French, all forced to share one room. They had no privacy, their beds were similar to camp beds and they only had one toilet and one shower between them. The food was atrocious. It was cold by the time they received it, because everything had to be cooked in the kitchen in the plant. The little bit of nutrition would always be floating about in a lake of grease. The occasional meat they were given was rancid. It was inedible. Derek lost two stones in weight in those weeks - and he was the type of man who would normally eat anything. They received virtually no fresh fruit or vegetables.

As well as Derek, the Britons were Norman Thompson, Steve Jones and David Pike. The four of them developed a friendship during their time together which has continued since they returned to Britain.

There was also a French woman who had decided to stay with her husband and not leave Iraq. Whilst the conditions in the bungalows outside the plant had not been too bad, when she found herself in this place it was too much for her. She also discovered she was pregnant and that proved too strong a reason to leave.

Like many hostages and people in hiding, couples found comfort in having children. It helped them feel they had something positive to look forward to. Children are a reaffirmation of life, especially in a time of darkness and death. Unfortunately, the woman lost the baby on the flight back. She had lost a lot of weight and was run down. The stress of the journey and leaving her husband proved too much for her body to cope with.

When she left, she took with her letters and phone numbers for relatives of all the men in the hut. She contacted them all. When she phoned Derek's wife, Cynthia, she was able to give her the first positive sighting of him for several weeks and to tell her that Derek was still all right. She painted a dire picture of their conditions, but said their spirits were high and Derek was feeling fine.

A few days after the French woman left, the men were ordered onto a bus again, but not told to pack. Instead, the Iraqi guards said it was for them to have their photographs taken. The men were more worried by this development than by any other journey. The reason seemed so spurious. Derek joked about it, but his humour hid worry. Worry that they were simply going to be taken into the desert and shot.

As it turned out, the Iraqis did take their photographs, for whatever reason, and promptly returned them to the chemical plant. Were they paranoid to imagine they would be killed? It's easy to think that now, or for the Iraqis to say they fully intended to treat their 'guests' well, but the fact was that these men had no idea when they would be released, if ever. They didn't know if they would be caught in the middle of a war with American cruise missiles targeted on the plant. They didn't know how intent Saddam was on using them. They were never told where they were going. They weren't allowed any contact with the outside world. At the time, being taken into the desert and left in a shallow grave seemed a strong possibility. Who would know any different?

Within a week, they were moved again. It was shortly after Mr Heath's visit. Derek ended up in Baiji, on the River Tigris. The hostages who had been held there were moved to al-Qaim to replace them. This installation was a 'fertiliser' plant, which made nitrates, amongst other things, to be used in gunpowder and explosives. He was there until he was eventually released in early December. Conditions were infinitely better than at the other chemical plant. The food was warmer and included vegetables and even cheese! They had a snooker table which kept them amused. It must have been one of the better camps because, during their stay, the Iraqis used it as a 'show camp'. An Iraqi film crew visited it and pictures of Derek playing snooker were beamed into British living rooms as part of *News at Ten* one night. This was towards the end of November. It gave a completely false picture of the general conditions the men in the installations were having to endure.

Stephen Mansell was only kept in the Melia al-Mansour for one night. The same day as his wife Anne and the children departed for Baghdad Airport and freedom, he and a group of other men were driven under armed guard to the large oil refinery at Basra. There were about twenty-five hostages in all, including Japanese, Germans, Americans and French.

They endured extremely bad conditions. They were put into aluminium and board nissan huts, which had no air-conditioning and were boiling hot. They had been an old camp for Indian contract workers and were filthy. The beds were thin foam mattresses on rusty springs. The hostages had to share their toilets, two showers and washing facilities with the guards. There was no proper washing facilities and they all had to do their own washing by hand. There was very little food and most of them went down with diarrhoea or dysentery at one time or another. The kitchen was filthy, but the Iraqis wouldn't give the hostages cleaning materials nor allow them to improve it. Stephen would feel sick just going into it. The British never received any food parcels at all, the whole time they were there.

The hostages were kept in the middle of the refinery, surrounded by gas flares, oil pipes, refining towers and storage tanks. One day, they were suddenly hurried to a fall-out shelter built nearby. Once inside, and thirty feet down, they heard a terrific explosion, rocking them and shuddering the shelter. The explosions continued, so their guards ordered them out of the shelter and took them further away. They were told that a nearby ammunition dump had blown up. Some of the hostages believed it was the British or American special military services, such as the SAS, but it seems more likely it was the Kuwaiti Resistance, which launched several operations around Basra, most notably the freeing of a large number of Kuwaiti prisoners from a jail.

Dark night, dark night, dark night. A tunnel, a light, a train, screeching brakes; no, no, NO! The camp. The wire. Tunnelling, falling earth, guards, shots, lights, no, NO! Watching. Night. Watching. Bribing guards. A few cigarettes, some chocolate. Oh, chocolate! Lights, officer, taken. Taken away. Questions, questions. No, NO! Taken, blind. Blinded, blindfolded, standing. Rifles, aiming. "Take aim. Fire!" No, no, no, NO! Aaaaaarrrggghhhh!"

He woke in a trembling sweat and lay there, in his rough, stinking bed, staring through the curtainless window at the wall of the chemical plant. It towered above the tiny hut as lights from the guard towers flickered across it. He rolled over and tried, yet again, to get some sleep.

"There was a group who moved into the embassy compound."

"That was Bechtel UK. It's a subsidiary of a United States company. They were British citizens working on a chemical installation. Immediately after the invasion the White House instructed American companies to stop work, so they were sitting around in hotels in Baghdad, not doing very much. They received information suggesting that the Iraqis might be about to round them up and send them to sites. In fact, that never happened to anybody in Baghdad, it had only happened to people in Kuwait. So they came to the embassy quite late one night in September and said they had been instructed to go to the embassy by their American boss. They said they would like to spend the night in the embassy to think things over. I said yes, and the next day they decided to stay.

"I was not at all sure their fears were well-grounded but I was not going to turn away British subjects who had a plausible fear of being rounded up and sent to sites, so we allowed them to stay. They remained until the end. One of them wrote a letter to *The Guardian* saying the British embassy was totally unhelpful and useless and subsequently said the same on the BBC World Service. However, I think he was working under a misconception of what the embassy was there for. They were employees of a large company. It was not up to us to supply them with food or even accommodation.

"They were allowed to bring in tents and would have been allowed to bring in anything for their own needs. Their basic building was what used to be the ballroom of the old ambassador's house. Then they had tents. At a fairly early stage, we said they could have portacabins, but there were technical difficulties over that. They were able to use our toilet facilities and the telephone. We had an extension through to the lounge. They could use the showers by the swimming pool and indeed the pool itself. They were skilled men and were very helpful to us. For example, we only had cold water showers and they rigged up a hot water shower. They were well organised. I appointed one member of my staff, Martin Hall, as liaison officer between the embassy and them, so it worked reasonably well, except that one or two were thoroughly cheesed off.

"We took them on shopping trips in a vehicle with a diplomatic number plate, to give them added assurance. They had plenty of money. They paid for their own food. It would have been quite wrong for the British tax-payer to open up a hotel for Bechtel people, people who had come in without well-grounded fears for coming in.

"The Bechtel people were less of an embarrassment, less trouble, than you might think. Of course, it was a great embarrassment in our relations with the Iraqis, and there was a famous occasion when the Iraqi Ministry of Foreign Affairs sent round a note to all foreign embassies in Baghdad which could be read as saying that, if foreign embassies did not declare the names of any foreigners they might be harbouring, the foreign ambassadors might be taken out and hanged. I think it was just bad drafting, but it was a fierce note. It was one of the occasions when a delegation from the diplomatic community went to see the Foreign Ministry and protested."

There were a great number of complaints from British people held in the hotels and at sites about the embassy in Baghdad. Many were very upset that they never received food or clothing parcels whilst the Japanese and Germans were getting them from quite early on. The same was true for mail. Very few men received letters, and those who did were given them only in the last few weeks before the general release. This, they felt, was the fault of the embassy. Those in the hotels were frequently disappointed that the embassy had not made greater efforts to visit them and, even when they were seen, seemed to have a far too casual and laid-back attitude to the crisis. It was as if those in Baghdad, themselves free from restrictions and hardships, had no idea whatsoever of the extreme danger and privations imposed upon the British in Kuwait, in the Melia al-Mansour and on the sites - a similar criticism to that against the Kuwait embassy officials, incarcerated behind their four walls and virtually cut off from the situation outside.

Many complaints were about little things, but they reflected a general feeling of being shabbily treated and virtually ignored. Many complained that they weren't given any money to buy necessities, some that they were refused entry to the embassy, were fobbed off with pleasantries, and weren't provided with clothes or toiletries, others that precious little was done to get them home and that other embassies were treating their nationals far better. The embassy seemed to many to be ill-organised, inefficient, and blasé about their plight.

I asked the ambassador why he felt there were so many complaints against the embassy in Baghdad, especially by the men who were sent to the strategic sites.

"There *were* hostages who were cheesed off and, in a way, I don't blame them. All these hostages, in their different categories, whether they were at sites or just members of the community, were all going through very, very difficult times. I think it's only human when you're going through difficult times to look around for someone to blame. It is only human to blame the British government and to find it hard to realise there might be others in difficulties as well. They only disappointed me on a number of occasions when they blamed the British embassy rather than the Iraqis. Some of the hostages said, 'We haven't got parcels like the Japanese have'. It didn't seem to occur to them that the Iraqis, in their policy of divide and rule, were discriminating against both the Americans and British and quite clearly not allowing the parcels to get through at one stage. Some of the hostages complained at us, but they should have realised our difficulties.

"Certainly, in September, and perhaps as early as August, Tug Wilson, who received an OBE in the honours list, did an absolutely marvellous job going down to the *souk* and buying things. He was from the British community, but he was not the only one. My staff did the same, buying whatever we could get that might be useful to the hostages, then making up parcels and sending them off. We tried various ways to get parcels to people but ended up using the Iraqi Red Crescent."

"The Iraqis were not letting British parcels through?"

"That's right. We know. We sent off so many and there were so many reports of them not getting through that it became quite obvious the Iraqis were discriminating - just stopping parcels getting through."

"What about mail?"

"There was quite a long period when nothing could be done about mail at all. I mean even *we* couldn't get mail out, and there was no question of us handling mail for anyone else. But, at a certain stage, we started sending mail out in small quantities in a sort of bag, which was not a diplomatic bag, but was carried by the same person. Those were letters from the British community in Baghdad. We didn't actually get any letters from hostages. We sent *out* a lot of letters to hostages, which were either stopped or took weeks and weeks to get through. We didn't get letters from hostages until very late, and then we used to put them into great big envelopes and send them off."

"So letters were coming via the Foreign Office to Baghdad and you were trying to distribute them through the Iraqis?"

"Yes. At one point the Iraqis gave people a PO Box number to write to. It never worked properly. We had many, many cases where we said we posted letters to that box number and the hostages said they never received them. Again, we finally settled on the Iraqi Red Crescent, who seemed very co-operative."

There were originally twenty-five staff at the embassy, but this number fluctuated. The commercial section, apart from one person, was sent home fairly early and the embassy advised its dependents to leave. But later eight Kuwait embassy staff came up to replace them. These staff were occupied in a number of areas. There was the day-to-day running of the embassy, but staff were also collating parcels to send out, handling mail, compiling lists of ill and elderly hostages, gathering information on those at the sites and trying to visit the hotels. Furthermore, the embassy staff were very restricted in their movements. In a tit-for-tat response to Iraqi officials in London being confined to a very limited radius of their embassy, the Iraqis didn't allow British officials out of Baghdad, and there was even worry at one time whether the distance limit excluded the airport. They were certainly never allowed to visit the installations, nor to go down to Basra or Kuwait. They were only ever allowed to visit one installation, but it proved to be a 'show' site. Similarly, they were continually refused entry to the hotels, especially the Melia al-Mansour, despite constantly demanding consular access.

The aim of this obstruction was to deny the embassy any information on its citizens, and thus make any selective bombing of targets impossible. In that they succeeded, but the embassy did try other methods of garnering data. There were five embassies representing countries with people held hostage, the British, American, German, French and Japanese. They regularly swopped information on hostages and people in transit. They made lists and gave them to each other. If a British official spotted a Frenchman or American, it was passed on and they had periodic meetings to discuss tactics, diplomatic issues, and the hostages.

It was an enormous problem trying to keep track of the hostages. They were moved around all the time. However, they usually went through the Melia al-Mansour and, occasionally, the embassy was allowed some access to the men held in transit there. As they came in, the consular staff would meet them and debrief them, but any information on their whereabouts was, of course, out of date. It was always about where they had been, not where they were going to. As there were, the ambassador estimated, some eighty strategic sites with hostages on board, this was a daunting task.

The embassy did a lot behind the scenes to help the people getting out. Under normal circumstances, if a British citizen is in distress or without money, the embassy is only under an obligation to buy them an air ticket against a promise to repay it when back in Britain. During this crisis, their hotel bills were paid, coaches were booked, planes chartered and flights paid for. It ran into millions of pounds.

The ambassador felt that every effort had been made both for the hostages and to get information back to their relatives. "When you think about it, the British government had a lot going on for the hostages. It had information coming from Kuwait via the wardens and embassy, and it had information coming from Baghdad. This was all channelled through the Emergency Unit to the relatives." In outline, it had the makings of an efficient system, but the problem was, this information was limited to what the embassies could gather, and that was always far less than the news being fed directly to the relatives via friends, people coming out of Iraq, and letters.

There were thirty men with Tom Colclough on the bus up to Baghdad, including Colin Eglington, in whose house he had been staying. Another bus followed with their bags, and two cars followed the buses. There were three guards and a driver on their coach. It stopped a few times for relief, but the journey was as awful as those for everyone else. It was late October. They had been in hiding for two and a half months before they were caught by the Iraqis.

Colin Eglington was Managing Director of the Kuwait Oil Tanker Company (KOTC), whilst Tom was Area Manager for ICL. Because he had been working on a computer system for the Kuwaiti security forces, he had access to all the names and addresses of the National Guard, police. army, navy and air force. When they were taken, they were both interrogated several times and both changed their identities. Colin's story was that he was just Personnel Manager for the offshore fleet, but the Iraqis brought out his file - about three inches thick - and told him who he *really* was. They also had a file on Tom. It was not so thick, but they were more interested in the information he might have. He was taken to a bare room with just a chair, his hands were tied behind his back with either steel or plastic wire in a dark room and he was questioned repeatedly. His interrogators would come and go, leaving him there to face a continuous barrage of intimidation, abuse, shouting, pleading, sympathy and brutality. He was beaten several times, especially in the kidneys, to get him to give them names and information. These interrogations followed him throughout his captivity, into the camps as well.

Tom and Colin were taken to the International Hotel, then driven up to the Melia al-Mansour where they were kept for seven days. They were put on the tenth floor. Above them, on the eleventh, were some sick and elderly men who hadn't gone back with Mr Heath, but who were being released as a result of his visit. Tom's wife Gilly managed to phone him at the hotel. It was their first direct contact for two months. Colin Eglington's teenage son Mark also reached his father, after ringing constantly for twenty-four hours. Such was the desperation and devotion of many of the children to their parents. Colin was really chuffed.

The floor of the hotel, like all the rest, comprised two corridors leading off a central stairwell, in which armed Iraqis sat at a table. The British men managed to acquire some cans and bottles of beer and there were several 'soirées' in the bedrooms and even in the corridor as the men passed the time in the best way they knew how.

By now, there were a wide variety of 'categories' of British in Iraq. As Harold Walker, the British ambassador, explained, "There were people in the embassy, mainly Bechtel, but at the end, one or two others. There were people at the sites. There were people in the community in Iraq, mainly Baghdad, who were 'free', but not allowed to leave. Then there was the curious, small bunch of males from Kuwait who, according to the strange system, should have been sent off to installations but were allowed to stay, mainly in the Melia al-Mansour, on the grounds that they were so obviously ill that even the Iraqis recognised they should not be sent off to sites." One such man was Mr Wilbraham, who had cancer, and who left with Mr Heath.

Whilst at the hotel, Tom and the other men received food parcels made up by a British businessman in Baghdad called Barry Cooper, who later received an OBE for this work. It was invaluable. Barry and another man, 'Tug' Wilson, sent messages around the British community in the city to send them a variety of clothes, games, items of food, books, toys, and toiletries. Other people donated money with which they were able to buy more essentials. A lot of the men only had one set of clothes. They needed clean underwear, shaving equipment, soap and toothbrushes. The community raised somewhere in the region of 17,000 Iraqi dinars in total for the hostages. An anorak cost about ID 175. They bought the men radios and they had shaving kits coming out of their ears.

"We had seven days with the British diplomats coming in," Tom Colclough explained, "but our biggest emotional supporter was the American Commercial Attaché, Steve Dieubault. He looked like Charlie Drake dressed as a typical 1960s hippy, with curly hair and a real sense of humour. He would come in and demand, 'What've those scumbags done to you guys today?', with the Iraqis around. He couldn't give a damn. He was brilliant. He'd come in with a rucksack and two twenty-four packs of beer. He only had three Americans to look after. It was embarrassing because the British diplomats would come in with their suits and ties, as if they were visiting people in hospital."

Tom felt that two of the embassy staff stood out from the rest and were excellent, a verdict supported by many other hostages. One was Caroline Cross, the other Julian Lyons. They both worked their hearts out for the hostages, but Caroline was a very junior official, a floater, not a permanent staff member. "She tried her best and really listened to us."

After seven days at the Melia al-Mansour, Tom was taken to his first installation. It was the al-Muldane military airport south-east of Salman Pak, on the Euphrates and thirty-eight kilometres south-west of Baghdad. The hostage camp was on the edge of an airfield, in a Nissan-type hut immediately adjacent to the runway. It was a prison camp, surrounded by three high fences topped with barbed wire, guard towers, guard dogs and an electric fence. He was there for ten days. His flatmate, Colin Eglington, was taken to the nearby Salman Pak nerve gas factory, where he was held in a building in its heart. He was treated very well there, with good food, good accommodation, and a relaxed atmosphere.

Tom's hut was about the size of a living room, bare apart from a mattress in the corner, with a few windows to give light. He was on his own. He took the risk of scouting around and listening to the guards, but couldn't get far because there were guards outside his door, at sentry posts, in the towers and by the fences. There were also packs of wild dogs. Rather than scaring him, they proved invaluable. They left tracks between the fences and had dug holes under them which the Iraqis were too lazy to fill in. He made his way through one fence and was climbing over another when he noticed insulators on it. He suddenly realised it was electrified and froze with panic. He tried to remember how he had got on it and whether he should stay put or jump off.

It didn't matter, the fence wasn't on. He was able to climb it at will. Once over it and under the next, he scouted around the perimeter of the airfield. He had no military training but knew how to keep out of sight of the guards. They weren't expecting him to get out anyway, so weren't looking for him. Most of them were asleep. All were very relaxed.

Tom made his way towards the military airfield and watched jets from the airfield take off in the distance as he hurriedly took bearings on them. He had managed to hide a compass in a bag, despite knowing it might mean he was severely beaten, tortured or shot if the Iraqis found them.

Tom was kept on his own because of his resistance and hostility to the Iraqis. It was to gain information from him on the Kuwaiti armed forces and to break him. But it was only a half-hearted attempt. Tom was used to being alone and to living rough. He had hunted gemsbok in South Africa, tracking an animal for days, sleeping in the bush. He was used to stalking at night, to being alone and to hardship. He had valuable memories and experiences to fall back on, which were of vital importance to him psychologically. He was able to accept suffering and hardship, rather than dwell on the unfairness of it all. He buckled down to life and made the most of it rather than moaning about what he could be doing and how his life was being ruined. Those who *did* dwell on their lot found it far harder to cope.

Tom adapted so well, he managed to draw a scale map of the airfield which he kept hidden on his person until he was able to send it out. He drew it to keep himself sane. The map proved so accurate that when the MoD later debriefed him, they were able to overlay an aerial photograph of the site and they matched virtually perfectly. There was an artillery range and even a water tower which matched the photograph. There was only one major geographical feature missing. He had included a lot of marshland around the airfield, but just out of sight, winding around the airfield on three sides was a major tributary of the great River Euphrates. He later saw pictures of the air base after the allied bombing. It had been totally destroyed.

The second site Tom found himself in was an animal experimentation area, still within the airfield compound, but further away from the runway. He joined a number of other hostages already there. The accommodation was amongst the laboratories. It was a suite of offices which had been converted into bedrooms, each with a wooden-framed bed and foam mattress. The toilet was disgusting, a hole in the ground with faeces all around. The windows of the offices had been welded shut and covered with reinforced wire mesh. The doors were shut most of the time and they were confined to their lounge and bedrooms.

The Iraqis were bringing in lorry loads of dogs, which they gassed or injected, then took away to be burned. They killed about sixty a day in a building just behind the hostages. Tom poked around enough to ascertain that they were conducting biological warfare experiments on the animals. He surmised that they were either using anthrax, nerve gas, toxic shock, or all three.

Tom was joined by a Japanese and three couples, a German and Syrian, a Palestinian and Briton, and two Americans. The German and Syrian had two children with them.Tom soon became suspicious of the two couples. They were a strange bunch and had an unusually friendly rapport with the guards. The German was a fanatical Muslim. "Everything was a bit iffy with them - strange. The guards were a bit too forward with the Syrian woman." They alone were getting phone calls out to their relatives. He became convinced all four were informers, passing information to the Iraqis.

Whilst he and the others were there, the German received tightly packed ration parcels which contained biscuits, apricot jam, chocolate, sugar, tuna fish, ham, sausage, coffee, tea and other goodies. The others received nothing. Their food was so unhygienic it contained mouse droppings. It created tensions between the German and the others. Once more, the aggression of a nation towards Iraq was reflected in the way the Iraqis treated their prisoners. The Germans were trying to mediate, so their food parcels were allowed through. The Palestinian and British couple were also getting German rations. They received so many, they had a stock of them in their rooms.

The four who were friendly with the Iraqis were allowed phone calls out, but not Tom. He grew steadily more angry about this, until it blew up into a fierce altercation with the guards. In retaliation, they stopped his cigarette ration. What they didn't know was that embassy had supplied him with two thousand before he left for the site, so he had enough for the lot of them hidden in his luggage. He used them as a form of currency, swopping them with the German for some of his special rations. Tom also used cigarettes to bribe the guards. The bribery worked and he was able to 'liberate' a whole stack of ration packets.

The American man, Don, had a cardiac problem. Both he and his wife Brenda had lost a lot of weight. They had been taken early in August and developed severe diarrhoea and dysentery. They were very sick. They were released fairly soon after Tom arrived. When they left, they took a letter from Tom to Gilly. It contained Tom's map of the site, which Gilly passed on to the MoD.

At night, Tom was able to climb out of a window and slip away from the hostage rooms to look around the other buildings of the establishment. The Iraqi lab technicians were working triple shifts, day and night, so Tom was able to walk outside and be taken for one of the workers. However, the Iraqis soon wanted to step up their experiments and needed the extra offices, so their guests had to be found alternative accommodation. They were all moved out.

About three kilometres away was the third site. It was the military airfield's fire station. In this final location, Tom had more freedom to roam the whole site than before. He went running during the day and at night, until he had a very good idea of the layout of the site.

Meanwhile, one of Tom's mates from the villa in Mushrif, Mike Southall, had been taken to a munitions factory on the Euphrates at ar-Ramadi, a hundred and twenty kilometres west of Baghdad.

The Iraqis tried to confuse this group as to their location. On the journey to the installation, they went along minor routes, made detours, turned back on themselves, and made off into the desert. None of it worked, but the Iraqis persisted. They were moved around the factory several times in the first forty-eight hours, until the Iraqis worked out where they were to stay. They ended up on the second storey of an office block in the factory complex, where fourteen of them had to share one toilet, one shower and one wash basin. None of the windows could be opened, nor was there any air-conditioning. The food was very poor; it had a very low nutritional level and there was very little of it. All of them lost a great deal of weight during their five week stay.

It was now the beginning of November, a time when many hostages found their situation began to get better and the food did improve after a week or so. They had meat and fresh fruit with their meals and were moved out of the office block into prefabricated huts previously used by the construction workers who had built the factory. One tremendous bonus was their access to a sports facilities nearby. They could use the tennis courts, play basketball and volleyball and relax quietly to ride out the crisis. They were even provided with brand new pin-stripe suits to keep them warm in the approaching winter. In another concession, they were allowed to phone their relatives in Britain to invite them over to Iraq for Christmas. The men were allowed to make calls about once a week, but used the chance to instruct their families *not* to come. It was the first real link they had made for four months.

Ron Duffy, from West Moor near Newcastle upon Tyne, was also on an installation. He was sixty-two years old. He had worked for Merz and McLellan as an engineer on a power station turbine contract. He was taken prisoner early on, driven up to Baghdad, then sent out to an installation. The weakness of months in captivity, of poor food, of loss of weight and continuous stress had played a big part in weakening his constitution. The plant had no proper medical facilities and the Iraqi health service in the area had insufficient expertise to deal with his problem. He suddenly had a coronary and died.

Given normal circumstances, living in Kuwait with its excellent medical services, there was no reason why Ron shouldn't have lived for many more years. He had been passed fit by an Iraqi doctor only a few days before his heart attack, but they frequently misdiagnosed everything from dysentery to migraines, doling out huge quantities of valium as a panacea. As his wife Christine said, he had no history of heart disease and it came as a complete shock to her. He died because he was part of the human shield.

KURDS SAY IRAQIS HAVE RELOCATED KEY ARMS PLANTS

Iraq has moved essential machinery and equipment from its arms production and chemical warfare plants to new locations as a precaution against possible air attack...

Among the first plants to be moved was the al-Taji armaments factory north of Baghdad on 16th October and parts of the Samara chemical plant on the Tigris, the [Kurdish Democratic Party] said. Other military plants have been evacuated, the exception being the al-Qaim chemical plant in western Iraq, near the Jordanian border.

The al-Qaim chemical plant, which is reputed to be a centre for the manufacture of binary chemical shells, is well protected by anti-aircraft weapons and ground troops and the presence of foreign hostages. The evacuation of military industry indicates that the Iraqi authorities do not believe that the holding of some seven hundred foreigners - including three hundred Britons - will be enough to deter air attack in the event of war. The fact that a considerable number of hostages, including almost all women, have now been released from strategic sites, may also have led the Iraqis to conclude that the security of the weapons plants has been compromised.

The Independent, 30th October

This was an important development. The Iraqis had recognised that their hostage policy would not protect their factories and were already looking for other ways of preserving them six weeks before the general release. The signs were there that the policy of the human shield would soon be over.

Mewling and Puking

"I'm sick of and tired of the mewling and puking of the relatives of hostages in the Gulf and of some of the hostages themselves. During the last war, we never heard the sobs of widows. Cannot these people keep a stiff upper lip and think of the country as a whole, instead of their own personal concerns?"

Kilroy Silk ran down between the banks of chairs seating relatives of Gulf hostages, microphone in hand. Anne and Joanna Mansell were sitting on the front row. Further back the people included Lesley Kerfoot and Josie and Stephen Brookes.

"Hello, good morning. Many French families will now be celebrating the return of their families from the Gulf. Nearly three hundred French hostages were released last night from Iraq and Kuwait. But what about the British hostages? Some wives haven't seen or heard from their husbands for months and they're now desperately anxious and feel that we've abandoned them.

"Brenda, when did you last hear from your husband?"

"On the seventh of the tenth," a demure, quietly spoken woman replied as Kilroy Silk perched himself on a seat beside her. She was clearly very upset as she clutched a letter tightly in her shaking hands. "A letter came through a diplomatic bag from Baghdad."

"How is he?"

"Very down."

"What does he say about how he's feeling? Where is he?"

"In an installation somewhere. No one knows where."

"How much do you know about what conditions are like there for him?"

"All I know is they get meals each day. I don't know much else."

"You say he's very down. What's he said to you that gives you that impression?"

"Well, he said that there's no one over here who's doing anything for them." She began to nervously read bits from the letter. "That he sincerely hopes more is being done to secure their release in the United Kingdom. There's nothing being done here. Nothing at all. And he wants me to keep it in the public eye, for the release of all of them."

....

"What about you Elaine? Your husband's in the Gulf as well, isn't he."

"Yes. He's in hiding in Kuwait. I last heard from him two weeks ago."

"How did you hear from him?"

"I had a letter from him. I don't know how it's come out. People are leaving, so they're bringing letters out with them... It actually says in the letter that there' people looting now, next door to where he is. People have been held at gunpoint, with knives and axes. They were let go, but they were held for two hours. Another man on his own, a friend of my husband, is petrified. Law and order has totally broken down. He's lucky. There' people in contact with the outside world where he's staying in Kuwait. They're free to move around and they're telling him what's going on. Things are going to get worse."

"Brenda says that her husband, Les, is down, depressed. Does your husband feel the same?"

"My husband is very frightened. He's normally a very calm sort of person. He finds now that every time an incident occurs, if they hear something explode or they hear looters in next door, he becomes very tense and feels very unwell."

"Is he not tempted to give himself up?"

"No. He doesn't want to become part of the human shield in Iraq."

"So he'd rather suffer that terrible fear, waiting for someone to knock on the door."

"It *is* a terrible fear. I sat there myself for four weeks, in the same situation, worrying. We used to blockade the door at night, worrying whether the soldiers were going to come in, what they were going to do to me, what they were going to do to my husband. We've got a small baby. It's constant fear. And I'm still living that all the time, I'm living that every day for him, because I went through it myself."

....

"I had two letters as recently as last Thursday from my husband."

"Where does he live?"

Lesley Bell told him. "He's in hiding in Kuwait. In his letters he describes in detail the continuous looting of our apartment block where there are five British people living. He witnessed the execution of a Kuwaiti at the back of our block. He describes conditions in Kuwait as, 'We're just hanging on to the grim thread of our existence', and he says, 'It's like being put in prison for a crime you haven't committed, without knowing what the length of the prison sentence is going to be'. He describes living on rations, 'Rationing our own food supply, we're down to one meal a day, which consists of rice and something'."

....

"Is it easier that you were there? You know what your husband's going through, because you can visualise it. Very often, if somebody's apart from you, part of the difficulty is visualising their daily life, what they're going through. The fact that you were there, you got married there in fact, does that help in any way to overcome your feelings at being apart from him now?" This question was directed at another woman, young, blonde, dressed in a black top.

"It did help quite a lot, but I have received a letter from my husband last week, through somebody who came out with Mr Heath. Reading between the lines, he's very, very depressed. He's been moved around, so they're not on the same camp and the routine's changed. They're living in a tin shack and food is very, very short."

"What's the effect on all of you of being apart like this?"

"It's terrible. It's devastating."

"Describe it to me."

The woman heaved a great sigh, as though the effort of delving into her emotions was proving too painful. Another woman saw her difficulty and answered instead. "I think the problem is you are constantly trying to remember what it was like, particularly for those of us who were there. I think it's easier for those of us who were there, because I can say, 'OK, it's three o'clock in the afternoon, my husband will be doing this'. I know his circumstances and that makes it much more comforting. For those people who have no idea what their husbands and loved ones are doing at any given time of the day, it must be devastating."

"It's a limbo existence we have here," a young Kuwaiti woman interrupted. "We are only existing, we aren't living."

"Where's your husband?"

"My husband's in Kuwait... My husband has stomach problems. I've had to get medication in to him. People are suffering because of the sheer length of time we're moving into - months and months."

"What's the worst effect on you?"

"It's the effect on the children."

"How does it effect the children?"

"Oh, my daughter is terribly upset. She's three and a half, old enough to know what was going on. She says to this day, 'The soldiers came into my house and took my toys'."

....

"It's not knowing what's actually happening to your husband," yet another woman said, barely able to control her emotions. "My husband was taken on the eighteenth of August and the Foreign Office rang me then to say he was taken as a hostage. The next time they rang me was the twenty-first of October, to say he'd been moved from one installation to another. That was over two months of not having any information at all on my husband. I had one letter out in that time which was written on the thirtieth of August. He'd only been a prisoner for twelve days and he said at the time, 'Please don't worry, I'm sure we will be released and I'm sure we will be all right. But I can't see us getting out until Christmas.' But the point is, I haven't heard anything for two months on how he is."

....

"My husband was taken hostage on the second of August, the day they invaded." Lesley Kerfoot leaned towards the microphone Kilroy Silk was pointing at her. "I found out the next day, the Friday, he was actually missing. Nobody knew where he was. Then on the Sunday I was told that he'd been taken hostage on his way home off the night shift and that he was actually down in Iraq, in the Melia al-Mansour Hotel. Since then I've had, at the beginning, one hastily written, censored letter. That's thirteen weeks ago. In this letter he was so sure it would only take a matter of days or weeks for sanctions to work and that the British government would do something to help him. It's heartbreaking to know that seemingly nothing's being done. I've now come to the conclusion, after thirteen weeks, that if my husband can't come to me, then I want to go to him."

Amidst a blaze of publicity in early November, a group of women finally decided to take matters into their own hands. They were going to Baghdad to get their husbands and sons released. They were not quite the first. Gilly Battersby had bravely gone out on her own at the same time as Edward Heath.

It was clear from the phone calls now coming from the installations that some men were in a terrible state. They were depressed, frightened, alone, and petrified of being either shot by the Iraqis or blown up by an American missile. Some were badly ill, especially with dysentery. The food was frequently appalling, and they were losing weight badly. Many thought they would never see their families again and some had suffered so severely they were verging on, or had gone over the edge of, a nervous breakdown.

The pressure on relatives was enormous. Many felt their husbands were dying. Others simply didn't know, but feared the worst. They *had* to take the risk of flying out to Iraq. They *had* to do their utmost to help their men. If they didn't go, and the men never came back, they would find it impossible to ever forgive themselves.

The first group of relatives to decide to go to Baghdad consisted of ten women: two mothers, a fiancée and seven wives, all of whose men were being held at sites in Iraq. They included Dorothy Goodwin, who had been a warden in Kuwait, had left with the women and children, and now took on the role of their spokeswoman. Her husband, Peter, who had worked for Kuwait Airlines, had tried to escape with the women, but been taken off by the Iraqis and sent to an installation at Basra.

The group decided on as much publicity as possible, both to keep the hostages in the news and to ensure that the Iraqis didn't try to detain them once they were in Baghdad. Two of the women, Dorothy Goodwin and Carol Cox, held a press conference on the sixth of November, just a couple of days before the group flew out. Carol commented that they were going out to request their men be released: "We think the only hope of their release is through us going out there and requesting - not begging - that they be allowed to come home." Dorothy Goodwin explained that they "were not trying to undermine the policies or work of the government or United Nations. We *do* urge all governments involved to exercise restraint, to work for peace, and to use less heated rhetoric." It was a desperate attempt to do something for their men which drove these women to go. And they were *driven*. The failure of governments and the remorseless, headlong tilt to war was obscuring their menfolk's tragic plight.

The two women were very careful not to criticise the government in public, but others in their party privately felt the government should, and could, have done far more for the hostages. Their trip was, of itself, a vote of no confidence in the government's efforts. They went with the blessing of the Iraqi embassy in London which promised that they would receive every possible assistance when they arrived and assured their personal safety. However, it was still a nerve-wracking experience, and all the women were filled with trepidation.

They flew out to Amman and then on to Baghdad. They were met at the airport and driven to the Melia al-Mansour Hotel, where they were accommodated free of charge. They went loaded with goodies for the men, including tinned fruit, chocolate, razor blades, clean clothes and newspapers. They knew the men would be desperate for little luxuries and for news. They had asked for an audience with Saddam Hussein, which they were granted. But first, they had to do the rounds of other visits, including to the Iraqi Women's Federation, to say how concerned they were for Iraqi mothers and children and how much they wanted peace. They were very courteously treated by the Iraqis, who gave them a 'minder' and insisted they see the sites of Iraq, going to the *souk* and offering to take them to the ancient ruins of Babylon. When they met Saddam, they handed him a list of hostages and a request that they be released on humanitarian grounds. If they couldn't be released, at least let them see them. One of the women even offered to replace her elderly parents trapped there.

The women were very unsure whether they would be successful. They arrived in the midst of piecemeal hostage releases and war-mongering bluster. On the one hand, the Japanese hostages had just left and the Germans were going, and it was announced that sixty British construction workers working on Saddam's palace, plus a nineteen-year-old Scottish lad, would be allowed home. On the other, Iraq continued with its threatening bluster, creating a very tense atmosphere in Baghdad. The Information Minister described Margaret Thatcher's latest remarks, that time was running out for Iraq, as "uninterrupted hysteria". She was an old hag who had lost her mental balance. The government newspaper *al-Jumhuriya* said, "If the fire of aggression is unleashed against Iraq... flames will cover everything, will be over everything and will burn everything in every direction. Nothing except ashes will be left... nothing except a sea of burning fire will be left from the oil they dream to control... The mother of all battles is near today... Nothing will be saved from the flames except the house of Allah [the Grand Mosque in Mecca] and the grave of the prophet of Allah [in Medina]."

There had been a great deal of doubt in Britain as to whether the women would be successful and heavy criticism that they would be used as propaganda tools by Saddam. The government was plainly against it, though muted its animosity to calling it "risky". Some members of the government were finally learning not to be too much against the efforts of the relatives, despite their own political views. The women knew they were stepping into danger, but were prepared to ignore criticisms and not to let their propaganda value to the Iraqis deter them. The women just kept on hoping and praying.

There had still been no indication that the women would be successful when, on the third day of their visit, their husbands suddenly turned up at the hotel, looking scruffy, unshaven and a lot thinner. At first, they were only allowed to stay together for a few days but were then given a four day extension. Whilst those days were marvellous for them all, the men were never sure they wouldn't be suddenly whisked back to the installations at five minutes notice. Several had nightmares during those days. Some refused to unpack their meagre possessions, or kept them neatly folded by the door in case they were suddenly ordered to leave. However, they were all due to have another audience with Saddam Hussein.

At the audience, they pleaded with Saddam to let them all return to the UK, both women and men. Imagine their delight and relief when they were told by him that they *could* all go. This was their finest answer to their critics. When they returned with their husbands, it acted as a huge spur to scores of other women to plan to go.

Sir John Stokes, Conservative MP for Halesowen, was sickened by the sight of relatives going out to Baghdad, criticising the government and calling for peace talks. He thought they were seriously undermining the united stand against Iraq by putting their own selfish interests before the interests of Britain and, indeed, the world. And he said so - to the media and frequently.

"I'm sick of and tired of the mewling and puking of the relatives of hostages in the Gulf and of some of the hostages themselves. During the last war, we never heard the sobs of widows. Cannot these people keep a stiff upper lip and think of the country as a whole, instead of their own personal concerns?"

The reaction of the Gulf Support Group was swift. It had to be. It was inundated with calls from furious or upset relatives. Joanna Copley appeared on the television and in the press in her olive dress giving her views on the MP. In an interview with Central News, Stephen Brookes laid what the relatives thought on the line. "It was highly insensitive. At first, we were getting calls from people full of annoyance, but once they realised the stupidity of the comment, all that went away. We've got too much else to do. We're trying to approach people, we're trying to get the relatives back and we have got a lot of work on."

"Do you think," the interviewer asked as Stephen sat in front of a computer screen, "the relatives should, as he says, 'keep a stiff upper lip'?"

"Oh yes, but you can only do that for so long. What's sad is, his remarks will soon reach the hostages. But they will realise it is just another set of stupid comments from someone who should know better."

Sir John stuck to his general attitude. The day after his speech, he did retract the words 'mewling and puking'. "I think I ought to have said 'crying and complaining', but 'mewling and puking' is good old Shakespeare." As he stood outside his red brick house in his tweed jacket, remembrance poppy in his buttonhole, and immaculately trimmed grey moustache, he expressed his very strong feeling that the relatives shouldn't cry in public. "They should do it privately. Terry Waite's family have behaved very dignifiedly. Why can't they?"

Sir John's comments had no effect on the relatives resolve to get their men back. In fact, it hardened it. Another group of wives and relatives prepared to fly out, with more to follow.

As if to confirm the worst fears of the relatives, more and more reports came out of atrocities being committed in Kuwait, frequently by eyewitnesses who had managed to escape across the desert. A British man, Douglas Moore, who had been a football coach in Kuwait, came out with a small group of British women and children in a flight mainly consisting of Americans. He emphasised the desperation those in hiding were facing. "...do something, for God's sake. They cannot hang on..." An American woman explained how she and her husband had come near to starvation. "We had no food and no one wanted to give us any because they were so scared of being found out." Another woman talked of the trauma inflicted upon her young children: "They kept saying to me, 'You're not going to die, are you Mummy?'"

BRITONS IN HIDING 'ARMING THEMSELVES'

Britons avoiding capture in Kuwait have begun to arm themselves against civilian looters, according to released wives and letters smuggled out by refugees. The wife of one man still in hiding said, "They are now prepared to kill any civilian who finds them, rather than be given up to the Iraqis"... dozens are at large, foraging for food... their attempts to avoid detection are being hampered by increasing numbers of looting raids... "We are fit and mentally prepared and [now] we have staves and knives in readiness. We have been subjected to two nights of assaults on the apartment by bands of looters...

[Another wrote] that his comrades had armed themselves with a sword-stick, knives, chemicals, staves and blinding aerosols... "They have been in hiding so long that they may be prepared to kill any civilian who finds them... They view the situation as a life and death struggle..." Preparations were also going on for chemical warfare.

The Independent, 12th November

In its continued rape of Kuwait, Iraq renamed Kuwait City Kathima and gave Kuwaitis a final deadline of 25th November to take up Iraqi identity cards in an attempt to extinguish any evidence of Kuwaiti nationality. Reports came out of the emirate that hundreds of thousands of Iraqis and Palestinians were being moved into vacated apartments and villas to swamp the Kuwaiti population with people sympathetic to Iraq, whilst those remaining Kuwaitis were being slowly exterminated. The Iraqi-imposed military government of Kuwait had replaced many road signs with Iraqi names, such as Freedom Street, Jerusalem Street and Hussein Street. The King Faisal Highway had been renamed Babylon Street and the Amiri Hospital in the centre of Kuwait City was now the Saddam Hospital. The Kuwaiti dinar and flag had long been banned. Possession of either could mean, and often did, summary execution. It was now illegal to have Kuwait number plates or identity cards. Everyone had to replace them with Iraqi ones.

More ominously, Saddam replaced the governor of Kuwait, Ali Hassan al-Majid, a cousin of his, with another hard-liner, Aziz Saleh al-Nouma, an adviser to the Ba'ath Party and former state minister. One of Saddam's half-brothers, Barzan Ibrahim al-Takriti was appointed above him as intelligence officer and was the holder of real power. Although al-Majid was particularly ruthless, the fact that Saddam had appointed his half-brother as well suggested an even more pathological approach to Kuwait was imminent. There were fears that the emirate would be totally dismantled and its population driven out or exterminated.

The Gulf Support Group was extremely anxious about the reports of attrocities emanating from Kuwait. Whilst the general tone was obviously accurate, of looting and appalling treatment for the Kuwaitis, many letters smuggled out talked of those in hiding feeling relatively safe, that they had adequate food stocks and were being helped by Kuwaitis. Many of the rumours of rapes seemed to have been exaggerated and unconfirmed. Notably, since the shooting of Douglas Crosgery in the first weeks of the occupation, there had been no shooting of a British citizen. One American had been shot in the arm trying to evade capture, but that was all. It was very difficult for the helplines. They wanted to tell the truth, but also wanted to reassure relatives as much as they possibly could about the situation in Kuwait, stressing the positive aspects rather than the horror stories.

Meanwhile, another meeting between relatives and government departments was held in Coventry. After it, a special evensong was arranged for the relatives, with the Provost of Coventry Cathedral in attendance, involving a candlelight vigil. They each received a personal blessing. The next day, Stephen, Josie and Joanna went to the Coventry cemetery where the dead from the blitz were buried and laid a wreath to the four Britons who, up until then, were known to have died during the hostage crisis: Doug Crosgery, shot trying to escape across the border; Alex Duncan, killed in a car crash on his way to join Edward Heath's flight; Bill Atack, who died of a perforated ulcer whilst alone in his flat in hiding; and Ron Duffy, who suffered a fatal heart attack whilst held in an installation in Iraq. It was a very emotional time.

Major political change was in the air. Margaret Thatcher seemed to be isolating herself both at home and abroad on a number of issues. She had already argued that sanctions against Iraq should continue even after it was expelled from Kuwait, in fact, until its chemical weapons and nuclear capability had been destroyed. Whilst this was supported by many people as showing strength and determination against a dictator, it was seen by others as further limiting Saddam Hussein's options and any prospect for peace. She argued that a war against Iraq didn't need the sanction of a special resolution from the United Nations and believed the alliance already had the legal authority to act, but every other permanent member of the Security Council disagreed with her position.

It was clear that, not only in her stance on Europe and monetary union - the issue on which Sir Geoffrey Howe, her Deputy Prime Minister, had resigned on 1st November - but also on the Gulf crisis, she was becoming increasingly isolated both at home and abroad. Only after pressure did she, in the interests of the unity of the alliance, agree to a resolution on possible military intervention, which was finally passed as Resolution 678 on 29th November. This long-awaited resolution passed by the United Nations Security Council set a final deadline for Iraqi withdrawal from Kuwait of 15th January, after which member states could use all necessary means to uphold and implement Security Council Resolution 660 (condemning the invasion of Kuwait and demanding immediate Iraqi withdrawal) and to restore international peace and security in the area. It further called on all member states to provide appropriate support for actions taken in pursuit of this resolution. From that date, the time bomb was ticking. Yet the hostages were still in out there.

Further controversy arose in the debate on the Queen's Speech at the opening of the new parliamentary session. Tony Benn MP announced that he, too, would be making a visit to Baghdad. It would be primarily concerned with trying to get a peaceful political solution to the crisis, but he made it plain he would also attempt to gain the release of *all* the hostages. To him, the two issues were unbreakably linked. As a result, he was criticised both for threatening the alliance by going to Baghdad, and for putting politics before the hostages. However, whilst political issues were top of his agenda, he undoubtedly did go with the intention of doing all he could for the hostages. His whole trip was to prove that.

In the Commons debate, Douglas Hurd, the Foreign Secretary, asked Mr Benn to reconsider. "I would like to ask him to think again. If he goes, he is joining in a game where the aggressor dictates the rules and selected human beings are the pawns. I hope it is not too late. I hope he will reflect on this and change his mind." It was a more intense form of the pressure put on Edward Heath, more intense because, being a radical socialist,

Tony Benn was regarded as a safer bet to attack. Mr Hurd continued, "There is only one outcome of this matter which has any decency in it and that is the release of all hostages and the ending of the policy of the human shield." Fine words, but unfortunately, few relatives saw the government doing anything to get them released. Many felt that politicians had no right to condemn others when they were doing nothing themselves.

Mr Hurd went on to list the estimated numbers of hostages held. He said there were about eight hundred British still in Iraq, three hundred of them at strategic sites. (This was still about fifty short of the real figure.) Over five hundred were still in hiding in Kuwait, facing "mounting danger". (Finally, the FCO had approximately correct figures on those in hiding.) He mentioned the attrocities that were taking place in Kuwait, including summary executions of "men, women and children, carried out in front of their children, routine torturing of detainees, rape, electric shock, and the breaking of limbs". He mentioned one particular incident. "On 18th October an eighteen-year-old boy was shot three times, once in the head. His family was forbidden to touch the body for five hours. The ambulance was kept away until the family had signed a document saying the boy had been killed by an unknown person."

At the same time, Britain was continuing its policy of backing the US military build-up. By the beginning of November, the alliance had 300,000 thousand troops in Saudi Arabia, from fifteen different countries. By the sixth, there were 330,000, a third of which were US forces. A further 100,000 American reservists were called up and it was confirmed that the SAS and American equivalent, the Delta Force, were operating in the region. On the sixteenth, the first major American-Saudi military exercise started, with the ominous name "Imminent Thunder". The six-day exercise included manoeuvres only forty kilometres south of the Kuwaiti border and an amphibious landing just a hundred and sixty kilometres from it. It was attacked by Iraq as a "clear act of provocation", which "demonstrated America's aggressive intentions". The Americans fobbed it off as "part of our Desert Shield training". It was clearly far more.

Tony Benn rejected the government's request for him not to visit Baghdad, to its dismay. This turned to anger when Bernie Grant, another Labour MP, announced he would be heading yet another delegation. It feared that an impression of a divided parliament would be given to Iraq and would further aid the Iraqi propaganda effort. The Labour leadership also opposed the visits, making it quite clear they were going without the Labour Party's sanction, and, indeed, despite its call for them not to go. Both men were unswayed by these attacks. Indeed Tony Benn promptly requested help from the embassy in Baghdad for his visit. This request was not greeted very favourably at all.

The EC continued to be divided over these visits by individuals. The German Foreign Minister, Herr Genscher, came under fire for his tacit support for the Brandt deputation. Denmark, Ireland, Luxembourg,

Belgium and Britain all criticised him. In response, Herr Genscher defended the Brandt mission, insisting the former chancellor had not entered into any negotiations or done any deal. Nor, he said, had the Bonn government backed him. This was only half true, as it had done a great deal to help him in the early planning stage.

As if to rub salt into the wound, an Italian, Amintore Fanfani, described as "a pillar of the Italian Christian Democratic Party", was planning yet another mission. He had been approached by relatives of hostages held in the Gulf to go. Many, if not a majority, of the Italian people already opposed military involvement and polls in France suggested that the French people were fast losing their taste for military action as well. Releasing hostages seemed to be working. It certainly undermined President Mitterand's stance and Brandt's mission continued to make it extremely hard for the German government to openly support a war.

In an effort to present a unified face, the EC agreed to ask other nations to put pressure on Iraq to release all the hostages. Those nations would include members of the Arab League, the Maghreb Arab Union (North-West Saharan countries), the Non-Aligned Movement, the USA, Japan and China. The EC would ask them to impress upon the Iraqi leadership the importance of receiving a visit from Perez de Cuellar, on behalf of the entire international community.

It was clear from initial responses to the EC initiative that Arab leaders were very divided. All were cautious on the hostage issue. Some, such as Sid-Ahmed Ghozali of Algeria, would not commit themselves to approaching Baghdad, but admitted that "All members of the [Maghreb Arab] Union are very concerned about the hostages and are doing everything they can to work towards a peaceful settlement."

Meanwhile, Iraq was refusing to accept a deputation from the United Nations. It was also about to strangle at birth plans for an Arab summit in Morocco hastily organised by King Hussain of Jordan. The summit had the support of many Arab leaders and was seen by them as the last chance for the Arab world to sort the crisis out itself. It failed. The Iraqi leadership said it had not been consulted about the summit and condemned it as a front for the United States. In reality, it feared there would be a majority at the summit against its policy. To stifle it, Iraq imposed the impossible condition that no summit should be held as long as foreign troops remained in Saudi Arabia, disputed the venue, and demanded that the Palestinian question be linked to that of Kuwait. Iraq also insisted that resolutions passed by the Arab League to send troops to join the alliance against Iraq be rescinded. This demand was viewed as yet another stalling tactic to avoid real dialogue on the crisis. It seemed as though the Iraqis, caught up in their own propaganda, believed they were invincible and could defeat the alliance forces. Reports from many of the human shield, when they returned, confirmed this conviction.

In Baghdad, pressure continued on the British embassy. Frequent and passionate demonstrations were organised outside its compound and that of the Americans. One member of the British staff, James Tansley, after a *contretemps* at the embassy gates during one such demonstration, was immediately deported by the Iraqis. It was a typically petty Iraqi response to its powerlessness in the face of the huge build-up of American forces. In reply, the British government summoned the Iraqi ambassador and expelled one of his staff.

On the twenty-second of November, Thanksgiving Day, Margaret Thatcher finally resigned, amidst tears and bitter internal Conservative Party strife. As might be expected, the Iraqi leadership claimed responsibility. The Information Minister, Latif Nassif al-Jassem, who had earlier condemned Mrs Thatcher as "unbalanced" and "a hag" said her resignation was a direct result of her hardline policy towards Iraq. "Anyone who takes hostile positions unjustly against Iraq will go to Hell". Another government spokesmen described how the Gulf crisis had "buried Mrs Thatcher". They were cock-a-hoop. "Mrs Thatcher's resignation is a terrible setback for Mr Bush. Without her support, he will find it very difficult to launch aggression against Iraq." In a peculiar cocktail of wishful thinking and complete ignorance of British public opinion, the Iraqi leadership expected Britain to suddenly become totally engrossed in other matters, notably Europe and solving the Poll Tax debâcle. "We know the new prime minister will be entirely occupied with domestic issues..." an Iraqi spokesman gloated.

It is impossible, without straying into the misty realms of Saddam Hussein's warped ego, to determine precisely the effect Mrs Thatcher's resignation had on the final release of the hostages. Probably little, as the Iraqi position was wilting by the day. But, to an Arab mind, having a man, Mr Major, as his opponent, a man whose style was much less combative, who seemed much closer in mood and attitude to Douglas Hurd, and to dialogue, and who encouraged working behind the scenes and the quick settlement of outstanding problems - note the almost immediate restoration of diplomatic relations with Syria - undoubtedly transformed the mood surrounding the hostage issue. Certainly, the great majority of relatives - and most of them were Conservative voters who supported Mrs Thatcher on a majority of issues - plus the hostages themselves heaved an collective sigh of relief which was probably heard in Baghdad. Whilst this was not true of them all - Hamish Ross supported Mrs Thatcher and felt she was their best chance of getting out; he was very sad when she resigned - many immediately felt their prospects of being released had significantly and dramatically improved. For example, and this feeling was virtually unanimous amongst the people I interviewed, the Bechtel employees trapped in the British embassy compound in Baghdad issued this joint statement:

"The consensus of opinion is that, even though we all come from different political persuasions and some of us are sad to see her go after such a long and largely successful period of time, we feel that this will greatly enhance our position for early release. Mrs Thatcher has probably been the most hawkish of all Western politicians and the policies of Iraq towards us have been directly linked to her comments and attitude. Now that she has gone, we can all feel a lot easier." Indeed, even government officials felt the Iraqis would try to woo the new prime minister with major concessions. Within two weeks the hostages' ordeal would be over.

As noted before, Iraq's position was steadily weakening. It is erroneous to think of the final release as a totally unexpected development. Some relatives began to sense a change in the wind weeks before. Certainly, Stephen Brookes is adamant that he grew more and more convinced that a general release was on the cards. Everything seemed to be moving that way.

On the eighteenth of November, Saddam had announced that all 'guests' would be allowed to return home between Christmas and 25th March. Of most significance to the relatives, this edict contained the first mention of *all* hostages being released. There was a possible end in sight. Saddam had finally set a deadline. Indeed, he had to. He was using it to undermine the military option against him and the announcement was carefully planned to coincide with the opening of the thirty-four nation Council on Security and Co-operation in Europe (CSCE), at which President Bush was trying to win support for a possible war.

The end of March marked the start of the holy Muslim month of fasting, Ramadan, after which the summer would have started and the heat been unbearable for American troops, so Saddam carefully pledged to release the hostages in batches "as a gesture of goodwill", stringing their ordeal out, with the threat of them not being released if something happened "to disturb the climate of peace". Saddam was also very aware of the impending UN Security Council resolution sanctioning the use of force and setting a deadline for Iraq's withdrawal from Kuwait. He hoped to dissuade some key countries from supporting it, or at least encourage them to water down the wording. He was anxious to appear as reasonable as possible; he suddenly became more conducive to negotiations and even said he was prepared to offer "sacrifices for the sake of peace".

Whilst the Foreign Office condemned the Iraqi announcement as a "cynical ploy" by attempting to close the alliance's 'window of opportunity', it did throw the alliance leaders into a quandary. The American military commander, General Schwarzkopf was preparing for a January offensive, but that was now threatened. It was one thing for a war which would kill hundreds of Western hostages if there was no prospect of them being released. But if they *were* being released? If a few more weeks delay would save hundreds of British and American lives - that was very tricky.

However, the hostages were also presenting Saddam with a dilemma. They were his last card against an allied offensive, but he realised the more he could be seen to be releasing them, the more likely he was to split the alliance and dissuade countries from supporting a war. He had to hold on to them, yet he had to release them. In the end, he hoped that significant releases every few days - and they were significant - would do the trick. It didn't. International solidarity against him remained firm.

On the twenty-first, seven Belgian MPs left for Baghdad to win the release of all thirty-two remaining Belgian hostages. The boxer, Mohammed Ali, flew to Iraq to spend Thanksgiving Day with some of the American hostages in Iraq and he later took some home with him. Also on the twenty-first, the Iraqis announced that all German hostages would be released in response to Chancellor Kohl's call for a peaceful solution to the crisis. Two hundred and fifteen dredging workers, mainly Dutch, and a hundred and sixty-nine Bulgarians were also allowed home and Iraq resumed the exchange of prisoners-of-war with Iran after a lengthy hiatus. Two hundred and thirty-eighty were flown out to Tehran.

On the twenty-second, a further hundred and nineteen hostages, including thirty-seven Britons, were allowed to leave as a result of appeals from two delegations, one Swiss, the other French. The latter was led by the extreme right-wing leader, Jean-Marie Le Pen. He had been in Iraq for several days and flew back with eighty-three hostages, including thirty-five Britons, fifteen Italians, fifteen Germans, and several Irish, Danes, Belgians, a Portuguese and a Greek. The Swiss party was smaller, just thirty-six, and mainly Swiss nationals, but included two Britons. Most of the Britons were contract workers resident in Baghdad. Only four were from the installations. *That* part of the strategy wasn't going to be changed yet. But further good news came from the PARC organisation, which was responsible for the two hundred and thirty-four medical staff at the Ibn al-Bitar Hospital in Baghdad. Iraq agreed to grant exit visas for all its Western staff before Christmas.

This latest Iraqi strategy seemed brilliant. It caught the allied military strategists on the hop. Once again, it demonstrated that, although the Iraqis had little control over the military situation and were just waiting for the Americans to appear over the sand dunes, they did have the hostages. Is this one area, the Iraqis retained at least some of the initiative.

However, the over-riding fact was that the hostage releases were not affecting the continued determination of the alliance to keep to its military deadline of mid-January. The UN resolution sanctioning the use of force was passed, clearly demonstrating to Saddam that the 'all released by the end of March' ploy would definitely not stop a January-February war. Iraq had failed to galvanise the Western peace movements sufficiently and there was still intense international pressure to release the hostages, especially from Arab countries. Furthermore, John Major, the successor to Mrs Thatcher, shared her determination neither to negotiate nor to offer concessions.

Suddenly, the political impasse over the hostages was dramatically broken, not by international diplomacy or belligerence, but by a tiny group of ordinary women. It was announced that Dorothy Goodwin and her party had secured the release of their men. It galvanised the relatives. Hundreds more decided they had to go to Baghdad, no just from Britain, but from America and Japan as well.

Cynthia Hill and Lynda Pickup heard the news whilst at a large meeting in Manchester between relatives and the Foreign Office, organised by the Gulf Support Group. The issue of whether relatives should visit their husbands in Baghdad hijacked the meeting. It sent an electrifying wave of anticipation and excitement through the relatives. Many, including Cynthia Hill, were for going out straight away.

"Well, can you imagine it?" she explained. "You'd got all these women in this place saying, 'I'm going too, I'm going too!' Straightaway, I said to Stephen Brookes, 'Well, that's it, I'm going. I want to discuss it with my family, but I'm really sure, I'm going.'"

Those, like Lynda Pickup, with husbands in hiding, were more cautious. They had no choice but to stay. They found the excitement of the others very hard to take. It was as though a cleaver had been driven right through the heart of the relatives, splitting them into two divergent camps. Would the men in the installations be let out whilst those in Kuwait were left to rot? Would those relatives who got their men out desert the rest of them?

"But why are you going out to Iraq? You're just undermining the united front against Saddam and playing into his hands."

"All the other countries are sending their ambassadors to talk and sending other people out there. They're talking to Saddam. It's no good waving a big stick at him. That's not going to get us anywhere. We've got to talk to the man and negotiate. It's no good us saying, 'I'm not discussing it', waving a big stick."

"You're becoming propaganda weapons for the Iraqis, letting the hostages go in dribs and drabs. As some are released, more are taken and the rest get more depressed than ever. You're not helping the situation. No more are going to come out if you go. He won't let them go. He's conning you, using you, he won't let them go. What guarantee've you got he'll even let you see your husband, eh?"

"I'll try to..."

"None. You've got none. He won't even see you. He might let a handful go, just to keep you begging him, but the rest'll still be there when the war starts. And I for one hope the war starts tomorrow. Today; I hope they start bombing the bastards right now."

"He's my husband. I've been married nineteen years and I love him and I'm not going to let him down. I'm going to fight to get him released. I can't bear the thought of him being alone out there. I just want to be with him, whatever. Mr Heath's got a few out. If he hadn't gone, those thirty-three would still been out there."

"No, no. All you're doing's diverting attention from the central issue of Iraq's rape of Kuwait. You're not interested in what happens to

Kuwait. You don't care about the Kuwaitis. All you're interested in's your husbands. The rest can go to Hell."

"Listen, my husband was taken in the first week of the invasion. He's been stuck out in installations in Iraq for three months. I've not spoken to him in all that time. I've only had a couple of letters and some phone calls from people, a Frenchman and a Japanese, who saw him on the installations. I can't bear it any longer. I want to be with him. He's the other half of me."

"I bet even your husband doesn't want you to go, does he."

"He phoned me a few days ago."

"What'd he say?"

"He was cut off."

"But what did he say? Did he want you to go out there?"

"No."

"Well then..."

"But he doesn't know how I feel. I'm torn two ways. Who else has he got if I don't try?"

"He's probably scared witless of you getting caught up in it. There could be a war any day. *You* could be caught right in the middle of it, not just your husband. Saddam'll have all you women for hostages as well. Then who'll look after your children? The state, I suppose."

But Cynthia was absolutely determined. "I *will* go to see my husband in December. Everyone has to consider their own circumstances. I've discussed it with my children. They're nearly grown up as it is. They're behind me a hundred and one per cent. They want me to go as much as I do. My circumstances mean I can go, so I'm going. And nothing the government can say will stop me."

"I think they should bomb the installations, even if there are hostages in them. There's only a couple of hundred in the human shield. What're they against the thousands of lives saved by destroying all Iraq's chemical weapons, munitions factories, airfields and nuclear weapons sites? You've always got to see it from the greatest good of the greatest number, from a world perspective."

"So, what you're saying is, they're just pawns. It doesn't matter what happens to them, they're not even worth considering in your 'world strategy'."

"That's right."

"They're the price of oil."

"Of stopping Saddam getting all the oil, yes."

"Well now, you've said it at last."

When Cynthia Hill first considered the possibility of going out to Baghdad, after Saddam announced they could visit their husbands for Christmas, she had been against the idea. She had three children. Already one of their parents was stuck over there. What if she was taken hostage or wasn't allowed to return? All three children were taking their father's absence very badly. Rachel and Nyree were both depressed and

Jeremy withdrawn. She could never leave them on their own.

It was the success of the first group of women and the emotionally charged atmosphere of the Manchester meeting which changed her mind. Suddenly, there was success and solidarity. Pretty soon there were a number of other women latching on to Cynthia, saying, 'I want to come, I want to come.' After months of waiting impotently, unable to do anything to help, these women suddenly had something positive they could do.

Cynthia drove home and told her kids what had happened at the meeting and what she was planning to do. But how could she tell them she'd decided to leave them? How could she say goodbye, when she might never see them again? She was walking into a war zone. It wasn't playing games, it was the real thing.

Cynthia was very unsure how they would take it. Nyree, at seventeen, would be all right, but it was the two youngest she was most concerned about. In the end, it was the youngest, Rachel, who swung it. She was the one who had gone through the most agony. She told her mother that she had to go, "because, if you don't go Mummy, you'll never have tried."

"What if I get stuck in Iraq as well?"

"But you'll have tried."

"Yes, but it's not out of the question that I'll get stuck there too. If this man has a change of heart and makes everyone stay, then you've got your Mummy and Daddy there."

"But you'll have tried."

They agreed she should go.

The Final Days

"He said to me, all the men will go. We can't cope with this. Every few days more women are coming. We don't want this."

Carolyn and Andrew Stevenson waited at the Melia al-Mansour Hotel as the women and children were flown out. Each time a convoy arrived, the new people would pile off and move into the rooms vacated by the last batch. It was chaotic. Carolyn knew some of them, especially Linda Frost and others who worked for the Ministry of Public Works in Kuwait. They all had stories about what had happened to them, their journeys up from Kuwait and the trauma of leaving their husbands behind.

As time passed, Carolyn had to decide whether to leave herself. She decided not to. She saw no reason. She and Andrew had no children to worry about and she knew that all she would do in Scotland was mope and be anxious about him. She much preferred to stay and share his experience. Even if he had ordered her to go, there was no way she would have gone. On reflection, both of them wished more wives had remained. "If more women had stayed, it would have been a lot more difficult for the Iraqis, because they just can't handle them. They're not used to strong women standing up for themselves or with women crying. They can't cope with it."

At five o'clock one afternoon, the Stevensons and their friends Ros and Dave Buchan heard knocks on their doors. An Iraqi instructed them to pack quickly as they were being taken to a resort, where they would be very well treated as guests of the Iraqi regime. They were told it was a much nicer place than the hotel, and only just outside Baghdad. Ten hours later, after a hot, sticky journey through the night, they arrived at the liquid petroleum plant at Basra.

I asked them whether this lying by the Iraqis was typical. "Oh yes, all the time. But by then we didn't believe anything they said. We knew within twenty minutes of setting off we were going back south. They took us down the road along the Tigris, through Basra, to the Shatt al-Arab waterway. There's a section of it with a power station, a 'fertiliser' plant, big docks and a huge refinery complex, and then there's 'our place'."

The Shatt al-Arab runs through the very southernmost tip of Iraq, flowing into the north of the Arabian Gulf. It was a hotly disputed region during the Iran-Iraq war and Iran was plainly visible across the waterway. 'Our place' was the liquid petroleum plant. It consisted of five enormous propane and butane storage tanks. The 'guests' were put in a compound at one end of this complex, within a hundred metres of a huge concrete tank. There were about twenty-five of them altogether, a dozen Japanese, ten British, a German, two Americans. Later, two Frenchmen joined them.

"What was your accommodation like?"

"Absolutely appalling. It's very difficult to describe how it was. We arrived very early in the morning. There were guards to meet us. When we got off the bus they showed us this cabin, this room. Filthy wouldn't describe it." Andrew wrinkled his face in disgust at the memory.

Carolyn interrupted him. "You went bananas."

"I wasn't happy."

"You went crazy at the guards. And there were all these wild dogs running around, so it was terrifying."

"In the end, we found one cabin with a reasonable bed."

"The mattresses were just like this." She raised her hands three or four inches apart.

"They were five-foot beds, so my feet were sticking out the end. They were steel framed with springs and a thin foam mattress, but absolutely disgustingly filthy."

"We had to sleep with our clothes and footwear on in case we had to get up in the night."

"It was crawling with cockroaches, flies, beetles, spiders; you name it, it had it."

"You would open the door and the wall would be completely black, covered with flies, masses of flies. The watermelon we had, we didn't know if they were seeds or flies. Ugh, disgusting."

"There were scorpions, geckoes, and wild dogs. Some of the beetles were huge, the size of cigarette packets. Then there were bats as well."

The hut was a flimsy, wooden-sided portacabin with an air-conditioning system which didn't work.

"Describe to me the toilet."

"It was a very small room. It had a shower base which was so filthy, you couldn't see it. There was a shower thing which hung over. It was so clogged up, the water couldn't come out. There was also a sink. We had to chisel off the dirt to turn the taps round. The toilet was a proper low-level one, but was covered in a black and brown slime. It was filthy. And we had nothing to clean it with."

They shared the hut with another couple for three days, during which time they protested vociferously, until they were moved to another, more reasonable hut. "One we could clean." Even so, it was still filthy. Andrew described the toilet there. "It took me a day and a half with a Swiss army knife to clean up the bathroom, scrapping off the muck."

They still weren't provided with any cleaning materials, but Carolyn managed to steal some scourer pads and a bottle of scouring powder to clean some of the mess.

This hut was also very basic. The front door was in the middle of one side. As you went in, the toilet was in front of you, with one room either side. Each room was tiny, half the size of an average kitchen, just large enough to fit a couple of five-foot beds. That was it - for four people during the first three days, and for two during the rest of their stay. There was no regular running water. It only came on for about an hour a day and, if they missed it, that was that. They couldn't flush the toilet, use the sink or take a shower. When the water did come on, it was brown, hot and undrinkable. They used a large plastic bin to store it and used it to swill down the toilet. Towards the end of their time there, the water supply improved and they were able to start taking showers. However, with more water came more leaks and whenever the bathroom was used, water would flood everywhere. As a result, the hut began to smell terribly.

Around the huts was an eight-foot high wire fence surmounted with blade wire which formed a compound, to which they were restricted. They weren't allowed out of it at all. There were guards on the gate and inside, chatting to each other in small groups. It was a prison camp.

"Going by what you see on the telly," Carolyn told me, "of those concentration camps during the war, it was very, very similar. Everywhere we turned, there was a guard. We couldn't do anything without there being a guard behind us."

Mind you, with packs of wild dogs roaming outside, they didn't want to go out anyway. These animals would occasionally find their way through the fence during the day and shelter in the shade under the cabins, so it wasn't even safe to walk in the compound. Whenever they did venture forth, Carolyn would carry a brick in her hand to chase the dogs away. The workers in the kitchen made it worse by feeding them with the hostages' food, probably the better bits.

Together with Ros and Dave Buchan, they pinched some furniture from a nearby rubbish tip. It contained the remains of some old cabins which had been demolished. They found a couple of whole tables and a few odds and ends. Meanwhile, Carolyn was stealing sheets and cleaning materials whenever she could. She stole them from the Arab *haji* woman who came round to clean the cabins. 'Cleaning' simply involved opening the front door of the cabin and throwing a bucket of water over the floor. That was all. It was worse than useless. "So we didn't let her in at all. I said I'd do it. They used to take the guards' sheets and wash them, then hang them on the line, so I would go out and steal them from the line. We had to. We weren't even given a towel."

Just as they were getting settled, they were moved again. Similarly to most other hostages, they had been kept outside the plant at first but, at the end of September-beginning of October, they were moved inside the plant. It was a direct result of the intensifying political and military situation.

The camp inside the liquid petroleum plant was only a few hundred metres away, but was in a slightly better condition that the one outside.

There had been some German contractors living in the huts until a few weeks before the hostages moved in. The cabins were a little better constructed and furnished, but not much. Some were boarded up with the Germans' possessions and equipment stored away. The rest were the worst of the bunch. Andrew and Carolyn moved into one which hadn't been lived in for months. There was a thick layer of dust over everything. The beds were better, almost divan types, but it was out with the Swiss army knife again. One single bed was lower than the other so, when they pushed them together, Carolyn would roll over and literally fall into Andrew's arms in the middle of the night. Who said romance was dead?

By now, their group had grown smaller as one by one people, especially the Japanese, disappeared. No one was ever told when they were going or where they were being taken. Fortunately, someone in the group which remained had a short-wave radio, so they were able to keep track of the days and weeks as they passed, as well as of world news.

They ate in a canteen hut which was nothing more than a very old portacabin equipped with decrepit plastic chairs and formica-topped tables. The food always consisted of two or three courses. The first was a very thin, watery soup covered in a layer of fat, with a few tomato skins and the odd bone floating around in it. The main course usually consisted of rice, together with some exotic variety of bone and gristle and a salad. The salad was good, and sometimes included a few slices of hard-boiled egg, tomatoes, cucumbers and onions. Usually this was followed with watermelon, which was always good. Frequently, the first two courses were so bad they would leave a lot. The 'guests' grew thinner, less healthy and more prone to diarrhoea, but the Iraqis never seemed concerned.

Their food plates were never very clean. They had to rinse them themselves before they ate. They had no hot water so everything, all the cutlery, plates and cooking utensils, were washed in the dirty water which reached their cabins. The Iraqi guards fared little better for hygiene, though they had their own, superior supplies of food, probably supplemented by creaming off (can you 'cream off' rancid meat and rice full of weevils?) some of their 'guests' supplies. They discovered that the camp commander was given enough money each month to have fed them a great deal better.

Their first cook was an Iraqi who didn't care at all about what he served up or how, so long as he got it out. The kitchen was a health inspector's nightmare. Every surface was covered in hundreds or flies. "It's hard to imagine, but the surfaces would be black with them." The cook would be quite unconcerned as he and his helpers 'prepared' the meals. Occasionally, one of the hostages would go in whilst he was doing it, to ask for hot water for a cup of tea. Raw meat and vegetables would be lying about, covered in flies. The floors were never washed, just occasionally swabbed down with cold water. The meat was always lamb and always on the bone, as they were the cheapest cuts they could get.

"One day, Juhad, one of the canteen helpers, was observed with this bone with a little piece of meat on the end of it. He picked the bone up and ripped the meat off it and ate it raw, before putting it back on the counter. That bone was for our soup."

"It was another one, Wadi, who found our jar of coffee. Carolyn had stolen it and hidden it in the fridge. At that time, we were only getting this horrible Arabic coffee. Wadi opened the fridge, found the coffee, poured a pile into the lid and swallowed it."

On one occasion, some officials from a government ministry turned up and the hostages complained about the state of the kitchen and the food. The officials agreed with them and there was an immediate improvement. They actually used some disinfectant on the kitchen floors for a few days, and they had table cloths provided. Another, older cook arrived. They knew there had been a change because they suddenly had scrambled egg one morning. It came as quite a shock! They sat there, staring at it, unable to quite believe it.

"What's this?"

"I'm not sure."

"Looks like scrambled egg to me."

"Can't be. We've eaten all the chickens in Iraq already."

The new cook spoke quite good English. He even asked them how they wanted their eggs done. He cooked them with milk and fried them in butter. Carolyn chatted with him and discovered he had worked for an English family and an Italian family. He could make pasta dishes and even do roasts. Although the guards would never give him enough money to get better food, Carolyn used her charm to get some extra cheese triangles and bread. Later, the cook provided her with alternative food, to help her with a special diet.

The hostages treated the guards with a mixture of respect and disdain. They never struck up any relationship with them and only talked to them when they had an ulterior motive - if they wanted information or a bit more food, for example. The Japanese kept themselves to themselves, except for one friendly one. Some tension did arise between them and the other nationals. They received food parcels every day whilst the British and Americans never saw any. Denying some hostages food parcels was a petty way of getting their own back. The policy had the added effect of dividing the hostages and causing deep resentment in many of the camps.

Thus, the Iraqi tactic of trying to drive a wedge between the alliance ranged against them extended even to the prison camps - to denying or allowing food parcels and clothing to reach the hostages depending on the attitude of their government. In many cases, the Japanese and Germans shared their ration packs, thus building bonds rather than breaking them but, unfortunately, in this Basra camp the Japanese chose to keep their supplies to themselves, watching the British and Americans suffer whilst they enjoyed boxes of chocolate, butter, jam, sugar, powdered milk and similar necessities-turned-luxuries, and received warm clothing such as track suits, sweaters and shoes for the approaching winter months. These parcels came from the men's relations and companies, such as Mitsubishi. They were sent via the Japanese embassy to the Red Crescent for delivery in trucks around the camps.

None of the British or Americans at the plant ever received any letters or phone calls from anyone. They were completely out of contact, isolated from their relatives and friends. All Andrew and Carolyn had were two messages over Gulf Link, one of which was from Andrew's parents, Betty and Andrew Stevenson. When he heard it, Andrew cried, such was the pent up emotion and frustration he was trying to contain.

The morale of the hostages differed greatly. The Stevensons managed to cope fairly well, but one man in particular became very depressed. "Jim's way of getting over the situation was to do his washing five or six times every day - and night. He would visit the communal washing machine at three o'clock in the morning, then come back for breakfast. After breakfast, when people asked him where he was off to, he'd say, 'Oh, I'm just going to do my washing.' He would put one item in the machine every time. It was his escape."

Andrew and Carolyn were fortunate in having each other. One would keep the other going. If one was down, the other would try to cheer him or her up. There were tensions though, and they did have their arguments, many of them reactions to stress the camp was imposing on them. Often silly little things would blow out of proportion, although even in the camp they managed to argue over money. The women needed toiletries and medicines and the guards were getting bored so they took groups of hostages into Basra to visit the *souk*. These escorted trips began with visits to the hospital. Carolyn had become pregnant and was getting attacks of diarrhoea and sickness and others were suffering from dysentery.

In the end, the Iraqis would regularly ask them who wanted to go. The journey by army bus to the city centre was an hour each way. The guards were always armed as they escorted them to the hospital, then around the bazaar and street shops.

On these trips, the hostages were able to appreciate the general standard of housing, food and merchandise the Iraqi people had to endure. It was a real eye-opener. The people were very poor and the shops badly stocked with shoddy goods. The wealth of Kuwait must have seemed like all their *Eids* come at once. They met some British Gas employees who were hostages but who had known Basra before the invasion of the emirate. They had told them that things like coffee, chocolate, decent trainers or clothes had simply not been available before, but that after the invasion the shops were full of such goods. The shopkeepers had simply followed the army down in their battered trucks, looted everything in sight, and hauled it back to Basra. They, at least, made a killing.

The Iraqi people had to suffer appalling standards of hygiene in their hospitals. With so much wealth diverted into armaments and the rich military-political élite, the health service was still at a very haphazard level. Some clinics and wards of the hospitals were excellent, but so many other parts of them were filthy and overcrowded. The floors of the corridors and wards at the women's hospital were just dirty, untiled concrete. As they walked into the reception they passed Arab women sitting on the floor in their black *abayas*, many of them pregnant, many of them holding new-born babies wrapped in swaddling bandages. Because they were 'guestages' the Westerners were escorted straight past these waiting women.

As they walked past the wards, they saw the food being dished out. The hospital staff were ladling rice straight into patients' hands. There were no plates or cutlery. The watermelons they were given were covered in flies. It was real poverty they were observing. In one room they saw a woman who had miscarried and been left on her own. The door to her room was open, so people could see all the blood, fluid and operating instruments lying around her.

There were wards off the main corridor, and a pharmacy, but the walls of all of them were in a shocking state. Once with a doctor, Carolyn had to first tell the guard what was wrong with her, and he would then tell the doctor. On one occasion, she had to go into a ward to be examined. The sheets hadn't been changed and women in nearby beds were lying on bloody stains. The nurses broke out a pair of clean sheets for her and asked her to lie up on a couch. As she lay there, a woman popped out from under the couch. She was a cleaner who'd been having a nap under the bed. Carolyn nearly died with fright. On another occasion, she was asked to get onto a bed which hadn't been changed. A woman had obviously just given birth on it. It was covered in blood and fluid stains, and was still damp. She refused to use it, but it demonstrated to her once again what appalling conditions the Iraqi people had to endure.

On another trip, Carolyn had to give a urine sample. She was told to use a toilet in one of the post-natal wards. There were about a dozen women with newborn babies in the ward. The toilet was so bad she couldn't go into it, but gave her sample standing in the middle of the ward.

After several weeks, some Frenchmen arrived at the camp. One of the them had kidney stones, which required another visit to Basra, this time to a teaching hospital. Andrew and Carolyn happened along as well. There were four in the group, each with his or her own problem, but they had to stay together and so attend four different hospitals or clinics and wait as each received treatment. At the teaching hospital, they were taken up in the lift. It stopped before their floor and two *haji* women pushed a trolley into the lift with a dead body on it. At their floor, the hostages and their guards exited to find their department. The trolley came out after them and followed them around the corridors, waited whilst they were treated, then followed them back into the lift and down to the ground floor. They wandered on, but the trolley still followed them, round and round, with the dead body on it. They ended up in the main reception, with the body right behind them. They went into an office to get away from it. When they came out, the body was still there on the trolley. The *haji* women had grown tired of pushing it and left it there, by the main door.

In the camp, the guards had similar huts to their hostages, although theirs were outside the compound and some way from the storage tanks. Apart from the towering concrete containers, the landscape was barren desert and wild dog. They were in the middle of nowhere. The hostages had a certain freedom to wander about the tanks and stroll around the plant but there was nothing to do and little to see. They couldn't escape the camp, and would have nowhere to go if they did. They were aware of the American and British military build-up and discussed what to do if there was a war. Interestingly, neither Andrew nor Carolyn believed it would come to war. But they did realise they were living in the middle of a prime military site. Whilst Andrew tried to put such thoughts out of his mind, Carolyn wavered between hope and fear. "Everyday I was saying, 'We're going to die here', then the next day I'd say, 'No, we're going to be OK, we'll be all right'. If we died, I wanted us to be buried together."

"How did you cope with that? Did you try to switch off and say, 'If it happens, it happens'?"

"Yes. I think that's what you've got to do." Andrew replied. "I think I found it quite easy to do that. I don't have problems switching off. I can think about other things."

"You didn't get angry?"

"Only when Carolyn left"

"Yes," his wife interrupted. "He changed completely when I left."

When she started to receive phone calls from her husband Stephen, also in an installation near Basra, Anne Mansell found herself with a problem. There were three calls in all. During the first one he was very upset. It lasted about a minute before he was cut off. He didn't say anything, he was in such a state. "He was extremely upset. His words told me he was clearly in distress."

Anne suddenly realised what he was going through. It was thrust before her in the starkest possible terms. Getting him released quickly was a matter of life or death. In the second and third calls he kept telling her he was going to die and would never see them again. Anne had to keep shouting to him over the phone that, "Yes, we'll get you out, I'll come over to get you out. It'll all be over soon", in an attempt to calm him down. It was awful to hear him like that.

Anne was plunged into a real dilemma. Some women had already gone to Baghdad to see their husbands and she had the difficult decision whether to go out as well. When she had left Kuwait she had promised herself never to go back and had stuck to that. It had been a tremendous relief to Stephen to know that she and the children were safe. He didn't want her to risk herself again. But he was in such a desperate state, she had to do something. She decided she had to go to see him.

Her son Stuart, aged fifteen, was supportive, but very worried about her going. "Mum," he told her, "I've already lost one parent, I don't want to lose two."

The other women in her conclave weren't in the same position. Ann Hill, Lollo Murthwaite and Marcia Griffiths had husbands in hiding and weren't getting any phone calls at all. Lollo for one found it very upsetting. She had little choice but to stay. There was no point in her going. It could only endanger her husband's life. Even if she had sent a message through Gulf Link that she was coming over, she didn't think he would have ventured out of hiding and was very unsure whether he would want her to risk herself in the process. But it was extremely distressing for her to watch groups of women going out and successfully bringing their menfolk back. Saddam hoped to split the women in Britain and increase the pressure on the British government, and he succeeded. He raised the emotional stakes considerably, as well as winning for himself world headlines. What sickened the relatives was that he was portraying a more humanitarian face by actually intensifying the suffering of the hostages and their relatives.

Anne Mansell left London for Iraq on Saturday 25th November. She went discreetly. Although the Six O'Clock Live programme followed her out there, she didn't make a big thing of it. She didn't want to go with a group, so went with just one other woman, Hilary Jones, daughter of the Reverend Michael Jones, who was in Baghdad. She did not intend to bring Stephen back with her; that seemed out of the question. They took stocks of medicines, food and other items the men might need. They had to fly via Amman and on the trip from the Jordanian capital to Iraq she met Tony Benn, who happened to be on the same flight. They sent a note to him and he came down the plane to speak to them. Although they disagreed with his politics, they found him an extremely pleasant man. His assistant came with him and took their particulars and the names of their detainees, to raise them with the Iraqis.

Tony Benn had immediately been against a war in the Gulf. Throughout August, he fought to get Parliament recalled to discuss the issue, without success and he joined the Committee to Stop the War in the Gulf. When Parliament was recalled in early September, he wanted a vote on the issue of a war, but was denied. He wrote a whole series of letters, to Neil Kinnock, Margaret Thatcher, Perez de Cuellar, Jesse Jackson, and many others, as well as writing articles and addressing conferences, protesting at what he saw was a headlong plunge towards war.

At the beginning of November, the Iraqi ambassador, Dr al-Salihi, went to see Tony Benn at his home in Kensington and told him that, after his speeches against the war, a visit by him would be acceptable to the Iraqi government. He was reluctant, because he feared being used by the Iraqis. As it was after Mr Heath's visit to Baghdad, Mr Benn went to see the Conservative MP to seek his advice. Mr Heath told him to go, so he decided to accept.

Mr Benn had two objectives. The first was to gain political support from as many people as possible to take to Saddam Hussein, calling for Iraqi withdrawal from Kuwait and for peace in the region. He eventually took with him messages of support from Nelson Mandela, Willy Brandt, President Mitterand, MEPs, Labour MPs, Commonwealth representatives, Lambeth Palace, Mr Papandreou, the ex-Greek prime minister, and a great many more. The second objective, and Mr Benn is quite specific on this, was to argue for the release of *all* the hostages trapped in Iraq and Kuwait. He rejected the distinction between 'humanitarian' objectives and 'political' objectives. "Nothing could be more humanitarian than the political objective of stopping the war. After all, two hundred thousand Iraqis were reportedly killed in the war."

Originally, his trip was planned for Sunday 18th November, but it was postponed for a week to sort out some final details. His office needed to organise visas and flight links. In that time, he received hundreds - whole sacks full - of letters from relatives of hostages asking him, not just to release their particular relative, but to argue for the release of all the hostages. "The letters and accounts in the letters were really very, very moving," Mr Benn told me. He was receiving in the region of two hundred a day on the Gulf generally, plus hundreds more a day specifically on the hostages. He was swamped.

The phone was also ringing non-stop. "We were flooded with phone calls," Kathy Ludbrook, Tony Benn's private secretary, explained. "They were asking for their friend or relative to be put on Tony's list. It meant a massive processing exercise, as well as the haranguing..."

"Haranguing?" I interrupted.

"Oh yes, because people were phoning up in a very emotional state sometimes, really hysterical, because they were so desperate, so frightened about what was happening out there. They knew of the build-up of troops, they knew there was a chance of war breaking out whilst their relatives were still out there. Sometimes they were screaming at us for not doing enough. 'Why aren't you doing more?' 'Why aren't you getting these people out?', not understanding Tony's lack of political power in that sense. Some were in a very, very upset state. There were some terrible stories. I cried at some of them and found it very difficult to cope with them. We were getting appeals from companies, which sent us lists, and we recorded all phone calls on photocopied forms." She dumped a great pile of forms on her desk in front of me. "But many were calm and understood our situation. It was enough for most of them to be reassured that their friend or relative would be on Tony's list when he went out there, that somebody was trying to do something about it."

Mr Benn promised he would try and see everyone he could when in Baghdad, both hostages and Iraqi government leaders. He and his staff spent days going through the letters and making a full list of names. He had six volunteers working on them. Like Mr Heath, he refused to prioritise them "because I didn't want to have to decide who should come and who should not."

"We went through and through the names, sorted them and put notes beside them," Kathy Ludbrook explained. "He also received names from Mr Heath, others from Rob Hayward of the Gulf Support Group, many from firms with employees in Kuwait and Iraq, and some from the Foreign Office. Even Conservative MPs were secretly coming up to him and asking him to help their constituents, whilst openly condemning his visit in Parliament or the press." The Gulf Support Group gave Mr Benn its full support and worked with him to assemble the list. Not only did his office amass names and personal details, but also which installations they were at and their distance from Baghdad, vital for the Iraqis to find them. Because the hostages had been able to make phone calls since early November, many relatives knew at least some details of the installation.

Unfortunately, the Foreign Office only gave Mr Benn's office their list reluctantly. According to Tony Benn's private secretary, the Foreign Office was unco-operative. "We didn't get much help. We had to keep asking for it. As soon as they knew Tony was going to Baghdad, we were not contacted. We had to keep making contact. It took us at least a week to get their list of hostages."

Kathy explained how, when she advised people to contact the Foreign Office and told them she was trying to contact it as well, they told her not to bother. "They said you're wasting your time. So many of them said that to us."

Mr Benn decided to discuss the Foreign Office's attitude with Douglas Hurd, the Foreign Secretary. According to Mr Benn, Mr Hurd told him that he was afraid his visit may give Saddam the message that the British government was not serious about getting the Iraqis out of Kuwait. Mr Benn told Mr Hurd that, in fact, he would emphasise the determination of the British and Americans to attack him if he didn't withdraw. He also asked formally for help from the embassy in Baghdad, but without response, other than a curt letter from the Foreign Secretary, which included the following extract:

"I will certainly ask our ambassador in Amman to brief you... I cannot however offer you the secretarial communications you have asked for. These are not services which we would normally offer to overseas visits by members of parliament. Like you, we continue to hope a peaceful solution to the crisis in the Gulf will be possible. We do not see any scope for a compromise solution to the Iraqi invasion to Kuwait..."

To deny Mr Benn the services of the Amman and Baghdad embassies through such a paltry excuse - we don't normally do it, so we're not going to do it for you (It's our ball and you can't have it) - ignored the dire straights the hostages were in and verged on the appalling. The extent to which the government was out of step with the views of the relatives was reflected in the letters of support Mr Benn received from them and from people across the world - 13,000 in all!

Due to the lack of support from the British government, and refusal to make the services of the British embassy in Baghdad available to him, Mr Benn went to the Indian High Commission and persuaded them to give him the support of their embassy in Baghdad. Furthermore, Mr Benn received a letter from Richard Branson saying he would make a plane available for any hostages he was able to bring out. It was a jumbo jet, the one permanently at a state of readiness at Gatwick Airport.

Mr Benn left for Amman on Sunday 25th November with just one other person, Paul Lalor, an Irishman who was an Oxford graduate and spoke fluent Arabic. They took a video camera, lent by ITN, but unfortunately camera work was not Paul's strong point. They also took a small present of medicines for Iraqi hospitals as a 'peace offering' and brought letters, both to Saddam from relatives, and to the hostages known to be in Baghdad - and Kuwait - which he was able to hand out on his travels.

The suitcase full of aspirins highlighted another issue. Mr Benn's office, realising the importance the Iraqi leadership put on visitors bringing medical supplies for its people, asked the Foreign Office if he could take a large supply of medicines out with him. It also requested, at the behest of the Iraqi Women's Federation, to take some baby milk powder. The Foreign Office refused, saying that it was against sanctions and that all such items were being distributed by the Red Cross. That was true, but such gifts oiled the cogs, turned the wheels of Arab circles, let them save face. But no, he was to be allowed nothing. He even had to sign a pledge that his bag of aspirins was strictly for British citizens!

In contrast, Saddam agreed to free a further seventy Italians on 25th November, after the Italian government had sent an aircraft loaded with twenty-five tons of medical supplies to Baghdad. Herr Brandt also took a very large consignment of medical supplies with him when he secured the release of his hostages. What if the British government had offered medical supplies? They were not a serious threat to sanctions. Would a sizeable number of British hostages have been released earlier?

When Mr Benn arrived in Baghdad, he was met at the airport by three leading Iraqis and gave an interview to Iraqi news inside the airport complex. He and Paul Lalor were then led out of the airport to give a much larger press conference to the assembled journalists from every major country in the world. From there, they were taken in an Iraqi car to the ar-Rashid Hotel, a plush establishment occupied by many of the press.

Mr Benn gave countless press statements and conferences in the four days he was in Baghdad, as well as keeping his own video record and diary of events. He is very aware of history, and of his personal part in it. His house in Kensington is packed with memoirs and diaries and notes and letters. In his four days in Iraq, which were historical days, he taped every meeting he was allowed to and would lie in bed last thing at night - actually, first thing in the morning - to dictate the day's events into a dictaphone. He is a meticulous keeper of records.

That first evening he had dinner at the hotel with several leading Iraqis, who assured him Saddam would see him and, when asked how many hostages would be released with him, said it would be on the same scale as for Willy Brandt. Mr Benn gave them his lists of hostages. In the hotel he met two members of the PARC medical staff working at the Ibn al-Bitar Hospital, with whom he talked, and two of the Bechtel employees holed up in the canvas village in the embassy compound. He arranged to visit the compound first thing the next morning. He contacted the British embassy to request permission. The ambassador, Harold Walker, agreed and Mr Benn saw them the following morning.

"They were living in appalling conditions" he told me. "They had these tents by the side of the river. They were washing in the open. It was really awful, although they were very jolly and taking it all in their stride. It was like a prisoner-of-war camp, really. But they were very cheerful."

This was not the view shared by Harold Walker, who emphasised that the Bechtel employees were there through their own choice and were free to leave at any time for the hotels. The Baghdad community was under no threat of arrest. The men had free use of the embassy swimming pool and a lounge-bar with a TV and a variety of games equipment. They had access to an embassy phone and to toilets. They had plenty of food, medical care and were otherwise looked after. He strongly refuted suggestions that it was a 'prisoner-of-war camp'.

As we spoke, Mr Benn showed me the video he took of the compound. It showed lines of tents with a few tables and chairs outside them, pitched across the grass. It was getting colder in the late November nights, and they needed warm clothing. One of the men described it as "our shanty town". In the first few days, they had used cardboard and wood to make shelters, then had bought the tents and bedding themselves. The temperatures were falling at night and the rainfall threatened to turn the camp into a muddy quagmire. In the sense that they were actually on British soil, they were refugees rather than hostages, and the camp was described as that - a refugee camp. It was very basic, the men sleeping on the ground or on camp beds, but the occupants did seem jovial and in good spirits.

The men assembled to listen to Mr Benn in the large lounge they were using as a bar and social area. The MP wrote down their particulars and their feelings and mentioned that he had received a lot of letters from their relatives giving details about them. Above all, he was able to tell them that people back in the UK were taking a great interest in their plight and doing everything they could to get them out. He explained fully to them what he would be saying to President Saddam: that the Iraqi leader was in a corner and should let all the hostages go immediately. There followed a question and answer session which covered most options surrounding the release of the hostages. The men all looked healthy. They were getting plenty of food. Their only real concern was when they would be allowed home.

"What I realised when I was out there was that the hostages were very convenient to the British government. They were pawns in the *British* government's game, as much as in Saddam's. The British felt that, while they were there, it could build up all the terrible conditions for the hostages without making much of an effort to get them released."

Mr Benn felt that the British embassy had been effectively told not to give him any help, and they did give him very little. But the ambassador, from his viewpoint, felt he tried to help Mr Benn in every way he could. He did give Mr Benn a supplementary list of hostages, but no car, or interpreter, or use of embassy facilities or staff. In contrast, a leading Canadian politician, Svend Robinson, shadow Canadian Foreign Secretary, who was part of an all-party Canadian delegation which had been in Baghdad for a week without seeing Saddam, had use of a Canadian embassy car, an interpreter, embassy facilities and staff, and was very well looked after. Mr Benn relied upon an Iraqi car and Iraqi hospitality. But then, so had Mr Heath.

The mood of people held in Baghdad, though not part of the human shield, was very bitter towards the British government. Three of them visited Tony Benn in his suite on the first evening. They were traditional British businessmen, but they were, in Mr Benn's words, "very, very angry at the behaviour of the British government."

Baghdad was a real centre of world affairs in those last days of November. Every leader or shadow-leader in the world seemed to be present. Daniel Ortega was there from Nicaragua, as was Yasser Arafat of the PLO. "The place was really buzzing." There were also about twenty British women and the occasional American woman out there, trying to see their husbands. Dorothy Goodwin was there with her party, as they prepared to leave for the UK and Anne Mansell was gathering a group around her. Dozens more were applying for visas. The hotels were full of Westerners debating the crisis and demanding to go home. Tony Benn was the first senior British politician they had serious access to. Mr Heath had only limited time for them, whereas Mr Benn made himself much more accessible. As a result, he found himself in constant demand. Significantly, the British trapped there were not only asking him to put their case to Saddam but, even more urgently, wanted him to put their case to the British government. That was where their overweening concern lay - to change *its* attitude. They saw *that* as the main obstacle to their release. Once the British government became more conciliatory and started dialogue, they felt sure they would be on their way home.

Every day was packed and pressured. Every moment was taken up with meeting Iraqi leaders, talking to hostages, doing press statements or preparing what he was going to say to Saddam. That second evening Mr Benn met the Speaker of the Iraqi Parliament, as part of the obligatory round of diplomatic meetings every important visitor had to go through. The media in Baghdad was much more interested in his visit than that at home. They followed him everywhere.

On the morning of the third day of his visit, Wednesday 28th November, Mr Benn spent three hours with Saddam Hussein. He went alone, but faced nine Iraqis in all. They included several cabinet ministers, Tariq Aziz, reporters and interpreters. The reporters and TV crew soon left them to talk in private.

To Mr Benn's consternation, Saddam was in military uniform and was wearing a pistol on a belt around his waist. The Labour MP introduced himself, then asked whether he could speak his mind, which Saddam said he could, so he did. "The first main point I made was, 'I have *not* come just to get British hostages - my quota. I've come to persuade you to restore freedom of movement to *all* foreign residents in Iraq. They're *all* ambassadors for peace and when they return home they will press their governments for peace.'

Mr Benn was not allowed to record the conversation, but made detailed briefing notes beforehand and detailed notes of the replies immediately afterwards. These are his notes regarding the hostages:

Danger and opportunity. Time is against us. The world is opposed to the status quo in the Gulf and doesn't want war. On Thursday, the UN Security Council meets. There will be a deadline and ultimatum set at it... My task is to encourage hope, to campaign for peace. Then I told him of the letters I'd received. I believe it is time for a major new Iraqi peace initiative, in three parts. The first is the free movement of residents; they will be ambassadors for peace; they are no protection to you from war; the US and UK are using the hostages for their own interests, and they have shown no real interest in them; the hostages in Kuwait want the liberation of Kuwait and to protect their Kuwaiti friends; they are being used as a main argument for war. Therefore, you should make an historic statement. 'All residents can come and go.' They will be ambassadors for peace. They will transform the political situation, reaffirm traditional Arab hospitality and open the way to peace talks. I hope I may take our people home.

There were five minute 'chunks' of argument each way. Mr Benn's other main points were to do with general political concerns, such as respecting UN resolutions and Palestine. One of his strongest arguments was that Saddam should pre-empt the UN debate and stave off the ultimatum and deadline of war. But to every point, Saddam replied, "If I do that, how do you know the Americans aren't going to attack me anyway?"

Mr Benn had to play the game of pretending the hostages were 'guests'. Whilst he used the term 'foreign resident' rather than waste time quibbling over the term 'hostage', Saddam Hussein persisted in calling them guests, to which Mr Benn replied, "In that case, why don't you restore their freedom of movement? With the best will in the world, imagine a friend of Iraq in Britain. Two years ago, Kuwait is a friendly country, helping you against Iran. Last July, it was an unfriendly state. Then in August, you tell us that there's a new Kuwaiti government which is friendly to us. Now you tell us Kuwait has always been part of Iraq. You're a lawyer. How can you expect anyone to believe four legal interpretations of your relationship to Kuwait in the last year?" At that stage, according to Mr Benn, Saddam Hussein admitted to him that he hadn't really wanted to go into Kuwait.

It was a rivetting discussion during which Mr Benn put his case as well as he could. "Saddam Hussein was a very interesting person. I've met a lot of dictators in my life. I spent hours with the Shah of Iran and I was with Ceaucescu, but it was a very, very intelligent, interesting, intense, exciting discussion. I worked for days on my brief, every night, deciding how to present the argument. It was a very, very intelligent discussion. It was a very tight, intellectual argument. He is a very clever person. He addressed my arguments and then allowed me to make my points. And I was absolutely blunt with him. He's a lawyer, not a soldier. At one stage, he took off his pistol which he had on his belt, and I thought I'd gone too far. But he put it on the couch beside him...

"His explanation of the invasion of Kuwait was a very skilful one. During the war with Iran, the Kuwaitis moved the frontier eighty kilometres north and took the Rumillah oilfield from Iraq. He said, 'I would be happy to withdraw from Kuwait if I thought the Americans weren't going to move in and attack me from there anyway'." By remaining in Kuwait, Saddam felt he was protecting Iraq as well, because he feared an American invasion or bombing war to destroy his military power anyway. "The arguments he used were very credible and he was very friendly. Of course, the brutality of the regime is unquestionable."

Amazingly, during the discussion, Saddam told Mr Benn that, "Within a week every 'foreign resident' could have freedom of movement restored." !

Mr Benn felt his arguments had made some impact on Saddam's thoughts. His interpreter came up to him afterwards and explained how pleased Saddam had been with the discussion. Whether that was merely politeness or reflected an honest opinion is anyone's guess and, obviously, strategic interests were the overwhelming reason Saddam changed his tactics.

On the second day, Mr Benn had visited a large group of hostages assembled in the Melia al-Mansour Hotel. They had only recently been moved up from Kuwait and, when they heard they would be meeting Mr Benn, had high hopes of being the ones he would take home. Indeed, Mr Benn received that distinct impression from the Iraqis himself.

One of the hostages just up from Kuwait, who was expecting to be released with Mr Benn, seemed to be speaking for all the others when he asked a question. "I know we don't want to talk about the stress on the families at the moment. We know that. In fact, we have people here with wives who've had nervous breakdowns, about whom we're very concerned. What we as a group want to focus on now is the future. The future being your visit here, the future being your meeting with the President, what you are going to propose to the President. Speaking as a group, we are all completely disgusted with the British government. Completely disgusted. It is the only word we can use for it. What Maggie Thatcher's said has let us all down and kept us all here. You are our greatest chance at the moment and will be in the near future. We are all for peace, without doubt. Will you be discussing with Saddam Hussein the disgust of us with the British government's attitude? Will that be one of your points?"

"The British government are using you as pawns in their game." This was met with nods of approval, 'Hear, Hear' and a round of applause. "If the British government is really quite happy to have you stranded here and in difficulties, how can it be in the interests of the Iraqi government that they should be helping the British government by leaving you here?"

Mr Benn reassured the men - and those women visiting their husbands and sons - about how he would try to do things for them when he went back as well. They were obviously very cheered by his visit. There was humour and laughter at the end of it and they were on a high. For most, it was the first time they had met a leading politician who cared about their plight. They were very grateful and also hopeful.

That evening, rather than going with Mr Benn, they were nearly all moved out to strategic sites. The reporter for *The Times* described the scene:

> Amid scenes of despair and anger, scores of plain-clothes Iraqi security men last night arrived at the Melia al-Mansour Hotel in Baghdad and told sixty-two Britons, many of them British Airways staff, to prepare to leave for strategic installations to become part of Iraq's human shield against attack. The order was a blow for the hostages, who had been brought from similar sites in Kuwait, believing they were to be freed as a result of Tony Benn's visit to Iraq. In fact, the order came just minutes after Mr Benn, Labour MP for Chesterfield, had met them...
>
> Harold Walker, the British ambassador, condemned hostage taking and said the men had earlier been given to understand that they would be freed either soon or in time for Christmas.
>
> *The Times, Wednesday 28th November*

It was awful. Mr Benn felt quite dismayed and made his feelings plain to the Iraqis. He only heard about their fate as he was preparing to leave Iraq and felt "utterly betrayed". He argued bitterly with Saddam's office over the phone and continued to press for the release of as many as he could. One was Don Majors. Three of his family had contacted his office before he left, emphasising Don's poor medical state and his weak heart. Mr Benn stressed his case, as he did those of several other seriously ill hostages, but to no effect. Don was to die two days after Mr Benn left Baghdad, just a week before the general release.

Overall, Mr Benn spent more time with the hostages in Baghdad than doing anything else. That last night of his visit, Mr Benn went to a final meeting, held at the Novotel, of everyone he had met; the Baghdad workers, the men in the embassy compound, some of the construction workers who were working on Saddam's palace, reporters, businessmen and some from the hotels. Again, the discussion revolved around their future and the prospects for war.

Mr Benn rejected the idea that he, or other 'missionaries' were simply being used by Saddam as propaganda weapons. The Iraqi leader was certainly glorying in being a magnet for high-level visits and Mr Benn admitted Saddam was very astute: "You were dealing with an extremely clever person. A very brutal one, but a very clever one. From that point of view, you could argue that he was [using us]." However, Mr Benn believed that, despite being used, he was able to put his point of view across very strongly to the President. And he turned the question on its head, to criticise his critics. "Why didn't others go? Why were there no negotiations going on? Why was there no dialogue? During the Cuban Crisis, Kruschev and Kennedy were in constant and direct contact on a hot line. But there was no contact at all during this crisis. And that was what persuaded me that the Americans were determined to go to war anyway."

Mr Benn did not secure the release of a great many hostages, only about fifteen. Nor did he fly out with the men he had secured the release of, simply because he did not want to 'exploit' the ones who returned, as Jesse Jackson had done. There was a great deal of confusion around who was coming out and when, and he was only planning to stay in Baghdad for four days, so he had no alternative but to leave without them. They followed on a few days later, on ordinary flights out of Iraq. Six came out on the second and a further nine came out a few days later. But by then Saddam had decided on a complete release, so how many went as 'his' batch was far less important than for previous missions.

It seems evident that such arguments as Mr Heath, Herr Brandt and Mr Benn presented must have emphasised to Saddam the folly of keeping the hostages, rather than encouraged him to hang onto them. Despite the media campaign and genuine fear of many people, including relatives and hostages, that the missions would simply string out the hostage releases and give Saddam welcome ammunition, in practice the visits had a cumulative propaganda effect upon the Iraqi leadership itself, which served to undermine its policy and make it aware of its miscalculation.

"When did you leave?"

"About the third or fourth of December."

"Why did you decide to leave then?"

"Women like Dorothy Goodwin had started flying from Britain to Baghdad to get their men out. They succeeded. So I thought, if I could fly out to Britain, get a visa and fly back again, I could get Andrew out as well."

During the last weeks of November the Stevensons had noticed an easing of camp discipline and an improvement in their food and conditions. The Iraqi leadership was increasingly sensitive to criticism of the camps and was moving towards releasing the hostages. They had been allowed to make two phone calls, one to Andrew's parents and one to Carolyn's. They were only given a few minutes, then were cut off in mid-sentence, but things were definitely relaxing. They decided to give their plan a go.

Carolyn was driven through Basra and up to Baghdad in a stolen Kuwaiti vehicle, so every time the driver stopped, he had to hot-wire it to start it again. It was a large four-wheel drive, filled in the back with hi-fi equipment purloined from Kuwait. She was alone with one Iraqi soldier who was carrying an AK47 and a revolver. She was terrified to go to sleep in case he attacked her. They left Basra at three in the afternoon and arrived in Baghdad at about midnight. On the way, the guard visited his mother's and his aunt's to drop off videos, televisions and other goodies for them.

When she arrived at the Melia al-Mansour, she was shown up to a room. It was two o'clock in the morning. She looked at herself in a mirror. She was in a real mess. Her hair hadn't been washed in clean water or with shampoo for months, she had been given nothing to wash with other than the dirty warm water of the camp and bars of cheap soap. Her clothes were worn out and unironed. Her shoes were on their last legs. But she was too tired to care. That night, she slept in a decent bed for the first time in three months.

The next day, Carolyn met Dorothy Goodwin, who advised her not to return to Britain, but just to go to Amman, then return to Baghdad. She also met Anne Mansell. She was wonderful to Carolyn. She had arrived stocked with tins of food, great pork pies, toiletries, medicines, everything she thought the men might need. When she saw Carolyn, she invited her up to her room to join a party that night. Once there, she showed Carolyn the stuff she and the other women had brought with them. When she heard she was pregnant, she instructed her to take a cod liver oil pill and an iron pill, then a multi-vitamin pill. That night, she tried to eat her first proper meal for three months, but had to leave most of it. Her stomach had shrunk.

Carolyn decided she would take Dorothy Goodwin's advice and fly to Amman. She flew out, stayed one night, then flew back the following day. She booked back into the Melia al-Mansour and demanded to see Andrew. The Iraqis were not sympathetic. They complained that she had played a trick on them and delayed sending for him. Carolyn was extremely distressed and pleaded with the Iraqis. Through her guard, she was eventually allowed to phone Andrew in the camp and tell him what was happening.

Andrew had missed Carolyn far more than he had expected. He found it very difficult suddenly being on his own and became depressed, anxious and withdrawn. He had expected her back within two days, but even four or five days later, the Iraqis were telling him that she still wasn't back. When he heard from Carolyn on the phone about her trip to Amman and back and how the Iraqis were now prevaricating and objecting, he went mad. He blew his top at the guards. "I threatened to take this Iraqi apart. They had been really messing me and Carolyn about, so I said, 'Right, either you get me up to Baghdad tomorrow or I'm walking out the gate, and you ain't big enough to stop me.' John Wayne would have been proud of him.

Andrew's bravado hid a frustration and an anger which had been pent up for months, ready to explode. He was at boiling point. The thought of what the Iraqis might be putting Carolyn through made it even worse. "We had been so close all the way through. We have always been very close, even more so now we're back and it's all over. We went everywhere together."

"We would even go to the loo together," Carolyn added, smiling, "because I was afraid they'd take Andy away when I wasn't there. You could never trust them."

It was two weeks before Cynthia Hill's flight was confirmed. Those days brought back the worst of the early times. She had an awful lot of organising and worrying to do. Her sleeping at night went completely haywire. She couldn't relax. She was constantly worrying about Derek and throwing herself around the bed over her decision to go. If the worst came to bear, who could she trust to bring her children up?

The hardest thing would not be the actual trip. That would be relatively straight-forward. The trauma lay over deciding *whether* to go and making all the arrangements for the children. Eventually, she decided to entrust them to her mother, who would move into the house to look after them. Then there was their food to consider. She went to the supermarket and bought everything she could think off until the freezer was packed. She purchased a turkey and Christmas pudding and all the trimmings for the Christmas meal. She filled a number of cardboard boxes with more food. "Don't let anyone tell you, you can't do your Christmas shopping in forty-eight hours!" Cynthia told me, throwing back her blonde hair and laughing. "Usually, Derek and I go Christmas shopping together, but this time I had to do it all myself. I was constantly wondering whether I'd ever see him again."

Another worry was when to come back. Her return flight was booked for 21st December, but Saddam had announced he would start releasing the hostages after Christmas and she was determined that, once out there, she was not going to return without Derek. So she had to plan for the children to be on their own over Christmas. She had to explain that to them as well, but they accepted it without any qualms. In fact, Rachel thought it was a better solution. She felt that then she would have Grandma with her for Christmas and Daddy would have Mummy with him. It seemed fairer that way.

Cynthia knew the guilt she would suffer if she didn't go. "I could not have sat here with my children on Christmas Day and watched on that television other people being released. It's a terrible feeling because I had a double guilt complex: the guilt at leaving my children if I did go, and the guilt that, if it had come off for other people and I hadn't chanced my arm, how could I face the children then? I was absolutely torn down the middle over what to do."

The wife of Norman Thompson, who was on the installation with Derek, wanted to go with her. Another woman, Val Ireland, who had been with Derek in the SAS Hotel when Iraq invaded said she would go as well. Gradually, a group built up as more women contacted her. In the end there were nine of them planning to go. They each had to go through the process of getting visas from the Jordanian and Iraqi embassies. The Iraqis insisted none of the women flew straight from London. They had to spend at least one night in Jordan and fly on.

By now, the Jordanian embassy had developed a reputation amongst the wives for tardiness, with its 'Come back tomorrow, come back tomorrow' attitude. "Can I tell you about the Jordanian embassy?" Cynthia glared. "I'd arranged for my Iraqi visa first and I'd got their embassy to courier it round to the Jordanian embassy the day before I went to pick it up, so it would be there for my collection. I was meeting two other ladies there. All of us had gone in personally and especially. But the ambassador wasn't there to put his rubber stamp on mine. The other two ladies had theirs done and were handed their passports but I was still sat there. 'You'll have to come back tomorrow,' they said. 'But I've only called in to collect it. It was brought in yesterday.' I had to insist on staying there until he'd gone back and found it."

The women bravely decided to contact the press. They were not going to sneak into Baghdad by the back door. They wanted to get as much publicity for their trip as possible. It would put pressure on the British and Iraqi governments to do something and they would feel much safer if people knew they were out there. It was the first time Cynthia had contacted the media. Until then, she had completely avoided it, mainly for the sake of the children. Now she felt differently, although it meant attending a press conference at the Palace of Westminster and inviting all their MPs to attend, as well as Douglas Hogg from the Foreign Office.

Even at this late stage, only a few days before the announcement of the general release, Britons in hiding were still being arrested, sent up to Baghdad and despatched to the strategic sites. Cliff Lindley was one of them. He had been caught late in November, spent some time in a hotel in Kuwait, then been driven up to the Melia al-Mansour Hotel. The place was buzzing with women demanding their husbands, pressmen and hostages. Many of the men were hoping to be released and the whole atmosphere of the hotel was fraught with tension. However, the only release Cliff had was when he contracted severe diarrhoea. "Most people in the Mansour had food poisoning. Very few survived there without getting a dose."

Late one night, about the fifth of December, Cliff's group were suddenly ordered to pack their things and be downstairs in quarter of an hour. There was no point resisting. They were ordered onto a bus with a number of others. The coach had its curtains drawn to prevent them knowing where they were going, but Cliff surreptitiously opened his. They passed under the huge crossed swords memorial to the martyrs of the Iran-Iraq War. Dave Fitzmorris was with him, who knew Iraq very well, and they had met up with Chris Haig-Prothero at one of the hotels, who also knew Iraq well. They were taken about eighty kilometres south, towards ancient Babylon - modern al-Hillah.

The installation was not as bad as Cliff feared. It manufactured shells and bullets and was a very large complex of camouflaged buildings, with five groups of hostages on the one complex. "We had comfortable beds in the rooms. There were two of us in each. I was sharing with Chris." It was an office block positioned in the middle of the enormous hangar-type factory buildings. It was surrounded by a high, corrugated aluminium fence to prevent any hostage seeing what was happening in the factory. The guards were living in the offices as well. They tended to be armed with pistols rather than rifles and seemed very relaxed. There were three couples, plus two Americans who were returned to Baghdad as soon as Cliff's group arrived because their wives had returned to Iraq to visit them. Some of the other groups were actually inside the factory buildings. One group was stuck up in some offices in a corner of one of the hangars.

"The Iraqis were very good. They were interchanging us between groups, letting us visit each other. They weren't completely mean. We could go over to one group and have a booze-up, then come back to ours and have another booze-up. The Iraqis weren't stopping us. In the main, the run-of-the-mill soldiers didn't want the situation." However, by now the men's final release was very much on the cards, so the hostages' treatment and conditions had dramatically improved. In fact, Cliff and Chris were only on the site one day before the release was announced and, two days after that, they were back in Baghdad. They had very nearly survived the entire period up to their release in hiding.

Their stay at the site was so brief, it was more of an interesting interlude than harrowing experience. The food was good and there was "tons of it". Speaking to other people who had been on the site for a while, it had improved greatly. "From what I was told, the conditions were awful until the French were released. The toilets weren't very good. They were proper lavatories, but they were smelly, with water all over the floor and an old-fashioned sink. It was like an old, derelict brew house or an outside loo. There were proper pans, but not in good condition or particularly clean. They did have regular visits from doctors and once the French were let out, conditions did get better. I think it was because the French got up a petition and protested for the conditions to be improved." As the French release was part of the overall build-up to the general release, it is difficult to be precise on the affect they had. But those British on the site were generally very grateful for the efforts the released Frenchmen put in for them and it demonstrated the camaraderie which had built up between the nationalities on the sites.

A great deal had happened in the time Carolyn had been in Jordan. A couple of days after Hilary Jones and Anne Mansell arrived in Baghdad, another two women flew in and joined them at the Melia al-Mansour. There were also a few women who had remained with their husbands in the installations but who had now come up to Baghdad to see if they could get their husbands out. What with the husbands of Dorothy Goodwin's party, plus the men in transit to the camps like Cliff Lindley, the Baghdad hotels were filling up. Meanwhile, the Iraqi embassy in London was being swamped with women applying for visas, all of whom would be demanding to see the Iraqi leaders and further filling up the hotels. Some members of the Iraqi government were starting to panic about this prospect. As many British had already noticed, the Iraqis found it extremely difficult to deal with stubborn, angry and determined Western women.

When in Baghdad, it became apparent to the British women that they had to play the Iraqi's game. They had to play with words. They had to say they wanted peace in the Gulf and had come on a mission of sisterly friendship. They had to visit women's organisations and members of the Iraqi parliament. They had to drape the mantle of a Peace Movement over their shoulders. They had to play the game shamelessly, simply to get the sympathetic ear of the Iraqis.

"I went around to see everybody and anybody," Anne Mansell recalled with a smile. "Oh, I'm from this peace movement in Britain and we want peace. Christmas is a time for giving and goodwill, the dove of peace, and so on. Heavens, anything!" She laughed as she remembered. "But we didn't just want *our* husbands. We said they should let everybody go, although we couldn't push it too much in case they turned against us."

The Iraqi security men who accompanied the groups of women didn't know what had hit them. They respected these women and treated them very well. When they asked for something, they tried to comply, but they were *constantly* demanding things, *perpetually* requesting to see people and *time and again* pestering everybody they could think of. They were angry and determined women who were not going to be put off easily. They were fighting for their husbands. It was too much for the Iraqis.

Anne, Hilary Jones and the other women were like agony aunts to the men. They would be surrounded as they sat in the hotel lounge by men wanting to experience female company again. They were of all ages and hadn't spoken to women for a very long time. They were full of anxieties and problems, and desperate for someone to talk to about their experiences. They were uptight, they were thin; some had thick beards, many looked pale and grey; more were ill with diarrhoea or recovering from dysentery.

There was so much tension, frustration and anger about. Many of the men were drinking heavily after months without alcohol, until they were paralytic. In that state, all their bitterness against the Iraqis boiled to the surface and they couldn't control it. Several times fights broke out as

British men tried to attack Iraqi soldiers. The women found themselves having to calm down the belligerent talk and arguments which erupted continually. The men were having to deal with very frustrating phone calls as well. Not only were they cut off after a few minutes, but sometimes the news from home was upsetting. One man was told by his wife that she had left him. He was so distraught he smashed up his room and ripped the wallpaper off, though he later came down and apologised to the hostages and to the hotel staff. The Melia al-Mansour was not a nice place to be in.

The British men were all kept on the top floors of the hotel, well away from any embassy officials or pressmen who might try to get in. In effect, the hotel was *incommunicado* for long periods. If the men wanted to go down to the dining room, they had to be accompanied by a guard. So too when they went up again. It was harder for the men to get to the dining room alone than for the women to get out of Iraq. It was ludicrous - so absurd, it became a joke.

Before she had come out, Anne Mansell had been involved in preparing for international Yellow Ribbon Day, due for Sunday the second of December, to mark the fourth month of the Iraqi occupation of Kuwait. News of the event had spread from the USA and Britain to the Gulf. Being a Sunday, the Reverend Michael Jones decided to hold a service for all those involved in the Gulf conflict - the hostages, the people in hiding, and those Iraqis, Kuwaitis and others caught up in it. The service was held in a reception room at the Melia al-Mansour Hotel which was converted into a chapel with an altar. Reverend Jones had been held in Baghdad ever since he had arrived with the British embassy convoy, ministering as best he could to the Anglican community there. His daughter Hilary helped organise the service. There were about forty or fifty British men in the hotel at the time and most of them turned up, along with the women present. They made everybody, including the Iraqis, wear yellow ribbons. They were happy to, as it served to promote the idea of peace.

In a further effort to raise morale, Hilary, Anne and the other women invited people into their room for gatherings. Officially there was just coffee drunk, but usually beers and spirits would find their way in. During these soirées, the two women would open their suitcases full of medicines and tins of food. Anne had come fully prepared. She had tea, coffee, dried milk and sugar. They had taken chocolate and cakes and tins of ham. She even had her kettle, so their room was like a café. The men read the English newspapers they had brought out with them. They all asked whether the women had seen their wives, and frequently they were able to say they had. "If we did nothing else, we did a lot during those few days for those men to see and talk to women about themselves and what they'd been through. They gave us messages to take out, letters, all sorts of things."

Whilst in the Melia al-Mansour, the men were treated like prisoners, yet the women could leave the hotel whenever they wished to go shopping, visit the *souk*, or meet Iraqi officials. That was very hard for the men. They had to let the women go and negotiate for their release. They were also very frustrated about the embassy. The overwhelming feeling was that it was a largely a waste of time and space during this period and did very little to improve the men's situation, even in little ways, or to get them released. Anne felt it as well. She had time for only two of its officials, both lowly ones, Julian Lyons and Caroline Cross, who were both 'floaters', moving from embassy to embassy and both in their early twenties.

By now, there were five other women with Anne Mansell and Hilary Jones. They had arrived in ones or twos, but soon realised they could get more done as a group. One of them was Carolyn Stevenson, who had arrived back in Baghdad just in time to join them. They were given a 'minder', a man from the security services who acted as their interpreter. He was a very nice man who even brought his small children up to see them. He had obviously been given instructions to ensure they went through the right channels and saw the right people. There was clearly a set procedure all the women had to follow. Those who had arrived with Dorothy Goodwin had been taken along the same route. Those groups of British, Japanese, French, American and Filipino women who followed went along it as well.

The minder arranged transport for them and appointments to see people. He also arranged for Iraqi television to come and film them for propaganda purposes. It was getting near Christmas and they were constantly asked what their message was to the people of Iraq. "They kept trying to make us say what they wanted to hear. But all we would say was that Christmas was a time for giving and for peace. 'Have you got nothing else to say?' they would ask. 'No, just that Christmas is a peaceful time.'" Anne laughed as she remembered the games the women and media had to play, each trying to get what they could from the other. "They kept coming round and round with the same question and we were keeping giving them exactly the same answer."

The first visit had to be to the Iraqi Women's Federation. Their minder warned them that, if they wanted the women's federation to support their case, they should bribe them with gifts for the mothers and children in Iraq. Taking the hint, they descended on the *souk* and bought nappies, baby clothes, baby food, dried milk, toys and everything else they could think off, and wrapped them in yellow ribbons as presents for Iraqi children. There was a whole bus full of gifts for them. Their visit to the women's federation was a massive exercise in fawning.

Following the success of that visit, they met the Speaker of the Iraqi Parliament, a powerless and ineffectual man, as it was Saddam who made all the decisions that were rubber-stamped by that body. He, too, was very polite and welcoming. The friendliness of their reception was an encouraging sign. One woman, Carolyn Hughes, acted as spokesperson. She was extremely placatory towards the Iraqi, telling him that, if their menfolk died, they were sure it wouldn't be by the Iraqis, but by the Americans. That seemed to please the Speaker. She said how they had children and how much they loved all children, especially Iraqi children, and spoke about their desire for peace and the warmth they felt for the Iraqi people and how they didn't want war or to harm the Iraqi people in any way. To their joy, the Speaker told them their husbands had been given permission to join them in Baghdad.

Soon after their audience with the Speaker, another group of about thirty British women arrived in Baghdad. They were followed by a group of fifty Japanese women. So many were flying in that the Iraqis stopped issuing visas from their embassy in London. Their promise to all the wives to visit their husbands over Christmas was turning into a bureaucratic nightmare. Moving men to and from the installations, putting them up in the hotels, trying to guard them but letting the women go free, dealing with all their requests and petitions and demands for meetings, was swamping them. They had clearly bitten off more than they could chew.

Anne's minder confirmed this impression. "He said to me, all the men will go. We can't cope with this. Every few days more women are coming. We don't want this." Anne was certain that the prospect of thousands of wives descending on them was a nightmare. Even now, she is positive that one of the reasons the Iraqis let all the men go was the hundreds of women applying for visas to return. They couldn't handle the few already out there. "There was just no way Iraq could cope with it."

It soon became clear to the women that criticisms of them going out to Iraq were unfounded. At home, the government and much of the press was arguing strongly against them going. They were splitting the alliance, they were allowing themselves to be used for propaganda and were playing into Saddam's hands by diverting attention from his occupation of Kuwait to the side issue of the hostages. To the government, other issues were more important. It was scathing about a parallel diplomacy which they feared would undermine both the UN's call for unconditional Iraqi withdrawal from Kuwait and the growing military pressure on Saddam.

However, Anne insists they were right to take matters into their own hands. "If we hadn't gone out, they might still have released the men, but a lot later. I felt they might release the men *because* we went out. Who knows? And who's to say? Just because Bush is President of America doesn't mean to say he's right. From a wife's point of view, two thousand hostages were only a drop in the ocean to him, so it was on the cards that he would send the troops in whether the hostages were out or not. I knew that. We all knew that. I was prepared for that to happen. But, I thought, Bush and Thatcher can't do anything for the men, so I have to try. The situation was changing day to day. When I left I had no intention of bringing Stephen back but when out there the Iraqis told me that, if I did as I was asked, I would get him out. So, was I supposed to say I wasn't going to do it? Every day was different. Stephen was in such a state I needed to get out to see him. If I hadn't, he might have done anything. I had no choice in the end. When it comes down to someone you love, there can never be any doubt in your mind."

In Britain, things were bumping along very much as they had been throughout the crisis. There was moderate coverage of Tony Benn's visit, interspersed with condemnations by both US and British governments. One Western diplomat said, "In a civilised world you normally punish kidnappers, you do not pander to them. The presence of these women only adds to the Iraqi inventory of human shields". Even Dan Quayle, US Vice-President, added his half-penny's worth - and that's about all it *was* worth.

None of this deterred the relatives who wished to go to Baghdad. Even more women were applying for visas. The Iraqis tried to channel this deluge by saying they would organise a huge Christmas party for them all, which only underlined that they had no idea of the extent of the response. The Iraqi and Jordanian embassies were being swamped by a flood of women, all determined to demand their men be immediately released. More were applying in the United States. It was getting out of hand. The hostages were rapidly slipping from the Iraqis' grasp and their strategy was falling apart at the seams. Undoubtedly, the prospect of thousands of women flocking to Baghdad was a significant cause of the sudden decision to let all the men go.

Unfortunately, at the most crucial moment, when Saddam and the Iraqi leadership was coming round to the idea of releasing all the hostages, the hostages disappeared from the news. On 29th November, the United Nations Security Council passed Resolution 678 setting a final deadline for Iraqi withdrawal from Kuwait of 15th January. The week before had been dominated by American diplomatic pressure to secure the passing of the resolution, Mrs Thatcher's resignation, and the battle for leadership of the Conservative Party. The hostages virtually disappeared from the news, apart from snippets on the humanitarian visits. That was why, when the general release was announced, it came as such a surprise. Not because it was a sudden change of heart by the Iraqis, but because the media simply hadn't been interested - and the British government had been effectively paralysed.

The passing of the resolution had the final effect of making plain to the Iraqi government that the hostages were, as Edward Heath, Willy Brandt, Tony Benn and all the others had explained, simply not going to deter the American and British governments from war. All Iraqi pressure had achieved was to postpone the deadline from 1st January, as wanted by the Americans, to the fifteenth, thereby appeasing the Soviet Union. The Christmas-to-March strategy had failed. Saddam had no realistic option other than to use the release of all the hostages as a final gamble to win over world public opinion. As the president said on the twenty-fifth of November, he would put his faith in averting conflict by appealing to Western public opinion rather than political leaders.

Stephen Mansell finally arrived at the Melia al-Mansour after being driven up from Basra. He was in an awful state, very depressed and thin. He looked terrible. As the days passed, he thought more and more about his imminent return to the refinery. It petrified him. He kept telling Anne he would never see her or the children again. Anne tried to comfort him and said she would try to get him an extension on his stay. Meanwhile, he had to cope with both Iraqi guards and other hostages cruelly pulling his leg about how they were about to take him away again.

Every other woman, apart from Carolyn Stevenson, was allowed to see her husband. They arrived in varying stages of exhaustion or elation. Carolyn was growing increasingly anxious, but on the evening of the fifth a guard called to her as she sat in the lounge of the Melia al-Mansour. She turned round and there was Andrew standing by the doorway. He was the last of the husbands to meet his wife. The next day, on Thursday 6th December, Saddam announced the release of all the men.

Release!

"a victory for humanity"

"We have found that the reasons that... prevented the travel of foreigners have weakened and been replaced by... good transformations in American public opinion that are restricting the intentions and decisions of evil-doers led by the enemy of God, Bush. For these reasons I call upon you, brothers, [*ie* the Iraqi Parliament] to adopt your just decision to lift the travel ban on all foreigners with our apologies for all harm and forgiveness from God Almighty... the time has come when our forces are fully prepared if they had to fight against the atheist, treacherous people and in defence of nationalistic and humanitarian gains."

Saddam Hussein in a letter to the Iraqi Parliament, 6th December

SADDAM SENDS HOSTAGES HOME FOR CHRISTMAS

President Saddam Hussein yesterday ordered the release of all foreigners held in Iraq and Kuwait "with our apologies for all harm". He said they had given great service to the cause of peace, but were no longer needed and could be home for Christmas...

President Saddam said he was bringing forward the release of other foreigners because Iraq no longer needed the "human shield" since its forces were sufficiently dug-in to counter any attack...

Holding the hostages "has given a great service to the cause of peace" [Saddam] said, "and because God has taught us that prohibitions should only be used in extreme cases, it is our duty not to prolong these emergency measures".

The Times, 7th December

The day book for the London helpline starts usually enough. A man phoned at 9.30am saying he was going to Baghdad to get his son and wanted details of how to go about it. Quarter of an hour later a woman phoned. She too was going to Baghdad and wanted the names of others, to form a group. Two packages arrived, and someone enquired about the Green Party. It was a casual, even routine morning until, about twelve, the phones suddenly went wild. Sue Dorrington was in the Gulf Support Group offices when the announcement of the men's release came through. She took the first phone call.

"Hello, London Gulf Support Group."

"Have you heard, on the news?"

"Heard what?"

"It's just been announced on the news. Saddam's agreed to let everyone go, all foreigners who want to leave."

"Has he?" Sue had heard nothing about it, so was sceptical. Was this another distressed caller raising her hopes too high? She looked across at Jocelyn, the shift supervisor. By now, all the other phones were ringing and the other volunteers were taking identical messages. It was true! Saddam had announced the hostages could all go free! A few minutes later, the Reuter line confirmed the news. Yet it seemed too good to be true. It couldn't be true. Could it? Not after so long?

Sue made the mental leap and decided it *was* true. It had to be! Once she accepted it, it was a big release. "Wheeeee!" She stood up and hugged the nearest woman to her. It was a wonderful moment. Someone scrawled across the day book: BERSERK! and MAYHEM! as relatives continued to jam the switchboard. There was another call for Sue. She picked up the phone. To her amazement, it was her husband, Dave, calling from the East German embassy in Baghdad.

"Have you heard?" he asked

"Yes, all hell's broken loose over here. Everything is total confusion. I'm so excited I can't get my breath."

"It's true then?" His voice came through crackly and barely audible. The noise and excitement in the Ops Room didn't help, with people screaming and laughing with delight.

"Can't you hear our celebrations?"

"Don't celebrate too early, it might be a trick. But I have to go now. Hopefully, I'll see you soon, Love."

"Oh yes. Love you."

And he was gone.

Then the press calls started. Sue Nicholson from World at One phoned, then the *Guardian*, then John Gurnett from the Jimmy Young Show, followed by the *Bristol Evening Post*, Greater London Radio, the Green Party, the *Financial Times* and many, many more.

In the midst of all this media attention a few relatives managed to get through with their regular problems, many of whom hadn't heard the news. One "wanted help with his phone bill" and was delighted to be told what had happened; another "has a three-bedroomed house and is happy for a family coming to the airport to stay a night. No charge." A woman phoned to thank Joanna Copley for her comments on the news. But an anonymous caller demanded bitterly "why there's such a fuss being made about the hostages when they've been earning so much money".

The Coventry day book was as busy. The volunteers there were inundated. People were phoning for confirmation of the news - ecstatic, worried, sceptical, joyous, yet having to withhold their joy in case it was another false dawn. The phones were so busy, Stephen was called back from work and arrived at about two o'clock. The media were all over him. At one point there were six television news teams in his house, plus a radio crew.

That Wednesday, December the fifth, Josie had decided to visit London. She was in a desperate state physically, with her back causing her agony. She had not taken a break for weeks and wrote in her diary: "Went to London for a break. Emotionally drained." She booked into a hotel in Knightsbridge for a two day break. It had a swimming pool, which allowed her to take exercise for her back and relieve her spinal pain.

Once she had booked in, all thought of rest vanished and she made her way to the London Support Group. She was addicted to it. The plight of the relatives never left her mind. She was constantly aware she may be needed at any time, that she had a duty to the relatives, that she must never let them down. By now, the needs of her 'family' had become so interwoven with her own emotional needs that even 'getting away' led her sub-consciously to the very heart of activity and pressure.

At Alexandra House she met Joanna Copley and told her she was down for two days. Joanna hadn't had a break from the helpline for a month herself and asked Josie where she was staying. Josie told her.

"Look, we both need a break," Joanna suggested. "Let me come over tomorrow and we'll have a day off together. How about that? We could have a swim and a good chat, about everything except the helpline."

Josie was delighted with the idea and laughed her pleasure.

So the next day, Thursday the sixth, Joanna brought her swimming costume to Josie's hotel and they decided to take things easy around the hotel's pool. In Josie's words, "We were two girls playing. We were going to talk about anything except serious matters, anything to take ourselves out of the situation."

They changed and bought some drinks at the bar, then swanned over to a table by the pool. After sitting and talking about who they were and what they had done with their lives, and about their families and husbands, they slipped into the warm, relaxing water and floated.

Josie describes what happened next.

"We had just got into the pool and were swimming and messing about when my portable phone rang. The manager came up and told me. So I got out of the pool and picked the phone up. It was Stephen from Coventry."

"Hi, Stephen, what's the matter?" Josie was annoyed at having been disturbed.

"It's Saddam. He's releasing all the hostages."

"He's not?"

"He is. It's just come over the fax. Now it's on Ceefax as well. He's releasing them all. "

"He's not?"

"He is. It's all over. It's all over!"

"Oh, Stephen, can it be? Can it finally be true?" There were tears in Josie's eyes as relief mixed with joy, as emotional let-down mixed with amazement and ecstasy. She turned to Joanna and shouted, "Joanna, Saddam's letting them all go!" As Stephen went on telling her details, her mouth fell, her eyes opened wide and her spare hand nervously pushed back her dripping red hair. As Joanna climbed out of the pool, Josie kept repeating, "They're free, they're free! He's letting them go! Saddam's letting them go!"

"When?" Joanna asked.

"When?" Josie asked Stephen, but he didn't know. No details had emerged yet. Scepticism swept over Josie. Was it another of Saddam's games, another way of heartlessly tormenting the relatives and hostages? She sighed with anguish.

Joanna, meanwhile, had become completely transformed. The little girl had gone and the organising woman had returned as she furiously dried her hair with a towel. She realised their intended day of peace was about to become the most intense day of the crisis so far. She knew the media would fly around to the London Support Group. She had to be there. Images of press teams and cameras madly packing into the rooms at Alexandra House filled her with trepidation - and determination. She was steeling herself and clenching her fists.

They were in a real tizzy by now, trying to get changed as fast as they could, throwing clothes around the changing room floor, scrambling for bras, tights and dresses, their wet hair flaying around. Still trying to get her shoes on, Josie followed Joanna out. She was already on her way through the entrance doors. Josie hurried after her, still clasping her wet bathing suit and towel. There was no time to go back to her room. They burst into the cold street and Joanna hailed a passing cab.

Josie described the journey and their arrival at the support group. "We were putting our make-up on as we were going along, so we'd look bright-eyed and bushy-tailed for the cameras. When we arrived at the helpline, it was all hell let loose. Television crews, reporters, cameramen. radio newsmen, lights, tape-recorders, sound equipment; it was mayhem. The big room was absolutely full of journalists and television crews. They were up the walls. And there, waiting for us, was one of Joanna's volunteers with the Reuter message giving the text of Saddam's letter."

Some of the volunteers had found it very hard to accept the news and Josie felt the same. They had become so utterly immunised against Saddam over months of false promises and inhumane actions, and he had played games of cat and mouse with them so many times before, they just didn't believe him.

"We have to go along with it," Joanna argued.

"OK," Josie replied, "so they're coming out, but when? When? I don't believe him."

However, Joanna was already briefing the helpline counsellors, deciding on the approach they should take with the relatives. "When people phone, tell them the news is unconfirmed as yet, that we don't know when or who or how many are involved. Saddam has said all those *held in Iraq*. Does that mean Kuwait as well? Does it mean those in hiding? We think it probably does, since Saddam sees Kuwait as Iraq's forty-ninth province. But we can't be certain on that. OK. That's what we'll say."

Josie watched Joanna cope with the pressure as she vigourous followed through interview after interview. Andy Charles, the press officer, handled other reporters and relatives such as Sue Dorrington did yet more, but it was Joanna's personality in full flow organising, ordering, trying to keep control. There was a job to be done, people were relying on her, lives were in her hands.

Despite the official caution, volunteers at the helpline were becoming more certain and more ecstatic as their pent-up nervous energy began to be released. One of the relatives, Linda Grant, told the press, "I have been in tears all morning. If Saddam Hussein was here at this minute, I would kiss him." And Sue Dorrington told a journalist, "I'm over the moon. It's what we've prayed and prayed for - that they're *all* coming home. It's what we all wanted and have been fighting for, not just one or two, but *all* of them."

Through their stunned disbelief and halting joy, the relatives tried to work out just why Saddam had so suddenly announced the release. In his letter to the Iraqi Parliament, Saddam Hussein alluded to four reasons for the release:

- that prohibitions should only be used in extreme circumstances and this was no longer an extreme circumstance;

- visits from "people of goodwill, men and women from various nationalities and political inclinations," and from Arab delegations, arguing strongly against holding hostages; (The announcement of the release on Iraqi news also stressed the role recent visits by Arab delegations had played, but this may well have been an attempt to butter them up.)

- "the decision by the Democratic majority in the American Congress and the invitation to our Foreign Minister for dialogue with the European parliament"; and

- "good transformations in American public opinion that are restricting the intentions and decisions of evil-doers led by the enemy of God, Bush".

Saddam also stated that the hostages were no longer needed because Iraq was now ready to repel any military attack on Kuwait. However, protection from attack was never a fundamental reason for the human shield, although it was always the moral justification employed by the Iraqis. Throughout August to October, the Iraqis had overwhelmingly superior forces to the Americans. Indeed, in the first two months, the danger was far more of an Iraqi invasion of Saudi Arabia than of Iraq being invaded.

The hostage policy began that very first weekend in August, in direct response to the UN resolution condemning the invasion and to the first American troops moving into the area. The idea constantly peddled by the Iraqis that the hostages had "kept the peace" was nonsense. They hadn't stopped a single troop being deployed - on either side. They were not intended to prevent direct military intervention, but to force America and Britain to the negotiating table *before* they posed an overwhelming military threat. Only when that had failed - in fact, precisely when Iraq could *no longer* defend itself against allied attack - were the hostages given up.

It was not until November that the military balance of forces began to shift decisively towards the allies. If the hostages had been kept to allow for Iraq to prepare its defences, they were held at the wrong time and let go at precisely the moment they were becoming most useful. It is this misconception which leads to problems over why Iraq gave the hostages up when war and defeat seemed so likely. It is because they were never, ever, kept primarily to stall direct military attack.

Many hostages tell of how the Iraqis had plans to rush them to air-raid shelters in the event of war, hardly the sort of thing to do if the Iraqis were prepared to let them be blown to pieces. The Iraqis realised the enormous world outcry there would be if the hostages were killed. They went out of their way to provide them with plenty of medical treatment to ensure they stayed alive. The few deaths in installations were acutely embarrassing for the Iraqi authorities, one reason why they were quite happy for the sick and elderly to be released with Mr Heath and Jesse Jackson. No, the hostages were intended to stall diplomatic preparations for war and to force the Americans, British and UN to the negotiating table *before* the military threat became too great. Their use was to forestall the military build-up, not protect against it. Thus, once hundreds of thousands of American troops were deployed, the strategy had failed.

Playing to the world gallery had been an essential part of Saddam's strategy. The hostage crisis was one long public relations exercise: a mixture of threats, bluffs, appeals, offers to negotiate, deals and diplomatic manoeuvres, interwoven between an incredible series of visits by foreign dignitaries, stroking Saddam's ego and keeping him firmly in the limelight. Everything was aimed at stoking up enough opposition to war in the West and Arab world to force their governments to the negotiating table, something the British and Americans consistently refused to contemplate.

Saddam was constantly playing to Western and Arabic public opinion throughout the hostage crisis. He was trying to calculate the effect his actions would have and trying to stir the British, American and Arabic peoples to in some way rise up and demand their governments withdraw their forces from Saudi Arabia. That was why he constantly exaggerated the human cost of war. Of course, part of this was undoubtedly Iraqi bravado, but it was also far more. Saddam realised the deep fear Americans had over becoming embroiled in another Vietnam. He played heavily on their horror of a long, drawn-out conflict which neither camp could win, but which would result in huge casualties on both sides. He threatened to use chemical and biological weapons of mass destruction, he threatened that his men would fight to their last drop of blood, all to resurrect the spectre of Vietnam and young American boys returning in body bags. And it did have a tremendous effect. The ghost of that Sixties fiasco raised itself in large peace demonstrations in Washington and a very strong anti-war lobby in Congress. It was only the fear of being weak in the face of aggression that kept many Senators and Representatives from completely opposing President Bush's military build-up. At times, Saddam totally miscalculated Western public opinion, as with the Stuart Lockwood affair, but at others he could be masterful.

At the time, Saddam was accused of trying to break the alliance ranged against him. Now, in what way was he trying to break it? Did he want to break it militarily? Of course not. There were only ever three countries with really significant forces in Saudi Arabia, the Americans, British and Saudis. None of these would ever withdraw their troops of their own free will. They had to be made to pull back by breaking the diplomatic alliance around the headlong dash to war. They had to be compelled to the negotiating table. What the British and American governments feared most was not that other countries would demand they pull out their forces, but that they would demand they stop and negotiate. It was the "no negotiations under any circumstances" stance which was so vulnerable and which was the centre of Iraq attack.

As the UN was the organisation which provided the moral shield and justification for the allied military effort, it was primarily key members of the UN which Saddam targeted. Those were France, the Soviet Union and China. The greatest error Saddam made was to totally misjudge the changed situation in the Soviet Union. He must have undoubtedly counted on the support of his old military and diplomatic ally and must have been bewildered and extremely disappointed when it backed the American position. However, President Gorbachev was anxious to distance himself from total acquiescence with the Americans and to be seen as an international leader in his own right, able to negotiate and pursue his own international initiatives. Thus, he was keen to play a mediatory role throughout the crisis, a factor Saddam was able to use to his advantage. The Soviet President's envoy, Yevgeny Primakov, was extremely active in shuttle diplomacy.

Iraq desperately wanted the Soviet Union to force America and Britain to negotiate for a peaceful solution. That was why he kept three thousand Soviet nationals in Iraq. Again, they were not intended as a shield against military attack, but as a lever - this time to push the Soviet Union into pressurising America and Britain. But, once again, Saddam miscalculated. Gorbachev would not be intimidated. Holding his citizens merely furthered angered him and eventually forced him to give Saddam an ultimatum that it would deploy troops unless they were released - significantly, on the 3rd December, only days before the general release of the hostages - to which Saddam replied on the fourth by granting the Soviet nationals their visas.

The Iraqi stance explains its peculiar action in releasing all the French hostages in late October, at the very time when France was sending more troops to the Gulf. As described above, this release occurred at the very moment Presidents Gorbachev and Mitterand were meeting in Paris to discuss the Gulf crisis. Both countries had significant popular movements for peace. Part of the reason the Soviet Union refused to get militarily involved in the Gulf was the effect it would have on its large Muslim population in its central Asian republics, and the opposition it would engender amongst Russians who would resent their troops being used to promote American and British 'imperialist' interests.

France, too, was fundamentally spilt over the prospect of war. The majority of the French people wanted negotiations and President Mitterand had to do his utmost to juggle between UN solidarity and his own countrymen. At times, he very nearly cracked. He refused to send a large force to the Gulf and, for most of the crisis, insisted those men he did send never took part in any military operations. He tried to pursue his own diplomatic initiatives to give the impression of seeking alternatives to war. In fact, keeping President Mitterand in the fold was clearly a worry for the British and Americans. He and Mr Gorbachev were the two weak links. They would both have favoured a line of more dialogue.

The British and American governments had to fight an intensive diplomatic battle to counteract these manoeuvres to break the alliance against, not Iraq, but against *dialogue with Iraq*. It cost the Americans a great amount in secret diplomatic deals during those days. A lot of foreign debts were written off. A lot of money was promised. A lot of schemes were sanctioned and pariahs, such as President Assad of Syria and the Iranian government, brought in from the cold. The diplomatic game, the struggle for international public opinion, was the very body of the period August to December. And at the heart of this body were the hostages.

Once the UN had passed its resolution at the end of November calling for all necessary means to be employed to free Kuwait, implicitly sanctioning the use of force and setting the 15th January deadline for Iraqi withdrawal, the role of the hostages was over anyway. As stated above, they were never intended to be a shield against attack, only to be a bargaining counter to start negotiations. Thus, their usefulness had evaporated once that resolution had been passed. In fact, the passing of that resolution was a very significant factor in creating the right climate for the general release of the hostages.

Accordingly, by the first week in December, Saddam seemed to have lost the race to split the UN and force the Americans and British to the negotiating table. However, another development cut across that situation. Suddenly, during the final days of November, President Bush dramatically changed his stance on dialogue with Iraq. The President had faced consistent and sometimes loud opposition to his position on the crisis from Congress. The Democratic majority in the Senate had instigated a hearing on the President's Gulf policy which opened in the last days of November and was very critical of the President's approach. Numerous 'expert' witnesses testified to the enormous casualties that would be suffered during a ground war, and that President Bush's recent decision to send a further 200,000 troops to the Gulf was a gross error. They even cast serious doubt over whether the United States could actually carry out its first major ground war since Vietnam.

This on-going criticism from Congress forced Mr Bush onto the defensive for a few days as his whole policy came under attack. Significantly, Mrs Thatcher was toppled at this time, leaving him vulnerable internationally and uncertain of her successor. He felt he had to be seen to be making more of an effort to get a peaceful solution. In a dramatic announcement on 30th November, he made an offer of direct talks with President Saddam to find a peaceful solution. He was prepared to send James Baker, his Secretary of State, to Baghdad anytime between 15th December and 15th January. [These were the infamous 'talks' which were haggled over for weeks as Baghdad wanted them postponed until after the 15th January deadline.] Mr Bush also invited Tariq Aziz to Washington for talks sometime after 10th December. It was a clear reversal of policy and a major concession to Iraq, although his rhetoric still made it clear that "time is running out" for Iraq.

Iraq was ecstatic at the prospect of talks at long last and claimed "it is not only a victory for the Iraqi people, it is a victory for humanity". The announcement sent Wall Street soaring. It was welcomed by the Foreign Office and, significantly, by the new British Prime Minister, Mr Major. Together with an offer by the European Parliament to enter into dialogue with Tariq Aziz, Saddam saw this as a decisive shift by the West towards a peaceful solution.

As if to complete the picture, visiting dignitaries and delegations had emphasised repeatedly to Saddam that the hostages, rather than encouraging Western peace movements, had become the major moral justification for war, so *that* reason for holding them had *also* become discredited. The last of these emissaries had been from Saddam's closest allies in the Arab world, King Husain of Jordan and Yasser Arafat of the Palestine Liberation Organisation, both of whom asked him to make a concession. That these missions did play an important role is clear from Saddam's letter to his Parliament. "People of goodwill, men and women from various nationalities and political inclinations have arrived in Iraq and dear brothers from Jordan, Yemen, Palestine, Sudan and the Arab Maghreb Union have consulted with us on this issue as well as other issues and we felt, in the light of our humanitarian feeling, that the time has come to give our decisive view on this issue." Thus, a central concern, as expressed by the Iraqi leader, was the pressure put on him by 'peace missions' and Arab delegations.

Finally, the moves in the American Congress and the pressure they were putting on President Bush at home, where he was deeply unpopular, suggested that a daring and total release would be seen by the American and international communities as a very significant gesture towards peace and completely cut the feet from under him. Saddam was looking for a way out of the hostage mess and the offer of dialogue was the perfect opportunity. He jumped at it.

One final event swung it. The BBC World Service, of all organisations, announced that the US had made a fundamental shift in its policy towards the Middle East by proposing an international peace conference at the UN Security Council. It turned out to be a misquote and was strenuously denied later by James Baker, but it was made the very day Saddam announced the general release. By the time Mr Baker had refuted the reports, the 'good' had been done and Saddam's letter to the Iraqi Parliament was in motion.

It could be argued that, put together, these factors clearly point to one over-riding conclusion: a willingness to enter dialogue, whether by individual statesmen or by governments, was of fundamental concern to the Iraqi leadership and was the central reason for the release of the hostages. If that dialogue had begun four months earlier, the human shield may very well have been released four months earlier. It was the total unwillingness of the American and British governments to enter dialogue which meant that, in retaliation, Saddam kept the hostages for so long.

On the other hand, it has been forcefully argued that the Western governments' refusal to discuss the invasion of Kuwait, and their complete determination to pursue the military option without entering into any dialogue at all was the real key to the release of the 'human shield'. It unequivocally demonstrated to the Iraqis that innocent civilians couldn't be treated as pawns, that they weren't going to be negotiated over under any circumstances, and that there would be a war whether or not the Iraqis released the hostages. Certainly, the unrelenting military build-up of the allies made it clear that the hostages were ineffective as a human shield and rapidly reduced Saddam's room for manoeuvre. The firmness of the British and American governments *was* crucial. They refused to let the hostages become bargaining counters, refused to do deals and refused to compromise. Without that, Saddam would have continued to use the human shield as bargaining chips during any dialogue that took place. Dialogue without strong military force would have been even more disastrous.

How can these arguments be reconciled? Most hostages and relatives supported the military build-up. None felt Saddam should be allowed to get away with what he had done. But, on the whole, they felt there should have been talking as well - dialogue from a position of strength. They felt the correct position was neither to just negotiate, nor to just have a military build-up. It was to pursue both at the same time.

'GUESTS' OF IRAQ DANCE WITH JOY AT RELEASE PLEDGE

The new British club in Baghdad never saw a party like it when the remaining Western detainees celebrated the news of their imminent release at a farewell party last night in their favourite watering hole. Irish nurses danced with British builders to a live rhythm-and-blues band and embassy consular staff toasted the end of four months of intensive and often frustrating work. Across Iraq at fifty [there were nearer eighty] installations, ranging from chemical weapons facilities to power stations, hundreds of British, American and Japanese "guestages", as they now call themselves, huddled around short-wave radios to hear the news on the BBC World Service.

Nowhere, however, was the announcement greeted with more relief than in the make-shift hide-outs of those stubborn expatriates who continue to remain in hiding in Kuwait more than four months after Iraq had invaded its tiny neighbour."

The Times, 7th December

Eric Watson and a few other BA passengers from the IBI camp in Kuwait had been moved up to Baghdad late in November, then moved down to a military airfield at Shu'aiba, near Basra. The hostages at the air base heard news of a release *before* Thursday 6th December when two Japanese lads in the camp were on the phone to their girlfriends in Japan. One of the women was watching the television at the same time and suddenly said, 'You're free!' Eric described the scene. "The two Japanese rushed around saying 'We're going home!'. We didn't believe them, so we went upstairs in the block to listen to the news on the World Service. There was no confirmation. It wasn't headlines, nor did it come as a later item." In fact, Saddam had only announced that the Japanese could go home.

Their disappointment was overwhelming. Another Iraqi trick. They had been told they were going home so many times in an attempt to undermine their morale that they had put it firmly out of their minds. But a spark of hope had been ignited and, on the sixth, they were all huddled around the radio for the three o'clock World Service bulletin. There was a short announcement at the beginning of the broadcast of a general release, but then nothing, no follow-up in the news itself. Excitement rose. People were still sceptical, but began praying it was true. They all huddled around the four o'clock bulletin. This time, it was headlines. They were glued to the radio, holding their breath as they listened, their stomachs turning over at the news and at the uncertainty. Would the Iraqis keep their word? *Was* it an elaborate hoax?

A few days before, Eric had been out jogging around the camp with a group of other hostages, including Don Majors. Don had suffered from the poor food and conditions at the IBI camp. He was thin and looked drawn, but he felt he had to keep his strength and fitness up. It was hot that morning and he began to perspire more than usual. They ran alongside the wire fence, taking it easy as always, but Don felt tired, as though his legs wouldn't work. They felt leaden, his knees like rubber. He felt faint, hot, sweaty, desperately short of breath. Suddenly, his chest exploded into searing pain and he collapsed into the desert dust. Eric rushed over to him as the others crowded round.

"Get the guards, quick, he's suffered a heart-attack."

Two of the men rushed off, but it was too late. Don had already died, his head cradled in Eric's arms.

Eric thought of Don as the news of their release was confirmed by the camp officer. It seemed such a waste. But, perhaps Saddam had heard of his death, and it had been another reason why he had let them all go. Perhaps he hadn't died in vain.

Gradually, over the next few days, Eric allowed his hopes to rise. Over the four previous months he had deliberately suppressed them. He had treated all good news with caution because it was so often stolen from him again, like a bully first gives, then steals back, sweets from a smaller child. If he'd allowed his hopes to rise, and then be smashed, he wouldn't have lasted psychologically. It had been a war of nerves where the only way to survive was to suppress all emotion. No fear, no worry, no anger, no hope, no bitterness, no sympathy, no joy. Just get through each day as calmly as possible.

But now his hopes did rise. The signs were good and finally, a few days after the announcement, they were ordered to pack their things and climbed aboard a coach for Baghdad.

When the people in the Melia al-Mansour heard from Julian Lyons of the British embassy that Saddam had announced a general release, there were great cheers. It was like a holiday camp. "It was how I imagined VE Day to be," Anne Mansell beamed. "Everyone was going berserk. They were sticking two fingers up at the Iraqi guards, they were singing and laughing. They were all drunk, going to the bar, demanding more beer. The atmosphere was electric. It was really good. Even the Iraqi soldiers were joining in with the party." Suddenly, it was all over.

The hotel was already full of arriving wives and departing Italians and Japanese, but now it was overflowing as more and more British and American men came in from the installations. Everyone was meeting friends they hadn't seen for months. It was like a huge reunion party, full of emotion and relief. It was too much for Anne. She had to retire to her room to get away from the tension. "I found it all too much. It was all getting out of hand."

Gilly Colclough was one of the women who had come back to Iraq from the UK. She had planned to go to Baghdad once before, with

Dorothy Goodwin, but her husband Tom had told her not to. The second time he was allowed a phone call, she told him she was coming out, whether he liked it or not. She travelled the familiar route, obtaining visas for Jordan and Iraq, flying to Amman and on to Baghdad, where she arrived on the 3rd December. She travelled with Gilly Battersby, who was returning for a second time, but on this occasion to get her husband released. They met up with another group when in Amman and decided to describe themselves as part of a peace movement. They were met at the airport by the Iraqi Women's Federation, which turned out to be extremely friendly and helpful. The Iraqi women looked after them, took them shopping around the *souk* and showed them the sights of Baghdad and Babylon. Everything had to be done through them. In gratitude, and to gain their support for the release of their men, the British women bought the Iraqis clothes, toys and toiletries for their children. They even had to sign letters disassociating themselves from the policies of the British and American governments and demanding peace. "We had to be seen to be appeasing them." In effect, they were subjected to constant moral blackmail.

Gilly's group were accommodated in the Melia al-Mansour. The night they arrived, the third, the Japanese hostages were bussed into Baghdad. There were hundreds of them in the hotels. Meanwhile, more women flew in and the Iraqis began the process of finding their men and bringing them in to meet their wives and mothers. Gilly was at the hotel two nights before Tom arrived on the fifth. The next day was the announcement of the release, and four days after that they obtained their visas and left for the UK. Those four days together in Baghdad were marvellous. "It was a very emotional time. All the guys were being brought into the Melia al-Mansour from outside. That was amazing. About three hundred and forty guys were brought in. There were guys we hadn't seen for months. One of our friends had been picked up early in August. He'd gone so thin. Another guy had been very badly treated, Ray [-]. That was pretty emotional. He had been shot up on the border trying to escape with his wife and kids. Their vehicle was machine-gunned eight kilometres from Saudi. He was taken to the Regency Palace Hotel, then up the road to Shuwaikh Port, where a group of BA stewards were being kept. His family left in the last days of August with one of the Iraqi convoys."

Gilly had brought with her a large suitcase full of food, clothes, cigarettes, medicines and chocolate. She had asked Tom over the phone what he needed. Medicines for diarrhoea, pre-cooked chicken legs, Christmas puddings, Christmas cake, large bottles of vodka and rum, and hams. Her room was like Marks and Spencer's delicatessen.

Roy Willatt had been on Tom's camp. When he came into the hotel a couple of days after Tom, Gilly invited him up their room and gave him some of this wealth of food. Roy had been really ill on the camp, poisoned by rodent faeces in the food. He had lost a lot of weight and been badly dehydrated at one time. Tom believed he had been close to death. So, when he saw thirteen bars of dairy milk chocolate staring up at him from

Gilly's suitcase, his face was a picture. His mouth dropped, his eyes stared, a smile grew across his lips. "Chocolate," he mumbled, running a finger along one bar, hardly daring to touch it. "And rum. Chocolate and rum. Rummmm..." his lips lingered into a kiss on the cool glass of the bottle. His eyes closed as he pressed it to his cheek. He was in heaven!

Gilly had put Tom in the bath. She had run it for him, undressed him and helped him into it. It was not only his first bath for six weeks, but the first time he had experienced hot water in that time. His favourite food is mango and she had brought him one from England. She peeled it and scooped out the stone, then brought it to him as he sat in the bath. As he lay there, his eyes closed, steam rising above him, she handed him a glass of rum and he too was in paradise.

Carolyn Stevenson's general impression of the detainees as they arrived at the hotel was of thin bodies, drawn and tired faces, and ragged clothes. They looked awful. Suddenly having access to alcohol again didn't help. Some spent their days at the hotel in a permanent state of inebriation which accompanied them onto the flights and stayed loyal to them all the way to London, amply helped by free miniatures on the British Airways plane. So, they were all in good spirits, and in good beer.

There weren't many depressed or sad faces. They were over the moon to be going home and ecstatic to be on their way back to their families at last. Most were meeting people they hadn't known were still alive, hugging each other and swapping ordeals. The drink flowed. One man brought out a Union Flag he had kept hidden throughout his incarceration. He threw it over his shoulders and refused to take it off until he reached the UK. The rest of his outfit was a real hotch-potch. During his time in hiding he had slipped from house to house searching for food and clothes. He had shoes from one villa, trousers from another and an ill-fitting shirt from another. He looked bedraggled but full of fun.

One person wasn't so happy. Stewart Griffiths had been released on the ninth of December and driven to the Melia al-Mansour Hotel in Baghdad, but he had no passport. He was plagued by worry in case he couldn't get a visa and was unable to catch the flight. There were several embassy officials at the hotel, taking people's details and getting them visas. He approached one and told him his problem. The official promised to get him a passport and took his photograph as he sat in the lounge.

The first the waiting British knew of their flight out of Baghdad was when Julian Lyons and Caroline Cross came in on the ninth and asked them to hand in their passports. Every ex-hostage I have talked to has nothing but praise for those two members of the embassy staff. Their dedication, tireless work and personal sacrifice deserves a special mention.

Unfortunately, all the passports had been given to the Iraqis, so the guards had to be persuaded to fetch them. They brought them into the hotel in boxes and asked everyone to find their own. They were dumped into a small room, in no sort of order and each person had to sort through the pile of blue, red and green booklets to find his or her document. Once they had found them, they had to hand them to the pair from the embassy who took them away to get exit visas. The two staff were given a room in the hotel where they worked right through the night to get them ready for the next day.

There had also been problems with the flight. The Iraqis wouldn't permit either the Virgin Atlantic jumbo or the British Airways plane waiting at Amman to enter Iraqi airspace. They had to leave on an Iraqi aircraft. Nor would they let them fly to Amman and then transfer; they had to fly to somewhere in Europe. This caused a great deal of consternation amongst the ambassadors with nationals still in Iraq and meant they each had to do their best to charter Iraqi jets.

The British embassy was not able to acquire any for the Monday but, fortunately, there were seats on a jet the Americans had chartered to take their people to Frankfurt. Because the plane would be two-thirds empty, they agreed to fill it with British. The BA jet in Amman would have to follow it to Germany, pick up the British passengers there, and fly them on to Heathrow.

By Monday, a large number of hostages from the sites had arrived and many of them had received their visas. The night before, those with visas had been told to be ready at eight o'clock in the morning to leave the hotel. They were instructed to assemble in the foyer and wait for the buses for the airport. It was several hours before the coaches eventually turned up and drove them to their destination. There, they disembarked and went into the concourse to be processed, but were delayed for several more hours. As the aircraft had been chartered by the Americans, their nationals were allowed on first.

Meanwhile, Stewart Griffiths still hadn't been given his passport or visa. He had caught the bus to the airport and stood waiting anxiously as the other men and women were led through to the departure lounge. Finally, when there was just him and one other man left, he spotted the British ambassador, Harold Walker, pacing up and down the terminal, so approached him for help.

"Excuse me, are you the British ambassador?"

"I am, how do you do."

"Not so well, actually. My name's Stewart Griffiths. I'm due to go out on this next flight, but I haven't got a passport. All the others've been let through, but not me. One of them's even taken my case through. Am I going on the flight or not?"

"Tell me how I can help."

"Well, you've got my passport. You've taken my photograph, but I've not got a visa or anything. I haven't even got any money for a drink."

"We've been giving out money."

"I know, but I didn't get any. I haven't got anything." Stewart was feeling very agitated. He'd had enough of everything and everyone. His patience had completely run out. He was on the verge of anger or tears - or both. "I don't think I'm going to get out of here."

Harold Walker asked one of his officials to get Stewart a coke to calm him down, which the man did. It was eight o'clock in the evening by now. The plane, due to leave at half past four, was about to depart.

"I'm not going to make it," Stewart complained to the ambassador. He was at the end of his tether, verging on nervous and physical collapse. The thought of being taken back to the hotel and staying in Iraq for days or weeks filled him with dread. He couldn't cope with it. He'd long ago had enough. He sat nervously on the edge of a chair next to the other man, who was also waiting for his passport and visa, and waited.

A few minutes later, the pilot of the aircraft appeared. The ambassador spoke to him about the two men left. Stewart rose and walked over.

"Don't go without us."

"Oh no, don't worry. If you stay here, we'll stay here. We won't leave without you."

Maybe an hour later, a embassy official drove up to the terminal and ran across the large, modern, air-conditioned foyer waving two passports. He had a great smile on his face. They had been stamped with visas and were ready to go. Stewart almost cried with relief. He thanked the man and the ambassador as he and the other ex-hostage were led through the departure lounge, out across the tarmac, and into the waiting plane. He was so relieved as he sat down in that seat it was as though every bone and muscle in his body collapsed with fatigue and joy. Oh, was his nightmare finally over?

When the other passengers had boarded the plane, they discovered that no proper meal was going to be provided on the journey. The Iraqi flight crew were dour and unhelpful and there were armed guards on board. All the passengers were offered on the three hour journey was a cup of tea and three slices of cold meat. Some had a slice of inedible cheese. One or two passengers had brought a few packets of biscuits which they shared out, but the atmosphere on board was very subdued and tense. It was not celebratory at all. The passengers understood that, being an Iraqi jet, it could receive orders at any moment to return to Baghdad. They had come to so distrust Saddam that they believed he was quite capable of such an act. This feeling stayed with them throughout the flight. Even when the plane approached Frankfurt airport it remained with them. They still couldn't believe it was over.

Tom Colclough described the feeling of the passengers: "The atmosphere on the flight was quite freaky. It was a packed flight, we were really packed in the seats." Gilly remembered it as "quite subdued. The air hostesses obviously didn't want to be there. They went through the safety routine, and that was it, we didn't see them again."

There were ninety-three British on the flight, along with a hundred and seventy-five Americans, thirty-two Canadians, twelve Irish and a handful of other nationalities - about three hundred in all. Many of the Americans had been flown up from Kuwait, preceding the British from there by one day. The British were men and women already in Baghdad, such as Anne and Steven Mansell and Tom and Gilly Colclough, some from the installations, such as Stewart Griffiths, Frank Kerfoot, George Parkin, Clive Stringer and David Shattock, and some of the married couples who had stayed together on the installations during the crisis, such as Carolyn and Andrew Stevenson. They didn't include any of the people who had been in hiding in Kuwait.

The stomach of fate gave out one final burp. As the pilot approached the runway at Frankfurt, coming down low, dropping the undercarriage and descending to only a few feet over the runway, he suddenly panicked, thought he was going to overshoot and pulled back on the throttle and flaps. As the jet screamed off again, the passengers hearts were in their mouths. Many of them thought they were going to die right there. Others visualised being flown all the way back to Iraq. As the plane rose over the Germany countryside and began to bank, they had no idea what was going to happen. Again, Tom Colclough described what it was like. "When we came into Frankfurt, we were coming in to land - and we missed! We heard the stall warning, then the pilot applied full power again; the passengers were all saying their Hail Maries. It seemed as though the Iraqis were squeezing the last ounce of resolve out of us. It was the last straw."

The aircraft circled whilst the pilot regained his composure. Then he approached the runway again and was brought in by ground control. The plane slowed and fell towards the runway once more. The airport lights could be clearly seen from the windows, though many weren't daring to look. The jet screamed over the tarmac, then its wheels touched and the engines went into reverse thrust. Gradually, the plane reduced speed, turned, then taxied towards the arrival terminal. Still, most of the passengers held their breath, for fear it would suddenly turn around and fly off again. Even when it drew up at the terminal and they were told to collect their hand luggage, most refused to celebrate. One man shouted out, "France has just invaded Germany!" which caused laughter, but it was not until they were actually off the plane and in the departure lounge that they allowed themselves the luxury of relaxing and believing they were finally free.

Representatives of some of the large firms working in Kuwait were present to meet their employees. Anne Mansell's next-door neighbour in Hampshire, a manager for British Airways, was there and they greeted him with glee. There were also a lot of press about. The airport provided the passengers with free food and soft drinks and the British passengers had plenty of time to relax and talk as they waited for the British Airways flight to arrive. Faces visibly relaxed and broke into smiles. The mood finally broke into joy.

The passengers' treatment changed dramatically on the British Airways plane. It was like Christmas. BA had stocked the plane with four hundred bottles of champagne and plenty of cases of food, thinking the people were going to be on it for hours. There were many more stewards and stewardesses than usual as the plane had flown to Amman with a spare crew, plus ticket staff and maintenance crew and they'd had to bring them all back. There were about forty BA staff altogether, including nurses and a doctor. ITN had a crew on board taking pictures.

The passengers were served with the champagne and as much food as they could eat. The atmosphere was absolutely fantastic - like a party. Nobody cared any more. They knew they were finally free. The BA crew handed each passenger a large black bag and told them to fill it with whatever they wanted. There were track suits, Mars Bars, cigarettes, miniatures, shaving kits and toiletries. When they reached Heathrow they were laden down with free gifts as if they'd just visited Santa's grotto.

However, the passengers were also exhausted. By now, it was early Tuesday morning. They had been up since 8am the previous day and had had no sleep or proper food for sixteen hours. Andrew Stevenson for one felt a let-down response, as if the flight was an anti-climax. The flight crew had been briefed about the emotional state some of the passengers might be in and they spent a lot of time talking to them, letting them get things off their chest or just relate what had happened.

Meanwhile, a second aircraft had followed them out of Baghdad. This was a Boeing 747 with a hundred and seventy-six Italians, fourteen Dutch, eleven Britons and nine Irish on board. It took off at 7.30pm local time and landed in Rome. The Italians were those freed by Roberto Formigioni, the Vice-President of the European Parliament.

The Foreign Office's Emergency Unit began to receive lists of names from the Iraqis once the jet had left Saddam Airport in Baghdad. Not only were they late, but they were in Arabic and had to be translated as best the Foreign Office could. The names were often indecipherable and had to be checked against lists of hostages held by the Gulf Support Group. The lists ran into pages of close type in alphabetical order, with passport numbers and ages.

Once the FCO had decided who was on board, it contacted the family of everyone on the list by phone. Earlier, it had sent instructions to every family by post on the procedure for meeting the flights. There were details on which car park to use at the airport, train directions and security measures. They were told that only two relatives were allowed per passenger, that they were not to bring cameras or tape-recorders, nor large bags, and to carry ID such as passports.

Josie and Stephen Brookes made their way down to London that night, booked into a hotel, then rose at 3am to go to Heathrow to meet the flight. Before making their journey, they had worked closely with the Foreign Office on the passenger lists and phoned dozens of families to tell them their relatives were on the flight. One of the last things Stephen had done was to phone Betty Stevenson in Coventry to check she knew about the flight and could make it. He was surprised when she broke into tears and told him she and her husband couldn't come. The Midlands was in the grip of the heaviest snowfall for ten years. The M6, M1, M5 and M40 were all blocked. Betty felt she couldn't risk the drive. Stephen told her he would try to help. He phoned CWR, Coventry's local BBC radio station and asked them to take her, offering an interview in exchange. They readily agreed and said they would contact Betty and her husband and bring them down to Heathrow.

After dressing, and it being far too early for breakfast, Josie and Stephen made their way to Heathrow. They arrived and parked, then walked over to the arrival lounge, where they met Betty and Andrew Stevenson and the CWR radio reporter with them. They did a short interview then walked up the gentle slope, through the security check, and into the arrival lounge. The press were not allowed in, so the CWR man had to stay behind. But he would get another interview later.

The arrival lounge was packed to the brim. There were children and grandparents, people with champagne and bouquets, groups laughing and joking, others talking wildly. The atmosphere was totally different to when the women and children had come out. This crowd included those women and many of those children, but this time they were ecstatic, though tense and hardly able to believe their ordeal was finally over. When they had arrived in September, they had been leaving their menfolk behind. Now they were being reunited. They were joyous, excited, high with anticipation. Josie went over to the support group stall with Stephen and talked to the London people beside it, including Andy Charles, Sue Dorrington and Joanna Copley, then went off to meet as many of the relatives as she could. She felt overjoyed to be with them.

Cynthia Hill was there to meet her husband Derek. She couldn't bear the crush of people and the waiting press. "I couldn't stand it. It was awful." Above all, she disliked the hordes of TV crews and press hounding them for gory stories of what they'd been through. She simply wanted to pick Derek up and be on her way home.

The day before, Cynthia had received a phone call from the Foreign Office to confirm that Derek was due to come out, but neither could they be absolutely certain nor did they know which flight he would be on. So Cynthia had to make the journey down to London from north of Manchester unsure when he would be arriving. Like every other relative, she had to go, stand around waiting, and hope for the best. It was actually Stephen Brookes, who had a flight list at the airport, who was able to tell her Derek was on the first flight, not the Foreign Office.

Cynthia was not pleased with the organisation at the airport. It felt like a cattle market. Nothing seemed to be planned. It was chaos in the departure lounge as people waited for coaches to take them across to the arrival suite. "I couldn't believe they'd only got about a hundred chairs for five hundred people." There was nothing for them to eat, although many people had been travelling all day to get there, had been messed about at the airport, and might well have to stay all night and into the morning. All they were provided with was a cup of tea. "People were crammed in like cattle. It was so hot we were perspiring until it was coming down the walls." The airport staff had no idea when the plane would land. No accommodation had been provided at the airport hotels and they were expected to sit there and wait. "It was a case of: find your own way there, find somewhere to stay yourself while you're there, and find your own way back. It wasn't very good really. I believe the French were treated a lot better."

Cynthia finally reached the lounge where the passengers would come through from the plane. There were sandwiches provided there, but by then it was too late. They were all on tenterhooks, knowing the plane was about to drop out of the night sky at any moment.

Not only was the organisation poor for the relatives, but nothing was done for the returnees. Those who had no one to meet them seemed to be given no help whatsoever. They had no winter clothes and no money to get to their nearest relative. The DSS stall was ineffective. There were forms to fill out for travel grants of up to £500 and resettlement grants of up to £2,500 (which was only a loan), but very, very few of them received either grant. The Gulf Support Group had a stall and gave what help it could but it had no money to give out. Cynthia went up to Stephen Brookes and told him she was appalled by the way the men coming back were treated. He agreed. They were given nothing.

As the plane touched down on the runway at 5am, a tremendous cheer went up in the arrival lounge. The relatives waited anxiously as the plane came up to the terminal and the passengers disembarked. As they emerged from the tunnel into the arrival lounge the reception was incredible. The cheers raised the roof. Josie Brookes recalls seeing the first man come through, then the next, then the next. Each was greeted with a huge round of applause. Stephen Brookes described the scene: "A British Airways announcer said over the tannoy, 'Ladies and gentlemen, we would like to welcome you, on behalf of the British government and British Airways, back to the United Kingdom'. There was an almighty cheer! The chill went down my back. We all dissolved into tears. None of us could hold back any more. It was amazing."

One man was still draped in his Union flag, smiling broadly, a bottle in one hand and bag of presents in the other. None of them cared how they looked, they were so pleased to be home. People rushed into each other's arms. Wives and husbands who had been apart since August or even earlier were hugging and kissing each other. Everyone was crying. Some youngsters were jumping up and down with the excitement and release of tension.

Another man walked through with plastic bags of presents from British Airways in both hands. Suddenly, two little blonde girls ran towards him. He dropped his bags and sank to his knees as they jumped onto his lap and hugged and kissed him. Then one looked up at him and said, "Daddy, your hair's long."

Grandparents clasped their children with all the love in their hearts. It was relief, ecstasy, sadness - mixed into a great potpourri of emotion. Nothing else in the world mattered. The tears shed that day were more special than any others for those people.

Betty and Andrew Stevenson waited as close to the barrier as they could, trying to spot their son and daughter-in-law as they came out, but they couldn't see them. More and more passengers came through, yet there was still no sign of them. Josie and Stephen came alongside Betty, who was becoming more and more anxious. Had they missed the flight? Had they been delayed in Baghdad at the last moment?

Suddenly someone tapped Betty on the shoulder.

"What're you doing here?"

Betty turned. It was her son Andrew. She collapsed into his arms with delight and nerves, hugging the breath out of her son, reunited after four and a half months of pain. Andrew's wife Carolyn was just behind him. She hugged her father-in-law and blurted out that she was pregnant. From then on, everything became a blur of excitement and tears. For Josie, it was the culmination of months of hearing about Andrew and Carolyn, of seeing their photographs, learning about their lives and sharing Betty and Andrew's love for them. For months she had shared their joys and sadness, their letters and phone calls. And for there to be news of a baby seemed to cap it all. For something so wonderful, symbolising life and love and hope, to have come out of the crisis seemed incredible. Stephen described what went through his mind at that moment. "I think it was the real emotional break for me when Andrew and Carolyn came through. We sat down together and we looked at each other and we couldn't stop crying. That was the tension breaker for us. The very first of 'our' lot who came out. We'd been involved in the airport for some of the earlier flights; they had been great, but were awfully sad reunions. This was something very, very special."

As Josie stood back and let the Stevensons talk, she suddenly felt alone. All around her, families were reunited; they all had somebody to share the moment with. As she stood there crying, her tears turning into sobs, Sue Dorrington came up to her and hugged her and tried to calm her. "I was so grateful to feel someone's comforting arms. I felt so alone as I watched all those relatives I knew so well finally reunited."

Stephen felt the same. "Josie and I just held each other and we sobbed. That was the break of the tension for us. Five months of waiting, of worrying whether people would ever get back together again. We also knew that Saddam had lost that element of the war. The human shield policy was finally broken. They were back without any conditions. That moment will never, ever, go from my life."

Anne and Stephen Mansell were met by Stephen's mother. Their children weren't there. Stephanie was at home asleep with her Grandad. The other two, Joanna and Stuart, were away at boarding school.

Derek Hill was met by Cynthia, who was delighted to be together with him again, but wanted to get away as quickly as possible. She said hello to the guys he had been with, collected his bag and hurriedly left.

"What was Derek like when he walked into the arrival lounge?"

"Very thin. He phoned me from Baghdad airport and told me to be ready for him, he was going to be the first one off the plane. Usually, he never rushes, but this time he was one of the first. I couldn't believe it. I was at the back of the crowd and didn't see him at first. Then the BA staff started calling people's names out, but I didn't hear Derek's. It was pandemonium in the arrival lounge, it really was. Everyone was everywhere. Then we saw him. The first thing I thought was, 'My God, where's this man gone?' He used to be fifteen stone, but had lost at least three of them. I think I'd lost quite a lot of weight as well."

Stewart Griffiths was met by his daughter, but at first she didn't recognise him. He had lost three and a half stone and aged twenty years.

As the reunions went on, Josie and Stephen stayed with the Stevensons as they did an interview for CWR and left in the radio car. By then it was mid-morning and they were exhausted, but they stayed on, along with other members of the Gulf Support Group, to speak to other families, to share in their joy and offer any help they could. It was clear from those brief chats that the returnees problems were far from over. Many had no homes to return to, no money and no jobs. Once the ecstasy of their welcome and relief at being free were over, they would come down to earth with one hell of a crash.

At about two in the afternoon, Josie and Stephen returned to their hotel, where they planned to collapse into bed. However, when Stephen called the London helpline it was obviously inundated with the press. He told them he would come over to help out. So, though very tired, he made his way across to Alexandra House where he spent the afternoon giving interviews and discussing the situation with Joanna Copley. Josie, meanwhile, had received a phone call. It was more press. The line was burning with calls and she had to deal with them as best she could, despite being very, very tired. Finally, they eased up, Stephen returned, and they were able to sleep solidly for a few hours.

The alarm woke them at nine. They had two hours to get dressed, have something to eat and drive to Gatwick for the second flight, on which they expected Eric Watson. Wen Li would also be there. She wouldn't miss it for anything.

500 OF SADDAM'S HOSTAGES FLY TO FREEDOM

Two aircraft carried more than five hundred Western hostages, including an estimated hundred and four Britons, to freedom yesterday as Saddam Hussein dismantled his 'human shield' defence. The exodus from Iraqi is expected to continue today and tomorrow with an airlift of around seven hundred Britons, including many who have spent four months in hiding in Kuwait... Most looked pale and thin, after living in secrecy on limited rations for several months. "It's going to be the greatest Christmas of all!" said John Healey, from Hitchin, Herts.

> **Andy Hall, a computer programmer from Wiltshire, said he was taken at gunpoint in Kuwait in October and later moved to a factory in Iraq. He said his Iraqi guards were "almost ashamed" to be holding hostages, although they supported the invasion... another Briton... said he had spent more than four months in the same house, sometimes hiding in air-conditioning ducts to escape detection by Iraqi patrols.**
>
> **The great majority of the three hundred and forty-two Britons held at Iraqi strategic sites were taken to Baghdad over the weekend... the four hundred and thirty-seven Britons in hiding in Kuwait had been asked to gather at Kuwait international airport tomorrow morning to board two aircraft to take them to Baghdad for exit visas.**
>
> ***The Independent*, *10th December***

On the sixth, Mike and Ben were still in hiding in the Muthanna Complex in central Kuwait City. They heard the announcement of the general release over their radio at 3 o'clock in the afternoon. It was a short statement merely saying that Saddam had agreed to let all hostages held in Iraq go. Neither of them could believe it was true. The immediate question they asked was, "Does that include us?" Were they classed as 'hostages' and was Kuwait included in the definition of Iraq? Then the phone started going with people ringing to spread the word. They listened to subsequent announcements, still not knowing whether they were included. They thought it could well be a trick to get them out of hiding, only to incarcerate them for disobeying Iraq edicts to give themselves up.

Jim McAlindin recorded the events of that day: "At 3pm on Thursday 6th December, the BBC stated that 'Before we read the news, it has just been announced that all travel restrictions on foreigners within Iraq have been lifted'. At that precise moment, I was lying on the settee waiting for the news. I had difficulty controlling myself in order to listen and make sure I hadn't misheard the statement. I had to lie still for a few seconds and wait to hear the cheers from one of my friends who I thought must be listening - but nothing happened. It was not a main item in the news at that point, but I decided I had not dreamt it and rushed to tell the others.

"I found two of them on the roof and I burst onto it beaming, 'OK lads, let's pack, we're going home!' At first, they thought I meant the Iraqi soldiers had arrived to pick us up, but I soon put them right. For the next hour, we sat around the radio waiting for the news. We couldn't understand why it continued with its normal service. It wasn't until four o'clock that it confirmed the news.

"That night, some friends, whom we hadn't seen for nearly four months, despite living only two hundred yards away, came round.

'Celebration' is an understatement! The relaxing of the tension which had built up cannot be described. The following evening was the first time I stepped outside my door for nearly four months. To look at the building, which I had not seen from the outside for so long, was very strange. I felt a strong sense of agoraphobia. The whole situation was very strange and we were all still very wary, in case the common Iraqi soldier was not aware of the declaration."

By the seventh, the World Service was advising people in hiding to stay put until the news was confirmed, although it also stated that people in hiding *were* included in the release. However, it still had to be ratified by a special session of the Iraqi Parliament being held that day, and it would take a day or two to filter down to the soldiers on the streets. The Foreign Office also recommended people stay indoors because a few British had been picked up the previous day. It had learnt the lesson of the women's journeys up to Baghdad by coach and told those in hiding to wait for two planes it was organising to transport them to the Iraqi capital.

Bernice and Lawrence MacDonald listened religiously to the World Service every hour, on the hour. When they heard of the general release on the 3 o'clock bulletin on the sixth, they were as cautious and sceptical as everyone else. Immediately, people started phoning each other, wondering if it was an Iraqi lie. Many phoned the embassy, but it knew no more than them.

Only a few days before, they had still been making plans to escape. They had been considering acquiring some aqualungs and an inflatable dinghy from somewhere and working their way through the sewerage system to the sea.

Even on the seventh, people still didn't believe the news and, apart from a few foolhardy groups, certainly weren't going out. Yet, now more than ever, the tension was impossible to bear. "By then we'd had enough. We'd come to the end of our tether, the limit of our endurance." On Saturday the eighth, Lawrence and Bernice decided they might as well take the risk. If they were arrested, they would resign themselves to their fate.

When they ventured out for the first time, they had little idea what to expect. In fact, they were stunned at the extent of the looting and destruction of the city. Cars were burnt out or had their tyres missing and were propped up on piles of bricks. Everywhere, shops were looted, burnt out or boarded up.

"We felt so exposed. Oh God, the big outdoors. It was weird. What would happen if the Iraqis walked past?" Lawrence smiled as he looked back and remembered how white their skins had become. They had been without natural sunlight for four months. "The feeling of sunlight on our faces was amazing. So much had changed. The Kuwaitis had brought in their cows, chickens, camels and goats from the desert to protect them from the Iraqis. There was a mini farm in the garden of every villa. Some

Kuwaitis ignored us, they didn't want to know, but others shouted to us 'Glad you are free!'."

The couple were really chuffed at having survived. They had beaten the Iraqis, they had taken all they could hand out and emerged undefeated. Even some Iraqi soldiers waved at them and hooted their horns, pleased for them. They visited four BA people in hiding nearby and persuaded them it was safe to come out and then reported back to the embassy. They even drove to the embassy, but the Iraqi soldiers outside wouldn't let them through.

Ian Barrett remembers 'coming out' well. He had remained in hiding in one of the small towns along the coast, supplied with food by friendly Arabs. The first thing he did when he emerged from his apartment was to have a haircut and shave off his beard. It was incredible to be able to walk around after such a long incarceration. The following night the other guys in the block organised a barbecue with kebabs on the roof to celebrate and got thoroughly drunk.

Mike Devey, in Rawda, recalled that no one really moved around the first day but, on Friday night, people began to emerge and some held parties. On the Saturday, the British in his area began to venture to neighbours' villas. "On the Sunday I went out, drove down to Salwa and saw that my house was full of Iraqi soldiers. They'd been living in it for three months." However, he had taken too much of a risk. "I went to Mel Gage's house to drop a suitcase off. As I drove through a roadblock I stupidly asked a newspaper seller in English for a newspaper. A soldier overheard me and ordered me out of the car.

"*Englesias*. Out! Out!"

Mike swore at himself for being so stupid, for having relaxed his guard for just a few seconds. He was taken to a telephone exchange which had been converted into a local military headquarters, then on to the Araby Stadium, which the Iraqi Special Forces were using as an interrogation and torture centre, then on to Kazmir Stadium, another 'interrogation' centre, and from there to Jaywan, where the Army Headquarters was located. He was seen by a brigadier of the Special Forces, before being taken to Gazali, where political prisoners were being held in an old agricultural building under the guard of a special Iraqi unit known as M16.

In all the previous centres, he had been questioned, though not harshly and not as if under interrogation, but at Gazali nothing happened. He was told to wait outside and then an officer came up, apologised and let him go. Stupidly, the Iraqis had shown an ex-British army man and key warden a whole series of military headquarters, plus their central intelligence base. Until then, Mike had been planning on staying in Kuwait, but he knew the information he now had must be got out.

On Monday the tenth, the World Service broadcast a Foreign Office statement that two aircraft would be ready the next day to take every

Briton wishing to leave up to Baghdad, to connect with a flight out to the UK. It urged everyone to use the opportunity.

One person who decided to stay was Jeff French. When Tuesday came, he and Mike Devey ran men up to the international airport. Even on that last day, they were stopped at a roadblock and ordered out of their car. Dave actually grabbed a passing Iraqi intelligence officer and asked him to tell the soldiers the situation. He was desperate, as it was shortly before 9am, when the plane was due to leave.

The Iraqis received quite a shock that day. They had no idea so many British were in hiding, certainly not the two hundred and thirty who emerged from their foxholes into the glaring sunlight.

Mike and Ben didn't emerge from the Muthanna Complex until the day of the flight. They didn't want anyone to see them leave because of the repercussions it might have for the Kuwaitis and other Arabs who had harboured them. They simply locked the apartment door behind them and slipped out through an underground car park. Imad, who had looked after them for months, had already taken their luggage down to a car which he had waiting for them. The driver was a friend of his. They arranged to meet him outside a nearby mosque and he took them to the international airport. The two young British men passed twenty or so road checks on the way. The Iraqi soldiers merely asked them where they were going, but didn't arrest them. They demanded their watches and money, but the British refused and the point wasn't pushed. They also wanted to know where they had been staying, so they could go and loot it. "Every roadblock we came to, they slowed the car down, realised we were going to the airport, then waved us on. There were just hundreds of British. I think the Iraqis were shocked to see so many of us. They didn't know what to do with us."

Jim McAlindin's group from Salwa was taken to the international airport in a bus supplied by an Arab friend, Khalid. Jim's maid went with them and said a tearful goodbye at the airport. "At the terminal, we all checked in. To say the Iraqis were surprised at the number of Brits is an understatement."

Groups were coming in from every area of the country. There were thirteen men left in Ahmadi by December, including Henry Hill, Don Murthwaite and Lawrence Griffiths. They travelled to the airport together. Others came up from Fahaheel, Shuaiba and Mahbola, still more from villas and apartments in the suburbs of Kuwait City such as Salwa, Salmiya, Jabriya, Rawda and Andalous. Barry Pickup came in with his group. Many of the wardens were there as well.

Quite a few British decided to stay. Now they were free to move around the country again, there seemed little point in leaving. War didn't seem immediate, and some were prepared to stay through the conflict anyway. Many had nothing to return to in the UK.

As the British assembled at Terminal 2 of the international airport, it developed into one big reunion. People hadn't seen each other for months. They went around looking for friends, talking, laughing, hugging, exchanging stories and getting to know each other again. It was also like a menagerie, because everyone had brought their animals with them. "At the airport everyone was jubilant," Bernice MacDonald smiled. "Some people we hadn't seen for months looked very thin and ill. There was one poor man on crutches. Everyone looked a lot thinner, a lot paler, but still their humour was high. People were joking. A Scotsman in kilt was playing bagpipes. That was magic. People were swopping stories as we waited for hours in a queue waiting to go." Bernice had dressed up in jewellery and a beautiful pink dress and had done her hair for the occasion, to look proud and undefeated. One man was in evening dress and Lawrence was in a three-piece suit, but under a duffel-coat, because he knew he was going back to a British winter. "We were determined not to look as though our spirit had been crushed. A lot of people had jeans and tee-shirts on, but we wanted to go out with an act of defiance."

Eventually, they were told the international airport was closed because the Kuwaiti Resistance had shot down an Iraqi aircraft with a ground-to-air missile and they would have to be bussed up to the Ali al-Salem military airfield near Jahra. They had arrived at the airport at about eight in the morning, and by now it was midday. It was two o'clock before the coaches arrived. They had waited at the airport for six hours.

Mike told me what happened then. "After checking in we proceeded through to get the bus to the plane. Surprisingly, they charged us 3 Iraqi dinars for the bus fare. People were just throwing money at them." The bus journey up to the Ali al-Salem military air field took over an hour. They disembarked and were shown into a large hangar.

"It was like a big, empty warehouse," Bernice MacDonald explained. "There were no toilet facilities other than a revolting room. I had to squat in the corner of an empty office."

"I thought there were toilets there, but wasn't it just another form of humiliation for you, not allowing you to use them?" her husband interrupted.

"It was certainly a humiliation," Bernice agreed.

They weren't offered any drinks as they waited for another two hours for their planes to be made ready. All their hand luggage was searched thoroughly as a further humiliation and they were told to remove batteries from radios in case they were bombs, though why they should want to blow themselves up was beyond the British. They were even made to pay the airport tax! By now, it was late afternoon. Eventually, they were let out of the hangar in groups of twenty to pick up their bags and walk across the apron to the two planes. They had to load their luggage onto the planes themselves.

The atmosphere on the planes was fairly muted. Again, they weren't offered anything to eat or drink. People were very tired and used the one-hour flight to rest. They were quiet, perhaps fearful that it might yet be an Iraqi trap and they would be despatched to installations once they reached Baghdad. However, one passenger remembered the flight as more joyful: "people were singing songs, making up their own words or using words they'd made up whilst in hiding, all the way from Kuwait to Baghdad." Perhaps one plane was more subdued than the other.

When the flights arrived at Baghdad airport, the passengers were ushered straight through to departure lounge. The place was teaming with people as there were a lot of other nationalities waiting for their flights, including Americans, Australians and Japanese. Then there were hundreds of reporters with cameras and microphones, wanting stories of where people had been hiding.

Some organisation, possibly the British embassy, had thoughtfully provided a buffet for the passengers. It was their first food for twelve hours and seemed wonderful. They hadn't seen many of the things on offer for months. "There was all this food and drink laid on, chocolate, biscuits, whisky, beer. We just went and helped ourselves." The atmosphere was suddenly more relaxed and noisy, with laughter and a lot of talking. "We started a bit of singing. Somebody had some bagpipes and he started up. The whisky and beer helped. Once we'd got our exit visas, we finally knew we were going." They were relieved to be departing so quickly, as most had feared they would be kept in Baghdad for days whilst their plight was drawn out for propaganda purposes.

Their wait was only for a couple of hours. On the embassy stall along one wall, they found mail which had been delivered to the embassy but not found its way down to Kuwait. Donald Macaulay and Harold Walker were both there, chatting, trying to deal with problems and settle anxieties. People were being hassled by the Iraqis for all their foreign currency and for their Kuwaiti and British addresses. At first, they refused to comply but, in the end, they started giving false addresses. Lawrence MacDonald told them his was 10 Downing Street. He also had to fill in a FCO form, but was suspicious of that as well. He was assured it was only for FCO purposes but, even then, he wouldn't put down a lot of the information asked for. At one time, the Iraqis had been ringing up the relatives of hostages in Britain, demanding to know why they hadn't got in touch with the British government. "Do you want your husband to be kept here? We have your husband. Why don't you get in touch with your government?" Imagine the effect of this on desperately worried relatives! News of this intimidation had been relayed back to those in hiding over the World Service.

"As the plane took off from Baghdad, there was just one massive cheer," Lawrence MacDonald told me. "As soon as we felt the wheels lift off the tarmac, it was all 'Here we go! Here we go!' That went on for ten minutes, but then it went quiet as everyone relaxed and got some sleep." Henry Hill remembers the scene vividly. "The relief as we walked onto the plane was immense and the atmosphere from then till we took off was electric. There was singing, shouting and plenty of noise, culminating in a crescendo of 'Here we go! Here we go!' as we thundered along the runway. That is one thing I shall never forget."

Once the jet rose to cruising height, the passengers settled down. They were very tired and the flight was with Iraqi Airways, so they were never quite sure it wouldn't be turned back at the last minute. There was only a very poor meal served on board and nothing to drink, unless they asked for it, and then it was only given grudgingly. The Iraqi crew were abrupt and unco-operative and the passengers suspected there were Iraqi secret service personnel on board. They had been warned of the possibility by the embassy, so said nothing about their experiences until they were back in the UK. "We were all professional survivors. We had all survived and had tales to tell and we were not going to foul it up on the last furlong. We were wanting to get home successfully. People were happy, but they were not letting their hair down until we got into London. We were all still quite cool and calculating. We were all thinking of surviving.

Lawrence recalled that "The Iraqi air stewardesses were obnoxious and nasty. One passenger asked for some orange juice for his son. 'For you people,' the stewardess replied, 'we have nothing'." Lawrence asked for a drink himself. He was offered tea. It came without milk or sugar.

"Do you have any beer?"

"No, the beer is for our people. For you we have nothing."

After that, the stewardesses disappeared. They didn't get thanks from the passengers, just anger. There was a lot of swearing and threats directed at them. People were bitter after suffering for so many months, and told them precisely what they thought of the Iraqi government.

For most of the flight, the passengers settled back and tried to sleep. There was no alcohol available, nothing to celebrate with, although many had drunk a lot in the airport and were well oiled before they boarded the plane. Even on the approach to Gatwick, the atmosphere was subdued. However, the closer they got, the more confident they became and, when the plane's tyres finally hit the tarmac at Gatwick, there was one massive cheer. People forgot about their seat belts and rose to demonstrate their feelings. Lawrence was one of them. He stood up and shouted, "Up yours, Saddam!" But some other passengers wanted him to keep quiet. Even on British soil, they were still worried that the plane might turn back.

The men disembarked to the welcoming arms of airport staff, who ushered them to waiting coaches. Ian Barrett recalled how "everybody seemed very pleased. They couldn't do enough for us, to make sure we were OK and to keep us away from the press. They took us straight to our families. Everything went very smoothly." However, for some, it was an anti-climax. Unlike the returning BA flight, these men were been given no champagne party, they had no reception waiting for them, no official welcome home. They missed that final climax, that appreciation of what they had been through. "The psychological impact of a proper reception would have been incredible. We were so disappointed about it. Just to have someone there from the government to say, 'Welcome back', something like that, some recognition, would have had a tremendous effect."

When Cathy Willis heard the news on the TV, she thought it was too good to be true. Did the release include people in hiding in Kuwait? Would Lawrence and Bernice have heard about it? Would they ignore it as another trick?

After being on a high for a few hours, she came down with a bang as she became convinced it was just another Iraqi ploy. It took several days to get her doubts cleared up. "No words can describe how we felt when we knew they were coming home. But, even then, up until the day they were coming home, we didn't know for sure." Like every other relative, Cathy wasn't told which flight her people would be on until a few hours before they arrived. She knew there were two flights coming out, one on Monday, the other on Tuesday, but she had no idea which would include Lawrence and Bernice. Like many others, she spent Sunday watching every news bulletin, phoning friends, trying to find definite news and attempting to calm her nerves. That day was dreadfully tense for everyone. They were all living on their nerves.

Cathy waited all Monday for the Foreign Office to call. She phoned the Emergency Unit, but it had no details and told Cathy it wouldn't have a flight list until the plane had actually taken off. She waited and waited, getting more and more tense, desperate for the phone to ring, but it refused to. She called the Gulf Support Group, but it had no details either. Finally, she decided Lawrence and Bernice couldn't be on the Monday flight and reconciled herself to another day's anxious wait.

On the Tuesday, Cathy decided not to wait for a call from the Foreign Office. She would take the risk that Bernice and Lawrence were on the next flight. She phoned the Foreign Office and was told the flight would take off at three o'clock in the afternoon, and was due in at five. She should ring up at four o'clock to check, but as she lived in Skelmersdale, that would be far too late. She decided to leave before she knew they were on board, get to Birmingham, and phone the Emergency Unit from there. She left with two other members of her family but, even at Birmingham, the FCO still didn't know the flight list, as the plane had been delayed for several hours and was now due in at 7.45pm.

The weather was awful through the Midlands. There was heavy sleet and snow and it took them another four hours to get to London. Once there, they phoned the Emergency Unit again. By then, it had received the manifest, translated it from the Arabic, and was able to tell Cathy that both Lawrence and Bernice were on board. However, there was no need for them to hurry as the flight had been further delayed, and was now due in at nine-thirty. Cathy and her two relatives had just bought some chips, but they were so excited by the news that they couldn't eat a thing. Their appetites vanished as they drove south around the M25 towards Gatwick, their stomachs churning, unable to believe their ordeal was finally about to be over.

At lunch time on Thursday December 6th, Marcia Griffiths phoned her friend Lollo Murthwaite in Birkenhead.

"Lollo, Saddam's just said all the hostages in Iraq can go free. They're free! All of them! Oh, Lollo..."

"Marcia, calm down. Don't get too high. Let's wait and see what happens."

"But it sounds very official this time. Oh, Lollo, I can't believe it's finally over, they're finally coming home." She was crying with joy.

"Don't believe it. I won't believe it until I see it." Although trying to be cautious, Lollo too was filling with relief and a joy she could barely control. "Remember, Marcia, our husbands are both in hiding. It might be more difficult for them to get out."

"I *couldn't* believe it," Lollo told me later. In fact, for her and thousands of other relatives, at first it was *impossible* for her to believe it; her mind wouldn't let her. Saddam had said 'hostages' and 'in Iraq'. Don was neither a hostage nor in Iraq. Even if he was allowed out, he would be amongst the last to make the journey. The first ones would be those already in Baghdad. She suspended any hope and refused to get elated, fearful of being let down again. The higher you get, the harder you fall, so don't get high! That was the principle by which the hostages and relatives kept their emotional integrity. Even with the news, she rang the Foreign Office "every day, every minute of the day, to find out if they had lists of names."

The Foreign Office didn't have the lists and told her they wouldn't have them until the flights actually took off. Only then could they sort out the mess the Iraqis were sending them. On the Tuesday, they told her that two flights had been chartered to fly to Kuwait to pick up those coming out of hiding and bring them up to Baghdad for the trip home. However, as far as they knew, only one had taken off from Kuwait, so they couldn't be sure Don was on his way home.

Lollo decided to go down to London anyway. She couldn't take the chance of missing him. "I thought, I have to go. If he's not on the flight, I'll stay over another two nights and he may be on one of the next flights." That afternoon she went down to London by train. When she arrived at Euston, she phoned her son in Stoke-on-Trent. He had recently called the Foreign Office which had, at last, been able to confirm that Don was on the plane. After crossing London and catching the Gatwick link train, she arrived at the airport late in the evening. Her son decided to catch a train as well and managed to join her at the airport before the flight landed.

As they arrived, the relatives checked in with the airport staff. After the usual security controls, they were directed to the Sir Winston Churchill Suite, where they waited to be shown onto an airport coach. To their relief, the press were kept miles away. The airport staff and government had learnt their lessons from the chaos of the first flight and processing the relatives was much smoother this time. Both food and drink were provided free and the coach which took them across to the arrival lounge was luxurious, with a drinks server, toilet, lounge area and TV screens.

At the arrival lounge, the relatives were allowed to make free phone calls, so many people phoned their friends and relatives to tell them they had arrived safely. The mood was elated, ecstatic, but very, very tense. Would the plane land, or would it be turned back to Iraq? "None of us could believe it was nearly the end," one young woman explained. "Then they announced that the plane had been delayed, and we thought, 'Oh no, not another set-back'. Later, they put this big barrier up where the men were going to be coming out, so I went and placed my seat next to the first barrier to wait for them. Then, at a quarter to twelve, they announced that the plane had landed safely, and the whole room erupted. There was champagne popping and everyone was kissing and hugging each other. There was one woman with two children. This little boy, about six, said to her, 'Mummy, I want to go to the toilet', but she told him he'd just have to wee on the floor. I was in stitches.

"One of the first passengers through was a man loaded down with bags, looking very tired as he struggled up the steps. He wasn't looking and had no idea of the reception waiting for them at the top of the stairs. He looked up and was gob-smacked as he stared at his family shouting down to him. It was so emotional. Every time someone came up, we were all clapping and then Mike just seemed to appear out of the crowd. He was like a ghost. I just jumped over the barrier. It was dead emotional. Everybody was hugging and kissing each other." Her husband was spell-bound by it all. "It was just like somebody had come out of hospital after a big operation and needed rehabilitating."

Some of the men who arrived looked fine, but some appeared to be quite ill. Barry Pickup was as brown as a berry, because he'd been sun bathing on the roof of his apartment block whenever he could. Don Murthwaite was also fine. "It was like being in a dream really," Lollo said, shaking her head. "I was expecting Don to be haggard and not feeling very well. But he wasn't. That was another surprise. He didn't have any problems at all. He hadn't lost any weight. It was the best Christmas present ever!" He had shaved and had a haircut and looked surprisingly smart.

It was very emotional for them all. Ian Barrett "just burst into tears with the joy of seeing people again and the relief that I was finally away from it. Getting back to Rugby, I woke my daughter at three in the morning, just to see her." Ian was on the verge of tears as he recalled the time. "I couldn't sleep that night, getting on the telephone to friends and relatives."

Cathy Willis remembers it as "a happy time, but it was also a terribly sad time. Men with haunted expressions, looking for people to meet them. To see some of them was terribly sad."

Henry Hill recalled it through the eyes of a returnee. "The atmosphere as we came through to the arrival lounge was incredible. It was absolutely brilliant, something I shall always remember. As we came into the room everybody was applauding as if we were national heroes. We had all tried to tidy ourselves up. It was ever so strange. I had never seen such a peculiar set of haircuts in all my life, where guys had tried to cut their own hair with razors or paper-scissors. We were a really motley crew. There were guys who had packed their dinner suits and one guy was in his dickie-bow and tuxedo. There was a Scotsman dressed in his kilt, with his bagpipes. Everybody came off the airplane in style and was greeted in style. I don't know; we were a bit phased by it all. We hadn't met anyone for months and all of a sudden we were meeting dozens of people, people we had never seen before." His wife Anne was there to meet him and make his joy complete.

Jim McAlindin was equally bowled over. "The scene at London could not be described. Before meeting our families, we were asked to fill in a short form - after four months nobody cared how many forms we filled in - we were out! While standing filling in the form, I spotted a telephone. Not having any money, I obtained 20p from a passing official. I phoned my mother-in-law to be told that my wife, Jane, was at the airport waiting for me! When we met, after exactly ninety-nine days of separation, I simply broke down. Everybody did. That night, we didn't sleep. It was spent talking. In the morning, we found that other people likewise had spent the whole night talking. I think everyone was simply too excited and needed to get things off their chests."

Lynda Pickup was there to meet her husband Barry. She had booked a flight back to Manchester, but he didn't want to fly again, so she drove him back to Lancashire. He wanted to take his time and be alone with his wife after such a long time apart. He talked all the way home, trying to catch up on how she and the children were and what they'd been doing. The one thing they didn't talk about were his experiences in hiding.

Thus, it was far from a celebration for all the returnees. Ron Barker and his wife were in a bad way. "We arrived here homeless, with no relatives. I was in hiding in Kuwait until 11th December with my wife, when we left together. My wife is an insulin-dependent diabetic and we'd lost everything in Kuwait. They had to put us up in a hostel and we had to exist on Income Support. We're still hardly any better off now, a year later."

Amongst the people on this flight were many of the BA Flight 149 passengers and crew, including Eric Watson. Because of this, British Airways had booked the nearby Hilton Hotel for a large reception and reserved rooms for them all.

Rob Hayward MP was there waiting for his close friend, Phil Long. He was in jubilant spirits. So were Josie and Stephen at the prospect of meeting Eric. It was a glorious coincidence and enabled them to share each other's happiness. This was *their* time; *their* hostages were coming out. At last, they could share in their own joy. It filled them with elation.

Instead of being taken to the Hilton, where the other relatives, including Wen Li, were waiting, the three of them were allowed through security, through the Sir Winston Churchill Suite, through the main arrival lounge which acted as a gathering point for the families, and into a much smaller arrival lounge.

Half of this special lounge was set aside for the BA flight passengers and half for the crews, where they could be met as a whole by a senior British Airways manager. Douglas Hogg and James Tansley, both junior Foreign Office officials, were there to represent the government. Josie, Stephen and Rob were the only relatives.

They suddenly heard that the plane was flying in. They ran to the window to watch it land, cheering as it touched down, its lights flashing amongst the lights of the runway. It slowly taxied towards the terminal, where it stopped. Nothing happened for several minutes. Then the doors were opened and the passengers began to descend to the tarmac. Josie strained to see Eric. She had no idea how he would look. Would he have lost much weight? Would he be thin and tired?

The men came through a set of double doors and walked upstairs towards them. Josie searched keenly for Eric. She was filled with disbelief and expectation. Every face seemed so tired and drawn. Could it really all be over?

They suddenly heard Rob Hayward yell out. He'd seen Phil Long. As Phil pushed his way into the arrival room, Rob ran up to him and held him. They both began to cry with relief and let out joyful screams of happiness, not caring what anyone else thought.

More men came through, but still no Eric. Josie peered down at the moving walkway below them. The rest of the passengers were making their way up to their relatives in the main arrival lounge. She could see their faces very clearly. They all had gaunt, staring eyes. Their eyeballs seemed about to pop out of their sockets. Some were inebriated, most were crying, and all were thin, bedraggled and scrawny. It was bizarre. They looked like they had come back from the dead.

Josie was beginning to give up hope when Eric suddenly appeared through the double doors. He calmly walked towards her and Stephen, looking as disorientated as all the others, his eyes wide in wonder at finally being home. Josie ran towards him to hug him. As she kissed him on the cheek, he turned to Stephen and said one, simple sentence: "You've no idea how bloody wonderful it is to see you."

Stephen smiled and clasped him. All three held each other in tight embrace as the tears flowed. They hugged for what seemed like hours. It felt so good to be together again. "It felt so wonderful, I couldn't help stroking Eric's arms and head, wondering if he was an illusion," Josie told me, tears in her eyes even a year later. "Was he really home? Was he really back with us? I didn't realise how much we loved him."

"Where's Wen?" Eric asked as they disengaged.

"She's waiting for you at the Hilton."

"Where's that?"

"Nearby. We don't know what's happening. I think they're taking us all over there straight away. All the BA relatives are over there."

"I wondered why we were separated from the others."

"They've organised a reception for you."

Eric smiled. Behind him came a rather pathetic looking figure. It was John Chappell. He was in ill-fitting clothes he had scrounged from the wreckage of the IBI camp and had a pronounced limp. Josie described him as "a gorgeous, cuddly, warm and friendly man." She introduced herself by giving him a big, comforting hug.

The British Airways staff on hand helped those who needed it. Quite a few of the men had drunk too much and the joy of the occasion had gone to their heads. One stewardess chatted with Josie. She mentioned that she had escorted Eric's son, Tim, off his plane in September to meet his mother. She said how Tim had talked to her about his experience in Kuwait. It had made her feel very close to him. The stewardess wanted to meet Tim's father and tell him how he was.

Josie could see John Chappell was anxious to find his wife Maureen. She suddenly thought she might not be waiting for him at the Hilton but have gone to the main arrival lounge. She told him she would go and look for her. Leaving Eric, she ran up the stairs. The main lounge was in absolute pandemonium. It was chock-a-block with people reuniting. The noise was incredible as people whooped and cheered. There was some laughter but a lot of crying. Everywhere, children were climbing into their fathers' arms, as if they would never let them go. It was exhilaration, tears, hugs and relief. Once again Josie noticed the thin, tired bodies and staring eyes of the returnees, and their expressions of disbelief and disorientation.

Members of the Red Cross and Salvation Army were walking between the groups of relatives asking whether they needed accommodation, clothing, medication or taxis to get home. The DSS was handing out hotel vouchers for people to use if they needed them and had forms to claim the £500 resettlement grant. But it was almost impossible for them to do their job. They hadn't anticipated the huge numbers of people who would turn up. The room was packed. No one really knew what was going on. Everyone seemed cocooned in their own, very private, very warm and secure space, oblivious to the rest of the world. It was a room filled to the brim with euphoria.

Josie tried to push through the crowd to find Maureen, until she realised it was useless. She returned to the small waiting group in the other lounge. By now, most of the BA passengers and crew had left for the Hilton, so they decided to follow. Josie took one of Eric's plastic bags for him. It was full of cigars and miniature bottles of spirits. He had someone else's clothes on and was carrying someone else's suitcase, all salvaged from the IBI camp.

It was now after midnight. They were all feeling very tired as they caught a coach to the champagne reception at the Hilton. It was only a short journey. Disembarking, they made their way into the hotel and up the stairs to the large party.

Suddenly, Wen Li appeared. She pelted towards Eric and leaped onto him, jumping clear of the ground into his arms. Their love for each other overflowed after being separated for so long. Josie and Stephen left them to be alone and walked with John Chappell into the packed reception. Maureen saw them and ran over to be with her husband. They embraced and kissed as their children, John and Jennifer, watched. Jenny was crying, but her brother John was trying to not let his feelings show as his father hugged him warmly. Maureen's mascara was running down her face, but she was far too happy to care. They were so full of deep relief and joy that their ordeal was finally over.

Unfortunately, for many, their troubles had only just begun. For the Gulf Support Group, the work increased rather than diminished. As Stephen Brookes explained, "It was the busiest period we ever had." The initial euphoria of their return and the Christmas period soon wore off and the reality of unemployment, post-traumatic stress and life on social security hit them hard. Over Christmas, Josie and Stephen received several calls from people desperate about their situation. Some were verging on suicide, many were severely depressed. There was little prospect of finding new jobs. Many firms were very supportive over the next months, but some ex-hostages were so emotionally distraught they found it impossible to hold their jobs down.

Whilst the London helpline closed down shortly after the men returned, Coventry went on helping people for another eighteen months. Two clinics were set up for them, after much struggle by the Gulf Support Group. Andy Charles and Sue Dorrington set up Hostages Of the Middle East (HOME) to try to recover some of the property they lost and give them assistance in registering claims against the Iraq government for compensation, but that struggle is still going on eighteen months after they returned, with no immediate prospect of success.

Let me try to put their problem into perspective. You are now sitting reading this book, perhaps at home on your settee, or in bed, or over a cup of coffee in a café somewhere. Your family is on holiday in France, having a whale of a time. Life has never been so good. Enjoy it. For within six hours you are in occupied Britain. Foreign tanks are rolling down your street and soldiers are setting up roadblocks at the cornershop, which is already being looted. You have no food, so try to get some. But you've no money, so go to the bank. It's shut. You try to use the cashpoint, but it's closed too. With what little money you've got you rush to the nearest Sainbury's, but find a huge queue of people there and most of the food gone.

Within a few days, you're forced into hiding. You cannot go *anywhere*. You try to escape, but come upon thousands of occupying soldiers and troops, who warn you to turn around. You return to life in darkness and fear. A few days later, the invading army threatens to shoot you and all your neighbours if you don't give yourself up. Just to prove it, Mrs Brown's son Tony is dragged out onto the street. He's tortured before your eyes, then shot. The junior school where your children attend is now a military barracks. You can't use the hospital, because it's now a military hospital. Mrs Smith's daughter across the road is raped by an army patrol. The local library is now a torture chamber. More friends are taken off and shot. Your chemist, bakery, opticians, greengrocers, butchers, and local clothes shops are all looted. The town centre is decimated. You can't even get a button. You can't go outside your front door, or risk letting your dog loose in the back garden. The telephone doesn't work. You can't get any letters out, nor mail in. No one knows if your safe. You have no idea where your family is or how they are. You know they've only enough money to last a week. What are *they* going to do? Where are *they* going to stay?

Four four months you are incarcerated in your own front room. You can't turn more than a single light on or watch the television with the sound up. The programmes are all propaganda anyway. Your one link with your family is a short message over the radio every two weeks. You have to eat stale bread and rice crawling with weevils, and only have one hot meal a day. You see no one for weeks on end. You have to barricade your front door as soldiers bang their rifles on it. You wake up one day to find looters in your house and try to scare them away, but they take your car and strip your garage. For four months you lie in fear of being picked up, terrified, yet bored out of your mind, with nothing to do but worry about your family.

Eventually, you're allowed to go free, but you can't stay in your house, or your street, or your town. You can't even stay in Britain. No, you have to go to Paraguay or Nepal or somewhere, where your aged mother happens to live. You finally meet your family after a horrendous three-day journey, amidst hundreds of relatives and press, and make it to you mother's house. You have left everything, and you know that what you have left will be looted.

Look around you. Look at your furniture, your TV and hi-fi, your ornaments and pictures, your books and photographs. Go into the kitchen and touch the new cooker or kitchen units you've saved hard for all these years. Go upstairs to your bedroom and open your wardrobe. Look at your dresses or suits. Now, all that is gone. Everything. Not a carpet, not a photograph, not a shoe or sock remains of everything you ever had. Gone, the lot.

Then your money. Oh no, you can't use your savings. They're tied up in the National Westminster bank in your home town. You can't get your hands on any of it. No, it's the Nepalese employment exchange for you, queueing for ten hours for a pittance, only to be told you're in the wrong queue or aren't eligible. Your children have to go to the local school, but you can't afford a new uniform. You have to buy the family new clothes, because you have none left. You, your partner and two or three children are sharing a two-bedroomed house with your mother. It is impossible. No money, no job, no house, no possessions, no future, no help, no hope. Nothing. Just sit and try to imagine that lot and you might realise what some - not all, but some - of the returnees and their families had to go through.

Whilst many ex-hostages had homes to return to, did not lose their jobs and did not have their flats looted, *all* of them have suffered *some* elements of the above scenario. None have completely escaped.

Appendix

List of Strategic Sites in Iraq and Kuwait Where British Hostages Were Held Captive

It has been extremely difficult to ascertain all the strategic sites where British hostages were held, because of the secrecy the Iraqis cloaked them in. However, Harold Walker [now Sir Harold], the British ambassador in Baghdad, and perhaps the person closest involved in gathering a detailed list, estimated there were 80. Including hotels used as holding points for hostages, I have managed to find 75; 17 in Kuwait and 58 in Iraq, a few of which are tentative.

The sites seem to fall into the following eight groups: Dams; Air bases; Refineries and oil installations; Chemical and biological plants; Armaments factories; Power stations; Ports; and Hotels.

Many hostages believed the Iraqis allocated each of them to one of these groups, so that when they were moved, they were moved within their category, *ie* always to ports or always to power stations.

Kuwait

Abdaly army camp
Ali al-Salem military air base
al-Wafra military air base
Bayan Palace
Dora power station
IBI camp
Jahra military camp
Kuwait City electricity sub-station
Misila Palace
Shuwaikh port and hydro-electric plant
The University complex (parts of)

Hotels

Airport Hotel (to guard the international airport)
International Hotel (where Iraqi and puppet Kuwaiti government officials stayed)
Meridien Hotel
Misila Beach Hotel
Regency Palace Hotel (which was wired up with explosives)
SAS Hotel

Iraq

Dams

al-Hadithah Dam (Qadissiya Dam) - on the Euphrates 200 kilometres north of Baghdad
Bakhma Dam - in the mountains close to the Turkish and Iranian borders
Darbandikhan Dam - ditto
Dukan Dam - in the mountains north-west of Baghdad, close to the Iranian border
Eski Mosul Dam
Hemrim Dam - 160 kilometres north of Baghdad
Saddam Dam - north of Mosul (this is possibly the same as Eski Mosul Dam)

Air bases

al-Hadithah airbase - 200 kilometres north-west of Baghdad
al-Muldane military air base - at Salman Pak, on the Euphrates south of Baghdad
al-Nassiriya air base - on the Euphrates, half way between Basra and Baghdad
Arbil air base - west of Mosul
ar-Rashid air base - just south of Baghdad on the Tigris
ar-Rutba air base - near al-Qaim, towards Jordan
Habbaniya air base - on the Euphrates, west of Baghdad
Kirkuk air base
Mosul air base
Shu'aiba air base - Basra

Refineries and oil installations

Basra liquid petroleum plant
Basra oil refinery
Daura oil refinery - half way between Mosul and Baghdad
Fallujah pipeline - running from Basra to Turkey
Khor Abdulla marine loading terminal - near Basra
Khosrowabad gas loading terminal - on the Shatt al-Arab
Kirkuk gas refineries (two)
Kirkuk oil installation
Mina Bakr oil terminal - on the Shatt al-Arab
Rumillah oil field - on the Kuwaiti border
Zakho oil installation - north of Mosul, right on the Turkish border

Chemical and biological plants

al-Fallujah chemical and biological installation - on the Euphrates, west of Baghdad
al-Khalis/Ba'qubah chemical bomb factory, 35 kilometres north of Baghdad
al-Qaim chemical plant - western Iraq, towards Jordan
ar-Ramadi chemical plant
Baija chemical weapons plant - on the Tigris, halfway between Baghdad and Mosul
Basra chemical plant
Karbala chemical weapons plant - on the Euphrates, south-west of Baghdad
Salman Pak chemical and biological installation - on the Euphrates, south of Baghdad
Samarra chemical and biological plant - on the Tigris, north of Baghdad

Armaments factories

al-Khalis/Ba'qubah T72 tank factory, 35 kilometres north of Baghdad
al-Taji armaments factory - north of Baghdad
ar-Ramadi munitions factory - 120 kilometres west of Baghdad

Kerbala munitions factory - south-west of Baghdad
Mosul defence complex (a number of installations)
Zubaidnah steel works - south-east of Basra

Power stations

al-Nasiryah power station
Baiji power station - north of Baghdad, halfway to Mosul
Basra power station
Daura power station - on the Tigris, halfway between Mosul and Baghdad

Ports

al-Fawr, on the Shatt al-Arab
Basra naval base
Umm Qasr naval base - south of Basra

Hotels (all in Baghdad)

ar-Rashid Hotel
Melia al-Mansour Hotel
Novotel Hotel
Sheraton Hotel

One perplexing question is whether any hostages were taken to nuclear processing plants. The fact that they were highly secret and the Iraqis wouldn't want anyone to know about them strongly suggests they weren't. I have not come across any hostages who were knowingly kept at a installation involved with Iraq's nuclear programme. However, there was a nuclear processing plant at **al-Atheer** just south of Baghdad, where some may have been held.